D0251080

The Book of

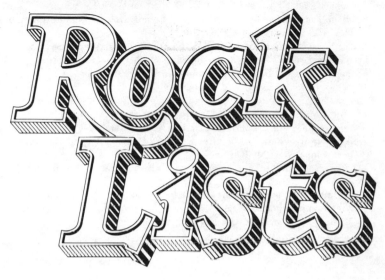

Rock Lists

BY DAVE MARSH
AND
KEVIN STEIN

A DELL/ROLLING STONE PRESS BOOK

1981

Song Lyric Credits:

"Brown Eyed Girl" by Van Morrison, © 1967 Web IV Music Co.

"Don't Pass Me By" by Ringo Starr, © 1968 Nida Music Publishing Co.

"Double Shot of My Baby's Love" by Vetter & Smith, © 1966 Windsong Music Co.

"Greenback Dollar" by Fred Fisher, © 1963 Davon Music Co.

"Hold On, I'm Comin'" by David Porter & Isaac Hayes, © 1966 East Memphis
    Music Corp. and Cotillion Music Inc.

"I Hear Voices" by Screamin' Jay Hawkins, © 1962 Rightsong Music Co.

"Locomotive Breath" by Ian Anderson, © 1971 Chrysalis Music Corp.

"Mamacita" by Clint Ballard, Jr. & Larry Kusik, © 1975 Bourne Co.

"Miracles" by Marty Balin, © 1968 Diamond Music Co.

"Money" by Roger Waters, © 1973 Hampshire House Publishing Corp.

"The Out Crowd" by A. Resnick & D. Young, © 1965 T. M. Music Inc.

"Rhapsody in the Rain" by Christie & Herbert, © 1966 Rambed Music Publishing Co.

"Walk on the Wild Side" by Lou Reed, © 1972 Oakfield Avenue Music Co.

"(Angels Wanna) Wear My Red Shoes" by Elvis Costello, © 1977 Street Music Co.

"You Look Good in Blue" by Jimmy Destri, © 1976 Jiru Music Co./Monster Island
    Music Co.

"Glass Onion" by Paul McCartney and John Lennon, © 1968 Maclen Music Co.

"The Ten Commandments of Love" Words & Music by M. Paul, © 1958, 1981 Arc
    Music Corp., New York. Used by Permission.

Book Design by Vincent and Martine Winter

Dell ® TM 681510, Dell Publishing Co. Inc.

PRINTED IN THE UNITED STATES OF AMERICA

First printing—October 1981

Library of Congress Cataloging in Publication Data

Marsh, Dave.
    The book of rock lists.

    1. Rock music—History and criticism.   I. Stein, Kevin.
II. Title.
ML3534.M37   784.5'4   81-9778
ISBN: 0-440-57580-X (pbk.)   AACR2

This book is dedicated to Rick Whitesell,
without whom it would not have been
possible; and to Keith Moon, without
whom it would not have been conceivable.

NOTE: All references to chart positions contained herein are based on *Billboard* magazine chart surveys, as collected in Joel Whitburn's excellent *Record Research* compilations.

The entries on the lists in this book are presented in alphabetical or chronological order, except for those that represent the usual arbitrary value judgments.

CONTENTS

Chapter Seventeen—GROUPS, 265

Chapter Eighteen—ELVIS, 287

ACKNOWLEDGMENTS

It's no exaggeration to say that the key moment in this book's creation was the day we met Rick Whitesell. Rick was more than a collector, researcher, and historian. He lived close to the heart of rock and roll, and his presence can be felt on almost all of these pages, not only on those to which he contributed facts and ideas. He was with us from near the beginning of the project to very near the end, and it saddens us that he won't be with us to share in the joy of its publication. But we'll never be able to see this book without remembering him.

Debbie Geller first came to us to help with typing and filing. She wound up researching, writing, and performing a wide variety of tasks that come under the broad category of simple heroism. Even that may not quite do her justice—we only hope that she knows how much we appreciate her contributions.

We'd also like to extend special thanks to our editors, Sarah Lazin at Rolling Stone Press and Sandra Choron at Dell, for bearing with us and contributing their own useful suggestions. Also, Jane Karr for her tireless copyediting efforts, which she completed without once being hospitalized.

We appreciate, as well, all those individuals identified in the text who contributed various personal lists. We'd also like to thank the following people who contributed lists and additions, often without attribution: Bud Kliment for the disco basics; Cathy Mallon for a good deal of the punk section; Rod Granger for the bulk of The Beatles entries; Malu Halasa for items too numerous to specify. Also, Lee Stein, George Monoogian, Christopher Connelly, Alan Betrock, John Swenson, Jeff Tamarkin and Andy Edelstein of *Relix* magazine, John Koenig of *Goldmine*, and Tom Kelly.

Vicki Sufian and Jim Nettleton led a voracious team of fact checkers, which included Jeff Howrey. Fran Pelzman supervised the photo research, along with photo consultants Peter

Kanze and Michael Zagaris. Among those around the Rolling Stone Press office who deserve our thanks are Carol Sonenklar, Pauline Finkelstein, Sam Weizman, Jane Mendelsohn, Linda Breitstein, kenn løwy, and Peter Bunche.

Debbie Gold did a great job of contacting and wearing down the resistance of many celebrities, performers, and industry people. We thank her and Neal Preston and Jimmy Wachtel, who helped her, and all the many people who were contacted, even if they couldn't always contribute. Also the law firm of Barovick, Konecky, Schwartz, Kay and Schiff.

For their help with various aspects of research, we'd like to thank Todd Anderson, Michael Ochs, Peter Hogan, Chet Flippo, Joe Enright, Don Rosen, Phil Goldberg, Stuart Linder, Beth Filler, Mark Norton of *Creem*, John Gehron at WLS in Chicago, Rhonda Keifer at WMMS in Cleveland, Jay Clark at WABC in New York, Richard Price, Joel Whitburn, Dan Friedman of the Victoria and Albert Museum, Neil Spencer of *New Musical Express*, the Hollywood Chamber of Commerce, James Patton of Coca-Cola, Nigel Dick, the Liverpool City Council, Michael Barker, Joel Selvin, Little Elliot Lloyd, and Greil Marcus.

Also, Mary Kelly and Ray Breault, Bob Chirmside, Stash Records, Karen Rose at Rock Read, Richard S. Glassman Productions, Electric Factory Concerts, Irv Zuckerman, Alex Kipfer, Ken Braun, Gordon Chilvers, Carrie Dorsch, Nancy Siebenthal, James Karnbach, Ron Furmanek, Penny Valentine, Mike Shaw, Neil Aspinall, Keith Altham, Barry Bell, Betty Cornfeld, Erik and Bruce Murkoff, Craig Waltcher, Albert Poland, Mark Bernolak, Randy Tuten, and Dan and Barbara Dunn.

Last but hardly least, Frank and June Barsalona, Sätty, New World Pictures, Cinemabilia, John Dempsey, Mitch Dancik, Elizabeth Enos, the Change of Hobbit Bookstore (L.A.), Suzan Crane of *Country Music* magazine, Lou Dumont, Ben Friedman at the Postermat, San Francisco, Peter Grendysa, Tom Grasso, Bob Gruen, Robert Pruter of *Goldmine*, Tania Grossinger, Jon

Goodchild, John Hodgeman, Ron Shafran, Andy Gellis, Caesar Glebbeek and Dan Foster of the Hendrix Information Center, Amsterdam, Jack Hart, Avi Hersh, Jonathan Kalb, Bill Solly, Paul Fishkin of Modern Records, Kevin Sadlier, Eddie Kirkland, Ed Rothkowitz, Fred Schruers, Gloria Stavers, "Irish" Jack Lyons, Jeff Pollack, Peter Nevard, Alyse Newman, Jaime Rivman, Mike Post, Glen Roven, Tom Sleight, Robert L. Green, Arthur Whitelaw, and Steve Leeds. Now *that's* a list.

Dave Marsh would like to extend very special personal thanks to Ted Nussbaum, Jim Dunning, Jeep Holland (for all the years of swiping and swapping ideas), Obie, Ralph Schuckett and Ellen Shipley, John Cafferty and the guys in Beaver Brown for keeping me on my toes, Miami Steve for being beyond research, and always, Barbara, Sasha, and Kristen.

Kevin Stein would like to offer special personal thanks to Howard and Sondra Green, Rose Harris, Dr. Elsimar and Micheline Coutinho, Susan and Marc Strausberg, Stuart A. Hersch, Burton I. Monasch, Joan Stewart, Dr. George W. Goethals, Richard Rosen, Carl A. P. Ruck, Alvin Granowsky, Dennis Tedlock, Michael Ragussis, Charles J. Brucia, Michael Joseph, Brian Lynch, Christian Alderson, Isabel Hickey, Nola Sheehan, Lisa Dreishpoon, Robin O'Hara, Vikki Nielsen, Barry Axelrod, Scott Ference, Vickie Shafran, Olivia Cheever, Anne Roof, Mac McAllister, Phyllis Whitesell, and Jeff Stein.

PSYCHOTIC REACTION
An Apologetic Introduction

"Print the legend, not the fact."—JOHN FORD

Somewhere along the line, the wrong impression has been left. Experts as diverse as Pete Townshend, brats off the street, pop culture pedants, and even my own kin all agree that I take rock too seriously. For the past decade, such taunts have plagued me.

But they've never really hit home. For one thing, it's too much fun to annoy so many people so effortlessly and consistently. For another, there's no doubt that rock is worth taking seriously, if just because the good stuff is so ridiculously good and the bad so totally aggravating.

However, the time has clearly come for corrective action. You're holding it in your hand. If some readers feel that anyone involved in the production of these pages has taken rock—or anything else—too seriously, that's their problem. (Maybe they take books too seriously.)

Undeniably, and probably unfortunately, there is some straightforward and utilitarian material contained here. Judging from the monumental ignorance and sheer neglect rock has suffered over the years, one trusts these facts won't interfere with the process of trivialization at hand. As an additional precaution, we have taken the liberty of making our standards as murky as possible. We have chosen, for instance, not to regard such minor musical cretins as Bobby Rydell and such obvious lames as John Denver as part of our rock universe— except when it suits our purpose. It wouldn't be fair to say that *The Book of Rock Lists* is written in code, but it wouldn't be unfair to say that no one is going to get all of the jokes and inside references. Tough trivia, in my opinion; there's nothing more disgusting than a book that hasn't got the courage of its own contradictions. Call us obtuse, call us elitist, but never call us obsequious. (There are even items here of which *the editors* have not divined the meaning. Naturally, we're not telling which ones, though I'll give you a hint: If you can figure out how *anybody* can do the Twist to *Katy Lied*, please write.)

If we remain in danger of misimpressing anyone, it is probably wise to assure all readers, right from the start, that any relevant material here is filler, pure and simple, and is in no way as significant as the outright lunacy and fanaticism that make up the bulk of the volume. Although it does strike me that even some of the factual material is pretty absurd. At least that's how we felt when we discovered that the ultimate singles band of all time, Creedence Clearwater Revival, had never had a Number One single. Or when confronted with the undeniable evidence that Linda Ronstadt has more platinum records than The Who and Elvis Presley combined. (This was not the situation that inspired the immortal Elvis Costello couplet, "I used to be disgusted/Now I try to be amused." But it could have been.)

When Kevin Stein and I first planned this book in the winter of 1979, we characterized it as "an act of revenge." (Kevin's brother, Jeff, who directed *The Kids Are Alright*, also thinks we take this stuff too seriously, and he's probably right, since we both liked the movie.) For far too long, Kevin and I, as fans and critics, had witnessed the ludicrous disintegration of rock; and its hardiness in the face of all attempts (many self-inflicted) to kill it off simply seemed stupid if all rock boils down to is Chuck Berry on the *Tomorrow* show and some underweight, overage limey yapping about "ant people." At the time, it seemed that rock, while not dead, was decrepit beyond hope. And that, since we somehow still found ourselves caring about it, the only solution was to dance right about where its grave should have been.

Of course, like Dracula, if not the angels, rock is immortal, which we discovered (not necessarily to our chagrin) as we dived ever deeper into the project. One of the first lists we created was the best singles of 1962, which led us to Little

Eva's "Keep Your Hands Off My Baby," the sequel to "The Loco-Motion" and one of those rare instances in which a totally off-the-wall hit has inspired a successor of equal quality and weirdness. Someone proposed Duane Eddy's "Some Kinda Earthquake" for the shortest songs lists, and we were enlightened once again. Over and over, we found music we had forgotten about or never knew, most of it quite insipid on any terms but its own, and all of it inspiring.

That, in the end, is what keeps us going—not so much a sense of revenge for all the years of boredom, but the awareness that because rock is so completely (hopelessly) disorganized and ambiguous, its pleasures are bottomless and can never be completely taken over by the merchants and the pundits. If we are in any way responsible for making this position less impregnable, at least we have the grace to regret it.

This doesn't mean we take rock seriously, just that we take it as it comes. In fact, right now, my favorite memory is of the night someone came up with an idea for a list of songs for "The Dictionary of Rock and Roll." "Songs about furniture," he said, decisively. "What'll be on it?" we wondered. "Well," he said with a killer's smile, "how about 'I'm a Rocker'?"

Some people never learn.

—Dave Marsh

ONE:
WISDOM

Chairman Townshend onstage at San Francisco's Cow Palace in 1968.

IRV ZUCKERMAN'S LIST OF 50 ROCK AND ROLL EXCUSES FOR ALL OCCASIONS

IRV ZUCKERMAN *is the leading concert promoter in St. Louis and Kansas City. He has also been involved in personal management, most notably with Head East. This list originally appeared as an advertisement in* Performance Magazine *and was compiled by Zuckerman, Steve Schankman, and Steve Litman.*

1   The check's in the mail.
2   He's in a meeting.
3   He's out to lunch.
4   He's got two calls waiting.
5   I'll call you on Monday.
6   Hold on for just a second.
7   I'll get right back to you.
8   The check should have been with the contracts.
9   He was supposed to get right back to me.
10 I've never met a girl like you before.
11 Didn't you get my message?
12 I lost my pass.
13 Of course I remember you.
14 We'll make it up to you next time.
15 Your name's on the list.
16 The mail must really be screwed up.
17 If only the album had come out sooner.
18 There's been a ton of shows in the market.
19 The record company is totally supporting this.
20 We're definitely buying strong support for the tour.
21 There's none in town.
22 It wasn't in the deal.
23 It's a last-minute town.
24 It's the best album they've ever made.
25 That's what everyone's paying.
26 Didn't you get the new rider?

27   They're going into ARBs.*
28   They're just coming out of ARBs.*
29   They said we're getting the bullet back next week.
30   He said it's in heavy rotation.
31   Of course you'll get a completed contract before the gig.
32   Of course they'll do interviews.
33   Our set never runs over.
34   There are T-shirts for everyone.
35   These jackets run really small.
36   The hall sounds a lot better when the kids are inside.
37   It sounds great out front.
38   You should see 'em live.
39   They said they don't have much equipment.
40   But they're huge in England.
41   It's an easy load-in.
42   They sound much better with the new singer.
43   They never do sound checks.
44   There's plenty of power.
45   He swore he'd bring the limo back in five minutes.
46   Nobody reads the reviews anyway.
47   We're losing on the sound and lights.
48   There's no place open this late.
49   They always do it this way.
50   It's a union rule.

*ARB is a radio rating service, similar to television's Nielsen ratings. The rating samples are taken only a few weeks each year; these periods are also commonly referred to as ARBs.

CUB KODA'S 10 RULES OF ROCK AND ROLL

1   The best gig in the world is a packed bar on a Friday night. Reason: Everybody gets paid and everybody wants to get laid. Any band that can't go over on a Friday night should be shot.

2   Rock and roll operates on the beat of the Geedus. Put the money in the Cubmaster's hand and the Cub will rock (i.e., no Geedus, no rockus).

3   There *is* a difference between rock and rock and roll; beware of inferior imitations (avoid contact with any musician who doesn't know how to play Chuck Berry music).

4   Junk food will keep you alive on the road; eat at White Castle and Krystal's as often as possible.

5   When you're out of Schmuzz, you're out of buzz; a day without Schmuzz is like a day without rock and roll.

6   Don't believe everything written about you. (Especially avoid fat, cigar-chewing record execs who keep telling you you're a genius; these guys never pay up.)

7   When you've got it to spend, everybody's your friend; if you're gonna blow all your money, at least leave a beautiful corpse.

8   Rock and roll musicians are the Men of the Great Indoors; avoid sunlight whenever possible and develop your moon tan.

9   Never give a roadie anything of value. (I have a large box of toothpicks in my kitchen cupboard that used to be a Les Paul.)

10   In the world of rock and roll, some gigs go fantastically, some are total crap. My best advice to young rock and rollers who find themselves in a crappy situation is to stare at the ceiling and scream at the top of their lungs: "Please, Reverend Jim, more Kool-Aid!"

Singer, guitarist, and songwriter CUB KODA *made his mark on the rock and roll charts with Brownsville Station, most notably with "Smokin' in the Boy's Room." A consummate record collector and author of the column "The Vinyl Junkie" in Gold-mine magazine, he has recorded two fine solo albums on the Baron label.*

ROBERT HUNTER'S 10 COMMANDMENTS OF ROCK AND ROLL

1   Suck up to the top cats.
2   Do not express independent opinions.
3   Do not work for common interests, only factional interests.
4   If there's nothing to complain about, dig up some old gripe.
5   Do not respect property or persons other than band property or personnel.
6   Make devastating judgments about persons and situations without adequate information.
7   Discourage and confound personal, technical, and/or creative projects.
8   Single out absent persons for intense criticism.
9   Remember that anything you don't understand is trying to fuck with you.
10   Destroy yourself physically and mentally and insist that all true brothers do likewise as an expression of unity.

ROBERT HUNTER *is a longtime lyricist for The Grateful Dead and has made several solo recordings.*

-◄❙❚►-

15 QUOTATIONS FROM CHAIRMAN TOWNSHEND

1   "People say, 'You've gotta go on, man, otherwise all those kids, they'll be finished, they'll have nothing to live for.' That's rock and roll!"
2   "Rock and roll is all that counts. I'll tell you, in ten years, you'll know. 'Cause ten years are past and we know."
3   "I think the thing really is that there's a certain honor attached to it because of the fact that rock has said: 'We will do it right. You've all done it wrong. We will do it right. We will show you

that not only can we write a song like 'My Generation' where we write off the Establishment, where we write off the politicians, where we write off the group, but we write off the whole lot of you! We will get it right!'"

4 "I am not a leader. Neither yours nor anyone else's. I am a rock musician, a mirror. You see yourself when you see The Who."

5 "Pop has become solemn, irrelevant, and boring. What it needs now is more noise, more size, more sex, more violence, more gimmickry, more vulgarity. Above all, it desperately needs a new messiah who will take things right back to the glamour, power, and insanity of the Elvis Presley age."

6 "I wrote the lines of 'My Generation' without thinking, hurrying them—scribbling on a piece of paper in the back of a car. For years I've had to live by them, waiting for the day when someone says, 'I thought you said you hoped you'd die when you got old. Well, now you are old. What now?' Of course, most people are too polite to say that sort of thing to a dying pop star. I say it often to myself."

7 "I realized that the only way I was ever going to fit into society and have a role was via the guitar."

8 "Let's face it, you can't worship a guy for destroying an instrument in the name of rock."

9 "I think that without having the stage and the guitar—the weapon of the guitar—I don't think I would have gone on."

10 "I smash guitars because I like them."

11 "I think you should keep on playing rock for as long as you have an axe to grind, and if you haven't got an axe to grind, you should go into cabaret."

12 "Rock is art and a million other things as well: It's an indescribable form of communication and entertainment combined, and it's a two-way thing with very complex but real feedback processes."

13 "Sometimes I really do believe that we're the only rock band on the face of this planet that knows what rock and roll is all about."

14   "Quite simply, I feel that The Stones are the world's best rock and roll band."

15   "Audiences are very much like the kids at Tommy's Holiday Camp: They want something without working for it."

PETE TOWNSHEND *has been rock's Supreme Pontiff since writing "My Generation" in his early teens. These are only the cream of his many critical pronouncements and outlines of rock philosophy.*

-◄▐▐►-

ROCK AND ROLL REFLECTIONS

1   "Middle-class kids make the best rock and roll."—ELLIOTT MURPHY

2   "Rhythm & blues? It's nothing but rock and roll without the movements."—MICKEY ASHMAN

3   "It's the music that kept us all intact . . . kept us from going crazy. You should have two radios in case one gets broken."—LOU REED

4   "Too many people are obsessed with pop music. The position of rock and roll in our subculture has become far too important, especially in the delving for philosophical content."—MICK JAGGER

5   "We like this kind of music. Jazz is strictly for the stay-at-homes."—BUDDY HOLLY

6   "It's not music, it's a disease."—MITCH MILLER

7   "We like to look sixteen and bored shitless."—DAVID JOHANSEN

8   "If I could find a white man who had the Negro sound and Negro feel, I could make a billion dollars."—SAM PHILLIPS

9   "I want to tell the world how the guy in the filling station feels."—JOHN D. LOUDERMILK

10   "Given the choice between accomplishing something and just lying around, I'd rather lie around. No contest."—ERIC CLAPTON

11   "Really, it's kind of like winning the football pools."—VAN MORRISON

12   "Rock and roll is a means of pulling the white man down to the level of the Negro. It is part of a plot to undermine the morals of the youth of our nation."—SECRETARY OF THE NORTH ALABAMA WHITE CITIZENS COUNCIL, circa 1956

13   "The Mersey Sound is the voice of 80,000 crumbling houses and 30,000 people on the dole."—The *Daily Worker*, 1963

14   "Rock and roll is phony and false, and it's sung, written, and played for the most part by cretinous goons."—FRANK SINATRA, 1957

15   "It's all soul."—JUNIOR WELLS

16   "Don't forget, the penis is mightier than the sword."
—SCREAMIN' JAY HAWKINS

17   "Rock and roll meant fucking, originally—which I don't think is a bad idea. Let's bring it back again."—WAYLON JENNINGS

18   "Rock is so much fun. That's what it's all about—filling up the chest cavities and the empty kneecaps and elbows."—JIMI HENDRIX

19   "Let's face it, rock and roll is bigger than all of us."—ALAN FREED

20   "It has no beginning and no end, for it is the very pulse of life itself."—LARRY WILLIAMS

21   "It's primarily not an intellectual thing. It's music, that's all."—JANN WENNER

22   "Pop music is sex, and you have to hit them in the face with it."—ANDREW LOOG OLDHAM

23   "It's just entertainment, and the kids who like to identify their youthful high spirits with a solid beat are thus possibly avoiding other pursuits that could be harmful to them."—BILL HALEY

24   "Rock and roll is an asylum for emotional imbeciles."
—RICHARD NEVILLE

25   "Rock and roll is simply an attitude. You don't have to play the greatest guitar."—JOHNNY THUNDERS

26   "It's better than fighting."—WILKO JOHNSON

27   "Rock and roll motivates. It's the big, gigantic motivator, at least it was for me."—BRUCE SPRINGSTEEN

-◀❚▶-

NORMAN PETTY'S INSTRUCTIONS TO THE CRICKETS

Producer NORMAN PETTY *gave The Crickets the following list of advice as they set out on their first tour away from their West Texas home. We discovered it in the booklet accompanying* The Complete Buddy Holly Story *album set. Much of it still seems relevant more than twenty years later.*

1   Be at the Amarillo air terminal by at least 6:30 to check reservations and check baggage.
2   Take enough cash to pay for excess weight and meals between flights. (He recommended thirty or forty dollars in cash, the rest in traveler's checks.—Eds.)
3   Be sure to take all available identification for each member of the group.
4   Sign only engagement contracts and nothing more.
5   Take extra sets of guitar strings, drumsticks, heads, etc.
6   Take out floater insurance for the entire group with everyone's name on the contract.
7   Be sure to pack records with clothes to take on trip.
8   Take all available clean underwear . . . and other articles for use on the trip.
9   When you get to New York . . . take a cab directly to the Edison Hotel and check in there.
10   Get at least two dozen Dramamine tablets . . . and take one tablet at least fifteen minutes before departure.
11   Make out trip insurance to your parents.
12   Take at least twenty-five feet of extension cord.
13   Take small shine kit.
14   Toilet articles of your choice.
15   Get telephone credit card and carry with you.

16   Take a small Bible with you and READ IT!
17   Get hotel credit cards or at least make applications for them.
18   Be sure to get and keep receipts for all money spent.
19   Be sure to send money to Clovis for bank account.

A MANAGER LISTS 10 REASONS WHY OUR RECORD ISN'T OUT YET

1   We haven't finished writing the music.
2   We haven't finished the lyrics.
3   We haven't finished the tracks.
4   We haven't finished mixing.
5   We haven't picked the takes.
6   We haven't got a title.
7   We haven't finished sequencing.
8   We haven't got a cover.
9   We don't like anything we've done; we're starting over.
10   Repeat all of above as needed.

NOTE: For obvious reasons, the manager in question prefers to remain anonymous.

MALCOLM McLAREN'S 10 LESSONS OF ROCK SUCCESS

1   Manufacture your group.
2   Establish the name.
3   Sell the Swindle.
4   Do not play. Do not give the game away.
5   Steal as much money as possible from the record company of your choice.
6   Become the world's greatest tourist attraction.

7   Cultivate hatred. It is your greatest asset.

8   Diversify business.

9   Take civilization to the barbarians.

10   Who killed Bambi?

MALCOLM MCLAREN, *manager of The Sex Pistols, is star of the posthumously released movie about the band,* The Great Rock 'n' Roll Swindle. *The picture elaborately presents McLaren's rules of promotional acumen, ostensibly those he used for the allegedly talentless Pistols.*

-◄▮►-

SLOGANS—UNFORGETTABLE AND REGRETTABLE

1   "Kill ugly radio."—The Mothers of Invention

2   "Disco sucks."—Rock and rollers, 1975 to 1978

3   "Happy Xmas, war is over if you want it."—John Lennon and Yoko Ono

4   "The man can't bust our music."—CBS Records

5   "Kick out the jams, motherfuckers."—The MC5

6   "Music, love, and flowers"—The Monterey International Pop Festival

7   "Three days of peace and music"—The Woodstock Festival

8   "The revolutionaries are on CBS."—CBS Records

9   "Kill for peace."—The Fugs

10   "I saw rock and roll future and its name is Bruce Springsteen."—Jon Landau

11   "On Warner/Reprise, where they belong."—Warner Bros. Records

12   "The sound of young America"—Motown Records

13   "Tomorrow's sound today"—Philles Records

14   "If it's a hit, it's Amazin'."—Amazin' Records

15   "We love you Beatles, oh yes we do."—Beatlemaniacs, 1964 to 1980

STIFF RECORDS' SLOGANS

Stiff Records is the renegade English label founded by Jake Riviera, manager of Elvis Costello, and David Robinson, manager of Graham Parker; it was started in the mid-seventies as a tongue-in-cheek but surprisingly successful alternative to the major labels' pomp and happenstance marketing. Over the years, the company has used a variety of revealing, satirical slogans to express its attitude.

1   "If it ain't Stiff, it ain't no use to no one." (Sanitized version, used on a T-shirt; the original was: "If it ain't Stiff, it ain't worth a fuck.")
2   "Reversing into tomorrow."
3   "If they're dead—we'll sign 'em."
4   "Undertakers to the industry."
5   "The world's most flexible record label."
6   "Trivia for the collector."
7   "The shape of things that win."
8   "Where money makes money."
9   "We came, we saw, we left."
10   "Be Stiff."
11   "Surfing on the New Wave."
12   "Preplanned deletions."
13   "Where industry aids nature."

Two: MONEY

"You know," muses a cheery Don Van Vliet, a.k.a. Captain Beefheart, shortly after cashing a royalty check, "It's things like this that make it all seem worthwhile."

SHAKE YOUR MONEYMAKER

1    $230 Million: promoter Sid Bernstein's estimated gross for a single Beatles reunion concert, 1980

2    $25 Million: amount of insurance policy taken out by MCA Records with Lloyd's of London on Elton John's life, 1975

3    $10 Million: alleged value of Elvis Presley's estate, 1977

4    $1 Million: cost of recording Fleetwood Mac's *Tusk*, 1979–1980

5    $110,000: advance paid by Atlantic Records for Led Zeppelin, 1969

6    $100,000: cost of recording The Beatles' *Sgt. Pepper's Lonely Hearts Club Band*, 1967

7    $75,000: initial advance paid by Polydor on signing The Who, 1965

8    $40,000, plus $5000 bonus: paid to Elvis on signing with RCA Records, 1956 ($35,000 also paid to Sam Phillips for Presley's Sun contract)

9    $30,000: annual royalties to Paul Anka for the "Tonight Show Theme"

10    $18,000: cost of producing The Knack's first album, *Get the Knack*, 1979

11    $3200: Lorne Michael's final bid to The Beatles to perform on *Saturday Night Live*, 1978

12   £1400: damage done by The Who and entourage to Bonaventure Hotel in Montreal, 1973

13    $2500: bail bond posted by Bill Graham for release of Roger Daltrey and Pete Townshend, who were thrown in jail after kicking a policeman during a Fillmore East concert, 1969

14    $2400: paid to The Beatles for their *Ed Sullivan Show* appearance, February 9, 1964

15    $50: paid to Bob Dylan for performing on harmonica on a Harry Belafonte album, 1960

CAREER OPPORTUNITIES
20 Songs about Working

1 "Big Boss Man," JIMMY REED
2 "Chain Gang," SAM COOKE
3 "Don't Look Now (It Ain't You or Me)," CREEDENCE CLEARWATER REVIVAL
4 "Factory," BRUCE SPRINGSTEEN
5 "Five O'Clock World," THE VOGUES
6 "Found a Job," TALKING HEADS
7 "Friday on My Mind," THE EASYBEATS
8 "Get a Job," THE SILHOUETTES
9 "Got a Job," THE MIRACLES
10 "A Hard Day's Night," THE BEATLES
11 "If We Make It Through December," MERLE HAGGARD
12 "Keep on Working," PETE TOWNSHEND
13 "Luxury," THE ROLLING STONES
14 "Maggie's Farm," BOB DYLAN
15 "Night Shift," BOB MARLEY AND THE WAILERS
16 "Sixteen Tons," TENNESSEE ERNIE FORD
17 "Summertime Blues," EDDIE COCHRAN
18 "Welcome to the Working Week," ELVIS COSTELLO
19 "Workin' for the Man," ROY ORBISON
20 "Working in the Coal Mine," LEE DORSEY

-◄❚▮❚►-

REALLY BIG RECORD DEALS

1 **PAUL SIMON with Warner Bros.,** 1979
   Partly a result of a bidding war between Warner and Columbia, Simon's former company, this pact resulted in Simon being paid $14 million for seven albums. Simon also managed to gain some money from Warner toward the promotion of any future film and theatrical projects.

2   **PAUL MCCARTNEY with CBS,** 1979
We know it's a big deal, and talk in the trade suggests it's at least of the dimensions of Paul Simon's Warner Bros. contract. However, neither CBS nor McCartney's representatives will confirm any details.

3   **STEVIE WONDER with Motown,** 1975
Wonder has threatened to leave Motown several times; he first made noises in that direction in 1971, when he reached twenty-one. But he's never departed, probably because the company has always come through for him. In 1971, the issue was artistic control; Stevie got it, and it paid off beyond anyone's wildest expectations. Four years later, he signed a contract said to be worth about $13 million.

4   **ELTON JOHN with MCA,** 1975
When Elton John made his $8 million deal, he was perhaps the biggest recording star in the world. The bubble has since burst, and he now sells far fewer records than he once did.

5   **THE ROLLING STONES with Atlantic,** 1976
Not too much is known of this deal. RSO withdrew from the bidding at $8 million, but perhaps this figure reflected worldwide rights. Atlantic Records reportedly secured The Stones for U.S. and Canadian distribution at $7 million for seven albums. However, The Stones also contracted at the same time with EMI for the rest of the world. Since the U.S. represents less than half of the worldwide market, the total amount The Stones received must be considerably higher.

6   **BOB DYLAN with CBS,** 1975
No one knows how much Dylan got for returning to CBS after a two-album visit with Asylum. His publicist says he receives $1 million per album, but industry practice suggests that Dylan also received retroactive royalty increases for his back catalog.

7   **NEIL DIAMOND with Columbia,** 1972
It doesn't seem like much now, but when Clive Davis signed Diamond and guaranteed him $400,000 per album shortly before Davis' demise as CBS Records president, it looked like the height of folly. CBS, of course, almost immediately made

all its money back with the dire but highly successful *Jonathan Livingston Seagull* soundtrack, which sold 7 million copies. Diamond then renegotiated to an advance of $1 million per album.

8   **RAY CHARLES with ABC-Paramount,** 1960
Charles probably got between $50,000 and $100,000 for leaving Atlantic, where he'd become enormously successful. The industry was outraged at the amount, and disaster was predicted. Charles then created a series of country-soul hits—"Hit the Road Jack," "Georgia on My Mind" and "Your Cheating Heart"—that established him as a greater star than ever, and the deal was vindicated.

9   **CLYDE MCPHATTER with Mercury,** 1960
McPhatter got about the same amount as Charles did for leaving Atlantic in the lurch, but this time, the results were less positive. Although he had some hits, he was never again as big as he was under Atlantic's guidance.

10   **JOHNNY WINTER with CBS,** 1969
Winter had been touted in a *Rolling Stone* feature, but almost no one had heard his music when this deal was made. To put matters in perspective, although this deal was considered outrageous at the time, Winter's guarantee per album was only about $100,000, a pittance by today's standards.

11   **CHICAGO with CBS,** mid-1970s
The size of the band's advance is not especially notable, but Chicago, during its glory days, was rumored to be the first act to achieve a royalty of more than one dollar per record sold.

12   **THE EAGLES with Asylum,** 1975–1980
The Eagles originally signed with David Geffen, who is known for making parsimonious advances while offering luxurious royalties. But since the band became an enormous international success, the contract has been renegotiated and extended so many times that what it might now be worth (if the group records long enough to cash in on all of it) is unfathomable.

REALLY DUMB RECORD DEALS

1 **DELANEY AND BONNIE with Columbia,** 1972
When Delaney and Bonnie decided they wanted out of their
contract with Atlantic, to whom they'd turned after making one
record for Stax and one for Elektra, they chose Columbia—and
Clive Davis—as their next option. Or target. In his autobiography, *Clive: Inside the Record Business*, Davis says that he
signed the group to a contract for seven years and $600,000.
He doesn't mention the hefty amount paid to Atlantic for the
contract, including a substantial override on Columbia's income. Didn't matter, anyhow: Delaney and Bonnie broke up
almost immediately, without ever making an album for their
fourth label.

2 **THE SEX PISTOLS with A&M,** 1977
After The Pistols were dropped by EMI for their licentious
behavior during an appearance on the BBC, A&M Records (a
company as staid in West Coast terms as EMI is in British
ones) decided to pick them up. The deal lasted about a week,
engendered heavy protest from more conventional A&M artists, and, of course, The Pistols walked off with a bundle
without recording a note for the label.

3 **Sale of ELVIS PRESLEY to RCA,** 1955
Sam Phillips sold Presley's Sun Records contract for $35,000,
flat. He retained no royalty percentage for Presley's future
work, a miscalculation worth millions. Legend says that
Phillips thought Carl Perkins would be bigger, anyhow.

4 **GAMBLE AND HUFF with Atlantic,** 1971
When Kenneth Gamble and Leon Huff were getting started as
record producers, their closest relationship was with Atlantic,
where they produced Archie Bell and the Drells, among
others. But when Gamble and Huff created Philadelphia
International Records in 1971, Atlantic passed on their
distribution deal as too expensive. Their new label went on to
become one of the major successes of the decade, of course.

This deal (actually, the absence of one) just about makes up for . . .

5 **STAX WITH CBS,** 1973

Stax Records was distributed by Atlantic almost from the company's beginnings in the early sixties. But in 1973, Clive Davis, desperate to shore up CBS' weak position in black music, lured Stax away from Atlantic for considerable bucks. Unfortunately, the tide in black pop taste was turning, the company was in ruinous financial condition, and Stax was a complete bust during its tenure with CBS distribution.

6 **DAVID CROSBY and GRAHAM NASH with ABC,** 1974

Crosby and Nash were signed to Atlantic Records as part of Crosby, Stills, and Nash. Both had also made solo albums, as well as one duet record, for Atlantic. In 1974, Crosby and Nash were signed to ABC, but Atlantic retained a hefty position. The label kept all tape rights—about one-fourth of the potential sales volume of their music. Naturally, ABC footed all the promotion and advertising expenses for the Crosby and Nash LPs but got only three-fourths of the reward it should have.

-◄❙❙►-

ANNUAL RECORD AND TAPE SALES

These figures are somewhat deceptive, because the Recording Industry Association of America (RIAA), which began compiling them in 1921, calculates sales volume on the basis of list price, but records and tapes are almost never sold at more than about 80 percent of that mythical figure. Nonetheless, because RIAA figures don't account for the enormous amount of money spent on concert tickets and other music-related purchases, the proportions are fairly correct for the music business as a whole. It's also worth noting that the more than $4 billion gross depicted in 1978 is a spectacular illusion, since that year proved to be more disastrous than prosperous because of a vast upsurge in the number of unsold records and tapes returned to producers. The 1979 total, then, indicates some return to sanity, at least as far as manufacturers' shippings and returns policies are concerned.

Year	Records ($ figures in millions)	Tapes ($ figures in millions)	Total ($ figures in millions)
1921	$105.6	—	$105.6
1930	$46.2	—	$46.2
1940	$48.4	—	$48.4
1945*	$109	—	$109
1950	$189	—	$189
1954**	$213	—	$213
1955	$277	—	$277
1956†	$377	—	$377
1957	$460	—	$460
1958	$511	—	$511
1959	$603	—	$603
1960	$600	—	$600
1961	$640	—	$640
1962	$687	—	$687
1963	$698	—	$698
1964††	$758	—	$758
1965	$862	—	$862
1966	$959	—	$959
1967‡	$1051	$122	$1173
1968	$1124	$234	$1358
1969	$1170	$416	$1586
1970	$1182	$478	$1660
1971	$1251	$493	$1744
1972	$1383	$541	$1924
1973	$1436	$580.6	$2016.6
1974	$1550	$650.2	$2200.2

Year	Records ($ figures in millions)	Tapes ($ figures in millions)	Total ($ figures in millions)
1975	$1696	$692	$2388
1976	$1908	$829	$2737
1977	$2440.2	$1060.6	$3500.8
1978	$2733.6	$1397.8	$4131.4
1979	$2411.2	$1264.9	$3676.1

* After the Depression and World War II, sales volume finally catches up to 1921 level.

**Beginning of rock and roll era

† Elvis' first big year

††The Beatles arrive in America.

‡ This is the first year in which the RIAA separates tape sales from album volume—just as cassettes and eight-track tapes begin to catch on. By the end of the seventies, record sales volume would triple (partly through price increases), but tape volume would increase by ten times, with far fewer price increases to account for the dramatic surge.

-◄▮►-

THIS MAGIC MOGUL
Rock Businessmen Worth Their Percentages

1 **COLONEL TOM PARKER**

He may not have had much artistic sense, but he maximized the profits of his one and only client from 1955 onward—Elvis Presley, of course.

2 **SAM PHILLIPS**

Not a great businessman, perhaps (he did sell Elvis' recording contract to RCA for only $35,000, which makes buying Manhattan for twenty-four dollars look like a stroke of genius on the part of the Indians), but he was as creative a figure in the studio as the world has known. And if Carl Perkins hadn't had that car accident, things might have been somewhat different.

3   **FRANK BARSALONA**

As the first booking agent to realize that you didn't have to have hit records to do successful concerts, Barsalona virtually invented the modern concept of the rock and roll tour. Indeed, working with acts as diverse as Mitch Ryder, Herman's Hermits, The Who, and a flood of English middleweights (Yes; Emerson, Lake, and Palmer; Ten Years After), he reversed the process and for a time made touring more profitable than recording for many acts. His Premier Talent Agency spawned heavy-metal music.

4   **BILL GRAHAM**

Infuriating, patronizing, simply obnoxious Graham is also the very best concert promoter rock has known. He was the genius of the rock ballroom, and was slick enough to make a big deal over folding the Fillmore East and West when their demise became inevitable; his monument is his assortment of tirades during the closing of the San Francisco club in the 1972 film *Fillmore*. You don't have to like him, but respecting him is unavoidable—which is all he's ever asked.

5   **AHMET ERTEGUN**

Though he couldn't have built Atlantic Records without partners like his brother Nesuhi, Jerry Wexler, and Herb Abramson, Ertegun looms more and more as the record executive all the rest strive to emulate. A patrician with a yen for the greatest gutter delicacies, he nonetheless has exquisite tastes, even if Atlantic's releases don't always reflect it these days. Besides which, Ahmet is the only record executive of major stature, except for Sam Phillips and Wexler, to have had substantial impact as a creative figure, both for his productions and songwriting. If all he had done was write "The Mess Around," the great Ray Charles piano tune, Ahmet Ertegun would still be a legend.

6   **DAVID GEFFEN**

The prince of Hollywood pop, Geffen created an enormous number of careers—Jackson Browne, The Eagles, Laura Nyro, and Joni Mitchell are only the most obvious ones. As a manager, agent, and record executive (Asylum Records was his original brainchild), Geffen is, among other things, Ertegun's most brilliant student. He returned to the record business in 1980, with Geffen Records, whose initial artist roster included Donna Summer, John Lennon, and Elton John.

7   **BERRY GORDY JR.**

America's most successful black businessman as founder of Motown, one of rock's two greatest record companies (the other is Atlantic, with Asylum a close third), Gordy is a major songwriter and producer in his own right.

8   **DON KIRSHNER**

Yes, he looks like a fool as the host of a TV show. But who do you think ran the songwriting mills that produced Carole King and Gerry Goffin, Neil Diamond, Barry Mann and Cynthia Weil, and so many others in the early sixties? No class, but *mucho dinero*.

9   **MICHAEL TANNEN**

Lawyer Tannen has become the best contract negotiator in the contemporary music world; he made Paul Simon's eight-figure pact with Warner Bros., renegotiated Bruce Springsteen's Columbia contract, represents Billy Joel, and represented John Lennon and The Rolling Stones. Low-key, *very* tough.

SHREWD INVESTORS

1   PAUL ANKA, music publishing, modern-art collection
2   FRANK BARSALONA, owns one of America's best art collections
3   JAMES BROWN, real estate
4   DICK CLARK, film, TV, and other holdings
5   DAVID GEFFEN, art collection, among other things
6   DON KIRSHNER, music publishing, broadcasting
7   JOHN LENNON, YOKO ONO, cattle, real estate
8   PAUL McCARTNEY, music publishing

9   THE MILLS BROTHERS, own substantial holdings in blue-chip stock
10   TED NUGENT, owns one of the ten largest mink ranches in the world
11   THE RAVENS, own Ravenwood Turkey Farm, Maryland
12   PAUL SIMON, music publishing

-◄❚❚▶-

ROCK'S RAREST 45s

It is impossible to accurately pinpoint the dollar value of these singles. Most of them are so rare that they show up infrequently in sales and auctions, and most prices quoted in the various price guides have been wildly overstated. However, it's certain that none of these records is worth less than $200 in near mint condition.

1   "That's All Right," ELVIS PRESLEY (Sun 209)
2   "Good Rockin' Tonight," ELVIS PRESLEY (Sun 210)
3   "Milkcow Blues Boogie," ELVIS PRESLEY (Sun 215)
4   "Baby, Let's Play House," ELVIS PRESLEY (Sun 217)
5   "My Bonnie," TONY SHERIDAN AND THE BEAT BROTHERS, a.k.a. THE BEATLES (Decca 31382, U.S.)
6   "I Really Don't Want to Know," THE FLAMINGOS (Parrot 811)
7   "Tell the World," THE DELLS (Vee Jay 134)
8   "No One to Love Me," THE SHA-WEEZ (Aladdin 3170)
9   "Yes Sir, That's My Baby," THE CLOVERS (Rainbow 122)
10   "My Baby's Gone," THE FIVE THRILLS (Parrott 796)
11   "These Foolish Things," THE FIVE KEYS (Aladdin 3190)
12   "Inebriated Surfer," THE HOLLYWOOD TORNADOES (Aertaun 102)
13   "Pittery Pat," DAVEY HOLT AND THE HUBCAPS (United Artists 110)

Rock's 10 rarest albums

1   *Speedway*, Elvis Presley, original soundtrack (RCA Victor LPM-3989, mono), $1200
2   *The Beatles and Frank Ifield* (VeeJay LPS 1085, stereo), $600
3   *Yesterday . . . and Today*, The Beatles, butcher-block cover (Capitol ST2553, stereo), $400
4   *Johnny Burnette and the Rock and Roll Trio* (Coral CRL 57080, mono), $400
5   *Elvis' Christmas Album*, Elvis Presley, deluxe edition with picture booklet and gold sticker (RCA Victor LOC-1035), $400
6   *The Freewheelin' Bob Dylan*, containing "Let Me Die in My Footsteps" (Columbia CL 1936, mono), $200
7   *Impact*, Kenny and the Kasuals (Mark LP5000, mono), $200
8   *Joyride*, The Four Lovers, later named The Four Seasons (RCA LPM 1317, mono), $150
9   *The Avons* (Hull HLP 1000, mono), $100
10 *That'll Be the Day*, Buddy Holly (Decca DL 86707, mono), $100

NOTE: Prices are approximations depending on condition.

-◄❙▮▶-

Bankrupt

1   Mitch Ryder, 1970
2   Martha Reeves, 1972
3   Isaac Hayes, 1976
4   Marvin Gaye, 1978
5   Tom Petty, 1979

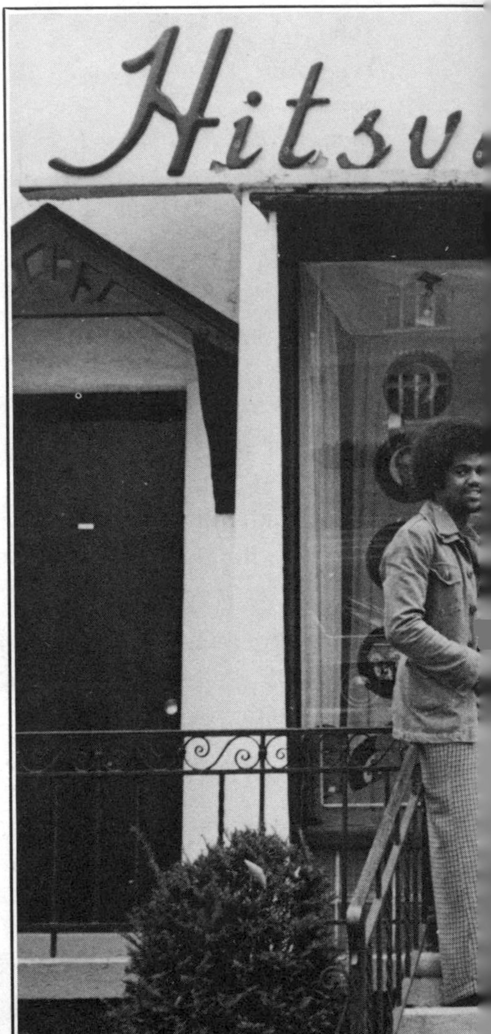
Hitsv

THREE:
RECORD COMPANIES

15 PROBLEMS ARTISTS HAVE WITH RECORD COMPANIES

1 Being put on hold
2 Getting someone to listen to your tape or come to your show
3 Verbal agreements that end with the words *trust me*
4 Not being able to work until the advance is paid off
5 Lack of tour support
6 Deliberate miscount on number of records sold
7 Royalties withheld as a "provision for returns"
8 Counterfeiting within the company
9 Salesmen dumping promo copies instead of distributing them
10 Publishing swindles as a condition of release from bad contracts
11 Inappropriate packaging
12 Failure to distribute records effectively
13 Loss of interest after initial signing period
14 Insistence on using staff producers or company-owned studios
15 Ruthless and premature record deletion policies

THE 5 MOST INNOVATIVE RECORD COMPANIES

1 **Sun**
   Invented rock and roll as we know it. Founded in the early fifties by Memphis talent scout and recording studio owner Sam Phillips, Sun nurtured as much talent as any label in history: Rufus Thomas, Carl Perkins, The Prisonaires, Jerry Lee Lewis, Charlie Rich, Johnny Cash, Billy Lee Riley, and biggest and best of all, Elvis Presley. Indeed, in the case of Presley, it might be said that Elvis supplied the talent and Sam Phillips provided the vision.

2   **Atlantic**

Proved that an independent company could compete on an equal footing with the majors. Formed in the late forties by two young Turkish aristocrats, Ahmet and Nesuhi Ertegun, and their dentist partner, Herb Abramson, Atlantic created a very appealing style of rhythm & blues, culminating in recordings by The Drifters (featuring Clyde McPhatter), The Coasters, and Ray Charles, all of which helped bring authentic black voices into the American musical mainstream. Without the capital resources of the major labels, Atlantic made its stand and continued to grow with a mixture of soul and British rock acts through the late sixties, when it was sold to Warner Bros.

3   **Motown**

Obliterated the marketing distinctions between pop and soul. Former Detroit record-store owner Berry Gordy Jr. created a veritable hitmaking machine that spewed dozens of unforgettable smashes by such stars as Smokey Robinson and the Miracles, Diana Ross and the Supremes, Marvin Gaye, The Four Tops, Stevie Wonder, Martha Reeves and the Vandellas, and The Temptations. These artists split their appeal between black and teenage white audiences, living up to the label's motto: "The sound of young America."

4   **Stiff**

Proved that an independent company did not have to compete on an equal basis with the majors. By the mid-seventies, when Jake Riviera and Dave Robinson, a pair of minor-league English music businessmen, gathered their forces (Nick Lowe, Elvis Costello, Ian Dury) to form Stiff, the majors had backed independent labels into a corner, driving up artist prices and marketing costs to a point where it was all but unimaginable for canny entrepreneurs without great capital resources to survive. Stiff stood such equations on their head by creating an environment that determinedly opposed such strategies, attracting marginal but profitable renegades.

5   **Rough Trade**

With such acts as The Slits, The Delta Five, The Young

Marble Giants, and others, Rough Trade, an English consortium of groups and support personnel, was the first successful collective in the rock business.

-◄❙▶-

SUN RECORDS' 20 GREATEST HITS

1   "Whole Lot of Shakin' Going On," JERRY LEE LEWIS, 1957
2   "Good Rockin' Tonight," ELVIS, SCOTTY AND BILL, 1954
3   "Blue Suede Shoes," CARL PERKINS, 1956
4   "Mystery Train," ELVIS, SCOTTY AND BILL, 1955
5   "Milkcow Blues Boogie," ELVIS PRESLEY, 1955
6   "Ooby Dooby," ROY ORBISON AND THE TEEN KINGS, 1956
7   "Red Hot," BILLY RILEY AND THE LITTLE GREEN MEN, 1957
8   "Lonely Weekends," CHARLIE RICH, 1960
9   "Dixie Fried," CARL PERKINS, 1956
10   "Great Balls of Fire," JERRY LEE LEWIS, 1957
11   "Flyin' Saucers Rock & Roll," BILLY RILEY AND THE LITTLE GREEN MEN, 1957
12   "Ubangi Stomp," WARREN SMITH, 1956
13   "That's All Right," ELVIS PRESLEY, 1954
14   "Just Walkin' in the Rain," THE PRISONAIRES, 1954
15   "High School Confidential," JERRY LEE LEWIS, 1958
16   "Breathless," JERRY LEE LEWIS, 1958
17   "Devil Doll," ROY ORBISON AND THE ROSES, 1960
18   "Who Will the Next Fool Be," CHARLIE RICH, 1960
19   "Mona Lisa," CARL MANN, 1959
20   "Bear Cat (the Answer to Hound Dog)," RUFUS THOMAS, 1953

-◄❙▶-

MOTOWN'S TOP 40

1   "I Heard It Through the Grapevine," MARVIN GAYE, 1968
2   "Reach Out I'll Be There," THE FOUR TOPS, 1966

3   "The Tracks of My Tears," SMOKEY ROBINSON AND THE MIRACLES, 1965
4   "I Want You Back," THE JACKSON 5, 1970
5   "Money," BARRETT STRONG, 1960
6   "Dancing in the Street," MARTHA AND THE VANDELLAS, 1964
7   "Ain't No Mountain High Enough," MARVIN GAYE and TAMMI TERRELL, 1967
8   "I Wish It Would Rain," THE TEMPTATIONS, 1968
9   "You Keep Me Hangin' On," THE SUPREMES, 1966
10   "Fingertips—Pt. 2," LITTLE STEVIE WONDER, 1963
11   "Ain't That Peculiar," MARVIN GAYE, 1965
12   "My Girl," THE TEMPTATIONS, 1965
13   "The Love I Saw in You Was Just a Mirage," SMOKEY ROBINSON AND THE MIRACLES, 1967
14   "My Whole World Ended (the Moment You Left Me)," DAVID RUFFIN, 1969
15   "Let's Get It On," MARVIN GAYE, 1973
16   "Papa Was a Rollin' Stone," THE TEMPTATIONS, 1972
17   "Do You Love Me," THE CONTOURS, 1962
18   "You've Really Got a Hold on Me," THE MIRACLES, 1963
19   "Stop! In the Name of Love," THE SUPREMES, 1965
20   "Heat Wave," MARTHA AND THE VANDELLAS, 1963
21   "What Becomes of the Brokenhearted," JIMMY RUFFIN, 1966
22   "Superstition," STEVIE WONDER, 1973
23   "My Guy," MARY WELLS, 1964
24   "Every Little Bit Hurts," BRENDA HOLLOWAY, 1964
25   "Shotgun," JR. WALKER AND THE ALL STARS, 1965
26   "I Can't Help Myself," THE FOUR TOPS, 1965
27   "The Way You Do the Things You Do," THE TEMPTATIONS, 1964
28   "What's Going On," MARVIN GAYE, 1971
29   "Ooo Baby Baby," THE MIRACLES, 1965
30   "Uptight (Everything's Alright)," STEVIE WONDER, 1966
31   "I Second That Emotion," SMOKEY ROBINSON AND THE MIRACLES, 1967

32   "Signed, Sealed, Delivered I'm Yours," STEVIE WONDER, 1970
33   "It Takes Two," MARVIN GAYE and KIM WESTON, 1967
34   "Three Times a Lady," THE COMMODORES, 1978
35   "Since I Lost My Baby," THE TEMPTATIONS, 1965
36   "If I Were Your Woman," GLADYS KNIGHT AND THE PIPS, 1971
37   "Bernadette," THE FOUR TOPS, 1967
38   "The Hunter Gets Captured by the Game," THE MARVELLETTES, 1967
39   "Leaving Here," EDDIE HOLLAND, 1964
40   "Love Is Here and Now You're Gone," THE SUPREMES, 1967

-◄▮▶-

THE 25 GREATEST STAX/VOLT HITS

1   "Soul Man," SAM AND DAVE, 1967
2   "Knock on Wood," EDDIE FLOYD, 1966
3   "(Sittin' on) the Dock of the Bay," OTIS REDDING, 1968
4   "In the Midnight Hour," WILSON PICKETT, 1965
5   "These Arms of Mine," OTIS REDDING, 1963
6   "When Something Is Wrong with My Baby," SAM AND DAVE, 1967
7   "Time Is Tight," BOOKER T. AND THE MGs, 1969
8   "Everybody Loves a Winner," WILLIAM BELL, 1967
9   "Hold On! I'm A Comin'," SAM AND DAVE, 1966
10   "634-5789," WILSON PICKETT, 1966
11   "Who's Making Love," JOHNNIE TAYLOR, 1968
12   "Green Onions," BOOKER T. AND THE MGs, 1962
13   "I've Been Loving You Too Long," OTIS REDDING, 1965
14   "Private Number," JUDY CLAY AND WILLIAM BELL, 1968
15   "Tramp," OTIS AND CARLA, 1967
16   "Respect Yourself," THE STAPLE SINGERS, 1971
17   "Your Good Thing (Is About to End)," MABLE JOHN, 1966
18   "Mr. Pitiful," OTIS REDDING, 1965
19   "Walking the Dog," RUFUS THOMAS, 1963

20   "Born under a Bad Sign," ALBERT KING, 1967
21   "You Don't Miss Your Water," WILLIAM BELL, 1962
22   "Last Night," THE MAR-KEYS, 1961
23   "Raise Your Hand," EDDIE FLOYD, 1967
24   "You Don't Know Like I Know," SAM AND DAVE, 1966
25   "Fa-Fa-Fa-Fa-Fa," OTIS REDDING, 1966

NOTE: Wilson Pickett recorded "In the Midnight Hour" and "634-5789" at Stax Studios, with the house musicians, but they were issued on the Atlantic label.

·◄▐▐►·

THE 10 GREATEST ARTIST- AND PRODUCER-OWNED RECORD LABELS

1   Apple, THE BEATLES (Jackie Lomax, Badfinger, Billy
     Preston, Doris Troy, among many others)
2   Philles, PHIL SPECTOR (The Crystals, The Ronettes, The
     Righteous Brothers, Darlene Love)
3   Red Bird and Blue Cat, JERRY LEIBER, MIKE STOLLER,
     GEORGE GOLDNER (The Shangri-Las, The Dixie Cups, The
     Ad Libs, The Trade Winds)
4   Bang, BERT BERNS, AHMET ERTEGUN, NESUHI ERTEGUN,
     JERRY WEXLER (Neil Diamond, Van Morrison, The McCoys,
     The Strangeloves)
5   Philadelphia International, KENNETH GAMBLE, LEON HUFF
     (Teddy Pendergrass, The O'Jays, MFSB, McFadden and
     Whitehead)
6   UK, JONATHAN KING (10cc, First Class, Jonathan King)
7   Curtom, CURTIS MAYFIELD (The Impressions, Leroy Hutson)
8   SwanSong, LED ZEPPELIN (Bad Company, Dave Edmunds)
9   Invictus/Hot Wax, HOLLAND-DOZIER-HOLLAND (Chairmen of
     the Board, Laura Lee, 8th Day, Freda Payne)
10   Bizarre/Straight, FRANK ZAPPA (Alice Cooper, Captain
     Beefheart, Wildman Fischer, The GTOs)

OFFSHOOTS OF APPLE CORPS.

1   **Apple Records**
    The record company was set up by The Beatles to distribute both their own records and associated acts (among the first were James Taylor, who left in a huff, and the Iveys, who became Badfinger).

2   **Zapple Records**
    Apple's first and only subsidiary label released only two albums: John Lennon and Yoko Ono's *Unfinished Music No. 2: Life with the Lions* and George Harrison's *Electronic Sound,* both in 1969.

3   **Apple Foundation of the Arts**
    Formed in conjunction with the record label, the foundation was established "for the encouragement of unknown talents."

4   **Apple Electronics**
    A branch of the larger Apple tree, specializing in sophisticated, often impractical developments in audio and visual technology, Apple Electronics featured Magic Alex, the supposed electronics wizard who persuaded Lennon to spend large sums of money on Alex' "inventions," most of which were psychedelic flights of fancy.

5   **Apple Films**
    Let It Be was the film branch's only notable production.

6   **Apple Publishing**
    The music publishing house was set up partly to give the band an out in the protracted dispute with Associated Television over control of the Northern Songs publishing company owned by Dick James, Lennon, and Paul McCartney.

7   **Apple Boutique**
    This London clothing store was opened on December 5, 1967. On July 30, 1968, the entire stock was given away when The Beatles decided that "the retail business wasn't our particular scene."

25 ARTISTS WHO WERE ON APPLE RECORDS

1   BADFINGER (The Iveys)
2   THE BEATLES
3   THE BLACK'DYKE MILLS BAND
4   BRUTE FORCE
5   THE ELASTIC OZ BAND
6   ELEPHANT'S MEMORY
7   GEORGE HARRISON
8   CHRIS HODGE
9   MARY HOPKIN
10 HOT CHOCOLATE
11 JOHN LENNON
12 JACKIE LOMAX
13 PAUL McCARTNEY
14 THE MODERN JAZZ QUARTET
15 DAVID PEEL
16 BILLY PRESTON
17 RADA KRISHNA TEMPLE
18 RONNIE SPECTOR
19 RINGO STARR
20 THE SUNDOWN PLAYBOYS
21 JOHN TAVENER
22 JAMES TAYLOR
23 TRASH
24 DORIS TROY
25 LON AND DEREK VAN EATON

-◄╫►-

HOW BANG RECORDS GOT ITS NAME

From its owners, of course, who were:

1   BERT BERNS, record producer extraordinaire
2   AHMET ERTEGUN, producer, executive, and songwriter
3   NESUHI ERTEGUN, producer, executive, and soccer expert
4   GERALD WEXLER, more familiarly known as Jerry, producer, executive, and writer

GREAT CHICAGO BLUES LABELS

1, 2 and 3 Aristocrat; Chess; Checker
These labels were owned by the Chess brothers, Leonard and Phil. Aristocrat, their original, featured Muddy Waters, who moved with them to Chess, where he joined Howlin' Wolf as the label's initial big sellers. Checker was the logical spinoff; its biggest star in the blues (prerock) years was Little Walter, the singer and harpist who'd started his Checker career in Muddy's band.

4 J.O.B.
Co-owned by singer-pianist St. Louis Jimmy, J.O.B.'s most celebrated records were made by the great J. B. Lenoir. The label lasted only briefly during the fifties; its masters were bought up by Chess and have been lost in confusion since that label's subsequent demise.

5 Chance
The original label of J. B. Hutto and his various Hawks also recorded Sunnyland Slim, John Lee Hooker, and for a time Little Walter.

6, 7 States; United
Junior Wells first cut "Hoodoo Man" for States; Robert Nighthawk was sister label United's most imaginative performer.

8 Parrot
Both John Brim, Jimmy Reed's sometime sidekick, and J. B. Lenoir recorded for this label, which had nothing to do with the London Records subsidiary for which Savoy Brown and Tom Jones would later cut sixties and seventies pop sides.

9 Vee-Jay
Primarily a soul label, Vee-Jay made its blues reputation with the seminal Jimmy Reed boogie and Billy Boy Arnold's marvelous "I Wish You Would."

10   **Cobra**
This was the leading label for the West Side blues players of the fifties, particularly Otis Rush.

11   **Artistic**
Buddy Guy got his start here.

12   **Chief**
Magic Sam's best early work was recorded for Chief, as well as Junior Wells' and the late Earl Hooker's.

13   **Alligator**
Currently doing a magnificent job of documenting what remains of the Chicago scene, especially through the fine albums of Hound Dog Taylor and Son Seals' music that it has issued.

FOUR: PROMOTION

CAPITOL RECORDS

Capitol Records enshrined Grand Funk Railroad high above Times Square during the costly promotion of their album Closer to Home *in 1970. At that time, the billboard cost approximately $33,500 for the paint job and $7,000 a month for the space.*

STEVE LEEDS OFFERS 48 REASONS WHY RADIO STATIONS WON'T PLAY YOUR RECORD

1   It's not for us (or our sound).
2   No room.
3   No label support.
4   We want to give the record the best shot, so we will have to wait until we have more room.
5   No local sales.
6   No national action.
7   We're considering.
8   We're watching and waiting.
9   It's the wrong image.
10   It's not modal.
11   We need another copy.
12   Poor reaction when we featured it.
13   The jocks don't like it.
14   No phone reaction.
15   We played the import.
16   We're gonna wait and see what the competition does.
17   We'll wait for the single.
18   The record's not in the stores yet.
19   We need approval from headquarters.
20   The program director doesn't like it.
21   It was vetoed in the music meeting.
22   It's too hard.
23   It's too soft.
24   It's wimpy.
25   It's not as good as the last record.
26   It needs to be relistened to.
27   It's too disco.
28   It's too pop.
29   We didn't get the copromotion of the live date.

30   Trade chart numbers don't merit airplay.
31   It sounds like everything else.
32   It's not a good record.
33   I don't like it.
34   It's warped (or broken).
35   There's a scratch in the vinyl on that track.
36   The wrong LP was in the jacket.
37   We're saving room for scheduled new releases.
38   Going into the book (station's ARB rating period).
39   We're already playing too many women.
40   We don't have the album yet.
41   No tip-sheet advertising.
42   Nothing hits me.
43   Don't like the mix.
44   Not enough guitar.
45   Too many strings.
46   Overproduced.
47   Underproduced.
48   Don't like the album cover.

STEVE LEEDS *is a well-known independent album promoter in the Northeast. He has worked for Atlantic/Atco, Stiff, Rounder, and a variety of other labels and artists. Leeds has also been a disc jockey at WHFS in Washington and WOUR, Utica, New York.*

10 PROMOTIONS THAT BACKFIRED

1   **The Rolling Stones Free Concert at Altamont,** 1969
It was meant to be the culminating event of their 1969 tour, a free concert in San Francisco that would permanently re-establish The Stones as the world's premier rock act and also solidify them as the standard-bearers of the Woodstock nation. Alas, as a result of site changes and general disorganization, the eventual one-day festival held at Altamont Speedway was a catastrophe, featuring dozens of bad trips, a crazed fan

punching out Mick Jagger, a Hell's Angel punching out Marty Balin of The Jefferson Airplane, and ultimately, the murder of a young black fan, Meredith Hunter, at the hands of the Angels.

2   **The Bosstown Sound,** 1968
The concept here was not so much to put the Boston rock scene on the map but to establish MGM Records, which sponsored the Bosstown hype, as a major music-industry force. Unfortunately, Ultimate Spinach and most of the other Bosstown Sound bands were far from the cream of the crop, in Boston or elsewhere. After a series of scathing reviews (led by Boston native Jon Landau's in *Rolling Stone*), the promotion sank without a trace. MGM never recovered its hip credentials.

3   **Mike Curb's drug purge at MGM Records,** 1970
Mike Curb spent the sixties making schlock-rock soundtracks for cheapo drive-in movies. But by the early years of Richard Nixon's regime, he had risen to the presidency of MGM, then on its last legs as a label. In a public-relations move, Curb vowed that he had dropped several dozen "drug-related" acts from the company's artist roster. He was never able to substantiate his claim, and he looked really insipid when it turned out that Eric Burdon and the Animals, the most explicitly drug-oriented band on MGM, had not been given their release. Curb had the last laugh: He became a Ronald Reagan protégé and was eventually elected lieutenant governor of California.

4   **The Concert for Bangladesh,** 1971
Ravi Shankar asked George Harrison to organize a benefit concert to raise money for Bangladesh, which had been devastated by famine and its war for independence from Pakistan. Harrison put on a spectacular show at Madison Square Garden, featuring himself, Ringo Starr, Leon Russell, Eric Clapton, and most impressive, Bob Dylan. But nearly ten years later, little of the money has reached the United Nations channels designed to help the folks in Bangladesh.

5   **Woodstock II,** 1979
As the tenth anniversary of Woodstock rolled around, various promoters made attempts to restage the event. But legislative and economic realities stymied their efforts. The closest anyone came to staging a second Woodstock was a pathetic and poorly attended weekend concert at a Long Island race track, which had the name but none of the music or spirit of the original.

6   **The Byrds reunion,** 1973
The most legendary West Coast rock band of all time, the original Byrds made only two albums before attrition set in when Gene Clark left to pursue a solo career. By the early seventies, only Roger McGuinn was left of the original members. So it was regarded as a major coup when Asylum Records announced that the original Byrds—McGuinn, Clark, Chris Hillman, Mike Clarke, and David Crosby—were re-forming to do another album for the label in 1973. The result, depending on one's degree of devotion to and confidence in the band, was a laughingstock or an embarrassment, full of flabby music that lacked cohesion or even a hint of the trademark sound of the band's early days.

7   **Kiss solo albums,** 1978
Kiss were riding the crest of an incredible wave of teen popularity in 1978, with sold-out concerts and multiplatinum albums, thanks to their flamboyant heavy-metal music, their cartoon-style makeup, and concert special effects. When Casablanca Records announced plans to simultaneously release four solo albums, one by each member of the group, it almost made sense—might even have been a workable concept if the label hadn't shipped more than anyone could possibly have wanted. In the end, the label admitted taking more than 1 million returns on the four LPs.

8   **The Knack as the new Beatles,** 1979
With New Wave artists beginning to feel more and more compromised in their attitude toward the conventional record

business, the time was ripe for a New Wave promotion by a major label. In early summer 1978, Capitol Records struck first with The Knack, a four-piece group whose debut album sleeve, meticulously copied from *Meet the Beatles!*, told their whole story. The group did have a major hit single, a piece of sexist swill called "My Sharona," before fading into obscurity like half a hundred "new Dylans" and "new Beatles" before them, their credibility and talent exhausted.

9   **The *Rolling Stone* Tenth Anniversary TV Special,** 1977
CBS gave Steve Binder Productions and *Rolling Stone* magazine $1,150,000 to produce a two-hour special celebrating the magazine's tenth anniversary, hoping that the publication's reputation would attract some stars not ordinarily seen in prime time. Unfortunately, not only were the stars wary of *Rolling Stone* and the network, but the narrow minds of the network brass bowdlerized *Rolling Stone*'s original intent and the script. The result was a noticeable absence of rock figures (featured stars of the show included Donny Osmond, Bette Midler, Gladys Knight, Art Garfunkel). The most remarkable visual display of the evening was a group of dancing strawberries parading around in a medley of Beatles hits. The result was ludicrous and the ratings showed that by the second hour most viewers had switched to other networks.

10   **The Brinsley Schwarz American junket,** 1970
A mild-mannered harmony group named Kippington Lodge was signed by a new British management company, Famepushers, was given a new name (its lead guitarist's), and was sent to make its debut at the Fillmore East in New York. Famepushers made a major strategic error, however, when it decided to fly the fickle British press to the States to witness the show. The result was reams of reportage about the hype and barely a line about the music, which wasn't bad. Brinsley Schwarz never recovered from this promotion, a circumstance doubly unfortunate because the group not only made some fine music later on, but also contained two crucial figures of the New Wave: guitarist Schwarz, who joined The Rumour,

Graham Parker's band; and bassist Nick Lowe, who earned a considerable reputation as Elvis Costello's producer, as a solo artist, as a member of Rockpile, and as the husband of postpunk debutante Carlene Carter.

-◄❙▮❙►-

15 HITS THAT BECAME COMMERCIALS

1   "Anticipation," CARLY SIMON, Heinz ketchup
2   "Barefootin'," ROBERT PARKER, Spic and Span
3   "Bend Me Shape Me," AMERICAN BREED, Pepsodent
4   "Calendar Girl," NEIL SEDAKA, Purina Cat Chow
5   "California Girls," THE BEACH BOYS, Clairol Herbal Essence
6   "Good Vibrations," THE BEACH BOYS, Sunkist
7   "Jackson," NANCY SINATRA AND LEE HAZELWOOD, Dodge
8   "Just One Look," DORIS TROY, Mazda
9   "Personality," LLOYD PRICE, K Mart Photos
10 "Pretty Woman," ROY ORBISON, Tone Soap
11 "Splish Splash," BOBBY DARIN, GTE Flip Phone
12 "Summertime, Summertime," THE JAMIES, Ken-L Ration
13 "Tie Me Kangaroo Down, Sport," ROLF HARRIS, Wallaby Squirt
14 "Up-Up and Away," THE 5TH DIMENSION, TWA
15 "Woman," PETER AND GORDON, Enjoli cologne

-◄❙▮❙►-

HITS BASED ON COMMERCIALS

1   "Book of Love," THE MONOTONES; based on the melody to a fifties Pepsodent commercial
2   "I'd Like to Teach the World to Sing (in Perfect Harmony)," THE NEW SEEKERS; followed the Coca-Cola commercial word for word, note for note
3   "The Jolly Green Giant," THE KINGSMEN; based, in hilarious fashion, on the vegetables commercial, with the band's instinct

for fratrock raunch transforming the giant into the world's largest horny human

4   "No Matter What Shape (Your Stomach's In)," THE T-BONES; a mid-sixties Alka Seltzer commercial with a sufficiently mnemonic melody to become one of the era's more memorable instrumental smashes

-◀▮▶-

ARTISTS WHO MADE COMMERCIALS

1   RAY CHARLES, Craig Car Stereo
2   BILL GRAHAM, milk
3   DEBORAH HARRY, Gloria Vanderbilt jeans
4   THE JEFFERSON AIRPLANE, Levi's
5   B. B. KING'S GUITAR LUCILLE, Memorex
6   ELVIS PRESLEY, Southern Maid Doughnuts
7   STEVIE WONDER, TDK cassettes
8   THE YARDBIRDS, Great Shakes

-◀▮▶-

THINGS GO BETTER WITH . . .
A Case of Great Coke Commercials

1   ASHFORD AND SIMPSON
2   FONTELLA BASS
3   THE BEACH BOYS
4   JAMES BROWN
5   RAY CHARLES
6   THE COASTERS
7   LEE DORSEY
8   THE DRIFTERS
9   THE FOUR SEASONS
10   THE FOUR TOPS
11   ARETHA FRANKLIN
12   MARVIN GAYE
13   THE IMPRESSIONS
14   ROY ORBISON
15   OTIS REDDING
16   DIANA ROSS
17   THE SHIRELLES
18   THE SPINNERS
19   THE STYLISTICS
20   THE SUPREMES
21   THE TEMPTATIONS
22   TAMMI TERRELL
23   THE TROGGS
24   VANILLA FUDGE

COURTESY PETER KANZE

THEY'D LIKE TO TEACH THE WORLD TO SING
A Second Case, Just in Case

1	THE BEE GEES	13	JAN AND DEAN
2	BOYCE AND HART	14	GLADYS KNIGHT AND
3	THE BOX TOPS		THE PIPS
4	JERRY BUTLER	15	LITTLE MILTON
5	THE CHI-LITES	16	LULU
6	JACKIE DESHANNON	17	LORETTA LYNN
7	THE EVERLY BROTHERS	18	THE MOODY BLUES
8	WAYNE FONTANA	19	THE POINTER SISTERS
9	CAROLYN FRANKLIN	20	JOE SIMON
10	FREDDIE AND THE	21	SISTER SLEDGE
	DREAMERS	22	B. J. THOMAS
11	LESLEY GORE	23	CARLA THOMAS
12	THE GUESS WHO	24	CONWAY TWITTY

FIVE:
PRODUCTION

JANICE BELSON

Phil Spector photographed at home shortly after producing an album by The Ramones.

BEST PRODUCERS

The producer's position in rock and roll masks a variety of functions, ranging from purely technical assistance to complete responsibility for selection and arrangement of material. In recent years, the producer has become a celebrity in his own right, a phenomenon that began with the emergence of Phil Spector, a producer more famous than the majority of artists with whom he worked. The producer's stature reached its peak in the late seventies, when picking the producer became a top priority in the record-making process. In soul music, particularly, the producer has often been the dominant figure in the studio. While it is hard to define what a producer does do, these twenty men epitomize what a producer can do.

1   **SAM PHILLIPS**
As much as any single nonperformer, Sam Phillips deserves credit as a father of rock and roll. In 1954–1955, he spent the better part of a year working at his Sun Records Studio in Memphis with Elvis Presley, Scotty Moore, and Bill Black, creating what stands as the most remarkable musical outpouring of the past forty years. Their sound owes at least as much to Phillips' vision as to their own talents. In later work with Jerry Lee Lewis, Charlie Rich, and especially Carl Perkins, Phillips helped capture a sound (dubbed rockabilly) that helped define rock. His work with echo alone marks him as a master.

2   **JERRY LEIBER and MIKE STOLLER**
Known primarily as songwriters, Leiber and Stoller perfected the three-minute pop song with their bright, effects-laden Coasters hits—"Yakety Yak," "Searchin'," "Charlie Brown," etc. It was Leiber and Stoller who taught Phil Spector the rudiments of record-making. In the late 1950s and early 1960s, with The Drifters, they helped take rhythm & blues into a new dimension, namely soul, through their use of habanera rhythm and funky string sections.

3   **PHIL SPECTOR**

"Tomorrow's sound today" was the slogan of the Philles label, and even though that tomorrow has come and gone, the statement seems more a fact than a boast. Spector's Wall of Sound, amassed volume of instruments creating a semiorchestral effect, had tremendously immediate impact, and it's had an incalculable influence, reaching from Brian Wilson and The Beatles to Bruce Springsteen and The New York Dolls. The records of The Crystals, The Ronettes, and The Righteous Brothers define not only the essence of rock romanticism, but also the most craftily detailed pop music ever made.

4   **BRIAN HOLLAND and LAMONT DOZIER**

In the early and middle 1960s, Motown was a hotbed of songwriting, performing, and production talent. The pop potential of soul music was defined with the help of Smokey Robinson, William Stevenson, Motown owner Berry Gordy Jr., and a bit later, Nickolas Ashford and Valerie Simpson. But Motown's definitive production unit was also two-thirds of its best songwriting team, Holland-Dozier-Holland—the additional Holland being Brian's brother, Eddie. Holland-Dozier productions run the gamut from the teen-dream froth of the early Supremes singles to the operatic grandeur of The Four Tops scarifying "Reach Out I'll Be There." Later, they'd go on to form Invictus/Hot Wax and score more hits on their own with Freda Payne, Laura Lee, The Chairmen of the Board, and others.

5   **ISAAC HAYES and DAVID PORTER**

Another songwriting team, Hayes and Porter were sometimes overshadowed at Stax, which was also home to such estimable production talent as Otis Redding, Steve Cropper, Eddie Floyd, Al Bell, and Jim Stewart. Hayes and Porter, however, typified Stax/Volt's sound—so much earthier and more adult than Motown's—with their grand, exciting series of Sam and Dave hits. Later, as a performer, Hayes would place himself in the forefront of the emerging black pop avant-garde with "By the Time I Get to Phoenix," "Theme from Shaft," and "Never Can Say Goodbye."

6   **LEE "SCRATCH" PERRY**
The current top man among Jamaican producers, Perry is best known for his production of Junior Murvin's "Police and Thieves" and for working briefly with punk maestros The Clash, according to him the only white band that plays reggae acceptably. He's also perfected reggae "dub" recordings with several artists. Perry's predecessor, Leslie Kong, is the other important name to know among Caribbean record-makers.

7   **KENNETH GAMBLE and LEON HUFF**
Soul in the seventies reached its peak at Sigma Sound Studios in Philadelphia. The principal label was Philadelphia International, owned and operated by Gamble and Huff. Like Motown and Stax, PI has a family of producers, writers, and performers, but here, the owners are also the top artists, at least in the control room. Gamble and Huff made hits with Jerry Butler, Archie Bell and the Drells, and The Intruders, among others, before forming PI in the early seventies. Since then, they've simply perfected what they started, chiefly through the vehicles of The O'Jays and Teddy Pendergrass (with Harold Melvin and the Blue Notes and later on his own).

8   **BRIAN WILSON**
Wilson learned his tricks from Phil Spector but added an affinity for limpid, white pop harmony, which lent glorious naiveté to such records as "Don't Worry Baby," "California Girls," and "Kiss Me, Baby," even before he embarked on such song-cycle epics as *Pet Sounds*. The latter, however, brought the intense detail of his music into clearer focus; in his heyday, Wilson was perhaps ahead of almost everyone else in rock, predicting the psychedelic pop extravaganza vogue that came along soon after.

9   **GLYN JOHNS**
The king of the British engineer-producers, Johns cut his spurs working with some of the biggest bands of English rock—The

Who and The Stones—so it's no surprise that he later went on to produce the former's greatest LP, *Who's Next*, or that his other hard-rock albums have amazing power and sophistication. What's more impressive is that Johns has also worked effectively with a diverse lot of artists, most notably Joan Armatrading and The Eagles. This range and empathy with the artist is what makes Johns stand out so dramatically over other British engineer-producers, even the current darling, Roy Thomas Baker (Queen, The Cars).

10 JERRY WEXLER, TOM DOWD, ARIF MARDIN, and AHMET ERTEGUN

The central figures here are Wexler and Dowd. Wexler because of his catalytic personality, which pushed Aretha Franklin to her best work. He galvanized his production teamings, first with Ertegun (they made Ray Charles' Atlantic hits) and later with Dowd and Mardin (Wilson Pickett, Franklin, etc.). Dowd is crucial because he virtually invented rock and roll engineering, and because he went on to develop a distinctive hard-rock style while working with Lynyrd Skynyrd, Eric Clapton (*Layla*, among many others), Rod Stewart (everything since *Atlantic Crossing*, except for his 1980 album, *Foolish Behaviour*), and others too numerous to mention. Ertegun hasn't been as active lately, but as both writer and producer, he's most important to Atlantic's fifties records; he's a white man with genuine soul. Mardin's approach is closer to the middle of the road, and he's enjoyed his greatest success with The Bee Gees (he invented their disco methodology), Judy Collins, and Carly Simon.

11 THE BEATLES and GEORGE MARTIN

They would be landmark figures if they had *only* created *Sgt. Pepper's Lonely Hearts Club Band*, an inexhaustible source of production style and subtlety. Add to it such masterpieces as *Revolver*, *The White Album*, and *Abbey Road*, and you have a body of work that's formidable simply for what it sounds like, much less for what it says. It's hard to say what George Martin's role was. On the basis of subsequent events, it may have been minor, but then on the basis of the four solo careers, maybe it was *all* chemistry.

12   **JIMMY MILLER**
This veteran English rock producer is especially notable for his work with The Spencer Davis Group, Traffic, and The Rolling Stones (*Exile on Main Street* and *Sticky Fingers*). Miller is a percussionist, so it's probably not surprising that he gets unbelievably fantastic drum sounds.

13   **PETE TOWNSHEND and KIT LAMBERT**
Townshend's sonic innovations as a guitarist tend to over-shadow what he could do with tape itself, but "My Genera-tion," *The Who Sell Out*, *Tommy*, and *Quadrophenia* are pure studio creations of unmistakable complexity and sophistica-tion. The same goes in spades for *Who's Next*. And Town-shend's demos offer convincing evidence that he deserves the credit. Kit Lambert was an indispensable foil for the young Townshend, pushing him to create the miniopera ("A Quick One While He's Away") on The Who's second album and to develop his more adventurous sonic concepts on *Quadro-phenia*.

14   **PETER ASHER**
King of the singer/songwriters, Asher produces cool and elegant pop-rock, typified by Linda Ronstadt's *Heart Like a Wheel* and James Taylor's *JT*. The intricate arrangements and pristine recording make up for what such music lacks in punch—and that's making up for a lot.

15   **STEVIE WONDER**
Wonder has done only a bit of outside production work, with Labelle and ex-wife Syreeta Wright, but even there, he is the very essence of sophisticated soulfulness. His productions are as eclectic as his music, blending elements not only from soul, but also from rock and roll, straight pop, reggae, and Elling-tonian jazz.

16   **BERNARD EDWARDS and NILE RODGERS**
Edwards and Rodgers have made enough hits with Chic to qualify as the foremost American disco producers on sales

power alone. But they have an ability to adapt rock licks to
their dance music that surpasses any of the competition; they
also have the hottest mixes in the business (courtesy of
engineer Bob Clearmountain), precise arrangements, and a
general lack of clutter that makes their work nonpareil in any
idiom.

17 **GIORGIO MORODER**
Yes, Moroder's Eurodisco, exemplified in his work with Donna
Summer, was a formula. But that formula gave rise to some
tremendously exciting records: big, bold, and worthy of the
boogie on which its rigid beat insisted.

18 **JIMMY IOVINE**
Iovine is the best of the American engineer-producers, even
though he has been in the spotlight only a short time. Although
his records with English rockers (Dire Straits, Graham Parker)
haven't worked out, Iovine has an exceptional knack for
drawing the best from Anglo-influenced American hard rock
(Patti Smith, Tom Petty, even Meat Loaf). His sound, at best,
is dense, big, and explosive, which figures, since he learned
his trade engineering for Bruce Springsteen and John Lennon.

19 **RICHARD PERRY**
Perry represents the mainstream pop producer as seventies
auteur. Since his production of Fats Domino's fine comeback
album, *Fats Is Back* (1969), Perry has stepped more and more
into the forefront of his projects, overshadowing many of the
artists with whom he works, in the mold of Phil Spector. When
he finds equilibrium (most especially on Carly Simon's amazing "You're So Vain"), Perry's music can have a pop grandeur
and wonderfully light touch that is unmatched by peers such as
Lenny Waronker.

20 **WILLIE MITCHELL**
Mitchell was a solid engineer at Hi Studios for years, until he
and Al Green started working together around 1969, at which
point his abilities as the last great soul producer became
evident. In addition to all of Green's hits, Mitchell has
produced Otis Clay, and Ann Peebles.

GREAT ENGINEERS

Unlike record producers, engineers are unsung heroes. Yet the two roles are intertwined to the extent that some producers work only with specific engineers, taking the technicians with them from studio to studio. Unfortunately, most early rock and R&B engineers went uncredited. As a result, the men who actually rolled the tape at such labels as Chess, Motown, and King are still unknown. Even today, album-cover photographers are more consistently given recognition than engineers. It is only in more recent years that engineers have received credit, partly because of a better understanding of their importance and, one suspects, because this year's engineers are likely to be next year's fledgling producers. The listing here reflects the best we've known about.

1   **TOM DOWD**
In the late forties and early fifties, working with Ahmet Ertegun and crew, Tom Dowd virtually invented rock and roll engineering. In Charlie Gillett's *Making Tracks*, Ertegun recalls their first meeting, in 1948: "We recorded at Apex, and the first engineer we had was a little middle-aged German doctor, who didn't know anything about popular music but was technically reliable. For the second session, a kid walked into the studio. I said, 'Where's the engineer?' He said, 'I'm the engineer.' I kicked up a great fuss, saying, 'I will not have this child ruin my records.' But the owner insisted that this kid, Tommy Dowd, was fine—and of course, since then, Tom engineered almost everything we did." Until well into the seventies, Dowd worked on virtually every important Atlantic R&B session, helping to perfect stereo and capturing beautiful balances and a "live" ambiance. Since then, Dowd has gone on to become a producer, working with Derek and the Dominos, Rod Stewart, and many more.

2 **GLYN JOHNS**
Johns pioneered the massive English hard-rock sound, working with the best bands to achieve a bigger-than-life power and clarity. *Who's Next* (which he also produced) and The Rolling Stone's *Beggar's Banquet* are his best. His later work as producer of The Eagles and Joan Armatrading reflects his passion for streamlined sound.

3 **LARRY LEVINE**
Levine, as engineer of all Phil Spector's important hits, was the technical architect of the Wall of Sound. 'Nuff said.

4 **BOB CLEARMOUNTAIN**
An ace recordist, especially known as a mixer and remixer (of The Stone's "Miss You," among others), Clearmountain works out of New York's Power Station, using his wimp filter on all manner of music, from Chic's postdisco funk to Bruce Springsteen's power-pop "Hungry Heart." The sound of today, today.

5 **JOE TARSIA**
Tarsia gets the sounds for the Philadelphia International complex of artists and producers, as well as most outsiders who go to Philly's Sigma Sound to record, which makes him one of the most important figures in seventies soul and disco.

6 **BUNNY ROBYN**
Robyn captured the intricacies of the great Coasters hits of the fifties with remarkable detail and fidelity. He also pioneered using multiple microphones. Robyn originally worked at Universal Studios, but in 1952, he moved to his own L.A. Master Recorders, perhaps the first studio specially designed to enhance cutting R&B masters. In addition to working with Leiber and Stoller, Robyn was also at the board for Little Richard's "Long Tall Sally," and Johnny Otis' "Willie and the Hand Jive."

7 **JIMMY JOHNSON**
Johnson is the greatest of the Southern rock and soul engineers. The other important engineers of Muscle Shoals, Alabama, were Rick Hall, at his own Fame Studio, and Larry Hamby, at both Fame and Muscle Shoals Sound. In Atlanta,

the man to see is Rodney Mills, who began working at Lefevre, the city's gospel studio, but later moved into rock and roll with Lynyrd Skynyrd's "Saturday Night Special." Mills now operates from the more rock-oriented Studio One in Atlanta.

8   **EDDIE KRAMER**
Kramer was Jimi Hendrix' most sympathetic partner, and by the time of *Electric Ladyland*, he was working in technical areas as yet untouched by others. Kramer went on to work on some of the best early-seventies Rolling Stones records, and with Kiss.

9   **RON CAPONE and JIM STEWART**
Capone and Stewart were the principal controllers of the board for such Stax/Volt hits as "Respect," "Gee Whiz," and "In the Midnight Hour." Stewart, of course, was an owner of the label. Interestingly, guitarist Steve Cropper, when producing sessions there, sometimes did his own engineering.

10   **DAVE HASSINGER**
Hassinger cut the great Los Angeles sides of The Rolling Stones, including "(I Can't Get No) Satisfaction." He was already a veteran engineer then, and remains one today, putting all manner of music on tape.

11   **BILL SZYMCZYK**
Best known for working with American hard rockers, a group generally not well served technically, Szymczyk is limited as a producer but is one of the finest engineers. He's always delivered marvelous punch with such artists as The James Gang, The Eagles, The J. Geils Band, and The Who.

12   **VAL GARAY and GREG LADANYI**
They're the kings of the control room in Los Angeles and environs. Garay is Peter Asher's technical right hand. The almost sterile precision of their work together, especially on Linda Ronstadt's hits, is a marvel. Ladanyi delivers a much tougher sound, found on such albums as Jackson Browne's *Running on Empty* and *Hold Out* (which he coproduced) and Warren Zevon's *Bad Luck Streak in Dancing School*.

13   **TONY VISCONTI**
Working with David Bowie and others at the arty end of the
British pop spectrum, Visconti has created a detailed complexity that, while never as powerful as the sound Glyn Johns
gets, has an openness Johns' hasn't.

14   **RON ALBERT, HOWARD ALBERT, and KARL RICHARDSON**
This trio has recorded hits ranging from "Layla" to the Bee
Gees disco smashes.

15   **ROY CICALA and PHIL RAMONE**
Cicala and Ramone work for a variety of artists, Cicala from
his Record Plant studio, Ramone from his A&R facility.
Together, they've been involved with most of New York's
important music in the past fifteen to twenty years. Cicala is
best known for recording the early John Lennon solo LPs, but
he's also recognized for training such superior hard-rock
engineers as Jimmy Iovine, Shelly Yakus, and Jack Douglas.
Ramone works in more varied styles, preferring the eclectic
pop-rock of Paul Simon and Billy Joel, whom he also produces. Ramone is perhaps the best live recording engineer in
the business as well.

-◄▮▮►-

BOB CLEARMOUNTAIN'S FAVORITE PRODUCERS AND THEIR BEST ALBUMS

1   TODD RUNDGREN, *A Wizard, a True Star*, Todd Rundgren
2   NICK LOWE, *Armed Forces*, Elvis Costello
3   ROGER BECHIRIAN, *Stateless*, Lene Lovich
4   ROY THOMAS BAKER, *A Night at the Opera*, Queen
5   DAVID GILMOUR, ROGER WATERS, JAMES GUTHRIE and BOB
     EZRIN, *The Wall*, Pink Floyd
6   ROBERT JOHN LANGE, *The Fine Art of Surfacing*, The
     Boomtown Rats

7   JIMMY MILLER, *Let It Bleed* and *Sticky Fingers*, The Rolling Stones

8   DAVID BOWIE and TONY VISCONTI, *Scary Monsters*, David Bowie

9   JIMMY IOVINE, *Damn the Torpedoes*, Tom Petty and the Heartbreakers

10   GEORGE MARTIN, *Meet the Beatles!*

NOTE: To maintain objectivity, I have omitted the names of any producers with whom I have worked professionally.

Current enfant terrible *of New York engineers and producers,* BOB CLEARMOUNTAIN *has recorded or mixed all of the hits by the Chic organization, "Miss You" by The Rolling Stones, and Bruce Springsteen's "Hungry Heart," among many others.*

ROCK BANDS THAT EMERGED FROM SESSION WORK

1   **AREA CODE 615**
This short-lived group, led by Charlie McCoy, featured the cream of Nashville's country session players.

2   **ATLANTA RHYTHM SECTION**
ARS was formed from a variety of Georgia sessionmen, several of whom had aided producer Buddy Buie in creating The Classic IV's great sixties hit, "Spooky." On their own, of course, they've reached greater heights.

3   **BAREFOOT JERRY**
This band was formed by veteran Nashville sessionman Wayne Moss, whose many credits include guitar work on *Blonde on Blonde*. Other band members—Jim Colvard, Russ Hicks, Si Edwards, Terry Dearmore, and Warren Hartman—are also well-respected Nashville session players.

4   **DELANEY AND BONNIE AND FRIENDS, MAD DOGS AND ENGLISHMEN and DEREK AND THE DOMINOS**
Delaney Bramlett was a top Los Angeles session guitarist when

he and his wife, Bonnie, decided to form a band in 1969. The group they assembled included several other top Hollywood studio names, including Leon Russell, Jim Price, Bob Whitlock, Bobby Keys, Carl Radle, and Jim Keltner. Unfortunately, while these performers were well known for their musicianship, they were somewhat less notorious for their loyalty. Soon after the group opened for Blind Faith on its American tour and was joined by Eric Clapton on a European tour of its own, Whitlock and Radle left to help form Derek and the Dominos. And not long after, Russell took several of the others to help form Joe Cocker's big band, Mad Dogs and Englishmen, while the Bramletts, left high and dry, disintegrated musically as well as maritally.

5 JO MAMA

Various permutations of Los Angeles session players from the generation after the Delaney and Bonnie bunch, Jo Mama mostly featured the stalwart Danny Kortchmar on guitar.

6 KING CURTIS AND THE KING PINS

Curtis, of course, was the greatest of the New York sax session players, after Sam "the Man" Taylor. His first group was King Curtis and the Noble Knights, but it was as the King Pins that they toured behind Aretha Franklin and recorded "Memphis Soul Stew."

7 MFSB

The Sound of Philadelphia owes a lot to the sound of the unheralded sessionmen who play on the records made by The Three Degrees, The O'Jays, McFadden and Whitehead, and Harold Melvin and the Blue Notes. MFSB had a Number One hit on its own in 1974 with "T.S.O.P. (The Sound of Philadelphia)."

8 THE MEMPHIS HORNS

All veterans of Memphis recording sessions, Wayne Jackson, Andrew Love, Lewis Collins, Jack Hale, and James Mitchell have gone on to record several albums for RCA.

9 THE METERS

New Orleans' finest.

10   **THE MUSCLE SHOALS HORNS**

Less acclaimed than The Muscle Shoals Rhythm Section, The Muscle Shoals Horns have made several well-received funk albums for Bang and Ariola/America Records. Band members include Harrison Calloway, Harvey Thompson, and Charles Rose.

11   **RONIN**

Linda Ronstadt's band, led by Waddy Wachtel, has so far made only one album, a self-titled Rolling Stones-style mélange that is better than the aimless funk made by The Section and Stuff, if not necessarily as hot as the straight rock of Jo Mama and The Atlanta Rhythm Section.

12   **THE SECTION**

The musicians who brought you the unmistakable sounds of southern California rock bring you their own jazz-rock offerings on albums for Capitol Records. Russ Kunkel, Leland Sklar, Danny Kortchmar, and Craig Doerge have recorded with James Taylor, Jackson Browne, Carly Simon, Nicolette Larson, and others of that ilk.

13   **STUFF**

The seventies New York equivalent of The Section, Stuff is best known for its appearances as the house band on *Saturday Night Live*.

14   **TOTO**

Steve Porcaro, David Paich, Steve Lukather, David Hungate, Jeffrey Porcaro, and Bobby Kimball hold the line.

JERRY WEXLER'S LIST OF SONGS HE PRODUCED THAT WERE NOT NECESSARILY HITS BUT LOVELY MOMENTS IN THE STUDIO

1 "Deep in the Night," ETTA JAMES
2 "Amazing Grace," ARETHA FRANKLIN
3 "Breakfast in Bed," DUSTY SPRINGFIELD
4 "Giving Up," DONNY HATHAWAY
5 "Tennessee Blues," DOUG SAHM
6 "I Still Can't Believe You're Gone," WILLIE NELSON
7 "Soul Dance #3," WILSON PICKETT
8 "Why Am I Treated So Bad," THE SWEET INSPIRATIONS
9 "Tonight's the Night," SOLOMON BURKE

JERRY WEXLER *is best known as one of the key figures in the history of Atlantic Records, where he served as an executive for more than twenty years and produced fundamental R&B and soul records by Ray Charles, Aretha Franklin, Solomon Burke, Wilson Pickett, and many others. More recently, Wexler and Barry Beckett have produced Bob Dylan's Christian albums and Dire Straits'* Communiqué. *Wexler is now an executive vice-president of Warner Bros. Records.*

-◄▮▮►-

THE 10 RECORDS WILLIE DIXON IS PROUDEST TO BE ASSOCIATED WITH

1 "Hoochie Coochie Man," MUDDY WATERS (writer and session musician)
2 "Shake for Me," HOWLIN' WOLF (writer and producer)
3 "I Just Want to Make Love to You," FOGHAT (writer)
4 "Little Red Rooster," THE ROLLING STONES (writer)
5 "Wang Dang Doodle," KOKO TAYLOR (writer and producer)
6 "You Shook Me," LED ZEPPELIN (writer)
7 "My Babe," RAMSEY LEWIS (writer)

8   "You Can't Judge a Book by Its Cover," BO DIDDLEY (writer and session musician)
9   "Run Rudolph Run," CHUCK BERRY (session musician)
10   *Johnny Winter* (session musician)

WILLIE DIXON has been deeply involved in the Chicago music scene since the forties, when he was a member of several swing vocal groups, including the popular Big Three Trio. During the fifties, he was a cornerstone of Chess Records as composer, A&R man, session player (bassist), and artist. Dixon is perhaps best known as a songwriter; since the British Invasion, rock acts have borrowed extensively from Dixon's impressive catalog of tunes.

-◄❚❚▶-

BILLY PRESTON LISTS HIS 10 MOST MEMORABLE SESSIONS

1   "Let It Be," THE BEATLES (George Martin, producer)
2   "Get Back," THE BEATLES (George Martin, producer)
3   "That's the Way God Planned It," BILLY PRESTON (George Harrison, producer)
4   "Stoney End," BARBRA STREISAND (Richard Perry, producer)
5   *Goat's Head Soup*, THE ROLLING STONES (Jimmy Miller, producer)
6   *Black and Blue*, THE ROLLING STONES (The Glimmer Twins, producers)
7   *Aretha Franklin Live at Fillmore West* (Jerry Wexler, Arif Mardin, Tom Dowd, producers)
8   "My Sweet Lord," GEORGE HARRISON (George Harrison, Phil Spector, producers)
9   "I Wrote a Simple Song," BILLY PRESTON (Quincy Jones, producer)
10   "Let's Go Get Stoned," RAY CHARLES (Ray Charles, Joe Adams, producers)

BILLY PRESTON has been a touring and recording sideman for more than twenty years, appearing as vocalist and keyboardist with Little Richard, The Beatles, and The Rolling Stones. He has also recorded a string of hit records, including "Outta Space."

10 GROUPS PRODUCED BY SHEL TALMY
1964–1967

Shel Talmy, an American, made his name during the British Invasion as producer of the earliest recordings by The Kinks and The Who.

1	THE KINKS	7	DAVID JONES, a.k.a.
2	THE WHO		BOWIE
3	THE EASYBEATS	8	GOLDIE AND THE
4	CREATION		GINGERBREADS
5	CHAD AND JEREMY	9	LANCASTRIANS
6	THE BACHELORS	10	NICKY HOPKINS

-◄◗►-

10 NON-BEACH BOY PRODUCTIONS BY BRIAN WILSON

As bassist, songwriter, vocalist, and producer, Brian Wilson has been the guiding genius of The Beach Boys since "Surfin' U.S.A." twenty years ago. His production work outside that band is less well known but often just as bright and pleasing.

1 "He's a Doll," THE HONEYS
2 "The One You Can't Have," THE HONEYS
3 "Run-Around Lover," SHARON MARIE
4 "Thinkin' 'Bout Your Baby," SHARON MARIE
5 "Sacramento," GARY USHER
6 "She Rides with Me," PAUL PETERSON
7 "I Do," THE CASTELLS
8 "Pamela Jean," THE SURVIVORS
9 "Guess I'm Dumb," GLEN CAMPBELL
10 *Spring*

ARRANGEMENTS BY JOHN PAUL JONES

Before joining Led Zeppelin, John Paul Jones was one of the leading session bassists and arrangers on the British rock scene.

1   "Sunshine Superman," DONOVAN
2   "Mellow Yellow," DONOVAN
3   "Hurdy Gurdy Man," DONOVAN; features Jimmy Page on lead guitar, the first time Page and John Bonham played together
4   "She's a Rainbow," THE ROLLING STONES
5   "Little Games," THE YARDBIRDS; cello arrangement
6   *Their Satanic Majesties Request*, THE ROLLING STONES; a substantial part of the orchestration

-◄◖►-

JIMMY PAGE AS SESSIONMAN

Before forming Led Zeppelin and joining The Yardbirds, Jimmy Page was one of the hottest guitar players on the London recording scene.

1   **"I Can't Explain,"** THE WHO
Page plays rhythm guitar, doubling Pete Townshend.
2   **"You Really Got Me,"** THE KINKS
Page definitely played on these and perhaps other tracks from the first Kinks album. Whether it is Page or Kinks guitarist Dave Davies who plays the ground-breaking fuzz-tone solo on the single is a matter of much dispute, however: Ray Davies says Page didn't, but did play tambourine, at the insistence of producer Shel Talmy.
3   **"With a Little Help from My Friends,"** JOE COCKER
Page plays lead guitar.
4   **"Gloria" and "Here Comes the Night,"** THEM
Page plays second guitar on both.

Songs on Which Phil Spector Performs

1   **"To Know Him Is to Love Him,"** THE TEDDY BEARS
Spector was a singing member of the group. He also produced
and wrote the song, taking the title from the inscription on his
father's grave.

2   **"My Sweet Lord,"** GEORGE HARRISON
Sings background vocals.

3   **"Play with Fire,"** THE ROLLING STONES
Plays guitar.

4   **"On Broadway,"** THE DRIFTERS
Plays the guitar solo.

-◄❙❙►-

Arrangements Ralph Schuckett Wishes He'd Done

1   **"Seconds,"** Gladys Knight and the Pips, arranged by BURT
BACHARACH
This is probably the most obscure thing on the list, but it's my
all-time favorite.

2   **"I'll Be Around,"** The Spinners, arranged by THOM BELL
There are only two chords in the whole song, but so many
things are done with them.

3   **"I Want You Back,"** The Jackson 5, arranged by THE
CORPORATION

4   **"Jenny Jenny,"** Little Richard, arranged by BUMPS
BLACKWELL
The saxes here are practically a part of the rhythm section;
there are only two of them, but they sound like about eight.

5   **"What'd I Say,"** Ray Charles, arranged by RAY CHARLES

6 **"There Goes My Baby,"** The Drifters, arranged by STAN APPLEBAUM

7 **"Walk on By,"** Dionne Warwick, arranged by BURT BACHARACH

8 **"Cold Sweat,"** James Brown, arranger not listed

9 **"Respect Yourself,"** The Staple Singers, arranged by THE MUSCLE SHOALS RHYTHM SECTION and THE MEMPHIS HORNS

11 **"Ninety-nine and a Half (Won't Do),"** Wilson Pickett, arranged by STEVE CROPPER and BOOKER T. JONES

12 **"Dance to the Music,"** Sly and the Family Stone, arranged by SLY STONE

13 **"Goodbye Yellow Brick Road,"** Elton John, arranged by PAUL BUCKMASTER
The strings are barely audible, yet they make the track breathe and their deletion in the second verse really brings the vocal into focus.

14 **"Lady Marmalade,"** Labelle, arranged by ALLEN TOUSSAINT
The drum beat, though very clever and hip, is simple and never stops grooving.

NOTE: Some of these—i.e., "What'd I Say," "There Goes My Baby," and "Dance to the Music"—were selected for their originality at the time of release and their subsequent influence on other records (trends, moments, schools of thought). Most were chosen for their simplicity and spaciousness but most of all, for their *feel*.—R.S.

RALPH SCHUCKETT, *a veteran keyboard player, has worked with such groups as Todd Rundgren's original Utopia and Jo Mama; he's recorded with a variety of performers, notably Carole King and James Taylor. Schuckett is currently playing and writing with Ellen Shipley and her band, The Numbers.*

NORMAN PETTY LISTS 5 SPECIAL BUDDY HOLLY RECORDS

"All recordings we made of Buddy Holly are favorites of mine, each very different in musical content as well as providing fond memories of things that took place in the studio at the time each recording was made," said Petty in reply to our question. "It would be very difficult to select only five recordings as 'the favorites,' but the following list would comprise special recordings that stand out in my mind."

1   **"Peggy Sue"**
The sound experimentation is interesting and rather advanced considering the recording-studio experience at that time. It resulted in a meeting of minds between the engineer and recording artist, producing very successful results for all concerned.

2   **"Everyday"**
Here again, absolute freedom in choosing musical instruments, as well as sound experimentation, produced very pleasing results, and that freedom is reflected in the easygoing, nice sound from the artist.

3   **"Early in the Morning"**
This was one of the first times we ventured into the "big" sound of other musicians and arrangers. Dick Jacobs did a fantastic arrangement, and his direction of the orchestra shows that he and the artist really felt what each was trying to do. It was great fun and interesting to be in a New York control room—in much different surroundings than I have been used to working in.

4   **"True Love Ways"**
Again in New York, under the expert direction of Dick Jacobs, this recording became a fine example of the "extremes" we felt we could take with the artist. The song was not written for Buddy, but was to be shown to artists known for recording

ballads. It was not until later that he decided to record it. Vi Petty was the first artist to record the song, followed by Jimmy Gilmer, Peter and Gordon, and others; there are many good recordings of the song, but the only big sales figures were from the ones made by Peter and Gordon and, lately, Mickey Gilley.

5   **"Love Is Strange"**
This is one of the most interesting recordings in my mind, for it was completely restructured and rerecorded after the demise of Buddy Holly. Several edits were made; instruments were retuned; musicians attempted to match the varying tempos and pitch on the artist's original mono recording, which was never released. (Other interesting things that took place during the completion of this "built" recording will be described in a forthcoming book.)

NORMAN PETTY *helped invent rock and roll by working as producer at his studios in Clovis, New Mexico, with such artists as Buddy Holly, Roy Orbison, Buddy Knox, and Jimmy Bowen.*

-◄❙▮❙►-

RECORDS THAT SHOULD BE IN STEREO BUT AREN'T

1   **"Dawn (Go Away),"** THE FOUR SEASONS, 1964
On their early Phillips albums, this song was rechanneled. Later, greatest-hits LPs used an alternate take, a stereo recording with a widely different intro from the original. Where is the stereo original?

2   **"Good Vibrations,"** THE BEACH BOYS, 1966
This song was recorded in stereo but not mixed that way, as Brian Wilson's partial deafness made him partial to mono. It has only appeared on albums in mono or electronic rechanneling.

3   **"I Think We're Alone Now,"** TOMMY JAMES AND THE
    SHONDELLS, 1967
    This mono single was on The Shondells' third album, though
    their previous hits were in stereo (except for "Hanky Panky,"
    which had been cut much earlier). Where did the stereo go on
    this one?

4   **"I Want to Hold Your Hand,"** THE BEATLES, 1963
    Recorded in stereo and released that way in many other
    countries, this song has yet to appear on any U.S. album in
    true stereo.

5   **"Mr. Tambourine Man"** and **"Turn! Turn! Turn!"** THE
    BYRDS, 1965
    These two big hits, by a group that sounds positively fabulous
    in stereo, were rechanneled on every Columbia album on
    which they appeared, yet even the *Preflyte* version of "Mr.
    Tambourine Man" sounds true stereo. What happened?

6   **"Proud Mary,"** CREEDENCE CLEARWATER REVIVAL, 1969
    Technically, this song is in true stereo, but it takes electronic
    testing to prove it. The mix has no separation at all, which
    means it might just as well be mono.

7   **"(I Can't Get No) Satisfaction,"** THE ROLLING STONES,
    1965
    Put together at RCA Studios in Hollywood, which makes it all
    but certain that recording was multitrack, this song has yet to
    appear in true stereo on any LP.

8   **"Suspicious Minds,"** Elvis Presley, 1969
    This song was recorded in 1968, very late for a mono track.
    And considering Elvis' popularity, it's incredible that no stereo
    version has turned up. On the albums released to date, it has
    always been monaural.

9   **"She's the One,"** BRUCE SPRINGSTEEN, 1975
    If you think you've been hearing it in stereo, check again. This
    number from *Born to Run* is in mono, though it was probably
    recorded under the same circumstances as "Proud Mary."

10   **"Why Can't We Live Together,"** TIMMY THOMAS, 1973
A giant hit, this song was just rechanneled on the album. By 1973, almost everyone in the world was recording in true stereo. So what's the story here?

-◄❚▶-

10 OF THE EARLIEST ROCK AND ROLL HITS RECORDED IN STEREO

1   "Don't Let Go," ROY HAMILTON, January 1958
2   "(I Don't Wanna) Hang Up My Rock and Roll Shoes,"
CHUCK WILLIS, April 1958
3   "What Am I Living For," CHUCK WILLIS, May 1958
4   "Yakety Yak," THE COASTERS, May 1958
5   "Born Too Late," THE PONI-TAILS, July 1958
6   "Chariot Rock," THE CHAMPS, August 1958
7   "Summertime, Summertime," THE JAMIES, August 1958
8   "It's All in the Game," TOMMY EDWARDS, August 1958
9   "I Wish," THE PLATTERS, September 1958
10   "It's Only Make Believe," CONWAY TWITTY, September 1958

-◄❚▶-

MIKE CALLAHAN LISTS UNLIKELY SONGS RECORDED IN STEREO

1   **"Born Too Late,"** THE PONI-TAILS, 1958
This song did not show up in stereo until just a few years ago, and then in the most unlikely place, on a K-Tel reissue album.
2   **"Duke of Earl,"** GENE CHANDLER, 1962
This song has been reissued so often in rechanneled stereo that the message should be coming through loud and clear that it doesn't exist in true stereo. But on the original Vee-Jay album, *Duke of Earl*, true stereo it is.

3   **"Hushabye,"** THE MYSTICS, 1959
It is unusual to find "Hushabye," an early rock song recorded
for a minor label, in true stereo. But like many other songs on
the Laurie label, it is authentically stereo and, in fact, was
issued as a stereo single as well as on a various-artists album,
Laurie Golden Goodies, some years later.

4   **"Lonely Teardrops,"** Jackie Wilson, 1958
Brunswick has put a rechanneled version of this track on all of
Wilson's albums; only on a various-artists album, *Hitsville*,
can a true stereo version be found.

5   **"Louisiana Man,"** RUSTY AND DOUG, 1961
Hickory, a small country label in Nashville, is hardly a likely
place to find true stereo recording. But this country hit was
stereo and later appeared on the LP *Rusty and Doug*.

6   **"A Lover's Question,"** CLYDE MCPHATTER, 1958
Atlantic was a relatively small label in 1958, but surprisingly
enough, a number of their hits that year were cut in stereo.
This one can be found on *History of Rhythm and Blues, Volume
Four*.

7   **"No Particular Place to Go,"** CHUCK BERRY, 1964
Like "Duke of Earl," this has been issued so many times in
rechanneled stereo that one usually doubts that it was ever
recorded in stereo. But on the LP *St. Louis to Liverpool*, it's
authentic.

HONORABLE MENTION:

1 and 2 **"Moonglow and Theme from Picnic,"** MORRIS STO-
LOFF, 1956; **"True Love,"** BING CROSBY and GRACE KELLY,
1956
Since true stereo on records wasn't introduced until early
1958, one wouldn't usually look for it on such early pop songs.
But these were recorded as part of stereo soundtracks and
then issued later on stereo albums.

3   **"Old Cape Cod,"** PATTI PAGE, 1957
Record labels were experimenting with stereo long before it
was commercially viable. The stereo version of this song,

without one of the vocal overdubs, is on a Mercury reissue album of Page material.

-◄❚▮❚►-

LES PAUL LISTS THE MOST IMPORTANT TECHNOLOGICAL INNOVATIONS IN RECORDED MUSIC

1	Solid-body electric guitar	5	Electro-magnetic pickup
2	Echo	6	Reverb
3	Flanging	7	Time delay
4	Phase-shifting	8	Sound-on-sound

LES PAUL *is, of course, either the inventor or one of the most important figures in innovating all of these devices. He is a unique character, with a wry wit and nonstop mind. He's a guitarist par excellence, and his milestones in the field of recording and electronics are many. Most folks still remember him as the guy who did "How High the Moon" with Mary Ford, though.*

-◄❚▮❚►-

SONGS THAT MADE FEEDBACK FAMOUS

1   "Train Kept a-Rollin'," JOHNNY BURNETTE AND THE ROCK AND ROLL TRIO, 1958
2   "Anyway, Anyhow, Anywhere," THE WHO, 1965
3   "Juke," LITTLE WALTER, 1952
4   "My Generation," THE WHO, 1965
5   "I Feel Fine," THE BEATLES, 1965
6   "Purple Haze," THE JIMI HENDRIX EXPERIENCE, 1967
7   "Train Kept a-Rollin'," THE YARDBIRDS, 1966
8   "Weasels Ripped My Flesh," THE MOTHERS OF INVENTION, 1970

NOT SO FAST
15 Songs with False Endings

1 "All by Myself," ERIC CARMEN
2 "Bernadette," THE FOUR TOPS
3 "Born to Run," BRUCE SPRINGSTEEN
4 "Do You Love Me?" THE CONTOURS
5 "Good Lovin'," THE YOUNG RASCALS
6 "Good Vibrations," THE BEACH BOYS
7 "I've Got You under My Skin," THE FOUR SEASONS
8 "I Need Your Loving," DON GARDNER AND DEE DEE FORD
9 "Keep on Dancing," THE GENTRYS
10 "Let Me," PAUL REVERE AND THE RAIDERS
11 "The Little Girl I Once Knew," THE BEACH BOYS
12 "Monday Monday," THE MAMAS AND THE PAPAS
13 "Rain," THE BEATLES
14 "She's the One," THE CHARTBUSTERS
15 "Some Kind-a Earthquake," DUANE EDDY

-◄▐▐►-

DO YOU HEAR WHAT I HEAR?
10 Songs with Moments You May Have Missed

1 **". . . And the Gods Made Love,"** THE JIMI HENDRIX
   EXPERIENCE
   At 78 rpm, a voice says, "emit erom eno," which is, in
   reverse, the gods pronouncing that you should make love just
   "one more time."
2 **"All Mine,"** THE FIVE SATINS
   In the background, a truck can be heard rumbling past the
   studio.
3 **"Ballad of John and Yoko,"** THE BEATLES
   John Lennon can be heard calling hello to Peter Brown, from
   Brian Epstein's office, during the song.

4   **"Blue Moon,"** ELVIS PRESLEY
Soda can be heard coming out of the studio vending machine.

5   **"Bob Dylan's 115th Dream,"** BOB DYLAN
Dylan cracks up after the band blows its cue.

6   **"Happy Jack,"** THE WHO
Pete Townshend shouts "I saw ya" at the end. He was speaking to the late Keith Moon, who had been banished from the vocal booth because he couldn't sing. Moon was hiding behind the recording console and making the group laugh during the take.

7   **"Strawberry Fields Forever,"** THE BEATLES
John Lennon says "cranberry sauce" at the end.

8   **"Stranded in the Jungle,"** THE JAYHAWKS
A telephone is ringing in the background.

9   **"Third Stone from the Sun,"** THE JIMI HENDRIX EXPERIENCE
Played at 78 rpm, an entire dialogue between "Starship" and "Star Command" will reveal itself.

10   **"Wendy,"** THE BEACH BOYS
A cough can be heard at the beginning of the instrumental break.

-◄❙❙►-

GREAT ROCK ALBUMS YOU MAY NEVER HEAR

1   ***The Everlasting First,*** JIMI HENDRIX and ARTHUR LEE
The title track was released on Love's *False Start*, but for legal reasons, Lee, the group's lead singer, has never been able to put out the rest of the material. This song only hints at the capabilities of Lee and Hendrix, who were both at their peak during this celebrated collaboration in 1970.

2   ***Smile,*** THE BEACH BOYS
This 1967 album was completely prepared, down to the cover art, when Brian Wilson decided it would not be proper to release it. According to Wilson acolytes, though, the material is his masterpiece. The reasons for his refusal to put it out

seem to be based in the deep insecurities that have virtually immobilized him since the late sixties. Various fragments from the work, however, have shown up on *Smiley Smile* and *Surf's Up*.

3   ***The Million Dollar Quartet,*** ELVIS PRESLEY, JERRY LEE LEWIS, CARL PERKINS, and JOHNNY CASH
Recorded in Memphis on December 3, 1956, when Presley happened to drop by Sun Studios and meet up with three other rockabilly greats, this two-and-a-half-hour session of gospel harmonizing has long been thought to be merely a rumor. It is now certain that the three tapes do exist. But because they were never officially presented to RCA, and because of the splintering contractual situations of the artists involved, the release of a *Million Dollar Quartet* LP is highly unlikely.

4   ***Live in the U.K.,*** BOB DYLAN
Dylan recorded all the dates on his 1966 tour, including the often-bootlegged Royal Albert Hall show in London, for a live album. But for whatever reasons, CBS did not release the record at the time, and it is now doubtful the planned LP will ever make an official appearance. But then, that's what everybody thought about *The Basement Tapes*, too.

5   ***The Rolling Stones and Stevie Wonder***
Recorded in the studio during The Stones 1972 American tour, on which Stevie opened most of the dates, the album was tied up, probably permanently, by litigation with former manager Allen Klein.

6   ***Homegrown,*** NEIL YOUNG
Young has described this studio album, recorded around 1974, as "the other side of *Harvest*." But, like some of Young's other projects, it molders while he moves spontaneously onward to new material.

7   ***Live Yardbirds (Featuring Jimmy Page)***
Taped during the final Yardbirds tour, at New York's Anderson Theatre in 1968, this album was released in 1971 on Epic, The Yardbirds' American label. But one week later, it was

withdrawn from circulation because of litigation threats from unspecified parties. The original package had liner notes by future Patti Smith Group guitarist Lenny Kaye.

8   ***Buffalo Springfield***
Eleven tracks that the band recorded some time in 1966 are reported to exist but were never released, presumably because the group was in one of its periodic snits of not speaking to one another.

9   ***David Bowie Live at the Santa Monica Civic***
Recorded in 1972 by RCA as the intended followup to *Ziggy Stardust and the Spiders from Mars*. Plans to release it were scrapped when *Aladdin Sane* was recorded. This live album has been heavily bootlegged.

10   ***Black Gold*, JIMI HENDRIX**
Jimi recorded this musical autobiography on a cassette at his Twelfth Street apartment in New York City just months before his death. After he died on September 18, 1970, in England, the tape was stolen from his apartment and never seen again.

11   ***Fillmore East '68*, and *Cow Palace '72*, THE WHO**
The Who recorded dates at both halls for release as live albums. The former record was canceled and *Live at Leeds* issued instead. One cut from the shows at San Francisco's Cow Palace did surface: A version of Marvin Gaye's "Baby Don't You Do It" was issued as the B-side of The Who's "Join Together."

12   ***John McLaughlin/Jimi Hendrix Jam Session***
Recorded at the New York City Record Plant in 1969. Alan Douglas was extremely enthusiastic about the tapes when he took over control of the Hendrix musical estate in the mid-seventies. However, he has been unable to release an album because McLaughlin was reportedly dissatisfied with his performance.

SIX: AWARDS

Bobby Roberts (left) and producer Lou Adler present Johnny Rivers with a gold record for "Memphis" in 1964.

THE BOOK OF ROCK LISTS DUBIOUS RECORDING ACHIEVEMENT AWARDS

1 **Most negative song to hit the Top Forty**
"Nobody but Me," by The Human Beinz, uses the word *no* over 100 times in a mere 2:16. In addition, the word *nobody* is used forty-six times. For balance, they throw in the word *yeah* once. Runner-up: "Tell Her No," by The Zombies, uses the word *no* sixty-three times in 2:08.

2 **Most obnoxious song to hit a jukebox**
"Aaah-Ah, Yawa Em Ekat Ot Gnimoc Er'yeht," by Napoleon XIV, is the B-side of "They're Coming to Take Me Away, Ha-Haaa!" The song is reputed to have completely cleared a restaurant of forty patrons in two minutes flat.

3 **Most tasteless song to hit the Top 100**
In "I Want My Baby Back" (a narrow victory over numerous competitors), singer Jimmy Cross has an auto accident in which his girlfriend is splattered all over the highway. Three months later, he decides he can't live without her, digs her up, and joins her in the pine box. Honorable mention: Warren Zevon's "Excitable Boy."

4 **Shortest record to make the Top Forty**
"Some Kind-a Earthquake," a 1959 instrumental by Duane Eddy, clocked in at 1:17. Several artists have cut flip sides just as short: for instance, The Beach Boys' "You're Welcome" (the flip side of "Heroes and Villains"). "John's Music Box," the flip side of "Dancing Bear," by The Mamas and the Papas, was timed at one minute flat. (But flip sides aren't eligible for this award, because they aren't listed on the Top Forty.)

5 **The "throw-in-an-extra-preposition-and-call-it-artistic-license" award**
Moby Grape, for the lyric to "Funky Tunk" (on the 1968 LP *Wow*): "How come you ain't got on your clothes on?"
Paul McCartney, for the lyric to 1973's "Live and Let Die": "In this ever-changing world in which we live in."

6 **Most unlikely surfer**
Bo Diddley, for his album *Surfin' with Bo Diddley* (*Bo Diddley is a Gunslinger* was bad enough, but *surfer?*).

7 **Longest album version of a Top Forty hit**
At 22:30, Kraftwerk's *Autobahn* exceeds Rare Earth's "Get Ready" by exactly one minute.

8 **Worst song issued by a major record label**
The only real competition to "Paralyzed" is its flip side. The Legendary Stardust Cowboy is a one-man band incapable of playing any instrument, singing in tune, or holding a steady beat. There are rumors that Mercury released an album by this guy, and that certain outlaw country fans consider this record a camp classic. Oh, God! Please don't let it be true. . . .

9 **The "Who-cares-what-the-album-sounds-like—did-you-see-the-cover?" award**
Mom's Apple Pie wins for its first album, or to be more exact, its jacket. The original cover featured "mom" holding a pie with one slice removed. Hidden among the apples was a drawing of a vagina. After retailers protested, subsequent copies of the album had the slice bricked up, with barbed wire around it, and tears in "mom's" eyes. Has anyone ever bothered to listen to this album?

10 **Worst guitar solo on a Number One record**
Scotty Moore, for Elvis Presley's "Heartbreak Hotel": Stan Freberg wasn't too far off when he said, "That's close enough for jazz."

11 **Longest pause for breath in a Top Forty record**
"Surfin' Bird," by the Trashmen: Was there ever a doubt?

12 **Longest final chord**
At twenty-four seconds, the end to The Beatles' "A Day in the Life" gets a little flaky; the engineers turned the sound level so high that the room's air-conditioners are audible.

13 **Most off-color line in the LP version of a Number One hit**
Jefferson Starship's "Miracles," for the line, "I got a taste of the real world when I went down on you girl." Runners-up

include the classic lyric from Lou Reed's "Walk on the Wild Side": "But she never lost her head, even when she was giving head"; and Blondie's "I'll give you some head—and shoulders to cry on." But these songs didn't make Number One.

14   **Longest note held**
Shortly after Jay and the Americans released "Cara Mia," WTRY in Troy, New York, aired a "special version" in which Jay held the long note near the end for just over a minute, and then continued without missing a beat. The award goes jointly to the group and the WTRY production staff.

15   **Artist with the most records containing studio talk**
The Beach Boys dwarf all competition. They made more than a dozen songs that contain extraneous talking in the background, most of it easily audible.

-◄▮▶-

3 LASHES WITH A WET NOODLE
The Wimp-Rock Top 40

1	THE COWSILLS	16	THE DUPREES
2	THE CARPENTERS	17	ZAGER AND EVANS
3	THE OSMONDS	18	BREAD
4	EVERY MOTHER'S SON	19	ABBA
5	BARNABY BYE	20	THE HUDSON BROTHERS
6	THE ASSOCIATION	21	MARK-ALMOND
7	SEALS AND CROFTS	22	JAMES TAYLOR
8	CROSBY, STILLS, AND NASH	23	GARY LEWIS AND THE PLAYBOYS
9	JOHN DENVER	24	LIGHTHOUSE
10	IT'S A BEAUTIFUL DAY	25	BILLY J. KRAMER AND THE DAKOTAS
11	PABLO CRUISE		
12	THE SEEKERS	26	GERRY AND THE PACEMAKERS
13	THE CHORDETTES		
14	DONOVAN	27	FREDDIE AND THE DREAMERS
15	THE MOODY BLUES		

28 AMBROSIA
29 THE CYRKLE
30 THE BABYS
31 BREWER AND SHIPLEY
32 CECILIO AND KAPONO
33 THE ROYAL GUARDS-
     MEN
34 LOGGINS AND MESSINA
35 THE UNION GAP

36 JONATHAN RICHMAN
     AND THE MODERN
     LOVERS
37 THE LITTLE RIVER
     BAND
38 THE EAGLES
39 FIREFALL
40 ART GARFUNKEL

-◄▮▮►-

THE 10 MOST FORGETTABLE PERFORMERS

1 FRANKIE AVALON
2 PAT BOONE
3 THE CARPENTERS
4 TOMMY SANDS
5 FABIAN
6 PAUL WILLIAMS

7 THE OSMONDS
8 NANCY SINATRA
9 THE CAPTAIN AND
    TENNILLE
10 LINDA RONSTADT

-◄▮▮►-

THE FIRST 10 ROCK RECORDS TO WIN GOLD DISCS

1 "Hard Headed Woman," ELVIS PRESLEY, 1958
2 *Pat's Greatest Hits,"* PAT BOONE, 1960
3 *Elvis*, ELVIS PRESLEY, 1960
4 *Elvis' Golden Records*, ELVIS PRESLEY, 1961
5 *Encore—Golden Hits*, THE PLATTERS, 1961
6 *Blue Hawaii*, ELVIS PRESLEY, 1961
7 "Can't Help Falling in Love," ELVIS PRESLEY, 1962
8 "I Can't Stop Loving You," RAY CHARLES, 1962
9 *Modern Sounds in Country and Western Music*, RAY CHARLES, 1962
10 "Hey Paula," PAUL AND PAULA, 1963

NOTE: Perry Como received the Recording Industry Association of America's (RIAA) first gold record, for "Catch a Falling Star," on March 14, 1958. Gordon MacRae's *Oklahoma* LP and Laurie London's "He's Got the Whole World in His Hands" also scored before "Hard Headed Woman," making it the fourth disc to go gold in any musical category.

The initial criterion for receiving a gold award was $1 million in sales, at retail list price. For singles, which then listed for about $1 each, this represented an equivalent number of units sold. For LPs, the criterion was based on wholesale price, which initially made sales of about 400,000 albums equivalent to gold status. But as LP list prices rose, the quantity of sales necessary to receive the award continuously shrank, necessitating revision in the mid-seventies.

THE FIRST 10 PLATINUM SINGLES

1   "Disco Lady," JOHNNIE TAYLOR, 1976
2   "Kiss and Say Goodbye," THE MANHATTANS, 1976
3   "Play That Funky Music," WILD CHERRY, 1976
4   "Disco Duck," RICK DEES AND HIS CAST OF IDIOTS, 1976
5   "Car Wash," ROSE ROYCE, 1977
6   "You Light Up My Life," DEBBY BOONE, 1977
7   "Boogie Nights," HEATWAVE, 1977
8   "Stayin' Alive," THE BEE GEES, 1978
9   "Emotion," SAMANTHA SANG, 1978
10   "We Are the Champions," QUEEN, 1978

NOTE: Platinum singles were not officially issued by the RIAA until 1976. Sales of 2 million units are required to merit the award. The platinum single remains fairly rare; to date, the only artists to win more than one of them are The Bee Gees (four), Donna Summer (two), and Queen (two).

ARTISTS WHO HAVE NEVER HAD A GOLD SINGLE

1	THE BYRDS	7	GENE PITNEY
2	SAM COOKE	8	SMOKEY ROBINSON AND
3	BOB DYLAN		THE MIRACLES*
4	MARVIN GAYE*	9	THE SUPREMES*
5	THE KINKS	10	THE WHO
6	JERRY LEE LEWIS	11	STEVIE WONDER*

*Motown did not ask that the RIAA certify its artists or those with its subsidiary labels until 1979.

-◄◖▮◗►-

ARTISTS WITH 5 OR MORE GOLD SINGLES
Through 1980

NOTE: The gold disc is awarded only if the company requests an audit, so the list is skewed.

1	THE BEATLES*	19	11	CREEDENCE CLEAR-	
2	ARETHA FRANKLIN	14		WATER REVIVAL	6
3	DONNA SUMMER	13	12	THE MONKEES	6
4	THE BEE GEES	9	13	DR. HOOK AND THE	
5	ELTON JOHN	9		MEDICINE SHOW	5
6	OLIVIA NEWTON-		14	EARTH, WIND, AND	
	JOHN**	9		FIRE	5
7	ELVIS PRESLEY	9	15	THE O'JAYS	5
8	AL GREEN	8	16	THE ROLLING STONES	5
9	THREE DOG NIGHT	7	17	THE SPINNERS†	5
10	PAUL MCCARTNEY AND				
	WINGS	7			

* Includes one with Billy Preston
** Includes two with John Travolta
† Includes one with Dionne Warwick

ARTISTS WITH 10 OR MORE GOLD ALBUMS
Through 1980

1	ELVIS PRESLEY	28	12	SANTANA**		11
2	THE BEATLES	22	13	THREE DOG NIGHT		11
3	THE ROLLING		14	NEIL YOUNG		11
	STONES	19	15	PAUL MCCARTNEY		
4	BOB DYLAN	18		AND WINGS†		11
5	ELTON JOHN	16	16	THE JEFFERSON AIR-		
6	JOHN DENVER*	16		PLANE/STARSHIP††		11
7	THE BEACH BOYS	14	17	THE DOORS		10
8	CHICAGO	13	18	KISS		10
9	NEIL DIAMOND	13	19	LINDA RONSTADT		10
10	JETHRO TULL	12				
11	GRAND FUNK RAIL-					
	ROAD	11				

* Includes one album with the Muppets
**Includes one album with Buddy Miles and another with John McLaughlin
† Includes two McCartney solo albums
††Includes five albums by the Jefferson Airplane and six by the Jefferson Starship, its successor

-◄❚❚►-

ARTISTS AWARDED THE MOST PLATINUM ALBUMS
Through 1980

1	THE BEE GEES*	7	5	PAUL MCCARTNEY	
2	BARBRA STREISAND	7		AND WINGS	5
3	KISS	6	6	KENNY ROGERS	5
4	NEIL DIAMOND	5	7	LINDA RONSTADT**	5

* The RIAA credits The Bee Gees with the *Saturday Night Fever* soundtrack because they are the dominant artists on it, and it is included in their total.
**Linda Ronstadt appears on the soundtrack for the film *FM*, but is not credited with its platinum LP award because she contributed only one track.

8	EARTH, WIND, AND FIRE	4	9	TED NUGENT	4
			10	WILLIE NELSON†	4

† Willie Nelson is credited, as Willie Nelson and Family, on the soundtrack to *Honeysuckle Rose*, and that album is included in his total, as is his collaborative LP with Waylon Jennings.

ROCK AND ROLLERS IN THE 'PLAYBOY' HALL OF FAME

1	BOB DYLAN, 1970	10	ERIC CLAPTON, 1973
2	JOHN LENNON, 1970	11	DUANE ALLMAN, 1974
3	PAUL MCCARTNEY, 1970	12	ELTON JOHN, 1975
4	JIMI HENDRIX, 1971	13	STEVIE WONDER, 1976
5	JANIS JOPLIN, 1971	14	RINGO STARR, 1977
6	ELVIS PRESLEY, 1971	15	LINDA RONSTADT, 1978, 1979
7	MICK JAGGER, 1972	16	KEITH MOON, 1980
8	JIM MORRISON, 1972	17	BRUCE SPRINGSTEEN, 1980
9	GEORGE HARRISON, 1972	18	JOHN BONHAM, 1981

ROCK-ERA PERFORMERS WHO WON THE MOST GRAMMYS

Through 1980

1	STEVIE WONDER	15	8	THE BEATLES	4
2	RAY CHARLES	10	9	CAROLE KING	4
3	ARETHA FRANKLIN	10	10	SIMON AND GARFUNKEL	4
4	PAUL SIMON	10			
5	MUDDY WATERS	6	11	ART GARFUNKEL	4
6	PAUL MCCARTNEY*	6	12	ROY HALEE	4
7	THE BEE GEES	5	13	ROBERTA FLACK	4

NOTE: Henry Mancini is the overall leader, with twenty Grammys won since 1958, when the awards began.

*Includes one with Wings

10 ARTISTS WHO'VE NEVER WON A GRAMMY

1   THE BEACH BOYS
2   CHUCK BERRY
3   CREEDENCE CLEAR-
       WATER REVIVAL
4   MARVIN GAYE
5   JIMI HENDRIX
6   JERRY LEE LEWIS
7   SMOKEY ROBINSON
8   SLY AND THE FAMILY
       STONE
9   THE WHO
10 NEIL YOUNG

THE MOST PATHETIC GRAMMYS

1   **Elvis Presley's Bing Crosby Award,** 1971
    The Crosby award is a special Grammy presented to "members
    of the recording industry who, during their lifetimes, have
    made creative contributions of outstanding artistic or scientific
    significance." Elvis apparently won for science, since he never
    won a Grammy for the artistry of any of his pop recordings. He
    did win—in 1967, 1972, and 1974, respectively—for his
    gospel recordings, *How Great Thou Art* (twice, for some reason)
    and *He Touched Me*.

2   **Best Rhythm & Blues Performance,** 1958
    In the first year of the Grammys—which was also the year that
    Jerry Butler and The Impressions recorded "For Your Precious
    Love," The Elegants graced us with "Little Star," and Chuck
    Berry created "Johnny B. Goode"—the Best Rhythm & Blues
    Grammy went to The Champs' instrumental, "Tequila." So
    whadda they know? It got worse. . . .

3   **Best Rock and Roll Recording,** 1962–1963
    The winners: Bent Fabric's tame piano instrumental, "Alley
    Cat," and Nino Tempo and April Stevens' hardly rockin'
    ballad, "Deep Purple."

4   **Record of the Year,** 1964
    This was, of course, the year of The Beatles. But in all their
    wisdom, the Grammy voters selected Stan Getz and Astrud

Gilberto's "Girl from Ipanema" as the Record of the Year. More outrageous, the Best Rock and Roll Recording was Petula Clark's forgettable pop quickie, "Downtown." The Beatles did win for Best New Artist, and for Best Performance by a Vocal Group. Ironically, the song that garnered them the latter award was "A Hard Day's Night," even though the year's winner for Best Motion Picture Score was . . . *Mary Poppins*.

5 **Best Rock and Roll,** 1966

Just as rock was rolling again, rock and roll was dropped as a Grammy category—although the travesties picked from 1962 to 1966, when "Winchester Cathedral" was one of the victors, made it obvious that the Best Rock and Roll slot was a fraud from the start. There was no rock and roll category again until 1979, when Bob Dylan collected his first Grammy for the gospel song "Gotta Serve Somebody." Other winners that year: Best Rock Vocal Performance, Female, Donna Summer; Best Rock Vocal Performance by a Duo or Group: The Eagles; Best Rock Instrumental Performance: Wings.

6 **Best Album Notes,** 1975

Pete Hamill won this award for his essay on the back cover of Dylan's *Blood on the Tracks*, a screed so patently embarrassing it was deleted from the jacket after the first pressing.

∙▪◗▐◖▪∙

ROCKERS WITH STARS ON HOLLYWOOD BOULEVARD

1	THE BEACH BOYS	7	ARETHA FRANKLIN
2	THE BEE GEES	8	THE JACKSON 5
3	NATALIE COLE	9	ELTON JOHN
4	CROSBY, STILLS, NASH, AND YOUNG	10	ELVIS PRESLEY
5	FLEETWOOD MAC	11	NEIL SEDAKA
6	PETER FRAMPTON	12	THE SPINNERS

SEVEN: FIRSTS AND DEBUTS

The Nitty Gritty Dirt Band, the first American band to play the Soviet Union.

25 RECORD AND RECORDING FIRSTS

1   First sound recording on a machine: "Mary Had a Little Lamb," Thomas Edison, December 6, 1877

2   First gramophone: United States patent obtained by Emile Berliner, September 26, 1887

3   First LP: developed by Thomas Edison (twelve inches in diameter, one-half-inch thick, weighing two pounds and played with a diamond stylus), 1926

4   First record chart: John G. Peatman's "Weekly Survey" (an English chart that ranked records on the basis of airplay), 1932

5   First recorded song called "rock and roll": The Boswell Sisters, 1934

6   First pop-record sales chart: *Billboard*, January 4, 1936

7   First Number One recording artist: Joe Venuti, January 4, 1936

8   First 45 rpm record: RCA, 1949

9   First use of an echo chamber: "Foolish Heart," Junior Mance (used a boom mike in a bathroom), 1950

10   First Sun recording: "Blues in My Condition"/"Selling My Whiskey," Jackie Boy Kelly and Little Walter Horton (never released), 1952

11   First eight-track recorder: built by Les Paul, 1954

12   First rock and roll song on *Billboard* chart: "Crazy, Man, Crazy," Bill Haley and His Comets, 1953

13   First black artist to record: The Dinwiddie Quartet (six one-sided discs for Monarch label), October 1902

14   First 78 rpm disc by a black artist: "Crazy Blues," Mamie Smith (Okeh label), 1920

15   First record to make pop, R&B, and C&W charts simultaneously: "Heartbreak Hotel," Elvis Presley, 1956

16   First Jamaican record released in U.K.: "Little Sheila," Laurel Aitken, 1953

17   First major R&B record with strings: "There Goes My Baby," The Drifters, 1959

18   First song to make *Billboard* chart without being issued as a single: "Love Me," Elvis Presley, 1956

19   First album with no artist name on cover, front or back: *For LP Fans Only*, Elvis Presley, 1959

20   First British group to have Number One hit in U.S.: The Tornadoes, "Telstar," 1962

21   First rock two-disc set: *Freak Out*, The Mothers of Invention, 1966

22   First gold record awarded to Chuck Berry: "My Ding-a-ling," 1972

23   First rock group to receive Russian record royalties: The Rolling Stones (as a result of Russian copyright law changes), June 4, 1975

24   First platinum cassette: *Frampton Comes Alive!* Peter Frampton, 1977

25   First picture-disc 45: "Hold the Line," Toto, 1978

-◄▮▮►-

BROADCASTING FIRSTS

1   First jukebox: installed at Palais Royal Hotel, San Francisco, November 23, 1899

2   First group on *American Bandstand:* The Chordettes, 1956

3   First song to be broadcast on BBC Radio One (the pop music station): "Flowers in the Rain," The Move, 1967

4   First national broadcast of *American Bandstand:* August 5, 1957

5   First all-rock radio station: WHB, Kansas City, 1958

6   First Rolling Stones TV Appearance: *Thank Your Lucky Stars,* June 7, 1963

7   First *Ready Steady Go* broadcast in Britain: August 9, 1963 (last broadcast, December 23, 1966)

8   First British pirate radio broadcast: Radio Caroline, March 28, 1964

PERFORMANCE FIRSTS

1   First American group to tour the U.K.: Freddie Bell and the Bellboys, 1956
2   First New York gig by Bob Dylan: Gerde's Folk City (played "House of the Rising Sun" and "Song to Woody," among others), September 11, 1961
3   First rocker nominated for an Oscar: Bobby Darin, for Best Supporting Actor in *Captain Newman M.D.*, 1963
4   First concert at the Fillmore Auditorium, San Francisco: The Grateful Dead, The Jefferson Airplane, The Charlatans (promoted by Bill Graham, who paid sixty dollars to rent the room), November 10, 1965
5   First official Ken Kesey and the Merry Pranksters Acid Test: Soquel, California, November 1965
6   First Be-In: Golden Gate Park, San Francisco, January 14, 1967
7   First time Jimi Hendrix burned his guitar: Finsbury Park, London, March 31, 1967
8   First use of lasers in a live performance: The Who, 1976 tour
9   First quadrophonic concert: Pink Floyd, Queen Elizabeth Hall, London, May 12, 1977
10   First American pop group to tour the U.S.S.R.: The Nitty Gritty Dirt Band, 1977

-◄►-

BEATLES FIRSTS

1   First appearance at Liverpool's Cavern Club: March 21, 1961
2   First appearance on *The Ed Sullivan Show:* February 9, 1964
3   First record to use reverse tapes: "Rain," June 10, 1966
4   First record on Apple label: "Hey Jude," August 30, 1968

5   First rumor that "Paul is dead": *Northern Star* headline
     "Clues Hint at Beatle Death," September 23, 1969
6   First solo album by a Beatle: *Wonderwall Music*, George
     Harrison, 1969
7   First solo single by a Beatle: "Give Peace a Chance," John
     Lennon, 1970
8   First official release in the U.S.S.R.: "Let It Be," 1972

-◄❙❙►-

THE 15 BEST DEBUT ALBUMS

1   *Are You Experienced?* THE JIMI HENDRIX EXPERIENCE, 1967
2   *With the Beatles* (U.K. title for *Meet the Beatles!*), 1963
3   *Elvis Presley*, 1956
4   *John Lennon/Plastic Ono Band*, 1970
5   *Here's Little Richard*, 1956
6   *Bob Dylan*, 1962
7   *The Clash*, 1977
8   *The Rolling Stones*, 1964
9   *Music from Big Pink*, THE BAND, 1968
10   *With a Little Help from My Friends*, JOE COCKER, 1969
11   *My Aim Is True*, ELVIS COSTELLO, 1977
12   *The J. Geils Band*, 1970
13   *The Doors*, 1967
14   *Pronounced Leh-Nerd Skin-Nerd*, LYNYRD SKYNYRD, 1973
15   *Jerry Lee Lewis*, 1958

-◄❙❙►-

THE 15 BEST DEBUT SINGLES

1   "I Want You Back," THE JACKSON 5, 1969
2   "That's All Right," ELVIS PRESLEY, 1954
3   "Anarchy in the U.K.," THE SEX PISTOLS, 1976
4   "I Can't Explain," THE WHO, 1965
5   "These Arms of Mine," OTIS REDDING, 1963

6   "Reet Petite (the Finest Girl You Ever Want to Meet),"
     JACKIE WILSON, 1957
7   "Ooby Dooby," ROY ORBISON, 1956
8   "Maybellene," CHUCK BERRY, 1955
9   "Be-Bop-a-Lula," GENE VINCENT AND HIS BLUE CAPS, 1956
10   "Mr. Tambourine Man," THE BYRDS, 1965
11   "Let's Go Trippin'," DICK DALE AND HIS DEL-TONES, 1961
12   "The Fat Man," FATS DOMINO, 1949
13   "Lawdy, Miss Clawdy," LLOYD PRICE, 1952
14   "I Don't Want to Go Home," SOUTHSIDE JOHNNY AND THE
     ASBURY JUKES, 1976
15   "I'm a Man/Bo Diddley," BO DIDDLEY, 1955

-◄❙▮▶-

THE 10 MOST DISAPPOINTING DEBUT ALBUMS

1   ***Blind Faith,*** 1969
     This was supposed to be the ultimate in supergroups, sporting
     a lineup that included Eric Clapton and Ginger Baker fresh
     from Cream and Steve Winwood of Traffic. Imagine the world's
     surprise when the music turned out to be tepid, uninspired,
     and uninspiring.
2   ***The Grateful Dead,*** 1967
     Supposed to be the granddaddy of psychedelic bands, the
     Dead debuted as a fourth-rate, pretentious blues band.
3   ***Big Brother and the Holding Company,*** 1967
     The word from the Monterey Pop Festival portrayed Janis
     Joplin as the new Bessie Smith. Unfortunately, the word didn't
     account for the fact that she was in a group of stoned
     stumblebums who had neither much sense of time nor much
     concept of melody.
4   ***Crosby, Stills, and Nash,*** 1969
     Another supergroup fiasco. Those who based their vision of
     what the music would be like on the fact that all three had been

in rock bands were stunned when what emerged was barbershop harmony.

5   ***Never Mind the Bollocks, Here's the Sex Pistols***, 1977

After their revolutionary set of hit singles, it seemed impossible that these rock and roll revolutionaries could make a record anything less than brilliant. But aside from the singles, what we got was pedestrian, and The Pistols were revealed as, of all things, a singles band. Best punk *album* honors go to *The Clash*, instead.

6   ***Wednesday Morning, 3 AM***, SIMON AND GARFUNKEL, 1965

Those who heard "The Sounds of Silence" and loved its folk-rock music were destined to be sadly surprised when they rushed out to buy the duo's first album, which was a straight and somewhat cloying folk set, all high harmonies and wimp prosody.

7   ***I Got Dem Ol' Kozmic Blues Again, Mama***, JANIS JOPLIN, 1969

So Joplin split from Big Brother and got herself a band of solid professionals. And then the leather-lunged singer's own technical limitations showed her up. She was better off with the high-spirited incompetence of Big Brother than this sterile drool.

8   ***McCartney***, PAUL McCARTNEY, 1970

How could the first pop-oriented, nonexperimental solo album by a Beatle miss? Easy, he played all the music himself, wrote about one and a half good songs, and revealed that it was not just an illusion that John Lennon was the group's intellectual *auteur*. Banal and dumb.

9   ***Song Cycle***, VAN DYKE PARKS, 1968

For months, the West Coast intelligentsia had been writing about the brilliance of Parks, a former collaborator on some Brian Wilson songs (none of them yet heard, of course). Turned out what he made was pretentious movie music.

10   ***Led Zeppelin***, 1969

Jimmy Page had been talking for nearly a year about the New

Yardbirds, and though this group didn't have that name, Zeppelin was his successor group to one of the most innovative bands rock ever knew. So what did we get? Recycled Jeff Beck Group.

-◄▐▌►-

THE 10 WORST DEBUT SINGLES

1   "Baby Kittens," CAROLE KING, 1959
2   "Baby Talk," JAN AND DEAN, 1959
3   "A Teenager's Romance," RICKY NELSON, 1957
4   "Long Tall Sally," THE KINKS, 1964
5   "Love to Love You Baby," DONNA SUMMER, 1976
6   "Movie Magg," CARL PERKINS, 1955
7   "My Bonnie," THE BEATLES, 1961
8   "Stormy Weather," THE FIVE SHARPS, 1954
9   "Suzie-Q," CREEDENCE CLEARWATER REVIVAL, 1968
10   "Taxi Blues," LITTLE RICHARD, 1951

-◄▐▌►-

THE FIRST BOOTLEG ALBUM

In the summer of 1969, Bob Dylan's Great White Wonder *made its first appearance in Los Angeles record shops as a blank-covered, unlabeled two-disc set. It was an immediate international sensation, featuring a variety of previously unissued, unknown, or only rumored Dylan music. It started a major bootlegging craze that was slowed down only when legitimate record companies went to great lengths to prevent it.* Great White Wonder *included:*

Side One
1   "Can You Please Crawl Out Your Window"
2   "It Takes a Lot to Laugh, It Takes a Train to Cry"

3   "She Belongs to Me"
4   "Love Minus Zero/No Limit"
5   "It's All Over Now, Baby Blue"
6   "That's Alright Mama"
7   "Hard Times in New York"
8   "Stealin'"

NOTE: The first six cuts are outtakes from official Dylan albums of the mid-1960s; the others are from a 1961 tape made in Minnesota.

Side Two
1   "I Was Young When I Left Home"
2   "Percy's Song"
3   "Corrina Corrina"
4   "In the Evening"
5   "Long John"
6   "Down in the Flood"

NOTE: Nos. 1, 4, and 5 are from the 1961 Minnesota tape; Nos. 2 and 3 are from album sessions; No. 6 is from *The Basement Tapes*.

Side Three
1   "Million Dollar Bash"
2   "Yea! Heavy and a Bottle of Bread"
3   "Please Mrs. Henry"
4   "Lo and Behold"
5   "Tiny Montgomery"
6   "Mixed Up Confusion"
7   "East Laredo"

NOTE: Nos. 1 through 5 are from *The Basement Tapes*; No. 6 was originally issued on *Freewheelin'* but subsequently deleted; No. 7 is an LP outtake.

Side Four

1 "Wade in the Water"
2 "Cocaine"
3 "I'll Keep It with Mine"
4 "Talkin' John Birch Society Blues"
5 "Who Killed Davey Moore?"
6 "Eternal Circle"
7 "Ramblin' Gamblin' Willie"

NOTE: Nos. 1 and 2 are from the Minnesota tape (No. 2 is incomplete); Nos. 3 and 6 are LP outtakes; Nos. 4 and 7 are from the original version of *Freewheelin'*; No. 5 is a live recording of Dylan's 1963 Carnegie Hall concert.

FAMOUS TURN-DOWNS

1 Elvis Presley was tossed out of the Grand Ole Opry in 1954 after a show. One of the Opry honchos reportedly suggested he go back to driving a truck. Elvis was also turned down by Arthur Godfrey's *Talent Scouts*.

2 Decca Records rejected The Beatles, as did several other labels, before producer George Martin finally saw some potential in them.

3 Stephen Stills flunked an audition to be in The Monkees; he joined Buffalo Springfield instead.

4 The Who were turned down by EMI Records. Later, American Decca would refuse the initial master of "My Generation" because it thought the feedback solo at the end was unplanned distortion.

5 Godfrey's *Talent Scouts* also spurned Sonny Til and the Orioles, who went on to hit with "Crying in the Chapel" and kick off the early-1950s bird-group craze.

6 The Sex Pistols were dropped by A&M Records without ever releasing a record. Actually, it was misbehavior at the band's signing party in the label offices that apparently caused the

dismissal, which cost A&M a pile of dough and enhanced The Pistols' outlaw imagery.

7   Boston's first demo tape, which was cut in Tom Scholz' basement but otherwise is almost identical to the group's first album, was turned down by virtually every major label in America. Finally, the tape returned for a second chance to Epic Records, which, on further listening, decided to sign them. The almost-identical album sold 8 million copies, the most commercially successful debut LP by a rock band in recording history.

PERFORMERS DISCOVERED BY JOHN HAMMOND

John Hammond has been a legendary talent scout for a variety of record companies, most notably Columbia, since the 1930s. In 1938, he organized the Carnegie Hall Spirituals to Swing concerts, which first brought the full scope of American black music to a sophisticated audience, and has nurtured a wide range of performers ever since. Among his discoveries:

1   BENNY GOODMAN, 1934
2   COUNT BASIE, 1935
3   CHARLIE CHRISTIAN, 1939
4   ARETHA FRANKLIN, 1960
5   BOB DYLAN, 1961
6   BRUCE SPRINGSTEEN, 1972

PERFORMERS DISCOVERED BY SAM PHILLIPS

Sam Phillips is the godfather of rock and roll, not only because he shepherded Elvis Presley, Scotty Moore, and Bill Black through their incredible early records for his Sun label, but also because of the performers he discovered and nurtured before and after that period. Some of them include:

1 WALTER HORTON, 1951
2 JUNIOR PARKER, 1951
3 ELVIS PRESLEY, 1954
4 JOHNNY CASH, 1955
5 CARL PERKINS, 1955
6 ROY ORBISON, 1956
7 JERRY LEE LEWIS, 1957
8 CHARLIE RICH, 1958

EIGHT: CRITICISM

Mick Jagger often finds it hard to measure up to legend. Here, he is seen in a typical pose carrying the weight of The Stones' famous stage act.

JOSEPH SIA

DISCREDITED ROCK THEORIES

1 **Elvis Presley's music was just imitation rhythm & blues.**
A canard of the worst kind. Presley, even in his first recordings, was influenced at least as much by country singers, pop vocalists like Dean Martin, and gospel music (white and black) as he was by R&B vocalists. In fact, some evidence suggests that Presley hadn't heard much R&B before Sam Phillips took him under his wing. The ultimate evidence that this theory is mistaken, however, is offered by the Sun singles themselves: All five contain nonoriginal material, and of the ten songs represented there, half are from country & western sources. "I Love You Because" and "I'm Left, You're Right, She's Gone" are nothing like R&B, but they have everything in common with country music. And both are rockers.

2 **Rock "died" between 1959 and 1964.**
This is thought to be true because during that period Elvis was in the army, Buddy Holly died, Jerry Lee Lewis was banned, Chuck Berry went to prison, and Little Richard entered a seminary. Fact is, however, that from 1959 to 1964, the following not only had hits but had Number One hits: Lloyd Price ("Stagger Lee"), Wilbert Harrison ("Kansas City"), The Drifters ("Save the Last Dance for Me"), Del Shannon ("Runaway"), Ernie K-Doe ("Mother-in-Law"), Roy Orbison ("Running Scared"), Gary "U.S." Bonds ("Quarter to Three"), Dion ("Runaround Sue"), Little Eva ("The Loco-Motion"), The Four Seasons ("Sherry," "Walk like a Man," "Big Girls Don't Cry"), The Crystals ("He's a Rebel"), The Chiffons ("He's So Fine"), Stevie Wonder ("Fingertips—Pt. 2")—not to mention a batch of other girl-group, Chicago soul, Motown, and surf hits. And if that ain't rock and roll. . . .

3 **Paul is dead.**
A dead person would never have sued to dissolve The Beatles'

partnership. However, it is true that when he reads his reviews, Paul sometimes *wishes* he were dead.

4 **All rock critics wear glasses.**
Lester Bangs doesn't.

5 **Rock lyrics are poetry.**
Rock lyrics are verse and generally rhyme, but they aren't poetic, except in the rarest cases, and certainly, the best of them have little or no emotional impact when laid out on the page, unadorned by music. Rock lyrics are doggerel, maybe.

-◄❙❙▶-

THE 10 BEST ROCK CRITICS

1 **Vince Aletti**
Contributor to *Rolling Stone*, *Creem*, and various other publications. The best writer, ever, about soul and disco music. Understands the genre emotionally, technically, formally, and theoretically. Fine stylist. Recently, he has been working as an executive at RFC Records.

2 **Lester Bangs**
Editor of *Creem*, contributor to a vast number of unlikely and likely publications in the United States and Britain. Most influential critic, best stylist, renegade taste that frequently doubles back on itself. Author of *Blondie* (Fireside, 1980), a scathing critical biography.

3 **Robert Christgau**
Music editor of the *Village Voice*, has also written regularly for *Esquire*, *Cheetah*, and *Newsday*. Champions bohemian chic, intellectually rigorous, can be infuriatingly obtuse, but is always at his most direct in his monthly "Consumer Guide" column, in which various current product is dissected and graded by letter. *Any Old Way You Choose It* (Penguin, 1973) is an anthology of his work.

4 **Nik Cohn**
England's best. Author of *Rock from the Beginning* (Stein &

Day, 1969), a jaundiced history, and the text for *Rock Dreams* (Popular Library, 1973). Primal fantasist and expert on all matters of style and nuance.

5   **Jon Landau**

Record-reviews editor of *Rolling Stone*, contributor to *Crawdaddy* as well as Boston's *Phoenix* and *Real Paper*. Now produces Bruce Springsteen. Ace theoretician and politician, specializing in Stax, Motown, Dylan. When he was passionate, no one was better. *It's Too Late to Stop Now: A Rock & Roll Journal* (Straight Arrow, 1972) is an anthology of his work.

6   **Greil Marcus**

Contributor, columnist, editor for *Rolling Stone*, *New West*, *Creem*. Author of *Mystery Train: Images of America in Rock 'n' Roll Music* (Dutton, 1975). As intellectually rigorous as Christgau, but a shade more academic. At the same time, possessed of an impish wit and thirst for genuine trash. Sees the big picture, with details.

7   **Dave Marsh**

Editor, contributor, columnist for *Rolling Stone*, *Creem*, *Newsday*, the *Real Paper*, *Musician: Player and Listener*. Author of *Born to Run: The Bruce Springsteen Story* (Doubleday, 1979). Instinctive purist, determined revisionist, gets lost easily outside the mainstream; emotionalism can turn into sentimentality.

8   **Paul Nelson**

Editor, contributor to the *Little Sandy Review*, *Sing Out!*, *Rolling Stone*, *Hullabaloo*, and *Circus*. With Bangs, the best stylist of the bunch. Perhaps too fascinated by heroic pulp mythology, devotee of the lyric sheet, but when it comes to feeling, he always gets it right.

9   **Robert Palmer**

Columnist, contributor to *Rolling Stone*, the *New York Times*, *Penthouse*, many more. Played in Insect Trust, an early avant-garde jazz-rock group with two LPs: *Insect Trust*, on Capitol, and *Hoboken Saturday Night*, on Atco. Scholarly and technical expertise shows up in his best writing, which is mostly about avant-rock, jazz, blues, and country performers. When his Southern roots don't overwhelm him, top-notch.

10 **Pete Townshend**

Townshend would be a great rock critic even if he hadn't written several intriguing articles over the years for various British and American publications. In both his songs and his interviews (which he has raised to an art form), his pronouncements on the meaning and state of rock are among the most probing to be read anywhere.

-◄❙❙▶-

GREIL MARCUS CHOOSES THE 10 WORST ROCK CRITICS

1 **Albert Goldman**

Closet rock-hater and formerly slick phrasemaker for *Life*, Goldman is now at work on the "definitive" biography of Elvis Presley. Look out, fans.

2 **Rory O'Connor**

Much worse than the Boston *Real Paper* scene-maker, much lower than the rock-crit type depicted in the film *Between the Lines*. O'Connor's radical chic makes him much lower, in his sleazy way, than the cretinous performers he promoted.

3 **Ellen Sander**

Star of the pages of the old *Saturday Review*, if you can believe that. So much of a star, in fact, that in her last days she took to signing liner notes with her first name only.

4 **Chris Van Ness**

Out of the pages of the preporno *Los Angeles Free Press*, and America's number-one sucker for sensitive singer/songwriters.

5 **Legs McNeil**

Avatar of *Punk* magazine. Precisely what *Creem* had in mind when, way back in the early 1970s, it predicted something called "Sopor Nation." (Sopors, for those unfamiliar with prepunk drug usage, are Quaaludes.)

6   **Ritchie Yorke**
    Canadian-based, international hustler. Author of a book on Van
    Morrison that is to rock criticism what *The Prophet* is to
    philosophy.

7   **Don Heckman**
    The *New York Times* jazz fan and rock know-nothing.

8   **Mike Jahn**
    When appearing in the *New York Times*, the first pop critic
    with his own publicist.

9   **Jonathan Eisen**
    Responsible for (in Robert Christgau's words) the worst rock
    column "in the history of Western Civilization" (it appeared in
    Circus), Eisen is best known for his now-out-of-print *Age of
    Rock* anthologies and their various spinoffs, each of which was,
    in its own special way, a triumph of merely snobbish one-
    upmanship.

10 **John Leonard**
    On the cultural pages of the *New York Times*, the arch defender
    of high culture against the subversion of the masses.

GREIL MARCUS *has been writing rock criticism since the late 1960s for publications
ranging from the* San Francisco Express-Times *and* Creem *to* Rolling Stone *and*
New West, *where he presently contributes "Real Life Rock." He is the author of*
Mystery Train: Images of America in Rock'n' Roll Music *(Dutton, 1975), which
was nominated for a National Book Critics Circle award.*

-◄▐▶-

FRANK ZAPPA'S FAVORITE ROCK CRITICS

1
2
3
4
5

THE LEAST PROMISING INTERVIEW OPENERS CAMERON CROWE HAS ENCOUNTERED

1 "This gun is loaded."—BUDDY MILES

2 "Let's do it in the bar."—STEPHEN STILLS

3 "Hold on, aren't you the one who called me the Liberace of Rock?"—ELTON JOHN

4 "You're too young to grasp my complete musical scope." —STEVE MILLER

5 "I changed my mind." PETE TOWNSHEND

6 "We don't believe in tape recorders."—ZZ TOP

7 "Is there any way you can write nice things about me without talking to me per se?"—RICHARD DREYFUSS

8 "There's nobody here except a few ghosts and I don't care. Let's rap."—BOB WEIR

9 "I think I just saw a body drop right outside that window. Did you just see a body drop? Let's go outside and see. I know I saw a body drop."—DAVID BOWIE

CAMERON CROWE *began contributing to such national rock publications as* Rolling Stone *and* Creem *while still attending junior high school in San Diego. (Despite the unpromising beginnings listed above, most of Crowe's interview and profiles turned out swell.) Now a full-fledged adult, Crowe recently spent a year in high school, as a student, for a book and a film project.*

-◄███►-

FROM THE PAGE TO THE STAGE—AND BACK
Performers and Producers Who Have Also Been Critics and Journalists

1	LAUREN AGNELLI, a.k.a. TRIXIE A. BALM	5	STEVE HARLEY
		6	CHRISSIE HYNDE
2	LESTER BANGS	7	LENNY KAYE
3	ROBERT FRIPP	8	CUB KODA
4	BOB GELDOF	9	JON LANDAU
		10	R. MELTZER

11 SANDY PEARLMAN   13 PETE TOWNSHEND
12 PATTI SMITH

-◄❚▶-

"WHEN I GET MY PICTURE ON THE COVER OF THE 'ROLLING STONE'"

Most Frequent Appearances on the Magazine's Cover

1	BOB DYLAN	9	12	ROD STEWART	4
2	JOHN LENNON*	8	13	ELTON JOHN	4
3	MICK JAGGER	6	14	FLEETWOOD MAC	4
4	JANIS JOPLIN	6	15	PETE TOWNSHEND	3
5	THE ROLLING STONES	5	16	RICHARD NIXON	3
6	PAUL McCARTNEY	5	17	JIMI HENDRIX	3
7	LINDA RONSTADT	5	18	JIM MORRISON	3
8	JAMES TAYLOR	5	19	JANE FONDA	3
9	THE BEATLES	4	20	MUHAMMAD ALI	3
10	CARLY SIMON	4	21	JEFFERSON AIRPLANE/ STARSHIP	3
11	JACKSON BROWNE	4			

NOTE: Dr. Hook make it to the cover of issue 131, March 29, 1973.

*Lennon appeared on the first cover of *Rolling Stone*, November 9, 1967.

-◄❚▶-

MOST APPEARANCES ON THE COVER OF "16" MAGAZINE

1	THE BEATLES	6	DONNY OSMOND
2	THE MONKEES	7	BOBBY SHERMAN
3	THE BAY CITY ROLLERS	8	SAJID KAHN
4	KISS	9	ELVIS PRESLEY
5	DAVID CASSIDY	10	RICK NELSON

PERFORMERS WHO MADE THE COVER OF "TIME"

1 THE BEATLES, 1967
2 ARETHA FRANKLIN, 1968
3 THE BAND, 1970
4 JAMES TAYLOR, 1971
5 JONI MITCHELL, 1974
6 BRUCE SPRINGSTEEN, 1975
7 CHER, 1975
8 ELTON JOHN, 1975
9 PAUL MCCARTNEY, 1976
10 LINDA RONSTADT, 1977
11 THE WHO, 1979
12 JOHN LENNON, 1980

-◄|▮►-

ROCK STARS WHO HAVE MADE THE COVER OF "NEWSWEEK"

1 THE BEATLES, 1964, 1969
2 JANIS JOPLIN, 1969
3 ARLO GUTHRIE, 1969
4 MICK JAGGER, 1970
5 BOB DYLAN, 1974
6 STEVIE WONDER, 1973
7 BRUCE SPRINGSTEEN, 1975
8 JOHN DENVER, 1976
9 THE BEE GEES and PETER FRAMPTON, 1978
10 WILLIE NELSON, 1978
11 DONNA SUMMER, 1979
12 LINDA RONSTADT,* 1979
13 JOHN LENNON, 1980

*Sitting next to California Governor Jerry Brown

THE 10 BEST ROCK PERIODICALS

1   *Rolling Stone*, 1969–1975
2   *Creem*, 1970–1973
3   *Let It Rock*, during its brief existence in the early 1970s
4   *Hit Parader*, as edited by Jim Delehant in the late 1960s
5   *New Musical Express*, 1975–1978
6   *16*, during the mid-1960s; when there were no "serious" rock publications, editor Gloria Stavers had the world to herself and took a chance on featuring the strangest psychedelic rockers as well as teen idols.
7   *Hullabaloo*, edited by Paul Nelson in the late 1960s-early 1970s
8   *Cheetah*, for the brief time during 1967 and 1968 that it lasted
9   *Goldmine*, 1978–1980, Rick Whitesell, editor; the best collector's magazine ever
10 *Who Put the Bomp*, early 1970s; midwifed the birth of punk rock

-◄▮▮►-

THE 5 WORST ROCK PERIODICALS

1   *Creem*, 1974-present; since the original staff (Lester Bangs, Dave Marsh) left
2   Any magazine issued since 1957 that is principally or solely concerned with Elvis Presley
3   *Circus*, 1975-present; redeemed only by an occasional perspicacious reviews editor (Paul Nelson, John Swenson)
4   *Rolling Stone*, 1977-present; consistently behind the trends and lackadaisical in its news and feature coverage
5   *Fusion*, during its late 1960s-early 1970s life span; attempted to bring sensibility of *Harper's* to a medium that is the antithesis of such bourgeois gentility

Nine:
ART

One of Andrew Gold's favorites.

MOST BEAUTIFUL RECORD LABELS

1   Sun
2   Motown (the original label with map)
3   J.O.B.
4   Checker
5   Roulette (original)
6   Old Town
7   End
8   States
9   Apple (red label)
10 Rama
11 Fire
12 Duke (purple and gold label)
13 RCA (with Nipper the Dog)

-◄▐▐►-

GREAT 45 COVERS

1   "Have You Seen Your Mother, Baby, Standing in the Shadows," THE ROLLING STONES
2   "God Save the Queen," THE SEX PISTOLS
3   "I Want You," BOB DYLAN
4   "All Shook Up," ELVIS PRESLEY
5   "All You Need Is Love," THE BEATLES
6   "Take Me to the River," TALKING HEADS
7   "Pressure Drop"/"English Civil War," THE CLASH
8   "Honky Tonk Women," THE ROLLING STONES
9   "Holidays in the Sun," THE SEX PISTOLS
10 "Mellow Yellow," DONOVAN
11 "Rough Boys," PETE TOWNSHEND

50 GREAT ALBUM COVER DESIGNS

1   *Sgt. Pepper's Lonely Hearts Club Band*, THE BEATLES
2   *Their Satanic Majesties Request*, THE ROLLING STONES
3   *Elvis Presley*
4   *Two Sides of the Moon*, KEITH MOON
5   *We're Only in It for the Money*, THE MOTHERS OF INVENTION
6   *Yesterday . . . and Today* (butcher-block version), THE
    BEATLES
7   *Born to Run*, BRUCE SPRINGSTEEN
8   *50,000,000 Elvis Fans Can't Be Wrong—Elvis' Gold Records,
    Volume 2*, ELVIS PRESLEY
9   *The Who Sell Out*
10 *The Velvet Underground and Nico*
11 *Weasels Ripped My Flesh*, THE MOTHERS OF INVENTION

*The original bad taste "butcher block" cover for The Beatles' Yesterday and
Today LP, which was recalled from the stores by Capitol Records after
numerous protests by meat packagers throughout the country. Today, it is
valued at several hundred dollars.*

Weasels Ripped My Flesh,
*Frank Zappa and the Mothers
of Invention.*

Cheap Thrills, *Big Brother and
the Holding Company.*

12 *Feats Don't Fail Me Now,* LITTLE FEAT
13 *Siren,* ROXY MUSIC
14 *Houses of the Holy,* LED ZEPPELIN
15 *Happy Trails,* QUICKSILVER MESSENGER SERVICE
16 *Who's Next,* THE WHO
17 *Are You Experienced?* THE JIMI HENDRIX EXPERIENCE
18 *How Dare You,* 10CC
19 *Argus,* WISHBONE ASH
20 *Lotus,* SANTANA
21 *Axis: Bold as Love,* THE JIMI HENDRIX EXPERIENCE
22 *Beggar's Banquet* (original men's room version), THE
    ROLLING STONES
23 *Ogden's Nut Gone Flake,* THE SMALL FACES
24 *Surf's Up,* THE BEACH BOYS
25 *Dark Side of the Moon,* PINK FLOYD
26 *A Nice Pair,* PINK FLOYD
27 *Aoxomoxoa,* THE GRATEFUL DEAD
28 *Kitsch,* HEAVY METAL KIDS
29 *Solution,* CORDON BLEU
30 *Tommy,* THE WHO
31 *Caravanserai,* SANTANA

32 *Mysterious Traveller,* WEATHER REPORT
33 *Cheap Thrills,* BIG BROTHER AND THE HOLDING COMPANY
34 *Tales from Topographic Oceans,* YES
35 *Gene Vincent and The Blue Caps*
36 *Pyramid,* ALAN PARSONS PROJECT
37 *Presence,* LED ZEPPELIN
38 *Dinosaur Swamps,* THE FLOCK
39 *King of the Delta Blues Singers,* ROBERT JOHNSON
40 *The Teenagers Featuring Frankie Lymon*
41 *Lumpy Gravy,* THE MOTHERS OF INVENTION
42 *Wish You Were Here,* PINK FLOYD
43 *I Wish It Would Rain,* THE TEMPTATIONS
44 *Two Steps from the Blues,* BOBBY "BLUE" BLAND
45 *Bringing It All Back Home,* BOB DYLAN
46 *Bo Diddley is a Gunslinger*
47 *Meet the Beatles!*
48 *Never Mind the Bollocks, Here's The Sex Pistols*
49 *The Kids Are Alright,* THE WHO
50 *Bare Trees,* FLEETWOOD MAC

-◄▐▶-

YOU CAN'T JUDGE A RECORD BY ITS COVER
10 Great Sleeves You Wouldn't Want to Open

1 *Child Is Father to the Man,* BLOOD, SWEAT, AND TEARS
2 *Climax,* THE OHIO PLAYERS
3 *Breakfast in America,* SUPERTRAMP
4 *Procol Harum Live*
5 *Workingman's Dead,* GRATEFUL DEAD
6 *The Stranger,* BILLY JOEL
7 *Hasten down the Wind,* LINDA RONSTADT
8 *Journey Through the Past,* NEIL YOUNG
9 *Brain Salad Surgery,* EMERSON, LAKE, AND PALMER
10 *Magic Bus: The Who on Tour*

ANDREW GOLD PICKS THE 10 BEST ALBUM GRAPHICS

1 *Rubber Soul*, THE BEATLES
2 *Blonde on Blonde*, BOB DYLAN
3 *Another Monty Python Record*
4 *One Man Dog*, JAMES TAYLOR
5 *The Roches*
6 *Walls and Bridges*, JOHN LENNON
7 *Who's Next*, THE WHO
8 *Electric Ladyland*, JIMI HENDRIX (U.S. version, side with Jimi's face)
9 *Wild Child*, VALERIE CARTER
10 *Actual Business Letters Dictated at Various Speeds*, STENODISC RECORDS

ANDREW GOLD *has been active in the West Coast folk-rock scene of recent years as a writer, recording artist, session player, and producer. His Asylum LP,* What's Wrong with This Picture?, *which contained the hit single "Lonely Boy," sported a unique cover that challenged listeners to spot visual incongruities planted there with malicious forethought.*

-◄◖►-

LESTER BANGS SELECTS THE WORST LP COVERS OF ALL TIME BY MAJOR ROCK ARTISTS

1 *Blank Generation*, RICHARD HELL AND THE VOIDOIDS
2 *Growing Up in Public*, LOU REED
3 *Saved*, BOB DYLAN
4 *Never Mind the Bollocks, Here's the Sex Pistols*
5 *Let It Bleed*, THE ROLLING STONES
6 *Hard Nose the Highway*, VAN MORRISON
7 Any JOURNEY cover

8   *On the Corner; In Concert; Big Fun; Water Babies*, MILES DAVIS
9   Any CHER cover, but most especially that album she made with Gregg Allman, *Allman and Woman*
10 *Lust for Life*, IGGY POP

LESTER BANGS *is an expert on all aspects of rock and roll. His wide-ranging commentary thereon has appeared in publications ranging from* Punk *to* Penthouse. *Bangs always walks it like he talks it, without missing a beat.*

-◄❙▮❙►-

FACES ON THE COVER OF 'SGT. PEPPER'S LONELY HEARTS CLUB BAND'

1   American Legionnaire
2   FRED ASTAIRE
3   AUBREY BEARDSLEY
4   THE BEATLES in wax
5   LARRY BELL
6   WALLACE BERMAN
7   ISSY BONN
8   MARLON BRANDO
9   BOBBY BREEN
10 LENNY BRUCE
11 WILLIAM BURROUGHS
12 LEWIS CARROLL
13 STEPHEN CRANE
14 ALEISTER CROWLEY
15 TONY CURTIS
16 MARLENE DIETRICH
17 DION
18 DIANA DORS
19 BOB DYLAN
20 ALBERT EINSTEIN
21 W. C. FIELDS
22 HUNTZ HALL
23 TOMMY HANDLEY
24 OLIVER HARDY
25 ALDOUS HUXLEY
26 C. G. JUNG
27 STAN LAUREL
28 T. E. LAWRENCE
29 RICHARD LINDNER
30 SONNY LISTON
31 DR. LIVINGSTONE
32 KARL MARX
33 MERKIN
34 MAX MILLER
35 TOM MIX
36 MARILYN MONROE
37 SIR ROBERT PEEL
38 EDGAR ALLAN POE
39 TYRONE POWER
40 SIMON RODIA
41 GEORGE BERNARD SHAW

42	TERRY SOUTHERN	48	JOHNNY WEISMULLER
43	KARLHEINZ STOCKHAUSEN	49	H. G. WELLS
		50	MAE WEST
44	ALBERT STUBBINS	51	OSCAR WILDE
45	STUART SUTCLIFFE	52	Three drawings of unidentified women
46	SHIRLEY TEMPLE		
47	DYLAN THOMAS	53	Five unidentified gurus

-◄❚▮❚►-

CAL SCHENKEL NAMES THE FACES ON "WE'RE ONLY IN IT FOR THE MONEY"

As a parody of Sgt. Pepper's Lonely Hearts Club Band *and the hippie mentality,* The Mothers of Invention *created* We're Only in It for the Money, *an equally adventurous concept album whose cover features faces even more fantastic and obscure than The Beatles' original.*

1	TOM WILSON	14	GAIL ZAPPA
2	DON PRESTON, plaster	15	MOON UNIT ZAPPA
3	BILLY MUNDI, plaster	16	CAL SCHENKEL
4	JIMMY CARL BLACK, plaster	17	LISA COHEN, daughter of Herb
5	IAN UNDERWOOD, plaster	18	JIMI HENDRIX
		19	?
6	FRANK ZAPPA, plaster	20	GABRIEL, Portrait of a Countess
7	ROY ESTRADA, Mother		
8	BILLY MUNDI, Mother	21	BIG MAMA THORNTON
9	BUNK GARDNER, Mother	22	CHESTER FIELD
10	JIMMY CARL BLACK, Mother	23	PHANTOM OF THE OPERA
11	DON PRESTON, Mother	24	FRANK ZAPPA SR.
12	IAN UNDERWOOD, Mother	25	BILLY PORTER
		26	JOE CASEY
13	FRANK ZAPPA	27	NANCY SINATRA
		28	BOB NORTON

We're Only in It for the Money, *Frank Zappa and the Mothers of Invention.*

29 DIAL SOAPMAN

30 H. BOSCH, Garden of
    Earthly Delights

31 COACH WARE

32 DAVID ST. JOHN

33 SANDY HURVITZ

34 LYNDON JOHNSON

35 MARY MARTIN

36 SUE COLE

37 BUNK GARDNER, plaster

38 MEDALO BOPS

39 Statue of Liberty

40 Dallas policeman

41 ?

42 JOHN ZACHERLE

43 ?

44 POPE PIUS IV

45 RODAN

46 ELROY PIE

47 HERB COHEN

48 ITALLO PAOLLOZI

49 ?

50 ELVIS PRESLEY

51 NOSFERATU

52 GEORGE LIBERACE

53 EDDIE HASKEL

54 ED WYNN

55 LLOYD PRICE

56 ROD SERLING

57 NOSFERATU

57a	RICK BLAUFELD	72	DAVID CROSBY
58	ERIC BURDON	73	L.B.J.
59	PAULINE BUTCHER	74	BUFFERINMAN
60	Sunbeam shaver	75	THEDA BARA
61	DON VAN VLIET, a.k.a.	76	JOHN SLOATMAN SR.
	CAPTAIN BEEFHEART	77	JACQUELINE BEER
62	ALBERT EINSTEIN	78	JEFF SKLAROW
63	CINDY	79	LEE HARVEY OSWALD
64	SUE GROSS	80	GRACIE ALLEN
65	TOMMY MARLOWE	81	DOTTIE DRIBBLE
66	HARRY S TRUMAN	82	?
67	ADMIRAL BYRD	83	METALMAN
68	LYNN LASCARO	84	BARBIE and KEN
69	SGT. FURY	85	LUDWIG VON
70	CAL SCHENKEL		
71	KATHERINE C. THURSTON		

NOTE: For the identity of Mystery People, Nos. 19, 41, 43, 49, and 82, write Cal Schenkel, Box 88, Roslyn, Pennsylvania 19001.

CAL SCHENKEL *is the designer of the* We're Only in It for the Money *cover.*

ARTY ROCKERS

1 BOB DYLAN: painted the *Self-Portrait* and *Music from Big Pink* covers

2 JOHN LENNON: did numerous line drawings, including some erotic ones published in *Rolling Stone* in the early 1970s.

3 JONI MITCHELL: paints album covers, notably her own *Court and Spark* and the Crosby, Stills, Nash, and Young collection *So Far*

4 CHARLIE WATTS: does cartoonlike drawings, the most public being the back cover of *Between the Buttons* and his book about Charlie Parker, *Ode to a High-Flying Bird*

Self-Portrait, *Bob Dylan*.

5   JOHN ENTWISTLE: did the sleeve for *The Who by Numbers* as a connect-the-dots puzzle drawing

6   DON VAN VLIET: sculpts, and has painted covers for several of his own LPs

7   RINGO STARR: designs furniture

8   COMMANDER CODY: studied painting at the University of Michigan and the University of Wisconsin

9   CAT STEVENS: painted his own *Teaser and the Firecat* cover

10   KLAUS VOORMAN: painted The Beatles' *Revolver* sleeve

11   DEAN TORRANCE: through his Kittyhawk Graphics, designed *Will the Circle Be Unbroken?* album cover for The Nitty Gritty Dirt Band

PETER WOLF LISTS HIS FAVORITE ROCK AND ROLL ARTISTS

1	GEORGE GROSZ	8	MARCEL DUCHAMP
2	MAX BECKMANN	9	ALBERT RYDER
3	CHAIM SOUTINE	10	JOHN SLOAN
4	EDVARD MUNCH	11	HENRI MATISSE
5	ELIZABETH SHREVE	12	PIERRE BONNARD
6	HENRI ROUSSEAU	13	FRANZ KLINE
7	EDOUARD VUILLARD		

PETER WOLF grew up in The Bronx and moved to Boston after hgh school to study painting. Somewhere down the line, his priorities changed, and for the past twelve years, he has been lead vocalist of The J. Geils Band. Wolf's greatest hits include "Must of Got Lost," "Give It to Me," "One Last Kiss," and his anthem, "Love Stinks."

15 GREAT ROCK POSTER ARTISTS

Rock posters emerged as an art form in San Francisco during the mid-1960s. Originally, they served as announcements for the concerts held at early psychedelic ballrooms like the Fillmore Auditorium and the Avalon Ballroom. Their creators were primarily painters and fine artists who developed a style of graphic and commercial art that stands with the great European poster art of the nineteenth century. Recently, posters from this era have become quite valuable; a complete set of Avalon Ballroom posters was auctioned in 1980 by Phillips in New York for thousands of dollars.

1	STANLEY MOUSE and ALTON KELLY	4	JOHN VAN HAMERSVELD
		5	VICTOR MOSCOSO
2	RICK GRIFFIN	6	WES WILSON
3	SATTY	7	BOB FRIED

An early Stanley Mouse poster for the Northern California Psychedelic Cattlemen's Association Ltd., 1966.

GREATEST ROCK PHOTOGRAPHERS

1	ANNIE LEIBOVITZ	7	PENNIE SMITH
2	DAVID GAHR	8	ETHAN RUSSELL
3	BARON WOLMAN	9	ED CARAEFF
4	LYNN GOLDSMITH	10	NEAL PRESTON
5	JIM MARSHALL	11	ERIC MEOLA
6	NORMAN SEEFF	12	BOB GRUEN

LESTER BANGS SELECTS THE 10 WORST "INNOVATIONS" IN RECORD PACKAGING

1   Unipak

2   Bar codes

3   RCA's Dynaflex

4   MCA Records' current repackaging of Impulse's classic jazz catalog as nongatefolds, in many cases without even line notes. So, for instance, John Coltrane's *A Love Supreme* is now a record in just a single sleeve with the same picture, the artist's name and the album title on front and back.

5   *Air Conditioning*, the first Curved Air album

6   MGM Records' endless repackages of Hank Williams, Billie Holiday, Oscar Peterson, The Velvet Underground, The Blues Project, etc. in every kind of embarrassing and heinously ugly camouflage known to man.

7   The blissfully forgotten singer/songwriter album released in 1971 or 1972 (I can't remember) that was dunked in patchouli oil. It stunk up the entire *Creem* office. We finally had to take it out in the field and bury it like a dead mongrel.

8   *Alone Together*, Dave Mason's multicolored (vomitone) solo album on Blue Thumb

9   All picture discs—P. T. Barnum snickers in the Ninth Circle

10   CBS Records' decision, along about the time it released The
      Byrds' *Ballad of Easy Rider*, to make some (all? how chosen?),
      in any case, a few of its new releases a wee tad taller than the
      standard twelve-by-twelve-inch, thus making shipping them
      even more of a headache. And this from the company that gave
      us Aorta—Goddard Lieberson shoulda hung his head in
      shame.

LESTER BANGS *is the rock critics' rock critic, a man gifted verbally in much the
same way that James Brown is gifted as a dancer. As an editor of* Creem, *and as
contributor to all manner of publications from the sublime to the sordid, Bangs is
not merely notorious but absolutely legendary. He is the author of* Blondie
(Fireside, 1980); is preparing a book, Rock Gomorrah, *a musical Hollywood*
Babylon; *and is collaborating with Paul Nelson on a book about Rod Stewart.
Bangs also sports a singing career that includes one single ("Let It Blurt"/"Live,"
on Spy Records) and an album (*Jook Savages on the Brazos, *on Live Wire), cut in
Austin. A San Diego native who makes his home in New York, Bangs has haunted
London, Los Angeles, and Detroit as well as Austin. His latest project is a book on
relationships between men and women in our age, to be titled* All My Friends Are
Hermits.

-◄❚▶-

Devo's FAVORITE MODERN CONVENIENCES

1   Voice stress analyzers
2   Chemotherapy
3   Recombinant DNA parlors
4   Taser guns
5   Aerosol air
6   Ankle grabbers
7   Short microwave heating units
8   Microwave food blenders

DEVO, *best known for their 1980 hit, "Whip It," are pioneers of techno-rock, as
befits their philosophy of the regression (de-evolution) of humanity. The above list
may be considered a representative sampling of the instruments of that decline.*

TEN:
FILM

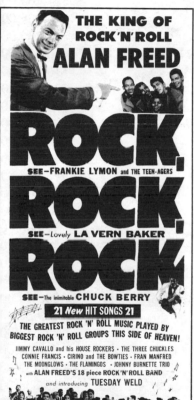

THE HIGHEST GROSSING ROCK FILMS
1955 to 1980

1	*Saturday Night Fever*, 1977	$74,100,000
2	*American Graffiti*, 1973	$55,886,000
3	*A Star Is Born*, 1976	$37,100,000
4	*Looking for Mr. Goodbar*, 1977	$16,900,000
5	*Woodstock*, 1970	$16,200,000
6	*Tommy*, 1975	$16,000,000
7	*Jesus Christ Superstar*, 1973	$13,291,000
8	*Sgt. Pepper's Lonely Hearts Club Band*, 1978	$12,958,000
9	*Xanadu*, 1980	$10,200,000
10	*Lady Sings the Blues*, 1972	$9,666,000
11	*More American Graffiti*, 1979	$8,177,000
12	*Thank God It's Friday*, 1978	$7,300,000
13	*Beyond the Valley of the Dolls*, 1970	$7,000,000
14	*Fame*, 1980	$7,000,000
15	*Hair*, 1969	$6,800,000
16	*Alice's Restaurant*, 1969	$6,275,000
17	*Bye Bye Birdie*, 1963	$6,200,000
18	*The Buddy Holly Story*, 1978	$5,900,000
19	*A Hard Day's Night*, 1964	$5,655,000
20	*American Hot Wax*, 1978	$5,532,000
21	*Wild in the Streets*, 1968	$5,500,000
22	*The Blackboard Jungle*, 1955	$5,459,000
23	*Help!* 1965	$5,335,000
24	*Viva Las Vegas*, 1964	$5,152,000
25	*Blue Hawaii*, 1961	$4,700,000
26	*G.I. Blues*, 1960	$4,300,000
27	*Love Me Tender*, 1956	$4,200,000

NOTE: Figures are for domestic (U.S./Canada) theater rentals only, according to *Variety* magazine's yearly totals.

BEST ROCK AND ROLL MOVIES

1   *King Creole*, directed by MICHAEL CURTIZ, 1958; stars Elvis
    Presley

2   *The Great Rock 'n' Roll Swindle*, directed by JULIEN TEMPLE,
    1980; stars The Sex Pistols

3   *Don't Look Back*, directed by D. A. PENNEBAKER, 1967; stars
    Bob Dylan

4   *A Hard Day's Night*, directed by RICHARD LESTER, 1964; stars
    The Beatles

5   *The T.A.M.I. Show*, directed by STEVE BINDER, 1965; stars
    James Brown, The Rolling Stones, Jan and Dean, The Su-
    premes, Marvin Gaye, Chuck Berry, and others

6   *The Girl Can't Help It*, directed by FRANK TASHLIN, 1956;
    features Little Richard, Gene Vincent, Eddie Cochran, and
    others

7   *The Harder They Come*, directed by PERRY HENZELL, 1972;
    stars Jimmy Cliff

8   *Monterey Pop*, directed by D. A. PENNEBAKER, 1968; stars
    Jimi Hendrix, Otis Redding, The Who, and others

9   *Privilege*, directed by PETER WATKINS, 1967; stars Paul Jones
    and Jean Shrimpton

10 *O Lucky Man*, directed by LINDSAY ANDERSON, 1973; stars
    Malcolm McDowell; score by Alan Price

11 *The Buddy Holly Story*, directed by STEVE RASH, 1978; stars
    Gary Busey

12 *Performance*, directed by NICHOLAS ROEG and DONALD CAM-
    MELL, 1970; stars Mick Jagger

13 *Superfly*, directed by GORDON PARKS JR., 1972; stars Ron
    O'Neal; score by Curtis Mayfield

14 *Beyond the Valley of the Dolls*, directed by RUSS MEYER,
    1970; stars Dolly Read, Edy Williams, and other forty-plus-
    inch busts; features The Strawberry Alarm Clock

15 *Wild in the Streets*, directed by BARRY SHEAR, 1968; stars
    Shelley Winters, Christopher Jones, and Richard Pryor

16   *The Kids Are Alright*, directed by JEFF STEIN, 1979; stars The Who

17   *Woodstock*, directed by MICHAEL WADLEIGH, 1970; stars a buncha bands and half a million hippies

18   *The Last Waltz*, directed by MARTIN SCORSESE, 1978; stars The Band, upstaged by Muddy Waters and Van Morrison

19   *Jailhouse Rock*, directed by RICHARD THORPE, 1957; stars Elvis Presley

20   *American Hot Wax*, directed by FLOYD MUTRUX, 1978; stars Tim McIntire as Alan Freed

21   *Mister Rock and Roll*, directed by CHARLES DUBIN, 1957; stars Alan Freed and friends

22   *Having a Wild Weekend*, directed by JOHN BOORMAN, 1965; stars The Dave Clark Five

23   *Shake, Rattle and R-O-C-K*, directed by EDWARD L. CAHN, 1956; stars Mike "Touch" Connors, Joe Turner, and Fats Domino

24   *That'll Be the Day*, directed by CLAUDE WHATHAM, 1974; stars David Essex, Ringo Starr, Billy Fury, and Keith Moon

25   *Yellow Submarine*, directed by GEORGE DUNNING, 1968; stars The Beatles

-◄❙▮❙►-

Worst ROCK AND ROLL MOVIES

1   *Sgt. Pepper's Lonely Hearts Club Band*, directed by MICHAEL SCHULTZ, 1978; stars The Bee Gees, Peter Frampton, Billy Preston, Steve Martin, Aerosmith, Earth, Wind, and Fire, and George Burns

2   *The Horror of Party Beach*, directed by DEL TENNEY, 1964; stars John Scott, Alice Lyon, Allen Laurel, Eulabelle Moore, and Marilyn Clark

3   *Renaldo and Clara*, directed by BOB DYLAN and HOWARD ALK, 1978; stars Bob Dylan, Joan Baez, Allen Ginsberg, Ronee Blakely, Sara Dylan, and The Rolling Thunder Revue

4   *The Song Remains the Same*, directed by PETER CLIFTON and
    JOE MASSOT, 1976; stars Led Zeppelin
5   *Celebration at Big Sur*, directed by BAIRD BRYANT and
    JOHANNA DEMETRAKAS, 1971; stars Joan Baez, Crosby,
    Stills, Nash, and Young, Joni Mitchell, John Sebastian, and
    Mimi Farina
6   *Xanadu*, directed by ROBERT GREENWALD, 1980; stars
    Olivia Newton-John, Gene Kelly, and Michael Beck; music
    by The Electric Light Orchestra
7   *Can't Stop the Music*, directed by NANCY WALKER, 1980;
    stars The Village People, Valerie Perrine, and Bruce Jenner
8   *Bye Bye Birdie*, directed by GEORGE SIDNEY, 1963; stars
    Janet Leigh, Dick Van Dyke, Ann-Margret, Paul Lynde, and
    Ed Sullivan; score by Charles Strouse and Lee Adams
9   *A Star Is Born*, directed by FRANK PIERSON, 1976; stars
    Barbra Streisand, Kris Kristofferson, and Gary Busey
10 *The Rose*, directed by MARK RYDELL, 1979; stars Bette
    Midler, Alan Bates, and Frederic Forrest
11 *Riot on Sunset Strip*, directed by ARTHUR DREIFUSS, 1967;
    stars Aldo Ray, Mimsy Farmer, Michael Evans, and Laurie
    Mock
12 *Roadie*, directed by ALAN RULDOLPH, 1980; stars Blondie,
    Meat Loaf, and Alice Cooper
13 *Journey Through the Past*, directed by NEIL YOUNG, 1973;
    stars Neil Young, Crazy Horse, and Buffalo Springfield
14 *Sympathy for the Devil (One Plus One)*, directed by JEAN-LUC
    GODARD, 1970; features The Rolling Stones
15 *Thank God It's Friday*, directed by ROBERT KLANE, 1978;
    stars Donna Summer and Jeff Goldblum
16 *Tommy*, directed by KEN RUSSELL, 1975; stars Roger
    Daltrey, Ann-Margret, Oliver Reed, Jack Nicholson, Eric
    Clapton, Tina Turner, Elton John, Robert Powell, and The
    Who
17 *Americathon*, directed by NEIL ISRAEL, 1979; stars John
    Ritter, Harvey Korman, and Zane Buzby; features Elvis
    Costello and The Beach Boys

18   *It's Trad, Dad,* directed by RICHARD LESTER, 1962; stars
     Chubby Checker and Dusty Springfield
19   *Rude Boy,* directed by JACK HAZANN, 1980; stars Roy Gange
     and The Clash
20   *Ladies and Gentlemen, the Rolling Stones,* directed by
     ROLLIN BINZER, 1975; stars The Rolling Stones, oddly
     enough
21   *FM,* directed by JOHN A. ALONZO, 1978; stars Martin Mull,
     Alex Karras, Cleavon Little, Michael Brandon; concert ap-
     pearances by Linda Ronstadt and Jimmy Buffett
22   *Rust Never Sleeps,* directed by BERNARD SHAKEY, a.k.a.
     NEIL YOUNG, 1979; stars Neil Young and Crazy Horse
23   *Sparkle,* directed by SAM O'STEEN, 1976; stars Philip M.
     Thomas, Irene Cara, Lonette McKee, Mary Alice, and Dwan
     Smith; music by Curtis Mayfield
24   *The Blues Brothers,* directed by JOHN LANDIS, 1980; stars
     Dan Aykroyd, John Belushi, and Aretha Franklin

-◄❙▐▶-

Best UNRELEASED ROCK FILMS

1   *Charlie Is My Darling,* stars THE ROLLING STONES, 1965
2   *Cocksucker Blues,* stars THE ROLLING STONES, 1972
3   *Something Is Happening,* stars BOB DYLAN, 1966
4   *Eric Clapton—Train Tour of Europe,* 1974–1975
5   *Feast of Friends,* stars THE DOORS, 1969
6   *Weird Scenes Inside the Gold Mine,* stars THE DOORS, 1969
7   *Jimi Hendrix Live at Albert Hall,* 1969
8   *Sweet Toronto,* stars JERRY LEE LEWIS, LITTLE RICHARD, BO
    DIDDLEY, and CHUCK BERRY, 1971
9   *David Bowie and the Spiders from Mars Live at Hammersmith
    Odeon,* 1972

WHO CARES WHAT PICTURE WE SEE?
The 10 Best Songs about the Movies

1 "Act Naturally," THE BEATLES
2 "Celluloid Heroes," THE KINKS
3 "Cool for Cats," SQUEEZE
4 "Emma," HOT CHOCOLATE
5 "Just Like in the Movies," THE UPBEATS
6 "Sad Movies (Make Me Cry)," SUE THOMPSON
7 "Saturday Night at the Movies," THE DRIFTERS
8 "Sittin' in the Balcony," EDDIE COCHRAN
9 "35 Millimeter Dreams," GARLAND JEFFREYS
10 "Western Movies," THE OLYMPICS

-◄❙❙►-

15 ROCK SONGS BASED ON FILM TITLES

1 "A Night at the Opera/A Day at the Races," QUEEN
2 "Black Sabbath," BLACK SABBATH
3 "Blue Angel," ROY ORBISON
4 "Ezy Ryder," JIMI HENDRIX
5 "Gone with the Wind," THE DUPREES
6 "Goodbye Girl," SQUEEZE
7 "Jools and Jim," PETE TOWNSHEND
8 "King Kong," THE JIMMY CASTOR BUNCH
9 "Night Moves," BOB SEGER
10 "Pretty Baby," SISTER SLEDGE
11 "The Thrill of It All," ROXY MUSIC
12 "Torn Curtain," TELEVISION
13 "Vertigo," SOUTHSIDE JOHNNY AND THE ASBURY JUKES
14 "Walk on the Wild Side," LOU REED
15 "Wild in the Streets," GARLAND JEFFREYS

THE 15 BEST FILM SCORES

1   *Mean Streets*, directed by Martin Scorsese, 1973; score by various artists

2   *The Harder They Come*, directed by Perry Henzel, 1972; score by JIMMY CLIFF and various artists

3   *Saturday Night Fever*, directed by John Badham, 1977; score by THE BEE GEES and various artists

4   *Pat Garrett and Billy the Kid*, directed by Sam Peckinpah, 1973; score by BOB DYLAN

5   *The Long Riders*, directed by Walter Hill, 1980; score by RY COODER

6   *Superfly*, directed by Gordon Parks Jr., 1972; score by CURTIS MAYFIELD

7   *American Graffiti*, directed by George Lucas, 1973; score by various artists

8   *O Lucky Man*, directed by Lindsay Anderson, 1973; score by ALAN PRICE

9   *Performance*, directed by Nicholas Roeg and Donald Cammell, 1970; score by JACK NITZSCHE, RANDY NEWMAN, and MICK JAGGER

10 *Shaft*, directed by Gordon Parks Jr., 1971; score by ISAAC HAYES

11 *The Valley (Obscured by Clouds)*, directed by Barbet Schroeder, 1972; score by PINK FLOYD

12 *Quadrophenia*, directed by Frank Roddam, 1979; score by THE WHO and various artists

13 *Car Wash*, directed by Michael Schultz, 1976; score by various artists

14 *Once upon a Time in the West*, directed by Sergio Leone, 1969; score by ENNIO MORRICONE

15 *Sorcerer*, directed by William Friedkin, 1977; score by TANGERINE DREAM

THE 10 WORST FILM SCORES

1   *Bye Bye Birdie*, CHARLES STROUSE and LEE ADAMS, 1963
2   *Phantom of the Paradise*, PAUL WILLIAMS, 1974
3   *Godspell*, STEPHEN SCHWARTZ, 1973
4   *Sgt. Pepper's Lonely Hearts Club Band*, THE BEE GEES, PETER FRAMPTON, and various artists, 1979
5   *The Idolmaker*, JEFF BARRY, 1980
6   *The Rocky Horror Picture Show*, RICHARD O'BRIEN, 1976
7   *Jesus Christ Superstar*, ANDREW LLOYD WEBBER and TIMOTHY RICE, 1973
8   *Grease*, THE BEE GEES and various artists, 1978
9   *The Rose*, AMANDA McBROOM and various artists, 1979
10 *Tommy*, PETE TOWNSHEND, 1975

-◄❙❚▶-

BEST FILM APPEARANCES BY ROCK PERFORMERS

1   RICK NELSON, *Rio Bravo*, 1959
2   MICK JAGGER, *Performance*, 1968
3   GARY BUSEY, *The Buddy Holly Story*, 1978
4   LEVON HELM, *Coal Miner's Daughter*, 1980
5   KRIS KRISTOFFERSON, *Cisco Pike*, 1972
6   RINGO STARR, *Candy*, 1968
7   ROY ORBISON, *The Fastest Guitar Alive*, 1968
8   ELVIS PRESLEY, *King Creole*, 1958
9   ADAM FAITH, *Stardust*, 1975
10 DAVID ESSEX, *That'll Be the Day*, 1974; *Stardust*, 1975
11 DIANA ROSS, *Lady Sings the Blues*, 1972
12 STEVE JONES, *The Great Rock 'n' Roll Swindle*, 1979
13 ART GARFUNKEL, *Carnal Knowledge*, 1971

WORST FILM APPEARANCES BY ROCK PERFORMERS

1 ELVIS PRESLEY, *It Happened at the World's Fair*, 1963
2 NEIL DIAMOND, *The Jazz Singer*, 1980
3 PAUL WILLIAMS, *Phantom of the Paradise*, 1975
4 ROGER DALTREY, *Lisztomania*, 1975
5 ART GARFUNKEL, *Bad Timing/A Sensual Obsession*, 1980
6 MICK JAGGER, *Ned Kelly*, 1970
7 RITA COOLIDGE, *Pat Garrett and Billy the Kid*, 1973
8 BARBRA STREISAND, *A Star Is Born*, 1976
9 THE VILLAGE PEOPLE, *Can't Stop the Music*, 1980
10 FRANK ZAPPA, *Baby Snakes*, 1980

-◄❙▐►-

FILMS FEATURING THE ROLLING STONES
With a Tip of the Hat to James Karnbach

1 *The T.A.M.I. Show*, 1964
2 *Charlie Is My Darling*, 1965*
3 *What's on the Flip Side*, 1966*
4 *Now Time*, 1967
5 *A Degree of Murder*, 1967**
6 *London in the Sixties*, 1968
7 *Rock and Roll Circus*, 1968*
8 *Tonight Let's All Make Love in London*, 1968
9 *Man to Man*, 1969
10 *Gimme Shelter*, 1970
11 *Ned Kelly*, 1970†
12 *Performance*, 1970†
13 *Sympathy for the Devil (One Plus One)*, 1970
14 *Invocation of My Demon Brother*, 1971

15 *Ladies and Gentlemen, the Rolling Stones* (at the Marquee Club) 1971
16 *Cocksucker Blues*, 1972*
17 *Ladies and Gentlemen, the Rolling Stones Are Back*, 1973
18 *Ladies and Gentlemen, the Rolling Stones*, 1974
19 *The Rolling Stones 1978 Tour Film*, 1978

* Unreleased
**Score by Brian Jones
† Mick Jagger only

JAMES KARNBACH *is a private rock and roll film archivist and collector with a special interest in Rolling Stones audio and visual materials. He was a consultant on* The Heroes of Rock 'n' Roll *and* The Kids Are Alright *and is currently working with David Dalton on a book called* Stones on Earth.

ROCK PERFORMERS WHO APPEAR IN THE ROLLING STONES' "ROCK AND ROLL CIRCUS"

The Rolling Stones' Rock and Roll Circus *was planned as a television special and filmed in December 1968 by Michael Lindsay-Hogg. Although it was never aired, various bootleg records of the musical performances have made it legendary.*

1 ERIC CLAPTON
2 MARIANNE FAITHFULL
3 JOHN LENNON
4 TAJ MAHAL
5 MITCH MITCHELL
6 YOKO ONO
7 THE ROLLING STONES
8 JETHRO TULL
9 THE WHO

Performers also included a classical pianist and violinist, and the Robert Fosset Circus with the Lovely Luna. Performers who were asked to appear, but did not, include:

1 JOHNNY CASH
2 DR. JOHN
3 THE ISLEY BROTHERS
4 TRAFFIC

ROLLING STONE

Jerry Lee Lewis seems to have forgotten his lines as Iago in this stage version of Catch My Soul, *a rhythm and blues version of Shakespeare's* Othello. *William Marshall (Othello) looks on in disbelief. Marshall was replaced by Richie Havens (below) in the screen version. The Metromedia Producers Corporation Presentation was directed by Patrick McGoohan and produced by Richard Rosenbloom and Jack Good. It was unleashed in 1974.*

COURTESY KEVIN STEIN

PERFORMERS WHO APPEARED AT WOODSTOCK BUT NOT IN THE MOVIE

1 THE BAND
2 BLOOD, SWEAT, AND TEARS
3 PAUL BUTTERFIELD
4 CREEDENCE CLEARWATER REVIVAL
5 THE GRATEFUL DEAD
6 KEEF HARTLEY
7 THE INCREDIBLE STRING BAND
8 THE JEFFERSON AIRPLANE
9 JANIS JOPLIN
10 MELANIE
11 MOUNTAIN
12 RAVI SHANKAR
13 BERT SOMMER
14 JOHNNY WINTER

·◄▐▶·

FILMS IN WHICH CHUCK BERRY HAS APPEARED

1 *Mister Rock and Roll,* 1957
2 *Rock, Rock, Rock,* 1957
3 *Go Johnny Go,* 1958
4 *Jazz on a Summer Day,* 1960
5 *The T.A.M.I. Show,* 1964
6 *Sweet Toronto,* 1971
7 *Let the Good Times Roll,* 1973
8 *American Hot Wax,* 1978

ELEVEN: BROADCASTING

Dr. Demento's number-one demented record.

Radio ROCK
The 15 Best Songs about Radio

1 "Capitol Radio," THE CLASH
2 "Caravan," VAN MORRISON
3 "FM (No Static at All)," STEELY DAN
4 "Heavy Music," BOB SEGER
5 "Mohammed's Radio," WARREN ZEVON
6 "On My Radio," THE SELECTER
7 "On the Radio," DONNA SUMMER
8 "On Your Radio," JOE JACKSON
9 "Radio Radio," ELVIS COSTELLO
10 "Road Runner," JONATHAN RICHMAN
11 "Rock and Roll," LOU REED
12 "Who Listens to the Radio?" THE SPORTS
13 "W*O*L*D," HARRY CHAPIN
14 "You Can't Say Crap on the Radio," STIFF LITTLE FINGERS
15 "You Turn Me On (I'm a Radio)," JONI MITCHELL

-◄▮▮►-

DJs WHO BECAME PERFORMERS

1 WAYLON JENNINGS, KLLL, Lubbock, Texas
2 B. B. KING, WDIA, Memphis
3 TERRY KNIGHT, CKLW, Detroit
4 JIM LOWE, WNBC, New York
5 WINK MARTINDALE, WHBQ, Memphis*
6 SOUPY SALES, WJW, Cleveland*
7 SLY STONE, KSOL, San Francisco
8 KIM WESTON, WCHB, Detroit

*Although both Sales and Martindale are best known as television personalities, they began their careers in rock and roll radio. In addition, both recorded minor hits; Sales had "Do the Mouse" in 1965 and Martindale made the Top Ten in 1959 with his cover of Tex Ritter's "Deck of Cards."

FABLED PIRATE RADIO STATIONS

Pirate radio was a phenomenon born of the British government's broadcasting monopoly. As English rock became more and more outrageous, the conservative mentality of the BBC found it increasingly difficult to cope. The result was that several enterprising capitalists established ships, staffed with American-style Top Forty DJs, in the English channel, just outside the three-and-a-half-mile limit, to blast the U.K. with high-powered transmitters and the latest pop music. The British government has since taken legal and bureaucratic measures against offshore broadcasting and made provisions for independent stations that can air the sort of music pirate stations were broadcasting. But in their mid-1960s heyday, pirate stations offered the best pop radio in Europe. About a dozen came and went. Among them:

1 Radio Caroline   5 Radio London
2 Radio Atlanta   6 Radio Scotland
3 Radio Sutch   7 Radio 390
4 Radio City

L.A.'S TOP 100 HITS

Guy Zapoleon of KRTH, Los Angeles, compiled this list, which is based on sales reports from 1956 and 1957, KFWB surveys from 1958 through 1963, KRLA surveys from 1964 and 1965, KHJ surveys for 1966 through 1976, and sales reports from 1977 through 1979.

1 "The Twist," CHUBBY CHECKER, 1960 and 1961
2 "Mack the Knife," BOBBY DARIN, 1959
3 "Exodus," FERRANTE AND TEICHER, 1961

4   "The Theme from 'A Summer Place'," PERCY FAITH, 1960
5   "Love Will Keep Us Together," CAPTAIN AND TENNILLE, 1975
6   "I'm a Believer," THE MONKEES, 1967
7   "Hey Jude," THE BEATLES, 1968
8   "You've Lost That Lovin' Feelin'," THE RIGHTEOUS BROTHERS,
       1965
9   "Stayin' Alive," THE BEE GEES, 1978
10   "I Can See Clearly Now," JOHNNY NASH, 1972
11   "Don't Be Cruel" / "Hound Dog," ELVIS PRESLEY, 1956
12   "Blue Bayou," LINDA RONSTADT, 1977
13   "The Hawaiian Wedding Song," ANDY WILLIAMS, 1959
14   "I Want to Hold Your Hand," THE BEATLES, 1964
15   "When Will I See You Again," THE THREE DEGREES, 1974
16   "Joy to the World," THREE DOG NIGHT, 1971
17   "Let's Get It On," MARVIN GAYE, 1973
18   "Limbo Rock," CHUBBY CHECKER, 1962
19   "My Sharona," THE KNACK, 1979
20   "We Can Work It Out" / "Day Tripper," THE BEATLES, 1966
21   "Seasons in the Sun," TERRY JACKS, 1974
22   "Bridge over Troubled Water," SIMON AND GARFUNKEL, 1970
23   "I'll Be There," THE JACKSON 5, 1970
24   "If You Leave Me Now," CHICAGO, 1976
25   "Bennie and the Jets," ELTON JOHN, 1974
26   "It's Too Late," CAROLE KING, 1971
27   "Night Fever," THE BEE GEES, 1978
28   "Love Rollercoaster," OHIO PLAYERS, 1976
29   "Sugar, Sugar," THE ARCHIES, 1969
30   "Love Is Blue," PAUL MAURIAT, 1968
31   "Raindrops Keep Fallin' on My Head," B. J. THOMAS, 1969
32   "Killing Me Softly with His Song," ROBERTA FLACK, 1973
33   "Alone Again (Naturally)," GILBERT O'SULLIVAN, 1972
34   "Boogie Oogie Oogie," TASTE OF HONEY, 1978
35   "Someday We'll Be Together," DIANA ROSS AND THE
       SUPREMES, 1969
36   "Handy Man," JIMMY JONES, 1960

37 "The Jerk," THE LARKS, 1964
38 "Be True to Your School," THE BEACH BOYS, 1963
39 "The Battle of New Orleans," JOHNNY HORTON, 1959
40 "Gloria," THEM, 1966
41 "You're So Vain," CARLY SIMON, 1973
42 "All Shook Up," ELVIS PRESLEY, 1957
43 "Light My Fire," THE DOORS, 1967
44 "Round and Round," PERRY COMO, 1957
45 "(You're My) Soul and Inspiration," THE RIGHTEOUS BROTHERS, 1966
46 "I Just Want to Be Your Everything," ANDY GIBB, 1977
47 "Blowin' in the Wind," PETER, PAUL, AND MARY, 1963
48 "Me and Mrs. Jones," BILLY PAUL, 1972
49 "It's Now or Never," ELVIS PRESLEY, 1960
50 "Baby Love," SUPREMES, 1964
51 "Emotion," SAMANTHA SANG, 1978
52 "Easy to Be Hard," THREE DOG NIGHT, 1969
53 "Big Girls Don't Cry," THE FOUR SEASONS, 1962
54 "Love Letters in the Sand," PAT BOONE, 1957
55 "Don't Go Breaking My Heart," ELTON JOHN and KIKI DEE, 1976
56 "Kung Fu Fighting," CARL DOUGLAS, 1974
57 "Wooly Bully," SAM THE SHAM AND THE PHARAOHS 1965
58 "Afternoon Delight," STARLAND VOCAL BAND, 1976
59 "I Can't Stop Loving You" / "Born to Lose," RAY CHARLES, 1962
60 "Mashed Potato Time," DEE DEE SHARP, 1962
61 "Rapper's Delight," THE SUGARHILL GANG, 1979
62 "Goodbye Cruel World," JAMES DARREN, 1961
63 "These Boots Are Made for Walkin'," NANCY SINATRA, 1966
64 "Please Mr. Postman," THE CARPENTERS, 1975
65 "Just My Imagination (Running Away with Me)," THE TEMPTATIONS, 1971
66 "Surfer Girl," THE BEACH BOYS, 1963
67 "Sugar Shack," JIMMY GILMER AND THE FIREBALLS, 1963

68 "Hey Paula," PAUL AND PAULA, 1963
69 "Jailhouse Rock," ELVIS PRESLEY, 1957
70 "Viva Tirado—Part 1," EL CHICANO, 1970
71 "Born to Be Wild," STEPPENWOLF, 1968
72 "Nel Blu Dipinto Di Blu (Volare)," DOMENICO MODUGNO, 1958
73 "How Deep Is Your Love," THE BEE GEES, 1978
74 "Aquarius" / "Let the Sun Shine In," THE 5TH DIMENSION, 1969
75 "Without You," HARRY NILSSON, 1972
76 "Play That Funky Music," WILD CHERRY, 1976
77 "My Guy," MARY WELLS, 1964
78 "Happy Together," THE TURTLES, 1967
79 "Moon River," HENRY MANCINI, 1961
80 "At the Hop," DANNY AND THE JUNIORS, 1958
81 "My Girl," THE TEMPTATIONS, 1965
82 "Le Freak," CHIC, 1979
83 "Ladies Night," KOOL AND THE GANG, 1979
84 "All I Have to Do Is Dream," EVERLY BROTHERS, 1958
85 "Cherish," THE ASSOCIATION, 1966
86 "Winchester Cathedral," NEW VAUDEVILLE BAND, 1966
87 "Theme from 'Shaft'," ISAAC HAYES, 1971
88 "Crystal Blue Persuasion," TOMMY JAMES AND THE SHONDELLS, 1969
89 "Lisbon Antigua," NELSON RIDDLE, 1956
90 "Get Down Tonight," KC AND THE SUNSHINE BAND, 1975
91 "Johnny Angel," SHELLEY FABARES, 1962
92 "There's a Kind of Hush" / "No Milk Today," HERMAN'S HERMITS, 1967
93 "Spirit in the Sky," NORMAN GREENBAUM, 1970
94 "Something" / "Come Together," THE BEATLES, 1969
95 "Chances Are," JOHNNY MATHIS, 1957
96 "Love Me Tender," ELVIS PRESLEY, 1957
97 "Help!" THE BEATLES, 1965
98 "Donna," RITCHIE VALENS, 1959
99 "Half-Breed," CHER, 1973
100 "Oh, Pretty Woman," ROY ORBISON, 1964

WABC-AM NEW YORK: NUMBER 1 HITS OF THE YEAR
1969–1980

1   "Aquarius" / "Let the Sunshine In," THE 5TH DIMENSION, 1969
2   "Raindrops Keep Fallin' on My Head," B. J. THOMAS, 1970
3   "Joy to the World," THREE DOG NIGHT, 1971
4   "Alone Again (Naturally)," GILBERT O'SULLIVAN, 1972
5   "Killing Me Softly with His Song," ROBERTA FLACK, 1973
6   "Rock the Boat," THE HUES CORPORATION, 1974
7   "The Hustle," VAN MCCOY, 1975
8   "Kiss and Say Goodbye," THE MANHATTANS, 1976
9   "I Just Want to Be Your Everything," ANDY GIBB, 1977
10 "Boogie Oogie Oogie," A TASTE OF HONEY, 1978
11 "I Will Survive," GLORIA GAYNOR, 1979
12 "Another One Bites the Dust," QUEEN, 1980

-◄❙❚►-

WLS-AM CHICAGO: YEAR-END PICKS
1964–1980

1   "I Want to Hold Your Hand," THE BEATLES, 1964
2   "(I Can't Get No) Satisfaction," THE ROLLING STONES, 1965
3   "Hanky Panky," TOMMY JAMES AND THE SHONDELLS, 1966
4   "Ode to Billie Joe," BOBBIE GENTRY, 1967
5   "Hey Jude," THE BEATLES, 1968
6   "Sugar, Sugar," THE ARCHIES, 1969
7   "Bridge over Troubled Water," SIMON AND GARFUNKEL, 1970
8   "Joy to the World," THREE DOG NIGHT, 1971
9   "First Time Ever I Saw Your Face," ROBERTA FLACK, 1972
10 "You're So Vain," CARLY SIMON, 1973
11 "Seasons in the Sun," TERRY JACKS, 1974

12   "Love Will Keep Us Together," CAPTAIN AND TENNILLE, 1975
13   "Don't Go Breaking My Heart," ELTON JOHN and KIKI DEE, 1976
14   "You Light Up My Life," DEBBY BOONE, 1977
15   "Stayin' Alive," THE BEE GEES, 1978
16   "My Sharona," THE KNACK, 1979
17   "Lost in Love," AIR SUPPLY, 1980

-◄❚❙❘►-

DR. DEMENTO'S 10 MOST DEMENTED RECORDS

1   "They're Coming to Take Me Away, Ha-Haaa!" NAPOLEON XIV
2   "Transfusion," NERVOUS NORVUS
3   "Purple People Eater," SHEB WOOLEY
4   "Fish Heads," BARNES AND BARNES
5   "Titties and Beer," FRANK ZAPPA
6   "Time Warp," from the soundtrack of *The Rocky Horror Picture Show*
7   "Monster Mash," BOBBY "BORIS" PICKETT
8   "Surfin' Bird," THE TRASHMEN
9   "Rubber Biscuit," THE CHIPS
10   "It's a Gas," ALFRED E. NEUMAN

DR. DEMENTO, *known to his mom as Barret Hansen, produced some superb R&B and gospel compilations for Specialty Records between 1969 and 1971. He then established a reputation as a purveyor of wacky wax (a.k.a. demented discs) on radio's nationally syndicated Dr. Demento Show. Having successfully transcended the bounds of sanity and good taste, the DJ has given air time to many songs and artists we'd never have heard otherwise. Thanks, Dr. D.?*

KID LEO'S 10 FAVE HEAVY-METAL SONGS

1   "How Many More Times," LED ZEPPELIN
2   "I'm Confused" (live), THE YARDBIRDS
3   "From a Dry Camel," DUST
4   "Dominance and Submission," BLUE ÖYSTER CULT
5   "Toxic Shadows," LUCIFER'S FRIEND
6   "War Pigs," BLACK SABBATH
7   "Radar Love," GOLDEN EARRING
8   "Runnin' with the Devil," VAN HALEN
9   "Black Diamond," KISS
10 "July Morning," URIAH HEEP

KID LEO *rules the airwaves in Cleveland as music director at WMMS-FM. A notorious character from coast to coast, Leo's style appropriates the best adrenaline of AM with solid FM taste and has helped Cleveland become one of the most important radio markets of the 1970s and 1980s.*

-◄❙❙▶-

TEST PATTERN BLUES
10 Songs about TV

1   "Along Came Jones," THE COASTERS
2   "However Much I Booze," THE WHO
3   "Johnny Carson," THE BEACH BOYS
4   "Sleeping with the Television On," THE DICTATORS
5   "Surrender," CHEAP TRICK
6   "Top of the Pops," THE KINKS
7   "TV Eye," THE STOOGES
8   "TV Mama," JOE TURNER
9   "T.V.O.D.," THE NORML
10 "Watching the Detectives," ELVIS COSTELLO

TV THEME SONGS BASED ON ROCK, COUNTRY, AND SOUL

1   "The Associates," performed by B. B. KING
2   "Baretta's Theme" (originally titled "Keep Your Eye on the Sparrow"), composed by STEVE BARRI and MICHAEL OMARTIAN
3   "The Beverly Hillbillies" (originally titled "Foggy Mountain Breakdown"), performed by LESTER FLATT and EARL SCRUGGS
4   "Chico and the Man," performed by JOSÉ FELICIANO
5   "The Courtship of Eddie's Father," composed by HARRY NILSSON and GEORGE TIPTAS; performed by HARRY NILSSON
6   "Happy Days," performed by PRATT AND McCLAIN
7   "Ironside," composed by QUINCY JONES
8   "The Mary Tyler Moore Show" (originally titled "Love Is All Around"), composed by SONNY CURTIS
9   "Maude," composed by DONNY HATHAWAY
10 "Movin' On," composed by MERLE HAGGARD
11 "Welcome Back, Kotter" (originally titled "Welcome Back"), composed and performed by JOHN SEBASTIAN
12 "Zorro," performed by THE CHORDETTES

-◄◗►-

THE 10 BEST ROCK TV SHOWS

1   *Shindig* (ABC), mid-1960s
2   *Ready, Steady Go!* (ITV), mid-1960s
3   *Hullabaloo* (NBC), mid-1960s
4   *Top of the Pops* (BBC), since the early 1960s
5   *The Old Grey Whistle Test* (BBC), since the early 1970s
6   *American Bandstand* (ABC), since the early 1950s
7   *Soul Train* (syndicated), since the early 1970s
8   *The Smothers Brothers* (CBS), in the late 1960s

9   *Hollywood a Go Go* (syndicated), in the mid-1960s
10 *Rock Palast* (West German), since the late 1970s

The 10 WORST ROCK TV SHOWS

1   *The Rolling Stone Tenth Anniversary Special* (CBS), 1977
2   *Dance Fever* (syndicated), contemporary
3   *Midnight Special* (NBC), from 1973 to 1981
4   *In Concert* (ABC), mid-1970s
5   *Where the Action Is* (ABC), mid-1960s
6   *The Ed Sullivan Show* (CBS), 1950s and 1960s
7   *Don Kirshner's Rock Concert* (syndicated), contemporary
8   *Fridays* (ABC), contemporary
9   *American Top 40* (syndicated), contemporary
10 *Saturday Night Live* (NBC), contemporary

Dick CLARK LISTS 40 PERFORMERS WHO MADE THEIR TV DEBUTS ON "AMERICAN BANDSTAND"

Clark, the show's host since 1956, tells us, "There have been more than 8500 musical appearances made by various artists on American Bandstand *since its debut in 1952. Among those thousands of performers, hundreds made their first national appearance on the program." Here is a partial list:*

1	PAUL ANKA	7	THE COASTERS
2	FRANKIE AVALON	8	SAM COOKE
3	CHUCK BERRY	9	CREEDENCE CLEAR-
4	JAMES BROWN		WATER REVIVAL
5	JOHNNY CASH	10	JIM CROCE
6	CHUBBY CHECKER	11	BOBBY DARIN

12	NEIL DIAMOND	25	BRENDA LEE
13	DION AND THE BELMONTS	26	JERRY LEE LEWIS
		27	THE MAMAS AND THE PAPAS
14	THE DOORS		
15	FATS DOMINO	28	THE PLATTERS
16	THE DRIFTERS	29	THE RASCALS
17	THE EVERLY BROTHERS	30	OTIS REDDING
18	THE FOUR SEASONS	31	MARTY ROBBINS
19	THE FOUR TOPS	32	SMOKEY ROBINSON AND THE MIRACLES
20	GLADYS KNIGHT AND THE PIPS		
		33	LINDA RONSTADT
21	BILL HALEY AND HIS COMETS	34	THE SHIRELLES
		35	SIMON AND GARFUNKEL
22	BUDDY HOLLY AND THE CRICKETS	36	THE SUPREMES
		37	THE TEMPTATIONS
23	THE JACKSON 5	38	THREE DOG NIGHT
24	THE JEFFERSON AIRPLANE	39	CONWAY TWITTY
		40	STEVIE WONDER

DICK CLARK *has also hosted* Where the Action Is, The $20,000 Pyramid, *and* The $50,000 Pyramid, *and has produced a wide range of dramatic and variety specials for television.*

Young teens on Dick Clark's American Bandstand *record review panel give candid reactions to Jimi Hendrix's "Purple Haze."*

COURTESY PETER KANZE

5 ROCK AND ROLL CARTOON SHOWS

1   *The Beatles*
2   *The Jackson 5*
3   *The Monkees*
4   *The Bay City Rollers*
5   *The Archies*

10 TELEVISION ENTHUSIASTS

1   THE BEE GEES
2   ALICE COOPER
3   ELVIS COSTELLO
4   JOHN LENNON and YOKO ONO
5   JOHN LYDON
6   PAUL MCCARTNEY
7   RANDY NEWMAN
8   THE RAMONES
9   TODD RUNDGREN
10 CHRIS STEIN

ALICE COOPER'S 10 FAVORITE TV SHOWS

1   *Monty Python's Flying Circus*
2   *Fawlty Towers*
3   *SC TV*
4   *The Untouchables*
5   *The Twilight Zone*
6   *The Prisoner*
7   *I Spy*
8   *The Man from U.N.C.L.E.*
9   *Taxi*
10 *The Many Lives of Dobie Gillis*

ALICE COOPER, *once the name of a band but now the sole pseudonym of the former Vincent Furnier, has recorded such hits as "I'm Eighteen," "School's Out," "Only Women Bleed," and "Welcome to My Nightmare." He is a recognized connoisseur of TV trivia.*

ROCK MUSICIANS WHO HAVE APPEARED ON "SATURDAY NIGHT LIVE" (THROUGH THE 1979–1980 SEASON)

1. ABBA
2. JOAN ARMATRADING
3. THE AMAZING RHYTHM ACES
4. ASHFORD AND SIMPSON
5. THE BAND
6. GEORGE BENSON
7. CHUCK BERRY
8. THE B-52's
9. BLONDIE
10. THE BLUES BROTHERS
11. DAVID BOWIE
12. JACKSON BROWNE
13. JIMMY BUFFETT
14. PAUL BUTTERFIELD
15. RAY CHARLES
16. CHICAGO
17. DESMOND CHILD AND ROUGE
18. JIMMY CLIFF
19. JOE COCKER
20. RY COODER
21. ELVIS COSTELLO
22. DEVO
23. THE DIRT BAND
24. THE DOOBIE BROTHERS
25. BOB DYLAN
26. MARIANNE FAITHFULL
27. KINKY FRIEDMAN
28. ART GARFUNKEL
29. THE J. GEILS BAND
30. THE GRATEFUL DEAD
31. GEORGE HARRISON
32. LEVON HELM
33. JANIS IAN
34. AL JARREAU
35. BILLY JOEL
36. RICKIE LEE JONES
37. THE KINKS
38. KRIS KRISTOFFERSON and RITA COOLIDGE
39. GORDON LIGHTFOOT
40. MEAT LOAF
41. TAJ MAHAL
42. THE McGARRIGLE SISTERS
43. THE METERS
44. PAUL and LINDA McCARTNEY
45. BETTE MIDLER
46. EDDIE MONEY
47. VAN MORRISON
48. RICK NELSON
49. WILLIE NELSON
50. RANDY NEWMAN
51. GARY NUMAN
52. THE PERSUASIONS
53. TOM PETTY AND THE HEARTBREAKERS
54. BILLY PRESTON
55. SUN RA
56. LEON REDBONE

57 MARTHA REEVES
58 LEON and MARY
    RUSSELL
59 BONNIE RAITT
60 EUGENE RECORD
61 THE ROCHES
62 THE ROLLING STONES
63 LINDA RONSTADT
64 SAM AND DAVE
65 SANTANA
66 LEO SAYER
67 BOZ SCAGGS
68 GIL SCOTT-HERON
69 JOHN SEBASTIAN
70 CARLY SIMON

71 PAUL SIMON
72 PATTI SMITH
73 PHOEBE SNOW
74 THE SPECIALS
75 STUFF
76 THE STYLISTICS
77 TALKING HEADS
78 JAMES TAYLOR
79 PETER TOSH
80 LOUDON WAINWRIGHT
    III
81 TOM WAITS
82 BRIAN WILSON
83 FRANK ZAPPA

TWELVE: LITERATURE

Patti addresses the faithful.

ROCK SONGS BASED ON LITERATURE, FAIRY TALES, AND NURSERY RHYMES

1 **"Darkness on the Edge of Town,"** BRUCE SPRINGSTEEN
   Based on lines from John Steinbeck's *The Grapes of Wrath*.

2 **"Games People Play,"** JOE SOUTH
   Title and concept taken from Eric Berne's best seller about transactional analysis.

3 **"Golden Slumber,"** THE BEATLES
   Based on a sixteenth-century poem by Thomas Dekker.

4 **"Gone with the Wind,"** THE DUPREES
   From Margaret Mitchell's novel of the Civil War.

5 **"The House at Pooh Corner,"** THE NITTY GRITTY DIRT BAND
   Based on A. A. Milne's *Winnie the Pooh*. (Also Jefferson Airplane's "Ballad of You, Me and Pooneil.")

6 **"The House That Jack Built,"** ARETHA FRANKLIN
   From the nursery rhyme "The House That Jack Built."

7 **"I Believe in Jesus,"** DONNA SUMMER
   Contains sections taken from "Mary Had a Little Lamb." (Paul McCartney has also recorded "Mary Had a Little Lamb.")

8 **"Little Miss Muffet,"** LEON T. GROSS
   Based on the nursery rhyme.

9 **"Little Star,"** THE ELEGANTS
   Based on the children's nursery rhyme and the melody created by the young Mozart.

10 **"Liar Liar,"** THE CASTAWAYS
    Based on the name-calling rhyme "Liar liar pants on fire/Nose is longer than a telephone wire."

11 **"Mother Goose,"** JETHRO TULL
    Features a panoply of childhood familiars.

12 **"My Mummy's Dead,"** JOHN LENNON
    Based on the melody to "Three Blind Mice." (Stevie Wonder has done "Three Blind Mice" in concert.)

13 **"Puddin' N' Tain,"** THE ALLEY CATS
Based on the children's rhyme.

14 **"Spy in the House of Love,"** THE DOORS
Taken from a novel of the same title by Anaïs Nin.

15 **"Sugar and Spice,"** THE CRYAN SHAMES
From the rhyme about what little boys and girls are made of.

16 **"Tomorrow Never Knows,"** THE BEATLES
Originally called "The Void." This song was inspired by Timothy Leary and Richard Alpert's *The Psychedelic Experience*, which was their interpretation of the *Tibetan Book of the Dead*.

17 **"White Rabbit,"** THE JEFFERSON AIRPLANE
From Lewis Carroll's *Alice in Wonderland*.

18 **"A Whiter Shade of Pale,"** PROCOL HARUM
Based on an old English poem of the same name.

19 **"Who's Been Sleeping Here,"** THE ROLLING STONES
From *Goldilocks and the Three Bears*.

HONORABLE MENTION: For the Beatles' "I Am the Walrus," John Lennon took the repeated phrase "goo goo boo joob" from Humpty Dumpty's last lines in *Finnegan's Wake* by James Joyce. The "walrus," of course, alludes to Lewis Carroll's character in *Alice in Wonderland*.

-◄❚▶-

MOST PROFOUND ROCK LYRICS

1 "Tutti Frutti," LITTLE RICHARD
2 "Da Doo Ron Ron," THE CRYSTALS
3 "Wooly Bully," SAM THE SHAM AND THE PHARAOHS
4 "Ooby Dooby," ROY ORBISON
5 "Sh-Boom," THE CHORDS
6 "Surfin' Bird," THE TRASHMEN
7 "Yakety-Yak," THE COASTERS
8 "Get a Job," THE SILHOUETTES

9   "Be-Bop-a-Lula," GENE VINCENT AND HIS BLUE CAPS
10 "Ooh Pooh Pah Doo, Part II," JESSIE HILL
11 "Rama Lama Ding Dong," THE EDSELS
12 "In-a-Gadda-da-Vida," IRON BUTTERFLY

-◄▐▐►-

THE 25 BEST ROCK BOOKS

1   *Any Old Way You Choose It: Rock and Other Pop Music, 1967–1973,* by ROBERT CHRISTGAU (Penguin, 1973)
    Contentious and rigorously theoretical criticism and reportage from the self-styled Dean of American Rock Critics.

2   *Apple to the Core,* by PETER MCCABE and ROBERT D. SCHONFELD (Pocket, 1972)
    Well-documented demise of the Beatles dynasty.

3   *Blondie,* by LESTER BANGS (Fireside, 1980)
    Scathing biography of New Wave icons; flamboyantly written and not without its moral tug.

4   *Bob Dylan: An Intimate Biography,* by ANTHONY SCADUTO (Grosset and Dunlap, 1971)
    Hasn't been updated since it first appeared in paperback in the early 1970s, and misses most of the highlights of the 1960 rock period, but the best Dylan bio nonetheless. (Jon Landau, Nik Cohn, and Greil Marcus cover the criticism.)

5   *Born to Run: The Bruce Springsteen Story,* by Dave Marsh (Doubleday, 1979)
    Perhaps overexuberant but detailed and analytical study of the life and career.

6   *Buddy Holly: His Life and Music,* by JOHN GOLDROSE (Quick Fox, 1975)
    Very well-researched study, and the best bio of any of the founding fathers.

7   *The Clash: Before and After,* photographs by PENNIE SMITH (Eel Pie Publishing Limited, 1980)

Hilarious, sometimes revealing photo study of the punk standard-bearers, with captions by the band members; unfortunately, unpublished in America.

8   ***Country: The Biggest Music in America,*** by NICK TOSCHES (Stein and Day, 1977)
    Rabelaisian history, not always notable for its accuracy, but good reading throughout.

9   ***Elvis Fifty-six: In the Beginning,*** photographs by ALFRED WERTHEIMER (Collier, 1979)
    Stunning collection of Elvis photos taken soon after he signed with RCA; captures the King in full-blooming innocence, long before the rot set in.

10 ***Feel Like Going Home: Portraits in Blues and Rock 'n' Roll,*** by PETER GURALNICK (Dutton, 1971)
    Finely drawn portraits of blues and rock and roll singers. Charlie Rich's piece is a classic, and not necessarily the only one.

11 ***The Gospel Sound: Good News and Bad Times,*** by TONY HEILBUT (Simon and Schuster, 1971)
    Not about rock per se, but in fully documenting the American gospel music scene (or at least its black half), Heilbut makes a compelling case for gospel as the true lost origin of rock and R&B.

12 ***Honkers and Shouters: The Golden Years of Rhythm and Blues,*** by ARNOLD SHAW (Collier, 1978)
    Exhaustive study of R&B from the mid-1940s through the rise and fall of Alan Freed. Not always factually correct, but priceless interview material.

13 ***It's Too Late to Stop Now: A Rock & Roll Journal,*** by JON LANDAU (Straight Arrow, 1972)
    Anthology by the seminal *Rolling Stone* and *Crawdaddy* critic, at its best on Otis Redding, Motown, The Rolling Stones, and Bob Dylan. Also tackles many important theoretical issues, both politically and artistically.

14 ***Lennon Remembers,*** by JANN S. WENNER (Popular Library, 1971)

The celebrated *Rolling Stone* interviews. As fine a job of question-and-answer give and take as anyone has ever done about anybody, and the most revealing look at Lennon and the Beatles available.

15　***Mystery Train: Images of America in Rock 'n' Roll***, by GREIL MARCUS (Dutton, 1975)

The most intellectually satisfying rock book, and justifiably the only one ever nominated for a National Book Critics Circle Award. Marcus traces the careers of five performers (Elvis, Sly and the Family Stone, Randy Newman, The Band, Robert Johnson, and Harmonica Frank) to show their interconnectedness with the mainstream of American culture.

16　***1988: The New Wave Punk Rock Explosion***, by CAROLINE COON (Hawthorn, 1977)

The best insider's chronicle of punk; well written and totally imbued (graphically, too) with the spirit of '68.

17　***Private Elvis***, by DIEGO CORTEZ (Two Continents, 1978)

Fantastically lurid photos of Elvis with B-girls in Germany during his sojourn in the service. Unpublished until after his death, and no wonder: Here we not only see the redneck boy that all the money in Vegas could never completely conceal, but also witness him in his true honky-tonk element for the first time.

18　***Rock Dreams*** by GUY PEELAERT and NIK COHN (Fawcett Popular Library, 1973)

Fantasy paintings of fifty rockers, with cogent captions from Cohn's acid-dipped pen.

19　***Rock from the Beginning***, by NIK COHN (Stein and Day, 1969)

Published in Britain under the title *A Wop Bop a Loo Bop, a Wop Bam Boom*. Arch but astute critical history of the music from Elvis to the late 1960s, Cohn is so aphoristic that not much of this commentary has dated.

20　***The Rolling Stone Illustrated History of Rock & Roll*** edited by JIM MILLER (Random House, 1980)

The most comprehensive and best-written study of the length and breadth of the music. Lavishly illustrated (if not quite so lavishly as the 1976 edition), provocative, and, best of all, factually trustworthy. Indispensable.

21 *'Scuze Me While I Kiss the Sky: The Life of Jimi Hendrix*, by DAVID HENDERSON (Bantam, 1981)

Avoid the original Doubleday hard-cover version, titled *Jimi Hendrix: Voodoo Child of the Aquarian Age* (1978), which is a raw manuscript. In the Bantam paperback revision, the poet-author not only collects more facts about Hendrix than anyone else, but also presents a convincing argument about what Jimi's real role and stature were about.

22 *Seventh Heaven*, by PATTI SMITH (Dynamic Learning Corporation, 1973)

Her first and best volume of poetry, enraptured in the rhythms of rock; in sensibility, inseparable from the music.

23 *Shooting Stars: The Rolling Stone Book of Portraits*, edited by ANNIE LEIBOVITZ (Straight Arrow, 1973)

Anthology of the best rock photographers, among whom Leibovitz is premier.

24 *The Sound of the City*, by CHARLIE GILLETT (Dutton, 1970)

Exhaustive, if clumsily written, history that traces the rise and fall of the regional R&B, pop, and country sounds that formed rock and roll.

25 *Star-Making Machinery: The Odyssey of an Album*, by GEOFFREY STOKES (Bobbs-Merrill, 1976)

Chronicles the making of one album, by Commander Cody and His Lost Planet Airmen, and in the process provides a neat, well-reasoned analysis of how the record business works and why the musicians are finally chattel.

THE 10 WORST ROCK BOOKS

1   *The Aesthetics of Rock,* by R. MELTZER (Something Else Press, 1970)
    Maybe not the worst, but it's hard to imagine anyone ever reading it—except for a pack of sycophantic critics who have completely misunderstood its satirical implications.

2   *Body Count,* by FRANCIE SCHWARTZ (Straight Arrow, 1972)
    Biography of a young woman whose chief life experience was a fling with Paul McCartney. How did this get published?

3   *Keith Richards,* by BARBARA CHARONE (Future, 1979)
    Sycophancy incarnate; a biography of The Rolling Stones guitarist that idolizes him for *all* the wrong reasons—and doesn't miss one.

4   *No One Here Gets Out Alive,* by DANNY SUGERMAN and JERRY HOPKINS (Warner Books, 1980)
    Muddled biography of Jim Morrison; a long-term national best seller that only serves to make clear how misanthropic and pretentious the Doors vocalist finally was.

5   *The Poetry of Rock,* by RICHARD GOLDSTEIN (Prentice-Hall, 1969)
    Theoretically inept and poorly selected lyric collection.

6   *Rock 'n' Roll Is Here to Pay: The History and Politics of the Music Industry,* by REEBEE GAROFOLO and STEVE CHAPPLE (Nelson Hall, 1978)
    Leftist diatribe against the record business; mangles fact snobbish tone. This might be hilarious if it weren't a botch o an important job.

7   *The Story of Motown,* by PETER BENJAMINSON (Grove 1980)
    Poorly researched, poorly written, poorly illustrated.

8   *Tarantula,* by BOB DYLAN (Macmillan, 1971)
    The first chink in his armor. A versified novel without plot o point.

9   ***Twenty Minute Fandangoes and Forever Changes***, by
     JONATHAN EISEN (Vintage, 1971)
     Smarmy anthology collects more trivia than one might have
     believed possible, even based on reading its predecessor
     volumes, *The Age of Rock* and *The Age of Rock II*.
10   ***The Boy Who Dared to Rock: The Definitive Elvis***, by
     PAUL LICHTER (Doubleday, 1978)
     Tossed together collection of obvious and uninteresting trivia.
     Belittles the life it ineptly celebrates.

-◄❚▶-

THE 10 BEST LINER NOTES

1   JOHN BEECHER and MALCOLM JONES, *The Complete Buddy
     Holly*
2   LENNY KAYE, *Eddie Cochran: Legendary Masters Series*
3   LESTER BANGS, *Them Featuring Van Morrison* (the London
     anthology, not the band's original LP of the same title)
4   JERRY WEXLER, *The Ray Charles Story, Vols. 1 and 2*
5   GREIL MARCUS, Bob Dylan and The Band's *The Basement
     Tapes*
6   PETER GURALNICK, Chuck Willis' *My Story*
7   STEVE CROPPER as told to JIM DELEHANT, Otis Redding's *Tell
     the Truth*
8   JON LANDAU, Otis Redding's *The Dock of the Bay*
9   PAUL ACKERMAN, Atlantic's *History of Rhythm and Blues,
     Vols. 5 and 6*
10   SEYMOUR STEIN, *18 King Size Rhythm and Blues Hits* and *18
     King Size Country and Western Hits*

THE 10 WORST LINER NOTES

1   PETE HAMILL, Bob Dylan's *Blood on the Tracks* (so bad they were quickly deleted, though Hamill *did* win a Grammy for them)
2   ROBERT FRIPP, his own *God Save the Queen/Under Heavy Manners*
3   JOHN SINCLAIR, The MC5's *Kick Out the Jams*
4   LEON ISAAC, *Smokey Robinson and the Miracles: Anthology*
5   DAVE MARSH, *Detroit*
6   ALLEN GINSBERG, Bob Dylan's *Desire*
7   BOB DYLAN, his own *Another Side of Bob Dylan* (not to mention the poetry he scribbled on the back of vintage Joan Baez and Peter, Paul and Mary albums)
8   MARVIN GAYE, his own *Let's Get It On*
9   RITCHIE YORKE, Aretha Franklin's *Soul '69*
10 JOHN MENDELSOHN, The Kinks' *Arthur (or the Decline and Fall of the British Empire)*

-◄▮►-

BEST LINER NOTES BY ARTISTS ON THEIR OWN ALBUMS

1   BOB DYLAN, *Highway 61 Revisited*
2   BOB DYLAN, *John Wesley Harding*
3   NEIL YOUNG, *Decade*
4   JIMI HENDRIX, *Electric Ladyland*
5   CHARLIE WATTS, *Between the Buttons*
6   BOB DYLAN, *Bringing It All Back Home*
7   JEFF BECK, *Truth*
8   STEVIE WONDER, *Talking Book* (in braille)
9   PETE TOWNSHEND, The Who's *Odds and Sods*

TRUMAN CAPOTE'S 10 FAVORITE ROCK PERFORMERS

1	BRUCE SPRINGSTEEN	6	THE EAGLES
2	THE WHO	7	THE GRATEFUL DEAD
3	THE ROLLING STONES	8	PAT BENATAR
4	ROD STEWART	9	THE CARS
5	THE DOOBIE BROTHERS	10	BLONDIE

TRUMAN CAPOTE *is one of America's leading novelists and talk-show celebrities. Among his novels are* Breakfast at Tiffany's, In Cold Blood, *and* Answered Prayers.

-◄▮▮►-

MIKE CALLAHAN'S ROCK AND ROLL SOAP OPERA
20 Tragic Tales

1 **"Teen Angel,"** MARK DINNING
   Mark's girlfriend is flattened by a train when she rushes back to the car, stalled on the tracks, to retrieve his high school ring. (With the price of gold what it is today, I can see why.) Mark is left singing to the sky, asking that his Teen Angel answer him, please. Tune in to No. 4 for the next installment.

2 **"Tell Laura I Love Her,"** RAY PETERSON
   Poor Tom can't support Laura in the way he'd like, but he sees

MIKE CALLAHAN *has been a record collector since 1954, specializing in early stereo rock and roll and Top Forty music. He was music director of WMOD-FM, an all-oldies station in Washington, D.C., where he also produced shows. Currently, Callahan is a columnist for* Goldmine *and* Classic Wax. *He also contributes information on stereo recordings to Jerry Osborne and Bruce Hamilton's* Price Guide, *the bible of record collectors.*

a way to make a quick buck by entering the local stock-car races. He flips his car in the heat of battle, killing himself. Heartbroken Laura later has a supernatural experience when she hears Tommy's voice in the chapel while she prays for his reckless soul.

3   **"The Water Was Red,"** JOHNNY CYMBAL

In this early *Jaws* thriller, Johnny and his true love enjoy a few lovely nights on the deserted beach, watching the last rays of sun turn the water red. One day, however, while Johnny's girl is swimming, unawares, a shark rips her to shreds. Johnny wades through the bloody waves and hauls her remains to shore, then materializes a knife and swims out to kill the shark. As the song ends, Johnny is wading back to shore, once more through red waves, carrying the shark's fin. *Ole!*

4   **"The Pickup,"** MARK DINNING

Mark simply doesn't have any luck with women. In this song, his friends dare him to date the town tramp, and after two years of singing to the sky, he figures he might as well. As luck would have it, Mark and The Pickup fall in love. Under normal circumstances, this would set the stage for a happy ending. But Mark can't stand the thought of telling his friends that he loves The Pickup, so instead, he dumps *her*, telling her that he doesn't care for her anymore, won't see her anymore, and so on. The poor Pickup is driven to leaping off a bridge and Mark is left to read about it in the paper the next day.

5   **"Patches,"** DICKEY LEE

Another suicide, this one with a surprise ending. Patches, the poor girl from Shantytown, has her hopes inflated when she dates Dickey, but soon he's forbidden by his dad to see her again. Despairing, Patches drowns herself in the dirty old river that runs by the coal yard. When he hears of the tragedy, Dickey just can't go on, and as the story ends, he's preparing to commit suicide, too.

6   **"Give Us Your Blessing,"** RAY PETERSON

The kids were in love, but their folks laughed and told them they were too young. After one final attempt at parental approval, the young couple drive off with tears in their eyes to elope, miss a detour sign, and total both the car and themselves. The next morning, in the rain, the parents kneel beside the bodies of their kids. From somewhere off in the great beyond, the kids are probably thinking, "Now I'll bet you're sorry."

7   **"Dead Man's Curve,"** JAN AND DEAN
Our hot-rod hero is cruising in his Sting-Ray late one night when a guy driving an XKE challenges him to a drag. They agree to come off the line at Sunset and Vine and race all the way to Dead Man's Curve. When they get to the curve, the singer loses, cracks up the car, and is hospitalized. But he recovers sufficiently to make a million seller telling his story.

8   **"Last Kiss,"** J. FRANK WILSON AND THE CAVALIERS
Yet another car crash. J. Frank crashes his daddy's car into a stalled vehicle and manages to cancel his date, permanently. He makes it up to her by giving her one last kiss after she's checked out, holding out strong hopes for a reunion in the next world.

9   **"The Leader of the Pack,"** THE SHANGRI-LAS
Jimmy, a leather-jacketed biker, meets Betty at the candy store (an updated version would probably be set in a head shop). Betty's parents forbid her to see her new, scruffy beau, and after a tearful breakup scene, Betty watches as Jimmy revs up and peels out, only to crash before her horrified eyes. Where is the Pack when you need it?

This song spawned several takeoffs, including the Detergents' "Leader of the Laundromat," in which the heroine meets her untimely demise under the wheels of a garbage truck, and Jimmy Cross' "I Want My Baby Back," which is sick, sick, sick. (See "The Book of Rock Lists Dubious Recording Achievement Awards," p. 80.)

10   **"I Can Never Go Home Anymore,"** THE SHANGRI-LAS
After her brief and unsuccessful fling with the Leader of the Pack, our heroine latches onto another boy, but once more, her mean, nasty parents demand a breakup. Not wanting another

bike crash on her hands, the girl leaves home with her guy, only to find that life in the real world can get pretty hairy. Pride keeps her from going home, however, and she's doomed to drift aimlessly and alone for the rest of her life. Her mother, who took her departure badly, finally dies of loneliness. As the episode ends, our heroine has become a counselor, devoting her life to preventing other young girls from repeating her errors.

11   **"The Hero,"** BERNADETTE CARROLL
Sue is pretty snooty about snaring the high school football hero, and lets everybody know that they'll be married after graduation. As the story opens, Sue is sitting at home, wondering why Johnny isn't back from the game, which is only thirty miles away. The telephone rings, Sue grabs it, and breathlessly answers, "Johnny? Johnny?" Alas, it's Patty, her girlfriend, who has just learned that the bus turned over and the entire team was killed. As the song ends, Sue has collapsed in a pool of self-pity, her dreams dashed to pieces. Doesn't anybody here care about the rest of the team?

12   **"A Young Girl,"** NOEL HARRISON
A girl from a filthy-rich neighborhood runs off with a vagabond, who seduces her with words she's never heard (?!?). In the end, he dumps her, and she's found by the side of the road, a girl of sixteen, child of springtime so green, dead. Tsk, tsk.

13   **"Billy and Sue,"** B. J. THOMAS
Everything was going fine for Billy and Sue when that evil Vietnam War cropped up and he got his ass drafted. He went off to war; Sue went off to party. For months, he wrote her religiously without receiving a reply. Finally, during an intense firefight (?), Billy gets a letter from Sue. It opens, "Dear John." Billy is so surprised that Sue has forgotten his name that he stands up in the trench and gets greased by a Charlie. A likely story.

14   **"Nightmare,"** WHYTE BOOTS
Everyone likes to see a good cat fight, and when one of the girls in school steals Bobby from Lori, Lori's friends egg her on.

Lori doesn't like the idea much, but she is swept up in the crowd as her friends chant, "Get her! Get her!" Lori kills her antagonist, and the police come to haul her off to jail. In the end, she proclaims: "I didn't want to fight, but what could I do? No boy is worth the trouble I'm in."

15 **"Ode to Billie Joe,"** BOBBIE GENTRY

Soap opera, down-home style, the pieces of a puzzle presented between dinner-table small talk. Bobbie and Billy Joe have evidently been having a secret affair, but it is only at dinner that Bobbie learns that Billy Joe has jumped off the Tallahatchee Bridge. This one is so complicated that they made a movie out of it; if you want to get all of the plot, see the flick.

16 **"Condition Red,"** THE GOODIES

A story similar to "The Leader of the Pack," but this time the parents disapprove because the boyfriend needs a haircut and a shave. Aside from being somewhat hilarious, this record is notable as the first tragedy song to feature the new police "yelp" siren rather than the old "whine" variety.

17 **"Mr. Turnkey,"** ZAGER AND EVANS

A sickie. Our boy is in prison for raping a woman who teased him in a Wichita Falls bar. After half a song of listening to him describe her beauty and how much he hates himself, we discover that he's nailed his left wrist to the cell wall and is hanging there bleeding to death. His last words are, "Tell her I'm sorry." This was Zager and Evans' followup to the hit "In the Year 2525."

18 **"D.O.A."** BLOODROCK

An unbelievably gruesome account of a plane crash victim's trip to the hospital in an ambulance. He describes, in graphic detail, seeing that his arm has been torn off, watching his girlfriend die next to him, hearing an attendant say he has no chance, the feeling of bleeding to death, and finally, death itself. This scandal sheet hit the Top Forty, too.

19 **"Emma,"** HOT CHOCOLATE

Emma's childhood dream was to become a movie star. Her boyfriend, who'd been with her from age five until they were married at seventeen, shared her conviction. But in her late teens, Emma finds the road to stardom too tough, and late one December, her husband finds her dead in their bedroom, a love letter in her hand. Merry Christmas.

20 **"Point Blank,"** BRUCE SPRINGSTEEN
Many of Springsteen's songs could fall into the soap-opera category, but in another way, his music is much more sophisticated and realistic. Looking over the list of tragedies from 1959 to 1980, there's an obvious progression from pure fantasy to more realistic events. "Point Blank" is perhaps the prototypical tragedy of the 1980s. We learn of a little girl saying her prayers at night, then follow her as she grows up, accepting what her elders teach, falling in Romeo-and-Juliet love, dancing at the clubs with her boyfriend. From there, in *Looking for Mr. Goodbar* fashion, her life unravels. She starts walking the streets, and finally, she's dead, shot point blank. But her spirit was killed long before.

-◄❚▶-

ROCK BOOKENDS

1   "The Book I Read," THE TALKING HEADS
2   "The Book of Love," THE MONOTONES
3   "Buying a Book," JOE TEX
4   "I Could Write a Book," JERRY BUTLER
5   "If You Could Read My Mind," GORDON LIGHTFOOT
6   "Life Is Just a Book," ERNEST LAWLARS
7   "My Little Red Book," LOVE
8   "Old Friends/Bookends," SIMON AND GARFUNKEL
9   "Paperback Writer," THE BEATLES
10 "The Snake and the Bookworm," THE COASTERS
11 "You Can't Judge a Book By Its Cover," BO DIDDLEY
12 "You're in My Book First," JIMMY MCCRACKLIN

THIRTEEN: FASHION

RETNA

Deborah Harry.

DEDICATED FOLLOWERS OF FASHION
The Rock and Roll Wardrobe

1   "The Angels Wanna Wear My Red Shoes," ELVIS COSTELLO
2   "Black Leatherette," THE SEX PISTOLS
3   "Black Slacks," JOE BENNETT AND THE SPARKLETONES
4   "Blue Jean Bop," GENE VINCENT AND THE BLUE CAPS
5   "Blue Suede Shoes," CARL PERKINS
6   "Blue Velvet," BOBBY VINTON
7   "Boots of Spanish Leather," BOB DYLAN
8   "Brown Shoes Don't Make It," THE MOTHERS OF INVENTION
9   "Chantilly Lace," THE BIG BOPPER
10 "Devil with a Blue Dress On," SHORTY LONG
11 "Hi-Heel Sneakers," TOMMY TUCKER
12 "Itsy Bitsy Teenie Weenie Yellow Polkadot Bikini," BRIAN HYLA
13 "Leopard-skin Pill-box Hat," BOB DYLAN
14 "Long Cool Woman (in a Black Dress)," THE HOLLIES
15 "Patches," CLARENCE CARTER
16 "Short Shorts," THE ROYAL TEENS
17 "Spanish Boots," JEFF BECK
18 "Sunglasses after Dark," THE CRAMPS
19 "Thirsty Boots," ERIC ANDERSEN
20 "Venus in Blue Jeans," JIMMY CLANTON

-◄❙▶-

ROCK STARS WHO HAVE MADE MR. BLACKWELL'S WORST DRESSED LIST

Mr. Blackwell is America's fashion arbiter, a self-appointed watchdog of the garment trade who each year issues his lists of the best and worst dressed celebrities, together with pithy comments about the latter. No rock performer has ever made the best dressed list. The comments below are from Blackwell.

1   **DAVID BOWIE,** 1973
     "A cross between Joan Crawford and Marlene Dietrich doing a glitter revival of New Faces!"

2 **CHER,** 1974
"Looks like a Hawaiian bar mitzvah!"

3 **DEBORAH HARRY,** 1979
"Ten cents a dance, with a nickel change!"

4 **ELTON JOHN,** 1975
"Would be the campiest spectacle in the Rose Parade!"

5 **LORETTA LYNN,** 1976
"The right dress in the wrong century!"

6 **BETTE MIDLER,** three-time award winner
1973: "Potluck in a laundromat." 1975: "Betsy Bloomer . . . didn't pantaloons go out with hoop skirts?" 1978: "She didn't go to a rummage sale, she wore it!"

7 **OLIVIA NEWTON-JOHN,** 1978
"The right dress in the wrong century!"

8 **YOKO ONO,** 1972
"A disaster area in stereo . . . oh, no, Yoko!"

9 **DOLLY PARTON,** another triple-award winner
1977: "Scarlett O'Hara dressed like Mae West in *My Little Chickadee!*" 1978: "Too many yards of Dolly poured into too few yards of fabric!" 1979: "A ruffled bedspread covering king-sized pillows!"

10 **THE POINTER SISTERS,** 1974
"Their fashion instinct is definitely *pointed* in the *wrong* direction!"

11 **HELEN REDDY,** two-time award winner
1974: "Isn't ready!" 1975: "She spent the year proving I was right . . . should have saved her costumes for the Bicentennial!"

12 **LINDA RONSTADT,** another two-time loser
1977: "Bought her entire wardrobe during a five-minute bus stop!" 1978: "Hits the high note in song, low note in fashion!"

13 **TAMMY WYNETTE and DONNA FARGO,** 1975
"Tied for yearly double . . . country magic dressed in circus tents!"

HONORABLE MENTION: Mr. and Mrs. Tiny Tim, 1969

10 ROCKERS WITH COSTUMES IN LONDON'S VICTORIA AND ALBERT MUSEUM

1 **MARC BOLAN**
Gold lamé jacket (made by Granny Takes a Trip) with black lamé collar and pocket flaps. Frayed and held together with safety pins on the left sleeve. Trousers to match. Made circa 1967–1968. A favorite suit of Bolan's, worn on his penultimate TV show in its held-together state, to appeal to punk tastes.

2 **WAYNE COUNTY**
Red nylon nightgown, pink lacy bed jacket, and beige woolly hat. The stage clothes of Wayne (now Jayne) County, of The Electric Chairs.

3 **BRIAN ENO**
Cream satin jacket with three-tiered stand-up collar trimmed in black with artificial blond hair fringing the front. Cream satin trousers with quilted design stitched in black and side pleat trimmed in black. Designed by Eno.

4 **JOHN ENTWISTLE**
Red and yellow jacket made from flag material. On back, red lions of Scotland; on front, yellow lions of England. Designed by Kit Lambert for the Who bassist.

5 **GARY GLITTER**
Jerkin in silver quilted vinyl, with stand-up collar and false zippered pockets. Silvered pendants on cuffs and pockets. Pair of trousers in silver Lurex edged with diamond-shaped sequins.

6 **DEBORAH HARRY**
Day-Glo orange and yellow striped minidress in synthetic jersey, with matching tights and headband. Worn on Blondie's 1979 European tour. Designed by Stephen Sprouse.

7 **ELTON JOHN**
Jacket with multicolored Lurex stripes, stud fastening, bell on front, mudguards on shoulders, and handlebar grips on sleeve cuffs. Pair of black trousers, sewn with reflectors in stripes.

Pair of black leather knee-high boots with platform soles and high heels, these studded with multicolored rhinestones. Designed by Bill Whitten. Worn on 1974–1975 American tour, during which Elton rode on stage on a bicycle encrusted end-to-end with red and white rhinestones.

8 **JOHN LENNON**
Gun-metal gray worsted, vented jacket with dark gray velvet collar and trousers to match. Worn onstage in 1963–1964.

9 **JIMMY PAGE**
One stage costume, known as "the Poppy." White cotton-backed satin jacket with Chinese-style frogging. Appliqué-embroidered poppy in red and green on right breast; velvet appliqué double-headed dragon entwined with poppy on back. Pair of matching trousers, flared, with chenille-embroidered dragon and appliqué poppy down left leg and astrological symbols and poppy down right leg. Pair of black-and-white moccasin-style shoes in imitation lizard and leather.

10 **BJORN ULVAEUS**
Blue satinlike bomber jacket, with blue-and-white wool trim and cotton embroidery. On back, multicolored pyramids above Abba logo; on front left breast, the name *Bjorn* in lower-case handwriting style. Worn on Abba's 1979 American tour.

·◀▐▐▶·

10 GROUPS THAT WORE UNIFORMS

1	THE BEATLES	7	KISS
2	THE BLUES MAGOOS	8	GARY PUCKETT AND THE
3	THE DAVE CLARK FIVE		UNION GAP
4	THE COMMODORES	9	PAUL REVERE AND THE
5	DEVO		RAIDERS
6	THE J.B.'S	10	THE YOUNG RASCALS

The Mods.

20 PERFORMERS KNOWN FOR THEIR HATS

1 CLARENCE CLEMONS
2 CHARLIE DANIELS
3 DR. JOHN
4 BOB DYLAN
5 KINKY FRIEDMAN
6 LOWELL GEORGE
7 JIMI HENDRIX
8 JANIS IAN
9 ELTON JOHN
10 JANIS JOPLIN
11 HARRY NILSSON
12 THE OHIO PLAYERS
13 PAUL REVERE AND THE RAIDERS
14 RAY SAWYER, a.k.a. DR. HOOK
15 SAM THE SHAM
16 SLY STONE
17 PETER TOSH
18 MIAMI STEVE VAN ZANDT
19 RONNIE VAN ZANT
20 CHRIS YOULDEN

THE 10 SKINNIEST ROCK STARS

1 STEVE WINWOOD
2 ROD STEWART
3 KEITH RICHARDS
4 GINGER BAKER
5 MICK JONES

6 SID VICIOUS
7 DAVID BYRNE
8 GRAHAM PARKER
9 STIV BATORS
10 MICK FLEETWOOD

TERENCE SPENCER/COLORIFIC

The Rockers.

THE 12 FATTEST ROCK STARS

1	LESLIE WEST	6	BUDDY MILES
2	RANDY BACHMAN	7	MEAT LOAF
3	HOWARD "FLO" KAYLAN, or is it MARK "EDDIE" VOLMAN?	8	CASS ELLIOTT
		9	CLARENCE CLEMONS
		10	BUBBA KNIGHT
4	ELVIS PRESLEY	11	BRIAN WILSON
5	DAVID CROSBY	12	CHRISTOPHER CROSS

-◄❚►-

BEST HAIRDOS

1 DAVID BOWIE
2 JAMES BROWN, circa 1965
3 BEACH BOYS, surfer look, 1963–1965
4 WAYNE COCHRAN
5 THE JIMI HENDRIX EXPERIENCE
6 THE BEATLES, circa 1964
7 BOB DYLAN, circa 1965–1966
8 THE B-52's
9 KEITH RICHARDS
10 THE WILD THING
11 JOHN LYDON
12 BRIAN JONES

-◄❚►-

PERFORMERS WITH THE LONGEST HAIR

1	ALICE COOPER	6	THE ROLLING STONES
2	SIR DOUGLAS QUINTET	7	THE HULLABALOOS
3	ZZ TOP	8	THE WILD THING
4	RICHARD AND THE YOUNG LIONS	9	THE SEEDS
		10	COUNT FIVE
5	BIG BROTHER AND THE HOLDING COMPANY	11	THE PEANUT BUTTER CONSPIRACY

BALDEST ROCK STARS

1	ED CASSIDY	6	THE PYRAMIDS
2	ISAAC HAYES	7	JOHN GOSLING
3	MAURICE GIBB	8	STEPHEN STILLS
4	ELTON JOHN	9	ART GARFUNKEL
5	DAVID CROSBY		

-◄❚▶-

FOUR EYES

1	PETER ASHER	13	PHIL LESH
2	JACK CASADY	14	CURTIS MAYFIELD
3	ELVIS COSTELLO	15	ROGER MCGUINN
4	BO DIDDLEY	16	RANDY NEWMAN
5	JERRY GARCIA	17	ROY ORBISON
6	BUDDY HOLLY	18	JOEY RAMONE
7	IAN HUNTER	19	DAVID RUFFIN
8	ELTON JOHN	20	LEON RUSSELL
9	PAUL KANTNER	21	SLY STONE
10	JOHN KAY	22	JOHN SEBASTIAN
11	AL KOOPER	23	WARREN ZEVON
12	JOHN LENNON		

-◄❚▶-

WORST TEETH

1	JOE STRUMMER	5	DAVID BOWIE
2	KEITH RICHARDS (now repaired)	6	TODD RUNDGREN
3	PETER ASHER (now repaired)	7	TOM PETTY
4	ROBERT PLANT (now repaired)	8	JOHNNY ROTTEN

BEST GROOMED

1 THE BEACH BOYS, up to *Pet Sounds* or so
2 THE CREWCUTS
3 JAN AND DEAN
4 THE EVERLY BROTHERS
5 PAT BOONE
6 THE COWSILLS
7 THE DIAMONDS
8 DICK AND DEEDEE
9 THE VILLAGE PEOPLE
10 EVERY MOTHER'S SON
11 KRAFTWERK
12 DINO, DESI, AND BILLY
13 PAUL AND PAULA
14 GRACE JONES
15 ELVIS COSTELLO AND THE ATTRACTIONS
16 JONATHAN RICHMAN
17 THE TALKING HEADS

-◄◗▮▶-

THE 10 TALLEST ROCK STARS

1 MICK FLEETWOOD
2 JOHN ENTWISTLE
3 CLARENCE CLEMONS
4 RANDY NEWMAN
5 CARLY SIMON
6 TODD RUNDGREN
7 LONG JOHN BALDRY
8 TEDDY PENDERGRASS
9 BRYAN FERRY
10 RIC OCASEK

-◄◗▮▶-

GOT NO REASON TO LIVE . . .
The 15 Shortest Rock Stars

1 ROGER DALTREY
2 PAUL SIMON
3 GRAHAM PARKER
4 IAN DURY
5 MARC BOLAN
6 ROY BITTAN
7 BRENDA LEE
8 VAN MORRISON
9 STEVE MARRIOTT
10 ALEXIS KORNER
11 GARLAND JEFFREYS
12 DOLLY PARTON
13 RONNIE SPECTOR
14 JOHN OATES
15 PHIL SPECTOR

FOURTEEN:
HISTORY

Mary Ford and Les Paul.

ROCK AND ROLL CELEBRATES ITSELF

Great Songs about the Birth, Death, and the Endurance of Rock and Roll

1   "It Will Stand," THE SHOWMEN
2   "Johnny B. Goode," CHUCK BERRY
3   "Hang Up My Rock and Roll Shoes," CHUCK WILLIS
4   "Rock and Roll," THE VELVET UNDERGROUND
5   "That Is Rock 'n' Roll," THE COASTERS
6   "Long Live Rock," THE WHO
7   "Do You Believe in Magic," THE LOVIN' SPOONFUL
8   "Rock and Roll Never Forgets," BOB SEGER
9   "Rock Therapy," THE ROCK AND ROLL TRIO
10 "Keep Playing That Rock 'n' Roll," EDGAR WINTER'S WHITE TRASH
11 "Rock and Roll," LED ZEPPELIN
12 "Rock and Roll Is Here to Stay," DANNY AND THE JUNIORS

-◄❙❙►-

ROOTS

Records That Used "Rock and Roll" in Their Titles Prior to the 1950s

1   **"My Daddy Rocks Me with One Steady Roll,"** TRIXI SMITH, 1922; THE SOUTHERN QUARTET, 1924; HAROLD ORT AND HIS OHIO STATE COLLEGIANS, 1925; JIMMY NOONE, 1929
2   **"Rocking and Rolling,"** BOB ROBINSON, 1930
    Recorded for Champion; unreleased at the time.
3   **"Rock and Roll,"** THE BOSWELL SISTERS, 1934; JOE HAYN AND HIS ORCHESTRA, 1934; JOHN LEE HOOKER, 1950
    The Boswell version is featured in the film *Transatlantic Merr Go-Round*.
4   **"Rockin' Rollin' Mama,"** BUDDY JONES, 1939
5   **"We're Gonna Rock, We're Gonna Roll,"** WILD BIL MOORE, 1947

This is usually acknowledged as the first rock and roll record. It provided the inspiration for Alan Freed's application of the term to the R&B genre. Moore redid it for Modern Record in 1949 as "Rock and Roll."

-◄❚❘►-

Broadway and Tin Pan Alley Standards That Have Been Converted to Rock and R&B Hits

1 "Are You Lonesome Tonight," Elvis Presley
2 "Baby Face," Wing and a Prayer Fife and Drum Corps
3 "Besame Mucho, Parts 1 and 2," The Coasters
4 "Blue Moon," The Marcels
5 "Danny Boy," Jackie Wilson
6 "Deep Purple," Nino Tempo and April Stevens
7 "Georgia on My Mind," Ray Charles
8 "I've Got You under My Skin," The Four Seasons
9 "It's All in the Game," Tommy Edwards (also cut by Van Morrison)
10 "Maria," P. J. Proby
11 "My Way," Sid Vicious
12 "Somewhere over the Rainbow," Jimi Hendrix
13 "Singin' in the Rain," Just Water
14 "Smoke Gets in Your Eyes," The Platters
15 "Till There Was You," The Beatles
16 "Try a Little Tenderness," Otis Redding
17 "Where or When," Dion and the Belmonts
18 "White Christmas," The Drifters
19 "Yes Sir, That's My Baby," The Clovers
20 "Zing Went the Strings of My Heart," The Trammps

PREHISTORIC ROCK AND ROLL
10 Records That Served as Important Stepping Stones

1   "Key to the Highway," JAZZ GILLUM, 1940
2   "Take Me Back to Tulsa," BOB WILLS' TEXAS PLAYBOYS, 1941
3   "Choo Choo Ch'Boogie," LOUIS JORDAN, 1946
4   "Good Rocking Tonight," ROY BROWN, 1947
5   "Old Man River," THE RAVENS, 1947
6   "Move It on Over," HANK WILLIAMS, 1947
7   "The Great Medical Menagerist," HARMONICA FRANK, 1951
8   "Rockin' Chair Daddy," THE FIVE KEYS, 1951, 1953
9   "Rock the Joint," BILL HALEY AND THE SADDLEMEN, 1952
10 "Feelin' Good," LITTLE JUNIOR PARKER'S BLUE FLAMES, 1953

-◄❚▶-

SONGS CARL PERKINS WOULD USE TO DESCRIBE ROCK AND ROLL TO SOMEONE WHO HAD NEVER HEARD IT

1   "Blue Suede Shoes," CARL PERKINS
2   "Honey, Don't," CARL PERKINS
3   "Match Box," CARL PERKINS
4   "That's All Right," ELVIS PRESLEY
5   "Blue Moon of Kentucky," ELVIS PRESLEY
6   "Kaw-Liga," HANK WILLIAMS

CARL PERKINS, *author of "Blue Suede Shoes," is one of the greatest rockabilly singers. Since the 1960s, he has also been a major country-music figure, both on his own and with close friend Johnny Cash.*

GREAT MULTIPART SONGS
Songs Whose Hit Versions Were Only Half the Story

1 "American Pie—Parts 1 and 2," DON MCLEAN
2 "Bad Luck (Part 1)," HAROLD MELVIN AND THE BLUE NOTES
3 "Fingertips—Pt. 2," STEVIE WONDER
4 "The Flying Saucer (Parts 1 and 2)," BUCHANAN AND GOODMAN
5 "Funky Broadway, Part 1," DYKE AND THE BLAZERS
6 "Honky Tonk (Parts 1 and 2)," BILL DOGGETT*
7 "I Like It Like That, Part 1," CHRIS KENNER
8 "(Not Just) Knee Deep, Part 1," FUNKADELIC
9 "Ooh Poo Pah Doo—Part II," JESSIE HILL
10 "Peppermint Twist—Part 1," JOEY DEE AND THE STARLITERS
11 "Rockhouse, Part 2," RAY CHARLES
12 "Shout—Part 1," THE ISLEY BROTHERS
13 "You Can't Sit Down, Part 2," PHIL UPCHURCH

NOTE: See "Multipart Hits by James Brown" (p. 396).

*"Honky Tonk, Part 2," was a hit twice.

-◄❚❙▮❙►-

ORIGINS OF 20 BAND NAMES

1 **ALICE COOPER**
Supposedly from a Ouija board reading that revealed that Vincent Furnier, the band's lead singer, was actually the reincarnation of a strange, seventeenth-century witch, Alice Cooper.

2 **THE BEATLES**
In honor of The Crickets.

3 **BUFFALO SPRINGFIELD**
From a steamroller, not an airplane, as is commonly thought.

4   **THE CHAMPS**
They recorded for Gene Autry's Challenge label. Autry named
them after his movie horse, Champion.

5   **THE DOORS**
From quotations of Aldous Huxley and William Blake
concerning "the doors of perception."

6   **THE FLEETWOODS**
After a Seattle telephone exchange, not the Cadillac, as is
commonly supposed.

7   **THE HOLLIES**
After Buddy Holly.

8   **THE JEFFERSON AIRPLANE**
From a convoluted joke about Blind Lemon Jefferson that was
made by San Francisco blues singer Steve Talbot, who was
talking about Blind Jefferson Airplane.

9   **JETHRO TULL**
From the eighteenth-century inventor of the seed drill.

10   **LED ZEPPELIN**
From a joke made by The Who's John Entwistle, who proposed
that Jimmy Page's new group would go over like the world's
largest lead balloon—a lead Zeppelin.

11   **THE LOVIN' SPOONFUL**
From the old blues lyric, "My baby loves me 'bout a lovin'
spoonful," which is also the supposed quantity of one male
ejaculation (the British equivalent: 10cc).

12   **THE O'JAYS**
From Cleveland disc jockey Eddie O'Jay, who gave them their
start.

13   **PINK FLOYD**
In honor of the Georgia bluesmen Pink Anderson and Floyd
Council.

14   **QUICKSILVER MESSENGER SERVICE**
From the fact that the original band members were Virgos,
which is ruled by the planet Mercury. Mercury is the chemical
name for quicksilver.

15 **RUFUS**

From the *Mechanix Illustrated* column "Ask Rufus," which is also the name of one of their albums.

16 **THE SEARCHERS**

After John Ford's famous western starring John Wayne, whose favorite expression in this 1956 film served as the title of Buddy Holly and the Crickets' first hit, "That'll Be the Day."

17 **THE SMALL FACES**

Because of the extreme lack of height of the group members, none of whom is taller than about five feet five inches. When the much larger Rod Stewart and Ron Wood replaced Steve Marriott, the band became The Faces.

18 **STEELY DAN**

From a dildo in William Burroughs' *The Naked Lunch*.

19 **THREE DOG NIGHT**

From an Australian aboriginal term for an especially cold evening: They bed down with their dogs, adding more animals as the weather grows harsher. A three-dog night is the coldest of the year.

-◄▌►-

ORIGINAL NAMES OF 15 FAMOUS BANDS

1 **AL AND THE SILVERTONES** (The Guess Who)

2 **THE BEEFEATERS** (The Byrds)

3 **CHICAGO TRANSIT AUTHORITY, THE BIG THING** (Chicago)

4 **THE DELTAS** (The Hollies)

5 **TOMMY FOGERTY AND THE BLUE VELVETS, THE GOLLIWOGS** (Creedence Clearwater Revival)

6 **THE HALLUCINATIONS** (The J. Geils Band)

They merged with another Boston blues band.

7 **THE HOURGLASS** (The Allman Brothers Band)

8 **KENNY AND THE CADETS, CARL AND THE PASSIONS** (The Beach Boys)

These were high school editions, before Dennis Wilson became fully committed to being in a band.

9   **THE PRIMETTES** (The Supremes)

10 **THE QUARRYMEN, THE SILVER BEATLES** (The Beatles)

11 **THE RED ROOSTERS** (Spirit)

12 **THE ROBINS** (The Coasters)

13 **THE SOFT WHITE UNDERBELLY** (Blue Öyster Cult)
As Soft White Underbelly, Blue Öyster Cult was highly praised in the pages of the early *Crawdaddy*. Few record companies agreed. Clive Davis, then president of CBS Records, turned down Underbelly, so they changed their name and submitted a new tape, which Davis liked. It took the band a year or so to tell Davis about the ruse.

14 **TOM AND JERRY** (Simon and Garfunkel)

15 **THE WARLOCKS** (The Grateful Dead)

The High Numbers (later to become The Who), demonstrate a dance favored by "blocked-up" pill-head Mods called the Block at London's Scene Club in 1964.

EXPELLED

15 People Who Quit or Were Fired Before Their Groups Became Famous

1 SIGNE ANDERSON, vocals, The Jefferson Airplane (quit)
2 PETE BEST, drums, The Beatles (fired)
3 ERIC CLAPTON, guitar, The Yardbirds (quit)
4 TORY CRIMES, drums, The Clash (fired)
5 PETER GREEN, guitar, Fleetwood Mac (quit)
6 AL JARDINE, guitar, The Beach Boys (quit—temporarily)
7 AL KOOPER, guitar, keyboards, vocals, Blood, Sweat, and Tears (quit)
8 VINNIE LOPEZ, drums, E Street Band (fired)
9 GLEN MATLOCK, bass, The Sex Pistols (fired)
10 DAVID SANCIOUS, keyboards, The E Street Band (quit)
11 DOUG SANDEN, drums, The Who (fired)
12 JEREMY SPENCER, guitar, Fleetwood Mac (quit)
13 IAN STEWART, piano, The Rolling Stones (fired; hung in as road manager)
14 STU SUTCLIFFE, bass, The Beatles (quit)
15 ROY WOOD, various instruments, Electric Light Orchestra (quit)

Eric Clapton performs with the Yardbirds on British television in 1965.

PREVIOUS CONVICTIONS
Former Occupations of Rock Stars

1 PAUL ANKA, movie theater usher
2 CHUCK BERRY, hairdresser
3 CILLA BLACK, Cavern Club hatcheck
4 MARC BOLAN, model
5 DAVID BOWIE, commercial artist for advertising agency
6 JOE COCKER, gas fitter (plumber)
7 ELVIS COSTELLO, computer programmer
8 ROGER DALTREY, steelworker
9 JOHN ENTWISTLE, tax clerk
10 DEBORAH HARRY, Playboy Club Bunny
11 SCREAMIN' JAY HAWKINS, prizefighter
12 ELVIS PRESLEY, truck driver
13 PAUL REVERE, barber
14 GRACE SLICK, model

-◄❚▶-

GREAT GIRL GROUPS AND THE HITS THAT MADE THEM FAMOUS

1 THE CRYSTALS, "Da Doo Ron Ron," "Then He Kissed Me"
2 THE RONETTES, "Be My Baby," "Baby, I Love You"
3 THE SHIRELLES, "Will You Love Me Tomorrow"
4 THE SHANGRI-LAS, "The Leader of the Pack"
5 THE SUPREMES, "Baby Love," "Stop! In the Name of Love"
6 THE MARVELETTES, "Please Mister Postman"
7 MARTHA AND THE VANDELLAS, "Heatwave," "Dancing in the Street"
8 THE COOKIES, "Don't Say Nothin' Bad (about My Baby)"
9 THE RAINDROPS, "The Kind of Boy You Can't Forget"
10 THE MURMAIDS, "Popsicles and Icicles"
11 THE ORLONS, "Don't Hang Up"

12 THE CHORDETTES, "Lollipop"
13 THE DIXIE CUPS, "Iko Iko," "Chapel of Love"
14 THE AD LIBS, "The Boy from New York City"
15 THE CHIFFONS, "He's So Fine," "One Fine Day"
16 THE JELLY BEANS, "I Wanna Love Him So Bad"
17 THE VELVELETTES, "Needle in a Haystack"
18 THE BOBBETTES, "Mr. Lee"
19 THE QUIN-TONES, "Down the Aisle of Love"
20 THE TEEN QUEENS, "Eddie My Love"
21 THE CHANTELS, "Maybe"
22 THE ANGELS, "My Boyfriend's Back"
23 THE JAYNETTS, "Sally, Go 'Round the Roses"

Cilla Black and friend at an early hours party in swinging London in January 1965.

PAUL NELSON PICKS THE FUNDAMENTAL FOLK-ROCKERS

1 and 2   BOB DYLAN; THE BYRDS
The fathers of folk-rock, of course, but that hardly rates more than a footnote because neither's career can be limited to one minor genre.

3   THE LOVIN' SPOONFUL
A crafty combination of infernal affability, cartoon costumes, rock and roll, and jug-band music.

4   BUFFALO SPRINGFIELD
Not really a folk-rock band, but Springfield deserves special mention for caring enough to preserve the very best qualities of the form and for conscientiously consolidating them into inspired if idiosyncratic rock and roll.

5   THE MAMAS AND THE PAPAS
What made this group was its haunting and sumptuous harmony singing; their message was surely the ultimate vocal message.

6   DONOVAN
From the vantage point of the present, it is hard not to regard Donovan's career as unnecessarily tragic, because, even while he was floating away into the lilac mist, there were traces of a solid and uncommon talent. "I think, therefore I shouldn' think" probably should have been Donovan's motto.

7   SONNY AND CHER
They cold-bloodedly pitted a whining teenage Romeo and Juliet against the authority of all grown-ups in their calculated classics, "I Got You, Babe" and "Laugh at Me."

PAUL NELSON, *currently record-review editor of* Rolling Stone, *was editor of* Little Sandy Review, Sing Out, *and* Hullabaloo *during the folk and folk-rock eras.*

GREAT FOLK-ROCK HITS

1   "Like a Rolling Stone," BOB DYLAN
2   "Hey Joe," THE LEAVES
3   "Norwegian Wood," THE BEATLES
4   "Mr. Tambourine Man," THE BYRDS
5   "Do You Believe in Magic," THE LOVIN' SPOONFUL
6   "I Want You," BOB DYLAN
7   "It Ain't Me, Babe," THE TURTLES
8   "Laugh at Me," SONNY BONO
9   "If I Were a Carpenter," TIM HARDIN
10 "Catch the Wind," DONOVAN
11 "Universal Soldier," BUFFY SAINTE-MARIE
12 "Just Like a Woman," MANFRED MANN

-◄❙❙►-

DAVID BROMBERG'S 10 FAVORITE ALBUMS

1   *The Real Bahamas**
2   *The Greatest Ray Charles*, RAY CHARLES
3   *Cry from the Cross*, RALPH STANLEY
4   *Penny Whistlers**
5   *Solo Flight—The Genius of Charlie Christian*
6   *The Pres de Paris*, PIERRE BEN-SUSAN
7   *Charlie Parker, Volume 5*, CHARLIE PARKER
8   *Uncle Pen*, BILL MONROE
9   *Blind Willie McTell*
10 *When I Die I'll Live Again*, REVEREND GARY DAVIS

DAVID BROMBERG *is best known for accompanying Bob Dylan as guitarist on* New Morning *and* Self Portrait. *But he has also distinguished himself as a session player with many other artists and with his own solo recordings and tours.*

*Part of the Nonesuch Explorer Series

GREATEST BANDS OF THE BRITISH INVASION

1   THE BEATLES
2   THE ROLLING STONES
3   THE DAVE CLARK FIVE
4   THE KINKS
5   MANFRED MANN
6   HERMAN'S HERMITS
7   THE ANIMALS
8   THE YARDBIRDS
9   FREDDIE AND THE
      DREAMERS
10 THE SEARCHERS
11 GERRY AND THE
      PACEMAKERS
12 THE HOLLIES
13 THE WHO
14 THE ZOMBIES
15 THE SPENCER DAVIS
      GROUP
16 THE MOODY BLUES
17 WAYNE FONTANA AND
      THE MINDBENDERS
18 THE PRETTY THINGS
19 THE HULLABALOOS
20 THE MERSEYBEATS

BEYOND THE BEATLES
The Mersey Groups

1   **THE SEARCHERS**
    Perhaps the best of the post-Beatles Liverpudlian rockers,
    "Needles and Pins," "When You Walk in the Room," and
    their other hits are first rate pop-rockers.

2   **THE MERSEYBEATS**
    They became the Merseys after personnel changes. Their
    original hit was "I Think of You," but they later scored with
    Pete Townshend's "So Sad about Us" and the great "Sorrow,"
    more recently redone by David Bowie.

3   **THE SWINGING BLUE JEANS**
    Most of these Liverpool groups were more aligned with
    pop-rock than blues. The Blue Jeans' "Hippy Hippy Shake"
    was a rare exception.

4 and 5 GERRY AND THE PACEMAKERS; BILLY J. KRAMER AND THE DAKOTAS

As part of Brian Epstein's large stable, Kramer hit with a version of Lennon-McCartney's "Do You Want to Know a Secret," among others, while Gerry and the Pacemakers' best-known hits were "How Do You Do It" and "Ferry Cross the Mersey." Both were rather wimpy, perhaps the way Epstein would have wished The Beatles to sound.

6 SCAFFOLD

Featured Mike McGear, Paul McCartney's younger brother; arty for the time.

7 RORY STORM AND THE HURRICANES

Best known for providing The Beatles with Ringo, Storm was apparently one hell of a showman, though his records don't amount to much.

8 KINGSIZE TAYLOR AND THE DOMINOES

This hard-line R&B band claimed to be the original Mersey group.

9 THE UNDERTAKERS

Best known for vocalist Jackie Lomax, who later cut the remarkable George Harrison-produced "Sour Milk Sea."

10 THE BIG THREE

Musicians' musicians, they were possibly the most respected players on the scene.

11 THE FOURMOST

Epstein-managed group with a flair for comedy.

12 THE ESCORTS

Provided The Hollies with Terry Sylvester.

13 THE CHANTS

A black vocal group.

14 THE MOJOS

Their best-known disc was "Everything's Alright."

15 TOMMY QUICKLY AND THE REMO FOUR

Pianist Tony Ashton went on to Ashton, Gardner, and Dyke, who hit with "Resurrection Shuffle" in 1971.

16   **THE RIOT SQUAD**
Claim to fame: toured in support of The Kinks in 1965.

17   **THE KUBAS**
Toured with The Beatles in 1965 and appeared in The
Pacemakers' movie, *Ferry Cross the Mersey*.

18   **FARON'S FLAMINGOS**
Best known for "Let's Stomp."

19   **THE FOUR PENNIES**
"Juliet" was their biggest disc.

20   **IAN AND THE ZODIACS**
They had one decent LP released in the States.

-◄❚▶-

THE LONDON R&B SCENE
And Its Mutations

1   **ALEXIS KORNER'S BLUES INCORPORATED**
(See "15 Veterans of Alexis Korner's Blues Incorporated,"
p. 205.)

2   **JOHN MAYALL'S BLUESBREAKERS**
(See "Veterans of John Mayall's Bluesbreakers," p. 204.)

3   **THE ROLLING STONES**

4   **THE ARTWOODS**
Featured Art Wood, Ron's older brother; Jon Lord of Deep
Purple; and Keef Hartley, later with Bluesbreakers and his
own band.

5   **GRAHAM BOND ORGANISATION**
Graduates: Dick Heckstall-Smith, Jack Bruce, Jon Hiseman,
and Ginger Baker.

6   **LONG JOHN BALDRY**
Veteran of Korner and Cyril Davies bands; had a couple of hits
as a vocalist; led Steampacket and The Hoochie Coochie Men
which also featured Rod Stewart.

7   **THE CHEYNES**
Graduates: Peter Bardens and Mick Fleetwood.

8   **BRIAN AUGER**
    Another member of Steampacket, Auger also led his own
    bands, Trinity and Oblivion Express.

9   **CYRIL DAVIES ALL STARS**
    Davies died of leukemia in 1964, just before the scene broke
    wide open. He was a remarkable harmonica player, legend
    says, though the recordings don't prove it. Graduates: Long
    John Baldry, Dick Heckstall-Smith and Nicky Hopkins.

10 **GARY FARR AND THE T-BONES**
    Contributed Keith Emerson to The Nice as well as Emerson,
    Lake, and Palmer.

11 **MARK LEEMAN FIVE**
    Drummer Brian Davison went on to The Nice.

12 **ZOOT MONEY BIG ROLL BAND**
    Money later recorded with Eric Burdon. The Big Roll Band
    produced Johnny Almond and the new Animals' Andy Somers.

13 **JIMMY POWELL AND THE FIVE DIMENSIONS**
    Rod Stewart's first band.

14 **THE PRETTY THINGS**
    Phil May and Rolling Stones refugee Dick Taylor led the
    original group. Mitch Mitchell was their drummer for a brief
    spell; their big hit was "Don't Bring Me Down," banned in the
    States.

15 **STEAMPACKET**
    Graduates: Long John Baldry, Brian Auger, singer Julie
    Driscoll, and drummer Mickey Waller.

16 **THE YARDBIRDS**
    The great R&B guitar band; produced Eric Clapton, Jeff Beck,
    and Jimmy Page.

17 **SHOTGUN EXPRESS**
    Featured Rod Stewart, Peter Bardens, and Peter Green; also,
    anomalously, Merseybeat singer Beryl Marsden.

18 **THE BIRDS**
    Ron Wood's first band.

19 **MANFRED MANN**
    More pop-jazz than blues, at least after the initial bunch of

hits. Graduates: Paul Jones, Tom McGuinness, Mike D'Abo, and Klaus Voorman.

20   **THE ZEPHYRS**
They're best known for their version of Bo Diddley's "I Can Tell," produced by Shel Talmy. Mick Jagger hated it, and said so a lot.

-◄▮▶-

10 FAVORITE BANDS OF THE MODS

1   **THE ACTION**
One of the earliest of the mod favorites (circa 1963) from the Kentish Town area. Despite their popularity in the clubs, none of their five singles ever hit the charts.

2   **THE BIRDS**
Another early 1964 mod band that specialized in American R&B covers, The Birds featured a young Ron Wood on guitar.

3   **THE CREATION**
Lead guitarist Eddie Phillips was so flash that Pete Townshend asked him to join The Who.

4   **GEORGIE FAME AND THE BLUE FLAMES**
Great mod dance band.

5   **CHRIS FARLOWE AND THE THUNDERBIRDS**
If Farlowe hadn't been so ugly, the fact that he numbered Keith Richards and Mick Jagger among his biggest fans—and sometime producers—might have made him a major star.

6   **JOHN'S CHILDREN**
The first of the glitter rock bands, its lead singer was Marc Bolan, later of T. Rex fame.

7   **THE KINKS**
Too Edwardian to really fit, but close enough in musical style.

8   **THE SMALL FACES**
Real mods.

9   **GENO WASHINGTON AND THE FAM JAM BAND**
The dancing band of the mods—terrible on records, though.

10 **THE WHO**
Dressed the part.

-◄❚▶-

THE BRITISH BLUES REVIVAL
Circa 1968

1 AYNSLEY DUNBAR RETALIATION
2 CLIMAX BLUES BAND
3 FLEETWOOD MAC
4 FREE
5 THE GROUNDHOGS
6 THE KEEF HARTLEY BAND
7 JUICY LUCY
8 JOHN MAYALL'S BLUESBREAKERS
9 SAVOY BROWN
10 STONE THE CROWS

-◄❚▶-

20 BRITISH FOLK ROCKERS

1 THE ALBION COUNTRY BAND
2 AMAZING BLONDEL
3 DONOVAN
4 NICK DRAKE
5 FAIRPORT CONVENTION
6 FOTHERINGAY
7 GRYPHON
8 THE INCREDIBLE STRING BAND
9 JACK THE LAD
10 LINDISFARNE
11 JOHN MARTYN
12 PENTANGLE
13 PLANXTY
14 JOHN RENBOURN
15 ALAN STIVELL
16 STEELEYE SPAN
17 AL STEWART
18 THE STRAWBS
19 RICHARD AND LINDA THOMPSON
20 TRAFFIC

PUB ROCKERS

These bands have little in common other than that they all played one form or another of the loose, easygoing music that was acceptable in British pubs in the early 1970s. Prior to 1972, pub music had been light jazz. But after an American band, Eggs over Easy, got a residency at the Tally Ho in Kentish Town, London, the way was paved for light rock to appear in such places, too. Brinsley Schwarz and Ducks Deluxe were the cream of the pub-rock crop, and it's no coincidence that guitarist Schwarz and Ducks Deluxe guitarist Martin Belmont formed the core of The Rumour after their earlier groups split.

1 ACE
2 BEES MAKE HONEY
3 BRINSLEY SCHWARZ
4 CHILLI WILLI AND THE RED HOT PEPPERS
5 DR. FEELGOOD
6 DUCKS DELUXE
7 EDDIE AND THE HOT RODS
8 EGGS OVER EASY
9 KILBURN AND THE HIGH ROADS
10 KOKOMO
11 THE KURSAAL FLYERS
12 ROOGALATOR

VETERANS OF JOHN MAYALL'S BLUESBREAKERS

1 JOHNNY ALMOND, sax (Mark-Almond)
2 JACK BRUCE, bass (Manfred Mann, Graham Bond Organisation, Cream, solo)
3 ERIC CLAPTON, guitar (Cream, Blind Faith, solo)
4 ROGER DEAN, guitar
5 AYNSLEY DUNBAR, drums (ubiquitous ever since, lately in The Jefferson Starship)
6 MICK FLEETWOOD, drums (Fleetwood Mac)
7 HUGHIE FLINT, drums (McGuiness-Flint)

8   ANDY FRASER, bass (Free)
9   PETER GREEN, guitar (Fleetwood Mac)
10 KEEF HARTLEY, drums (The Keef Hartley Band)
11 JON HISEMAN, drums (Graham Bond Organisation, Colosseum)
12 HARVEY MANDEL, guitar (Canned Heat)
13 JON MARK guitar (Mark-Almond)
14 JOHN McVIE, bass (Fleetwood Mac)
15 CHRIS MERCER, guitar, sax (Juicy Lucy)
16 TONY REEVES, bass (Colosseum)
17 LARRY TAYLOR, bass (Canned Heat)
18 MICK TAYLOR, guitar (The Rolling Stones, solo)

-◄❙❙►-

15 VETERANS OF ALEXIS KORNER'S BLUES INCORPORATED

1   GINGER BAKER, drums (Graham Bond Organisation, Cream)
2   LONG JOHN BALDRY, vocals (Steampacket)
3   GRAHAM BOND, sax, organ (Graham Bond Organisation)
4   JACK BRUCE, bass (John Mayall's Bluesbreakers, Graham Bond Organisation, Manfred Mann, Cream, solo)
5   ERIC BURDON, vocals (The Animals)
6   TERRY COX, drums (Pentangle)
7   DICK HECKSTALL-SMITH, sax (John Mayall's Bluesbreakers, Colosseum, solo)
8   LEE JACKSON, bass (The Nice, Jackson Heights)
9   MICK JAGGER, occasional vocals, harp (The Rolling Stones)
10 BRIAN JONES, guitar jams (The Rolling Stones)
11 PAUL JONES, vocals (Manfred Mann)
12 ROBERT PLANT, vocals (Led Zeppelin)
13 KEITH RICHARDS, guitar jams (The Rolling Stones)
14 DANNY THOMPSON, bass (Pentangle)
15 CHARLIE WATTS, drums (The Rolling Stones)

10 FLOWER-POWER RELICS

1 "All You Need Is Love," THE BEATLES
2 "Get Together," THE YOUNGBLOODS
3 "Good Vibrations," THE BEACH BOYS
4 "Harry Hippie," BOBBY WOMACK
5 "The Hippies Are Trying," JUNIOR WELLS
6 "Itchycoo Park," THE SMALL FACES
7 "Love City," SLY AND THE FAMILY STONE
8 "San Francisco (Be Sure to Wear Some Flowers in Your Hair)," SCOTT MCKENZIE
9 "San Franciscan Nights," ERIC BURDON AND THE ANIMALS
10 "Wear Your Love Like Heaven," DONOVAN

-◄❙▶-

YOU CAN'T SAY WE DIDN'T WARN YOU
40 of the Most Absurd Group Names of the Psychedelic Era

1 AFRICA CREEPS UP AND UP
2 AUTOSALVAGE
3 AUM
4 BALL POINT BANANA
5 BUBBLE PUPPY
6 CLEAR LIGHT
7 THE CHARGING TYRANNOSAURUS OF DESPAIR*
8 CHOCOLATE WATCHBAND
9 TRUMAN COYOTE
10 THE CRAB COMETH FORTH
11 DAISY OVERKILL
12 DR. ZOOM AND HIS SONIC BOOM
13 THE ELECTRIC RECTUM

*The name was later changed to Detroit Edison White Light Co., because the drummer refused to have anything to do with despair.

14   THE ELECTRIC PRUNES
15   EVERPRESENT FULLNESS
16   EVERYTHING IS EVERYTHING
17   THE FIFTY FOOT HOSE
18   FROSTED SUEDE
19   FRUMIOUS BANDERSNATCH
20   THE GRATEFUL DEAD
21   HMMM
22   THE HOLY MODAL ROUNDERS
23   IT'S A BEAUTIFUL DAY
24   THE JEFFERSON AIRPLANE
25   JESUS CHRIST AND THE NAILKNOCKERS
26   LOTHAR AND THE HAND PEOPLE
27   THE NITTY GRITTY DIRT BAND
28   THE ONLY ALTERNATIVE AND HIS OTHER POSSIBILITIES
29   THE PEANUT BUTTER CONSPIRACY
30   PH FACTOR JUG BAND
31   PURPLE EARTHQUAKE
32   RECURRING LOVE HABIT
33   THE STRAWBERRY ALARM CLOCK
34   13TH FLOOR ELEVATOR
35   THORSTEN VEBLEN BLUES BAND
36   THE TIME BEING
37   TINY HEARING AID COMPANY
38   TRANSATLANTIC CHICKEN WICKEN NO. 5
39   ULTIMATE SPINACH
40   UNCUT BALLOON

-◄❚▶-

10 SONGS EVERY 60s BAND HAD TO KNOW

1   "Foxy Lady," JIMI HENDRIX
2   "Gloria," THEM, THE SHADOWS OF KNIGHT
3   "Hey Joe," THE LEAVES
4   "(I Can't Get No) Satisfaction," THE ROLLING STONES

5   "In the Midnight Hour," WILSON PICKETT
6   "Little Latin Lupe Lu," THE RIGHTEOUS BROTHERS, MITCH
        RYDER AND THE DETROIT WHEELS
7   "Louie Louie," THE KINGSMEN
8   "Twist and Shout," THE ISLEY BROTHERS, THE BEATLES
9   "Walking the Dog," RUFUS THOMAS
10   "You Really Got Me," THE KINKS

-◄❙▶-

TIMOTHY LEARY LISTS THE TECHNO-EROTIC VECTOR BANDS

1   DAVID BOWIE
2   KING CRIMSON
3   MANUEL GOTTSCHING
4   THE JIMI HENDRIX
        EXPERIENCE
5   ROXY MUSIC (Brian
        Eno, Bryan Ferry)
6   KLAUS SCHULZE

TIMOTHY LEARY *was one of the foremost influences on popular culture in the
1960s. Today, he writes books about exo-psychology when he is not entertaining
audiences in nightclubs across the country.*

-◄❙▶-

25 U.S. ROCK FESTIVALS WITH THE LARGEST ATTENDANCE

The following information was gleaned from Robert Santelli's
Aquarius Rising: The Rock Festival Years *(Delta Books,
1980)*

1   Watkins Glen Summer Jam, New York, July 28,
     1973   600,000
2   Woodstock Music and Art Fair, Bethel, New York,
     August 15–17, 1969   400,000
3   Altamont, Livermore, California, December 6,
     1969   300,000

4	California Jam II, Ontario, California, March 18, 1978	250,000
5	Mount Pocono Festival, Long Pond, Pennsylvania, July 18, 1972	200,000
6	Atlanta Pop Festival, July 3–5, 1970	200,000
7	California Jam I, Ontario, California, April 16, 1974	200,000
8	Newport '69, Northridge, California, June 20–22, 1969	150,000
9	Atlanta Pop Festival, July 4, 5, 1969	140,000
10	Texas International Pop Festival, Lewisville, August 30– September 1, 1969	120,000
11	Atlantic City Pop Festival, August 1–3, 1969	110,000

150,000 people await Bob Dylan's performance at the first Isle of Wight Festival in England in 1969.

12	Newport Pop Festival, Costa Mesa, California, August 4, 5, 1968	100,000
13	Miami Pop Festival, Hallandale, Florida, December 28–30, 1968	100,000
14	Newport Jazz Festival, Rhode Island, July 3–6, 1969	78,000
15	Seattle Pop Festival, July 25–27, 1969	70,000
16	Monterey International Pop Festival, California, June 16–18, 1967	50,000
17	Denver Pop Festival, June 27, 28, 1969	50,000
18	Celebration of Life, McCrea, Louisiana, June 21–28, 1971	50,000
19	Powder Ridge Rock Festival, Middlefield, Connecticut, July 30–August 1, 1970	30,000
20	Randall's Island Rock Festival (New York Pop Concert), July 17–19, 1970	30,000
21	Mar y Sol, Vega Baja, Puerto Rico, April 1–3, 1972	30,000
22	New Orleans Pop Festival, August 31–September 1, 1969	25,000
23	Second Annual Sky River Rock Festival, Tenino, Washington, August 30–September 1, 1969	25,000
24	Human Be-In, San Francisco, January 14, 1967	20,000
25	Fantasy Faire and Magic Mountain Music Festival, Mount Tamalpais, California, June 10, 11, 1967	15,000
	ALSO: Sky River Rock Festival and Lighter than Air Fair, Sultan, Washington, August 31–September 2, 1968	15,000

ROBERT SANTELLI SELECTS THE 5 BEST ROCK FESTIVALS

1   **Monterey International Pop Festival,** California, June 1967
    The Summer of Love began at Monterey; 50,000 people gathered for the best of sixties rock and blues: The Who, The Jimi Hendrix Experience, Janis Joplin and Big Brother and the Holding Company, Aretha Franklin, Otis Redding, The Byrds, Eric Burdon and the Animals, Canned Heat, Quicksilver Messenger Service, The Jefferson Airplane, and The Grateful Dead. Monterey's success paved the way for festival fever in the late 1960s.

2   **Woodstock Music and Art Fair,** Bethel, New York, August 1969
    Jimi Hendrix, Creedence Clearwater Revival, The Band, Janis Joplin, The Jefferson Airplane, Sly and the Family Stone, Canned Heat, The Who, and The Grateful Dead, among others, played to 400,000 who flocked to Max Yasgur's upstate New York dairy farm. The day after it ended, the *New York Times* ran an editorial calling Woodstock a "Nightmare in the Catskills": "What kind of culture is it that can produce so colossal a mess?" The those who were there will remember it as the most idyllic event of their lives.

3   **Watkins Glen Summer Jam,** New York, July 1973
    This was the largest gathering of rock fans, 600,000, for a one-day show by The Grateful Dead, The Allman Brothers Band, and The Band.

4   **Miami Pop Festival,** Hallandale, Florida, December 1968
    The billing represented just about every form of contemporary pop music (Joni Mitchell, The Paul Butterfield Blues Band, Hugh Masekela). Miami was the first successful, large-scale rock festival on the East Coast and the first ever to use two stages.

5   **Atlanta Pop Festival,** July 1969
     This two-day festival attracted 140,000 fans to a Fourth of July
     extravaganza including Janis Joplin, Led Zeppelin, Creedence
     Clearwater Revival, Tommy James and the Shondells, and The
     Staple Singers.

ROBERT SANTELLI *is a critic, journalist, and author of* Aquarius Rising: The Rock
Festival Years, *published by Delta Books in 1980.*

-◄▐▐►-

ROBERT SANTELLI SELECTS THE 5 WORST ROCK FESTIVALS

1   **Celebration of Life,** McCrea, Louisiana, June 1971
     Billed as "the resurrection of the rock festival," Celebration of
     Life was one of death, leaving five dead and many hospitalized
     with wounds inflicted by marauding motorcycle gangs. Hun-
     dreds were also arrested and thrown into jail.
2   **Powder Ridge Rock Festival,** Middlefield, Connecticut,
     July-August, 1970
     Although shut down by a court injunction before it opened,
     30,000 people attended anyway.
3   **Altamont,** Livermore, California, December 1969
     Halfway through "Sympathy for the Devil," Meredith Hunter,
     an eighteen-year-old black from Berkeley, was stabbed to
     death by Hell's Angels hired as security by The Rolling Stones
     for the speedway.
4   **Mar y Sol,** Vega Baja, Puerto Rico, April 1972
     Four people died at Mar y Sol, the most violent death being
     that of a sixteen-year-old boy from St. Croix who was slashed
     with a machete in his sleep. (He was a coke dealer who'd run
     into trouble with local dealers.) The 30,000 festival-goers were
     also plagued by poor sanitary conditions and sleeping facili-
     ties, not to mention rip-off tactics employed by locals who
     sometimes charged seventy-five cents for a glass of water or
     twenty dollars for a ride to the airport.

5   **Newport '69,** Northridge, California, June 1969
This was the first rock festival where widespread property
damage occurred, most of it caused by gate crashers. Sixty-
seven crashers were arrested and fifteen cops wounded and
hospitalized. Thousands of dollars in personal property damage was assessed in the neighborhood adjacent to the festival
site.

PERFORMERS AT THE MONTEREY INTERNATIONAL POP FESTIVAL
June 16–18, 1967

1   THE ASSOCIATION
2   BOOKER T. AND THE MGs
3   BUFFALO SPRINGFIELD

4   ERIC BURDON AND THE ANIMALS
5   THE PAUL BUTTERFIELD BLUES BAND

© 1981 JIM MARSHALL

Brian Jones and Jimi Hendrix look for survivors during a stroll on the festival grounds at Monterey in June 1967.

6	THE BYRDS	16	THE MAMAS AND THE PAPAS
7	CANNED HEAT	17	HUGH MASEKELA
8	COUNTRY JOE AND THE FISH	18	THE STEVE MILLER BAND
9	THE ELECTRIC FLAG	19	MOBY GRAPE
10	ARETHA FRANKLIN	20	LAURA NYRO
11	THE GRATEFUL DEAD	21	THE PAUPERS
12	THE JIMI HENDRIX EXPERIENCE	22	QUICKSILVER MESSENGER SERVICE
13	THE JEFFERSON AIRPLANE	23	OTIS REDDING
14	JANIS JOPLIN AND BIG BROTHER AND THE HOLDING COMPANY	24	JOHNNY RIVERS
		25	RAVI SHANKAR
		26	SIMON AND GARFUNKEL
15	AL KOOPER	27	THE WHO

-◄▮►-

PERFORMERS AT WOODSTOCK
August 15–17, 1969

1	JOAN BAEZ	11	ARLO GUTHRIE
2	THE BAND	12	TIM HARDIN
3	BLOOD, SWEAT, AND TEARS	13	THE KEEF HARTLEY BAND
4	THE PAUL BUTTERFIELD BLUES BAND	14	RICHIE HAVENS
5	CANNED HEAT	15	JIMI HENDRIX
6	JOE COCKER	16	THE INCREDIBLE STRING BAND
7	COUNTRY JOE AND THE FISH	17	THE JEFFERSON AIRPLANE
8	CREEDENCE CLEARWATER REVIVAL	18	JANIS JOPLIN
9	CROSBY, STILLS, NASH, AND YOUNG	19	MELANIE
		20	MOUNTAIN
10	THE GRATEFUL DEAD	21	QUILL
		22	SANTANA

-◄❙❙►-

MICHAEL OCHS LISTS 12 OBSCURE RECORDS THAT SHOULD BE FAMOUS

1 **"Couldn't Hear Nobody Pray,"** THE WOMACK BROTHERS
Later recorded as "Looking for a Love" when they changed their name to The Valentinos (and covered by The J. Geils Band and Ry Cooder under that title), this song is the best gospel-to-pop crossover record.

2 **"Two Tone Brown,"** DAVID ALLEN COE
This song about mixed marriages is the best of seventies rockabilly.

3 **"Hymn #5,"** THE MIGHTY HANNIBAL
The best Vietnam song.

4 **"I Hear Voices,"** SCREAMING JAY HAWKINS
Best voodoo record. Sample lyric: "I wish I could be who I was before I was me."

5 **"Sam Cooke Interview"**
Interviewed by Los Angeles disc jockey the Magnificent Montague, Sam defines soul by humming the way John Coltrane plays sax.

6 **"Daddy Rollin',"** DION
The B-side of "Abraham, Martin and John" was never included on an album, but it's probably the best thing Dion ever did. A funky blues.

7 **"The Lord's Prayer,"** THE SWAN SILVERTONES
Possibly the best male vocal ever recorded in any field of music.

8   **"Stay with Me,"** LORRAINE ELLISON
     Possibly the best female vocal ever recorded.
9   **"Goodbye Sam,"** SHAD O'SHAY
     Great absurdist mini-opera about American history.
10   **"Old MacDonald,"** THE CHARGERS
     Best resurrection of a totally dead tune.
11   **"Home of the Brave,"** BONNIE AND THE TREASURES
     Rumored to be The Ronettes, singing about the injustice of
     making young men cut their hair.
12   **"CHAOS,"** ARBOGAST AND ROSS
     The definitive summation of fifties radio.

MICHAEL OCHS *grew up in Ohio and went on to become manager for his brother,*
Phil, and later a record executive. Today he lives in a California home crowded
with an immense collection of rock and roll records and memorabilia, from which
he runs the Michael Ochs Archives, which supplies music, photos, and data to all
manner of media projects.

-◄▮▶-

THE 10 MOST OBSCURE ROCK OPERAS

1   **"An Excerpt from a Teenage Opera,"** KEITH WEST
     West's single was released in 1967, well before The Who's
     Tommy kicked off the pop-opera craze; the whole thing
     captured on a single.
2   ***S. F. Sorrow***, THE PRETTY THINGS
     Another one released before *Tommy*, though this opera takes a
     full album to get across what isn't entirely clear once you've
     heard it, anyway.
3   ***The Giant Crab Cometh Forth***
     Mystical but dull.
4   ***The Golden Scarab***, RAY MANZAREK
     Mystical, ambitious, and dull.
5   ***Love Chronicles***, AL STEWART
     Romantic rather than mystical, but not any less dull.

6   **Keynsham,** BONZO DOG DOO DAH BAND
     The great comic opera, rock or otherwise. Takes the hot air out
     of everything from *Tommy* to Gilbert and Sullivan, traditional
     England to the American space age.

7   **666,** APHRODITE'S CHILD
     Satanic, mischievous, and dull.

8   **Joe's Garage, Act One and Act Two,** FRANK ZAPPA
     The story of a rock musician in a world in which music has
     been declared illegal. Pete Townshend proposed the story long
     before (as one of his many *Lifehouse* concepts), but it took
     Zappa (and the inspiration of Ayatollah Khomeini, no doubt) to
     bring this rancid vision to fruition. Utterly without charm or
     subtlety, in Zappa's usual mode, but also on the mark often
     enough to be whimsically hilarious.

9   **"The Gift,"** THE VELVET UNDERGROUND
     A macabre John Cale story from the *White Light, White Heat*
     album brings Edgar Allan Poe into the atomic age, with
     appropriate sound effects.

10   **Rock Justice,** MARTY BALIN
     Balin presents the story of a rock singer on trial for not making
     hits. Allegorical, absurd, not terribly listenable, but a nice
     metaphor for Balin's problems with the Jefferson Airplane/
     Starship complex, anyway.

-◄❚▮❚►-

THE 20 BEST ROCK OPERAS

1   *Tommy,* THE WHO
2   *Ogden's Nut Gone Flake,* THE SMALL FACES
3   "A Day in the Life," THE BEATLES
4   "Jungleland," BRUCE SPRINGSTEEN
5   *Keynsham,* THE BONZO DOG DOO DAH BAND
6   *Berlin,* LOU REED

7   "Bob Dylan's 115th Dream," BOB DYLAN
8   "Thank You for Talkin' to Me Africa," SLY AND THE FAMILY STONE
9   *Ziggy Stardust*, DAVID BOWIE
10   *Funkentelechy vs. the Placebo Syndrome*, PARLIAMENT
11   "Run Red Run," THE COASTERS
12   *Arthur*, THE KINKS
13   *Quadrophenia*, THE WHO
14   *S. F. Sorrow*, THE PRETTY THINGS
15   "A Quick One (While He's Away)," THE WHO
16   "Brown Shoes Don't Make It," THE MOTHERS OF INVENTION
17   "Celebration of the Lizard," THE DOORS
18   *The Wall*, PINK FLOYD
19   "Rael," THE WHO
20   *Schoolboys in Disgrace*, THE KINKS

-◀◗▶-

15 ROCK SONGS BASED ON CLASSICAL CONCEPTS

1   "Because," THE BEATLES; based on Beethoven's "Moonlight Sonata," played backward
2   "Beck's Bolero," JEFF BECK; based on Ravel's "Bolero"
3   "Brown Shoes Don't Make It," THE MOTHERS OF INVENTION; inspired by Holst's "The Planets"
4   "Deserts," FRANK ZAPPA; derived from Edgard Varese
5   "Farandole," DAVE EDMUNDS AND LOVE SCULPTURE; from a Bizet piece
6   "Forms and Feelings: Sabre Dance," DAVE EDMUNDS AND LOVE SCULPTURE; based on Khachaturian's "Sabre Dance" and Holst's "Mars"
7   "I'll Never Fall in Love Again," ERIC CARMEN; from a Rachmaninoff melody

8   "Joy," Apollo 100; based on a Bach melody
9   "Little Star," The Elegants; derived from Mozart's "Twinkle
     Twinkle Little Star," written when he was five years old
10   "Lover's Concerto," The Toys; from Bach's "Five Finger
     Piano Exercise"
11   "Night," Jackie Wilson; based on "My Heart at Thy Sweet
     Voice," from Saint-Saëns' *Samson and Delilah*
12   "Nut Rocker," B. Bumble and the Stingers, also
     Emerson, Lake, and Palmer; based on Tchaikovsky's
     "Nutcracker Suite"
13   "Ride of the Valkyries," Andy MacKay; from the Wagner
     melody
14   "Varese Ionization," Frank Zappa; inspired by Edgard
     Varese
15   "A Whiter Shade of Pale," Procol Harum; based on the
     Bach cantata "Sleepers Awake"

The 25 BEST INSTRUMENTALS

1   "Rumble," Link Wray and His Ray Men
2   "Pipeline," The Chantay's
3   "Wild Weekend," The Rockin' Rebels
4   "Wipe Out," The Surfaris
5   "Rebel 'Rouser," Duane Eddy
6   "Soul Twist," King Curtis
7   "Green Onions," Booker T. and the MGs
8   "Walk—Don't Run," The Ventures
9   "The Lonely Surfer," Jack Nitzsche
10   "Last Night," The Mar-Keys
11   "Out of Limits," The Marketts
12   "TSOP (The Sound of Philadelphia)," MFSB
13   "Night Train," James Brown

14 "Hide Away," FREDDY KING
15 "Shotgun," JR. WALKER AND THE ALL-STARS
16 "Harlem Nocturne," THE VISCOUNTS
17 "Walkin' with Mr. Lee," LEE ALLEN AND HIS BAND
18 "Memphis," LONNIE MACK
19 "Sleep Walk," SANTO AND JOHNNY
20 "Machine Gun," THE COMMODORES
21 "Let's Go Trippin'," DICK DALE AND HIS DEL-TONES
22 "Time Is Tight," BOOKER T. AND THE MGS
23 "Honky Tonk, Parts 1 and 2," BILL DOGGETT
24 "Soul Finger," THE BAR-KAYS
25 "Wiggle Wobble," LES COOPER AND THE SOUL ROCKERS

-◄▮▮►-

THE 10 WORST INSTRUMENTALS

1 "Hocus Pocus," FOCUS
2 "Outa-Space," BILLY PRESTON
3 "Classical Gas," MASON WILLIAMS
4 "Whole Lotta Love," C.C.S.
5 "Disco Lucy (I Love Lucy Theme)," WILTON PLACE STREET BAND
6 "A Fifth of Beethoven," WALTER MURPHY AND THE BIG APPLE BAND
7 "Dueling Banjos," ERIC WEISSBERG
8 "Mexican Hat Rock," THE APPLEJACKS
9 "Rock and Roll—Part 2," GARY GLITTER
10 "Love Is Blue," JEFF BECK

RICK WHITESELL SELECTS THE 10 BEST COVER VERSIONS

1 **"Adorable,"** THE DRIFTERS, 1955
The West Coast-based Colts, managed by Buck Ram, did this medium-tempo ballad first, but The Drifters' version was infinitely superior. The Colts were forgotten, though Buck Ram got lucky and discovered The Platters.

2 **"Crying in the Chapel,"** THE ORIOLES, 1953
This pop tune is a thinly veiled spiritual, originally written and recorded by Darrell Glenn, a country singer no one had heard of even then. Sonny Til, the Orioles' lead singer, was a friend of Glenn's, and his cover of the tune went right to the top. It's not known whether Glenn and Til remained friendly afterward.

3 **"Little Darlin',"** THE DIAMONDS, 1957
R&B purists will scream in pain at this contention, but in 1957, the rhythm & blues record buyers bought more copies of this Maurice Williams composition in its version by The Diamonds, a white quartet from Canada, than of the one by Williams' own Gladiolas, a black group that recorded for Excello. Why? Because The Diamonds did it better.

4 **"Sugar, Sugar,"** WILSON PICKETT, 1970
The Wicked Pickett displayed talent above and beyond the call of duty when he made this bubble-gum smash by The Archies sound like a real song. And he did a good job in 1969 on "Hey Jude," too . . . .

5 **"Girls Talk,"** DAVE EDMUNDS, 1979
Elvis Costello wrote it but couldn't sing it worth a damn. Linda Ronstadt covered it, but of course, she covers *everything*. Dave Edmunds clearly had the best and last word this time.

6   **"Fire,"** THE POINTER SISTERS, 1978
     Bruce Springsteen, the composer, gave this tune to Robert
     Gordon (Elvis had died, unfortunately) and it appeared on
     Fresh Fish Special, the LP Gordon recorded with guitar
     virtuoso Link Wray. But it was The Pointer Sisters' cover of
     "Fire" that burned up the hit parade and reminded AM radio
     listeners of what cruisin' around music once sounded like.

7   **"My Back Pages,"** THE BYRDS, 1967
     While the Byrds reinterpreted many of Bob Dylan's songs, this
     recording turned a nondescript acoustic tune into a rock gem.

8   **"Born to Run,"** ALLAN CLARKE, 1975
     The ex-Hollies lead singer did not top Springsteen, but Clarke
     did give us perspective on what "Born to Run" would have
     been like *without* Wall of Sound production. The only problem
     with Clarke's version is that it appeared only on a British
     eight-track tape.

9   **"Get a Job,"** THE MILLS BROTHERS, 1958
     After launching their career in 1931 with a series of recordings
     on which they imitated musical instruments with voices and
     cupped hands, The Mills Brothers drifted into a pattern of
     dreary pop tunes rendered in such a manner that each disc
     sounded like the one before it. But they did a surprisingly fine
     cover of The Silhouettes' sole hit, "Get a Job." It really rocks

10   **"Changes,"** JIM AND JEAN, 1966
     This duo did a fine, folk-rock cover of Phil Ochs' most
     sentimental composition, sparked by Al Kooper's accompani-
     ment on harpsichord.

RICK WHITESELL *was editor of* Goldmine, *the collector's magazine, and a noted rock
and R&B record collector and historian. He was one of the chief researchers of* The
Book of Rock Lists *before his death in January 1981.*

THE GREATEST CHUCK BERRY "REWRITES"

The following songs are modeled after the basic Chuck Berry guitar style.

1 "Surfin' U.S.A.," THE BEACH BOYS
2 "Brown Sugar," THE ROLLING STONES
3 "Jumpin' Jack Flash," THE ROLLING STONES
4 "Get Out of Denver," BOB SEGER
5 "Fun, Fun, Fun," THE BEACH BOYS
6 "Back in the U.S.S.R.," THE BEATLES
7 "I Knew the Bride," DAVE EDMUNDS
8 "Katmandu," BOB SEGER
9 "Come Together," THE BEATLES

THE SINCEREST FORM OF FLATTERY
Songs You'd Swear Were by Someone Else

1 "Crazy on You," HEART (Jefferson Starship)
2 "Horse with No Name," AMERICA (Neil Young)
3 "It's a Heartache," BONNIE TYLER (Rod Stewart)
4 "Jamie," EDDIE HOLLAND (Jackie Wilson)
5 "Let Me Roll It," PAUL McCARTNEY (John Lennon)
6 "Lies," THE KNICKERBOCKERS (The Beatles)
7 "Listen to Her Heart," TOM PETTY AND THE HEARTBREAKERS (The Byrds)
8 "Long Cool Woman (in a Black Dress)," THE HOLLIES (Creedence Clearwater Revival)
9 "A Public Execution," MOUSE AND THE TRAPS (Bob Dylan)
10 "Stuck in the Middle with You," STEALER'S WHEEL (Bob Dylan)
11 "Sub. Rosa Subway," KLAATU (The Beatles)
12 "Sultans of Swing," DIRE STRAITS (Bob Dylan)

GREAT CAMEO APPEARANCES

1 **DUANE ALLMAN**
Plays guitar on "Layla," Derek and the Dominos; "Hey Jude," Wilson Pickett; "Loan Me a Dime," Boz Scaggs; "The Road of Life," Clarence Carter.

2 **PAUL MCCARTNEY**
Sings backup on "Mellow Yellow," Donovan; "We Love You," The Rolling Stones.

3 **JOHN LENNON**
Sings backup on "We Love You," The Rolling Stones

4 **ERIC CLAPTON**
Plays guitar on "Good to Me as I Am to You," Aretha Franklin; *We're Only in It for the Money*, The Mothers of Invention; "While My Guitar Gently Weeps," The Beatles.

5 **BOB DYLAN**
Sings backup on "Buckets of Rain," Bette Midler; "Don't Go Home with Your Hard-on," Leonard Cohen.

6 **GEORGE HARRISON**
Plays guitar on "Badge," Cream.

7 **JIMI HENDRIX**
Plays lead guitar on *You Can Be Anything You Want to Be This Time Around*, Timothy Leary.

8 **MICK JAGGER**
Sings backup on "You're So Vain," Carly Simon.

9 **KEITH MOON**
Plays drums on "Ole Man River," The Jeff Beck Group.

10 **JIMMY PAGE**
Plays guitar on *The Kinks*, The Kinks' first LP; "I Can't Explain," The Who's first single.

11 **PHIL SPECTOR**
Plays piano on *Out of Our Heads*, The Rolling Stones.

12 **STEVIE NICKS**
Sings backup on "Gold," by John Stewart.

13 **BRUCE SPRINGSTEEN**
Provides backing voice on "Street Hassle," Lou Reed.

14 **DON HENLEY, GLENN FREY, TIM SCHMIT**
Provide backing voices on "Fire Lake," Bob Seger.

15 **CAPTAIN BEEFHEART**
Sings lead vocals on *Hot Rats*, Frank Zappa.

16 **STEPHEN STILLS**
Plays lead guitar on "Ain't No Sunshine," Bill Withers.

17 **THE CHIFFONS**
Provide backing voices on "Rock and Roll Lullaby," B. J. Thomas.

18 **BO DIDDLEY**
Plays rhythm guitar on several Chuck Berry fifties recordings.

19 **THE CRICKETS**
Sing backup on "Till I Kissed You," The Everly Brothers.

-◄❙❙►-

PETE FRAME'S 10 GREATEST ROCK FAMILY TREES

Pete Frame devotes a good deal of energy to conducting massive inquiries into the histories of rock bands and movements, which information he then assembles into extensively branched family trees. This list reflects what Frame feels are both his most interesting and most complex trees. "The longer it takes and the more research I have to do," says the founder of Zig Zag magazine, "the happier and more satisfied I am." Rock Family Trees, a book collecting many of his best trees, was published in 1980 by Omnibus Press. Volume two is currently being assembled.

1 **Savages, Crusaders, and Outlaws**
The publishers of my book were loathe to include this one because it was so obscure and uncommercial. It took me over a

year to complete and involved interviewing twenty-eight people, many of them pioneers of English rock and roll, which sprang out of the Two I's coffee bar in Soho during the late 1950s.

2   **Liverpool 1980: Eric's progeny**

This, a recent tree, does not appear in the book but has been published in *Sounds* and *Trouser Press*. I spent several days in Liverpool, working out the convolutions of this particularly incestuous scene. To my mind, some of the best rock music of 1980 is coming out of Liverpool. Great place, great people, wonderful atmosphere.

3   **Children of the revolution, 1976–1978**

This tree encapsulated the history of British punk . . . tied up all the loose ends into a neat package, which (I thought) explained it all. Took a lot of legwork and research because a lot of the musicians didn't want to talk to me on the grounds that I was a boring old fart or that they didn't want to be connected with other, lesser bands. That's a problem I encounter all the time: jumped-up musicians who feel they are too good or unique to be connected to a movement. Either that, or else they are scared of revealing details of their past. Needless to say, my attitude to such balkers is "Bollocks to you, you stupid little cunt," and I get the information from another source.

4   **Birmingham beatsters**

This traced the evolution of The Move, ELO, The Moody Blues, etc.—all of whom interconnect. Took a long time, but everyone I spoke to was nice as pie. Took more than thirty interviews to complete.

5   **San Francisco, part two**

My trees are crammed with facts and info, but the best ones are aesthetically pleasing also. I think this one looks as good as it reads. Whatever happened to Quicksilver Messenger Service?

6   **COMMANDER CODY AND THE LOST PLANET AIRMEN**

Rejected by the publishers of the book on the grounds of

commercial appeal (lack of) and size (too big). Cody's a damned nice chap, and Bill Kirchen's one of my favorite guitar players.

7   **CHUCK BERRY's "Promised Land"**
Another reject, this wasn't a tree but a map tracing Berry's cross-country journey from Norfolk, Virginia, to Los Angeles. Great song. I did it as a press handout when I was working at Stiff Records, which issued a version by Johnnie Allen. It's going to appear in volume two.

8   **GENE VINCENT AND THE BLUE CAPS**
Some of my favorite music is raw, unschooled, pioneer grist from the fifties. A lot of Gene Vincent's records were pretty duff, but his good ones were out of this world. He was only thirty-six when he died in October 1971. He was a destitute, confused, cheated, hounded, flabby, alcoholic, humiliated, broken wreck. He should have been a millionaire.

9   **ERIC CLAPTON: guitar and vocals**
I did Clapton's tour program for three years running but was never allowed to speak to the guy. I'm sure he's a reasonable enough geezer. Most of them are when they're not surrounded by a bunch of managers and publicists trying to isolate them from the real world. Anyway, RSO paid handsomely and I was broke at the time. Still am.

10   **MULDAUR, GARRETT, KEITH and ROONEY**
I toiled for weeks over the history of the Cambridge-Boston folk scene of the mid-1960s. It was forty-nine by thirty-four inches and contained more than 12,000 words. I couldn't find anyone to publish it, which may be why I like it so much. It'll be in volume two if I can reduce it enough and still retain its legibility.

PETE FRAME *is a magazine editor, publicist, and sometime surveyor who lives in the British countryside.*

FIFTEEN: WHO PUT THE BOMP?

The Writers

The Brill Building, 1619 Broadway, New York City.

10 BRILL BUILDING WRITERS

*Technically, most of these weren't true Brill Building compos-
ers, since few had offices in the ancient and decrepit Tin Pan
Alley office building itself. However, all of them represent the
flower of the Brill Building songwriting-machine concept, as it
burst forth in the period between Presley and The Beatles, for
girl groups, Spectorian superproductions, and, on occasion,
Elvis hits.*

1   **RICHARD BARRETT**
    He wrote "Maybe" and did much talent scouting and produc-
    tion work in New York as well as Philadelphia.

2   **NEIL DIAMOND**
    He wrote "I'm a Believer" and others when he was just getting
    started.

3   **ELLIE GREENWICH and JEFF BARRY**
    They were responsible for "Then He Kissed Me," "Walkin' in
    the Rain," and many other Phil Spector and Red Bird Records
    hits.

4   **CAROLE KING and GERRY GOFFIN**
    Their contributions included "The Loco-Motion," "Will You
    Love Me Tomorrow," "One Fine Day," and "Up on the Roof."

5   **JERRY LEIBER and MIKE STOLLER**
    After relocating to New York from their Hollywood home, they
    wrote various Drifters and Ben E. King hits, which they also
    produced.

6   **BARRY MANN and CYNTHIA WEIL**
    They wrote "Kicks," "Hungry," and others for such artists a
    Paul Revere and the Raiders as well as for many girl groups.

7   **SHADOW MORTON**
    Best known as the leading producer at Red Bird Records (The
    Shangri-Las, The Ad-Libs, The Jelly Beans), Morton collabo-
    rated with many others for his acts.

8 **GENE PITNEY**
Pitney wrote "Little by Little" and most of his own hits while employed by Aaron Schroeder, a major Brill-style music publisher.

9 **DOC POMUS and MORT SHUMAN**
The geniuses of this turf, they wrote "Save the Last Dance for Me," "This Magic Moment," "Little Sister," "Suspicion," and "Viva Las Vegas."

10 **NEIL SEDAKA and HOWARD GREENFIELD**
They wrote "Oh! Carol," "Breaking Up Is Hard to Do," as well as Sedaka's other hits.

-◄▮▮►-

CELEBRATED SONGWRITING TEAMS AND THEIR GREATEST HITS

1 **NICKOLAS ASHFORD and VALERIE SIMPSON**
"Ain't No Mountain High Enough," "Reach Out and Touch (Somebody's Hand)," "You're All I Need to Get By," "Let's Go Get Stoned"

2 **FELICE and BOUDLEAUX BRYANT**
"Bye Bye Love," "Wake Up, Little Susie," "Love Hurts," "Raining in My Heart," "All I Have to Do Is Dream"

3 **BERNARD EDWARDS and NILE RODGERS** (Chic)
"Le Freak," "Dance, Dance, Dance (Yowsah, Yowsah, Yowsah)"

4 **GERRY GOFFIN and CAROLE KING**
"Take Good Care of My Baby," "Up on the Roof," "Chains," "Will You Love Me Tomorrow," "The Loco-Motion," "Goin' Back," "(You Make Me Feel Like a) Natural Woman"

5 **ELLIE GREENWICH and JEFF BARRY**
"What a Guy," "Then He Kissed Me," "River Deep, Mountain High"

6 **ISAAC HAYES and DAVID PORTER**
"Hold On! I'm Comin'," "Soul Man"

7 **BRIAN HOLLAND, LAMONT DOZIER, EDDIE HOLLAND**
"Baby, I Need Your Lovin'," "Baby Love," "I Can't Help Myself (Sugar Pie, Honey Bunch,)" "It's the Same Old Song," "Heat Wave," "Nowhere to Run," "Reach Out I'll Be There," "Standing in the Shadows of Love," "Stop! In the Name of Love," "Where Did Our Love Go," "You Keep Me Hangin' On"

8 **MICK JAGGER and KEITH RICHARDS**
"(I Can't Get No) Satisfaction," "Tumbling Dice," "Get Off My Cloud," "Gimme Shelter"

9 **ELTON JOHN and BERNIE TAUPIN**
"Daniel," "Your Song," "Rocket Man," "Goodbye Yellow Brick Road"

10 **JERRY LEIBER and MIKE STOLLER**
"Jailhouse Rock," "Searchin'," "Yakety Yak," "Kansas City," "Hound Dog"

11 **JOHN LENNON and PAUL McCARTNEY**
"She Loves You," "I Want to Hold Your Hand," "Strawberry Fields Forever," "Penny Lane," "Ticket to Ride," "Hey Jude," "Let It Be"

12 **BARRY MANN and CYNTHIA WEIL**
"Kicks," "Hungry"

-◄❙❙►-

ALAN BETROCK LISTS 20 GOFFIN–KING SONGS YOU'VE NEVER HEARD
And Might Not Want To

1 "Can't Stop Talking about You," TOBIN MATTHEWS
2 "Carole," BILLY SCOTT
3 "Don't You Wanna Love Me Baby," THE OTHER TWO
4 "Everybody Go Home," EYDIE GORME

5   "Follow That Girl," VINNIE MONTE
6   "Good Buddies," THE CRAWFORD BROTHERS
7   "Hard Way to Go," ED TOWNSEND
8   "Harlem Tango," THE ORCHIDS
9   "I've Got Bonnie," BOBBY RYDELL
10   "I Was Only Kidding," MOLLY BEE
11   "Keep Your Love Locked Deep inside Your Heart," PAUL
     PETERSON
12   "Look Who's Talking," GINNY ARNELL
13   "Melodrama," THE KEYSTONE FAMILY SINGERS
14   "Short Mort," CAROLE KING
15   "So Did I," ANN-MARGRET
16   "They Should Have Given You an Oscar," JAMES DARREN
17   "Walking Proud," STEVE LAWRENCE
18   "When I Did the Mashed Potatoes with You," LARRY BRIGHT
19   "When I Was 15," MARY SNEED
20   "You Can't Sit Still," THE SEQUINS

ALAN BETROCK *founded* New York Rocker. *He has written books on girl groups and rock films, and currently runs Shake Records, whose artists include The Cosmopolitans and the dB's.*

-◄▐▌►-

20 PHIL SPECTOR SONGWRITING COLLABORATORS
And the Artists They Wrote For

1   PETER ANDREOLI and VINNIE PONCIA (The Ronettes, Darlene
     Love)
2   RITCHIE BARRETT (Ray Sharpe)
3   LEROY BATES (The Crystals)
4   PAUL CASE, VINNIE PONCIA, PETER ANDREOLI (Bonnie Jo
     Mason, a.k.a. Cher)
5   AHMET ERTEGUN and ? ADLUM JR. (Castle Kings)
6   GERRY GOFFIN and CAROLE KING (The Righteous Brothers)

7   ELLIE GREENWICH and JEFF BARRY (The Crystals, Darlene Love, The Ronettes, The Dixie Cups)
8   GEORGE HARRISON (Ronnie Spector)
9   HANK HUNTER (Connie Francis, Terry Day)
10 JERRY LEIBER (Ben E. King)
11 BARRY MANN and CYNTHIA WEIL (The Ronettes, The Righteous Brothers)
12 NANKER PHELGE* (The Rolling Stones)
13 TERRY PHILLIPS (Johnny Nash, Gene Pitney)
14 DOC POMUS (Ben E. King, Bobby Day)
15 TONY POWERS and ELLIE GREENWICH (Bob B. Soxx and the Blue Jeans)
16 BEVERLY ROSS (Timothy Hay)
17 CORRIE SANDS** (The Paris Sisters)
18 BOBBY STEVENS (The Checkmates Ltd.)
19 NINO TEMPO (Noreen Corcoran)
20 TONI WINE and IRWIN LEVINE (The Ronettes, The Checkmates Ltd., Carla Thomas)

* Nanker Phelge was a songwriting pseudonym for Mick Jagger and Keith Richards.
**Corrie Sands was a pseudonym for Annette Merar.

-◄❙▶-

SONGS BOB DYLAN WROTE BUT NEVER RECORDED

This list does not include any of those songs written by Dylan that have appeared on bootleg discs or tapes, but only songs he has never performed, or at least no version of them has ever turned up.

1   **"Ballad of Easy Rider"**
This was allegedly written with Roger McGuinn for the film *Easy Rider*. For one reason or another, Dylan left his name off the composing credit. The song has been recorded by The

Byrds and Fairport Convention, with Richard Thompson singing lead.

2   **"Catfish"**
Dylan wrote this with Jacques Levy in honor of the great Yankees pitcher Jim "Catfish" Hunter. (Hunter hated it.) Kinky Friedman is the only artist to record it.

3   **"Champagne Illinois"**
Recorded by Carl Perkins.

4   **"Coming from the Heart"**
Written with and recorded by The Searchers.

5   **"Farewell Angelina"**
Recorded by Joan Baez.

6   **"Golden Loom"**
Recorded by Roger McGuinn's post-Byrds band, Thunderbyrd.

7   **"I'd Have You Any Time"**
Written with George Harrison and released on his *All Things Must Pass* LP.

8   **"If I Don't Be There by Morning"**
Written with Helena Springs and recorded by Eric Clapton.

9   **"Jack of Diamonds"**
This is the poem that served as liner notes to *Another Side of Bob Dylan*. Set to music by Ben Carruthers, it was recorded by Carruthers and the Deep and by the original Fairport Convention.

10 **"Long Distance Operator"**
Recorded by The Band on *The Basement Tapes*.

11 **"Love Is Just a Four Letter Word"**
Recorded by Joan Baez.

12 **"Seven Days"**
Recorded by Ron Wood on his solo LP, *Gimme Some Neck*.

13 **"Sign Language"**
Recorded by Eric Clapton. Dylan sang lead with Clapton on the song, which makes its inclusion here marginally misleading.

14   **"Troubled and I Don't Know Why"**
Sung by Joan Baez in concert.

15   **"Up to Me"**
Recorded by Roger McGuinn.

16   **"Walk Out in the Rain"**
Written with Helena Springs and recorded by Eric Clapton.

17   **"Wallflower"**
Recorded by Doug Sahm.

18   **"Wanted Man"**
Recorded by Johnny Cash for the movie *Little Fauss and Big Halsey*.

-◄❚▶-

25 SONGS THAT THE BEATLES RECORDED BUT DID NOT COMPOSE
With Original Artists

1   "Act Naturally," BUCK OWENS, 1963
2   "Ain't She Sweet," PAUL ASH AND HIS ORCHESTRA, 1927
3   "Anna (Go to Him)," ARTHUR ALEXANDER, 1962
4   "Baby It's You," THE SHIRELLES, 1961
5   "Bad Boy," LARRY WILLIAMS, 1959
6   "Boys," THE SHIRELLES, 1960
7   "Chains," THE COOKIES, 1962
8   "Devil in Her Heart," THE DONAYS, 1962
9   "Dizzy Miss Lizzie," LARRY WILLIAMS, 1958
10   "Everybody's Trying to Be My Baby," CARL PERKINS, 1958
11   "Honey Don't," CARL PERKINS, 1956
12   "Kansas City," LITTLE WILLIE LITTLEFIELD, 1952*
13   "Long Tall Sally," LITTLE RICHARD, 1956
14   "Matchbox," CARL PERKINS, 1957
15   "Mr. Moonlight," DR. FEELGOOD AND THE INTERNS, 1962
16   "Money (That's What I Want)," BARRET STRONG, 1959
17   "Please Mr. Postman," THE MARVELETTES, 1961
18   "Rock and Roll Music," CHUCK BERRY, 1957

19   "Roll over Beethoven," CHUCK BERRY, 1956
20   "Slow Down," LARRY WILLIAMS, 1958
21   "A Taste of Honey," BOBBY SCOTT AND COMBO, 1960**
22   "Till There Was You," ROBERT PRESTON and BARBARA
      COOK, 1958†
23   "Twist and Shout," THE ISLEY BROTHERS, 1962
24   "Words of Love," BUDDY HOLLY, 1957
25   "You Really Got a Hold on Me," THE MIRACLES, 1962

NOTE: The Beatles also recorded several cover versions
with Tony Sheridan. They include: "My Bonnie," "Nobody's
Child," "Sweet Georgia Brown," "Take Out Some Insurance,
Baby," and "Why (Can't You Love Me Again)."

* The Beatles' arrangement seems to be based on Little Richard's "Hey Hey Hey,"
released in 1958.
**On the soundtrack of the movie of the same name
† From the play *The Music Man*, 1957

-◄▐▶-

ALAN BETROCK LISTS 10 RAY DAVIES SONGS NEVER RECORDED BY THE KINKS
And the People Who Did Record Them

1   "All Night Stand," THE THOUGHTS
2   "Emptiness," THE HONEYCOMBS
3   "I Go to Sleep," THE APPLEJACKS, THE TRUTH, PEGGY LEE
4   "King of the Whole Wide World," LEAPY LEE
5   "A Little Bit of Sunlight," THE MAJORITY
6   "Little Man in a Little Box," BARRY FANTONI
7   "Nobody's Fool," COLD TURKEY
8   "Oh What a Day It's Going to Be," MO AND STEVE
9   "This Strange Effect," DAVE BERRY
10   "Toymaker," WILD SILK, BASIL

ALAN BETROCK, *who runs Shake Records, founded* New York Rocker.

10 SONGS MICHAEL JACKSON WISHES HE HAD WRITTEN

1	"Respect"	6	"Living in the City"
2	"Bridge over Troubled Water"	7	"You Send Me"
3	"Walk on the Wild Side"	8	"Yesterday"
4	"Moon River"	9	"Fool on the Hill"
5	"For the Good Times"	10	"Eleanor Rigby"

-◄▮▶-

4 SONGS CARL PERKINS WISHES HE HAD WRITTEN

1	"The Star Spangled Banner"	3	"You Are My Sunshine"
2	"White Christmas"	4	"America the Beautiful"

CARL PERKINS is our best living proof of what good rockabilly music is all about. "Blue Suede Shoes," "Boppin' the Blues," and "Matchbox" were classics made for Sun Records in the 1950s, and their impact was felt again when the British Invasion groups put their versions of these songs back on the charts a decade later. Currently touring in a band featuring two of his sons, Perkins is bringing his music to yet another generation. "I've always got time to shake a fan's hand," Carl states. "That's why I'm here, isn't it?"

-◄▮▶-

5 SONGS EDDIE FLOYD WISHES HE HAD WRITTEN

1	"Another One Bites the Dust"
2	"By the Time I Get to Phoenix"
3	"Doggin' Around"
4	"Never Can Say Goodbye"
5	"Someone That I Used to Love"

EDDIE FLOYD was one of the key figures in Memphis rhythm & blues, both as a Stax recording artist, with "Knock on Wood," "Big Bird," and "Raise Your Hand," and as a songwriter, with "634-5789" and "Ninety-nine and a Half (Won't Do)."

KARLA BONOFF'S 10 FAVORITE SONGWRITERS

1 GERRY GOFFIN and CAROLE KING
2 BOUDLEAUX BRYANT
3 DON HENLEY and GLENN FREY
4 JOHN LENNON and PAUL MCCARTNEY
5 RANDY NEWMAN
6 JAMES TAYLOR
7 BUDDY HOLLY
8 J. D. SOUTHER
9 BRIAN HOLLAND, LAMONT DOZIER, and EDDIE HOLLAND
10 JACKSON BROWNE

KARLA BONOFF *is a West Coast singer/songwriter best known for "Hasten down the Wind," which became the title track on Linda Ronstadt's best album. She has also recorded two solo albums for Columbia.*

-◄◗▮◗►-

JOHN SEBASTIAN'S FAVORITE SONGWRITERS

1 CHUCK BERRY
2 GEORGE GERSHWIN
3 JOHN LENNON and PAUL MCCARTNEY (as a team)
4 COLE PORTER
5 SMOKEY ROBINSON
6 CHESTER BURNETT, a.k.a. HOWLIN' WOLF
7 FRED NEIL
8 MISSISSIPPI JOHN HURT
9 FELICE and BOUDLEAUX BRYANT
10 ARTHUR CRUDUP
11 JOHN D. LOUDERMILK
12 JIMMY REED
13 SAM COOKE

JOHN SEBASTIAN *wrote and recorded "Daydream," "Do You Believe in Magic," "Summer in the City," and countless other fine sides with The Lovin' Spoonful during the 1960s. Since the group disbanded, Sebastian's solo records have included the hit "Welcome Back," written as a theme for the popular television show* Welcome Back Kotter. *Today he lives in Woodstock, New York, and continues to record.*

4 FILMS AND 1 TV SHOW THAT FEATURE "ROCK AROUND THE CLOCK"

1 *The Blackboard Jungle*, 1955
2 *Rock around the Clock*, 1956
3 *American Graffiti*, 1973
4 *Happy Days**
5 *Superman*, 1979**

* The ABC show's original theme song
**In the background, but it's there

-◄▮▮►-

20 ANSWER SONGS
Songs Written in Response to Other Songs

1 **"Annie's Answer,"** HAZEL McCOLLUM AND THE EL DORADOS, 1955
   A retort to The Midnighters' successful mid-fifties string of allegations about Annie ("Work with Me Annie," "Annie Had a Baby," etc.).

2 **"Annie Pulled a Humbug,"** THE MIDNIGHTERS, 1955
   Obscure but blunt reply to "Annie Had a Baby" by a West Coast group in which the lead singer asserts that Annie's baby looks nothing like *him*, concluding, "That's not my kid!"

3 **"Aretha, Sing One for Me,"** GEORGE JACKSON, 1971
   Memphis writer-singer Jackson's lovely reply to Aretha's hit, "Don't Play That Song."

4 **"Ballad of the Yellow Berets,"** BOB SEGER, 1966
   A hilarious spoof of "Ballad of the Green Berets," in which Seger sings a tale of draft-dodger woe.

5 **"Can't Do Sixty No More,"** THE DU-DROPPERS, 1951
   A response to The Drifters' 1951 R&B smash, "Sixty Minute Man."

6   **"Come Back, Maybellene,"** BIG JOHN GREER, 1955
    The one-time Lucky Millinder Band vocalist responds to Chuck Berry's 1955 hit.

7   **"Copy Cat,"** GARY "U.S." BONDS, 1962
    In which the outer space Echo King severely chastises any number of competitors, not least Chubby Checker, for "trying to cop my groove." Gary is quite agitated about the injustice, although he assures himself in the last verse that copy cats don't last long.

8   **"The Dawn of Correction,"** THE SPOKESMEN, 1965
    Middle America's answer to the rad-lib sentiments of "Eve of Destruction."

9   **"Got a Job,"** THE MIRACLES, 1959
    The Miracles' Motown career began with this reply to the Silhouettes' "Get a Job," although Smokey and friends failed to achieve the originals' marvelous incoherence.

10 **"Hey Memphis,"** LaVERN BAKER, 1961
    Reply to Elvis Presley's "Little Sister," written by the same composing team, Doc Jerome Pomus and Mort Shuman.

11 **"I'll Bring It on Home to You,"** CARLA THOMAS, 1962
    Queen of Memphis soul replies to Sam Cooke's "Bring It on Home to Me."

12 **"I'm Just a Down Home Girl,"** THE AD LIBS, 1963
    Response to Arthur Alexander's "Down Home Girl" by the girl group that had a hit with "The Boy from New York City."

13 **"It Wouldn't Happen with Me,"** JERRY LEE LEWIS, 1961
    In which the Killer warns fans with roving eyes that neither Ricky Nelson nor Elvis deserves their adoration as much as he does. A monumental act of humility, and a perfect testament to why Jerry Lee's popularity is enduring: If you don't pay attention, he'll beat you up.

14 **"My Girl,"** THE TEMPTATIONS, 1965
    Smokey Robinson's answer to the charms proposed by his own "My Guy," written for Mary Wells. Both were major hits.

15 **"Roll with Me, Henry,"** ETTA JAMES, 1954
The great soul singer had her first hit with this response to The Midnighters' original "Annie" hit, "Work with Me Annie."

16 **"Son-in-Law,"** THE BLOSSOMS, 1961
Riposte to Ernie K-Doe's "Mother-in-Law," a significant 1961 hit. The lead singer is ultimate Phil Spector chanteuse Darlene Love.

17 **"Sweet Home Alabama,"** LYNYRD SKYNYRD, 1974
Ronnie Van Zant's brilliant retort to Neil Young's "Southern Man"; perhaps the greatest answer record of all time.

18 **"Tell Tommy I Miss Him,"** MARILYN MICHAELS, 1960
Ghostly reply to "Tell Laura I Love Her."

19 **"Your Boyfriend's Back,"** BOBBY COMSTOCK AND THE COUNTS, 1963
Tough reply to the Angels' "My Boyfriend's Back," in which the hero's return is to little or no avail.

20 **"Your Generation,"** GENERATION X, 1978
Punk reply to The Who's mod anthem, "My Generation," doesn't hold a candle to the original, but a great symbol of punk-rock rebellion anyhow.

SIXTEEN: MUSICIANS AND THEIR INSTRUMENTS

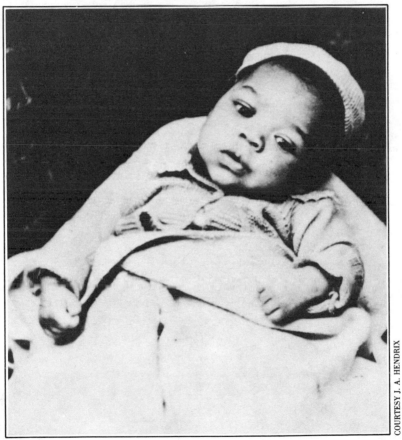

James Marshall Hendrix at age two, Seattle, 1944.

THE 30 GREATEST ROCK AND ROLL GUITARISTS

1 JIMI HENDRIX
2 CHUCK BERRY
3 MICKEY "GUITAR" BAKER (Mickey and Sylvia, sessions)
4 JAMES BURTON (Elvis Presley, Ricky Nelson)
5 PETER TOWNSHEND (The Who)
6 KEITH RICHARDS (The Rolling Stones)
7 SCOTTY MOORE (Elvis, Scotty, and Bill)
8 STEVE CROPPER (Booker T. and the MGs)
9 LINK WRAY
10 ERIC CLAPTON The Yardbirds, John Mayall's Bluesbreakers,
    Derek and the Dominos, Cream, solo)
11 CARL PERKINS
12 JEFF BECK (The Yardbirds, The Jeff Beck Group)
13 EDDIE VAN HALEN (Van Halen)
14 DUANE EDDY
15 CARL WILSON (The Beach Boys)
16 MICHAEL BLOOMFIELD (The Paul Butterfield Blues Band, Bob
    Dylan, The Electric Flag)
17 DUANE ALLMAN (The Allman Brothers Band, sessions)
18 BOBBY WOMACK
19 BO DIDDLEY
20 MARV TARPLIN (Smokey Robinson and the Miracles)
21 JOE WALSH (The James Gang, The Eagles, solo)
22 JIMMY PAGE (The Yardbirds, Led Zeppelin)
23 RY COODER
24 MICK JONES (The Clash)
25 STEVE JONES (The Sex Pistols)
26 ROY BUCHANAN
27 ROBBIE ROBERTSON (The Band)
28 BRUCE SPRINGSTEEN
29 MICK TAYLOR (John Mayall's Bluesbreakers, The Rolling
    Stones)
30 PETER GREEN (Fleetwood Mac, John Mayall's Bluesbreakers)

CHET FLIPPO PICKS THE 10 BEST STEEL-GUITAR PLAYERS

1 RALPH MOONEY
2 JIMMY DAY
3 SHOT JACKSON
4 TOM BRIMLEY
5 BUDDY EMMONS
6 BEN KEITH
7 WELDON MYRICK
8 DON HELMS
9 PETE DRAKE
10 LEON MCAULIFFE

CHET FLIPPO *has been a* Rolling Stone *editor and contributor for the past decade. His Texas roots are reflected in his knowledge of and passion for country & western music. He is the author of* Your Cheatin' Heart *(Simon and Schuster, 1981), a biography of Hank Williams.*

GREAT SLIDE GUITARISTS—ROCK AND ROLL STYLE

1 ELMORE JAMES
2 MICK TAYLOR (The Rolling Stones)
3 HOUND DOG TAYLOR
4 ERIC CLAPTON
5 JEREMY SPENCER (Fleetwood Mac)
6 MIKE BLOOMFIELD *(Highway 61 Revisited)*
7 BONNIE RAITT
8 RON WOOD (The Faces)

LES PAUL'S 10 FAVORITE GUITARISTS

1	GEORGE BENSON	7	DJANGO REINHARDT
2	PAT MARTINO	8	JIMI HENDRIX
3	AL DIMEOLA	9	GEORGE BARNES
4	JEFF BECK	10	EDDIE LANG
5	JAMES BURTON	11	SNOOZER QUINN
6	ANDRES SEGOVIA	12	WES MONTGOMERY

LES PAUL *is one of the greatest guitarists in American music. He was a pioneer in electrifying the guitar, creating multitrack recordings, and in using a wide variety of studio effects. The guitar he designed for Gibson in the 1950s remains one of the quintessential rock and blues instruments.*

JOHN CIPOLLINA'S GUITAR INFLUENCES

1 **SCOTTY MOORE**
The original pioneer rock guitar player.

2 **CHET ATKINS**
Truly the "Country Gentleman." I met him when I knew three chords. He said, "You look like a guitar player. Do you play?" I said, "No." I learned precision and finger work from him.

3 **JAMES BURTON**
Palming and cupping technique, especially for Dale Hawkins' "Suzie-Q."

4 **MICKEY BAKER**
Primal influence; electric guitar as an entity. When I heard Mickey and Sylvia's "Love Is Strange," I asked my mother what that sound was. She told me it was an electric guitar.

JOHN CIPOLLINA *was the guitarist with Quicksilver Messenger Service and one of the hottest, hardest rockers in the entire San Francisco scene.*

5   **MERLE TRAVIS**
He got me into the image of the guitar. I liked the pearl work on his, so when everybody else was putting lake pipes into their '57 Chevys, I was customizing my guitars.

6   **LINK WRAY**
He convinced me that you could swear without using words.

7   **MONTOYA**
Classical flamenco.

8   **SABICAS**

9   **PACO**

10   **MANITAS DE PLATA**
The punk of flamenco.

11   **JIMI HENDRIX**
He taught me how to resonate and carry tones. I still play the guitar he broke.

12   **LEADBELLY**
I still can't figure out what he was doing.

13   **DJANGO REINHARDT**
Guitar as violin.

-◄███►-

DANNY KORTCHMAR'S 10 FAVORITE GUITAR PLAYERS

1	DJANGO REINHARDT	6	KEITH RICHARDS
2	JIMI HENDRIX	7	PAUL BURLISON
3	JOSEPH SPENCE	8	JOHNNY MOORE
4	STEVE CROPPER	9	CHUCK BERRY
5	LEADBELLY	10	LIGHTNIN' HOPKINS

DANNY KORTCHMAR, *"Kootch" to his friends, has played guitar with everyone from The Fugs to Jackson Browne and was one of the key members of Jo Mama and The Section, among others. He's also recorded several solo albums.*

THE 30 GREATEST ROCK AND ROLL KEYBOARDISTS

1   JERRY LEE LEWIS, LITTLE RICHARD, tie
2   PROFESSOR LONGHAIR
3   JOHNNY JOHNSON (with Chuck Berry)
4   BOOKER T. JONES
5   RAY CHARLES
6   ARETHA FRANKLIN
7   NICKY HOPKINS (sessions)
8   STEVIE WINWOOD (Traffic, The Spencer Davis Group, etc.)
9   FATS DOMINO
10 ROY BITTAN (The E. Street Band, etc.)
11 GARTH HUDSON (The Band)
12 JACK NITZSCHE (sessions)
13 BILL PAYNE (Little Feat, etc.)
14 SLY STONE
15 HUEY "PIANO" SMITH
16 BARRY BECKETT (The Muscle Shoals Rhythm Section)
17 RICHARD TEE (sessions)
18 PAUL McCARTNEY (The Beatles, Wings)
19 KEITH EMERSON (The Nice, Emerson, Lake, and Palmer)
20 SETH JUSTMAN (The J. Geils Band)
21 IAN STEWART (The Rolling Stones)
22 IAN MacLAGLAN (The Faces, The Rolling Stones)
23 DANNY FEDERICI (The E Street Band)
24 RICHARD MANUEL (The Band)
25 CRAIG DOERGE (sessions)
26 LEON RUSSELL (sessions)
27 ART NEVILLE (The Meters, etc.)
28 RAY MANZAREK (The Doors)
29 AL KOOPER (Blood, Sweat, and Tears, The Blues Project, etc.)
30 MIKE STOLLER (sessions)

10 GREAT NEW ORLEANS PIANISTS

1 **PROFESSOR LONGHAIR**
The indisputable king of mardi-gras rhythm from whom all the rest stole their licks.

2 **ARCHIBALD, a.k.a. LEON GROSS**
Longhair's predecessor.

3 **FATS DOMINO**
The greatest New Orleans recording artist and Longhair's most adept student.

4 **HUEY "PIANO" SMITH**
Celebrated for his work with The Clowns—"Rockin' Pneumonia" and so forth—but a considerable player in his own right.

5 **EDWARD FRANK**
With the all-star band, Royal Dukes of Rhythm, and many sessions.

6 **JAMES BOOKER**
More strictly a jazz player, and more schooled than the rest, but a genius R&B figure for one record, the immortal "Gonzo," and as a member of Dave Bartholomew's sixties group.

7 **ART NEVILLE**
The Meters leader began as a session pianist, though he has since devoted more attention to playing organ.

8 **ALLEN TOUSSAINT**
Best known as songwriter and producer, but the mainstay of sixties New Orleans sessions with his keyboard playing.

9 **SALVADOR DOUCETTE**
Pianist with Dave Bartholomew's fifties band.

10 **TOMMY RIDGLEY**
On his own and in sessions.

Seth JUSTMAN'S KEYBOARD INFLUENCES

1 RED GARLAND
2 OSCAR PETERSON
3 OTIS SPANN
4 JIMMY SMITH
5 JERRY LEE LEWIS
6 HORACE SILVER
7 ALBERT AMMONS
8 RAY CHARLES
9 COUNT BASIE

SETH JUSTMAN *joined The J. Geils Band while he was still in his teens, and over the years he has become one of its guiding lights, not only playing keyboards but also writing much of the band's material and producing its gold album,* Love Stinks.

Ray MANZAREK'S KEYBOARD INFLUENCES

1 ALBERT AMMONS, boogie-woogie
2 LAFAYETTE LEAKE, Chuck Berry's one-time pianist
3 GLENN GOULD, classical
4 HORACE SILVER, funk jazz
5 JOE ZAWINUL, electric jazz
6 BILL EVANS, Debussy jazz
7 JERRY LEE LEWIS, rockabilly

RAY MANZAREK *was the keyboard player for The Doors. He still lives in Los Angeles, where he is involved in record and film production.*

The 25 GREATEST ROCK AND ROLL DRUMMERS

1 KEITH MOON (The Who)
2 CHARLIE WATTS (The Rolling Stones)
3 JERRY ALLISON (The Crickets)
4 AL JACKSON (Booker T. and the MGs)

5   HAL BLAINE (sessions)
6   EARL PALMER (sessions)
7   BENNY BENJAMIN (Motown)
8   LEVON HELM (The Band)
9   D. J. FONTANA (Elvis Presley)
10   ROGER HAWKINS (Muscle Shoals Rhythm Section)
11   MICKY WALLER (sessions)
12   BERNARD "PRETTY" PURDIE (sessions)
13   CHARLES "HUNGRY" WILLIAMS (New Orleans)
14   MICK FLEETWOOD (Fleetwood Mac)
15   RINGO STARR (The Beatles)
16   JIM KELTNER (sessions)
17   MAURICE WHITE (Earth, Wind, and Fire)
18   ZIGGY MODELISTE (The Meters)
19   ROY MILTON (his own band, The Solid Senders)
20   JIM GORDON (sessions)
21   MAX WEINBERG (The E Street Band)
22   JOHN BADANJEK (Detroit Wheels)
23   NAT KENDRIX (The Flames)
24   MITCH MITCHELL (Jimi Hendrix Experience)
25   RUSS KUNKEL (sessions)

-◄❚❚►-

5 GREAT NEW ORLEANS DRUMMERS

1   **EARL PALMER**
    A mainstay of the fifties scene down home, Palmer has since
    become a major sessionman in Hollywood and is widely
    regarded as the definitive New Orleans percussionist.

2   **CHARLES "HUNGRY" WILLIAMS**
    Palmer's successor, at least in the esteem of his fellow New
    Orleans sessionmen, Williams had stopped recording by the
    mid-1960s and moved to New York. He worked with Huey
    Smith and the Clowns.

3   **ZIGGY MODELISTE**
The drummer with The Meters (and The New Barbarians), Modeliste is possibly the most brilliant American funk percussionist of the contemporary era.

4   **JOHN BOUDREAUX**
Boudreaux drummed for Professor Longhair and Dr. John.

5   **JOE "SMOKEY" JOHNSON**
Johnson was the drummer with The Royal Dukes of Rhythm and Alvin "Red" Tyler.

-◄❙❙►-

MAX WEINBERG'S FAVORITE DRUMMERS IN BANDS

1   **RINGO STARR**
Most everything he did, but especially "Anytime at All," "Please Please Me," "I Want to Hold Your Hand," "She Loves You," "Dizzy Miss Lizzie," "Rock and Roll Music," "Slow Down" (great bass drum line), "Long Tall Sally" (especially the long fill in the guitar solo), "I Should Have Known Better," and "Tell Me Why."

2   **JOHN BADANJEK**
With Mitch Ryder and the Detroit Wheels on "Jenny Take a Ride," "Devil with a Blue Dress On," "Good Golly Miss Molly," and "Little Latin Lupe Lu." With Edgar Winter on "Free Ride" and live with Dr. John.

3   **DAVE CLARK**
On "Can't You See That She's Mine," "Anyway You Want It," "Because," "Glad All Over," "Bits and Pieces," and "Do You Love Me." His whole style of playing was built up from his snare drum.

4   **MIKE HUGG**
With Manfred Mann on "Sha La La," "Do Wah Diddy Diddy," "When You Walk in the Room," and "You Got to Take It."

5   **KEITH MOON**
Where do I stop? "The Kids Are Alright," "Out in the Street,"

"I Can See for Miles," "Happy Jack," "My Generation" (from *Live at Leeds*), "Young Man Blues," "Baba O'Reilley," "Won't Get Fooled Again," and "Pictures of Lily."

6 **BOBBY ELLIOTT**

With The Hollies on "Look Through Any Window," "On a Carousel," and "Don't Run and Hide."

7 **CHARLIE WATTS**

With The Rolling Stones on "19th Nervous Breakdown," "(I Can't Get No) Satisfaction," "Tumbling Dice," "Rip This Joint," "Jumpin' Jack Flash," "Around and Around," "Street Fighting Man," "Brown Sugar," and "Sway."

8 **LEVON HELM AND DOUG CLIFFORD**

Classic American rockers. Especially Levon on The Band's "Up On Cripple Creek," "Don't Do It," "Rag Mama Rag," "The Night They Drove Old Dixie Down," "Chest Fever," and "Life Is a Carnival." Doug sounded great on Creedence Clearwater Revival's "Lodi," "Proud Mary," "Travelin' Band," "Who'll Stop the Rain," and "Green River."

9 **D. J. FONTANA**

On all of Elvis' fifties material, but especially "Heartbreak Hotel," "Jailhouse Rock," "Don't Be Cruel," "Hound Dog," and "Wear My Ring (Around Your Neck)."

10 **DINO DANELLI**

With The Rascals on "Good Lovin'," "People Got to Be Free," "I Ain't Gonna Eat Out My Heart Anymore," "Groovin'," and "A Beautiful Morning."

11 **KENNEY JONES**

With Rod Stewart on "Maggie May" and with The Faces on "Stay with Me."

12 **JIM McCARTY**

With The Yardbirds on "Heart Full of Soul" and "Over Under Sideways Down."

MAX WEINBERG is the drummer with Bruce Springsteen and the E Street Band. He also an avid student of drumming and is in the process of preparing a book of interviews with his favorites.

MAX WEINBERG'S FAVORITE FREELANCE DRUMMERS

1 **BERNARD "PRETTY" PURDIE**
With Aretha Franklin on "Rock Steady," "Since You've Been Gone," "Respect," "(You Make Me Feel Like a) Natural Woman," "Day Dreaming," "Until You Come Back to Me," and on almost everything from his Atlantic Records dates in the fifties and sixties. Purdie virtually invented hi-hat "kicks."

2 **HAL BLAINE**
With The Byrds, The Beach Boys, and on so much sixties Los Angeles stuff, especially Phil Spector's "Baby, I Love You," and "Then He Kissed Me." Also with Simon and Garfunkel on "The Boxer" and "Bridge over Troubled Water."

3 **JIM KELTNER**
With Joe Cocker's Mad Dogs and Englishmen. On John Lennon's *Rock 'n' Roll* album, and his double drumming with Ringo Starr in the mid-1970s. Also with Phil Spector and Gary Lewis and the Playboys in the 1960s. Very tasteful drumming.

4 **RUSS KUNKEL and RICK MAROTTA**
Studio dates with Linda Ronstadt, Carole King, and Steely Dan. They epitomize L.A. rock drumming.

5 **BOBBY GREGG**
With Bob Dylan, especially on "Like a Rolling Stone," and much of his other mid-sixties recordings.

6 **ROGER HAWKINS**
On his Memphis and Muscle Shoals sessions particularly. Also on Percy Sledge's hits and misses, notably "Dark End of the Street," "Out of Left Field," and "When a Man Loves a Woman." *Unbelievable feel and time.*

7 **AL JACKSON**
With Booker T. and the MGs on "Born under a Bad Sign,"

(from the LP *Soul Limbo*) and on all Sam and Dave, Otis Redding, and other Stax hits.

8 **BENNY BENJAMIN and EURIEL JONES**
Any and all drumming by these two at Motown. They patented the intro pickup (for example, on "Tears of a Clown") that I use on "Hungry Heart." Their singles are simply too numerous to mention.

9 **GARY CHESTER**
On all Coasters records, especially "Little Egypt (Ying Yang)" and "Yakety Yak."

10 **BUDDY SALTZMAN**
With The Four Seasons on their Crewe-Gaudio productions and on some Spector records and sessions with Charlie Callelo.

11 **EARL PALMER**
On "You've Lost That Lovin' Feelin'" by The Righteous Brothers and on a dozen other Los Angeles and New Orleans classics.

-◄❙❙►-

MAX WEINBERG'S LIST OF 10 GREAT ANONYMOUS DRUMMERS
Whoever played on . . .

1 "Louie Louie," THE KINGSMEN
2 "Stay Awhile," DUSTY SPRINGFIELD
3 "Here Comes My Baby," THE TREMELOES
4 "Maybellene," "You Never Can Tell," "School Days," "Around and Around," CHUCK BERRY
5 "Lucille," LITTLE RICHARD
6 "Red River Rock," JOHNNY AND THE HURRICANES
7 "Denise," RANDY AND THE RAINBOWS
8 "The Wanderer," DION
9 "You Can't Sit Down," THE DOVELLS
10 "The Twist," HANK BALLARD and CHUBBY CHECKER

THE 25 GREATEST ROCK AND ROLL BASSISTS

1 JAMES JAMERSON (Motown Records)
2 ASTON BARRETT (Bob Marley and the Wailers)
3 DUCK DUNN (Booker T. and the MGs)
4 BILL BLACK (Elvis, Scotty, and Bill)
5 LARRY GRAHAM (Sly and the Family Stone)
6 JOHN ENTWISTLE (The Who)
7 BILL WYMAN (The Rolling Stones)
8 PAUL MCCARTNEY (The Beatles)
9 GARRY TALLENT (The E Street Band)
10 TOMMY COGBILL (The Muscle Shoals Rhythm Section)
11 BOOTSY COLLINS (Funkadelic, James Brown, etc.)
12 RICK DANKO (The Band)
13 VERDINE WHITE (Earth, Wind, and Fire)
14 JOHN MCVIE (Fleetwood Mac)
15 JOHN PAUL JONES (Led Zeppelin)
16 BRIAN WILSON (The Beach Boys)
17 RONNIE LANE (The Faces)
18 CHAS CHANDLER (The Animals)
19 NICK LOWE (Rockpile)
20 JOE MAULDIN (The Crickets)
21 NOEL REDDING (The Jimi Hendrix Experience)
22 JOHN WETTON (Roxy Music, etc.)
23 JACK CASADY (The Jefferson Airplane, Hot Tuna)
24 JACK BRUCE (Cream, etc.)
25 CARL RADLE (Delaney and Bonnie, Eric Clapton, etc.)

10 GREAT BASS SOLOS

1 "Another Man's Woman," Atlanta Rhythm Section; PAUL GODDARD
2 "Astral Weeks," Van Morrison; RICHARD DAVIS
3 "Dark Star," The Grateful Dead; PHIL LESH
4 "Dreaming from the Waist," The Who; JOHN ENTWISTLE
5 "Fat Angel," The Jefferson Airplane; JACK CASADY
6 "Mountain Jam," The Allman Brothers Band; BERRY OAKLEY
7 "Moon in June," Soft Machine; HUGH HOPPER
8 "My Generation," The Who; JOHN ENTWISTLE
9 "1983 . . . . (A Merman I Should Turn to Be)," Jimi Hendrix Experience; NOEL REDDING
10 "Spoonful," Cream; JACK BRUCE

-◄❚▮▶-

THE 20 BEST HARMONICA PLAYERS

1 SONNY BOY WILLIAMSON
2 LITTLE WALTER
3 BIG WALTER HORTON
4 CHARLIE MCCOY
5 TONY GLOVER
6 JAZZ GILLUM
7 MAGIC DICK
8 P. T. GAZELL
9 JIMMY RIDDLE
10 JAMES COTTON
11 SOUTHSIDE JOHNNY LYON
12 JIMMY REED
13 SONNY TERRY
14 PAUL BUTTERFIELD
15 DON VAN VLIET, a.k.a. CAPTAIN BEEFHEART
16 LEE OSKAR
17 JOHN SEBASTIAN
18 DELBERT MCCLINTON
19 NEIL YOUNG
20 BOB DYLAN

JOHN SEBASTIAN'S FAVORITE HARP PLAYERS

John Sebastian wanted it made clear that there is a difference between harmonica playing and blues-based harp playing, even though both forms use similar instruments. His favorite harmonica player, of course, is his father, the late John Sebastian Sr.

1 SONNY TERRY
2 SONNY BOY WILLIAM-
      SON II, a.k.a. RICE
      MILLER
3 PAUL BUTTERFIELD
4 WILL SHADE
5 BIG WALTER HORTON
6 CHARLIE MCCOY
7 PEGRAM AND PARHAM,
      banjo and harp duo

JOHN SEBASTIAN *wrote and recorded all of the great Lovin' Spoonful hits, including "Do You Believe in Magic?" and "Summer in the City." He has also had several solo hits, including "Welcome Back." Today, he lives in Woodstock, New York, and continues to make music.*

-◄▮▮►-

MAGIC DICK'S MUSICAL INFLUENCES

1 LITTLE WALTER
2 SONNY BOY WILLIAM-
      SON I and II
3 JUNIOR WELLS
4 ROY ELDRIDGE
5 LOUIS ARMSTRONG
6 MILES DAVIS
7 JOHN COLTRANE
8 ORNETTE COLEMAN
9 CHARLIE PARKER
10 STEVIE WONDER
11 PAUL BUTTERFIELD
12 TOOTS THIELEMANS

MAGIC DICK, *mystery figure that he is, needs no introduction to fans of The J. Geils Band or blues-harp playing, of which he is an acknowledged master.*

THE 10 BEST SCREAMS

1 "Beck's Bolero," The Jeff Beck Group; KEITH MOON
2 "The End," The Doors; JIM MORRISON
3 "Fire," ARTHUR BROWN
4 "Helter Skelter," The Beatles; JOHN LENNON
5 "Hey Jude," WILSON PICKETT
6 "I Feel Good," JAMES BROWN
7 "The Strain," Bonzo Dog Doo Dah Band; VIV STANSHALL
8 "Twist and Shout," The Beatles; PAUL McCARTNEY
9 "Won't Get Fooled Again," The Who; ROGER DALTREY
10 "Why," LONNIE MACK

-◄❙▮▶-

BARRY GIBB'S FAVORITE VOCALISTS

1 THE MILLS BROTHERS
2 THE EVERLY BROTHERS
3 THE BEATLES
4 OTIS REDDING

BARRY GIBB *is a member of The Bee Gees, who have been making hit records since the late 1960s, ranging from "New York Mining Disaster, 1941 (Have You Seen My Wife, Mr. Jones)" and "Massachusetts" to "Jive Talkin'" and "Stayin' Alive."*

-◄❙▮▶-

MICHAEL JACKSON'S 10 FAVORITE VOCALISTS

1	DIANA ROSS	6	ARETHA FRANKLIN
2	STEVIE WONDER	7	PAUL McCARTNEY
3	BARBRA STREISAND	8	SAM COOKE
4	JERMAINE JACKSON	9	SLIM WHITMAN
5	JACKIE WILSON	10	OTIS REDDING

MICHAEL JACKSON, *a former Motown wunderkind with the Jackson 5, is responsible for such top-selling solo ventures as* Off the Wall.

LIBERACE'S 10 FAVORITE ROCK PERFORMERS

1	BILLY JOEL	6	BLONDIE
2	DAVID BOWIE	7	THE EAGLES
3	BOZ SCAGGS	8	SUPERTRAMP
4	THE DOOBIE BROTHERS	9	LINDA RONSTADT
5	TEDDY PENDERGRASS	10	BOB SEGER

LIBERACE *has absolutely nothing to do with rock and roll, but he does his best to keep up, anyway.*

-◄❙▮❙►-

GENE VINCENT'S 5 FAVORITE SINGERS

Gene Vincent was one of early rock's grandest figures. Best known for "Be-Bop-a-Lula," Vincent continued to record prolifically in both rock and country styles until his death in 1972. The following list is contained in "Wild Cat": A Tribute to Gene Vincent, *edited by Eddie Muir.*

1	BROOK BENTON	4	JOHNNY CASH
2	LITTLE RICHARD	5	CLIFF RICHARD
3	CONNIE FRANCIS		

Gene Vincent and Darrell Glenn at the Sportatorium in Dallas, Texas, where they were appearing on the Big D Jamboree in early 1958. Darrell's father, Artie Glenn, wrote "Crying in the Chapel."

EDDIE COCHRAN'S FAVORITE SINGERS AND INSTRUMENTALISTS

Eddie Cochran was one of the greatest of the fifties rock and roll singers before his tragic death in a car crash in 1960. The following list is from Eddie Muir and Tony Scott's Somethin' Else: A Tribute to Eddie Cochran.

1	RAY CHARLES	3	DUANE EDDY
2	BRENDA LEE	4	JOE BROWN

ROBERT GORDON'S FAVORITE VOCALISTS

1   ELVIS PRESLEY
2   GENE VINCENT
3   JOHNNY BURNETTE
4   JACK SCOTT
5   HANK WILLIAMS
6   WANDA JACKSON
7   TAMMY WYNETTE
8   PATSY CLINE
9   JOHNNY CASH
10 GEORGE JONES
11 CONWAY TWITTY

ROBERT GORDON was lead singer of The Tuff Darts, one of the earliest New Wave groups to play New York's CBGB's. He is also a solo vocalist specializing in updated rockabilly material. He has one of the last perfect pompadours in existence.

-◄▮►-

MOST FREQUENTLY BORING INSTRUMENTAL GROUPS

1   KRAFTWERK
2   SALSOUL ORCHESTRA
3   FOCUS
4   DAVIE ALLAN AND THE ARROWS
5   THE VENTURES
6   THE METERS

-◄▮►-

FAMOUS LEFT-HANDED MUSICIANS

1   ELLIOT EASTON (The Cars)
2   JIMI HENDRIX
3   TONY IOMMI (Black Sabbath)
4   LEE JACKSON (The Nice)
5   ALBERT KING
6   BARBARA LYNN

7   PAUL McCARTNEY
8   PAUL SIMON*
9   RINGO STARR
10   JOE STRUMMER* (The Clash)
11   WADDY WACHTEL*
12   DAVE WAKELING (The [English] Beat)
13   CHARLES "HUNGRY" WILLIAMS (New Orleans drummer)
14   BOBBY WOMACK

*Play right-handed

-◄▮▶-

CHUCK BERRY'S SIDEMEN
1955–1966

Piano
1   JOHNNY JOHNSON
2   LAFAYETTE LEAKE
3   OTIS SPANN
4   PAUL WILLIAMS

Drums
1   FRED BELOW
2   EDDIE HARDY
3   ODIE PAYNE
4   JASPER THOMAS

Bass
1   WILLIE DIXON
2   G. SMITH

Maracas
1   JEROME GREEN

Second Guitar
1   MATT MURPHY
2   BO DIDDLEY
3   JIMMY ROGERS

Background Vocals
1   THE FIVE DIMENSIONS
2   MARTHA BERRY

SEVENTEEN: GROUPS

Ray Charles and the Raelettes.

20 BANDS THAT HAVE BEEN REINCARNATED

1 **THE ANIMALS**
First formed in Newcastle around 1962 as the Alan Price Combo, the original Animals enjoyed their greatest success during the British Invasion from 1964 to 1966. After Price left in 1966, continued attrition eventually saw the act evolve into Eric Burdon and the Animals, with none of the originals save Burdon for the psychedelic hits "Monterey" and "When I Was Young." But in 1976, the original members gathered together once more for an album, appropriately entitled *Before We Were So Rudely Interrupted*. Although a longer tenure was reportedly considered, the group has not performed together since.

2 **BIG BROTHER AND THE HOLDING COMPANY**
Originally, of course, Big Brother was Janis Joplin's group. After some scathing reviews focusing on Big Brother's reputed musical ineptitude, Joplin dumped the band, and at that point (circa 1969), it looked like the end of the road for Big Brother. But in the early seventies, the band did re-form for two decent last-gasp Columbia LPs and a tour, with Los Angeles session vocalist Kathi McDonald.

3 **BLOOD, SWEAT, AND TEARS**
This horn-based group was meant to be Al Kooper's ultimate expression of his art-pop ambitions. But after only one album in that vein, *Child Is Father to the Man*, Kooper was sacked and David Clayton-Thomas was brought in for the succeeding albums, which fostered the band's popularity within diluted big-band-rock circles. After the third album, *Three*, personnel changes became so frequent that at various points in the seventies, the current version of Blood, Sweat, and Tears had none of the original members on hand. Thus, this is perhaps not so much a tale of rock reincarnation as of parthenogenesis.

4 **THE BYRDS**
The original group, the pioneers of folk-rock, lasted for three albums, before Gene Clark left during the recording of the

fourth LP, *Fifth Dimension*. This left the band a quartet; two years later, in 1968, it became a trio when David Crosby absented himself. Leader Roger McGuinn added Gram Parsons and continued the group with ever-shifting personnel. The Byrds folded for good in 1972. In 1973, the original band was reincarnated for a disastrous one-shot album, *The Byrds*, on Asylum Records.

5   **CRAZY HORSE**

Neil Young found this band in the southern California boondocks. They hung in for a few albums of their own before guitarist-writer Danny Whitten split in 1972; the group disbanded after releasing *Crazy Horse at Crooked Lake* later that year. But in 1975, with Whitten dead of a drug overdose, Young re-formed the band as his backing group, this time with Frank Sampedro on guitar.

6   **THE DRIFTERS**

There are at least three distinct incarnations of The Drifters. The first began in 1953—with Clyde McPhatter as lead vocalist—and pioneered the merger of gospel and rhythm & blues with such hits as "Money Honey" and "White Christmas." When McPhatter left for a solo career in 1956, manager George Treadwell (who owned rights to the group's name) selected Johnny Moore as his replacement. But Moore was drafted, and the group didn't gel around a solid lineup until 1959, when Treadwell simply disposed of all the members and hired a group that had been performing in Harlem as The Five Crowns. The lead vocalist was Ben E. King, and their first recording, "There Goes My Baby," was an important, innovative hit that incorporated strings with R & B for the first time, thereby inaugurating one of the key changes that led to soul. But in 1961, King went solo, and Treadwell created a third version of the group, this time to support lead singer Rudy Lewis, who sang on The Drifters' best-known hits, including "On Broadway" and "Up on the Roof." When Lewis died in 1964, Moore returned, for "Under the Boardwalk" and a string of other hits. Managed by Fay Treadwell, George's widow, The Drifters are still active today and are especially popular in Europe, where *another* incarnation recut many of the old hits in 1972 with surprising success. Ironically, Johnny Moore is the oldest surviving member.

7　**THE ELECTRIC FLAG**

Mike Bloomfield was thinking along the same lines as his friend Al Kooper in 1967, and The Electric Flag became his version of a big rock band. The Flag debuted at the Monterey Pop Festival, but made only two albums before splitting up. In 1974, however, Bloomfield and several other original band members, including Buddy Miles, Barry Goldberg, and Nick Gravenites, reunited to cut one album for Atlantic. Its lack of success prevented them from continuing.

8　**FAIRPORT CONVENTION**

Fairport has made more than a dozen albums; hardly any have featured the same lineup. Judy Dyble was lead vocalist on the band's first album, in 1967, but was replaced by Sandy Denny for the second. Denny left in 1969 for a solo career and the band carried on without a lead singer, which led to a series of departures that found the group, in 1973, with no original members. Denny returned in 1974 but left in 1976. The group struggled onward until very late in the decade.

9　**FLEETWOOD MAC**

The group was originally formed in 1967 by Peter Green, John McVie, and Mick Fleetwood—all alumni of John Mayall's Bluesbreakers. But in 1970, Green, the acknowledged leader retired, and a year later, so did second guitarist Jeremy Spencer (for religious reasons). Having added guitarist Danny Kirwan, keyboardist Christine McVie, and American Bob Welch, the group carried on, until Kirwan was fired in '72. Various replacements occurred until 1975, when the addition of Californians Lindsey Buckingham and Stevie Nicks completely transformed the original blues-based sound into romanticized folk-rock. Thus, this is more a musical reincarnation

COURTESY PETER KANZE

The second incarnation of Fleetwood Mac seen in 1967. Members of the group were John McVie, Peter Green, Jeremy Spencer, and Mick Fleetwood. Only McVie and Fleetwood stayed with the group.

than one involving personnel changes or breakups and regroupings. (Although in the dark days of 1973, when the group *did* consider disbanding, former manager Clifford Davis formed a group on his own—à la Treadwell's many Drifters—for a short period.)

10 THE GUESS WHO

Formed in Winnipeg in 1959, the original Guess Who, under the name Chad Allan and the Expressions, didn't have a hit until 1965 with "Shakin' All Over." Allan then left to go to college, and guitarist Randy Bachman took over, with Burton

Cummings as lead vocalist, naming the group The Guess Who. They developed an altogether different pop-rock sound that led to many hits in the ensuing years, until Bachman quit after the band recorded "American Woman," in 1970. Bachman went on to more success with Bachman-Turner Overdrive; Cummings carried on with various replacements until 1975, when the group finally disbanded, no original players having been in the group for several years.

11 **THE HOLY MODAL ROUNDERS**

Peter Stampfel and Steve Weber formed this acid-folk group in the early sixties and have disbanded and re-formed it on a frequent basis ever since. Its best recent incarnations have featured the redoubtable Michael Hurley.

12 **LOVE**

This legendary L.A. band formed in 1964; by the next year, they had recorded their first album and had a minor hit, "My Little Red Book," that led to a certain cult notoriety on the psychedelic fringe. Personnel shifts were near constant—two members added after the first album, two subtracted after the second, and so on. The only constant was guitar-vocalist-writer Arthur Lee. By the end of 1967, Lee had gotten rid of all the other original members; the lineup thereafter lasted, more or less intact, through 1971. In 1974, Lee resurfaced with another incarnation of the group, for one album and a tour. But the original had all the magic.

13 **MANFRED MANN**

The group was named after one of its members, so personnel changes shouldn't matter much. But Mann is a keyboard player, not a lead vocalist, and it was the singing of Paul Jones that gave the band its British Invasion hits ("Do Wah Diddy Diddy," "5-4-3-2-1," etc!). The group first splintered in 1966 with Jones replaced by Mike D'Abo, who sang lead on "The Mighty Quinn." In 1969, Mann broke up the band altogether to form Manfred Mann Chapter Three (a jazz-rock–oriented outfit), and then Manfred Mann's Earth Band, which continued playing in a variety of styles.

14 **THE MOODY BLUES**

Formed in Birmingham, England, in 1964, The Moody Blues had a major international hit the next year with their second single, "Go Now." They promptly disappeared from the public eye until 1968, when they recorded *Days of Future Passed*, establishing a mock-orchestral style in which the group continued, prosperously, until well into the seventies. However, in the interim, two key members, Denny Laine (later of Wings) and Clint Warwick, left to be replaced respectively by Justin Hayward and John Lodge, who were effectively the leaders of the band thereafter.

15 **THE MOTHERS OF INVENTION**

Frank Zappa enjoys posturing as a misanthrope, and maybe there's a reality behind the pose. In any event, there have been at least as many editions of The Mothers of Invention as there have been Mothers albums, with Zappa the *only* constant.

16 **MOTT THE HOOPLE**

Formed in Herefordshire, England, the core of Mott moved to London in 1968 and cut its debut album in 1969. Three more followed, but none had any chart success. In March 1972, the group formally disbanded, but within a few weeks, Mott re-formed after David Bowie encouraged them to do so. The band went on to its successful *All the Young Dudes*, written and produced by Bowie. Although they continued to make some fine music, their commercial and artistic successes were limited. When vocalist Ian Hunter split in 1974 to go solo, the band was, for all practical purposes, finished, although some of the original members carried on for a time as Mott.

17 **THE MOVE**

Formed in 1965 in Birmingham, and almost instantly successful in Britain, The Move never had a hit in America. By 1968, two original members left, and so did the direction of the band, which became increasingly arty and conservative. By 1970, when vocalist Carl Wayne was replaced by Jeff Lynne, The Move was virtually a new group, symbolized by a name change in 1972 to The Electric Light Orchestra.

18 **THE PRETTY THINGS**

The Pretty Things were formed in 1963 by Phil May and Dick Taylor as a Stones-style R&B band, only dirtier. By the time they completed the rock opera *S. F. Sorrow* in 1968, May was the only original member left in the band; *he* finally left in 1976. The Prettys continued, feebly.

19 **THE SMALL FACES**

Archetypal sixties mods, The Small Faces had a rip-roaring heyday from 1965 until 1968. In 1969, leader Steve Marriott left to form Humble Pie, which was presumably the end of the tale. But shortly after, the other members found two Jeff Beck Group alumni, Ron Wood and Rod Stewart, to take his place. As The Faces, they went on to greater glories through the mid-seventies. In 1977, with Stewart gone solo and Wood a Rolling Stone, the group tried it again with the original membership minus bassist Ronnie Lane, who was replaced by Rick Wills. However, this version lasted for only one LP.

20 **THE SONS OF CHAMPLIN**

This second-rank San Francisco band was formed in 1965 by Bill Champlin. Despite a name change in the late sixties (to The Sons), and various hirings and firings, the band never had any real commercial success. They first broke up in early 1970, reformed later that year, changed their name to Yogi Phlegm, a Mahavishnu Orchestra-style outfit. This incarnation lasted only six months. With an expanded lineup, the band reverted to The Sons name and early funk sound, which they kept until 1977 when they finally disbanded. Bill Champlin went on to form a completely new band, Full Moon, in 1978.

-◄▮►-

10 BANDS THAT DIED BEFORE THEIR TIME

1 **THE BONZO DOG DOO DAH BAND**

Although they had some success in England (the Paul McCartney-produced "I'm the Urban Spaceman" was a Top Ten hit there), The Bonzos, with their mix of parodistic rock and surrealistic comedy, might have hit it really big worldwide if they had lasted past 1969. (After all, it is listening to The Bonzos that makes it easy to understand how puerile such "satiric" successors as Sparks and The Ramones ultimately are.)

2 BRINSLEY SCHWARZ

Schwarz was simply the best of the pub-rock bands. But disastrous hype for their first LP—and a public apathetic to all but boogie and bombast—doomed the band to a mid-seventies breakup. Its version of country was very like what became known as New Wave, partly because New Wave was inaugurated by producer-bassist Nick Lowe and guitarist Brinsley Schwarz himself (as a member of Graham Parker's Rumour).

3 BUFFALO SPRINGFIELD

Nothing more clearly demonstrates the fact that this group broke up too soon than the massive success of members Neil Young, Stephen Stills, Richie Furay, and Jim Messina both as solo artists and as members of such groups as Poco (which Furay joined); Crosby, Stills, Nash, and Young; and Loggins and Messina.

4 DUCKS DELUXE

This was another of the pub-rock bands that could not continue against the trend. Guitarist Martin Belmont later joined The Rumour.

5 THE ELECTRIC FLAG

The original version of this group never quite got its bearings. But the blues-band-with-a-horn-section concept it helped pioneer quickly became big business with such inferior groups as Blood, Sweat, and Tears and Chicago.

6 LYNYRD SKYNYRD

Guitarist Steve Gaines and singer-writer Ronnie Van Zant died in a plane crash in 1977 just as this group was about to reach its commercial zenith. Even with its career thus truncated, Skynyrd remains the best of the southern rock bands.

7　**THE MC5**

They pioneered what would later become known as punk rock with a political ferocity equaled only by The Clash. But because of drug problems and managerial contretemps, the group simply couldn't hold together long enough for its turn in the limelight.

8　**MOBY GRAPE**

A disastrous CBS Records hype for its first album, and the fact that the group played deceptively simple and straightforward rock and roll songs, obscured the genuine virtues of the one nonpsychedelic band to emerge from mid-sixties San Francisco. Like Brinsley Schwarz in England, Moby Grape would have seemed a natural in the New Wave context of the seventies.

9　**THE NEW YORK DOLLS**

Their semitransvestite appearance was so off-putting in their halcyon days of the early seventies that The Dolls never quite found an audience. But, like The MC5, this band was a progenitor of punk. The early Sex Pistols singles, for one thing, sound like Dolls remakes. Had they lasted into the punk moment, they might have been viewed as the semigeniuses they were.

10　**BARRY AND THE REMAINS**

Lead singer Barry Tashian had the fire and fervor of the classic rockers, to hear people in New England tell the tale. But their one album didn't reveal much of that, and they never got the chance to make another. Chances are, they're the great lost band of the sixties.

-◄▐▐►-

GREATEST DUOS

1　MARVIN GAYE and TAMMI TERRELL

2　THE RIGHTEOUS BROTHERS

3　SAM AND DAVE

4　THE EVERLY BROTHERS

5　SIMON AND GARFUNKEL

6　MEL AND TIM

7   IKE AND TINA TURNER
8   MARVIN GAYE and KIM
      WESTON
9   DARYL HALL and JOHN
      OATES
10 JAN AND DEAN
11 PEACHES AND HERB
      (seventies
      incarnation)

12 JAMES and BOBBY
      PURIFY
13 NICKOLAS ASHFORD and
      VALERIE SIMPSON
14 DON GARDNER and DEE
      DEE FORD

-◄◗►-

GREATEST TRIOS

1   CREAM
2   THE CRICKETS
3   ELVIS, SCOTTY, AND BILL
4   THE IMPRESSIONS
5   THE ISLEY BROTHERS
6   THE POLICE

7   THE JIMI HENDRIX
      EXPERIENCE
8   THE ROCK AND ROLL
      TRIO
9   THE SUPREMES

-◄◗►-

THE JORDANAIRES' 15 FAVORITE RECORDINGS

1   "Sugaree," THE JORDANAIRES
2   "Battle of New Orleans," JOHNNY HORTON
3   "Big John," JIMMY DEAN
4   "Gone," FERLIN HUSKEY
5   "Paper Roses," MARIE OSMOND
6   "Poor Little Fool," RICKY NELSON
7   "Lonesome Town," RICKY NELSON
8   "The Gambler," KENNY ROGERS
9   "I Can't Stop Loving You," DON GIBSON
10 "Four Walls," JIM REEVES
11 "Crazy," PATSY CLINE

The Jordanaires.

COURTESY DECCA 1978

12   "Coal Miner's Daughter," LORETTA LYNN
13   "Don't Be Cruel," ELVIS PRESLEY
14   "All Shook Up," ELVIS PRESLEY
15   "Young Love," SONNY JAMES

THE JORDANAIRES, *who helped to arrange or sang on the above records, are best known for providing harmonies for all of Elvis Presley's recordings from the time he joined RCA Records in 1956 until the end of the sixties.*

- ◄ | | ► -

THE GREATEST QUARTETS

1	THE BEATLES	5	THE KINKS
2	THE CLASH	6	LED ZEPPELIN
3	CREEDENCE CLEAR-	7	THE SEX PISTOLS
	WATER REVIVAL	8	THE RAVENS
4	THE FOUR TOPS	9	THE WHO

THE 10 GREATEST QUINTETS

1	THE ANIMALS	6	THE DAVE CLARK FIVE
2	THE BAND	7	THE JACKSON 5
3	THE BEACH BOYS	8	THE ROLLING STONES
4	BUFFALO SPRINGFIELD	9	THE TEMPTATIONS
5	THE DRIFTERS (the Ben E. King and Clyde McPhatter editions)	10	THE YARDBIRDS

·◄▐▐►·

THE GREAT SEXTETS

1	THE ALLMAN BROTHERS BAND	4	LITTLE FEAT
2	THE PAUL BUTTERFIELD BLUES BAND	5	PROCOL HARUM
3	LOUIS JORDAN AND THE TYMPANI FIVE	6	BOB SEGER AND THE SILVER BULLET BAND
		7	ROXY MUSIC

·◄▐▐►·

TWO DOZEN GREAT BACKUP BANDS

1 **The Attractions**
Elvis Costello's New Wave partners in crime.

2 **Big Brother and the Holding Company**
Unless you think that Joplin was Big Brother herself, or that the band was something more than support . . . .

3 **The Blue Caps**
Gene Vincent's great band.

4   **Crazy Horse**
     Neil Young found them playing bars in rural California and put
     them together with arranger Jack Nitzsche. Thereafter, Young
     had one of the greatest supporting bands ever (at least until
     Danny Whitten died).

5   **The Crickets**
     This floating assortment of West Texas hotshots backed Buddy
     Holly, and once even included Waylon Jennings. But mostly it
     was Jerry Allison, Sonny Curtis, Niki Sullivan, and Buddy
     himself.

6   **Elephant's Memory**
     True enough, they recorded on their own, but this group of
     New York politico-rockers made a name for itself only when
     backing up John Lennon on *Some Time in New York City*.

7   **The E Street Band**
     Bruce Springsteen's crew of cosmic East Coast hoodlums.

8   **The Famous Flames**
     James Brown's original collection of soul masters featured
     keyboardist Bobby Byrd and saxman Maceo Parker.

9   **The Grease Band**
     After starting out with Joe Cocker, pre-Mad Dogs and English-
     men, they turned to a freelance career backing various artists.

10   **Guam**
     Bob Dylan's combo for the Rolling Thunder Revue.

11   **The Hawks**
     You know them as The Band, but when they backed Ronnie
     Hawkins and then Bob Dylan, they were Levon and the
     Hawks—even made a couple of rare singles that way.

12   **The Heartbreakers**
     Tom Petty's, of course, not Johnny Thunder's.

13   **The JB's**
     James Brown's later assemblage of soul masters were led by
     the redoubtable Fred Wesley, who eventually took them solo

as The Horny Horns, part of George Clinton's Parliafunka-delicment.

14   The Kingpins

King Curtis' crew of ace New York session pros had one of the all-time steamiest sounds on record. They featured guitarist Cornell Dupree and the fabled drummer Bernard Purdie.

15   Mad Dogs and Englishmen

This massive rock and roll orchestra made up of Los Angeles heavyweights and relative unknowns was put together by Leon Russell for Joe Cocker.

16   The Noble Knights

King Curtis' original band of funk innovators.

17   The Pirates

They made their reputation backing early British rocker Johnny Kidd, and are most famous for the original version of "Shakin' All Over." But Kidd was never much of a singer: The real thrill was guitarist Mick Green's fretboard wizardry.

18   The Rhythm Rockers

Ike Turner used this band when he was a touring R&B showman (pre-Tina) and talent scout in the fifties.

19   Rockpile

Sometimes this group was led by Dave Edmunds, sometimes by Nick Lowe. Either way, it was the greatest oldies-influenced rock and roll band in history.

20   The Rumour

Graham Parker's backing band was formed from the splinters of two great pub-rock combos, Brinsley Schwarz and Ducks Deluxe.

21   The Silver Bullet Band

Maybe they'd be nothing without Bob Seger, but these journeymen Detroit rockers have outlasted everything else in Motown through sheer tenacity and ferocity.

22   **War**

Before they scored with "The World Is a Ghetto" and "Slippin' into Darkness," War was Eric Burdon's supporting cast for a couple of notable years, connecting with "Spill the Wine" and "They Can't Take Away Our Music," the funkiest Burdon ever got.

24   **Wonderlove**

Stevie Wonder's free-floating assemblage of modern funksters.

-◄❙▶-

IAN HUNTER'S DREAM BAND

1   JEFF BECK: guitar
2   LEON RUSSELL: keyboards
3   RICK MAROTTA: drums
4   DAVID SANBORN: saxophone
5   GORDON EDWARDS: bass

IAN HUNTER *was the leader of the fabled British group Mott the Hoople and author of most of its best songs. Since that group split up, Hunter has pursued a solo career, and with his partner, Mick Ronson, has produced such artists as Ellen Foley and The Iron City Houserockers.*

-◄❙▶-

5 BANDS WITH 2 DRUMMERS

1   THE ALLMAN BROTHERS BAND
2   JAMES BROWN
3   THE DOOBIE BROTHERS
4   THE EAGLES (onstage)
5   THE GRATEFUL DEAD

BEYOND PLUTONIUM
15 Great Heavy-Metal* Bands

1	BLUE ÖYSTER CULT	8	AEROSMITH
2	LED ZEPPELIN	9	GRAND FUNK RAILROAD
3	VAN HALEN	10	DUST
4	BLACK SABBATH	11	BLUE CHEER
5	THIN LIZZY	12	SIR LORD BALTIMORE
6	DEEP PURPLE	13	AC/DC
7	TED NUGENT AND THE (latter-day) AMBOY DUKES	14	IRON BUTTERFLY
		15	URIAH HEEP

*The term *heavy metal* comes from a phrase coined by William Burroughs in his novel *The Soft Machine*.

-◄▐▐►-

10 GREAT SURF BANDS
Not Including the Beach Boys, Jan and Dean, or Even Jack Nitzsche

1 THE CHANTAYS, "Pipeline"
2 DICK DALE AND THE DEL-TONES, "Misilou," "Let's Go Trippin'"
3 THE SURFARIS, "Wipe Out," "Surfer Joe"
4 THE TRASHMEN,* "Surfin' Bird"
5 THE PYRAMIDS, "Penetration"
6 THE WAILERS, "Tall Cool One"
7 THE SENTINALS, "Latinia"
8 THE MARKETTS, "Surfer's Stomp"

9   THE TRADE WINDS,** "New York's a Lonely Town"
10   THE REVELS, "Church Key"

* Okay, so they were from Minnesota. They still played real surf music, reverb guitars and all.
**Okay, so they were from Providence, Rhode Island, and mostly a vocal group, when the great surf bands were all-instrumental. But Narragansett Beach is the hottest surf spot on the East Coast, so at least they knew what they were talking about. And every landlocked Midwesterner who heard "New York's a Lonely Town" finally knew the truth about the music and himself. So how could we omit it?

The Surfaris, whose infamous "Wipe Out" rose to Number 2 on the charts in 1963.

RICK WHITESELL'S GREATEST DOO-WOP GROUPS

Black Groups

1 THE CADILLACS
2 THE DELLS
3 THE DRIFTERS
4 THE FIVE KEYS
5 THE FLAMINGOS
6 THE HARPTONES
7 FRANKIE LYMON AND THE TEENAGERS
8 THE MIDNIGHTERS
9 THE MOONGLOWS
10 THE ORIOLES
11 THE PENGUINS
12 THE PLATTERS
13 THE RAVENS
14 THE ROBINS

White Groups

1 DANNY AND THE JUNIORS
2 DION AND THE BELMONTS
3 THE DUPREES
4 THE EARLS
5 THE ELEGANTS
6 THE FOUR LOVERS, a.k.a. THE FOUR SEASONS
7 JAY AND THE AMERICANS
8 THE MYSTICS
9 THE REGENTS
10 THE RIVIERAS
11 THE SKYLINERS
12 VITO AND THE SALUTATIONS

RICK WHITESELL *was editor of* Goldmine *and* Classic Wax *and one of America's best-known historians and researchers on rock, rhythm & blues, and related music. His special interest was in harmony-group music. Whitesell, one of the chief researchers of this book, died in January 1981.*

15 A CAPPELLA GROUPS

1   THE CAMELOTS
2   THE DEL STARS
3   THE FIVE BLIND BOYS
      OF MISSISSIPPI
4   THE FIVE FASHIONS
5   THE FIVE SHADOWS
6   THE FOUR VAGABONDS
7   GINGER AND THE
      ADORABLES
8   THE NUTMEGS
9   DENNIS OSTRUM AND
      THE CITADELS
10 THE PERSUASIONS
11 THE SAVOYS
12 THE VELVET ANGELS
13 THE VI-TONES
14 THE YOUNG ONES
15 THE ZIRCONS

- ◄ ▮ ► -

15 NOTABLE INTERRACIAL BANDS

1   THE ALLMAN BROTHERS BAND
2   THE AVERAGE WHITE BAND
3   THE BUS BOYS
4   THE PAUL BUTTERFIELD BLUES BAND
5   THE DOOBIE BROTHERS
6   THE ELECTRIC FLAG
7   THE FOUNDATIONS
8   THE JIMI HENDRIX EXPERIENCE
9   RUFUS
10 THE SELECTER
11 SLY AND THE FAMILY STONE
12 THE SPECIALS
13 BRUCE SPRINGSTEEN AND THE E STREET BAND
14 TOWER OF POWER
15 THE VILLAGE PEOPLE

FAMOUS ROCK COMEDY GROUPS AND PERFORMERS

1 BLOW FLY, a.k.a. CLARENCE REID
2 THE BONZO DOG DOO DAH BAND
3 BUCHANAN AND GOODMAN
4 CHEECH AND CHONG
5 BILLY CONNOLLY
6 FLO AND EDDIE
7 FRUT
8 THE FUGS
9 LIVERPOOL SCENE
10 MONTY PYTHON
11 THE MOTHERS OF INVENTION
12 MARTIN MULL
13 NATIONAL LAMPOON'S LEMMINGS
14 NERVOUS NORVUS
15 THE PLASMATICS
16 THE RUTLES
17 SCAFFOLD
18 THE SENSATIONAL ALEX HARVEY BAND
19 SHA NA NA
20 THE TUBES
21 ZACHERLE

-◄❙❙►-

LOUDEST BANDS

1 THE WHO*
2 BLUE CHEER
3 THE MC5
4 THE CLASH
5 DEEP PURPLE
6 GRAND FUNK RAILROAD
7 THE JIMI HENDRIX EXPERIENCE

*Confirmed by *The Guinness Book of World Records*

8   CREAM
9   MOUNTAIN
10 THE VELVET UNDER-
        GROUND
11 LED ZEPPELIN
12 THE MOTHERS OF
        INVENTION (original
        incarnation)

13 BLUE ÖYSTER CULT
14 CREEDENCE CLEAR-
        WATER REVIVAL
15 XTC
16 QUEEN
17 KISS

·◄❙▶·

MOST BORING BANDS

1   RHINOCEROS
2   THE GRATEFUL DEAD
3   ELECTRIC LIGHT
        ORCHESTRA
4   QUEEN
5   PERE UBU
6   BLACK SABBATH

7   STEELY DAN
8   URIAH HEEP
9   BLUE CHEER
10 POCO
11 THE EAGLES
12 PABLO CRUISE

·◄❙▶·

MOST NARCISSISTIC BANDS

Groups That Have Claimed the Title of "Greatest Rock Band"

1   QUEEN: "We Are the Champions"
2   THE ROLLING STONES: See the introduction on *Get Yer Ya-Ya's Out*.
3   THE CLASH: "The Only Band That Matters"
4   THE WHO: See The Collected Apologies of Pete Townshend.
5   THE BEATLES: "We're more popular than Jesus Christ."
    —John Lennon
6   THE SEX PISTOLS: Claim made at the Longhorn Ballroom in San Antonio, Texas.
7   LED ZEPPELIN: They just got more money than anyone else.
8   ZZ TOP: Claimed to be the most popular touring band in the world.

EIGHTEEN: ELVIS

Elvis at eighteen.

QUOTATIONS FROM CHAIRMAN ELVIS

1   "I get lonesome sometimes. I get lonesome right in the middle of a crowd."
2   "Rhythm is something you either have or don't have, but when you have it, you have it all over."
3   "I was thinking about a Presley used-car lot."
4   "I know practically every religious song that's ever been written."
5   "When music starts, I gotta move."
6   "Rock and roll music, if you like it, if you feel it, you can't help but move to it. That's what happens to me. I can't help it."
7   "I want to entertain people. That's my whole life—to my last breath."
8   "I wanted to be a singer because I didn't want to sweat."
9   "I don't know anything about music. In my line, you don't have to."
10   "I hope I haven't bored you."

-◄❙▶-

ELVIS PRESLEY'S 20 GREATEST HITS

1   "Mystery Train"
2   "Heartbreak Hotel"
3   "Good Rockin' Tonight"
4   "Jailhouse Rock"
5   "All Shook Up"
6   "Suspicious Minds"
7   "Hurt"
8   "Hound Dog"
9   "One Night" (from the NBC special Elvis)
10   "Milkcow Blues Boogie"
11   "How Great Thou Art"
12   "Viva Las Vegas"

13   "Are You Lonesome Tonight?"
14   "Little Sister"
15   "Wear My Ring Around Your Neck"
16   "(You're So Square) Baby, I Don't Care"
17   "Blue Christmas"
18   "Blue Suede Shoes"
19   "Tryin' to Get to You"
20   "Bridge over Troubled Water"

-◄❚▶-

THE 20 GREATEST ELVIS TITLES

1   "How Great Thou Art"
2   "Rock-a-Hula Baby"
3   "All Shook Up"
4   "Song of the Shrimp"
5   "Playing for Keeps"
6   "(There's) No Room to Rhumba in a Sports Car"
7   "Return to Sender"
8   "Fort Lauderdale Chamber of Commerce"
9   "Wearin' That Loved On Look"
10   "Do the Clam"
11   "Wear My Ring around Your Neck"
12   "Poison Ivy League"
13   "(Marie's the Name) His Latest Flame"
14   "Queenie Wahine's Papaya"
15   "(You're So Square) Baby, I Don't Care"
16   "He's Your Uncle, Not Your Dad"
17   "A Fool Such as I"
18   "I'm Left, You're Right, She's Gone"
19   "I Forgot to Remember to Forget"
20   "Who Are You (Who Am I)?"

NOTE: These are titles of songs that were actually recorded and released on official RCA discs—with the dog and everything—by Elvis during his lifetime.

50 ELVIS SONGS AND WHERE HE FOUND TH.

Elvis Presley is the only important rock and roll star who did not write any of his own songs. Instead, he made his mark as an interpreter—although his interpretations could sometimes be so drastic that they amounted to a rewrite of the song (e.g., "Milk Cow Blues," "Baby, Let's Play House"). This list shows the sources of some of the more interesting tunes Presley recorded, with the names of the original artist and the year that the first version appeared.

1   "And I Love You So," BOBBY GOLDSBORO, 1971
2   "Baby, Let's Play House," ARTHUR GUNTER, 1955
3   "Big Boss Man," JIMMY REED, 1961
4   "Blue Suede Shoes," CARL PERKINS, 1956
5   "Bridge over Troubled Water," SIMON AND GARFUNKEL, 1970
6   "Don't Think Twice, It's All Right," BOB DYLAN, 1963
7   "Fever," LITTLE WILLIE JOHN, 1956
8   "Good Rockin' Tonight," ROY BROWN, 1948
9   "Green Green Grass of Home," PORTER WAGONER, 1965
10 "He'll Have to Go," JIM REEVES, 1960
11 "Hi Heel Sneakers," TOMMY TUCKER, 1964
12 "I Can Help," BILLY SWAN, 1974
13 "I Feel So Bad," CHUCK WILLIS, 1954
14 "I Got a Woman," RAY CHARLES, 1955
15 "I Need You So," IVORY JOE HUNTER, 1950
16 "I've Got a Thing about You, Baby," BILLY LEE RILEY, 1972
17 "Lawdy, Miss Clawdy," LLOYD PRICE, 1952
18 "Little Darlin'," THE GLADIOLAS, 1957
19 "Little Egypt," THE COASTERS, 1961
20 "Love Letters," KETTY LESTER, 1962
21 "Love Me," WILLIE AND RUTH, 1954
22 "Merry Christmas Baby," JOHNNY MOORE'S THREE BLAZERS, 1949
23 "Milk Cow Blues," KOKOMO ARNOLD, 1935

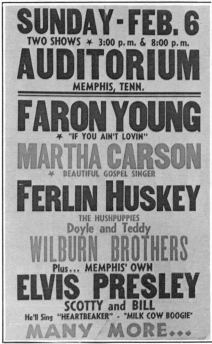

Announcement for one of Elvis' first public appearances in Memphis, 1955.

24 "Money Honey," THE DRIFTERS, 1953
25 "My Babe," LITTLE WALTER, 1955
26 "My Baby Left Me," ARTHUR CRUDUP, 1950
27 "My Boy," RICHARD HARRIS, 1971
28 "My Way," FRANK SINATRA, 1969
29 "Mystery Train," LITTLE JUNIOR'S BLUE FLAMES, 1953
30 "One Night," SMILEY LEWIS, 1956
31 "Pledging My Love," JOHNNY ACE, 1955
32 "Promised Land," CHUCK BERRY, 1964
33 "Reconsider Baby," LOWELL FULSON, 1954
34 "Shake, Rattle and Roll," JOE TURNER, 1954
35 "So Glad You're Mine," ARTHUR CRUDUP, 1946

36 "Soldier Boy," THE FOUR FELLOWS, 1955
37 "Steamroller Blues," JAMES TAYLOR, 1970
38 "Such a Night," THE DRIFTERS, 1954
39 "Tell Me Why," MARIE KNIGHT, 1956
40 "That's When Your Heartaches Begin," THE INK SPOTS, 1950
41 "There Goes My Everything," JACK GREEN, 1966
42 "Tomorrow Night," LONNIE JOHNSON, 1948
43 "Too Much," BERNARD HARDISON, 1954
44 "Too Much Monkey Business," CHUCK BERRY, 1956
45 "Tutti Frutti," LITTLE RICHARD, 1955
46 "Unchained Melody," ROY HAMILTON, 1955
47 "What'd I Say," RAY CHARLES, 1959
48 "White Christmas," BING CROSBY, 1942
49 "Witchcraft," THE SPIDERS, 1955
50 "You Don't Have to Say You Love Me," DUSTY SPRINGFIELD, 1966

-◄▮▮►-

ELVIS' MENTORS

1 THE BLACKWOOD BROTHERS
2 ARTHUR CRUDUP
3 THE GOLDEN GATE QUARTET
4 THE INKSPOTS
5 DEAN MARTIN
6 BILL MONROE
7 LITTLE JUNIOR PARKER
8 HANK SNOW
9 RUFUS THOMAS
10 HANK WILLIAMS
11 BOB WILLS AND THE TEXAS PLAYBOYS

-◄▮▮►-

ARTISTS WHO SANG ON ELVIS DEMOS

1 OTIS BLACKWELL
2 BRIAN HYLAND
3 P. J. PROBY

MUSICIANS WHO PLAYED WITH ELVIS

1 and 2 **SCOTTY MOORE, GUITAR; BILL BLACK, BASS**
Black and Moore were the original musicians to record with Elvis at Sun Records in Memphis, with Sam Phillips producing. On some of the later sessions, drummers were added, though they have never been identified.

3 **D. J. FONTANA, DRUMS**
Fontana joined Elvis as a touring musician, although he did record with him in Nashville for RCA, beginning with the January 1956 session that produced "Heartbreak Hotel."

4 and 5 **CHET ATKINS, GUITAR; FLOYD CRAMER, PIANO**
Atkins—who also served as the RCA producer—and Cramer were added as soon as Elvis began recording for RCA, in January of '56.

6, 7, and 8 **CARL PERKINS, GUITAR; JOHNNY CASH, GUITAR; JERRY LEE LEWIS, PIANO**
They performed with Elvis only on the fabled, and still unissued, Million Dollar Quartet sessions. Elvis reportedly plays piano and guitar on these sides.

9 **DUDLEY BROOKS, PIANO**
Brooks played on the West Coast studio sessions for many years.

10 **MIKE STOLLER, PIANO**
He appeared in the movie *Jailhouse Rock* and on at least some of the soundtrack recordings.

11 **"TINY" TIMBRELL, GUITAR**
Timbrell replaced Elvis as rhythm guitarist on Hollywood sessions beginning in February 1958.

12, 13, and 14 **HANK GARLAND, GUITAR; BOB MOORE, BASS; BUDDY HARMAN, DRUMS**
These are the Nashville cats who replaced Bill, Scotty, and eventually D. J. after Elvis joined the army and the original group was disbanded.

15 **BOOTS RANDOLPH, SAX**

16 **RAY SIEGEL,** BASS
17 **NEIL MATTHEWS,** GUITAR
Matthews was also a Jordanaire.
18 **HAL BLAINE,** DRUMS
19 **GORDON STOKER,** PIANO
He's another of The Jordanaires.
20 **JERRY KENNEDY,** GUITAR
Kennedy appeared on only two sessions and later went on to produce great sides with Jerry Lee Lewis and Charlie Rich.
21 **BARNEY KESSEL,** GUITAR
22 **GRADY MARTIN,** GUITAR
23 **HAROLD BRADLEY,** GUITAR
24 **DAVID BRIGGS,** ORGAN
25 **CHIP YOUNG,** GUITAR
26 **PETE DRAKE,** STEEL GUITAR
27 **JERRY SCHEFF,** BASS
Scheff, like Briggs, became a mainstay of Presley's touring band in the late sixties and throughout the seventies, although they both began recording with him earlier.
28 **CHARLIE McCOY,** GUITAR, KEYBOARDS, HARMONICA
29 **JERRY REED,** GUITAR
Reed dominated the singles "Guitar Man" and "U.S. Male."
30 **LARRY KNECTAL,** BASS
31 **TOM TEDESCO,** GUITAR
32 **DON RANDI,** KEYBOARDS
During the 1968–1969 "comeback," these and other Hollywood studio heavyweights frequently appeared on Elvis recordings. All were on the '68 TV special, for instance.
33 **TOMMY COGBILL,** GUITAR, BASS
34 **RONNIE MILSAP,** PIANO, VOCALS
35 **BOBBY EMMONS,** PIANO
Emmons is among the stalwarts featured on the epochal *Back in Memphis* sessions of 1969.
36 **JAMES BURTON,** GUITAR
Burton had made his reputation with Ricky Nelson. Beginning in 1969, he became the key figure in Presley's stage band.

37, 38, 39, and 40 **CHARLIE HODGE, GUITAR; JOHN WILKINSON, GUITAR; RONNIE TUTT, DRUMS; GLEN HARDIN, PIANO**
More stage-band mainstays.

41 and 42 **AL JACKSON, DRUMS; DONALD DUNN, BASS**
These two members of Booker T. and the MGs appear on only one finished and released track, "Girl of Mine."

43 **EMORY GORDY, BASS**

44 **DENNIS LINDE, BASS**
Linde is better known for writing "Burning Love" than for his instrumental work.

-◄❙▮❙►-

ELVIS' BACKING SINGERS

1 **THE JORDANAIRES**
They settled in as the backup vocal group on most sessions from 1956 until they split from Presley in 1969. The basic lineup was Gordon Stoker, Hoyt Hawkins, and Neal Matthews Jr. Hugh Jarrett was the bass singer until 1958, when Ray Walker replaced him.

2 **THE MELLO MEN**
The Mello Men backed Elvis on "Love Me Tender," his 1956 movie hit, which was recorded at a session for which The Jordanaires were unavailable.

3 **THE JUBILEE FOUR**
A black quartet made up of former members of The Jubalaires, a key forties spiritual group, they accompanied Elvis on "What'd I Say."

4 **THE GOLDEN GATE QUARTET**
Although they were never to record together, this greatest of all jubilee-style black·gospel groups sang with Presley during his army years in Germany. Certainly, those informal jam sessions must have made a major impact on Elvis, for when he returned to the U.S., he almost immediately recorded three of the eight songs the Golden Gates had released on a 1950 Columbia

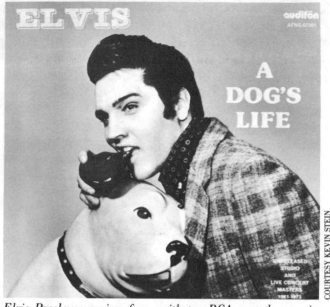

Elvis Presley currying favor with top RCA record executive, Nipper the Dog.

album: "I Will Be Home Again," "Swing Down, Sweet Chariot," and "Joshua Fit the Battle."

5 and 6 THE IMPERIALS; THE STAMPS QUARTET WITH J. D. SUMNER

Two outstanding white Southern spiritual groups who backed Elvis after The Jordanaires left.

7 and 8 MILLIE KIRKHAM; KATHY WESTMORELAND

They toured and recorded with Presley throughout the seventies.

9   VOICE

A studio and practice group, they were assembled by Elvis in the 1970s to play with him and be on twenty-four-hour call. They appear on some of his later sessions. Members included Donnie Sumner (J. D. Sumner's stepson), Sherrill Nielson (former lead singer of The Imperials), bass vocalist Tim Batey and pianist Tony Brown (who replaced Glen Hardin).

THE FILMS OF ELVIS PRESLEY
Graded and in Chronological Order

1   ***Love Me Tender*** (Twentieth Century-Fox), released November 1956; directed by Robert D. Webb, with Deborah Paget
Civil War yarn, lightweight romance, wimpy action—an appropriately inauspicious beginning: C

2   ***Loving You*** (Paramount), released July 1957; directed by Hal Kantor; with Lizabeth Scott, Wendell Corey, Dolores Hart
This set the mold: Scott discovers Presley and makes him a star. Elvis performs with more energy than he would later. There are some fine production numbers, especially the final one, in which his mother and father can be glimpsed in the audience, if you look hard: B

3   ***Jailhouse Rock*** (MGM), released October 1957; directed by Richard Thorpe; with Mickey Shaughnessy, Judy Tyler, Dean Jones, Vaughn Taylor
Elvis is jailed for assault, then meets Shaughnessy, who becomes his manager and makes him a singing sensation. High energy, perfect Leiber-Stoller score, decent script, marvelous choreography. One of the best: A −

4   ***King Creole*** (Paramount), released May 1958; directed by Michael Curtiz; with Carolyn Jones, Dolores Hart, Dean Jagger, Walter Matthau
This was based on the Harold Robbins novel *A Stone for Danny Fisher*. Given decent material (good script, snappy plot, several Leiber-Stoller songs) and a solid director (Curtiz did *Casablanca*), Elvis rises to the occasion, turning in his best performance in any of his flicks: A

5   ***G.I. Blues*** (Paramount), released October 1960; directed by Norman Taurog; with Juliet Prowse
A GI forms a combo. And the long descent begins. Now Presley will grind out his pictures, with hack directors like Taurog and inane plots like the above. Even The Presence

can't compensate, and it will soon wilt—through sheer boredom, perhaps: D

6   *Flaming Star* (Twentieth Century-Fox), released December 1960; directed by Don Siegel; with Barbara Eden, Steve Forrest, John McIntire, Delores Del Rio

One last gasp. This is overrated, both as a Siegel film and as a Presley vehicle: He looks lost, which helps in some scenes, but not all. Still, given Del Rio to act with, he comes through, proving that the boy could have been a contender. Alas, it wasn't in the cards: B

7   *Wild in the Country* (Twentieth Century-Fox), released June 1961; directed by Philip Dunne; with Hope Lange, John Ireland, Tuesday Weld, Gary Lockwood

Despite the anomaly of Elvis playing a writer, of all things, this shapes up pretty well: decent cast, adequate script, which as these things go, makes it above average: B −

8   *Blue Hawaii* (Paramount), released November 1961; directed by Norman Taurog; with Angela Lansbury, John Blackman, and Iris Adrian

The return of the hacks; his most successful picture, and not his worst, although it should have been: C −

9   *Follow That Dream* (United Artists), released March 1962; directed by Gordon Douglas; with Arthur O'Connell, Joanna Moore, Ann Helm

This was based on Richard Powell's *Pioneer Go Home*. Elvis and family migrate to Florida and try to homestead, despite opposition: C +

10 *Kid Galahad* (United Artists), released July 1962; directed by Phil Karlson; with Gig Young, Lola Albright, Charles Bronson, Joan Blackman

Remake of Michael Curtiz' 1937 version, which starred Edward G. Robinson and Humphrey Bogart. This is over-matched in comparison, and it wasn't one of the great boxing pictures to begin with. Still, Karlson's a good director, and the cast and script are above average for a Presley vehicle: B −

11   ***Girls! Girls! Girls!*** (Paramount), released November 1962; directed by Norman Taurog; with Stella Stevens, Jeremy Slate
Lives up to the title: F

12   ***It Happened at the World's Fair*** (MGM), released April 1963; directed by Norman Taurog; with Joan O'Brien, Gary Lockwood, Yvonne Craig
Taurog could ruin Alpo—but at least Alpo is all meat: D

13   ***Fun in Acapulco*** (Paramount), released November 1963; directed by Richard Thorpe; with Ursula Andress, Paul Lukas, Alejandro Ray
Thorpe did direct *Jailhouse Rock*, and despite the clichéd plot—you know, boy loses girl but has guitar to console him, but she comes back anyway, after both have suffered enough—this has a certain energy: C

14   ***Kissin' Cousins*** (MGM), released March 1964; directed by Gene Nelson; with Pamela Astin, Yvonne Craig, Arthur O'Connell
Elvis tries to convince yokel relative to allow a missile site to be placed on his homestead. Embarrassing and tedious: F

15   ***Viva Las Vegas*** (MGM), released April 1964; directed by George Sidney; with Ann-Margret, Cesare Denova, William Demarest
Oddly prophetic, with Elvis a reckless sports car racer in the town where he would squander even more of his talent than he did in Hollywood. Good score, though: C+

16   ***Roustabout*** (Paramount), released November 1964; directed by John Rich; with Barbara Stanwyck, Joan Freeman, Sue Ann Langdon
The usual plot, transferred to a carnival setting. Even Stanwyck can't save this one: C−

17   ***Girl Happy*** (MGM), released January 1965; directed by Boris Sagal; with Shelley Fabares, Mary Ann Mobley, Chris Noel, Joby Baker
Elvis chaperones Fabares, whose father is a mobster. What?! Stupid and dull: F

18 **Tickle Me** (Allied Artists), released June 1965; directed by Norman Taurog; with Jocelyn Lane, Julie Adams, Jack Mullaney

Dude ranch la-de-da. And I was about to say *Girl Happy* was enough to make you miss Norman Taurog. Wrong again: F

19 **Harum Scarum** (MGM), released December 1965; directed by Gene Nelson; with Mary Ann Mobley, Fran Jeffries

Even in the Middle East, the Presley plot grows boring. But at least this offers some variety: D −

20 **Frankie and Johnny** (United Artists), released July 1966; directed by Frederick De Cordova; with Donna Douglas, Harry Morgan, Sue Ann Langdon

The ballad set on a riverboat and fleshed out with girls, songs, and a couple of fights. Yawn: D

21 **Paradise, Hawaiian Style** (Paramount), released June 1966; directed by Michael Moore; with Suzanna Leigh, James Shigeta, Donna Butterworth

Sometimes, you had to wonder why Elvis didn't just quit. When he got around to recycling *Blue Hawaii*, as he did here, you realized (if you had any brains not turned to mush by what had come before) that he already had: F −

22 **Spinout** (MGM), released December 1966; directed by Norman Taurog; with Shelley Fabares, Deborah Walley

Maybe Elvis should have made one porno film, gotten laid for real, and then come back and gotten down to business. Could never have saved this, despite a decent soundtrack: D −

23 **Easy Come, Easy Go** (Paramount), released June 1967; directed by John Rich; with Elsa Lanchester, Pat Priest, Dodie Marshal

Elvis plays a frogman; even a fan could be forgiven for hoping that he did his own stunts: F

24 **Double Trouble** (MGM), released May 1967; directed by Norman Taurog; with Annette Day, John Williams, the Wiere Brothers

Set in mid-sixties London, it definitely does not swing: D −

25   *Clambake* (United Artists), released December 1967; directed by Arthur H. Nadel; with Shelley Fabares, Bill Bixby
Makes *Spinout* look like *Citizen Kane:* F

26   *Stay Away, Joe* (MGM), released March 1968; directed by Peter Tewksbury; with Burgess Meredith, John Blondell, L. Q. Jones
Social consciousness rears its ugly head! Stereotyped Indian rights flick with confused message and politics: F

27   *Speedway* (MGM), released June 1968; directed by Norman Taurog; with Nancy Sinatra, Bill Bixby, Gale Gordon
'Nuff said: F

28   *Live a Little, Love a Little* (MGM), released October 1968; directed by Norman Taurog; with Rudy Vallee, Eddie Hodges, Michele Carey
Good grief!: F

29   *Charro!* (National General Productions Inc.), released September 1969; directed by Charles Marquis Warren; with Lynn Kellogg
In which Elvis sings just one song, and we find out that bad music wasn't the only problem with the earlier pictures. Surprise, surprise: barely competent straight western action: C −

30   *The Trouble with Girls (And How to Get into It)* (MGM), released December 1969; directed by Peter Tewksbury; with Sheree North, Vincent Price, John Carradine
Elvis manages a Chautauqua company, in the 1920s. Above average: C +

31   *Change of Habit* (NBC-Universal), released January 1970; directed by William Graham; with Mary Tyler Moore
Icon meets icon, more so because Mary's a nun, torn between her vows and Elvis. Great last shot captures her indecision: C +

32   *Elvis: That's the Way It Is* (MGM), released December 1970; directed by Denis Sanders
Concert footage and backstage documentary: B −

33   ***Elvis on Tour*** (MGM), released 1972; directed by Pierre
     Adidge and Robert Abel
     Great concert footage, some historical intercutting. One of his
     best, and a worthy final theatrical fling: B+

-◄||►-

THE FATHER OF US ALL

1   "Without Elvis, none of us could have made it."—Buddy
     Holly
2   "It took people like Elvis to open the door for this kind of
     music, and I thank God for Elvis Presley."—Little Richard
3   "Gosh, he's so great. You have no idea how great he is, really
     you don't. You have no comprehension—it's absolutely impos-
     sible. I can't tell you why he's so great, but he is. He's
     sensational. He can do anything with his voice. He can sing
     anything you want him to, anyway you tell him. The unques-
     tionable King of rock 'n roll."—Phil Spector
4   "Elvis recorded a song of mine. That's the one recording I
     treasure most."—Bob Dylan
5   "I basically became a musician because of Elvis Presley."
     —John Lennon
6   "Elvis is my man."—Janis Joplin
7   "Elvis had animal magnetism. He was even sexy to guys. I
     can't imagine what the chicks used to think."—Ian Hunter
8   "He was the great living pop idol in the whole world."—Marc
     Bolan
9   "I grew up on a box of Elvis singles."—Tom Petty
10   "That Elvis, man, he is all there is. There ain't no more.
     Everything starts and ends with him. He wrote the book."
     —Bruce Springsteen

NINETEEN
THE BEATLES

The Beatles, 1969.

ON THE BEATLE TRAIL IN LIVERPOOL

The Beatle Trail is a tour suggested by the Liverpool City Council.

1   Take bus number 72, 73, or 80 along Princes Road to High Park Street, walk down to Ringo's house at 10 Admiral Grove.
2   Walk back to Princes Road and continue by bus number 72 along Menlove Avenue to Beaconsfield Road for Strawberry Fields. (As this is a children's home, we have been asked to request that visitors keep out of the home and off the grounds, which are private.)
3   Walk back to Menlove Avenue; 251 Menlove Avenue was John's house.
4   Continue along Menlove Avenue by bus number 72 to Mackets Lane; George lived at number 174.
5   Return to Penny Lane and take bus number 86 (destination Garston) along Mather Avenue to Forthlin Road. Paul lived at number 20.
6   Return to City Centre by bus number 86 (destination Pier Head).

-◀▮▶-

RECORD COMPANIES THAT TURNED DOWN THE BEATLES

1   Decca
2   Pye
3   Columbia
4   HMV
5   EMI

BEATLES TOURS
1963–1966

1963

The Helen Shapiro* tour of England with Danny Williams, Kenny Lynch, The Beatles, The Kestrels, The Red Price Orchestra

February 2	Gaumont, Bradford
February 3	Gaumont, Doncaster
February 4	Granada, Bedford
February 7	Odeon, Wakefield
February 8	ABC, Carlisle
February 9	Odeon, Sunderland
February 10	Embassy, Peterborough
February 23	Granada, Mansfield
February 24	Coventry Theatre, Coventry
February 26	Odeon, Taunton
February 27	Rialto, York
February 28	Granada, Shrewsbury
March 1	Odeon, Southport
March 2	City Hall, Sheffield
March 3	Gaumont, Hanley

The Beatles tour of Britain, with Gerry and the Pacemakers, Roy Orbison

May 18	Granada, Slough
May 19	Gaumont, Hanley
May 20	Gaumont, Southampton
May 22	Gaumont, Ipswich
May 23	Odeon, Nottingham
May 24	Granada, Walthamstow
May 25	City Hall, Sheffield
May 26	Empire, Liverpool
May 27	Capitol, Cardiff

*Shapiro, a British pop performer, headlined this tour.

May 28	Gaumont, Worcester
May 29	Rialto, York
May 30	Odeon, Manchester
May 31	Odeon, Southend
June 1	Granada, Tooting
June 2	Hippodrome, Brighton
June 3	Granada, Woolwich
June 4	Town Hall, Birmingham
June 5	Odeon, Leeds
June 7	Odeon, Glasgow
June 8	City Hall, Newcastle
June 9	King George Hall, Blackburn

The Beatles tour of Sweden (October 24–29)

The Beatles tour of Britain and Ireland, with Peter Jay and the Jaywalkers, The Brook Brothers

November 1	Gaumont, Cheltenham
November 2	City Hall, Sheffield
November 3	Odeon, Leeds
November 5	Adelphi, Slough
November 6	ABC, Northampton
November 7	Ritz, Dublin
November 8	Adelphi, Belfast
November 9	Granada, East Ham
November 10	Hippodrome, Birmingham
November 12	Guildhall, Portsmouth
November 13	ABC, Plymouth
November 14	ABC, Exeter
November 15	Colston Hall, Bristol
November 16	Winter Gardens, Bournemouth
November 17	Coventry Theatre, Coventry
November 19	Gaumont, Wolverhampton
November 20	Ardwick Apollo, Manchester

November 21	ABC, Carlisle
November 22	Globe, Stockton
November 23	City Hall, Newcastle
November 24	ABC, Hull
November 26	ABC, Cambridge
November 27	Rialto, York
November 28	ABC, Lincoln
November 29	ABC, Huddersfield
November 30	Empire, Sunderland
December 1	De Montfort Hall, Leicester
December 8	Odeon, Lewisham
December 9	Odeon, Southend
December 10	Gaumont, Doncaster
December 11	Futurist, Scarborough
December 12	Odeon, Nottingham
December 13	Gaumont, Southampton

1964

The Beatles at the Paris Olympia, with Trini Lopez and Sylvie Vartan (three weeks in January)

First American visit (February 7–21)

February 9	*The Ed Sullivan Show*
February 11	Coliseum, Washington, D.C.
February 12	Carnegie Hall, New York City
February 14	*The Ed Sullivan Show*
February 21	*The Ed Sullivan Show*

Denmark and Holland

June 4	Copenhagen
June 5	TV appearance, Amsterdam
June 6	Blokker Exhibition Hall, Amsterdam

Hong Kong, Australia, New Zealand

June 9	Hong Kong
June 12	Adelaide, Australia
June 15	Melbourne, Australia
June 18	Sydney, Australia
June 22	Wellington, New Zealand
June 23	Wellington
June 24	Auckland, New Zealand
June 25	Auckland
June 26	Christchurch, New Zealand
June 27	Christchurch
June 29	Brisbane, Australia

The U.S.A. and Canada

August 19	Cow Palace, San Francisco
August 20	Convention Hall, Las Vegas
August 21	Municipal Stadium, Seattle
August 22	Empire Stadium, Vancouver
August 23	Hollywood Bowl, Los Angeles
August 26	Red Rock Stadium, Denver
August 27	The Gardens, Cincinnati
August 28	Forest Hills Stadium, New York
August 30	Convention Hall, Atlantic City
September 2	Convention Hall, Philadelphia
September 3	State Fair Coliseum, Indianapolis
September 4	Auditorium, Milwaukee
September 5	International Amphitheatre, Chicago
September 6	Olympic Stadium, Detroit
September 7	Maple Leaf Gardens, Toronto
September 8	Forum, Montreal
September 11	Gator Bowl, Jacksonville
September 12	Boston Gardens, Boston
September 13	Civic Centre, Baltimore
September 14	Civic Arena, Pittsburgh

September 15	Public Auditorium, Cleveland
September 16	City Park Stadium, New Orleans
September 18	Memorial Coliseum, Dallas
September 20	Paramount Theatre, New York City

The Beatles tour of Britain and Northern Ireland, with Mary Wells, Tommy Quickly, Remo Four, Michael Haslam, The Rusticks, Bob Bain

October 9	Gaumont, Bradford
October 10	Leicester
October 11	Birmingham
October 13	Wigan
October 14	Ardwick
October 15	Stockton
October 16	Hull
October 19	Edinburgh
October 20	Dundee
October 21	Glasgow
October 22	Leeds
October 23	Kilburn, London
October 24	Walthamstow
October 25	Brighton
October 28	Exeter
October 29	Plymouth
October 30	Bournemouth
October 31	Ipswich
November 1	Finsbury Park
November 2	Belfast
November 4	Luton
November 5	Nottingham
November 6	Southampton
November 7	Cardiff
November 8	Liverpool
November 9	Sheffield
November 10	Bristol

1964–1965

The Beatles Christmas show at London's Hammersmith Odeon, with Freddie and the Dreamers, The Yardbirds, Elkie Brooks, Jimmy Saville, Mike Haslam, The Mike Cotton Sound (December 24 and January 18)

1965

Europe

June 20	Palais des Sports, Paris
June 22	Palais d'Hiver, Lyons
June 24	Velodromo Vigonelli, Milan
June 26	Palais des Sports, Genoa
June 27	Adriana Hotel, Rome
June 30	Palais des Fêtes, Nice
July 1	Jerez, Spain
July 2	Monumental Bullring, Madrid
July 3	Barcelona Bullring, Barcelona

America

August 14	*The Ed Sullivan Show,* with Cilla Black
August 15	Shea Stadium, New York City
August 16	Shea Stadium, New York City
August 17	Maple Leaf Stadium, Toronto
August 18	Atlanta Stadium, Atlanta
August 19	Sam Houston Coliseum, Houston
August 20	Comiskey Park, Chicago
August 21	Metropolitan Stadium, Minneapolis
August 22	Portland Coliseum, Portland
August 28	San Diego
August 29	Hollywood Bowl, Los Angeles
August 31	San Francisco

Britain

December 3	Odeon, Glasgow
December 4	City Hall, Newcastle

December 5	Empire, Liverpool
December 7	Ardwick Apollo, Manchester
December 8	City Hall, Sheffield
December 9	Odeon, Birmingham
December 10	Hammersmith Odeon, London
December 11	Finsbury Park Astoria, London
December 12	Capitol, Cardiff

1966

Germany, Japan, and the Philippines

June 24	Circus Krone, Munich
June 25	Grugahalle, Essen
June 26	Ernst Merck Halle, Hamburg
June 30	Budokan Hall, Tokyo
July 1	Budokan Hall, Tokyo
July 2	Budokan Hall, Tokyo
July 4	Araneta Coliseum, Manila

North America

August 12	International Amphitheatre, Chicago
August 13	Olympia Stadium, Detroit
August 14	Municipal Stadium, Cleveland
August 15	Washington Stadium, Washington, D.C.
August 16	Philadelphia Stadium, Philadelphia
August 17	Maple Leaf Gardens, Toronto
August 18	Suffolk Downs Racetrack, Boston
August 19	Memphis Coliseum, Memphis
August 20	Crosley Field, Cincinnati
August 21	Busch Stadium, St. Louis
August 23	Shea Stadium, New York City
August 24	Shea Stadium, New York City
August 25	Seattle Coliseum, Seattle
August 28	Dodger Stadium, Los Angeles
August 29	Candlestick Park, San Francisco

SONGS PERFORMED BY THE BEATLES AT THEIR FIRST U.S. CONCERT
Washington, D.C., February 11, 1964

1 "Twist and Shout"
2 "All My Loving"
3 "From Me to You"
4 "Roll over Beethoven"
5 "I Saw Her Standing There"
6 "This Boy"
7 "I Want to Hold Your Hand"
8 "Till There Was You"
9 "Please Please Me"
10 "I Wanna Be Your Man"
11 "Long Tall Sally"
12 "She Loves You"

·◄❙▮❙►·

NEW FACTS ON THE FAB 4
From "Fabulous Magazine," 1965

1 John flew to Hong Kong wearing pajamas.
2 John is a cat lover.
3 Ringo spent much of his childhood in a Cheshire hospital.
4 John used to envy his cousin Stanley's Meccano set.
5 Brian Epstein hesitated a long time before taking Ringo as a replacement for Pete Best.
6 George is afraid of flying.
7 George has bought a bow and arrow.
8 Patti Boyd didn't like The Beatles before she met them on the set of *A Hard Day's Night*.
9 John's father was a singer on prewar Atlantic liners.
10 Ringo's stepfather, Harry Graves, sings Beatles songs at family parties.

Life-lines of the BEATLES

	JOHN	PAUL	GEORGE	RINGO (STARR)
Real name :	John Lennon	Paul McCartney	George Harrison	Richard Starkey
Birth date :	October 9, 1940.	June 18, 1942.	February 25, 1942.	July, 7, 1940.
Birthplace :	Liverpool.	Liverpool.	Liverpool.	Liverpool.
Height :	5 ft. 11 in.	5 ft. 11 in.	5 ft. 11 in.	5 ft. 8 in.
Weight :	11 st. 5 lb.	11 st. 4 lb.	10 st. 2 lb.	9 st. 8 lb.
Colour of eyes :	Brown.	Hazel.	Dark brown.	Blue.
Colour of hair :	Brown.	Black.	Brown.	Dark brown.
Brothers, sisters :	None.	Mike.	Louise, Peter and Harry.	None.
Instruments played :	Rhythm guitar, harmonica, percussion, piano.	Bass guitar, drums, piano, banjo.	Guitar, piano, drums.	Drums, guitar.
Educated :	Quarry Bank Grammar and Liverpool College of Art.	Liverpool Institute High School.	Liverpool Institute High School.	Liverpool Secondary Modern, Riverdale Technical College.
Age entered show business :	20.	18.	17.	18.
Former occupation :	Art student.	Student.	Student.	Engineer.
Hobbies :	Writing songs, poems and plays; girls, painting, TV, meeting people.	Girls, songwriting, sleeping.	Driving, records, girls.	Night-driving, sleeping, Westerns.
Favourite singers :	Shirelles, Miracles, Chuck Jackson, Ben E. King.	Ben E. King, Little Richard, Chuck Jackson.	Little Richard, Eartha Kitt.	Brook Benton, Sam "Lightning" Hopkins.
Favourite actors :	Robert Mitchum, Peter Sellers.	Larry Williams, Marlon Brando, Tony Perkins.	Vic Morrow.	Paul Newman, Jack Palance.
Favourite actresses :	Juliette Greco, Sophia Loren.	Brigitte Bardot, Juliette Greco.	Brigitte Bardot.	Brigitte Bardot.
Favourite foods :	Curry and jelly.	Chicken Maryland.	Lamb chops, chips.	Steak.
Favourite drinks :	Whisky and tea.	Milk.	Tea.	Whisky.
Favourite clothes :	Sombre.	Good suits, suede.	Anything.	Suits.
Favourite band :	Quincy Jones.	Billy Cotton.	Duane Eddy group.	Arthur Lyman.
Favourite instrumentalist :	Sonny Terry, Luther Dixon.	None special.	Chet Atkins.	None special.
Favourite composers :		Goffin-King.	None special.	Bert Bacharach, McCartney and Lennon.
Likes :	Blondes, leather.	Music, TV.	Driving.	Fast cars.
Dislikes :	Stupid people.	Shaving.	Haircuts.	Onions and Donald Duck.
Tastes in music :	R-and-b, gospel.	R-and-b, modern jazz.	Spanish guitar, c-and-w.	C-and-w, r-and-b.
Personal ambitions :	To write musical.	To have my picture in the " Dandy."	To design a guitar.	To be happy.
Professional ambition :	To be rich and famous.	To popularise our sound.	To fulfil all group's hopes.	To get to the top.

COURTESY KEVIN STEIN

11   The Beatles never visit a barber.

12   Paul washes his hair every day.

13   The Beatles turned down the offer of an appearance on the 1964 *Royal Variety Show*.

14   Ringo cannot swim, except for a brief doggie paddle.

15   Brian Epstein made The Beatles have their hair cut short after he signed them in 1962.

16   They are never photographed with their hair "up."

17   Paul ate cornflakes and bacon and eggs at a champagne and caviar luncheon in London. Music publisher Dick James was host.

18   The Beatles didn't want to go to Australia without Ringo when he was ill. But Brian Epstein persuaded them to change their minds.

19   Paul has a Mini as well as an Aston Martin DB 4.

20   George's personal Christmas card was a photograph of him scowling at a cameraman.

21   John never saw an audience properly until Dundee in Scotland. Then he wore contact lenses.

22   An American firm wrote to The Beatles asking if they could market The Beatles' bath water at a dollar a bottle.

23   They refused the offer.

24   Their road manager, Mal Evans, was once a bouncer at the Liverpool Cavern Club.

25   Neil Aspinall, their other road manager, was given a Jaguar last Christmas—a present from The Beatles.

26   Paul drinks coffee for breakfast. The other three drink tea—even in America.

27   Ringo had his new clothes designed by a woman, Caroline Charles.

28   Jane Asher bought Paul a record player for his Aston Martin.

29   Brian Epstein says, "America discovered Ringo."

30   Paul believes he is not a very good guitarist.

31   None of The Beatles drinks Scotch and Coke. They now dilute the occasional spirit with lemonade.

32   John told an American journalist that U.S. fashions were five years behind the U.K.

33   The Beatles never really liked jelly babies. They just said they did for a joke.

34   They carry a crate of pop in the trunk of their Austin Princess.

35   Their new chauffeur, Alf Bicknell, used to drive for David Niven and Cary Grant.

36   Burt Lancaster has sent Ringo a set of pistols. They became friends in Hollywood.

37   Burt let them use his home for a showing of *A Shot in the Dark*.

38   Edward G. Robinson and his grandchild twice joined the queue to shake hands with The Beatles at their Hollywood garden party.

39   So did Mrs. Dean Martin and her five children.

40   The Beatles have no pockets in their trousers and only two side pockets in their jackets. Paul designed them.

41   All they carry on them in the way of money is a few bank notes.

42   John has bought his mother-in-law a house near his own in Surrey.

43   None of The Beatles wears undershirts.

44   Paul wants to buy a farm.

·◄▮►·

THE BEATLES' TOP 40 GREATEST HITS

1   "She Loves You"
2   "Ticket to Ride"
3   "I'm Down"
4   "Money (That's What I Want)"
5   "Twist and Shout"
6   "Don't Let Me Down"

7   "I Saw Her Standing There"
8   "Strawberry Fields Forever"
9   "I Feel Fine"
10   "A Hard Day's Night"
11   "A Day in the Life"
12   "Long Tall Sally"
13   "Revolution" (45 version)
14   "Helter Skelter"
15   *Abbey Road* (side two)
16   "Help!"
17   "Back in the USSR"
18   "I Am the Walrus"
19   "We Can Work It Out"
20   "Paperback Writer"
21   "Got to Get You into My Life"
22   "Please Please Me"
23   "Norwegian Wood"
24   "Can't Buy Me Love"
25   "Boys"
26   "She Said She Said"
27   "Yer Blues"
28   "Lady Madonna"
29   "Get Back"
30   "Eight Days a Week"
31   "Penny Lane"
32   "Sgt. Pepper's Lonely Hearts Club Band"
33   "Slow Down"
34   "Dear Prudence"
35   "Anytime at All"
36   "Tomorrow Never Knows"
37   "Day Tripper"
38   "I've Just Seen a Face"
39   "You've Got to Hide Your Love Away"
40   "I Want You (She's So Heavy)"

BEATLES SINGLES THAT DIDN'T MAKE THE TOP 10

B-Sides Not Included

1 "Ain't She Sweet," 1964
2 "All My Loving," 1964*
3 "And I Love Her," 1964
4 "I'll Cry Instead"/"I'm Happy Just to Dance with You," 1964
5 "Matchbox"/"Slow Down," 1964
6 "My Bonnie," 1964**
7 "Roll over Beethoven," 1964*
8 "Sie Liebt Dich," 1964†
9 "Why?" 1964**

* Canadian releases that made the U.S. chart
**With Tony Sheridan
† German version of "She Loves You"

·◀▮▶·

GAMES BEATLES PLAY

1 **"Baby, You're a Rich Man,"** 1967
Rumor has it that at the end of this song, The Beatles sing, "Baby, you're a rich fag Jew," perhaps a slur on their manager, Brian Epstein, who was certainly Jewish, definitely wealthy, and probably gay.

2 **"Girl,"** 1965
The background singers are repeating the syllable *tit*.

3 **"I Am the Walrus,"** 1967
John Lennon included cryptic chanting and a portion of Shakespeare's *King Lear* at the end of the song.

4 **"I'm Only Sleeping,"** 1966
The guitar solo was recorded straight, then overdubbed onto the tape backward.

5   **"I Feel Fine,"** 1964
    Lennon claimed that at the beginning of this song, he plays the first deliberately recorded guitar feedback in history.

6   **"Norwegian Wood,"** 1965
    George Harrison debuts the sitar as a rock and roll instrument.

7   **"Paperback Writer,"** 1966
    The backing voices sing "Frère Jacques."

8   **"Rain,"** 1966
    Lennon used the vocal track for the last verse backward.

9   **"Strawberry Fields Forever,"** 1967
    Lennon says "cranberry sauce"; millions have believed he says "I buried Paul."

10 **"Yellow Submarine,"** 1966
    At the end of the section where the strange spoken voice repeats the lyrics, Ringo seems to sing "slubmarine."

-◄▐▐►-

25 SONGS ABOUT THE BEATLES

1   **"All I Want for Christmas Is a Beatle,"** DORA BRYAN
    Amazingly enough, the surge of Beatlemania that erupted on their arrival in the U.S. in February 1964 lasted long enough to produce this Beatles-oriented Christmas disc the next winter.

2   **"The Beatles' Barber,"** SCOTT DOUGLAS
    A real weeper.

3   **"Beatle Beat,"** ELLA FITZGERALD
    An old-timer tries to catch up.

4   **"Beatle Flying Saucer,"** ED SOLOMON
    This punch-in pastiche takes up where Buchanan and Goodman's original "Flying Saucer" left off. Buchanan had his own say. (See No. 16.)

5   **"A Beatle I Want to Be,"** SONNY CURTIS
    A tribute from one of Buddy Holly's Crickets.

6   **"Bring Back The Beatles,"** DAVID PEEL
The weird denizen of New York's Lower East Side recorded this after his short-lived association with John Lennon (which resulted in one album by Peel for Apple Records).

7   **"Early 1970,"** RINGO STARR
The B-side to "It Don't Come Easy" is Ringo's tribute to his mates, in which he describes his relationship to each of the others in musical terms. It's lovingly mournful and the one disc here that isn't exploitative.

8   **"Frankenstein Meets The Beatles,"** JEKYLL AND HYDE
Another "Flying Saucer"-style parody disc.

9   **"The Guy with the Long Liverpool Hair,"** THE OUT-
SIDERS
From the frat-rock band, which the British Invasion was about to render outmoded.

10 **"I Hate The Beatles,"** ALLAN SHERMAN
The most famous of the anti-longhair songs. History has told the story: Paul McCartney got a bigger obituary than Allan Sherman without dying.

11 **"I Love You, Ringo,"** BONNIE JO MASON
The most interesting thing about this curio of the past is that Mason went on to stardom as Cher.

12 **"I Wanna Be a Beatle,"** GENE CORNISH AND THE UNBEAT-
ABLES
Cornish and friends made it, too. Within a year, they were stars as The Young Rascals.

13 **"I Want to Kiss Ringo Goodbye,"** PENNY VALENTINE
Valentine was and is a British pop journalist.

14 **"I'll Let You Hold My Hand,"** THE BOOTLES
Answer song to a question never asked.

15 **"I'm Better Than The Beatles,"** BRAD BERWICK AND THE
BUGS
Sheer megalomania.

16 **"The Invasion,"** BUCHANAN AND GREENFIELD
The original flying saucer man (Dickie Goodman) strikes again.

17   **"Little Beatle Boy,"** THE ANGELS
      Beatles tribute from the "My Boyfriend's Back" bunch.

18   **"A Letter from Elaina,"** CASEY KASEM
      Unctuous sentimentality from one of the world's lamest Top
      Forty DJs.

19   **"My Boyfriend Got a Beatle Haircut,"** DONNA LYNN
      Arguably the best of the Beatles fan songs, because Lynn
      could sing a little bit. Also a prime example of how show biz
      devours its own: This Beatles exploitation effort was issued on
      Capitol, The Beatles' own label.

20   **"My Girlfriend Wrote a Letter to The Beatles,"** THE
      FOUR PREPS
      This pop singing group probably wished this were the full
      extent of their problems.

21   **"Saga of The Beatles,"** JOHNNY AND THE HURRICANES
      Tribute from the famous instrumental group.

22   **"Treat Him Tender, Maureen,"** ANGIE AND THE CHIC-
      LETTES
      Premature bubblegum group mourns Ringo's marriage.

23   **"We Love The Beatles,"** THE VERNON GIRLS
      Inferior attempt to copy No. 24.

24   **"We Love You Beatles,"** THE CAREFREES
      The only about-The-Beatles disc to make the Top Forty, this
      hit Number Thirty-nine in April 1964. It was a recorded
      version of the chant Beatlemaniacs sent up outside the Plaza
      Hotel, where the group stayed on their first New York visit.

25   **"Yes, You Can Hold My Hand,"** THE BEATLETTES
      Further evidence that it was going to take the music business
      awhile to adjust.

20 BEATLES SONGS WRITTEN ABOUT OR INSPIRED BY REAL PEOPLE AND PLACES

1   **"And I Love Her"**
Written by Paul about Jane Asher, his girlfriend during the mid-1960s.

2   **"Baby, You're a Rich Man"**
Written by Paul and John about Beatles manager Brian Epstein.

3   **"Blue Jay Way"**
Written by George while waiting for Derek Taylor to come to the house he was staying at in Los Angeles (on a street called Blue Jay Way) in the early summer of 1967.

4   **"A Day in the Life"**
John was inspired by the death of a friend, Tara Brown, who "blew his mind out in a car"; it has also been said that Lennon read a newspaper item about such a person, but not someone he knew.

5   **"Dear Prudence"**
Written by John for Mia Farrow's sister.

6   **"Dr. Robert"**
Written by John and Paul about a doctor they had heard of who supposedly prescribed pills freely for his star clients.

7   **"For the Benefit of Mr. Kite"**
John and Paul were inspired by British carnival figures.

8   **"Hey Jude"**
Written by Paul about John's son Julian.

9   **"I Am the Walrus"**
The Walrus was Paul. (We're pretty sure.)

10   **"I'm Looking Through You"**
Another song Paul wrote about Jane Asher.

11   **"Julia"**
Written by John and Paul for Julia Lennon, John's mother, who died while he was still a teenager. She also would inspire the *Plastic Ono Band* song "Mother."

7   **"Martha My Dear"**
     Written by Paul about Martha, his English sheep dog.

13   **"Norwegian Wood"**
     Written by John about a woman with whom he had had an affair; he was afraid to tell Cynthia, his first wife, but decided he had to get the story out somehow.

14   **"Penny Lane"**
     Written by Paul and John about people they had known on the Liverpool street of the same name.

15   **"Sgt. Pepper's Lonely Hearts Club Band"**
     John and Paul were inspired by British carnival figures.

16   **"Sexy Sadie"**
     Written by John about Maharishi Mahesh Yogi, the original lyric was more direct, but when it came time to record the song, Lennon changed the words.

17   **"She Said She Said"**
     John and Paul were inspired by a comment made by Peter Fonda while he and Lennon were tripping on acid: He said, "I know what it's like to be dead."

18   **"Taxman"**
     Written by George about the general economic situation in Britain but with special emphasis on the two most recent prime ministers, Edward Heath and Harold Wilson, both of whom are mentioned in the song.

19   **"When I'm Sixty-four"**
     Written by John and Paul for James McCartney, Paul's father.

20   **"You Never Give Me Your Money"**
     Considered to be a McCartney reference to the debacle with Allen Klein.

10 CELEBRITIES WHO SIGNED JOHN LENNON'S IMMIGRATION PETITION

In the early seventies, when the Nixon regime denied John Lennon status as an important artist, which would have allowed him permanent residency in the U.S., Lennon entered into a legal dispute that dragged on until October 9, 1975, John's thirty-fifth birthday and also the birth date of his son Sean. Among those who signed the petition sent to the U.S. Immigration and Naturalization Service attesting to the value of Lennon's artistic achievements were the following:

1	FRED ASTAIRE	6	ALLEN GINSBERG
2	SAUL BELLOW	7	JACK LEMMON
3	LEONARD BERNSTEIN	8	HENRY MILLER
4	BOB DYLAN	9	VIRGIL THOMSON
5	LAWRENCE FER-LINGHETTI	10	KURT VONNEGUT JR.

-◄▮►-

GEORGE HARRISON'S RECORDING PSEUDONYMS

1 **L'Angelo Misterioso**
   "Badge," CREAM; plays rhythm guitar, wrote song with Eric Clapton
   "Never Tell Your Mother She's Out of Tune," JACK BRUCE; plays rhythm guitar

2 **Son of Harry**
   "If You've Got Love," DAVE MASON; plays guitar

© JÜRGEN VOLLMER/CHAMBERS AGENCY

George Harrison in Hamburg, Germany, 1961.

3   Hari Georgeson

China Light, SPLINTER; plays acoustic guitar, mandolin

"Costafine Town," SPLINTER; plays bass, eight-string bass

"Drink All Day," SPLINTER; plays six- and twelve-string guitar, Dobro

"Elly-May," SPLINTER; plays acoustic guitar

"Gravy Train," SPLINTER; plays guitar

"Haven't Got Time," SPLINTER; plays guitar

"The Place I Love," SPLINTER; plays acoustic and electric guitar

Shankar Family and Friends; plays acoustic and electric guitar, autoharp

"Situation Vacant," SPLINTER; plays guitar
"Somebody's City," SPLINTER; plays six- and twelve-string guitar, electric guitar
"That's Life," BILLY PRESTON; plays guitar
"Lonely Man," SPLINTER; plays guitar

4   George O'Hara Smith
"I'm Your Spiritual Breadman," ASHTON, GARDNER, AND DYKE; plays electric swivel guitar

5   Jai Raj Harisein
"Costafine Town," SPLINTER; plays percussion
"Drink All Day," SPLINTER; plays percussion
"Haven't Got Time," SPLINTER; plays percussion
"The Place I Love," SPLINTER; plays percussion
"Somebody's City," SPLINTER; plays percussion

6   George Harrysong
"You're Breaking My Heart," HARRY NILSSON; plays slide guitar

7   George H.
"I Wrote a Simple Song," BILLY PRESTON; plays lead guitar

8   P. Roducer
"Costafine Town," SPLINTER; plays harmonium
"Drink All Day," SPLINTER; plays harmonium and jew's harp
"Elly-May," SPLINTER; plays Moog synthesizer

9   The George O'Hara-Smith Singers
All Things Must Pass, GEORGE HARRISON; overdubbed vocals under pseudonym

10   George O'Hara
"Banana Anna," NICKY HOPKINS; plays guitar
"Edward," NICKY HOPKINS; plays guitar

Footprint, GARY WRIGHT; plays guitar and slide guitar
"Speed On," NICKY HOPKINS; plays lead guitar
"Waiting for the Band," NICKY HOPKINS; plays slide guitar

-◄❚▶-

WE CAN WORK IT OUT
Musical Comments on the Breakup

1   **"Early 1970,"** RINGO STARR, 1971
    The B-side of "It Don't Come Easy," describes the band members' willingness to play music with Ringo when he sees them. He seems most distanced from Paul, closest to John, miserable about the entire situation.

2   **"Too Many People,"** PAUL MCCARTNEY, 1971
    John Lennon, at least, interpreted these lyrics as a subtle attack on him and as McCartney's way of shifting the blame for the breakup onto John's shoulders. It's from the album *Ram*.

3   **"How Do You Sleep?"** JOHN LENNON, 1971
    A direct hit on McCartney, this song was included on *Imagine,* which features a picture of John pulling a pig's ears, an apparent reference to McCartney's photo on the cover of *Ram*. Not exactly subtle.

4   **"Back Off Boogaloo,"** RINGO STARR, 1972
    This single was taken by many to be Ringo's attempt at conciliating the Lennon-McCartney feud. It didn't help much.

5   **"Sue Me, Sue You Blues,"** GEORGE HARRISON, 1973
    George, of all people, has the last word on the breakup with this song about legal entanglements and resulting bad vibes.

TWENTY: DYLAN

Young Bob Dylan.

BOB DYLAN'S 20 GREATEST HITS

1   "Like a Rolling Stone"
2   "Ballad of a Thin Man"
3   "Visions of Johanna"
4   "Just Like Tom Thumb's Blues" (live version—B-side of "I
    Want You")
5   "Most Likely You Go Your Way and I'll Go Mine"
6   "All along the Watchtower"
7   "I Shall Be Released"
8   "Stuck Inside of Mobile with the Memphis Blues Again"
9   "This Wheel's on Fire"
10 "A Hard Rain's A-Gonna Fall"
11 "Subterranean Homesick Blues"
12 "Positively 4th Street"
13 "I Want You"
14 "Please Crawl out Your Window"
15 "Mr. Tambourine Man"
16 "I Shall Be Free #10"
17 "I Don't Believe You" (electric concert version)
18 "Tangled Up in Blue"
19 "She's Your Lover Now" (unreleased)
20 "When I Paint My Masterpiece"

-◄❙▮❙►-

35 BOB DYLAN PROTEST SONGS

1   "A Hard Rain's A-Gonna Fall"
2   "The Ballad of Donald White"
3   "The Ballad of Emmett Till"
4   "Blowin' in the Wind"
5   "Chimes of Freedom"
6   "Cuban Blockade (World War No. 3)"
7   "The Gates of Eden"

8   "George Jackson"
9   "Hollis Brown"
10   "Hurricane"
11   "I Shall Be Free"
12   "I Shall Be Free #10"
13   "I'd Hate to Be You on That Dreadful Day"
14   "Idiot Wind"
15   "It's All Right Ma (I'm Only Bleeding)"
16   "Let Me Die in My Footsteps (I Will Not Go Down under the
       Ground)"
17   "The Lonesome Death of Hattie Carroll"
18   "Maggie's Farm"
19   "Masters of War"
20   "My Back Pages"
21   "North Country Blues"
22   "Only a Pawn in Their Game"
23   "Oxford Town"
24   "Paths of Victory"
25   "Percy's Song"
26   "Slow Train"
27   "Talkin' John Birch Society Blues"
28   "Talking Bear Mountain Picnic Massacre Disaster Blues"
29   "Talking World War III Blues"
30   "The Times They Are A Changin' "
31   "Walls of Redwing"
32   "When the Ship Comes In"
33   "Who Killed Davey Moore?"
34   "With God on Our Side"
35   "Ye Playboys and Playgirls"

-◄▮►-

BOB DYLAN'S 25 BEST SONG TITLES

1   "Absolutely Sweet Marie"
2   "A Hard Rain's A-Gonna Fall"

3   "All along the Watchtower"
4   "Ballad of a Thin Man"
5   "Please Crawl out Your Window"
6   "I Dreamed I Saw St. Augustine"
7   "It Takes a Lot to Laugh, It Takes a Train to Cry"
8   "Just Like Tom Thumb's Blues"
9   "Killing Me Alive"
10 "Leopard-skin Pill-box Hat"
11 "Like a Rolling Stone"
12 "Stuck Inside of Mobile with the Memphis Blues Again"
13 "Mixed Up Confusion"
14 "Motorpsycho Nightmare"
15 "Most Likely You Go Your Way and I'll Go Mine"
16 "Nothing Was Delivered"
17 "Obviously 5 Believers"
18 "Positively 4th Street"
19 "Subterranean Homesick Blues"
20 "Talking Bear Mountain Picnic Massacre Disaster Blues"
21 "Tears of Rage"
22 "Temporary Like Achilles"
23 "This Wheel's on Fire"
24 "Turkey Chase"
25 "Yazoo Street Scandal"

-◄►-

SHE'S YOUR LOVER NOW
The 15 Best Bob Dylan Cover Versions

1   "All along the Watchtower," JIMI HENDRIX
2   "The Mighty Quinn," MANFRED MANN
3   "Mr. Tambourine Man," THE BYRDS
4   "Tears of Rage," THE BAND
5   "It's All Over Now, Baby Blue," THEM
6   "Blowin' in the Wind," STEVIE WONDER
7   "Percy's Song," FAIRPORT CONVENTION

8   "Like a Rolling Stone," JIMI HENDRIX
9   "A Hard Rain's A-Gonna Fall," BRYAN FERRY
10   "Only a Hobo," ROD STEWART
11   "Tomorrow is a Long Time," ELVIS PRESLEY
12   "It Ain't Me Babe," THE TURTLES
13   "My Back Pages," THE BYRDS
14   "You Angel You," MANFRED MANN'S EARTH BAND
15   "Sign on the Cross," COULSON, DEAN, McGUINESS, FLINT

-◄❚▶-

BOB DYLAN ON OTHER PEOPLE'S RECORDS

1   HARRY BELAFONTE, *The Midnight Special;* plays harmonica on
     the title track
2   DAVID BLUE, *Com'n Back for More;* plays harmonica on "Who
     Love"
3   BOOKER T. and PRISCILLA JONES, *Chronicles;* plays harmonica
     on "Crippled Cow"
4   ERIC CLAPTON, *No Reason to Cry;* sings duet with Clapton on
     "Sign Language"
5   LEONARD COHEN, *Death of a Ladies' Man;* sings background
     vocals on two tracks
6   RAMBLIN' JACK ELLIOTT, *Jack Elliott;* plays harmonica on
     "Will the Circle Be Unbroken," under the name of Tedham
     Porterhouse
7   RICHARD FARIÑA and ERIC VON SCHMIDT, *Dick Farina and
     Eric von Schmidt;* plays harmonica and sings backing vocals on
     four songs under the name Blind Boy Grunt
8   STEVE GOODMAN, *The Essential Steve Goodman;* plays piano
     and sings backup vocals on "Election Year Rag" and "Some-
     body Else's Troubles" (the latter also on the album of the same
     name), with Dylan identified as Robert Milkwood Thomas
9   GEORGE HARRISON, "Miss O'Dell"; rumored to play harmon-
     ica; also did backing vocals on *All Things Must Pass*

© 1981 JIM MARSHALL

Dylan and Johnny Cash—a famous union.

10 CAROLYN HESTER, *Carolyn Hester;* plays harmonica on three tracks

11 ROGER MCGUINN, *Roger McGuinn;* plays harp on "I'm So Restless"

12 BETTE MIDLER, *Songs for the New Depression;* does backing vocals on "Buckets of Rain"

13 TOM RUSH, *Take a Little Walk with Me;* rumored to play piano on three songs under the name Roosevelt Cook

14 DOUG SAHM AND BAND, *Doug Sahm;* plays harp, organ, and guitar as well as sings with Sahm on five tracks, including the single, "San Antone"

15 EARL SCRUGGS, *Earl Scruggs: His Family and Friends;* jams on "Nashville Skyline Rag"

16 VICTORIA SPIVEY, *Three Kings and the Queen;* sings backup vocals and plays harp on "Sitting on Top of the World" and harp on "Wichita"; on *Two Kings and the Queen*, plays harp on "It's Dangerous," "Big Joe," and "Victoria"

"THE BASEMENT TAPES"

Recorded in the summer and early autumn of 1967, in the basement of the house now known as Big Pink, in West Saugerties, New York (near but not in Woodstock), The Basement Tapes remained unreleased until 1975. They are Dylan's final burst of sixties rock and roll, before the release of John Wesley Harding *steered him in other directions.*

1   "Million Dollar Bash"
2   "Yea! Heavy and a Bottle of Bread"
3   "Please, Mrs. Henry"
4   "Down in the Flood," also known as "Crash on the Levee"
5   "Lo and Behold"
6   "Tiny Montgomery"
7   "This Wheel's on Fire"
8   "You Ain't Goin' Nowhere"
9   "I Shall Be Released"*
10   "Too Much of Nothing" (released, but only one of two takes)
11   "Tears of Rage"
12   "The Mighty Quinn"* (two takes available; "Quinn" does appear on LP cover)
13   "Nothing Was Delivered" (another take exists)
14   "Open the Door, Homer" (two other takes exist)
15   "Apple Suckling Tree"
16   "Clothes Line Saga," also known as "Talkin' Clothes Line Blues"
17   "I'm Not There,"* (unreleased probably because the song was never finished)
18   "Odds and Ends"
19   "Get Your Rocks Off"*
20   "Sign on the Cross"*
21   "Don't Ya Tell Henry"
22   "Going to Acapulco"

*Still unreleased

23 "Orange Juice Blues (Blues for Breakfast)" (Richard Manuel, lead vocals)
24 "Yazoo Street Scandal" (Levon Helm, lead vocals)
25 "Katie's Been Gone"** (Richard Manuel, lead vocals)
26 "Bessie Smith" (Rick Danko and Robbie Robertson, lead vocals)
27 "Ain't No More Cane" (Levon Helm and Richard Manuel, group vocals; Rick Danko, lead vocals)
28 "Ruben Remus" (Richard Manuel, lead vocals)
29 "Don't Ya Tell Henry" (Levon Helm, lead vocals)
30 "Long Distance Operator" (Richard Manuel, lead vocals)
31 "Ferdinand the Imposter"* (Richard Manuel, lead vocals)

-◄❙▶-

Bob DYLAN'S BACKING BANDS

1 *Freewheelin'*, 1963
   Dylan isn't usually considered to have gone "electric" until his fifth album, *Bringing It All Back Home*, but two songs on his second album, *Freewheelin'* (as well as several outtakes), feature backing groups led by guitarist Bruce Langhorne. The other players included pianist Dick Wellstood, bassists George Barnes and Gene Ramey, guitarist Howie Collins, and drummer Herb Lovelle. Incidentally, one of the outtakes, "Mixed Up Confusion," makes fair claim to being Dylan's first recorded rock and roll number. It's a sort of Little Richard tune.

2 *Bringing It All Back Home*, 1964
   Side one is almost all electric, but aside from Bruce Langhorne on guitar, the musicians are unknown, though it is possible that some of the musicians on *Highway 61 Revisited* are also featured here, since producer Tom Wilson was instrumental in assembling both bands.

3 *Newport Folk Festival*, 1965
   Dylan did several songs with The Paul Butterfield Blues Band

(Mike Bloomfield, guitar; Sam Lay, drums; Mark Naftalin, keyboards; and Jerome Arnold, bass) until he was booed off the stage by folk purists.

4   ***Highway 61 Revisited,*** 1965

This time, the musicians are credited: Bloomfield and Charlie McCoy, guitar; Al Kooper and Paul Griffin, organ and piano; Frank Owens, piano; Harvey Goldstein and Russ Savakus, bass; and the redoubtable Bobby Gregg, drums. Bloomfield was surely Dylan's choice; he knew him from the Butterfield band. The others are session pros, probably brought aboard primarily by Tom Wilson, the producer.

5   **1965–1966 tour**

Dylan toured with The Hawks, but not with Levon and the Hawks. Drummer-vocalist Levon Helm resented the intrusion of the upstart folk-rocker into *his* band and went back to Arkansas for the duration of The Hawks' work with Dylan. His place was taken by Bobby Gregg and/or Mickey Johns. For the rest, this was The Band as we now know it (minus Levon, of course): Richard Manuel and Garth Hudson, keyboards; Rick Danko, bass; and Robbie Robertson, guitar.

6   ***Blonde on Blonde,*** 1966

It's hard to trust this album's credits. Although Robbie (then Jaime) Robertson is the only Hawk listed, that's almost certainly The Hawks on "One of Us Must Know (Sooner or Later)." The other players are mostly Nashville studio pros: Kenneth Buttrey, drums; Charlie McCoy, harmonica, guitar, and maybe something else; Henry Strzelecki and Jerry Kennedy, keyboards; Wayne Moss and Hargus Robbins, bass; and Joe South and Bill Aikens, guitars. Also present is Al Kooper, who might have played almost anything, versatile scamp that he is.

7   ***The Basement Tapes,*** 1967

The Hawks again, but still without Levon. Richard Manuel filled in as the drummer. Unless Robbie Robertson did.

8 ***John Wesley Harding,*** 1968

More Nashville pros: Charlie McCoy on bass, Kenneth Buttrey on drums, plus Pete Drake on steel guitar on the final two songs.

9 ***Nashville Skyline,*** 1969

Same Nashville pros, only more of 'em.

10 **Isle of Wight Pop Festival,** 1969

The Hawks return, this time as The Band, doing their own set and with Levon back on drums.

11 ***Self-Portrait,*** 1969

Half of Nashville is listed on the sleeve, in addition to Al Kooper, all of The Band, and the up-and-coming David Bromberg, whose reputation seems based on having played on this, the most embarrassing record of Dylan's checkered (musically speaking) career. It's a wonder any of them can still hold their heads up, especially The Band, who play at their worst on the live tracks from Isle of Wight.

12 **"New Morning,"** 1970

Al Kooper assembled this group (apparently hastily, to get the stench of *Self-Portrait* out of the air). The group includes guitarists Buzzy Feiten, Bromberg, and Ron Cornelius; with Kooper on keyboards, guitar, and French horn; Harvey Brooks and Charlie Daniels on bass; Russ Kunkel and Billy Mundi on drums; plus Hilda Harris, Maretha Stewart, and Albertine Robinson as backing singers.

13 ***Pat Garrett and Billy the Kid,*** 1973

Dylan first recorded this material in Mexico City during a weekend break from shooting the film of the same name. "Billy 4," which features Dylan accompanied only by bassist Terry Paul, is the sole surviver of those sessions. The rest of this odd soundtrack seems to have been done in Hollywood, at the Burbank Studios. Players include Booker T. Jones, Bruce Langhorne, Russ Kunkel, Roger McGuinn, Carol Hunter, Byron Berline, Jim Keltner, Carl Fortina, Gary Foster, Fred Katz, and Ted Michel, although only a few are given specific instrumental credit. Backing vocalists are Donna Weiss, Priscilla Jones, Byron Berline, Brenda Patterson, and Terry Paul. Despite haste and the motley crew, this is probably Dylan's most underrated LP. (It's interesting to note that none of the other musicians in the film—Kris Kristofferson, Rita Coolidge, and Donnie Fritts—plays on this record. Director Sam Peckinpah said he would have preferred Charlie Rich or Roger Miller to Dylan, anyhow.)

14 ***Planet Waves*** **and the 1974 tour**
Back to The Band again. Richard Manuel's name is misspelled on the LP cover.

15 ***Blood on the Tracks*,** 1974
This LP was recorded with a band led by Eric Weissberg in New York and also recorded with unknown players, who were assembled by Dylan's brother, David Zimmerman, in Minneapolis. No one is identified on the album cover.

16 ***Desire*** **and The Rolling Thunder Revue,** 1976
The *Desire* sessions featured Ronee Blakley and Emmylou Harris, vocals; Rob Stoner, bass; Scarlet Rivera, violin; Howard Wyeth, drums; Vincent Bell, bellzouki; Dom Cortese, mandolin; and Steve Soles and Luther Vandross, guitars. Stoner, Wyeth, Soles, T-Bone Burnette, and David Mansfield came together as Guam (later, Soles, Burnette, and Mansfield formed The Alpha Band) for The Revue's basic backing ensemble. See "Members of the Rolling Thunder Revue," p. 338.

17 ***Street-Legal*** **and the 1978 tour**
The album features former Elvis Presley sideman Jerry Scheff, bass; Steve Soles and Billy Cross, guitars; Ian Wallace, drums; Bobbye Hall, percussion; Alan Pasqua, keyboards; David Mansfield, violin, steel guitar, and mandolin; Steve Douglas, sax; Steve Madaio, trumpet; plus backing vocalists Carolyn Dennis, Jo Ann Harris, and Helena Springs. Cross, Pasqua, Wallace, Mansfield, Soles, Douglas, Hall, and Springs all made the tour, with the addition of Rob Stoner on bass and Jo Ann Harris and Debi Dye doing vocals.

18   **The Gospel Days,** 1979–1981
     The first gospel album, *Slow Train Coming*, features Dire
     Straits guitarist Mark Knopfler and drummer Pick Withers,
     plus keyboardist Barry Beckett (who produced, with Jerry
     Wexler), bassist Tim Drummond, The Muscle Shoals Horns,
     and backing vocalists Carolyn Dennis, Helena Springs, and
     Regina Havis. The players with whom Dylan briefly toured in
     1979 are essentially the same as those on *Saved*, the second
     Jesus album. The band is Jim Keltner, drums; Drummond,
     bass; Fred Tackett, guitar; Spooner Oldham, Terry Young, and
     probably Beckett, keyboards; plus Clydie King, Regina Havis,
     and Mona Lisa Young doing vocals. Dylan's 1980 touring
     ensemble also included some of the above, Keltner in particu-
     lar.

-◄▮►-

MEMBERS OF THE 1976 ROLLING THUNDER REVUE

1   JOAN BAEZ, singer, actress, longtime friend
2   RONEE BLAKELY, singer, actress
3   DAVID BLUE, singer, stand-up comic
4   T-BONE BURNETTE, guitarist, Christian
5   BOB DYLAN
6   SARA DYLAN, wife, actress
7   RAMBLIN' JACK ELLIOTT, legendary Brooklyn cowboy folk
     singer
8   ALLEN GINSBERG, poet, spiritual observer
9   BARRY IMHOFF, producer, straw boss
10   LOU KEMP, fisherman, boyhood friend, road manager
11   JACQUES LEVY, songwriter, playwright, coconspirator
12   DAVID MANSFIELD, keyboardist, nice guy
13   ROGER MCGUINN, guitarist, singer
14   JONI MITCHELL, singer, artist
15   DAVE MYERS, cameraman

16   BOBBY NEUWIRTH, musician, instigator
17   PETER ORLOVSKY, poet, pal
18   KEN REGAN, photographer
19   SCARLET RIVERA, violinist, mystery figure
20   LUTHER RIX, additional guitarist
21   ROLLING THUNDER, Indian medicine man
22   MICK RONSON, guitarist, English pop star
23   SAM SHEPARD, writer, playwright, actor
24   LARRY SLOMAN, reporter, sycophant
25   STEVE SOLES, lonesome guitarist
26   ROB STONER, bassist, bandleader
27   HOWIE WYETH, drummer, grandson of famous painter

-◄❙▶-

BIBLICAL CHARACTERS WHO APPEARED IN BOB DYLAN'S LYRICS BEFORE HE BECAME A CHRISTIAN

1   ABRAHAM, "Highway 61 Revisited"
2   ADAM and EVE, "Talking World War III Blues"
3   CAIN and ABEL, "Desolation Row"
4   DAVID, "If I Could Do It All over Again, I'd Do It All over You"
5   DELILAH, "Tombstone Blues"
6   ELI, "The Wicked Messenger"
7   GOLIATH, "When the Ship Comes In"
8   THE GOOD SAMARITAN, "Desolation Row"
9   THE GOOD SHEPHERD, "Changing of the Guard"
10   JESUS, "Masters of War"
11   JEZEBEL, "Tombstone Blues"
12   ST. JOHN, "Where Are You Tonight (Journey through Dark Heat)"
13   JOHN THE BAPTIST, "Tombstone Blues"
14   JUDAS, "Masters of War," "With God on Our Side," "The Ballad of Frankie Lee and Judas Priest"

15   THE KING OF THE PHILISTINES, "Tombstone Blues"
16   LUCIFER, "New Pony"
17   NOAH, "Desolation Row"
18   PHARAOH, "When the Ship Comes In"
19   ST. PETER, "I'd Hate to Be You on That Dreadful Day"
20   SAMSON, "If I Could Do It All over Again, I'd Do It All over You"

NOTE TO WISE GUYS: St. Augustine lived several hundred years *after* the Bible was written.

-◄▮►-

BOB DYLAN'S GARBAGE'S GREATEST HITS
Collected by A. J. Weberman

1   A half-finished, handwritten letter from Dylan to Johnny Cash
2   Several disposable diapers
3   Copies of *Crawdaddy*, *Rock*, and *Rolling Stone*
4   A used airline ticket (L.A. to New York)
5   A photo of Jimi Hendrix (found the day after his death, ripped to pieces)
6   Invoices from Bloomingdales and the Book-of-the Month Club
7   Empty cans of Ken-L Ration
8   One note from his attorney
9   Blimpie wrappers
10 A post card from his grandmother

-◄▮►-

GREIL MARCUS' LIST OF "THE NEW DYLANS"

Since Bob Dylan first became a phenomenon, it has been obligatory for the music industry to create at least one new Dylan every year or two. In periods of great Dylan fertility, the manufacture of new Dylans can become a growth industry, as i did in the days of protest, folk-rock, and the singer/songwriter. In the music industry, being labeled a new Dylan is regarded as the kiss of death—only Bruce Springsteen has survived it. And then, of course, there are those who responded to one of the perpetual chameleon's more fetching stylistic changes, remodeling themselves in his image: thus, "Norwegian Wood," the electrified "All along the Watchtower," and so on. This list doesn't get everybody, but it presents a clear picture of a muddy situation.

1	BOB DYLAN	25	NEIL YOUNG
2	JOHN LENNON	26	ERIC BURDON
3	STEVE FORBERT	27	JOAN BAEZ
4	ELLIOTT MURPHY	28	JOHN DENVER
5	BRUCE SPRINGSTEEN	29	BOB DYLAN
6	JOHN PRINE	30	DONOVAN
7	ERIC ANDERSEN	31	ARLO GUTHRIE
8	BOB DYLAN	32	RICHIE HAVENS
9	ALBERT GROSSMAN	33	JIMI HENDRIX
10	ROBBIE ROBERTSON	34	JANIS IAN
11	KRIS KRISTOFFERSON	35	BOB LIND
12	JONI MITCHELL	36	DON McLEAN
13	THE BYRDS	37	BOB MARLEY
14	LOU REED	38	BOB DYLAN
15	JIM CARROLL	39	ALLEN GINSBERG
16	SKY SAXON	40	RANDY NEWMAN
17	BOB SEGER	41	SLY STONE
18	BOB DYLAN	42	DAVID ACKLES
19	DONALD BASKIN	43	SAL VALENTINO
20	PAUL SIMON	44	BOB DYLAN
21	LEVI STUBBS	45	PAT BOONE
22	IGGY STOOGE	46	TIM BUCKLEY
23	THE TURTLES	47	SONNY AND CHER
24	LOUDON WAINWRIGHT III	48	RICHARD FARIÑA
		49	TIM HARDIN

50	PHIL OCHS	54	SAMMY WALKER
51	MARC BOLAN	55	IAN HUNTER
52	MARK KNOPFLER	56	DAVID BLUE
53	WILLIE NILE	57	PETE SEEGER

GREIL MARCUS *is the author of* Mystery Train: Images of America in Rock 'n' Roll Music *(Dutton, 1976). He currently writes "Real Life Rock," a rock and roll column for* New West *magazine.*

TWENTY-ONE:
ON THE ROAD

"Have you ever had the feeling that you've been cheated?" With these words Johnny Rotten concluded the Sex Pistols' final performance as a band at San Francisco's Winterland on January 14, 1978.

"I'M ON THE GUEST LIST "

Shelly Lazar Lists Excuses People Use to Try to Get Backstage at Rock Concerts

1 I just flew in from L.A.
2 I work for the record company.
3 _____ is my brother (or cousin, sister-in-law, aunt, uncle, etc.).
4 I'm a songwriter.
5 _____ lives next door to me.
6 I'm a good friend of Ron Delsener's.
7 I'm a close friend of Ahmet Ertegun's and he said I could use his pass.
8 I'm Shelly Lazar's cousin.
9 I'm Shelly Lazar.
10 I'm Bruce Springsteen's hairdresser.
11 I design Rod Stewart's clothing.
12 I tune Billy Joel's piano.
13 I'm Barry Manilow's dance instructor.
14 I'm Freddie Mercury's wife.
15 I hitchhiked from Cleveland.
16 I'm just in the U.S. for a few days (delivered with an accent).

SHELLY LAZAR *is coordinator of backstage security for Ron Delsener Productions in New York and has heard variations on these lame excuses everywhere from the Palladium to Madison Square Garden.*

· ◄ ▮ ► ·

THE 20 GREATEST LIVE ALBUMS

1 ***Live in Europe,*** OTIS REDDING
   While it may be disputed that the live album is a good idea in the first place—since manipulating recording technology and working an audience are often mutually exclusive propositions—here's a grand example of a moment when everything clicks. The definitive soul music show.

2 **Live at the Apollo '62**, JAMES BROWN
More soul dementia: If you could see Brown dancing, this one would be perfect. Actually, the recording quality isn't so hot (although it's much improved on Solid Smoke's 1980 reissue). Nonetheless, this is as hot and danceable as it gets.

3 **It's Too Late to Stop Now**, VAN MORRISON
In which everybody's favorite Irish blues singer rips through a fine selection of his standard repertoire, demolishing the best of it with a surgeon's skill and a zealot's relish.

4 **Live at Leeds**, THE WHO
Paved the way for Led Zeppelin and the heavy-metal hordes. Hardly the best night The Who ever had, but it's an influential and gut-crunching document just the same.

5 **Kick Out the Jams**, THE MC5
Hard rock at its most trebly, interstellar, and punkesque: If this wasn't where The New York Dolls and The Sex Pistols got half their sonic ideas, it should have been.

6 **"Get Yer Ya-Ya's Out!"** THE ROLLING STONES
Recorded on a night when they really might have been the greatest rock band in the world.

7 **Band of Gypsys**, JIMI HENDRIX
This is prophetic funk with a band that included Billy Cox and Buddy Miles. It's not Hendrix at his happiest, but it represents a breakthrough toward the kind of funk/rock fusion he might have explored had he lived. George Clinton is still trying to catch up to it.

8 **Live! At the Star Club, Hamburg, Germany, 1962**, THE BEATLES
George Harrison says that The Beatles were never better than during their Reeperbahn tenure, and while there's much dross amid the nuggets here ("Red Sails in the Sunset"?), there's enough hot stuff to convince you that Harrison might be right.

9 **Hendrix/Redding at Monterey**, JIMI HENDRIX and OTIS REDDING
The only official LP released from the first and putatively greatest rock festival ever, this includes Hendrix' debut as an

American star, with grand—no, *majestic*—versions of "Like a Rolling Stone" and "Wild Thing," and with Otis singing his heart out to what he called "the love crowd" on the other side.

10 ***Live at Newport,*** RAY CHARLES
The genius is in full swing.

11 ***Woodstock,*** VARIOUS ARTISTS
Spotty, but the best performances—The Who, Joe Cocker, Jimi Hendrix, Sly Stone—are truly monumental.

12 ***Rock of Ages,*** THE BAND
The greatest example extant of the group's tension-and-release interplay, with the additional fillip of horn charts by Allen Toussaint.

13 ***That's the Way It Is,*** ELVIS PRESLEY
This is definitive spectacle, from the opening "Also Sprach Zarathustra" to the concluding "Bridge over Troubled Water" (which was probably recorded in the studio, and the applause overdubbed, but that's appropriate, too).

14 ***Made in Japan,*** DEEP PURPLE
Greatest live heavy-metal record ever made.

15 ***The Stax/Volt Revue Live in Europe,*** VARIOUS ARTISTS
Lesser lights from the same tour on which Otis Redding made his album—but when the cast includes Sam and Dave, *lesser lights* becomes a highly relative term.

16 ***Five Live Yardbirds***
This is the only really great recording of The Yardbirds with Eric Clapton ("Slowhand" of the intros) on lead guitar. They're at their most blues-wailing, with a genius version of "Too Much Monkey Business."

17 ***Running on Empty,*** JACKSON BROWNE
It's more audacious in concept than execution, but what a concept: a song cycle about life on the road, recorded in concert, and with a title track that's easily the greatest thing Browne has ever done.

18 ***Mad Dogs and Englishmen,*** JOE COCKER
The only big-band rock album that really works.

19 **The Allman Brothers Band at Fillmore East**
    The pinnacle of Southern rock and roll.

20 **Live at Pacoima Jr. High School,** RITCHIE VALENS
    Tinny sound, and a heart as big as all outdoors.

HONORABLE MENTION: BOOTLEGS:

1 **Royal Albert Hall,** BOB DYLAN AND THE HAWKS, 1966

2 **Live at the Roxy,** BRUCE SPRINGSTEEN AND THE E STREET
   BAND, 1978
   Neither of these has been officially released, but both have
   been bootlegged so frequently that it's hard to imagine a
   self-respecting fan who's still without them. Dylan and the
   Hawks (who would become The Band) are scintillating; they
   rock London as if to prove that one hour of folk-rock could
   conquer the world. The intro to "Like a Rolling Stone" alone
   ranks as one of the great recorded moments in rock history.
   Springsteen, meanwhile, proves on this tape why he was the
   greatest live performer of the seventies, running through his
   repertoire with uncommon (even for him) ferocity and adding
   an impromptu "Heartbreak Hotel" when his guitar strings
   snap.

-◄▮▮►-

THE WORST LIVE ALBUMS

*Choosing the worst live albums is actually more difficult than
picking the best. After all, really inept pop bands usually make
concert recordings no better than their usual junk, while better
performers may simply have been captured on the wrong night
(or in the wrong era). This list attempts to represent both.*

1 **Chicago IV—Live at Carnegie Hall**
   A four-record boxed set by the blandest of the supergroup horn
   bands: The shrink wrap is as interesting as the music.

2   *Live at Budokan,* BOB DYLAN
From his Vegas-style "and then I wrote . . ." period, this is as
soulless as any music he's ever made.

3   *Aloha from Hawaii (Via Satellite),* ELVIS PRESLEY
A pure rip-off, this recording was made from an internationally
broadcast TV concert. Presley was at his most bored, had no
interesting new material, and the sound quality suggests that
the discs were recorded from a transistor radio a couple of
rooms away from the mikes.

4   *Europe '72,* THE GRATEFUL DEAD
Dead fans consider this one of their definitive LPs, which
ensures its stature here.

5   *Four-Way Street,* CROSBY, STILLS, NASH, AND YOUNG
This is the personification of wimp, presumably offered as a
method of fulfilling a contractual obligation.

6   *Metallic K.O.,* IGGY POP
This is the personification of punk, offered as a method of
deifying self-destruction.

7   *Woodstock II,* VARIOUS ARTISTS
Leftovers from volume one, this features some of the lamest
bands to play for the mud-pie crowd: for Cactus fans only.

8   *Miles of Aisles,* JONI MITCHELL
Mitchell isn't particularly comfortable performing in public in
the first place, and she can't conceal her loathing of the hockey
arenas she played on the tour caught here. The sound of no
hands clapping.

9   *Love You Live,* THE ROLLING STONES
In which the World's Greatest Rock Band reveals itself as the
Over the Hill Gang. If the title is true, better hope your
insurance is paid up.

10 *Wheels of Fire* (live disc), CREAM
After Ginger Baker's drum-solo workout on "Toad," there
wasn't any question that this kind of power trio was dead. Not
that the band's breakup soon after this metallic slop was
released stopped the genre from proliferating.

11   *Live Album,* Grand Funk Railroad
        See what we mean?

12   *Welcome Back, My Friends, to the Show That Never Ends,* Emerson, Lake, and Palmer
        Lives up to the title: It's the definition of interminable.

13   *Live at the Copa,* The Supremes
        Supper-club soul, the aural equivalent of DiGel.

14   *11/17/70,* Elton John
        He may be Mr. Personality, but listening to him prove it with an overwhelming overlay of smugness and smarmy humor isn't exactly a privilege.

15   *Alive 2,* Kiss
        Owning this is like putting a bad joke on a tape loop and locking yourself in a closet with it. Once wasn't enough?

16   *Live with the Edmonton Symphony Orchestra,* Procol Harum
        This did more for Edmonton than it did for Procol Harum. Middle-brow classicism gone berserk.

17   *Joplin in Concert,* Janis Joplin
        Wretched shouting passed off as bluesy emoting. Stick with the mythology; actually listening to her sing is too painful.

18   *Eric Clapton's Rainbow Concert*
        A superstar gala falls flat on its face.

19   *The Live Adventures of Al Kooper and Mike Bloomfield*
        The spinoff of the successful, if stupid, *Super Session* LPs wasn't even successful.

20   *Coast to Coast: Overture and Beginners,* The Faces
        A splendid opportunity to witness the deterioration of a once-splendid rock band.

21   *Got Live if You Want It,* The Rolling Stones
        Very muddy tapes of teen-agers screaming.

THE 10 MOST VIOLENT STAGE ACTS

1   THE WHO
2   THE STOOGES
3   THE PLASMATICS
4   JERRY LEE LEWIS
5   ALICE COOPER
6   KISS
7   THE MC5
8   THE DEAD BOYS
9   THE MOVE
10 THE CRAZY WORLD OF
     ARTHUR BROWN

-◄◊►-

THE WEIRDEST CONCERT BILLS

1   THE BEATLES/STEVE LAWRENCE and EYDIE GORME, Paramount Theatre, New York City, 1964
2   JIMI HENDRIX/FERNANDO VALENTI and THE NEW YORK BRASS QUINTET, Philharmonic Hall, New York City, 1968
3   THE WHO/THE GRATEFUL DEAD, Oakland Coliseum, Oakland, California, 1976
4   JIMI HENDRIX/THE MONKEES, American tour, 1967

-◄◊►-

ITEMS THROWN ONSTAGE AT BRUCE SPRINGSTEEN'S MADISON SQUARE GARDEN CONCERT
December 18, 1980

Jim McDuffie, Springsteen's right-hand security man and Clown Prince, informs us that this night was not particularly notable, except for its array of Christmas-related items. "In Pittsburgh," he says, "we must have gotten a dozen pair of women's underpants."

1   One bedsheet painted with the words *Merry Christmas, Bruce Springsteen*

An early Wes Wilson poster done for The Family Dog in 1966.

2   One stuffed dog
3   Five Santa Claus hats, three of them stenciled *Bruce*
4   One box of one-dozen Twinkies
5   One box of one-dozen Hostess Cupcakes
6   Three two-foot Christmas stockings stenciled *Bruce Springsteen and the E Street Band*
7   One eighteen-inch Christmas card with four rubber gnome musicians taped onto it.
8   Two ordinary Christmas cards
9   One gift-wrapped package the size and shape of a shoe box
10 One rubber duck

-◄❚▶-

15 FAMOUS PSYCHEDELIC BALLROOMS

1   The Aragon, Chicago
2   The Avalon, San Francisco
3   California Hall, San Francisco
4   The Carousel, San Francisco; most famous site of the Fillmore West
5   Cheetah, Los Angeles
6   The Electric Circus, New York City
7   The Electric Factory, Philadelphia
8   Family Dog on the Great Highway, San Francisco
9   Fillmore Auditorium, San Francisco; original site of the Fillmore, prior to Fillmore East
10 Fillmore East, New York City
11 The Grande Ballroom, Detroit
12 Longshoreman's Hall, San Francisco; site of Bill Graham's first rock concert promotion
13 Shrine Auditorium, San Francisco
14 The Tea Party, Boston
15 Winterland, San Francisco

20 GREAT CLUBS

1   **The Agora,** Cleveland, Ohio
    In the 1970s, nearly everybody played here on the way up. Also, this is the first club to be franchised into a chain, which extends from Ohio throughout the South. (Paul Simon filmed part of *One-Trick Pony* at the Cleveland club.)

2   **The Bitter End,** New York City
    For more than twenty years, *the* New York showcase joint.

3   **The Bottom Line,** New York City
    The most prestigious mainstream-rock club of the seventies, it rules New York.

4   **CBGB's,** New York City
    The original home of punk rock: Television, Patti Smith, Richard Hell and the Voidoids, and The Ramones all got their start at this Bowery dump.

5   **The Cavern,** Liverpool, England
    The Liverpool home of The Beatles and Merseybeat, back before the beginning.

6   **Club 47,** Boston, Massachusetts
    Home of the Boston folk scene in the early sixties.

7   **Gerde's Folk City,** New York City
    Site of Bob Dylan's original gig, and thus one of the original bastions of folk-rock. Others: the Nite Owl, Cafe au Go Go, Cafe Wha?

8   **The Main Point,** Philadelphia
    Philadelphia's most important club of the sixties and seventies, the Main Point became a home away from home for the likes of Jackson Browne and Bruce Springsteen, among others.

9   **The Marquee,** London
    London's most celebrated mod venue, it's lasted well into the punk era.

10 **The Matrix,** San Francisco
    The most important San Francisco rock and folk club. Marty Balin of The Jefferson Airplane was part owner.

11 **The Mudd Club,** New York City
The original punk-rock chameleon club in New York: a rock disco one night, a venue for oddball fashion shows the next. Competitors include, the Ritz, the Peppermint Lounge, and Irving Plaza.

12 **100 Club,** London
The original London punk-rock mecca.

13 **The Peppermint Lounge,** New York City
New York's Home of the Twist in the early sixties, when Joey Dee and the Starliters ("Peppermint Twist") were the house band. Became a New Wave danceteria in the eighties.

14 **The Rat,** Boston
Home of Boston's New Wave scene.

15 **The Roxy,** Los Angeles
Los Angeles version of the Bottom Line.

16 **The Star Club,** Hamburg, Germany
Famous joint on the Reeperbahn where The Beatles, among others, got their European education.

17 **Steve Paul's The Scene,** New York City
The greatest after-hours club of the psychedelic sixties. Jimi Hendrix, Janis Joplin, Jim Morrison, Jeff Beck, and others showed up to jam all night.

18 **The Stone Pony,** Asbury Park, New Jersey
This club is the original home turf of Bruce Springsteen and other denizens of the Asbury Park scene. After Southside Johnny and the Asbury Jukes crawled out of town, the action shifted to the Fast Lane.

19 **The Troubadour,** Hollywood
Home to the West Coast singer/songwriter scene, from The Eagles to Warren Zevon.

20 **The Whiskey a Go-Go,** Los Angeles
Sunset Strip joint where the action was from The Byrds and Buffalo Springfield days on down to the punk present.

10 LEGENDARY AND INFLUENTIAL CONCERT PROMOTERS

1 **BILL GRAHAM**
   With his Fillmores East and West, Graham virtually invented
   the rock ballroom. Despite early-seventies "retirement," he
   has never stopped booking shows in the San Francisco area.
   Noted for professionalism, hard bargains, and a hot temper.

2 **TEDDY POWELL**
   The original soul promoter in the Southeast, Powell ran the
   Warner Theatre in Washington, D.C., that area's equivalent of
   the Apollo. He also booked week-long theater stints all over
   the South, and is known for driving hard bargains.

3 **ROBERT SCHIFFMAN**
   Owned and operated the Apollo Theatre in Harlem.

4 **SID BERNSTEIN**
   Promoted the first American Beatles concert date (at Carnegie
   Hall in 1964), as well as the Shea Stadium concerts of lore and
   yore. He never reached those heights again, although he did
   enjoy some success as manager of The Rascals, Laura Nyro,
   and Phoebe Snow.

5 **LARRY MAGID**
   One of the last of the original sixties ballroom operators (he
   owns the Electric Factory in Philadelphia), Magid was the
   target of a memorable lawsuit in 1979 alleging antitrust
   violations in bookings. The same year, he promoted The Who
   concert at Cincinnati's Riverfront Coliseum, where eleven fans
   were killed in a crush at the door. Well regarded despite his
   bad luck streak.

6 **JERRY WEINTRAUB**
   Pioneered the concept of taking national rock tours (Elvis
   Presley, Led Zeppelin, Eric Clapton, Bob Dylan) out of the
   hands of local promoters, booking the shows through his own
   cross-country organization. Handles only superstars, never

touches breaking acts. Bad for long-term business but great for biggies' bottom line.

7   **HARVEY GOLDSMITH**
The most celebrated U.K. promoter, Goldsmith has also handled some acts—notably Van Morrison—as manager.

8   **HOWARD STEIN**
Although he had a virtual monopoly in New York after Graham's departure, Stein blew it when he decided he was too "classy" to serve as a "caterer." Now runs a couple of discos.

9   **MIKE and JULES BELKIN**
Midwestern kingpins and superpros, the Belkins are also involved in management. Home base is Cleveland, where they were instrumental in the discovery of Joe Walsh.

10   **DON LAW**
Boston-based, Law is involved on every level of promoting from clubs to arenas and has dabbled in management. A tough negotiator, thoroughly professional, he's not very well liked at home, but well respected everywhere.

·◄❚❚►·

BILL GRAHAM'S MOST MEMORABLE CONCERTS

1   All the early JEFFERSON AIRPLANE and GRATEFUL DEAD concerts

2   OTIS REDDING at the Fillmore Auditorium, San Francisco December 20–22, 1966

3   LENNY BRUCE/THE MOTHERS OF INVENTION at the Fillmore Auditorium, June 24, 25, 1966

4   JIMI HENDRIX/JOHN MAYALL/ALBERT KING at the Fillmore Auditorium and Winterland, February 1–4, 1968

5   The Matrix Benefit (JANIS JOPLIN with BIG BROTHER AND THE HOLDING COMPANY/THE STEVE MILLER BLUES BAND/SANDY BULL/DAN HICKS/SANTANA) at the Fillmore Auditorium, June 16, 1968

6   ARETHA FRANKLIN/KING CURTIS AND THE KINGPINS/TOWER OF POWER at the Fillmore West, San Francisco, March 5–7, 1971
7   The Watkins Glen Festival (THE GRATEFUL DEAD/THE BAND/THE ALLMAN BROTHERS) in Watkins Glen, New York, July 28, 1973
8   S.N.A.C.K. Benefit (Students Need Activities, Culture and Kicks) (EDDIE PALMIERI/TOWER OF POWER/SANTANA/JOAN BAEZ/THE GRATEFUL DEAD/NEIL YOUNG/BOB DYLAN/THE JEFFERSON STARSHIP/WILLIE MAYS/MARLON BRANDO, etc.) at Kezar Stadium, San Francisco, March 23, 1975
9   The Last Waltz (THE BAND/BOB DYLAN/VAN MORRISON/NEIL YOUNG/JONI MITCHELL/NEIL DIAMOND/MUDDY WATERS/RONNIE HAWKINS, etc.) at Winterland, November 25, 1976
10 BRUCE SPRINGSTEEN at Winterland, December 15, 16, 1978
11 THE GRATEFUL DEAD at the Warfield Theatre, San Francisco, September 25–October 4, 1980

BILL GRAHAM *is the most celebrated concert promoter in rock. He earned his reputation with the greatest of the sixties ballrooms, the Fillmores East and West, and sustains it with frequent productions around his San Francisco Bay home base. Graham also manages such artists as Santana and Eddie Money.*

◄▮►

10 BANDS THAT HAVE OPENED FOR J. GEILS

1   THE CARS
2   THE EAGLES
3   EARTH, WIND, AND FIRE
4   PETER FRAMPTON
5   BILLY JOEL
6   LITTLE FEAT
7   TOM PETTY AND THE HEARTBREAKERS
8   BOB SEGER
9   VAN HALEN
10 YES

10 NOTED ROADIES AND ROAD MANAGERS

1   **IAN STEWART** (The Rolling Stones)
    One of the original members, cast out by an early manager as
    being too ugly (for The Stones?). Still fills in frequently as
    pianist onstage and, now and then, in the studio.

2   **BOBBY PRIDDEN** (The Who)
    Soundman and frequent target of abuse, both mental and
    physical, from the guitarist.

3   **RICHARD COLE** (Led Zeppelin, The Yardbirds, Eric Clapton,
    Jeff Beck)
    Cole is a notorious brawler.

4   **BOBBY NEUWIRTH** (Bob Dylan)
    A songwriter in his own right, Neuwirth made his name as
    Dylan's tour manager/sidekick. See the film *Don't Look Back*

5 and 6   **MAL EVANS; NEIL ASPINALL** (The Beatles)
    The original roadies. Evans later got himself killed in a
    shoot-out with Hollywood police; Aspinall has proceeded more
    placidly.

7   **BOBBY "RED" WEST** (Elvis Presley)
    A high school buddy of Elvis' who was fired, West turned
    renegade, along with a couple of his peers, by providing the
    information for the book *Elvis: What Happened?* a kind of
    Memphis-to-Vegas *Hollywood Babylon*.

8   **OTIS REDDING** (Johnny Jenkins and the Pinetoppers)
    Otis was their driver/roadie and once chauffeured them to Stax
    Studios in Memphis. When their session fizzled, his career
    began.

9   **BILL SIDDONS** (The Doors)
    Siddons became the group's manager, which is the pinnacle of
    success in this line of work.

10 **CHUCK MAGEE** (The Stones, The Faces)
    A pro's pro, tough and resilient. Magee handled Ron Wood's
    equipment needs for years and often staged entire Faces tours
    with three-man crews.

Ray MANZAREK'S MOST MEMORABLE DOORS CONCERTS

1 **Whiskey a Go-Go,** Los Angeles
When Jim first did "Father, I want to kill you, Mother, I want to fuck you!" We were fired that night.

2 **Fillmore West,** San Francisco
The weekend of the Human Be-In, the world's first love-in ever. We were the opening act. The first number was "When the Music's Over." We'd never opened with it before, or since.

3 **Singer Bowl,** New York
What a show! The Doors and The Who. And what a riot! One of the best riots I've ever been in.

4 **The Roundhouse,** London
The Doors and The Jefferson Airplane: Psychedelic West Coast comes to England.

5 **Miami**
I think we all know what happened there. Or do we? Did he really do it? If he did it, how long was it?

6 **Des Moines**
Thirty-four people in the audience. One of the last college gigs before "Light My Fire" hit the top of the charts. We were a little early for Des Moines. The promoters told us that the week before, more than 5000 people had come to the same auditorium to see The Association.

RAY MANZAREK *was the keyboard player for The Doors. He still lives in Los Angeles, where he is involved in record and film production.*

WILLIE DIXON LISTS THE 5 MOST INTERESTING PLACES AT WHICH HE HAS PERFORMED

1 A nudist camp just outside of Colorado Springs, 1949
2 American Folk Blues Festival, Berlin, 1964
3 Festival de Blues en Mexico, Mexico City, 1978, 1979, 1980
4 ChicagoFest, Chicago, 1978, 1979, 1980
5 Melbourne Dallas Brooks Hall, Melbourne, Australia, 1974

After moving from Mississippi to Chicago as a youngster, WILLIE DIXON *was a member of several Windy City swing vocal groups (The Five Breezes, Four Jumps of Jive, and the popular Big Three Trio) in the years before rock. During the 1950s, he was a cornerstone of the Chess Brothers' label organization as a composer, A&R man, session player, and blues artist* extraordinaire. *During the British Invasion and ever since, rock music acts have borrowed extensively from Dixon's catalog of tunes.*

- ◄❙❙►-

NOEL REDDING LISTS HIS 10 MOST MEMORABLE CONCERTS WITH THE JIMI HENDRIX EXPERIENCE

1 **Paris Olympia,** Paris, October 18, 1966
We supported French pop singer Johnny Halliday and really enjoyed playing those early gigs.
2 **Bag O'Nails,** London, November 25, 1966
Our launching pad. I was awed by the star-filled audience.
3 **Kiel,** West Germany, May 27, 1967
Jimi was so stoned that I had to tune his guitar for him.
4 **Monterey International Pop Festival,** California, June 18, 1967
My all-time favorite. Our first U.S. appearance, tension-filled as a result of following both The Who and a Brian Jones introduction.

5   **Minneapolis,** November 2, 1968
    I was so stoned I fell off the stage, knocking over the right P.A.
    stack; I cut my leg but kept on playing.

6   *Lulu Show,* BBC-TV, January 3, 1969
    Hilarious! A tribute to Cream with powerless TV directors
    going insane.

7   **Berlin,** January 23, 1969
    A highly political atmosphere complete with a riot in a packed
    hall.

8   **Royal Albert Hall,** London, February 18, 24, 1969
    A rare onstage jam with Traffic on the 18th. Everyone knew the
    group had really broken up and this would be the last English
    appearance, which made the shows exceptionally emotional. A
    good part of the audience ended up onstage. The Fat Mattress
    [Noel's solo group] backed The Experience for the first time.

9   **Devonshire Downs,** Los Angeles, June 20, 1969
    For the sheer heaviness of the vibes and persons who sur-
    rounded us.

10 **Denver,** June 29, 1969
    The last show of The Experience—and nearly the last of us. I
    suddenly realized there were three of us and 40,000 of them as
    the audience and the tear gas started coming.

NOEL REDDING *was the bassist in The Jimi Hendrix Experience. Since then, he has
played in a number of groups and has recently completed a book about his
experiences in The Experience.*

-◄❙❙►-

PARTICIPANTS AT THE FIRST L.A. "FREAK OUT"
March 1966

*The original "Freak Out" was a glorified jam session conducted
by Frank Zappa with a cast of characters that included most of
the personalities in the mid-sixties Los Angeles underground.*

The liner notes to the album, Freak Out, *which documented this session, described the art of freaking out as ". . . a process whereby an individual casts off outmoded and restricting standards of thinking, dress and social etiquette. . . ."*

1 **The Mothers of Invention**
JIM BLACK
RAY COLLINS
ROY ESTRADA
ELLIOT INGBER

2 **Conductor**
FRANK ZAPPA

3 **Producer**
TOM WILSON

4 **Guests**
PAUL BUTTERFIELD
LES McCANN

5 **The Mothers' auxiliary**
DAVID ANDERLE
BENJAMIN BARRETT
EDWIN V. BEACH
PAUL BERGSTROM
RAY CATON
EUGENE DI NOVI
GENE ESTES

VIRGIL EVANS
KIM FOWLEY
CARL FRANZONI
JOHN JOHNSON
PLAS JOHNSON
CAROL KAYE
RAYMOND KELLEY
NEIL LE VANG
ARTHUR MAEBE
GEORGE PRICE
KURT REHER
JOHN ROTELLA
EMMET SARGEANT
JOSEPH SAXON
VITO
KENNETH WATSON
DAVID WELLS

6 **Manager**
HERBIE COHEN

- ◄ ▮ ▶ -

FAREWELL CONCERTS

1 **THE BEATLES,** Candlestick Park, San Francisco, August 29, 1966

The band, of course, didn't know this was its last show. No did the crowd. But the next time a Beatle set foot on a concer stage with his own group was in 1971, when John Lenno appeared with the Plastic Ono Band at the Toronto Pop Festival.

2   **THE BAND,** Winterland, San Francisco, Thanksgiving 1976
A gala farewell performance, with guest appearances by everyone from Bob Dylan, Ronnie Hawkins, and Muddy Waters to Eric Clapton, Neil Young, and Joni Mitchell. The concert was filmed by Martin Scorsese and released as *The Last Waltz*, with additional studio music and footage.

3   **DAVID BOWIE,** Hammersmith Odeon, London, July 3, 1973
Bowie announced his retirement after this show but has since had several relapses.

4   **CREAM,** Royal Albert Hall, London, November 26, 1969
Filmed and recorded as *Goodbye Cream*

5   **JONI MITCHELL,** Royal Albert Hall, London, February 17, 1970
Mitchell announced her retirement, but like Bowie's, it didn't stick.

6   **THE ROLLING STONES,** the Roundhouse, London, March 14, 1971
Their final U.K. show before moving to France, a move at least partially prompted by England's excessive tax rates.

7   **THE SEX PISTOLS,** Winterland, San Francisco, January 14, 1978
Immediately after this gig, the last of their U.S. tour, Johnny Rotten announced that, due to a dispute with manager Malcolm McLaren, he was leaving the group. This effectively ended the Sex Pistols' career as *enfants terribles*, a.k.a. the world's greatest punk-rock band.

Rock's MOST ILL-FATED TOUR

The Winter Dance Party, January 23–February 3, 1959

The tour played its final engagement at the Surf Ballroom, in Clear Lake, Iowa, on February 2. Later that evening, Buddy Holly, Ritchie Valens, and J. P. Richardson (the Big Bopper) chartered a plane to take them to the next stop, so they would have some extra time to get shirts cleaned and could pick up their mail. The plane crashed, killing its passengers. The musicians on the tour were:

1 Buddy Holly and the Crickets   4 The Big Bopper
2 Dion and the Belmonts   5 Frankie Sardo
3 Ritchie Valens

-◄❚▶-

Complete ITINERARY FOR THE WINTER DANCE PARTY

1   January 23, George Devine's Ballroom, Milwaukee
2   January 24, Kenosha, Wisconsin
3   January 25, Kato Ballroom, Kankato, Minnesota
4   January 26, Eau Claire, Wisconsin
5   January 27, Fiesta Ballroom, Montevideo, Minnesota
6   January 28, Prom Ballroom, St. Paul
7   January 29, Capitol Theatre, Davenport, Iowa
8   January 30, Laramar Ballroom, Fort Dodge, Iowa
9   January 31, Armory, Duluth, Minnesota
10 February 1, Cinderella Ballroom, Appleton, Wisconsin (after noon); Riverside Ballroom, Green Bay, Wisconsin (evening)
11 February 2, Surf Ballroom, Clear Lake, Iowa
12 February 3, Armory, Moorhead, Minnesota
13 February 4, Shore Acres, Sioux City, Iowa
14 February 5, Val Air Ballroom, Des Moines

15	February 6, Danceland Ballroom, Cedar Rapids, Iowa
16	February 7, Les Buzz Ballroom, Spring Valley, Illinois
17	February 8, Aragon Ballroom, Chicago
18	February 9, Hippodrome Auditorium, Waterloo, Iowa
19	February 10, Melody Hill, Dubuque, Iowa
20	February 11, Memorial Auditorium, Louisville, Kentucky
21	February 12, Memorial Auditorium, Canton, Ohio
22	February 13, Stanbaugh Auditorium, Youngstown, Ohio
23	February 14, Peoria, Illinois
24	February 15, Springfield, Illinois

Twenty-Two: DANCING

Still twisting after all these years: Chubby Checker demonstrates a new sensation with full orchestral strength in this 1960 photo.

BEST SONGS ABOUT DANCING

1 "Nobody but Me," THE HUMAN BEINZ
2 "I Gotta Dance to Keep from Crying," SMOKEY ROBINSON AND THE MIRACLES
3 "Dancing in the Street," MARTHA AND THE VANDELLAS
4 "Land of 1000 Dances," CHRIS KENNER
5 "Dance This Mess Around," THE B-52's
6 "Yeah Man," SAM COOKE
7 "Keep on Dancing," THE GENTRYS
8 "Do You Want to Dance," BOBBY FREEMAN
9 "Dance, Dance, Dance (Yowsah, Yowsah, Yowsah)," CHIC
10 "Do You Love Me," THE CONTOURS
11 "Turn the Beat Around," VICKI SUE ROBINSON
12 "Dance, Dance, Dance," THE BEACH BOYS

-◄▮►-

THE 50 GREATEST DANCE HITS

1 "Land of 1000 Dances," CHRIS KENNER
2 "The Loco-Motion," LITTLE EVA
3 "Disco Inferno," THE TRAMMPS
4 "Doing It to Death," FRED WESLEY AND THE J.B.'s
5 "Boogaloo down Broadway," FANTASTIC JOHNNY C
6 "Do You Love Me," THE CONTOURS
7 "Funky Broadway," DYKE AND THE BLAZERS
8 "Slow Twistin'," CHUBBY CHECKER AND DEE DEE SHARP
9 "The Monkey Time," MAJOR LANCE
10 "Willie and the Hand Jive," JOHNNY OTIS
11 "The Stroll," THE DIAMONDS
12 "Dance, Dance, Dance (Yowsah, Yowsah, Yowsah)," CHIC
13 "Baby Workout," JACKIE WILSON
14 "Ain't That a Groove," JAMES BROWN
15 "Tighten Up," ARCHIE BELL AND THE DRELLS

16 "Barefootin'," ROBERT PARKER
17 "C'mon and Swim," BOBBY FREEMAN
18 "Walking the Dog," RUFUS THOMAS
19 "Whole Lot of Shakin' Goin' On," JERRY LEE LEWIS
20 "Do You Want to Dance," DEL SHANNON
21 "The Hustle," VAN MCCOY AND THE SOUL CITY SYMPHONY
22 "Nobody But Me," THE HUMAN BEINZ
23 "Licking Stick—Licking Stick," JAMES BROWN
24 "One Nation under a Groove," FUNKADELIC
25 "Shake," SAM COOKE
26 "Hitch Hike," MARVIN GAYE
27 "Ride Your Pony," LEE DORSEY
28 "Hollywood Swinging," KOOL AND THE GANG
29 "Mickey's Monkey," THE MIRACLES
30 "Hot Pastrami with Mashed Potatoes," JOEY DEE AND THE
   STARLITERS
31 "Shake a Tail Feather," JAMES AND BOBBY PURIFY
32 "Cool Jerk," THE CAPITOLS
33 "You Can't Sit Down," THE DOVELLS
34 "Turn the Beat Around," VICKI SUE ROBINSON
35 "(Do the) Mashed Potatoes," NAT KENDRICK AND THE SWANS
36 "Keep on Truckin'," EDDIE KENDRICKS
37 "Wiggle Wobble," LES COOPER
38 "Going to a Go-Go," THE MIRACLES
39 "The Wah Watusi," THE ORLONS
40 "Twine Time," ALVIN CASH AND THE CRAWLERS
41 "El Watusi," RAY BARRETTO
42 "Pop-Eye," HUEY "PIANO" SMITH AND THE CLOWNS
43 "The Walk," JIMMY MCCRACKLIN
44 "Hi-Heel Sneakers," TOMMY TUCKER
45 "Mashed Potato Time," DEE DEE SHARP
46 "The Popeye Waddle," DON COVAY
47 "The Philly Freeze," ALVIN CASH AND THE REGISTERS
48 "Cissy Strut," THE METERS
49 "Dance, Dance, Dance," THE BEACH BOYS
50 "Save the Last Dance for Me," THE DRIFTERS

THE TOP 40 DANCE STEPS

1	Barefoot	21	Mess Around
2	Bird	22	Monkey
3	Boogaloo	23	Moonwalk
4	Bristol Stomp	24	Philly Freeze
5	Bump	25	Pogo
6	Duck	26	Pony
7	81	27	Popcorn
8	Freddie	28	Pop-Eye
9	Frug	29	Reggae
10	Hand Jive	30	Shake
11	Hucklebuck	31	Shimmy
12	Hully Gully	32	Sissy Strut
13	Hustle	33	Slop
14	Jerk	34	Stroll
15	L.A. Hustle	35	Suzie-Q
16	Latin Hustle	36	Swim
17	Limbo	37	Temptation Walk
18	Locomotion	38	Twine
19	Madison	39	Twist
20	Mashed Potato	40	Watusi

·◄▮►·

20 TWIST RECORDS
The Wildest and the Weirdest

1 "Slow Twistin'," CHUBBY CHECKER AND DEE DEE SHARP
2 "Twist and Shout," THE ISLEY BROTHERS
3 "Let's Twist Again," CHUBBY CHECKER
4 "Twistin' the Night Away," SAM COOKE
5 "Dear Lady Twist," GARY "U.S." BONDS
6 "Peppermint Twist—Part One," JOEY DEE AND THE STAR-
   LITERS

7   "Soul Twist," KING CURTIS AND THE NOBLE KNIGHTS
8   "The Twist," HANK BALLARD AND THE MIDNIGHTERS,
    CHUBBY CHECKER
9   "Twistin' Postman," THE MARVELETTES
10 "Bristol Twistin' Annie," THE DOVELLS
11 "Twist, Twist Señora," GARY "U.S." BONDS
12 "Patricia Twist," PEREZ PRADO
13 "The Basie Twist," COUNT BASIE
14 "Tequila Twist," THE CHAMPS
15 "Twistin' Matilda," JIMMY SOUL
16 "(Let's Do) the Hully Gully Twist," BILL DOGGETT
17 "Twistin' Bells," SANTO AND JOHNNY
18 "Twistin' with Linda," THE ISLEY BROTHERS
19 "Twistin' U.S.A.," DANNY AND THE JUNIORS
20 "Percolator (Twist)," BILLY JOE AND THE CHECKMATES

-◄❙▮▶-

10 WHO MAKE CHUBBY CHECKER DANCE

1   THE BEATLES, *Sgt. Pepper's Lonely Hearts Club Band*
2   MARVIN GAYE, "Mercy Mercy Me (the Ecology)"
3   ELVIS PRESLEY, *G.I. Blues*
4   NAT KING COLE
5   STEELY DAN, *Katy Lied*
6   STEVIE WONDER, *Innervisions*
7   LEON RUSSELL at his 1974 Las Vegas concert with The Gap
    Band
8   HARRY BELAFONTE
9   CROSBY, STILLS, AND NASH (without Neil Young)
10 FATS DOMINO

CHUBBY CHECKER *is the* auteur *of dance music, especially through his "Twist" recordings, which created the greatest rock dance craze of all time. He continues to perform in nightclubs and on the oldies circuit, stretching sacroiliacs coast to coast with "The Twist," "Limbo Rock," and his other muscle-bending hits.*

DANCE HITS BY CHUBBY CHECKER
All of Which Made the Top 40

1	"The Twist"	9	"Birdland"
2	"Pony Time"	10	"The Hucklebuck"
3	"Limbo Rock"	11	"Let's Limbo Some More"
4	"Slow Twistin'"	12	"Dance the Mess Around"
5	"The Fly"	13	"Twist It Up"
6	"Let's Twist Again"	14	"The Class"
7	"Popeye the Hitchhiker"	15	"Let's Do the Freddie"
8	"Dancin' Party"		

DANCES MADE FAMOUS BY RUFUS THOMAS

One of the pillars of Memphis rhythm & blues since the late forties, RUFUS THOMAS fathered Carla Thomas and the following dance steps, based on his hit records of the same names.

1	The Breakdown	4	Funky Chicken
2	The Dog*	5	Funky Penguin
3	Funky Bird	6	The Push and Pull

*Not to mention the celebrated "Walking the Dog" and "Can Your Monkey Do the Dog," in which Rufus adapted the steps of others to his own devilish purposes.

BEST DANCERS

1	JAMES BROWN	7	RUFUS THOMAS
2	JACKIE WILSON	8	BRUCE SPRINGSTEEN
3	THE TEMPTATIONS	9	CHUCK BERRY
4	CHUBBY CHECKER	10	MICHAEL JACKSON
5	ELVIS PRESLEY	11	JOE TEX
6	JIMI HENDRIX	12	THE CADILLACS

10 HELPLESS DANCERS

1	IGGY POP	6	PETER WOLF
2	JOE COCKER	7	MICK JAGGER
3	JOHNNY ROTTEN	8	PETE TOWNSHEND
4	VAN MORRISON	9	THE B-52's
5	DONNA SUMMER	10	ROD STEWART

-◄▮▶-

THE 10 GREATEST DANCE BANDS

1 THE TRAMMPS
2 SLY AND THE FAMILY STONE
3 THE J.B.'s
4 JR. WALKER AND THE ALL STARS
5 CHIC
6 JOEY DEE AND THE STARLITERS
7 THE COMMODORES
8 FELA AND AFRIKA 70
9 THE ISLEY BROTHERS
10 PARLIAFUNKADELICMENT THANG

-◄▮▶-

GARY "U.S." BONDS' DREAM DANCE BAND

1 Bass: WILLIE WEEKS, GORDON EDWARD
2 Lead guitar: GEORGE BENSON, ERIC CLAPTON, JIMI HENDRIX
3 Rhythm guitar: JOHNNY WINTER
4 Piano: WILLIE TEE, EDGAR WINTER
5 Drums: BERNIE PURDIE, STEVE GADD

6   Saxophone: DADDY G, CLARENCE CLEMONS
7   Vocals: SAM COOKE, OTIS REDDING, B. B. KING, CLYDE
    McPHATTER, BRUCE SPRINGSTEEN

GARY "U.S." BONDS *created a series of unforgettable dance hits in the early sixties,
including "Quarter to Three," "Dear Lady Twist," and "Twist Twist Señora," in
addition to such other greats as "School Is Out" and "New Orleans." In early
1981, he released an album* Dedication, *with Bruce Springsteen and Miami Steve
Van Zandt producing.*

-◄❚▶-

TOP 20 DISCO HITS

1   "Bad Girls," DONNA SUMMER
2   "Dazz," BRICK
3   "Don't Stop Till You Get Enough," MICHAEL JACKSON
4   "Do Ya Wanna Get Funky with Me," PETER BROWN
5   "Good Times," CHIC
6   "Hot Stuff," DONNA SUMMER
7   "I Feel Love," DONNA SUMMER
8   "Mighty Real," SYLVESTER
9   "Rapper's Delight," THE SUGARHILL GANG
10 "Ring My Bell," ANITA WARD
11 "Running Away," ROY AYERS' UBIQUITY
12 "San Francisco (You've Got Me)," THE VILLAGE PEOPLE
13 "Searching," CHANGE
14 "Shake Your Body (Down to the Ground)," THE JACKSONS
15 "Shame," EVELYN "CHAMPAGNE" KING
16 "Shame, Shame, Shame," SHIRLEY AND COMPANY
17 "There but for the Grace of God Go I," MACHINE
18 "This Time Baby," JACKIE MOORE
19 "Victim," CANDI STATON
20 "We Are Family," SISTER SLEDGE

THE 15 BEST DISCO ALBUMS

1 *Bad Bad Boy*, THEO VANESS
2 *Bad Girls*, DONNA SUMMER
3 *Bionic Boogie*, BIONIC BOOGIE
4 *Dr. Buzzard's Original "Savannah" Band*
5 *Ecstasy, Passion and Pain*, ECSTASY, PASSION, AND PAIN
6 *From Here to Eternity*, GIORGIO
7 *Garden of Love*, DON RAY
8 *Les Plus Grands Success de Chic—Chic's Greatest Hits*, CHIC
9 *Nightbirds*, LABELLE
10 *Once upon a Time*, DONNA SUMMER
11 *Phoenix*, LABELLE
12 *Step Two*, SYLVESTER
13 *Supernature*, CERRONE
14 *The Village People*, THE VILLAGE PEOPLE
15 *We Are Family*, SISTER SLEDGE

-◄▐▐►-

TOP DISCO PRODUCERS

1 GIORGIO MORODER (DONNA SUMMER)
2 JACQUES MORALI (THE VILLAGE PEOPLE, THE RITCHIE FAMILY)
3 NILE RODGERS and BERNARD EDWARDS (CHIC)
4 H. W. CASEY (KC AND THE SUNSHINE BAND)
5 AUGUST DARNELL (DR. BUZZARD'S ORIGINAL "SAVANNAH" BAND)
6 KARL RICHARDSON and ALBHY GALUTEN (THE BEE GEES)
7 KENNY GAMBLE and LEON HUFF (THE O'JAYS, THE THREE DEGREES, MFSB)
8 ALEC CONSTANDINOS (LOVE AND KISSES)
9 BORIS MIDNEY (USA-EUROPEAN CONNECTION)
10 CERRONE (himself)
11 GREGG DIAMOND (BIONIC BOOGIE)

EARLY RUMBLINGS ON THE DANCE FLOOR
The First Disco Records

1 "Theme from 'Shaft,'" ISAAC HAYES, 1971
2 "Armed and Extremely Dangerous," FIRST CHOICE, 1973
3 . "Soul Makossa" MANU DIBANGO, 1973
4 "Under the Influence of Love," LOVE UNLIMITED, 1974
5 "The Player," FIRST CHOICE, 1974
6 "Dreaming a Dream," CROWN HEIGHTS AFFAIR, 1975
7 "Foot-Stompin' Music," BOHANNON, 1975
8 "Free Man," SOUTH SHORE COMMISSION, 1975
9 "Nice 'n' Nasty," SALSOUL ORCHESTRA, 1976
10 "Tangerine," SALSOUL ORCHESTRA, 1976
11 "We're on the Right Track," SOUTH SHORE COMMISSION, 1976
12 "Young Hearts Run Free," CANDI STATON, 1976

-◄▐►-

DISCO'S REVENGE
Disco Singers Make Rock Songs

1 "Bad Girls," DONNA SUMMER
2 "Dirty Minds," PRINCE
3 "Fame," IRENE CARA
4 "Hot Stuff," DONNA SUMMER
5 "The Wanderer," DONNA SUMMER

-◄▐►-

DONNA SUMMER'S 10 FAVORITE FEMALE VOCALISTS

1 IRENE CARA
2 ARETHA FRANKLIN
3 CHRISSIE HYNDE
4 BETTE MIDLER

5	Olivia Newton-John	8	Diana Ross
6	Dolly Parton	9	Barbra Streisand
7	Linda Ronstadt	10	Dionne Warwick

Donna Summer *ruled as the Queen of Disco, beginning with her first record, "Love to Love You Baby" and continuing with a remarkable string of hits. Summer has more recently turned her talents to dance-rock, with such records as "The Wanderer," "Hot Stuff," and "Cold Love."*

·◄▐▶·

THE SOUND OF PHILADELPHIA
Philadelphia's 20 Best Disco Records

1 "Ain't No Stoppin' Us Now," McFadden and Whitehead
2 "Ask Me," Ecstasy, Passion, and Pain
3 "Bad Luck," Harold Melvin and the Blue Notes
4 "Dirty Ol' Man," The Three Degrees
5 "Disco Inferno," The Trammps
6 "Do It Anyway You Wanna," The People's Choice
7 "Doctor Love," First Choice
8 "For the Love of Money," The O'Jays
9 "I Love Music," The O'Jays
10 "I'll Always Love My Mama," The Intruders
11 "Livin' for the Weekend," The O'Jays
12 "Love Epidemic," The Trammps
13 "Love Train," The O'Jays
14 "Only You," Teddy Pendergrass
15 "That's Where the Happy People Go," The Trammps
16 "The Love I Lost," Harold Melvin and the Blue Notes
17 "TSOP (The Sound of Philadelphia)," MFSB
18 "Turn the Beat Around," Vickie Sue Robinson
19 "When Will I See You Again?" The Three Degrees
20 "Where Do We Go from Here," The Trammps

MOTOWN'S 20 BEST DISCO RECORDS

1 "Bad Weather," THE SUPREMES
2 "Behind the Groove," TEENA MARIE
3 "Boogie Down," EDDIE KENDRICKS
4 "The Boss," DIANA ROSS
5 "Brick House," THE COMMODORES
6 "Dancing Machine," THE JACKSON 5
7 "Don't Leave Me This Way," THELMA HOUSTON
8 "Forever Came Today," THE JACKSON 5
9 "Girl You Need a Change of Mind," EDDIE KENDRICKS
10 "Goin' up in Smoke," EDDIE KENDRICKS
11 "Got to Give It Up," MARVIN GAYE
12 "Keep on Truckin'," EDDIE KENDRICKS
13 "Law of the Land," THE TEMPTATIONS
14 "Let's Get Serious," JERMAINE JACKSON
15 "Livin', Lovin', and Givin'," DIANA ROSS
16 "Love Hangover," DIANA ROSS
17 "Love Machine," THE MIRACLES
18 "Love Power," WILLIE HUTCH
19 "Slippery When Wet," THE COMMODORES
20 "Walk away from Love," DAVID RUFFIN

-◄▮▮►-

THE WORST DISCO RECORDS

1 "Disco Duck," RICK DEES AND HIS CAST OF IDIOTS
2 "Disco Lady," JOHNNIE TAYLOR
3 "No More Tears (Enough Is Enough)," BARBRA STREISAND and DONNA SUMMER
4 "The Hustle," VAN MCCOY
5 "I Got My Mind Made Up (You Can Get It)," INSTANT FUNK
6 "I Love the Nightlife," ALICIA BRIDGES
7 "In the Bush," MUSIQUE

8   "In the Navy," THE VILLAGE PEOPLE
9   "Kung Fu Fighting," CARL DOUGLAS
10   "Play That Funky Music," WILD CHERRY
11   "(Shake, Shake, Shake) Shake Your Booty," KC AND THE
     SUNSHINE BAND
12   "What's Your Name, What's Your Number," ANDREA TRUE
     CONNECTION

-◄▮►-

6 DISCO FLICKS
In Order of Awfulness

1   *Can't Stop the Music*   4   *Thank God, It's Friday*
2   *Xanadu*   5   *Car Wash*
3   *Roller Disco*   6   *Saturday Night Fever*

TWENTY-THREE: RHYTHM & BLUES

The Five Satins had a great hit with "In the Still of the Night," among others, including "Shadows" and "To the Aisle." Lead vocalist Fred Parris wrote "In the Still of the Night" while on guard duty in the Army.

100 GREATEST NUMBER 1 RHYTHM & BLUES HITS
1949–1980

All of these records made Number 1 on Billboard's *Top Rhythm & Blues (Soul) charts in the years indicated. No hits are listed for 1964, since* Billboard *did not have an R&B chart for that year.*

1   "Chicken Shack Boogie," AMOS MILBURN, 1949
2   "Saturday Night Fish Fry," LOUIS JORDAN, 1949
3   "I Almost Lost My Mind," IVORY JOE HUNTER, 1950
4   "Please Send Me Someone to Love," PERCY MAYFIELD, 1950
5   "Sixty Minute Man," THE DOMINOES, 1951
6   "Lawdy Miss Clawdy," LLOYD PRICE, 1952
7   "Juke," LITTLE WALTER, 1952
8   "(Mama) He Treats Your Daughter Mean," RUTH BROWN, 1953
9   "Crying in the Chapel," THE ORIOLES, 1953
10 "Money Honey," THE DRIFTERS, 1953
11 "The Things That I Used to Do," GUITAR SLIM, 1954
12 "Work with Me, Annie," THE MIDNIGHTERS, 1954
13 "Hearts of Stone," THE CHARMS, 1954
14 "Earth Angel," THE PENGUINS, 1955
15 "Pledging My Love," JOHNNY ACE, 1955
16 "My Babe," LITTLE WALTER, 1955
17 "Ain't It a Shame," FATS DOMINO, 1955
18 "Maybellene," CHUCK BERRY, 1955
19 "The Great Pretender," THE PLATTERS, 1955
20 "Long Tall Sally"/"Slippin' and Slidin'," LITTLE RICHARD, 1956
21 "Fever," LITTLE WILLIE JOHN, 1956
22 "Blue Monday," FATS DOMINO, 1957
23 "You Send Me," SAM COOKE, 1957
24 "It's All in the Game," TOMMY EDWARDS, 1958

25   "A Lover's Question," CLYDE MCPHATTER, 1958
26   "Lonely Teardrops," JACKIE WILSON, 1958
27   "Stagger Lee," LLOYD PRICE, 1959
28   "There Goes My Baby," THE DRIFTERS, 1959
29   "What'd I Say," RAY CHARLES, 1959
30   "Fannie Mae," BUSTER BROWN, 1960
31   "There's Something on Your Mind," BOBBY MARCHAN, 1960
32   "Save the Last Dance for Me," THE DRIFTERS, 1960
33   "Shop Around," THE MIRACLES, 1961
34   "I Pity the Fool," BOBBY BLAND, 1961
35   "Mother-in-Law," ERNIE K-DOE, 1961
36   "Stand by Me," BEN E. KING, 1961
37   "Ya Ya," LEE DORSEY, 1961
38   "Soul Twist," KING CURTIS AND THE NOBLE KNIGHTS, 1962
39   "You'll Lose a Good Thing," BARBARA LYNN, 1962
40   "Do You Love Me," THE CONTOURS, 1962
41   "You've Really Got a Hold on Me," THE MIRACLES, 1963
42   "Fingertips—Pt. 2," LITTLE STEVIE WONDER, 1963
43   "Heat Wave," MARTHA AND THE VANDELLAS, 1964
44   "It's All Right," THE IMPRESSIONS, 1964
45   "My Girl," THE TEMPTATIONS, 1965
46   "In the Midnight Hour," WILSON PICKETT, 1965
47   "Papa's Got a Brand New Bag," JAMES BROWN, 1965
48   "Uptight (Everything's Alright)," STEVIE WONDER, 1966
49   "When a Man Loves a Woman," PERCY SLEDGE, 1966
50   "It's a Man's Man's Man's World," JAMES BROWN, 1966
51   "Hold On! I'm Comin'," SAM AND DAVE, 1966
52   "Reach Out I'll Be There," THE FOUR TOPS, 1966
53   "Knock on Wood," EDDIE FLOYD, 1966
54   "You Keep Me Hangin' On," THE SUPREMES, 1966
55   "I Never Loved a Man (the Way I love You)," ARETHA
      FRANKLIN, 1967
56   "Respect," ARETHA FRANKLIN, 1967
57   "Cold Sweat," JAMES BROWN, 1967
58   "Funky Broadway," WILSON PICKETT, 1967

59 "(Your Love Keeps Lifting Me) Higher and Higher," JACKIE
    WILSON, 1967
60 "Soul Man," SAM AND DAVE, 1967
61 "I Second That Emotion," SMOKEY ROBINSON AND THE
    MIRACLES, 1968
62 "I Wish It Would Rain," THE TEMPTATIONS, 1968
63 "Cowboys to Girls," THE INTRUDERS, 1968
64 "Ain't Nothing Like the Real Thing," MARVIN GAYE and
    TAMMI TERRELL, 1965
65 "Stay in My Corner," THE DELLS, 1968
66 "Who's Making Love," JOHNNIE TAYLOR, 1968
67 "I Heard It through the Grapevine," MARVIN GAYE, 1968
68 "Everyday People," SLY AND THE FAMILY STONE, 1969
69 "Only the Strong Survive," JERRY BUTLER, 1969
70 "I Want You Back," THE JACKSON 5, 1970
71 "Thank You (Falettinme Be Mice Elf Agin)," SLY AND THE
    FAMILY STONE, 1970
72 "Love on a Two-Way Street," THE MOMENTS, 1970
73 "Just My Imagination (Running away with Me)," THE
    TEMPTATIONS, 1971
74 "What's Going On," MARVIN GAYE, 1971
75 "Trapped by a Thing Called Love," DENISE LA SALLE, 1971
76 "Family Affair," SLY AND THE FAMILY STONE, 1971
77 "Have You Seen Her," THE CHI-LITES, 1971
78 "Let's Stay Together," AL GREEN, 1972
79 "(If Loving You Is Wrong) I Don't Want to Be Right,"
    LUTHER INGRAM, 1972
80 "Back Stabbers," THE O'JAYS, 1972
81 "I'm Still in Love with You," AL GREEN, 1972
82 "If You Don't Know Me by Now," HAROLD MELVIN AND THE
    BLUE NOTES, 1972
83 "Superstition," STEVIE WONDER, 1973
84 "Could It Be I'm Falling in Love," THE SPINNERS, 1973
85 "One of a Kind (Love Affair)," THE SPINNERS, 1973
86 "Let's Get It On," MARVIN GAYE, 1973

87   "Lookin' for a Love," BOBBY WOMACK, 1974

88   "Rock Your Baby," GEORGE McCRAE, 1974

89   "Shame, Shame, Shame," SHIRLEY AND COMPANY, 1975

90   "Young Hearts Run Free," CANDI STATON, 1976

91   "Wake Up Everybody," HAROLD MELVIN AND THE BLUE
      NOTES, 1976

92   "Tryin' to Love Two," WILLIAM BELL, 1977

93   "Useta Be My Girl," THE O'JAYS, 1978

94   "Three Times a Lady," THE COMMODORES, 1978

95   "Le Freak," CHIC, 1978

96   "Hot Stuff," DONNA SUMMER, 1979

97   "Ain't No Stoppin Us Now," McFADDEN AND WHITEHEAD,
      1979

98   "We Are Family," SISTER SLEDGE, 1979

99   "Funkytown," LIPPS INC, 1980

100   "Master Blaster (Jammin')," STEVIE WONDER, 1980

-◄❙▶-

THE BLUES, A TO Z

1   "Atomic Blues," BERTHA HILL

2   "Big Stars Falling Blues," HUDSON WHITTAKER

3   "Constipation Blues," SCREAMIN' JAY HAWKINS

4   "Dying Crapshooter's Blues," WILLIE McTELL

5   "Evolution Blues," PLEASANT JOSEPH

6   "Future Blues," WILLIE LEE BROWN

7   "Grooving the Blues," VIOLA WELLS

8   "Hey Bud Blues," "BIG BILL" BROONZY

9   "Inflation Blues," J. C. BURRIS

10   "Jungle Man Blues," PEETIE WHEATSTRAW

11   "Keyhole Blues," PRINCESS WHITE

12   "Lonesome Desert Blues," BESSIE SMITH

13   "Mama Doo Shee Blues," IDA COX

14   "Never No Mo' Blues," JIMMIE RODGERS

15   "Organ Grinder Blues," VICTORIA SPIVEY

16   "**P**ast Forty Blues," JIMMY WITHERSPOON
17   "**Q**ueen Bee," JOHN LEE HOOKER
18   "**R**attle Snake Blues," CHARLEY PATTON
19   "**S**anta Claus Blues," WALTER DAVIS
20   "**T**ruthful Blues," LEROY CARR
21   "**U**nderworld Blues," BEULAH WALLACE
22   "**V**itamin B Blues," JOE LEE WILLIAMS
23   "**W**atergate Blues," JOHN JENKINS
24   "**X**-Rated Blues," LITTLE ELLIOT LLOYD AND THE HONEYMOON CATS
25   "**Y**o Yo Blues," "BLIND" LEMON JEFFERSON
26   "**Z**ombie Walkin' Blues," TOMMY "TEACHER MAN" GRASSO

THE DICTIONARY OF SOUL

This list includes only twenty-five titles, principally because there has never been a U.S. chart song whose title began with the letter X—nor did we choose to include "X Offender" by Blondie, which lacks a certain rhythmic style. A tip of the topper to Otis Redding, for the inspiration.

1   "**A**ce of Spade," O. V. WRIGHT
2   "**B**-A-B-Y," CARLA THOMAS
3   "**C**an I Get a Witness," MARVIN GAYE
4   "**D**oggin' Around," JACKIE WILSON
5   "**E**verybody Needs Somebody to Love," WILSON PICKETT
6   "**F**a-Fa-Fa-Fa-Fa (Sad Song)," OTIS REDDING
7   "**G**et Up, I Feel like Being a Sex Machine," JAMES BROWN
8   "**H**old On! I'm Comin'," SAM AND DAVE
9   "**I** (Who Have Nothing)," BEN E. KING
10   "**J**amie," EDDIE HOLLAND
11   "**K**nock on Wood," EDDIE FLOYD
12   "**L**ove Makes a Woman," BARBARA ACKLIN
13   "**M**y Girl," THE TEMPTATIONS
14   "**N**eed Your Love So Bad," LITTLE WILLIE JOHN

15   "Only the Strong Survive," JERRY BUTLER
16   "Precious, Precious," JACKIE MOORE
17   "Quicksand," MARTHA AND THE VANDELLAS
18   "Respect," ARETHA FRANKLIN
19   "S.Y.S.L.J.F.M. (The Letter Song)," JOE TEX
20   "Temptation 'Bout to Get Me," THE KNIGHT BROTHERS
21   "Um, Um, Um, Um, Um, Um," MAJOR LANCE
22   "Voice Your Choice," THE RADIANTS
23   "We're Gonna Make It, " LITTLE MILTON
24   "Yield Not to Temptation," BOBBY "BLUE" BLAND
25   "Zing! Went the Strings of My Heart," THE TRAMMPS

-◄❙❙►-

MIAMI STEVE VAN ZANDT'S FAVORITE 40 SOUL HITS

1   "John the Revelator," SON HOUSE
2   "Hellhound on My Trail," ROBERT JOHNSON
3   "Basin Street Blues," LOUIS ARMSTRONG
4   "I Just Want to Make Love to You," MUDDY WATERS
5   "Mardi Gras in New Orleans," PROFESSOR LONGHAIR
6   "Stagger Lee," LLOYD PRICE
7   "Blue Monday"/"Three Nights a Week," FATS DOMINO
8   "Money Honey," CLYDE MCPHATTER AND THE DRIFTERS
9   "Finger Poppin' Time," HANK BALLARD
10   "For Your Precious Love," JERRY BUTLER
11   "Why Do Fools Fall in Love," FRANKIE LYMON
12   "So Young," THE STUDENTS
13   "Let the Good Times Roll," RAY CHARLES
14   "Stand by Me," BEN E. KING; also: "There Goes My Baby,"
     with THE DRIFTERS
15   "Everybody Needs Somebody to Love," SOLOMON BURKE
16   "Shake"/"A Change Is Gonna Come," SAM COOKE; also:
     "The Last Mile of the Way," with THE SOUL STIRRERS
17   "Twist and Shout," THE ISLEY BROTHERS

18   "Loco-motion," LITTLE EVA
19   "I'll Go Crazy," JAMES BROWN
20   "Going to a Go-Go," THE MIRACLES
21   "I'm a Midnight Mover," WILSON PICKETT
22   "(Your Love Keeps Lifting Me) Higher and Higher," JACKIE WILSON
23   "Pretty Little Angel Eyes," CURTIS LEE
24   "He's a Rebel," THE CRYSTALS
25   "Will You Love Me Tomorrow," THE SHIRELLES
26   "Nowhere to Run," MARTHA AND THE VANDELLAS
27   "Walking the Dog," RUFUS THOMAS
28   "Mother-in-Law," ERNIE K-DOE
29   "Yakety Yak," THE COASTERS
30   "Holy Cow," LEE DORSEY
31   "Out of Left Field," PERCY SLEDGE
32   "Bernadette," THE FOUR TOPS
33   "I Could Never Love Another (After Loving You)," THE TEMPTATIONS
34   "(Sweet Sweet Baby) Since You've Been Gone," ARETHA FRANKLIN
35   "Just One More Day," OTIS REDDING
36   "Big Bird," EDDIE FLOYD
37   "Can I Get a Witness," MARVIN GAYE
38   "Born Again," SAM AND DAVE
39   "Let's Get It On," MARVIN GAYE
40   "Fool for You," CURTIS MAYFIELD, with the IMPRESSIONS; also "If Only I Were a Child Again"

NOTE: Miami Steve would like to apologize to Wynonie Harris, Joe Tex, Johnnie Taylor, The Supremes, Chris Kenner, William Bell, Huey Smith and the Clowns, and a million other great artists and records there wasn't enough room for.

MIAMI STEVE VAN ZANDT *is rhythm guitarist with Bruce Springsteen's E Street Band; he's also known for writing such soul gems as "I Don't Want to Go Home," "This Time It's for Real," and "Trapped Again," for Southside Johnny and the Asbury Jukes.*

SONNY ROLLINS LISTS HIS 10 FAVORITE RECORDS

1 *Amazing Grace*, ARETHA FRANKLIN
2 *Head Hunters*, HERBIE HANCOCK
3 *Songs in the Key of Life*, STEVIE WONDER
4 "Knock Me a Kiss," LOUIS JORDAN AND HIS TYMPANY FIVE
5 "Body and Soul," COLEMAN HAWKINS
6 "Lover Man," BILLIE HOLIDAY
7 "I Can't Get Started," BUNNY BERIGAN
8 "Ko-Ko," CHARLIE PARKER
9 "I'm Gonna Sit Right Down and Write Myself a Letter," FATS WALLER
10 "Afternoon of a Basie-ite," LESTER YOUNG

SONNY ROLLINS *is one of the all-time greatest jazz saxophonists. In his impressive career, which spans three decades, he has worked with some of the top names in music and recorded a series of brilliant albums. Currently, he records for Milestone.*

-◄❙❙►-

JOHN LEE HOOKER'S 10 FAVORITE RECORDING ARTISTS

1 MUDDY WATERS
2 B. B. KING
3 ALBERT COLLINS
4 BOBBY BLAND
5 OTIS SPANN
6 GEORGE BENSON
7 HOWLIN' WOLF
8 LITTLE WALTER
9 JIMMY REED
10 LIGHTNIN' HOPKINS

JOHN LEE HOOKER *has been recording blues since the Bihari brothers signed him to their West Coast-based Modern label in the late 1940s. Hooker still maintains an active touring schedule and enjoys widespread acclaim as one of the key blues guitarists.*

JAY COCKS SELECTS THE GREATEST NEW ORLEANS RHYTHM & BLUES HITS

1 "Big Chief," PROFESSOR LONGHAIR, 1964
2 "Down the Road," ROLAND STONE and DR. JOHN 1972
3 "The Fat Man," FATS DOMINO, 1950
4 "Holy Cow," LEE DORSEY, 1966
5 "I Hear You Knocking," SMILEY LEWIS, 1955
6 "I Like It Like That, Part 1," CHRIS KENNER, 1961
7 "It Will Stand," THE SHOWMEN, 1961
8 "Java," *Wild Sounds of New Orleans*, ALLEN TOUSSAINT, 1963
9 "Land of 1000 Dances," CHRIS KENNER, 1963
10 "Little Liza Jane," from *Rocking Pneumonia and Boogie Woogie Flu*, HUEY "PIANO" SMITH AND THE CLOWNS, 1959
11 "Mardi Gras in New Orleans," PROFESSOR LONGHAIR (listed as Roy "Boldhead" Byrd), 1950
12 "Mother-in-Law," ERNIE K-DOE, 1961
13 "Sea Cruise," FRANKIE FORD, 1959
14 "Tell It Like It Is," AARON NEVILLE, 1966
15 "There's Something on Your Mind," BOBBY MARCHAN, 1960
16 "The Things That I Used to Do," GUITAR SLIM, 1953
17 "Those Lonely, Lonely Nights," EARL KING, 1955
18 "Time Is on My Side," IRMA THOMAS, 1964
19 "Travelin' Mood," WEE WILLIE WAYNE, 1962 (recorded 1956)
20 "Waiting at the Station," from *Mother-in-Law*, ERNIE K-DOE 1961
21 "Walking to New Orleans," FATS DOMINO, 1960
22 "Wish Someone Would Care," IRMA THOMAS, 1964

23   "Working in the Coal Mine," LEE DORSEY, 1966
24   "You Always Hurt the One You Love," CLARENCE "FROG
      MAN" HENRY, 1961

JAY COCKS *is a screenwriter who writes about popular music for* Time, *where he was formerly film critic. Cocks lives in New York, where he hoards massive quantities of New Orleans R&B classics.*

-◀▮▶-

MOST UNLIKELY RHYTHM & BLUES HITS
All of Which Made the R&B Top 15

1   "Dede Dinah," FRANKIE AVALON
2   "Love Letters in the Sand," PAT BOONE
3   "Teen Angel," MARK DINNING
4   "Cathy's Clown," THE EVERLY BROTHERS
5   "The Theme from 'A Summer Place,'" PERCY FAITH
6   "Exodus," FERRANTE AND TEICHER
7   "It's My Party,"* LESLEY GORE
8   "Surf City," JAN AND DEAN
9   "If I Had a Hammer," TRINI LOPEZ
10   "Hey Paula," PAUL AND PAULA
11   "Pink Shoe Laces," DODIE STEVENS
12   "Calcutta," LAWRENCE WELK

*Number One on the charts

THE 15 MOST INFLUENTIAL BLUES PERFORMERS

1   MUDDY WATERS
2   B. B. KING
3   JIMMY REED
4   ROBERT JOHNSON
5   HOWLIN' WOLF
6   LITTLE WALTER
7   JOHN LEE HOOKER
8   "SONNY BOY" WILLIAMSON (RICE MILLER)
9   BESSIE SMITH
10 ELMORE JAMES
11 JUNIOR PARKER
12 FREDDIE KING
13 "BIG BILL" BROONZY
14 OTIS SPANN
15 SONNY TERRY AND BROWNIE MCGHEE

-◄❚▮►-

15 GREAT ELECTRIC BLUES GUITARISTS

1   B. B. KING
2   JIMMY ROGERS
3   T-BONE WALKER
4   FREDDIE KING
5   BUDDY GUY
6   ALBERT COLLINS
7   LEFTY BATES
8   OTIS RUSH
9   HUBERT SUMLIN
10 MUDDY WATERS
11 IKE TURNER
12 SON SEALS
13 HOUND DOG TAYLOR
14 J. B. LENOIR
15 ALBERT KING

MUDDY WATERS' DREAM BAND

1 Piano: OTIS SPANN
2 Harmonica: LITTLE WALTER
3 Drums: FRED BELOW
4 Bass: BIG CRAWFORD and WILLIE DIXON
5 Guitar: PAT HARE and JIMMY ROGERS

MUDDY WATERS *took the Delta blues from Mississippi to Chicago, electrified it, and became a legend. He has inspired an incredible number of rock performers, including The Rolling Stones, who took their name from one of his songs. He continues to tour and record prolifically.*

-◄▐▶-

THE MOST CHALLENGING AUDIENCES FOR WHICH MUDDY WATERS HAS PLAYED

1 Leeds, England, 1958; Waters' first overseas trip
2 Newport Jazz Festival, 1960
3 Canberra City, Australia, May 6, 1976; the date was played in a circus tent; this concert was particularly astounding because the elephants responded to the music by swaying, shaking and standing up on their back legs.
4 The Last Waltz, Winterland Auditorium, San Francisco, November 1978
5 White House Lawn Picnic, August 9, 1978

-◄▐▶-

REALLY THE BLUES

1 BOBBY "BLUE" BLAND
2 BLUE ASH
3 BLUE CHEER
4 BLUE MAGIC
5 BLUE ÖYSTER CULT
6 BLUE RIDGE RANGERS
7 BLUE SWEDE
8 DAVID BLUE
9 BLUES IMAGE
10 THE BLUES MAGOOS

11	THE BLUES PROJECT	14	ROOMFUL OF BLUES
12	B. B. ("BLUES BOY") KING	15	SUGAR BLUE
13	THE MOODY BLUES		

EDDIE FLOYD'S FAVORITE SOUL SINGERS

1	JOHNNY ACE	6	OTIS REDDING
2	WILLIAM BELL	7	JOHNNIE TAYLOR
3	JESSE BELVIN	8	JOE TEX
4	SAM COOKE	9	CHUCK WILLIS
5	LITTLE WILLIE JOHN	10	JACKIE WILSON

NOTE: "Tell Wilson Pickett to forgive me," says Floyd.

EDDIE FLOYD *is the author of such soul classics as "Knock on Wood," "634-5789," "Raise Your Hand," and "Ninety-Nine and a Half (Won't Do)," which have been hits for himself, Wilson Pickett, and other artists. He still actively tours and records.*

-◄❙❙►-

ALLEN GINSBERG'S FAVORITE BLUES RECORDS

1 "James Alley Blues," RICHARD "RABBIT" BROWN
2 "Washington D.C. Hospital Center Blues," "Drunken Spree," SKIP JAMES
3 "Jim Crow Blues" (a rare, sublime political blues), "Birmingham Jail," "Irene," "Black Girl," etc., LEADBELLY
4 "See See Rider Blues," "Jelly Bean Blues," MA RAINEY
5 "Baby Doll," BESSIE SMITH
6 "Don't Explain," "I Gotta Right to Sing the Blues," BILLIE HOLIDAY
7 "Long Tall Sally," LITTLE RICHARD
8 "Cannon Ball Blues," FRED HUTCHINSON
9 "Blueberry Hill," etc., FATS DOMINO

10   "I Got a Woman," "Georgia on My Mind," etc., RAY
     CHARLES
11   "Waiting for the Train," "Way Out on the Mountain," "Mule
     Skinner Blues," "T for Texas," "The Mystery of Number
     Five," JIMMIE RODGERS
12   "Cold, Cold Heart," "Your Cheating Heart," HANK WILLIAMS
13   "Absolutely Sweet Marie," "It's All Over Now, Baby Blue,"
     "Idiot Wind," "In the Garden," BOB DYLAN
14   Oeuvre, JOHN LENNON
15   Oeuvre, MICK JAGGER
16   "Dildo Song," "Raspberry Song," "Keep It Clean in
     Between" (see *Asshole Poems and Smiling Vegetable Songs*,
     City Lights, 1978), PETER ORLOVSKY

ALLEN GINSBERG *is America's leading bard. His interests have ranged from Tibetan
Buddhism to singing the blues.*

-◄▮▮►-

THE POINTER SISTERS' 10 FAVORITE HARMONY GROUPS

1	THE POINTER SISTERS	6	THE O'JAYS
2	SEALS AND CROFTS	7	QUEEN
3	THE TEMPTATIONS	8	GLADYS KNIGHT AND THE PIPS
4	THE JACKSONS	9	EARTH, WIND, AND FIRE
5	SISTER SLEDGE	10	THE OAK RIDGE BOYS

THE POINTER SISTERS *are best known for their pop hits "Yes We Can Can," "Fire,"
and "He's So Shy," but the Oakland-based trio sings in a wide variety of styles,
from modern rhythm & blues to forties pop.*

CARLA THOMAS' 5 FAVORITE SWEET-SOUL SINGERS

1 DINAH WASHINGTON
2 OTIS REDDING
3 LARRY GRAHAM
4 AARON NEVILLE
5 SAM COOKE

CARLA THOMAS *is best known for such hits as "B-A-B-Y" and "Gee Whiz (Look at His Eyes)," and for a series of duets with Otis Redding, especially "Tramp." The daughter of Rufus Thomas, Carla was one of the first acts signed to Stax Records.*

-◀▮▶-

THE 10 FUNKIEST JAMES BROWN SONG TITLES

1 "I Don't Want Nobody to Give Me Nothing (Open Up the Door, I'll Get It Myself)"
2 "Hot Pants (She Got to Use What She Got to Get What She Wants)"
3 "Say It Loud, I'm Black and I'm Proud"
4 "Get Up I Feel Like Being a Sex Machine"
5 "It's Too Funky in Here"
6 "It's a Man's, Man's, Man's World"
7 "Papa's Got a Brand New Bag"
8 "I Got Ants in My Pants and I Want to Dance"
9 "I Can't Stand Myself (When You Touch Me)"
10 "Let a Man Come in and Do the Popcorn"

-◀▮▶-

35 MULTIPART HITS BY JAMES BROWN

1 "Ain't It Funky Now," part one
2 "Ain't That a Groove," part one
3 "America Is My Home," part one

4   "Body Heat," part one
5   "Brother Rapp," parts one and two
6   "Cold Sweat," part one
7   "Escape-ism," part one
8   "Funky Drummer," part one
9   "Get It Together," part one
10   "Get on the Good Foot," part one
11   "Get Up Get into It Get Involved," part one
12   "Get Up I Feel Like Being a Sex Machine," part one
13   "Honky Tonk," part one
14   "Hot Pants (She Got to Use What She Got to Get What She Wants)," part one
15   "I Don't Want Nobody to Give Me Nothing (Open up the Door, I'll Get It Myself)," part one
16   "I Got Ants in My Pants and I Want to Dance," part one
17   "I'm a Greedy Man," part one
18   "It's a New Day," parts one and two
19   "Let a Man Come in and Do the Popcorn," parts one and two
20   "Make It Funky," part one
21   "Money Won't Change You," part one
22   "Mother Popcorn," part one
23   "Oh Baby, Don't You Weep," part one
24   "Papa Don't Take No Mess," part one
25   "Papa's Got a Brand New Bag," part one
26   "The Payback," part one
27   "Say It Loud, I'm Black and I'm Proud," part one
28   "Sex Machine," part one
29   "Soul Power," part one
30   "Spinning Wheel," part one
31   "Stoned to the Bone," part one
32   "Super Bad," parts one and two
33   "Talking Loud and Saying Nothing," part one
34   "There It Is," part one
35   "World," part one

TWENTY-FOUR:
LIFE—REAL & SURREAL

Grace Slick cools off during an outdoor concert at Gaelic Park in the Bronx during the summer of 1974.

25 SONGS ABOUT REAL PEOPLE

1 **"Abraham, Martin and John,"** DION
   Written by Dick Feller about Abraham Lincoln, Martin Luther King Jr., John—and Robert—Kennedy.

2 **"American Pie,"** DON MCLEAN
   Dedicated to Buddy Holly.

3 **"Angie,"** THE ROLLING STONES
   Written by Mick Jagger and Keith Richards about Angela Bowie, David's wife.

4 **"Claudette,"** ROY ORBISON
   About Roy's first wife, Claudette.

5 **"Crucifixion,"** PHIL OCHS
   About John Kennedy.

6 **"Dandelion,"** THE ROLLING STONES
   Written by Mick Jagger and Keith Richards about Richards' daughter.

7 **"Delta Lady,"** JOE COCKER
   Written by Leon Russell about Russell's then-heartthrob, Rita Coolidge.

8 **"Dolly Dagger,"** JIMI HENDRIX
   Written about Jimi's girlfriend, Devon Wilson.

9 **"Donna,"** RITCHIE VALENS
   Written about Valens' girlfriend, Donna Ludwig.

10 **"Frankie,"** CONNIE FRANCIS
   Written by Neil Sedaka, but it was Connie who had the crush on Frankie Avalon.

11 **"The Hustler,"** ERIC ANDERSEN
   Thinly veiled diatribe about Bob Dylan.

12 **"Sad-Eyed Lady of the Lowlands,"** BOB DYLAN
   About Dylan's wife, Sara Lownds.

13 **"Jennie Lee,"** JAN AND DEAN
   Written about a stripper appearing in downtown Los Angeles.

14 **"Just the Way You Are,"** BILLY JOEL
   Written as a birthday present for his wife (and then manager) Elizabeth.

15 **"Layla,"** ERIC CLAPTON
Written about his frustrated love for Patti Boyd Harrison, then married to his friend, Beatle George. True love won out, and Patti and Eric are today husband and wife.

16 **"Linda,"** JAN AND DEAN
Written in 1947 by Jack Lawrence for the daughter of his attorney, Lee Eastman. Linda Eastman is now married to Paul McCartney, who has written many other songs about her, including the celebrated "Cook of the House."

17 **"Long Time Gone,"** CROSBY, STILLS, AND NASH
Written by David Crosby for Robert Kennedy.

18 **"Oh! Carol,"** NEIL SEDAKA
About Carole King.

19 **"Peggy Sue,"** BUDDY HOLLY
For Peggy Sue Gerrow, who married Jerry Allison of the Crickets. Buddy almost chickened out and called this one "Cindy Lou."

20 **"Puppy Love,"** PAUL ANKA
Written about his crush on Annette Funicello

21 **"Shine on You Crazy Diamond,"** PINK FLOYD
Written by Roger Walters for the group's original leader, Syd Barrett.

22 **"Surfer Girl,"** THE BEACH BOYS
Written by Brian Wilson about his then-girlfriend, Judy Bowles.

23 **"Tonight's the Night,"** NEIL YOUNG
Written for two friends who had overdosed, roadie Bruce Berry and guitarist Danny Whitten of Crazy Horse.

24 **"You Gave Me the Answer,"** PAUL McCARTNEY
Dedicated to Gene Kelly, Fred Astaire, and Lenny Bruce.

25 **"You're So Vain,"** CARLY SIMON
There have been dozens of rumors about the subject of this vicious put-down, since writer-producer Simon has had numerous liaisons with the famous. But the consensus seems to be that the victim is Warren Beatty, although Mick Jagger probably still thinks it's about him—he sings on it, after all.

20 SONGS ABOUT PARENTS

1 "A Boy Named Sue," JOHNNY CASH
2 "Adam Raised a Cain," BRUCE SPRINGSTEEN
3 "Daddy Could Swear, I Declare," GLADYS KNIGHT AND THE PIPS
4 "Daddy's Song," JACKSON BROWNE
5 "Don't Cry Daddy," ELVIS PRESLEY
6 "Give Us Your Blessings," THE SHANGRI-LAS
7 "Got to See if I Can't Get Mommy (to Come Back Home)," JERRY BUTLER
8 "Have You Seen Your Mother, Baby, Standing in the Shadows?" THE ROLLING STONES
9 "I'm Bugged at My Old Man," THE BEACH BOYS
10 "Independence Day," BRUCE SPRINGSTEEN
11 "My Idaho Home," RONEE BLAKELY
12 "My Old Man," IAN DURY
13 "Papa Was a Rollin' Stone," THE TEMPTATIONS
14 "Patches," CLARENCE CARTER
15 "She's Leaving Home," THE BEATLES
16 "So Young," THE STUDENTS
17 "Society's Child," JANIS IAN
18 "Surrender," CHEAP TRICK
19 "Teach Your Children," CROSBY, STILLS, NASH AND YOUNG
20 "Was I Right or Wrong," LYNYRD SKYNYRD

-◀❙▶-

TWO DOZEN ROCKERS WITH FAMOUS PARENTS

1 **ROCKY and BILL BURNETTE**
These two, who began their recording careers in the late seventies, are the sons of brothers Dorsey and Johnny Burnette, respectively. Their dads were in one of the firs

important rockabilly groups, The Rock and Roll Trio, in the fifties.

2 **RANDY CALIFORNIA**

Randy played guitar with his step-father, drummer Ed Cassidy, in Spirit. Cassidy was also a member of Taj Mahal and Ry Cooder's Rising Sons for a time.

3 **SHAUN and DAVID CASSIDY**

They are the sons of the late actor Jack Cassidy. Shaun's mother is actress Shirley Jones, who played David's mother in the TV series *The Partridge Family*. Offstage, she was David's real-life step-mother.

4 **NATALIE COLE**

She is the daughter of Nat "King" Cole.

5 **MARK DINNING**

His mother was one of The Dinning Sisters, who were famous in the 1940s and 1950s. The others, of course, were the "Teen Angel" lad's aunts.

6 **DINO, DESI, AND BILLY**

The first two are the sons of Dean Martin and Desi Arnaz, respectively; Billy's brother-in-law is Carl Wilson; and the group's manager, Bill Howard, is the son of Dorothy Lamour.

7 **KIM FOWLEY**

His father, Douglas, played Doc Holliday on TV's *The Life and Legend of Wyatt Earp*. Myron Healey, however, was the one who made the role famous.

8 **ANDREW GOLD**

Gold's father, Ernest, writes movie scores. His mother is singer Marni Nixon, best known for dubbing famous voices in *West Side Story*, *The King and I*, and *My Fair Lady*.

9 **LOUISE GOFFIN**

Louise is the daughter of famed songwriters Carole King and Gerry Goffin.

10 **JOHN PAUL HAMMOND**

The white blues singer is the son of legendary talent scout and record producer John Hammond.

11 **BUDDY HOLLY**
His mother, Ella Holley, wrote the lyrics to "Maybe Baby," although she was not credited.

12 **PAUL KOSSOFF**
The guitarist's father, David, is a noted British actor.

13 **GARY LEWIS**
The Playboys' leader is the son of comedian and philanthropist Jerry Lewis.

14 **PETER LEWIS**
The Moby Grape guitarist is the son of Loretta Young.

15 **TERRY MELCHER**
The record producer and session-group maven (The Fantastic Baggys, The Rip Chords, etc.) is the son of Doris Day.

16 **JIM MORRISON**
His father, Stephen, is an admiral in the U.S. Navy.

17 **RICK NELSON**
Nelson is the son of Ozzie and Harriet of the TV show, which is where he got his start.

18 **MICHAEL NESMITH**
His mother invented Ko·Rec·Type.

19 **SHUGGIE OTIS**
The guitarist is the son of bandleader Johnny Otis.

20 **MACKENZIE PHILLIPS**
Formerly of the TV series *One Day at a Time*, is the daughter of John Phillips of The Mamas and the Papas.

21 **BILLY PRESTON**
His mother, Ernesta Wade, played Saffire in both the radio and television versions of *Amos 'n' Andy*.

22 **HUNT and TONY SALES**
Soupy Sales' sons have recorded with David Bowie, Iggy Pop, and Todd Rundgren.

23 **CARLY SIMON**
Her father, Richard, founded the publishing house Simon and Schuster.

24 **NEIL YOUNG**
His father, Scott, is perhaps the best-known sports (and now general interest) columnist in Canada.

20 SONGS ABOUT CHILDREN

1   "Another Brick in the Wall," PINK FLOYD
2   "As Tears Go By," THE ROLLING STONES
3   "Baby Talk," JAN AND DEAN
4   "First Born Son," THE MCGARRIGLE SISTERS
5   "Forever Young," BOB DYLAN
6   "Growin' Up," BRUCE SPRINGSTEEN
7   "I Am a Child," NEIL YOUNG
8   "Little Children," BILLY J. KRAMER AND THE DAKOTAS
9   "Memphis," CHUCK BERRY
10   "Ob-La-Di, Ob-La-Da," THE BEATLES
11   "Our House," CROSBY, STILLS, NASH, AND YOUNG
12   "Ready or Not," JACKSON BROWNE
13   "Rufus Is a Tit Man," LOUDON WAINWRIGHT III
14   "Someday Never Comes," CREEDENCE CLEARWATER REVIVAL
15   "Teddy Bear," ELVIS PRESLEY
16   "When I Grow Up to Be a Man," THE BEACH BOYS
17   "Yellow Submarine," THE BEATLES
18   "You Angel You," BOB DYLAN
19   "You Better Sit Down Kids," SONNY AND CHER
20   "Younger Generation," THE LOVIN' SPOONFUL

-◄▮►-

THE KIDS ARE ALRIGHT
50 Famous Rock and Roll Siblings

1   **DUANE and GREGG ALLMAN**
The late guitarist of The Allman Brothers Band and keyboardist-vocalist Gregg (who married Cher) are brothers.

2   **RON and SCOTT ASHETON**
The original Stooges (later called Rock Action) included brothers Ron on guitar and Scott (later of Rock Action) on drums.

Don and Phil Everly.

3   **RANDY and ROBBIE BACHMAN**
    Guitarist Randy and drummer Robbie of Bachman-Turner
    Overdrive are brothers.

4   **JOAN BAEZ and MIMI FARIÑA**
    Joan and folk singer-activist Mimi (ex-wife of Richard Fariña)
    are sisters.

5   **BILL and JOHNNY BLACK**
    Elvis Presley's original bassist was the brother of Johnny
    Black, who joined The Rock and Roll Trio after Dorsey
    Burnette quit. (See No. 7.)

6   **EDGAR AND STEVE BROUGHTON**
    The vocalist-guitarist of The Edgar Broughton Band was joined
    by his brother, Alex, on drums.

7   **JOHNNY and DORSEY BURNETTE**
    The Rock and Roll Trio featured these brothers. (See No. 5.)

8   **ERNIE AND EARL CATE**
    The Cate Brothers Band members are twins.

9   **LESTER, GEORGE, and JOE CHAMBERS**
    The Chambers Brothers were just that.

10 **HARRY, TOM, and JIM CHAPIN**
    Harry often worked with his two brothers.

11 **BILL and B. B. CUNNINGHAM**
    The two brothers from Memphis went on to rock and roll
    success—Bill in The Box Tops ("The Letter"), B.B. in The
    Hombres ("Let It Out [Let It All Hang Out]").

12 **RAY and DAVE DAVIES**
    The Kinks' Ray Davies (songwriting, vocals, guitar) and Dave
    (lead guitar) are brothers.

13 **RICK and RANDY DERRINGER (originally Zehringer)**
    Guitarist Rick played in The McCoys with his brother on
    drums.

14 **RODNEY and DOUG DILLARD**
    The Dillards consisted of brothers Rodney on guitar and Doug
    on banjo.

15 **PHIL and DON EVERLY**
    The vocalists *extraordinaire* are brothers.

16   **JOHN and TOM FOGERTY**
Songwriter-vocalist John shared guitar-playing chores with his brother in Creedence Clearwater Revival.

17   **SIMON and FRED FRITH**
The rock critic's brother, Fred, is an avant-garde guitarist (Henry Cow, Art Bears, et al.).

18   **MIKE and PETER GILES**
Robert Fripp's first recording group, Giles, Giles and Fripp, featured brothers Mike on drums and Peter on bass.

19   **ADRIAN and PAUL GURVITZ**
Adrian (guitar) and brother Paul (bass) were featured in both the Bronx heavy-metal band Gun and The Baker-Gurvitz Army with former Cream drummer Ginger Baker.

20   **JIMMY, JACK, and DONNA HALL**
Wet Willie vocalists Jimmy and Jack were joined by their sister, Donna, on occasional backing vocals.

21   **LES and ALEX HARVEY**
The late guitarist of Stone the Crows (he was electrocuted in midperformance by an improperly grounded microphone) was the brother of Alex Harvey of The Sensational Alex Harvey Band.

22   **RONALD, RUDOLPH, KELLY, ERNIE, and MARVIN ISLEY**
Originally, The Isley Brothers consisted of Ronald, Rudolph, and Kelly. In the seventies, they added much younger brothers Ernie (guitar, drums) and Marvin (bass), as well as their cousin, keyboardist Chris Jasper.

23   **MICHAEL, TITO, JACKIE, MARLON, and JERMAINE JACKSON**
The Jackson 5 were all brothers. The core of the group left Motown for Philadelphia International (and further success as The Jacksons), but Jermaine stayed behind. Reason: He married Motown president Berry Gordy Jr.'s daughter.

24   **BILLY J. KRAMER and ELKIE BROOKS**
Merseybeat singer Kramer is the brother of Brooks (Vinegar Joe).

25 ALVIN and RIC LEE
Ten Years After featured Alvin on guitar and brother Ric on drums.

26 NILS and TOM LOFGREN
The guitarist-keyboardist added his brother Tom to Grin as an additional guitarist.

27 DARLENE LOVE and EDNA WRIGHT
Love ("Today I Met the Boy I'm Gonna Marry"), the best of the Phil Spector singers, is the sister of Wright of The Honey Cone ("Want Ads").

28 RON and RUSSELL MAEL
The members of Sparks are brothers.

29 KATE and ANNA McGARRIGLE
The Canadian art-folkies are sisters.

30 JUNE and JEAN MILLINGTON
June played guitar and her sister, Jean, played bass for Fanny.

31 AARON, ART, and CYRIL NEVILLE
Spearheaded by the Neville brothers, The Meters are undoubtedly the funkiest combination on this list.

32 ANITA, BONNIE, JUNE, and RUTH POINTER
Originally, The Pointer Sisters featured all four artists. But Bonnie later split to a solo career at Motown; the others continued as a trio.

33 SUZI and MICHAEL QUATRO
Quatro, of English rock fame ("Can the Can"), has a brother who specialized in particularly excruciating classical rock keyboard playing and once was a concert promoter in their native Detroit.

34 SUZZY, MAGGIE, and TERRE ROCHE
These bohemian harmonizers are sisters.

35 PETER and CARL ROWAN
These Marin County hippie-brothers had their own group, The Rowans.

36 HUNT and TONY SALES
Soupy Sales' sons have backed David Bowie, Todd Rundgren, and Iggy Pop.

37 **JIMMY and DAN SEALS**
Jimmy Seals, of Seals and Crofts, is the brother of Dan Seals of England Dan and John Ford Coley.

38 **CARLY and LUCY SIMON**
Sister Lucy also sings.

39 **SLY, FREDDIE, and ROSIE STONE**
Sly and the Family Stone was accurately named; in addition to cousin Larry Graham on bass, the band included Sly's brother Freddie on guitar and sister Rosie on vocals and piano.

40 **JOE and LEVI STUBBS**
Joe Stubbs, of The Falcons, is the brother of The Four Tops' lead singer.

41 **RALPH, POOCH, CHUBBY, BUTCH, AND TINY TAVARES**
An all-brother band that began performing around New England in the fifties, backing their father.

42 **JAMES, ALEX, LIVINGSTON, and KATE TAYLOR**
James is only one of four members of his family to make pop-rock records: The others are his two brothers and sister.

43 **PETE and SIMON TOWNSHEND**
Simon has made occasional records with and without his brother's assistance.

44 **MARY and BETTY WEISS; MARY ANN and MARGE GANSER**
Shangri-Las lead singer Mary and vocalist Betty are sisters; the Gansers, also of The Shangri-Las, are twins.

45 **ANN and NANCY WILSON**
Heart is led by the Wilson sisters, who would be the queens of heavy metal if heavy metal were not ruled by male primogeniture.

46 **BRIAN, CARL, and DENNIS WILSON**
Beach Boys Brian (bass, keyboards, vocals, songwriting), Carl (guitar), and Dennis (drums) are brothers. Mike Love (vocals) is their cousin; and their former manager, Murry Wilson, was their father.

47 **RICK and CINDY WILSON**
The B-52's singers are brother and sister.

48 **JOHNNY** and **EDGAR WINTER**
    Both brothers are albinos.

49 **STEVE** and **MUFF WINWOOD**
    Not only was Steve the real musical leader of The Spencer
    Davis Group, but his brother, who's now an A&R man in
    England, played bass for the band.

50 **BOBBY** and **CECIL WOMACK**
    The Womacks and three other singing and guitar-playing
    brothers formed The Valentinos, a gospel group backing their
    father, a minister.

·◄❙▶·

TWINS

1 MARGE and MARY ANN GANSER, of The Shangri-Las
2 MAURICE and ROBIN GIBB, of The Bee Gees, of course
3 MICK and KEITH GLIMMER, of The Glimmer Twins
4 SCOTT and THOMAS HERRICK, of The Arbors
5 THE KALIN TWINS (their only hit: "When," 1958)
6 JOHN and PAUL NURK, of The Nurk Twins
7 CHARLES and JOHN PANOZZO, of Styx
8 ELVIS and JESSE PRESLEY (Jesse died, altering history in
   unfathomable ways.)

·◄❙▶·

5 DISTANT RELATIONS

1 **JAMES BROWN**
   Barbara Mason ("Yes I'm Ready") is his cousin.

2 **SAM COOKE**
   R. B. Greaves ("Take a Letter Maria") is his nephew.

3 **HARVEY FUQUA**
   The lead singer of many Moonglows hits and later a force at
   Motown, Harvey was the cousin of Charlie Fuqua of the

original Ink Spots. Harvey Fuqua later married Motown president Berry Gordy Jr.'s sister.

4 **JERRY LEE LEWIS**
Mickey Gilley is his cousin.

5 **RANDY NEWMAN**
His uncles, Alfred and Lionel, were famous composers of movie scores.

-◄❚▮▶-

THE 15 MOST ELIGIBLE BACHELORS

1	BRUCE SPRINGSTEEN	9	JOHN LYDON
2	DAVID LEE ROTH	10	MICHAEL JACKSON
3	TEDDY PENDERGRASS	11	CLARENCE CLEMONS
4	J. D. SOUTHER	12	CHUCK BERRY
5	CHRISSIE HYNDE	13	LINDA RONSTADT
6	DAVID BYRNE	14	DON HENLEY
7	JOE STRUMMER	15	PETER WOLF
8	TOM ROBINSON		

-◄❚▮▶-

GUESTS AT MICK AND BIANCA JAGGER'S WEDDING
May 12, 1971, St. Tropez Town Hall

1	MR. and MRS. PAT ARNOLD	9	DAVID BROWN
2	SHIRLEY ARNOLD	10	DES BROWN
3	JOHN BATTGES	11	MR. and MRS. RICKY BURNS
4	JO BERGMAN	12	DONALD CAMEL
5	JEAN MARIE BERIER	13	MARSHALL CHESS
6	BERNARD DE BOLLSON	14	MR. CHRYSOSTOM
7	DEREK BOLTON	15	HOIMA CHURCHILL
8	JEAN BOUQUIN	16	TREVOR CHURCHILL

17   ERIC CLAPTON
18   MR. and MRS. OZZIE CLARK
19   NATALIE DELON
20   MR. and MRS. TONY DOMINGUES
21   AHMET ERTEGUN
22   MISS C. FINDLEY
23   LIZ GARRETT
24   CHRISTOPHER GIBBS
25   MYRIAM GIBRIL
26   JIM GORDON
27   ALICE ORMSBY GORE
28   JULIAN ORMSBY GORE
29   VICTORIA ORMSBY GORE
30   MR. and MRS. NICKY HOPKINS
31   CHRIS JAGGER
32   MR. and MRS. JOSEPH JAGGER
33   DAVE JEFFRIES
34   IAN JEFFRIES
35   MR. and MRS. RONNIE JONES
36   BOBBY KEYES
37   EDDIE KRAMER
38   DOMENIQUE LAMBLIN
39   MR. and MRS. RONNIE LANE
40   MR. and MRS. SANDY LEIBERSON
41   D. LINDLEY
42   PATRICK LITCHFIELD
43   MRS. B. LEWIS
44   JULIAN LLOYD
45   CHRISTIAN MARQUAND
46   HEATHER and MARY MCCARTNEY
47   MR. and MRS. PAUL MCCARTNEY
48   ANNA MENZIES
49   LEE MILES
50   JIMMY MILLER
51   MARK PALMER
52   MR. and MRS. LES PERRIN
53   CAROLINE PFEIFFER
54   Police chief (St. Tropez)
55   MARC PORCEL
56   MR. and MRS. JIM PRICE
57   MR. and MRS. TERRY REID
58   MICHAEL SHRIEVE
59   CHRISTOPHER SYKES
60   MR. and MRS. RICHARD STARKEY
61   STEPHEN STILLS
62   IAN STEWART
63   MALDIN THOMAS
64   FRED TROWBRIDGE
65   DORIS TROY
66   ROGER VADIM
67   JOHN WALKER
68   MR. CHRIS WOOD
69   MAUREEN WOODHAM
70   VIVIAN ZARVIS

I'VE GOT 2 LOVERS AND I AIN'T ASHAMED
Women Who Have Married More Than 1 Celebrity

1   PATTI BOYD (George Harrison, Eric Clapton)
2   BARBARA CAMPBELL (Sam Cooke, Bobby Womack)
3   BONNIE CAMPBELL (Merle Haggard, Buck Owens)
4   CHER (Sonny Bono, Gregg Allman)
5   JESSI COLTER (Duane Eddy, Waylon Jennings)
6   SARA DAVIS (Mac Davis, Glen Campbell)
7   BILLIE JEAN ESHLIMAR (Hank Williams, Johnny Horton)
8   MIRIAM MAKEBA (Hugh Masekela, Stokely Carmichael)
9   KIM MOON (Keith Moon, Ian MacLagan)

AMERICAN INDIAN PERFORMERS

1   JIMMY CARL BLACK ("He's the Indian of the group," said The Mothers of Invention on their early album covers.)
2   JOHNNY CASH
3   JESSE ED DAVIS
4   JIMI HENDRIX (one-quarter Cherokee)
5   BUFFY SAINTE-MARIE
6   PATRICK SKY
7   THE THUNDERBIRDS
8   PAT and LOLLY VEGAS (Redbone)
9   LINK WRAY

25 ITALIAN-AMERICANS

1   FRANKIE AVALON
2   SONNY BONO
3   FREDDY CANNON
4   THE CAPRIS
5   LOU CHRISTIE
6   BOBBY DARIN
7   JOEY DEE
8   DION AND THE BELMONTS
9   THE ELEGANTS
10 FABIAN

11	EDDIE FONTAINE	19	BOBBY RYDELL
12	ANNETTE FUNICELLO	20	JOHN SEBASTIAN
13	THE GAYLORDS	21	BRUCE SPRINGSTEEN
14	MARIA MULDAUR	22	THE THREE CHUCKLES
15	FELIX PAPPALARDI	23	FRANKIE VALLI AND
16	GENE PITNEY		the FOUR SEASONS
17	THE RASCALS	24	MIAMI STEVE VAN ZANDT
18	THE REGENTS	25	FRANK ZAPPA

NICE JEWISH BOYS

1	MICHAEL BLOOMFIELD	5	DICK DALE
2	MARC BOLAN (T. Rex)	6	BOB DYLAN
3	RANDY CALIFORNIA (Spirit)		(born Zimmerman)
4	LEONARD COHEN	7	ART GARFUNKEL

UPI

"You Gotta Serve Somebody": Bob Dylan visits the Wailing Wall in Jerusalem on his thirtieth birthday, May 24, 1971. The singer/songwriter's later work from his "born again" period attests to the fact that the yarmulke was adjustable.

8   PETER GREEN
     (Fleetwood Mac)
9   HOWARD KAYLAN
     (Flo and Eddie)
10   AL KOOPER
11   MANFRED MANN
12   PHIL OCHS
13   JOEY RAMONE (The Ramones)
14   PAUL SIMON
15   GENE SIMMONS (Kiss)
16   PHIL SPECTOR
17   PAUL STANLEY (Kiss)
18   MARK VOLMAN (Flo and
19   LESLIE WEST (Mountain)
20   PETER WOLF (The J. Gei
21   ZAL YANOVSKY (Lovin' S
22   WARREN ZEVON

-◄▮▶-

NICE JEWISH GIRLS

1   KARLA BONOFF
2   LOTTE GOLDEN
3   LESLEY GORE
4   ELLIE GREENWICH
5   JANIS IAN
6   CAROLE KING
7   LEAH KUNKEL
8   LINDA EASTMAN
9   CAROLYNE MAS
10   BETTE MIDLER
11   GENYA RAVEN
12   ELLEN SHIPLEY
13   CARLY SIMON
14   PHOEBE SNOW
15   RACHEL SWEET

-◄▮▶-

GOOD CATHOLIC BOYS

1   EDDIE BRIGATI (The Rascals)
2   FELIX CAVALIERE (The Rascals)
3   ELVIS COSTELLO
4   DION DIMUCCI
5   BOB GELDOF (The Boomtown Rats)
6   JOHN LYDON (Public Image Ltd.)
7   BRUCE SPRINGSTEEN

8   THE UNDERTONES
9   MIAMI STEVE VAN ZANDT
10   JAH WOBBLE (Public Image Ltd.)

-◄❚❙►-

JEHOVAH'S WITNESSES

1   LESTER BANGS
2   GEORGE BENSON
3   ORNETTE COLEMAN
4   LARRY GRAHAM (Sly and the Family Stone, Graham Central
    Station)
5   HANK MARVIN (The Shadows)
6   THE MODERN JAZZ QUARTET
7   VAN MORRISON
8   HUEY "PIANO" SMITH
9   DAVID THOMAS (Pere Ubu)

-◄❚❙►-

PAST AND PRESENT RELIGIOUS PERSUASIONS AND PECCADILLOES OF THE HIGH AND MIGHTY

1   BOB DYLAN, fundamentalist Christian
2   ROBERT FRIPP, Gurdjieff and a J. G. Bennett Sherbourne
    monastery survivor
3   ARLO GUTHRIE, Roman Catholic convert
4   GEORGE HARRISON, Krishna
5   KEITH JARRETT, Gurdjieff
6   RONNIE LANE, Meher Baba
7   LITTLE RICHARD, Seventh-Day Adventist
8   ROGER MCGUINN, Subud
9   ELVIS PRESLEY, Assembly of God (Pentecostal Christians)
10   CARLOS SANTANA, Sri Chinmoy

11   SEALS AND CROFTS, Bah'aism
12   JEREMY SPENCER, Children of God (fundamentalist
     Christians)
13   PETE TOWNSHEND, Meher Baba

-◄❚▶-

PERFORMERS CONNECTED WITH THE MAHARISHI MAHESH YOGI AND TRANSCENDENTAL MEDITATION

1   THE BEACH BOYS
2   THE BEATLES
3   DONOVAN
4   MARIANNE FAITHFULL
5   MIA FARROW
6   PAUL HORN
7   MICK JAGGER (The Rolling Stones)
8   BRIAN JONES (The Rolling Stones)
9   ROBBIE KRIEGER (The Doors)
10 RAY MANZAREK (The Doors)
11 SKIP SPENCE (Moby Grape)
12 MAURICE and VERDINE WHITE (Earth, Wind, and Fire)

-◄❚▶-

THEY SAW THE LIGHT
Born-Again Rockers

1	ROY BUCHANAN	7	ROBIN LANE
2	T-BONE BURNETT	8	LITTLE RICHARD
3	JOHNNY CASH	9	CARL PERKINS
4	BOB DYLAN	10	P. J. PROBY
5	AL GREEN	11	JEREMY SPENCER
6	PETER GREEN	12	DONNA SUMMER

PREACHERS
Rock and Rollers Who Are Ordained Ministers

1 **SOLOMON BURKE**
Burke became a minister at age nine. Billed then as the "Wonder Boy Preacher," he returns to the cloth every now and then.

2 **LITTLE RICHARD**
He returns periodically to the church to cleanse his soul and denounce his decadent former lifestyle.

3 **AL GREEN**
Since retiring around 1976 to devote time to studying for the ministry, Green has recorded only rarely and now has a flock at a Memphis parish.

4 **JOHNNIE TAYLOR**
Taylor was ordained but is not practicing.

5 **JOE TEX**
Tex was ordained as a Muslim minister.

6 **HANK MIZELL**
Mizell is a nonpracticing ordained minister.

7 **JIM RISSMILLER**
Rissmiller, a Los Angeles concert promoter, was ordained as an evangelist in his youth.

-◄❚❚►-

SON OF A PREACHER MAN
And His Daughter, Too

1 JESSI COLTER
2 RITA and PRISCILLA COOLIDGE
3 SAM COOKE
4 ALICE COOPER
5 PAUL DAVIS
6 MARK DINNING

7   ERNIE K-DOE
8   ARETHA, CAROLYN, and ERMA FRANKLIN
9   MARVIN GAYE
10   CLYDE MCPHATTER
11   THE POINTER SISTERS (both parents)
12   OTIS REDDING
13   LINK WRAY (both parents)

-◄▮►-

DANCIN' WITH MR. D.

1   "Black Sabbath," BLACK SABBATH
2   "Burning Hell," JOHN LEE HOOKER
3   "The Devil," EDDIE KIRKLAND
4   "The Devil Went Down to Georgia," THE CHARLIE DANIELS BAND
5   "Devil's Daughter," JOHNNY SHINES
6   "Devil in Her Heart," THE BEATLES
7   "Devil or Angel," THE CLOVERS
8   "Devil with a Blue Dress On," MITCH RYDER
9   "The Devil's Gonna Get You," BROWNEE MCGHEE
10   "Downbound Train," CHUCK BERRY
11   "Friend of the Devil," THE GRATEFUL DEAD
12   "Prelude: Fanfare-Fire," THE CRAZY WORLD OF ARTHUR BROWN
13   "Sleeping with the Devil," JOHN YOUNG
14   "Sympathy for the Devil," THE ROLLING STONES
15   "(You're the) Devil in Disguise," ELVIS PRESLEY

MOST INFLUENTIAL GOSPEL SINGERS

1   SISTER ROSETTA THARPE
2   THE GOLDEN GATE JUBILEE QUARTET
3   THE NORFOLK JUBILEE QUARTET
4   THE SWAN SILVERTONES
5   REVEREND JAMES CLEVELAND
6   THE PILGRIM TRAVELERS
7   THE SOUL STIRRERS
8   MAHALIA JACKSON
9   THE SENSATIONAL NIGHTINGALES
10   MIGHTY CLOUDS OF JOY
11   THE CLARA WARD SINGERS
12   THE STAPLE SINGERS

-◄❙❙►-

EDDIE FLOYD'S FAVORITE SPIRITUAL ARTISTS

1   THE BROOKLYN ALL-STARS
2   REVEREND JAMES CLEVELAND
3   THE FIVE BLIND BOYS OF ALABAMA
4   THE FIVE BLIND BOYS OF MISSISSIPPI
5   THE HIGHWAY QC'S
6   THE JACKSON SOUTHERNAIRES
7   MAHALIA JACKSON
8   THE SOUL STIRRERS (with SAM COOKE)
9   THE SWAN SILVERTONES
10   THE SWANEE QUINTET
11   THE VIOLINAIRES
12   CLARA WARD

EDDIE FLOYD *recorded the soul classics "Knock on Wood" and "Raise Your Hand," among many others, and wrote a number of hits for Wilson Pickett and other artists. Today, the former Stax artist continues to tour and record.*

CARL PERKINS' 5 FAVORITE SPIRITUALS

1   "Down by the Riverside"
2   "Give Me That Old Time Religion"
3   "How Great Thou Art"
4   "What a Friend We Have in Jesus"
5   "Daddy Sang Bass"

CARL PERKINS *is the greatest living rockabilly artist. His hits include "Blue Suede Shoes," "Matchbox," and "Boppin' the Blues." Since the sixties, he's recorded in country and gospel styles as well as rock. Today, he tours with a band that features two of his sons.*

-◄▮►-

THE BLACKWOOD BROTHERS CHOOSE 10 POP ARTISTS WHO CAN SING THE GOSPEL WELL

1   PAT BOONE
2   JOHNNY CASH
3   THE DOOBIE BROTHERS, for "Jesus Is Just Alright with Me"
4   LARRY GATLIN
5   EMMYLOU HARRIS
6   MARGUERITE PIAZZA
7   BILLY PRESTON
8   THE RASCALS, for "People Got to Be Free"
9   THE STATLER BROTHERS
10   B. J. THOMAS

THE BLACKWOOD BROTHERS *have been leaders in the gospel field for four decades. Their harmonic blend inspired scores of rock, country, and pop artists. Elvis Presley himself auditioned for the Blackwoods in 1954; he was turned down.*

10 SONGS ABOUT SCHOOL

1 "Another Brick in the Wall," PINK FLOYD
2 "Be True to Your School," THE BEACH BOYS
3 "Charlie Brown," THE COASTERS
4 "I Wish," STEVIE WONDER
5 "My Old School," STEELY DAN
6 "School Days," CHUCK BERRY
7 "School Days," LOUDON WAINWRIGHT III
8 "School's Out," ALICE COOPER
9 "Smoking in the Boys' Room," BROWNSVILLE STATION
10 "Rock 'n' Roll High School," THE RAMONES

-◄❙▐►-

SARAH LAWRENCE GIRLS

1 LINDA EASTMAN
2 LESLEY GORE
3 YOKO ONO
4 CARLY SIMON

·◄❙▐►·

ROCK PERFORMERS WHO REALLY PUMPED GAS

1 GENE CLARK (The Byrds)   4 GRAHAM PARKER
2 ROGER MCGUINN (The Byrds) 5 BRUCE SPRINGSTEEN
3 BOB MOSLEY (Moby Grape)   6 TONY WILLIAMS (The Platters)

Rockers Who Really Worked the Assembly Line

1 CHUCK BERRY
2 SONNY BONO
3 JOHNNY CASH
4 BERRY GORDY, JR.
5 BOB MARLEY
6 JACK SCOTT
7 THE SPINNERS

Alumni of the Crown Electric Company
Memphis, Tennessee

1 ELVIS PRESLEY
2 DORSEY BURNETTE
3 JOHNNY BURNETTE

Baby You Can Drive My Car
Chauffeurs

1 TYRONE DAVIS, for bluesman Freddie King
2 BOBBY "BLUE" BLAND, B. B. King's chauffeur and valet
3 LARRY WILLIAMS (of "Bony Moronie" fame), for Lloyd Price
4 BILLY SWAN, for country star Webb Pierce

6 ROCKERS YOU WOULDN'T WANT TO DRIVE WITH

Stars Who Drive Race Cars

1	JEFF BECK	5	GEORGE HARRISON
2	JOHN BONHAM	6	TED NUGENT
3	ERIC CLAPTON	7	JOHN OATES
4	PETER FRAMPTON	8	BRUCE SPRINGSTEEN

-◄▮►-

20 ROCK JOCKS

1 **MUHAMMAD ALI**
When his name was still Cassius Clay, he released "Stand by Me," the Ben E. King song, as a single in 1964.

2 **JAMES BROWN**
Brown was a professional bantamweight fighter (sixteen wins, one defeat) before becoming a singer.

3 **JOHNNY BURNETTE**
Before becoming a Memphis Golden Gloves champion fighter, Burnette played on the football team at L. C. Humes High School in Memphis, where Elvis Presley was a bench warmer.

4 **DAVE CLARK**
Clark, of The Dave Clark Five, was a soccer player in his British youth.

5 **LEE DORSEY**
Under the name Kid Chocolate, Dorsey was a light heavyweight championship contender.

6 **BERRY GORDY JR.**
He fought both as a Golden Gloves and professional boxer in Detroit from 1948 to 1951.

7 **SAMMY HAGAR**
Hagar, whose father was a fighter, also tried boxing.

Elton John, Rod Stewart, and Michael Parkinson at the Goaldiggers Charity Football Match in London, September, 1974.

8   BOBBY HATFIELD
The Righteous Brothers member had a tryout with the Dodgers.

9   BILLY JOEL
Joel had twenty-two amateur boxing bouts, accounting for the somewhat disheveled state of his nose.

10   KRIS KRISTOFFERSON
Kristofferson was a star football player in high school and college, which helped earn him his Rhodes scholarship.

11   NILS LOFGREN
As a trained gymnast, Lofgren has at times used a trampoline as part of his stage act.

12   BOB LUMAN
Luman turned down a Pittsburgh Pirates baseball contract.

13   LAMONT MCLEMOR
McLemor, of The Fifth Dimension, played for a Los Angeles Dodgers farm team.

14   LEE MAY
The baseball player recorded many singles, both during and after his professional career.

15   JIMMY MCCRACKLIN
Prior to his hit with "The Walk," McCracklin had twenty-two professional fights.

16   ELVIS PRESLEY
Elvis was ranked as a karate "master."

17   CHARLEY PRIDE
A prospect in the San Francisco Giants organization, Pride took up singing professionally only after being cut from a farm team.

18   MARTY ROBBINS
Robbins ran a Dodge in the 1972 Daytona 500 and totaled it when he hit a wall at 150 miles per hour.

19   BOB SEGER
Seger ran a mile in 5:05 in high school, a most respectable high school time for the early sixties.

20 **ROD STEWART**
Stewart thought about becoming a professional soccer player prior to beginning his singing career. He was reportedly good enough to have a serious shot at English football stardom.

-◄❚▐▶-

GOLDEN GLOVES CHAMPIONS

1   WILLIE DIXON
2   JOHNNY BURNETTE
3   SCREAMIN' JAY HAWKINS
4   BILLY WARD
5   JACKIE WILSON

Other Golden Gloves fighters
1   BERRY GORDY JR.
2   PETER CRISS
3   KRIS KRISTOFFERSON
4   TOMMY TUCKER

-◄❚▐▶-

ROCKERS WHO REALLY SURFED

1   JAN BERRY (Jan and Dean)
2   EDDIE BERTRAND (The Belairs, Eddie and the Showmen)
3   JOHN CAFFERTY (Beaver Brown)
4   DICK DALE (of course)
5   DICKEY DODD (The Belairs, Eddie and the Showmen, The Standells)
6   JIM FULLER (The Surfaris)
7   RUSS KUNKEL (Los Angeles session drummer)
8   BOB MOSLEY (Moby Grape)
9   BOB SPICKARD (The Chantays)
10 BRUCE SPRINGSTEEN

New York is a lonely town: Joey Ramone can often be seen early in the morning after a gig stalking the perfect wave and looking for someone to help carry his "stick" on the South Shore of Long Island, New York.

11 DENNIS WILSON (The Beach Boys)*
12 RON WILSON (The Surfaris)

*Dennis was the only one of The Beach Boys who surfed.

·◄❙❙▶·

15 FAMOUS RECORD COLLECTORS

1 **PAUL BURLISON**
The guitarist with The Rock and Roll Trio (and also the man who made guitar distortion chic with "Train Kept a-Rollin'"),

Burlison collects all sorts of records and has more than 150,000 discs in his collection.

2 **ROBERT CRUMB**

The underground cartoonist par excellence and occasional novelty recording artist collects all manner of 78s.

3 **DAVE EDMUNDS**

The Rockpile guitarist, vocalist, and erstwhile record producer has a major stockpile of rockabilly discs at his home in Wales.

4 **BOB HITE***

One of the biggest collectors in existence, Hite has been collecting blues and rhythm & blues records since his teens in the early fifties; he now has a collection of more than 100,000 records. He won't say exactly how many, but it is reported that he has at least 10,000 *doubles*. Hite was, of course, lead vocalist of Canned Heat, whose guitarist, Alan Wilson, was also a respected blues collector and scholar.

5 **ELTON JOHN**

John is a generalist: He's mostly interested in rock records, but also soul and all kinds of modern pop.

6 **CUB KODA**

Koda, the leader of Brownsville Station and now a solo artist, is the author of a column in *Goldmine* called "The Vinyl Junkie," which about sums it up. Included in his vast archives are healthy doses of rock, blues, and novelty records. Haunts junk shops and Goodwill stores like the fanatic he is.

7 **JOHN LYDON**

The Sex Pistols and Public Image Ltd. singer is a major-league reggae collector. He has also reportedly bought up all the various albums he could find of the Pope John Paul II world tour.

8 **JOHNNY LYON and GARRY TALLENT**

The Asbury Jukes singer and the E Street Band bassist have a combined collection (parts stored in each of their houses) that focuses on rhythm & blues and rockabilly records.

*Bob Hite died in early 1981.

9   EDDIE MONEY
Believe it or not, the former Brooklyn cop turned San Francisco rocker specializes in collecting Brian Hyland discs.

10   DAVE PEVERETT
Peverett is the guitarist in Foghat, but he is also very well known in collectors' circles as a blues and R&B specialist.

11   ROBERT PLANT
Plant often indulges himself on American visits with heavy splurges of a cappella 45s.

12   RINGO STARR
Starr collects Beatles memorabilia, what else? He had a massive collection, until his Hollywood home burned in 1979.

13   CARLA THOMAS
Thomas is the daughter of bluesman Rufus Thomas, so perhaps it makes sense that she expresses her connection to the tradition by collecting blues and soul discs.

14   PETER WOLF
The lead singer of The J. Geils Band has an apartment jammed with records, mostly blues, soul, and rock and roll, although it includes many novelty items as well.

15   FRANK ZAPPA
As those who have heard *Ruben and the Jets* (or any of his other more directly rock influenced albums) probably already suspect, Zappa is a major doo-wop fiend.

-◄❚❚►-

GIMME BACK MY BULLETS
Rock Marksmen

1   JOHN CIPPOLINA (Quicksilver Messenger Service)
2   JOHN ENTWISTLE (The Who)
3   MARK FARNER (Grand Funk Railroad)
4   TED NUGENT
5   WILSON PICKETT
6   ELVIS PRESLEY
7   RONNIE VAN ZANT (Lynyrd Skynyrd)

ROCK STARS WHO SERVED IN THE ARMY

1   THE BIG BOPPER
2   BILLY COX (Band of Gypsys)
3   JERRY GARCIA (The Grateful Dead)
4   JIMI HENDRIX
5   KRIS KRISTOFFERSON
6   FRED PARRIS (The Five Satins)*
7   ELVIS PRESLEY
8   LLOYD PRICE
9   DEL SHANNON
10 LINK WRAY

* Parris wrote The Satins' biggest and most beautiful song, "In the Still of the Nite," while serving on guard duty late one night. This is perhaps the loveliest doo-wop ballad ever made.

-◄▮►-

ROCKERS WHO SERVED IN THE AIR FORCE

1   JOHNNY CASH   5   CLYDE MCPHATTER
2   THE DEL-VIKINGS*   6   MICHAEL NESMITH (The Monke
3   MARVIN GAYE   7   BILL WYMAN (The Rolling Ston
4   ROY HARPER**

* Entire group
**Served in the Royal Air Force in Britain

-◄▮►-

ROCKERS WHO SERVED IN THE MARINES

1   The Essex*   4   Tim Hardin
2   Don Everly   5   Bob Mosley (Moby Grape)
3   Phil Everly

*The entire group served in the Marines around 1963, when they created their hit "Easier Said Than Done"; the band was formed at a military base in Okinawa.

ROCK STARS WHO SERVED IN THE NAVY

1	JOHNNY ACE	3	GENE VINCENT
2	BOYD BENNETT*	4	BILL WITHERS

*Served in World War II

10 VEGETARIANS

1 THE CAPTAIN AND TENNILLE
2 THE CLASH
3 BOB DYLAN
4 GEORGE HARRISON
5 CHRISSIE HYNDE (The Pretenders)
6 JOHN LENNON and YOKO ONO
7 MIKE LOVE (The Beach Boys)
8 RANKING ROGER and ANDY COX (The [English] Beat)
9 SMOKEY ROBINSON
10 YES (except for Rick Wakeman)

BLIND

1 CLARENCE CARTER
2 RAY CHARLES
3 JOSÉ FELICIANO
4 THE FIVE BLIND BOYS OF ALABAMA
5 THE FIVE BLIND BOYS OF MISSISSIPPI
6 BLIND LEMON JEFFERSON
7 RONNIE MILSAP
8 EDGAR WINTER (legally)
9 JOHNNY WINTER (legally)
10 STEVIE WONDER

DAVID BOWIE'S 5 FAVORITE UNUSUAL PEOPLE

1 THE WILD BOY OF AVEYRON, the French boy raised by wolves on whom François Truffaut based his film *The Wild Child*

2 THE PAW PAW BLOWTORCH, a 1930s Chicago black youth who set fire to his hospital sheets and pillow by breathing on them

3 SEAN BEANY, a seventeenth-century Scottish highwayman and cannibal.

4 JOHN MERRICK, the Elephant Man

5 THE FARTER OF MOULIN ROUGE, a turn-of-the-century cabaret artist (Le Petomane; real name, Joseph Pujol) reknowned for his melodious asshole and candle-extinguishing routine

DAVID BOWIE *has been a rock musician, a mime, and most recently, a Broadway actor (in* The Elephant Man*). He has also made several movies, notably* The Man Who Fell to Earth *and* Just a Gigolo. *Bowie's hits include "Fame," "Young Americans," and "Space Oddity." In addition to his own records, he has produced Lou Reed, Iggy Pop, and Mott the Hoople's "All the Young Dudes," which he wrote.*

Twenty-Five: POLITICS

James Brown, noted Republican, is shown here being introduced to the joys of the Democratic Party by Lester Maddox in Augusta, Georgia in 1970.

ENEMIES LIST

1   **STEVE ALLEN**
    Allen first entered the ranks of rock and roll infamy when he
    made Elvis Presley wear a white tie and tail and sing "Hound
    Dog" to a basset sitting on a stool. Since then, this celebrated
    video has-been and third-rate jazz pianist has watched his
    career slowly sink, but he's never relented in his hatred for
    rock, abusing it whenever he's given the opportunity.

2   **MITCH MILLER**
    As chief A&R man for Columbia Records during the early rock
    era, Miller preferred to record his own banal barbershop
    harmonies, refusing to allow the label to record *any* rock,
    much less rhythm & blues or rockabilly. When rock did not
    disappear, as Miller predicted, his career took a nose dive
    from which it has never recovered.

3   **BILLY JAMES HARGIS**
    Hargis is a Tulsa-based preacher famous for his antirock
    tirades, which have from time to time taken the form of tracts
    claiming that The Beatles, for instance, were the product of a
    Satanist/Communist conspiracy. Hargis has been less widely
    heard of since his well-publicized scandal in the middle
    seventies for allegedly sexually abusing several members of
    the student body at his church-run university.

4, 5 and 6 **REPRESENTATIVES OREN HARRIS, FRANK HOGAN,
    JOSEPH STONE**
    The chief conspirators of the 1959-1960 payola witch hunt, an
    antirock crusade spearheaded by the Tin Pan Alley publishers
    represented by ASCAP, these three contended that only
    corrupt, bribe-taking broadcasters could possibly play such
    vile trash and make it successful. Harris chaired the House
    Legislative Oversight Subcommittee, which did little but
    establish that disc jockeys were so underpaid they needed the
    extra dough. Hogan, the New York City district attorney,

appointed his assistant, Stone, to crack down on New York jocks, particularly the king of 'em all, Alan Freed. Freed never denied his income was supplemented but insisted that this had little to do with what records he played; Freed also consistently refused to become a state's witness, which cost him his job and eventually drove him to alcoholism and an early grave. But it is Alan Freed, not any of the above-mentioned politicians, whose name lives on.

7 **KAL RUDMAN**

Rudman runs the tip sheet *Friday Morning Quarterback*, a mimeographed listing of schmoozy hype and AM-station play-lists that is allegedly extremely influential with important Top Forty programmers. At least, enough record companies think so to keep the issues stuffed with ads. In this capacity, the tip sheet and its proprietor are largely responsible for the general godawful blandness of American Top Forty radio.

8 **MIKE CURB**

Curb, the lieutenant governor of California, has also been a producer of exploitative soundtracks for trash movies, entre-preneur of such bubblegum sensations as Debby Boone, Leif Garrett, Shaun Cassidy, and The Osmond Family, and once ran MGM Records. At MGM, Curb announced in 1970 he was cutting from the label's roster all acts with any "drug orienta-tion"—a ploy designed to rid him of the company's many lame acts. It backfired, however, when Eric Burdon, then one of the MGM stars, cheerfully admitted his drug use and petitioned Curb for his release; it wasn't forthcoming. Soon after, Curb released an album of Grateful Dead outtakes that epitomized psychedelic excess. None of this has stopped the Ronald Reagan protegé's political career, though it must be said that there are many in the record industry who were not sorry to see Curb attain a position wherein he could do considerably less damage to American culture. (Oh, yes, Curb also handled the entertainment for Richard M. Nixon's first inaugural ball.)

9 **LEE ABRAMS**

Abrams pioneered the "Superstars" format, which mathematically justifies FM rock radio's decline into an LP-track Top Forty. He then moved on to produce such bathetic bathwater as the "progressive" rock band Gentle Giant, a conflict of interest that is legal only because Abrams is not officially an employee of any broadcaster, just a "consultant" who happens to give advice on hiring, firing, and programming to more than 100 U.S. stations. Gentle Giant's first Abrams-produced LP stiffed, of course.

10 *The New York Times*

The *Times* played up both the payola investigation of 1959-1960 and the abortive one that lasted from 1972 to 1974. But the paper never mentioned the latter's lack of results or the inaccuracies of its own reporting on it. Citadel of the most patronizing rock criticism in existence, the *Times* refuses to run articles on rock in its Sunday Music page, relegating the subject to a special page (Recordings) when it deigns to cover it at all. Naturally, record ads have until recently been the dominant revenue source of the paper's Sunday Arts and Leisure section, proving conclusively that rock's worst enemy is the people who run the recording industry. The latest insult was Sidney Zion's *Sunday Times* magazine piece attacking rock for squeezing Good Music off the air waves. Believe it or not, this article appeared in 1981.

-◄▮▶-

MUSICIANS UNITED FOR SAFE ENERGY
Performers at the MUSE Concerts for a Non-Nuclear Future, Madison Square Garden, September 19-24, 1979

1 JACKSON BROWNE
2 RY COODER
3 CROSBY, STILLS, AND NASH
4 THE DOOBIE BROTHERS
5 JOHN HALL

6   CHAKA KHAN
7   GRAHAM NASH
8   TOM PETTY AND THE HEARTBREAKERS
9   BONNIE RAITT
10   GIL SCOTT-HERON
11   CARLY SIMON
12   BRUCE SPRINGSTEEN AND THE E STREET BAND
13   SWEET HONEY IN THE ROCK
14   JAMES TAYLOR
15   JESSE COLIN YOUNG

-◄❙❙▶-

APOCALYPSE NOW
15 Songs of Nuclear Anxiety

1   "Before the Deluge," JACKSON BROWNE
2   "Eve of Destruction," BARRY MCGUIRE
3   "The Great American Eagle Tragedy," EARTH OPERA
4   "A Hard Rain's A-Gonna Fall," BOB DYLAN
5   "I Come and Stand at Every Door," THE BYRDS
6   "It Came Out of the Sky," CREEDENCE CLEARWATER
     REVIVAL
7   "London Calling," THE CLASH
8   "Morning Dew," TIM ROSE
9   "Mushroom Clouds," LOVE
10   "1983," JIMI HENDRIX
11   "Plutonium Is Forever," JOHN HALL
12   "Roulette," BRUCE SPRINGSTEEN (unreleased)
13   "Uranium Rock," WARREN SMITH
14   "We Almost Lost Detroit," GIL SCOTT-HERON
15   "Wooden Ships," CROSBY, STILLS, NASH, AND YOUNG

GREATEST 50s PROTEST SONGS

1   "Almost Grown," CHUCK BERRY
2   "Get a Job," THE SILHOUETTES
3   "I've Had It," THE BELL NOTES
4   "Money (That's What I Want)," BARRETT STRONG
5   "Money Honey," THE DRIFTERS
6   "Riot in Cell Block No. 9," THE CLOVERS
7   "School Days," CHUCK BERRY
8   "Summertime Blues," EDDIE COCHRAN
9   "Too Much Monkey Business," CHUCK BERRY
10 "Well All Right," BUDDY HOLLY
11 "What about Us," THE COASTERS
12 "Yakety Yak," THE COASTERS

-◄◗►-

GREATEST 60s PROTEST SONGS

1   "Abraham, Martin and John," DION
2   "Alice's Restaurant," ARLO GUTHRIE 1967
3   "Bad Moon Rising," CREEDENCE CLEARWATER REVIVAL
4   "Big Boss Man," JIMMY REED
5   "Blowin' in the Wind," STEVIE WONDER
6   "A Change Is Gonna Come," SAM COOKE
7   "Choice of Colors," THE IMPRESSIONS 69
8   "Don't Call Me Nigger, Whitey (Don't Call Me Whitey, Nigger)," SLY AND THE FAMILY STONE
9   "Don't Look Now (It Ain't You or Me)," CREEDENCE CLEARWATER REVIVAL
10 "Everyday People," SLY AND THE FAMILY STONE
11 "For What It's Worth (Stop, Hey What's That Sound)," BUFFALO SPRINGFIELD
12 "Fortunate Son," CREEDENCE CLEARWATER REVIVAL

13 "Games People Play," JOE SOUTH
14 "Get Together," THE YOUNGBLOODS
15 "Give Peace a Chance," THE PLASTIC ONO BAND
16 "A Hard Rain's A-Gonna Fall," BOB DYLAN
17 "I Ain't a-Marchin' Anymore," PHIL OCHS
18 "I Don't Live Today," THE JIMI HENDRIX EXPERIENCE
19 "If I Can Dream," ELVIS PRESLEY
20 "If 6 was 9," JIMI HENDRIX
21 "Is It Because I'm Black," SYL JOHNSON
22 "Laugh at Me," SONNY
23 "The Lonesome Death of Hattie Carroll," BOB DYLAN
24 "My Generation," THE WHO
25 "People Get Ready," THE IMPRESSIONS
26 "People Got to Be Free," THE RASCALS
27 "Pride of Man," QUICKSILVER MESSENGER SERVICE
28 "Revolution," THE BEATLES
29 "Street Fighting Man," THE ROLLING STONES
30 "Something in the Air," THUNDERCLAP NEWMAN
31 "Thank You Falettinme Be Mice Elf Agin," SLY AND THE
    FAMILY STONE
32 "This Is My Country," THE IMPRESSIONS
33 "The Under Assistant West Coast Promotion Man," THE
    ROLLING STONES
34 "Universal Soldier," DONOVAN
35 "Viet Nam," JIMMY CLIFF
36 "We Gotta Get Out of This Place," THE ANIMALS
37 "We're a Winner," THE IMPRESSIONS
38 "Who'll Stop the Rain," CREEDENCE CLEARWATER REVIVAL
39 "With God on Our Side," MANFRED MANN
40 "The Young Mod's Forgotten Story," THE IMPRESSIONS

GREATEST 70s (AND 80s) PROTEST SONGS

1 " 'A' Bomb in Wardour Street," THE JAM
2 "Anarchy in the U.K.," THE SEX PISTOLS
3 "Before the Deluge," JACKSON BROWNE
4 "Bring the Boys Home," FREDA PAYNE
5 "Brother Louie," THE STORIES
6 "The Call Up," THE CLASH
7 "Complete Control," THE CLASH
8 "Feel Like a Number," BOB SEGER AND THE SILVER BULLET BAND
9 "George Jackson," BOB DYLAN
10 "Geronimo's Cadillac," MICHAEL MURPHEY
11 "Gimme Some Truth," JOHN LENNON
12 "Glad to Be Gay," THE TOM ROBINSON BAND
13 "God Save the Queen," THE SEX PISTOLS
14 "Had Enough," THE WHO
15 "Holidays in the Sun," THE SEX PISTOLS
16 "I'm So Bored with the U.S.A.," THE CLASH
17 "Imagine," JOHN LENNON
18 "Inner City Blues (Make Me Wanna Holler)," MARVIN GAYE
19 "Less Than Zero," ELVIS COSTELLO
20 "London Calling," THE CLASH
21 "Mercy, Mercy Me (the Ecology)," MARVIN GAYE
22 "Miss-tra Know It All," STEVIE WONDER
23 "Night Rally," ELVIS COSTELLO
24 "Ohio," CROSBY, STILLS, NASH, AND YOUNG
25 "Respect Yourself," THE STAPLE SINGERS
26 "Right to Work," CHELSEA
27 "Sandinista!" THE CLASH
28 "Southern Man," NEIL YOUNG
29 "Sweet Home Alabama," LYNYRD SKYNYRD
30 "Thank You for Talkin' to Me Africa," SLY AND THE FAMILY STONE

31   "There but for the Grace of God Go I," MACHINE
32   "Volunteers," THE JEFFERSON AIRPLANE
33   "Waiting for the End of the World," ELVIS COSTELLO
34   "Wake Up Everybody," HAROLD MELVIN AND THE BLUE NOTES
35   "War," EDWIN STARR
36   "Welcome to the Working Week," ELVIS COSTELLO
37   "(What's So Funny 'Bout) Peace, Love and Understanding," ELVIS COSTELLO
38   "White Riot," THE CLASH
39   "Won't Get Fooled Again," THE WHO
40   "The World Is a Ghetto," WAR

-◄❙❙►-

THE ANTIWAR TOP 40

1   "Alice's Restaurant," ARLO GUTHRIE
2   "Ball of Confusion," THE TEMPTATIONS
3   "Blowin' in the Wind," STEVIE WONDER
4   "Bring the Boys Home," FREDA PAYNE
5   "The Call Up," THE CLASH
6   "English Civil War," THE CLASH
7   "Fortunate Son," CREEDENCE CLEARWATER REVIVAL
8   "Fox Hole," TELEVISION
9   "Give Peace a Chance," THE PLASTIC ONO BAND
10   "Happy Xmas (War Is Over)," JOHN LENNON AND YOKO ONO
11   "A Hard Rain's A-Gonna Fall," BOB DYLAN
12   "He Looks a Lot like Me," DION
13   "Hymn #9," THE PERSUASIONS
14   "Feel-Like-I'm-Fixin'-to-Die-Rag," COUNTRY JOE AND THE FISH
15   "Imagine," JOHN LENNON
16   "Izabella," JIMI HENDRIX
17   "Life During Wartime," THE TALKING HEADS

18   "Lost in the Flood," BRUCE SPRINGSTEEN
19   "Machine Gun," THE JIMI HENDRIX EXPERIENCE
20   "Monster," STEPPENWOLF
21   "Ohio," CROSBY, STILLS, NASH, AND YOUNG
22   "Oliver's Army," ELVIS COSTELLO
23   "Peace Train," CAT STEVENS
24   "Rompin' Through the Swamp," THE HOLY MODAL
     ROUNDERS
25   "Sky Pilot," ERIC BURDON AND THE ANIMALS
26   "Sam Stone," JOHN PRINE
27   "Super Bird," COUNTRY JOE AND THE FISH
28   "2 + 2 = ?," BOB SEGER
29   "Universal Soldier," DONOVAN
30   "The Unknown Soldier," THE DOORS
31   "Viet Nam," JIMMY CLIFF
32   "Vietnam Rag," COUNTRY JOE AND THE FISH
33   "War," EDWIN STARR
34   "War Pigs," BLACK SABBATH
35   "We've Got to Have Peace," CURTIS MAYFIELD
36   "What's Going On," MARVIN GAYE
37   "(What's So Funny 'Bout) Peace, Love and Understanding,"
     ELVIS COSTELLO
38   "With God on Our Side," MANFRED MANN
39   "Yes Sir, No Sir," THE KINKS
40   "Your Flag Decal Won't Get You into Heaven Anymore,"
     JOHN PRINE

-◄❚▶-

10 SONGS THAT WERE ALTERED DUE TO CENSORSHIP

1   **"Stagger Lee,"** LLOYD PRICE, 1959
    The original version features a murder in which Stagger Lee
    shoots fellow gambler Billy. Bowing to antiviolence sympa-

thies, Price recut the song in a nonviolent version. The two are immediately distinguishable. In the opening line of the original, Price says, "The night was Claire," while in the remake he sings, "The night was clear."

2   **"Greenback Dollar,"** THE KINGSTON TRIO, 1963
Originally, the line was "I don't give a damn about a greenback dollar," but somebody had the bright idea that *damn* was offensive. The single was therefore pressed with the word edited out, allowing the listeners to mentally supply any word they chose (usually four letter).

3   **"Double Shot (of My Baby's Love),"** The Swinging Medallions, 1966
The original version has the lyrics "the worst hangover I ever had" and "She loved me so long and she loved me so hard/I finally passed out in her front yard." Gasp! How immoral! The lyric was changed to "the worst morning after I ever had" and "She kissed me so long and she kissed me so hard . . . ." The original version is on the mono LP, while the "clean-up" one is on the stereo LP.

4   **"Rhapsody in the Rain,"** LOU CHRISTIE, 1966
Oh, the flak on this one! Such lyrics as "On our first date, we were makin' out in the rain" and "In this car, our love went way too far" were the subject of radio call-in shows. Christie pleaded innocent to writing "a dirty song" but agreed that maybe the lyrics could be open to misinterpretation. The "new" version toned it down to "On our first date, we fell in love in the rain" and "In this car, love came like a falling star."

5   **"Brown Eyed Girl,"** VAN MORRISON, 1967
How could we ever allow such smut on the radio as the line, "Making love in the green grass, behind the stadium"? To make matters worse, the next time he meets her, he remarks, "My, how you have grown." (Around the middle, I suppose.) Change that offensive line to "laughin' and a-runnin', behind the stadium." The censored version, which was the only one

played on many stations, appears on the mono version of the *Blowing Your Mind* LP, but the stereo version has the more daring original.

6   **"Hold On,"** THE MAUDS, 1968

This Chicago rock-soul group couldn't get its rock and roll version of the Sam and Dave hit played on one of the big Chicago Top Forty stations until it provided the station with a version that changed "Hold on, I'm coming" to "Hold on, don't you worry, hold on, please."

7   **"Locomotive Breath,"** JETHRO TULL, 1971

This is perhaps the ultimate censorship job. Not satisfied with the line from the LP, "got him by the balls," Chrysalis spliced in a word from another part of the song, and the radio stations ended up with "got him by the fun." Do I detect a new euphemism being born here? A kick in the fun? Brass fun? Freezing his fun off? Maybe someday the radio stations and record companies will find the fun to play records like these.

8   **"Money,"** PINK FLOYD, 1973

Almost let this one get by, didn't we? When Harvest Records sent out the original promo copies, they contained the line "don't give me that goody-good bullshit." But just in the nick of time, the morals of the country were saved, and Harvest hurriedly issued a second DJ copy (the "bull-blank" version) with a desperate note to throw away the first one.

9   **"Mamacita,"** THE GRASS ROOTS, 1975

When this one came out in 1975, it raised a lot of eyebrows with the line "she's so sweet you could eat her." By the time the Haven label caught on that the record wasn't being played, and issued a new version with the line changed to "there ain't nobody sweeter," everybody had forgotten about the record anyway, and it died at Number Seventy-one.

10 **"The Devil Went to Georgia,"** THE CHARLIE DANIELS BAND, 1979

Even when you're talking to the devil, I guess it's inappropriate to call him a "son of a bitch" on AM radio. So the transistor crowd was treated to the reworded version with "son of a gun."

BEST SONGS TO PASS THE CENSOR

1   "Gloria," THEM
2   "Lola," THE KINKS
3   "Shake, Rattle and Roll," JOE TURNER
4   "Don't Eat the Yellow Snow," FRANK ZAPPA AND THE
    MOTHERS OF INVENTION
5   "Walk on the Wild Side," LOU REED
6   "Good Golly Miss Molly," LITTLE RICHARD
7   "Honky Tonk Women," THE ROLLING STONES
8   "Pictures of Lily," THE WHO
9   "Great Balls of Fire," JERRY LEE LEWIS
10 "Hanky Panky," TOMMY JAMES AND THE SHONDELLS
11 "Blinded by the Light," BRUCE SPRINGSTEEN
12 "Jools and Jim," PETE TOWNSHEND
13 "Love to Love You Baby," DONNA SUMMER
14 "Lido Shuffle," BOZ SCAGGS
15 "Miracles," JEFFERSON STARSHIP

- ◄▮▮► -

THE 10 MOST CONTROVERSIAL RECORD SLEEVES AND COVERS

1   *Two Virgins*, JOHN LENNON and YOKO ONO, 1969
    Lennon and Ono posed in the buff, full-frontal on the front
    cover, and from the rear on the back. On release, it sold in
    America in a brown paper bag in the rare stores that would
    carry it. Because this represented such a drastic departure
    from The Beatles' relatively clean-cut image, the *Two Virgins*
    sleeve even upset rock fans.
2   **"God Save the Queen,"** THE SEX PISTOLS, 1977
    The Pistols intended "God Save the Queen" as a blast at
    Queen Elizabeth's Silver Jubilee, and the 45 sleeve featured a
    defaced picture of HRH, engendering the usual protests from

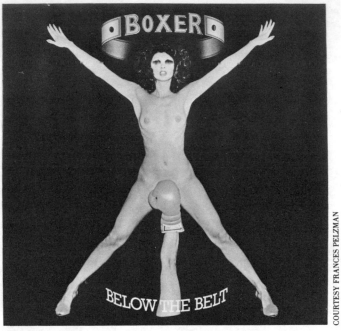

The Boxer album cover banned in the U.S. in 1976.

the guardians of taste and the usual banishment from shops o
dignified mien.

3 ***Yesterday . . . and Today,*** THE BEATLES, 1966
Throughout the sixties, Capitol Records adopted the policy o
leaving a British track or two off The Beatles' America
albums, and thus periodically had enough material left over t
make a separate album for U.S.-only release. By 1966, Th
Beatles were both bold and annoyed enough to take action, an
when Capitol announced plans for an LP to fill the space i
time between *Revolver* and *Sgt. Pepper's Lonely Hearts Clu
Band,* the group delivered a cover featuring the boys i
blood-smeared butcher smocks, surrounded by raw meat an
holding dismembered dolls. The cover was actually printe
and a precious few copies were delivered to stores befor

retailers' outrage forced their recall. Some of the sleeves were in fact only covered over, and today, a butcher sleeve pressing of *Yesterday . . . and Today* is one of the most valuable Beatles collectables.

4 **Beggar's Banquet,** THE ROLLING STONES, 1968
The original outside sleeve of this fold-out design featured a bathroom wall covered in fairly scatalogical graffiti. London and Decca, the band's American and British labels, refused to release the sleeve. The print has often been bootlegged.

5 **Mom's Apple Pie,** 1971
Grand Funk Railroad entrepreneur Terry Knight was responsible for this group. Their first album, unlistenable as it was, remains legendary for its cover, which featured an innocent-looking matron holding out a steaming pie with a single slice removed. But rather than an apple or cherry filling, what the slice revealed was a vagina. The cover was later reissued with the filling bricked up.

6 **Moby Grape,** 1967
The San Francisco group's first album featured Skip Spence holding his middle finger extended over a washboard. Columbia reissued the sleeve with Spence's digit sliced off.

7 **Blind Faith,** 1969
The original cover for this supergroup's first and only album showed a bare-chested, pubescent girl. Because of retailer reluctance to stock that sleeve, however, the album was also issued with a sleeve featuring a photo of only the band. Interestingly, when RSO reissued the album in the late seventies, only the censored sleeve was used.

8 **Some Girls,** THE ROLLING STONES, 1978
This cover was designed in the form of a pulp magazine advertising column with die cuts through which famous faces (Lucille Ball, Brigitte Bardot, Marilyn Monroe, Raquel Welch, Liza Minnelli) peered out from the inner sleeve. Protests from several of the women involved resulted in the sleeve being altered.

9   ***Below the Belt,*** BOXER, 1977

This album featured a boxing glove slamming into a nude female figure, squarely at the crotch. It engendered all manner of protest, with the result that the English sleeve was replaced in America by a more conventional photo of the band.

10   ***Electric Ladyland,*** THE JIMI HENDRIX EXPERIENCE, 1968

Hendrix' original sleeve, a swirling psychedelic photomontage of Jimi in action, was issued in the U.S. Polydor in England, however, released a sleeve featuring Hendrix surrounded by about a dozen very voluptuous and extremely naked women. The sleeve has been a U.S. collectors' item for years.

-◄▮▶-

CONTROVERSIAL ADVERTISING CAMPAIGNS

1   ***Black and Blue,*** THE ROLLING STONES, 1976

When this mid-seventies album was released, Rolling Stones Records bought the usual billboard on L.A.'s Sunset Strip, featuring an illustration of a woman bound and beaten, in "comic" reference to the title. Not too long after, an organization called Women Against Violence Against Women defaced the billboard and instituted a feminist boycott of all Warner Communications recordings. The boycott lasted for more than a year, until Warners agreed to leave the sexism off its packaging and advertising. (In addition, the *Black and Blue* ad copy was rejected by a number of magazines.)

2   **Fuck Hudson's,** THE MC5, 1968

Because of the line "Kick out the jams, motherfuckers," on the MC5's debut LP, Hudson's, the largest department store in the band's hometown, Detroit, refused to carry the album. Incited by the boycott, the band took out its own ad in an underground newspaper, reading, "Stay alive with The MC5—and fuck Hudson's." The ensuing controversy saw Hudson's refuse to carry any records from Elektra, the group's label, and led directly to Elektra dropping The MC5 from its artist roster.

Billboard above Sunset Strip for The Rolling Stones' Black and Blue *album, which caused a raised eyebrow, even in Los Angeles.*

National Lampoon's *answer to* The Rolling Stones' Black and Blue *controversy.*

3   ***Head Games,*** FOREIGNER, 1979
    The ad for this album, like its cover, featured women emerging from men's toilets and inspired feminist protests similar to those surrounding *Black and Blue*.

4   **CBS Records,** 1968
    CBS was a Johnny-come-lately to acid rock, thanks to the blind stewardship of Mitch Miller, and the label's slogans—"The man can't bust our music" and "The revolutionaries are on CBS"—were its way of trying to catch up and improve its image among hipsters. Written by self-styled radical Jim Fouratt, later a major force in the New Wave dance-club scene in New York, the slogans managed mostly to make CBS look insipid, but did anger many young leftists, who felt that the record industry was "co-opting" their rhetoric. (Not that the record industry wasn't.)

TWENTY-SIX: DRUGS, DEATH, AND ROCK AND ROLL

BURK UZZLE / MAGNUM

Duane Allman and Berry Oakley rest almost in peace at Rose Hill Cemetery in Macon, Georgia.

25 PIECES OF EVIDENCE PROVING THAT PAUL McCARTNEY IS DEAD

1   On the cover of *Yesterday . . . and Today*, "Paul" sits in a trunk. Turn it sideways, and he seems to be in a coffin.

2   On the cover of *Revolver*, "Paul" is turned to the side, as if he doesn't really fit in.

3   *Revolver* contains numerous references to death, such as in "She Said She Said."

4   On the cover of *Sgt. Pepper's Lonely Hearts Club Band*, a hand is held directly over "Paul's" head. This is a symbol of death.

5   On the same cover, "Paul's" bass is laid on flowers atop a coffin.

6   "Paul" is also holding a black musical instrument.

7   On the inside of the cover, "Paul" wears a black arm band with the letters *OPD*, which is a Canadian acronym for Officially Pronounced Dead.

8   On the back cover, "Paul's" back is turned to the camera.

9   Also on the back cover, the lyrics "Without You" (part of the title, "Within You and Without You") bloom from "Paul's" head.

10 "A Day in the Life" contains the line, "He blew his mind out in a car"; this is supposedly the manner in which Paul died.

11 On *The White Album* track "Revolution 9" there is a voice that repeats "number nine, number nine." If you play this segment backward, it becomes "turn me on, dead man." (John claimed that at the beginning of each take, an engineer would announce, "This is EMI Recording Studio Number 9." Lennon said that he simply took the end of the phrase and added it in the final mix. According to him, the "turn me on, dead man" revelation was a coincidence.)

12 On Lennon's song "Glass Onion," he says, "And here's another clue for you all/The Walrus was Paul." In some societies, the walrus is an image of death, but this is most important as Lennon's acknowledgment of the rumor.

13   Between the end of "I'm So Tired" and the beginning of "Black Bird," Lennon utters some nonsense syllables. Played backward, they say (approximately), "Paul is dead, miss him, miss him."

14   While George is wailing away at the end of "While My Guitar Gently Weeps," he says, "Paul, Paul."

15   "Don't Pass Me By" contains the line, "You were in a car crash."

16   The poster included with *The White Album* contains many references to McCartney's "death." For example, there is a picture of "Paul's" head lying back in a bath; this resembles what he may have looked like after "the car crash."

17   The pictures also show a scar on "Paul's" lip, which supposedly had never been there before.

18   At the end of "Strawberry Fields Forever," Lennon can be heard saying what sounds very much like "I buried Paul." (Lennon claimed that The Beatles would often say wild and crazy things while in the studio, and that what he was really saying was "cranberry sauce.")

19   On the cover of *Magical Mystery Tour*, the words of the title are written in stars. If you turn the album upside down, the letters reveal a phone number that some say you could call to find out details of Paul's death. Some say this number belonged to Billy Shears.

20   Inside the booklet accompanying *Magical Mystery Tour*, there is a picture of "Paul" sitting at a desk on which there is a sign that reads, "I was you."

21   In the "Your Mother Should Know" sequence of the *Magical Mystery Tour* movie, "Paul" wears a black carnation; the others wear white ones. ("Paul" has explained that they ran out of white carnations.)

22   At the end of the *Magical Mystery Tour* photo book, there is a picture of The Beatles interspersed with shots of many other people. There is a hand directly over "Paul's" head.

23   On the cover of *Abbey Road*, "Paul" is barefoot (corpses are often buried without shoes) and out of step with the other

Beatles. His eyes appear to be closed. He is also smoking. The other Beatles wear clothing contributing to the motif: John, all in white, is the preacher; Ringo, all in black, is the pallbearer; George, all in denim, is the gravedigger. There is also a Volkswagen with the license number "28 IF," symbolizing that McCartney would have been twenty-eight years old if he had lived.

24   On the back cover, immediately after the words *Abbey Road*, a skull-like drawing can be discerned.

25   In "Come Together," Lennon sings, "One and one and one is three." Three Beatles. What about Paul?

NOTE: We have used quotation marks to distinguish between the real Paul and the lookalike imposter who "replaced" him.—Eds.

-◄▐►-

DEATH ROCK

1   "The Bells," JAMES BROWN
2   "Cadillac Ranch," BRUCE SPRINGSTEEN
3   "Death of a Clown," DAVE DAVIES
4   "Endless Sleep," JODY REYNOLDS
5   "For a Dancer," JACKSON BROWNE
6   "For You," BRUCE SPRINGSTEEN
7   "Hand of Fate," THE ROLLING STONES
8   "I Don't Live Today," JIMI HENDRIX
9   "I Shall Be Released," BOB DYLAN
10   "I'll Never Get Out of This World Alive," HANK WILLIAMS
11   "July the 12th, 1939," CHARLIE RICH
12   "Long Black Limousine," ELVIS PRESLEY
13   "Mother and Child Reunion," PAUL SIMON
14   "Patches," CLARENCE CARTER
15   "Percy's Song," FAIRPORT CONVENTION
16   "Sky Pilot," ERIC BURDON AND THE ANIMALS

17   "Stagger Lee," LLOYD PRICE
18   "That Smell," LYNYRD SKYNYRD
19   "Tonight's the Night," NEIL YOUNG
20   "Wreck on the Highway," BRUCE SPRINGSTEEN

·◄❙❙▶·

THE JOHNNY ACE MEMORIAL LISTS
Rock and Roll Deaths

Suicides
1   JOHNNY ACE, 1929–1954
2   IAN CURTIS (Joy Division), 1959–1980
3   PETE HAM (Badfinger), 1947–1975
4   DONNY HATHAWAY, 1945–1979
5   PHIL OCHS, 1940–1976
6   RORY STORM (c. 1941–1974)
7   PAUL WILLIAMS (The Temptations), 1939–1973

Plane Crashes
1   JIM CROCE, 1943–1973
2   STEVE GAINES (Lynyrd Skynyrd), 1949–1977
3   BUDDY HOLLY, 1936–1959
4   OTIS REDDING, 1941–1967
5   J. P. RICHARDSON, a.k.a. THE BIG BOPPER, 1935–1959
6   RITCHIE VALENS, 1941–1959
7   RONNIE VAN ZANT (Lynyrd Skynyrd), 1949–1977

Automobile and Motorcycle Crashes
1   DUANE ALLMAN, 1946–1971
2   JESSE BELVIN, 1933–1960
3   MARC BOLAN (T. Rex), 1948–1977
4   EDDIE COCHRAN, 1938–1960
5   RICHARD FARIÑA, 1937–1966
6   EARL GRANT, 1931–1970

...A BIRD
FLYING HIGH
OVER The
SAN Andreas
FauLT...

BURK UZZLE/MAGNUM

Site of Gram Parsons' cremation in the Mojave Desert. He died on September 19, 1973.

7   Johnny Horton, 1927–1960
8   Berry Oakley (The Allman Brothers Band), 1948–1972
9   Billy Stewart, 1938–1970

Drug Overdoses and Related Circumstances
1   Tommy Bolin (Deep Purple, James Gang), 1950–1975
2   Tim Buckley, 1947–1975
3   Nick Drake, 1948–1974
4   Tim Hardin, 1940–1980
5   Jimi Hendrix, 1942–1970
6   Gregory Herbert (Blood, Sweat, and Tears), 1950–1978
7   Janis Joplin, 1943–1970
8   Frankie Lymon, 1942–1968
9   Robbie McIntosh (The Average White Band), 1944–1974
10   Keith Moon, 1946–1978
11   Gram Parsons, 1946–1973
12   Elvis Presley, 1935–1977
13   Sid Vicious (The Sex Pistols), 1958–1979
14   Danny Whitten (Crazy Horse), 1945–1972
15   Alan Wilson (Canned Heat), 1943–1970

Shootings, Stabbings, and Beatings
1   Sam Cooke, 1935–1964
2   King Curtis, 1934–1971
3   Meredith Hunter, 1951–1969
4   Al Jackson (Booker T. and the MGs), 1935–1975
5   Terry Kath (Chicago), 1946–1978*
6   John Lennon, 1940–1980
7   James "Shep" Sheppard, 19??–1970

*Self-inflicted

Asphyxiations and Drownings
1   Johnny Burnette, 1934–1964
2   Bobby Fuller, 1943–1966
3   Brian Jones (The Rolling Stones), 1944–1969

Heart Attacks and Strokes

1 FLORENCE BALLARD (The Supremes), 1943–1976
2 JOHN BONHAM (Led Zeppelin), 1945–1980
3 DORSEY BURNETTE, 1933–1979
4 BOBBY DARIN, 1936–1973
5 LOWELL GEORGE (Little Feat), 1945–1979
6 ROY HAMILTON, 1929–1969
7 SLIM HARPO, 1924–1970
8 BOB HITE, 1945–1981
9 CHRIS KENNER, 1929–1976
10 PAUL KOSSOFF (Free), 1950–1976
11 VAN McCOY, 1941–1979
12 CLYDE McPHATTER, 1931–1972
13 JIM MORRISON, 1943–1971
14 ELVIS PRESLEY, 1935–1977

Cancer and Other Diseases

1 GUITAR SLIM, 1926–1959
2 IVORY JOE HUNTER, 1911–1974
3 LITTLE WILLIE JOHN, 1937–1966: pneumonia; died in prison
4 FREDDIE KING, 1934–1976: ulcers
5 BOB MARLEY, 1945–1981
6 RON "PIGPEN" McKERNAN (The Grateful Dead), 1945–1973: cirrhosis
7 JUNIOR PARKER, 1932–1971: brain tumor
8 MINNIE RIPERTON, 1948–1979
9 CLARENCE WHITE (The Byrds), 1944–1973: stomach hemorrhage
10 CHUCK WILLIS, 1928–1958: stomach disease; delayed having an operation and died during surgery

Other Accidents

1 **Sandy Denny** (Fairport Convention), 1947–1978
   Fell down a flight of stairs at her home.
2 **Cass Elliott** (The Mamas and the Papas), 1943–1974
   Choked to death (in the same London flat where Keith Moon died in 1978).

3   **Les Harvey** (Stone the Crows), 19??–1972
    Died onstage at Swansea University as a result of a shock from
    a live microphone.

4   **Kit Lambert,** 1936–1981
    The Who manager died of injuries suffered when he fell down a
    flight of stairs at his mother's home.

5   **Tammi Terrell,** 1946–1970
    Fell down a flight of stairs, incurring brain damage.

6   **Gene Vincent,** 1934–1971
    Had a leg injured in the army and reinjured it in the same
    1960 car crash in which Eddie Cochran died. The wound
    became ulcerated and left Vincent in terrible pain, leading to
    his alcoholism and eventual death of a hemorrhage.

-◄❙▶-

THE 10 MOST SPECTACULAR DEATHS

1   **Johnny Ace**
    Died backstage on Christmas Eve 1954, at Houston City
    Auditorium, while playing Russian roulette.

2   **Sam Cooke**
    Cooke was shot to death under mysterious circumstances at a
    Los Angeles motel on December 10, 1964. The proprietor who
    shot him claimed that Cooke had appeared to be an intruder; a
    court returned a verdict of justifiable homicide.

3   **Les Harvey** (Stone the Crows)
    Killed onstage in 1972 at Swansea University in Wales when
    he was electrocuted by touching a live microphone.

4   **Buddy Holly, J. P. Richardson, and Ritchie Valens**
    Died in an airplane crash on February 3, 1959; they decided
    not to take the bus to Fargo, North Dakota, from Clear Lake,
    Iowa, so they'd have time to get their laundry done and pick up
    some mail before the next gig.

5   **Terry Kath** (Chicago)
    Died at the Los Angeles home of a friend in 1978, when the

gun he was playing with went off as it was pointed at his head. This occurred in full view of his wife and one of the band's sound crew.

6   **John Lennon**

On December 8, 1980, Lennon and his wife, Yoko Ono, arrived at New York's Dakota, the apartment house in which they lived, after an early-evening recording session. As they walked through the gates, a lone gunman stopped and fired five bullets into Lennon, killing him almost instantly. The gunman did not attempt to escape and was immediately apprehended. Lennon's death set off a week of worldwide mourning.

7   **Otis Redding**

On December 10, 1967, Otis Redding and his touring band, including members of The Bar-Kays, were on their way from Cleveland to Madison, Wisconsin, when the plane crashed and wound up at the bottom of Lake Monona, then frozen over. Ironically, Redding was just enjoying the benefits of his first major pop hit, "(Sittin' on) the Dock of the Bay." His body was never recovered.

8   **Keith Relf**

The former Yardbirds vocalist, who founded Renaissance, was found dead in his bathtub on May 14, 1976, the result of an electric shock from a guitar.

9   **Rory Storm**

The onetime Merseybeat bandleader (Ringo Starr was playing with Rory Storm and the Hurricanes when he joined The Beatles) was found dead in his home in 1974, with his head in the oven, the result of a suicide pact with his mother, whose body was found nearby.

10   **James "Shep" Sheppard**

The vocalist on both The Heartbeats' "A Thousand Miles Away" and Shep and the Limelites' long-delayed answer record, "Daddy's Home," was found beaten to death in a car parked at the side of the Long Island Expressway on January 24, 1970.

ROCK AND ROLL HEAVEN
A List of Probable Inductees

1 Master of Ceremonies: ALAN FREED
2 Singers: OTIS REDDING, SAM COOKE, ELVIS PRESLEY
3 Guitarists: JIMI HENDRIX, EDDIE COCHRAN, BUDDY HOLLY, BOB MARLEY
4 Bass: BILL BLACK
5 Drums: AL JACKSON
6 Horns: KING CURTIS AND THE BAR-KAYS
7 Harp: LITTLE WALTER, SLIM HARPO
8 Keyboards: JOHN LENNON
9 The Choir: THE BIG BOPPER, JOHNNY BURNETTE, JESSE BELVIN, BILL HALEY, FRANKIE LYMON, CLYDE McPHATTER, MINNIE RIPERTON, TAMMI TERRELL, RITCHIE VALENS, GENE VINCENT, CHUCK WILLIS

·◄◗►·

ROCK AND ROLL HELL
A List of Probable Inductees

1 Master of Ceremonies: KEITH MOON
2 Singers: RONNIE VAN ZANT, JOHNNY ACE, lead vocals; JIM MORRISON, JANIS JOPLIN, background vocals
3 Guitars: DUANE ALLMAN, LOWELL GEORGE, DANNY WHITTEN
4 Drums: JOHN BONHAM
5 Bass: BERRY OAKLEY
6 Keyboards: PIGPEN
7 Road crew: BRUCE BARRY, SID VICIOUS, MEREDITH HUNTER

PSYCHEDELIC TOP 40

1   "Are You Experienced?" THE JIMI HENDRIX EXPERIENCE
2   "Break on Through (to the Other Side)," THE DOORS
3   "The Crown of Creation," THE JEFFERSON AIRPLANE
4   "Dark Star," THE GRATEFUL DEAD
5   "A Day in the Life," THE BEATLES
6   "Eight Miles High," THE BYRDS
7   "The End," THE DOORS
8   "A Girl Named Sandoz," ERIC BURDON AND THE ANIMALS
9   "Hung Upside Down," BUFFALO SPRINGFIELD
10   "I Can See for Miles," THE WHO
11   "I Got a Line on You," SPIRIT
12   "I Had Too Much to Dream (Last Night)," THE ELECTRIC PRUNES
13   "In-a-Gadda-da-Vida," THE IRON BUTTERFLY
14   "Incense and Peppermints," THE STRAWBERRY ALARM CLOCK
15   "Itchycoo Park," THE SMALL FACES
16   "Journey to the Center of Your Mind," THE AMBOY DUKES
17   "Lucy in the Sky with Diamonds," THE BEATLES
18   "Magical Mystery Tour," THE BEATLES
19   "Open My Eyes," THE NAZZ
20   "Psychedelic Shack," THE TEMPTATIONS
21   "Psychotic Reaction," COUNT FIVE
22   "Purple Haze," THE JIMI HENDRIX EXPERIENCE
23   "Revelation," LOVE
24   "Room Full of Mirrors," JIMI HENDRIX
25   "St. Stephen," THE GRATEFUL DEAD
26   "See Emily Play," PINK FLOYD
27   "She's a Rainbow," THE ROLLING STONES
28   "She Said She Said," THE BEATLES
29   "Somebody to Love," JEFFERSON AIRPLANE
30   "Strange Brew," CREAM
31   "Strawberry Fields Forever," THE BEATLES

32   "Sunshine of Your Love," CREAM
33   "Time Has Come Today," THE CHAMBERS BROTHERS
34   "Tomorrow Never Knows," THE BEATLES
35   "2000 Light Years from Home," THE ROLLING STONES
36   "When the Music's Over," THE DOORS
37   "White Rabbit," THE JEFFERSON AIRPLANE
38   "You Keep Me Hangin' On," VANILLA FUDGE
39   "You Set the Scene," LOVE
40   "You're Gonna Miss Me," THE 13TH FLOOR ELEVATOR

·◀▮▮▶·

THE NEEDLE AND THE DAMAGE DONE

1   "Berkshire Poppies," TRAFFIC
2   "Chinese Rocks," THE RAMONES
3   "Heroin," THE VELVET UNDERGROUND
4   "Junker's Blues," MICHAEL BLOOMFIELD
5   "Kid Charlemagne," STEELY DAN
6   "The Needle and the Damage Done," NEIL YOUNG
7   "The Needle and the Spoon," LYNYRD SKYNYRD
8   "The Pusher," STEPPENWOLF
9   "Sam Stone," JOHN PRINE
10   "Tonight's the Night," NEIL YOUNG
11   "Waiting for the Man," LOU REED
12   "You Can't Always Get What You Want," THE ROLLING
     STONES

·◀▮▮▶·

WHITE-LINE FEVER

1   "A Blow for Me, a Toot for You," FRED WESLEY AND THE
     HORNY HORNS
2   "Casey Jones," THE GRATEFUL DEAD
3   "Cocaine," JACKSON BROWNE
4   "Cocaine Charley," THE ATLANTA RHYTHM SECTION

5   "Life in the Fast Lane," THE EAGLES
6   "Memo from Turner," MICK JAGGER
7   "Moonlight Mile," THE ROLLING STONES
8   "My Snowblind Friend," HOYT AXTON
9   "That Smell," LYNYRD SKYNYRD
10   "Witchy Woman," THE EAGLES

-◄▐▶-

REEFER MADNESS

1   "Comin' into Los Angeles," ARLO GUTHRIE
2   "Don't Step on the Grass, Sam," STEPPENWOLF
3   "Flying High," COUNTRY JOE AND THE FISH
4   "Itchycoo Park," THE SMALL FACES
5   "Let's Go Get Stoned," RAY CHARLES
6   "New Dope in Town," SPIRIT
7   "Okie from Muskogee," MERLE HAGGARD
8   "One Toke over the Line," BREWER AND SHIPLEY
9   "Panama Red," THE NEW RIDERS OF THE PURPLE SAGE
10   "Rainy Day Women #12 & 35," BOB DYLAN
11   "Taxi," HARRY CHAPIN
12   "Wacky Tobaccy," NRBQ

-◄▐▶-

THE ROCK AND ROLL BAR STOOL
Drinking Songs

1   "Alcohol," THE KINKS
2   "Cracklin' Rose," NEIL DIAMOND
3   "Drinkin' Wine Spo-Dee-O-Dee," STICK MCGHEE
4   "Letter to Johnny Walker Red," ASLEEP AT THE WHEEL
5   "One Bourbon, One Scotch, One Beer," AMOS MILBURN
6   "Sitting and Thinking," CHARLIE RICH
7   "Tequila Sunrise," THE EAGLES

8   "What's Made Milwaukee Famous (Has Made a Loser Out of Me)," JERRY LEE LEWIS
9   "White Port and Lemon Juice," THE FOUR DEUCES
10 "Wine," THE ELECTRIC FLAG

-◄▐►-

ANTIDRUG TOP 10

1   "Cold Turkey," JOHN LENNON
2   "Kicks," PAUL REVERE AND THE RAIDERS
3   "Tonight's the Night," NEIL YOUNG
4   "Speed Kills," STEVE GIBBONS BAND
5   "Little Billy," THE WHO
6   "Chinese Rocks," THE RAMONES
7   "The Needle and the Damage Done," NEIL YOUNG
8   "The Pusher," STEPPENWOLF
9   "Sam Stone," JOHN PRINE
10 "My Snowblind Friend," HOYT AXTON

-◄▐►-

WHITE LIGHT, WHITE HEAT
Former Heroin Users

1	GREGG ALLMAN	7	LOU REED
2	TIM BUCKLEY	8	KEITH RICHARDS
3	RAY CHARLES	9	JAMES TAYLOR
4	ERIC CLAPTON	10	JOHNNY THUNDERS
5	MARIANNE FAITHFULL	11	SID VICIOUS
6	FRANKIE LYMON	12	JOHNNY WINTER

CHRIS MORPHET

Pete Townshend—before.

DOWN ON DRUGS

1 JONATHAN KING
2 LITTLE RICHARD*
3 TED NUGENT
4 BRUCE SPRINGSTEEN
5 PETE TOWNSHEND*
6 FRANK ZAPPA

*Reformed drug-user

DRUGS PRESCRIBED TO ELVIS BY HIS PAL, DR. NICK

In its malpractice charges against Dr. George Nichopoulos, known to Elvis' intimates as Dr. Nick, the Tennessee Medical Board used eight full-sized legal pages to list the prescriptions he had written; these are only some of them. In the eighteen months before he died, thousands of pills were prescribed to Presley.

1	Amytal	10	Ionamin
2	Biphetamine	11	Leritine
3	Carbrital	12	Lomotil
4	Hydrochloride cocaine	13	Parest
5	Demerol	14	Percodan
6	Dexamyl	15	Placidyl
7	Dexedrine	16	Quaalude
8	Dilaudid	17	Tuinal
9	Hycomine	18	Valium

◄▮►·

TRIBUTE RECORDS

1 **"American Pie,"** DON MCLEAN
A tribute to Buddy Holly (among others) and "the day the music died." Major U.S. hit.

2 **"Dedicated to Otis,"** LUCILLE SPANN
Memorial to the great blues pianist Otis Spann by his widow.

3 **"Gold Records in the Snow,"** BENNY BARNES
Yet another tribute to Holly, J. P. Richardson, and Ritchie Valens.

4 **"Hound Dog Man (Play It Again),"** LENNY LEBLANC
Although it was actually released shortly before his death, it

was the best of the posthumous Elvis salutes. Also recorded by Roy Orbison.

5   **"Just Like Eddie,"** HEINZ
Memorializes Eddie Cochran; English hit.

6   **"Old Friend,"** WAYLON JENNINGS
Another about Buddy Holly, this time by a part-time Cricket, whose first record, "Jolé Blon," was produced by Holly.

7   **"The Real Buddy Holly Story,"** SONNY CURTIS
The former Cricket and Holly cowriter takes the film about his life to task and summons up better memories of the man.

8   **"Rock and Roll Heaven,"** THE RIGHTEOUS BROTHERS
Includes everybody from Bobby Darin to Brian Jones.

9   **"Song for a Dreamer,"** PROCOL HARUM
The English rock band mourns Jimi Hendrix; guitarist Robin Trower went on to make several albums clearly influenced by Jimi.

10 **"Three Stars,"** TOMMY DEE with CAROL KAY AND THE TEEN-AIRES
Another plane crash memorial.

11 **"Tribute to Buddy Holly,"** MIKE BERRY AND THE OUTLAWS
This tribute was a minor British hit, made distinctive because both music and vocals are such a strong evocation of Holly's sound.

12 **"Tribute to a King,"** WILLIAM BELL
The Stax memorial to Otis.

-◄▐►-

Bizarre Last Records

1   "A Change Is Gonna Come," SAM COOKE
2   "Three Steps to Heaven," EDDIE COCHRAN
3   "It Doesn't Matter Anymore," BUDDY HOLLY
4   "(Just Like) Starting Over," JOHN LENNON and YOKO ONO

5   "That Smell," LYNYRD SKYNYRD
6   *Who Are You*, KEITH MOON
    On the cover, Moon is sitting in a chair stenciled "Not to Be
    Taken Away."
7   "I'll Never Get Out of This World Alive," HANK WILLIAMS
8   "What Am I Living For?" CHUCK WILLIS

TWENTY-SEVEN
BORN TO BE WILD

Lou Reed takes a walk on the wild side at Winterland in 1974.

MICHAEL ZAGARIS

NIK COHN PICKS ROCK'S "THE GOOD, THE BAAAD, AND THE UGLY"

Nik Cohn says that his prime criterion was moral grace, rather than physical beauty or even musical talent.

The Good

1 ELVIS PRESLEY
2 SMOKEY ROBINSON
3 JIMI HENDRIX
4 ARETHA FRANKLIN
5 ARLENE SMITH (The Chantels)
6 JOHN LENNON
7 PROFESSOR LONGHAIR
8 BOB MARLEY
9 ROY ORBISON
10 BILLY FURY

The Baaad

1 JOE TEX
2 JERRY LEE LEWIS
3 JOHNNY ROTTEN
4 P. J. PROBY
5 LOU REED
6 MILLIE JACKSON
7 THE COASTERS
8 GATEMOUTH BROWN
9 CHUCK BERRY
10 THE BIG BOPPER

The Ugly

1 BOB DYLAN
2 FRANK ZAPPA
3 ROGER DALTREY
4 LEON RUSSELL
5 ELVIS COSTELLO
6 THE VILLAGE PEOPLE
7 TOM WAITS
8 LED ZEPPELIN
9 GEORGE HARRISON
10 PETER ALLEN

NIK COHN, *an Irishman from Londonderry, spent the sixties as the best pop reporter and critic in London, exemplified by his volume of rock history,* Rock from the Beginning *(Stein and Day, 1969), his editorial work on* Rock Dreams *(Fawcett/ Popular Library, 1973) and his novels* King Death *(Harcourt Brace Jovanovich, 1975) and* I Am Still the Greatest, Says Johnny Angelo *(Penguin, 1967). Since 1975, Cohn has lived in the U.S., where his most celebrated achievement was a New York magazine article, "Tribal Rites of the New Saturday Night," which became the film* Saturday Night Fever. *Cohn is currently a columnist for* Inside Sports.

PAUL BURLISON LISTS THE 5 WILDEST ROCK AND ROLL CATS OF THE 1950s

1   JERRY LEE LEWIS
2   BOBBY LEE TRAMMELL
3   THE JUDIMARS
4   SCREAMIN' JAY HAWKINS
5   LONNIE DONEGAN

PAUL BURLISON *played an important part in the development of early rock as the lead guitarist in The Rock and Roll Trio, with Johnny and Dorsey Burnette. Burlison is responsible for creating fuzz tone, with his distorted solo on "Train Kept a-Rollin'." He now lives in Memphis, where he has a record collection including more than 100,000 discs.*

- ◄❙▶ -

ATTITUDE PUNKS: ORIGINALS

Before the punk rock movement, there were men—adventurous, scruffy souls—who exemplified that rebel spirit precisely. Johnny Rotten would never have been imaginable without these pioneers.

1   LINK WRAY
2   JERRY LEE LEWIS
3   SKY SAXON
4   BILLY LEE RILEY
5   TED NUGENT
6   DAVID LEE ROTH
7   MARTY BALIN
8   RONNIE VAN ZANT
9   JOHN CIPOLLINA
10 JOE PERRY
11 DAVE DAVIES
12 PETER WOLF

- ◄❙▶ -

JIM MORRISON'S ARREST RECORD

1   **New Haven, Connecticut,** December 9, 1967
    Morrison had turned twenty-four only the day before. Prior to The Doors set, he was making out with a girl in a backstage

showerroom when they were rousted by a cop. Jim, of course, immediately harassed the cop, lipping off until he was maced. During the middle of "Back Door Man" in that night's show, Morrison launched into a tirade about the incident. The cops, retaliating, turned on the houselights, and Morrison was arrested onstage. He was charged with breach of peace and resisting arrest.

2   **Las Vegas,** early 1968
Morrison was with writer Robert Gover (author of *The $100 Misunderstanding)* outside the Pussy Cat Au-Go-Go, a topless joint. The pair had made the mistake of starting a fight with a security guard in the parking lot. Both Gover and Morrison were charged with public drunkenness, Morrison also being hit with accusations of vagrancy and failure to identify himself.

3   **Miami,** March 1, 1969
At Dinner Key Auditorium, Morrison was arrested for exposing his organ during a Doors performance that night. Morrison was not charged until some weeks later, when the incident had already become a media spat. He was charged with lewd and lascivious behavior (a felony carrying a maximum three-year sentence), indecent exposure, open profanity, and public drunkenness. After a lengthy trial, he was found guilty in 1970 of indecent exposure and profanity; he was sentenced to six months of hard labor with a $500 fine on the first charge, and sixty days hard labor on the second. The sentence was on appeal when Morrison died.

4   **Phoenix,** November 11, 1969
On a Continental Airlines flight from Los Angeles, on their way to see a Rolling Stones concert in Phoenix, Morrison and friend Tom Baker were arrested by the FBI. They were charged with drunk and disorderly conduct and interfering with personnel aboard a commercial aircraft, the latter carrying a federal skyjacking penalty of a $10,000 fine and/or ten years in prison. They were found innocent of the felony charge but guilty of "assaulting, threatening, intimidating, and interfering with the performance of" two stewardesses. However, the

The Lizard King and accomplice perform a Florida Duet onstage at the Dinner Key Auditorium in Miami Beach, Florida on March 1, 1969. A warrant for their arrest was issued several days later citing four counts: lewd and lascivious behavior, indecent exposure, open profanity, and drunkenness.

stewardess who made most of the accusations later changed her testimony, and the charges were dropped.

5   **Los Angeles,** August 4, 1970

Morrison was charged with public drunkenness after falling asleep on an old woman's porch in West L.A.; this occurred one day before the Miami trial began.

Slammer BLUES

1 "Alice's Restaurant," ARLO GUTHRIE
2 "Cell Number 7," JOHN ENTWISTLE
3 "Chain Gang," SAM COOKE
4 "Christmas in Prison," JOHN PRINE
5 "Electric Chair," SLEEPY JOHN ESTES
6 "Folsom Prison Blues," JOHNNY CASH
7 "Friend of the Devil," THE GRATEFUL DEAD
8 "George Jackson," BOB DYLAN
9 "Gonna Give Her All the Love I Got," JIMMY RUFFIN
10 "Have Mercy Judge," CHUCK BERRY
11 "Hollaway Jail," THE KINKS
12 "Hurricane," BOB DYLAN
13 "I Fought the Law," BOBBY FULLER FOUR
14 "Jail," BIG MAMA THORNTON
15 "Jailhouse Rock," ELVIS PRESLEY
16 "Long Black Veil," THE BAND
17 "Mama Tried," MERLE HAGGARD
18 "Penitentiary Blues," DAVID ALLAN COE
19 "Percy's Song," BOB DYLAN
20 "Sweet Lucy," MICHAEL HURLEY
21 "Take a Message to Mary," THE EVERLY BROTHERS
22 "There's Gonna Be a Jailbreak," THIN LIZZY
23 "Thirty Days in the Hole," HUMBLE PIE
24 "We Love You," THE ROLLING STONES

-◄❙▶-

Warden THREW A PARTY IN THE COUNTY J
Rockers Who've Done Time

1 **CHUCK BERRY**
   He did time twice, once in the late fifties on a Mann Ac
   violation, and again in the late seventies for income-ta
   evasion.

2　**JOHNNY BRAGG**
The leader of The Prisonaires, he served time first for rape, and later for parole violation. The parole violation apparently was a trumped-up charge for having sex with his wife in a car. While doing time, he and a group of inmates recorded "Just Walking in the Rain" and several other classics for Sun Records.

3　**JAMES BROWN**
Brown spent three years in a Georgia reform school.

4　**FREDDY FENDER**
Under his real name, Baldemar G. Huerta, Fender spent three years in a Louisiana prison on a marijuana-related conviction.

5　**LITTLE WILLIE JOHN**
After a manslaughter conviction, he did time in Washington State Penitentiary, where he died of pneumonia.

6　**EUGENE MUMFORD**
The leader of The Larks served a sentence for grass in 1949 and went on to write "When I Leave These Prison Walls."

7　**PHIL OCHS**
Ochs served a spell for vagrancy in Florida around 1960.

8　**RICK STEVENS**
The Tower of Power lead vocalist is currently doing time in California on three counts of first-degree murder.

9　**SID VICIOUS**
After serving several weeks in New York City jails for the alleged murder of girlfriend Nancy Spungen, Vicious overdosed on heroin before the case came to trial.

-◄❚❚►-

20 FAMOUS BUSTS

1　**THE ROLLING STONES,** March 18, 1965
They were fined five pounds each for public urination at a gas station after a gig at the Romford ABC in Essex, U.K.

2   **KEITH RICHARDS, MICK JAGGER, AND MARIANNE FAITH-
    FULL,** February 12, 1967
    At his home at Redlands, West Wittering, U.K., Richards was
    busted with Jagger, Faithfull, and art dealer Robert Fraser
    The celebrated drug orgy raid.

3   **MICK JAGGER and KEITH RICHARDS,** May 10, 1967
    In Chichester, U.K., they were arrested for drugs and sent to
    jail at West Sussex Quarter Session.

4   **BRIAN JONES,** May 10, 1967
    After a bust for possession of marijuana in England, Jones was
    released on £250 bail. He was sentenced to nine months in
    jail, which was later reduced to a £1000 fine and three years
    probation.

5   **THE GRATEFUL DEAD,** October 2, 1967
    Narcotics agents raided their house at 710 Ashbury Street in
    San Francisco, and arrested Pigpen, Bob Weir, and nine
    others, although the bust was ultimately meaningless because
    the cops had failed to obtain warrants before breaking down
    the door.

6   **MICK JAGGER and MARIANNE FAITHFULL,** May 24, 1968
    At their home in Cheyne Walk, London, they were arrested for
    possession of pot and released on fifty-pound bail.

7   **JOHN LENNON and YOKO ONO,** October 18, 1968
    At their flat in Montague Square, London, Lennon was fined
    £150, and £21 in court costs, for possession of marijuana.

8   **GEORGE and PATTI HARRISON,** March 12, 1969
    Their London home was raided and 120 joints found. Harrison
    claimed it was a frame-up, timed by police to coincide with the
    marriage of Paul McCartney.

9   **PETE TOWNSHEND and ROGER DALTREY,** May 16, 1969
    They were charged with assault after Townshend kicked a cop
    offstage at New York's Fillmore East. The plainclothesman
    was trying to clear the hall because of a fire next door. Bill
    Graham bailed them out.

10 **ARETHA FRANKLIN,** July 22, 1969
    In Detroit, Franklin was busted for causing a disturbance in

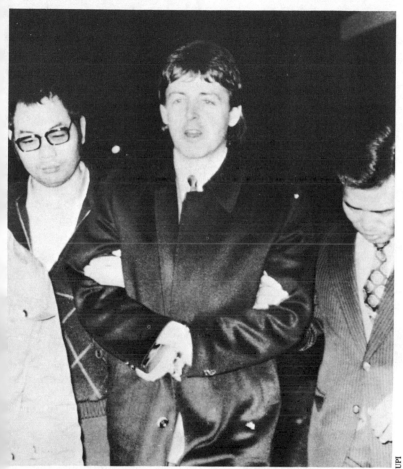

UPI

Paul McCartney is carted off to jail in Tokyo in January 1980. His alleged crime: bringing more than 200 grams (that's almost six ounces) of pot into Nippon. McCartney cooled his heels in jail for several days, forcing cancellation of his entire Japanese tour and creating an international incident.

parking lot. Released on a fifty-dollar bond, she ran down a street sign as she left the police station.

11   **JANIS JOPLIN,** November 15, 1969
In Tampa, Florida, Joplin was accused of vulgar and indecent language and later released on a fifty-dollar bond.

12   **THE GRATEFUL DEAD,** January 31, 1970
They were busted for narcotics (LSD and barbiturates) in New Orleans, along with the celebrated LSD chemist Stanley Owsley.

13   **PETER YARROW,** March 26, 1970
He pleaded guilty to charges of "taking immoral liberties" with a fourteen-year-old girl in Washington, D.C. (Peter, Paul, and Mary had just won a Grammy for Best Children's Record.)

14   **PHIL LESH,** January 14, 1973
The Grateful Dead bassist was busted for possession of drugs in Marin County, California.

15   **PAUL MCCARTNEY,** March 8, 1973
He was fined £100 for growing cannabis on his farm in Campbeltown, Scotland.

16   **JERRY GARCIA,** March 27, 1973
After stopping him for speeding on Interstate 295 near Philadelphia, the cops found grass, acid, coke, and prescription pills in a suitcase.

17   **KEITH RICHARDS,** February 27, 1977
Richards was originally charged in Toronto, Canada, for possession of heroin for the purposes of trafficking, and for possession of cocaine. The cocaine charge was later dropped and Richards pleaded guilty to the possession of twenty-two grams of heroin. Despite official protests, Richards was given a suspended sentence. The only stipulation asked by the court was that he give a benefit concert for the Canadian Institute for the Blind, which he did give on April 22, 1979, and which included a guest appearance by Mick Jagger.

18   **PAUL MCCARTNEY,** January 16, 1980
In Tokyo, customs inspectors discovered nearly a half a pound of marijuana he had absent-mindedly left in his suitcase

McCartney spent ten days in prison, had his Japanese tour canceled, and was forbidden from ever returning to that country.

19   **Chrissie Hynde,** March 1980
The Pretenders' lead singer spent the night in a Memphis jail, and was released the next day on a $250 bond, for drunken behavior, including kicking out a police car window outside a local bar.

20   **Wendy O. Williams,** January 18, 1981
The arrest, in Milwaukee, was initially for onstage obscenity, but after an officer allegedly made a sexual grab at her, a battle ensued. Williams was charged with resisting arrest and for battery of a police officer. She was released on a $2,000 bond. The Plasmatics' lead singer had seven stitches above her eye and spent the night in jail, as did the band's manager.

-◄▮▶-

Jailbait

1   "Brown Shoes Don't Make It," The Mothers of Invention
2   "Come Up the Years," The Jefferson Airplane
3   "I'm So Young," The Students
4   "It Hurts to Be Sixteen," Brenda Lee
5   "Jailbait," Andre Williams
6   "Only Sixteen," Sam Cooke
7   "Sent Up," The Falcons
8   "Sixteen Candles," The Crests
9   "Sweet Little Rock and Roller," Chuck Berry
10   "Sweet Little Sixteen," Chuck Berry
11   "Sweet Sixteen," The Colts
12   "Teenage Wildlife," David Bowie
13   "Young Blood," The Coasters
14   "You're Sixteen," Johnny Burnette

Frankie Lymon and the Teenagers in a still from the 1957 release, Rock, Rock, Rock. *Frankie was 15 years old.*

PERFORMERS WHO REACHED STARDOM BEFORE TURNING 18

1 FABIAN, "I'm a Man," 1959 (at age 16)
2 JANIS IAN, "Society's Child (Baby I've Been Thinking)," 196 (at age 15)
3 MICHAEL JACKSON, "I Want You Back," 1970 (at age 11)*
4 BRENDA LEE, "One Step at a Time," 1957 (at age 12)
5 LITTLE EVA, "The Loco-Motion," 1962 (at age 16)
6 FRANKIE LYMON, "Why Do Fools Fall in Love," 1956 (at age 14)**
7 RICKY NELSON, "A Teenager's Romance," 1957 (at age 17)
8 LITTLE ESTHER PHILLIPS, "Double Crossing Blues," 1950 (at age 15)

9   THE SCHOOLBOYS, "Please Say You Want Me," 1955†
10   RACHEL SWEET, "B-A-B-Y," 1979 (at age 16)
11   TANYA TUCKER, "Would You Lay with Me (in a Field of Stone)," 1973 (at age 14)
12   LITTLE STEVIE WONDER, "Fingertips, Part 2," 1963 (at age 12)

* With The Jackson 5
**With The Teenagers
† Ages unknown, but all attended Cooper Junior High School, Harlem

-◄❚▮❚►-

10 FAMOUS BUBBLE-GUM GROUPS

Buddah Records kicked off the bubble-gum rock craze in 1968 with a batch of synthetic groups (floating collections of session-men). The result was some of the most ludicrous, if occasionally transcendent, trash produced in the rock and roll age. Kasenetz-Katz is the cream of this crop, but that doesn't mean a lot.

1   THE ARCHIES, "Sugar, Sugar"
2   THE BANANA SPLITS, "The Tra La La Song"
3   CRAZY ELEPHANT, "Gimme Gimme Good Lovin'"
4   KASENETZ-KATZ SINGING ORCHESTRAL CIRCUS, "Quick Joey Small (Run Joey Run)"
5   THE LEMON PIPERS, "Green Tambourine"
6   THE MUSIC EXPLOSION, "Little Bit o' Soul"
7   THE 1910 FRUITGUM COMPANY, "Simon Says"
8   THE OHIO EXPRESS, "Yummy Yummy Yummy"
9   THE ROCK AND ROLL DUBBLE BUBBLE TRADING CARD COMPANY OF PHILADELPHIA, 19141, "Bubble Gum Music"
10   STEAM, "Na Na Hey Hey (Kiss Him Goodbye)"

ONAN'S GREATEST HITS
The 25 Greatest Songs about Masturbation

1   "All I Have to Do Is Dream," THE EVERLY BROTHERS
2   "The Beat," ELVIS COSTELLO
3   "Blinded by the Light," BRUCE SPRINGSTEEN
4   "Buttered Popcorn," THE SUPREMES
5   "Captain Jack," BILLY JOEL
6   "Cool Jerk," THE CAPITOLS
7   "Dancing with Myself," GEN. X
8   "Don't Treat Me Bad," MICHAEL HURLEY
9   "Fiddle About," THE WHO
10 "Going Home," THE ROLLING STONES
11 "Imaginary Lover," THE ATLANTA RHYTHM SECTION
12 "In My Room," THE BEACH BOYS
13 "Jamaica Jerk-Off," ELTON JOHN
14 "Love or Confusion," JIMI HENDRIX
15 "Only the Lonely (Know How I Feel)," ROY ORBISON
16 "Pictures of Lily," THE WHO
17 "Pump It Up," ELVIS COSTELLO
18 "Rattlesnake Shake," FLEETWOOD MAC
19 "Rocks Off," THE ROLLING STONES
20 "Rosie," JACKSON BROWNE
21 "Shake a Hand," FAYE ADAMS
22 "Slippery Fingers," GRIN
23 "Turning Japanese," THE VAPORS
24 "Whip It," DEVO
25 "Whole Lot of Shakin' Going On," JERRY LEE LEWIS

HONORABLE MENTION: "You'll Never Get Cheated by Your Hand," STUMBLEBUM; "Solo," ELLEN SHIPLEY; "When Something Is Wrong with My Baby," SAM AND DAVE; "Just Out of Reach (of My Two Empty Arms)," PERCY SLEDGE; "Move It on Over," HANK WILLIAMS

20 PUNK GROUPS OF THE 1960s

*Between the British Invasion and the full onslaught of psyche-
delia two or three years later, it seemed as if virtually every
American male with three friends and access to an electrical
outlet formed a band. Playing in basements and garages, for
beer blasts and at sock hops, these bands were characterized by
marginal competence, great naiveté and a willingness to try
anything: English accents, tough-guy looks, the longest hair in
the neighborhood. These were the original punk rockers, from
whom the more politicized and radical seventies version took its
name and inspiration. These groups are best memorialized on
Nuggets, an album compiled by Lenny Kaye for Elektra Records
(and later reissued on Sire). This list is a mere honor roll by
comparison.*

1 THE AMBOY DUKES, "Baby Please Don't Go"
2 THE BARBARIANS, "Are You a Boy or Are You a Girl?"
3 THE BLENDELLS, "La La La La La"
4 THE BLUES MAGOOS, "(We Ain't Got) Nothin' Yet"
5 CANNIBAL AND THE HEADHUNTERS, "Land of 1000 Dances"
6 THE CASTAWAYS, "Liar Liar"
7 THE COUNT FIVE, "Psychotic Reaction"
8 THE CRYAN' SHAMES, "Sugar and Spice"
9 THE GANTS, "Road Runner"
10 THE KINGSMEN, "Louie Louie"
11 THE McCOYS, "Hang on Sloopy"
12 THE MC5, "Kick Out the Jams"
13 MOUSE AND THE TRAPS, "Public Execution"
14 THE MUSIC MACHINE, "Talk Talk"
15 THE OUTSIDERS, "Respectable"
16 THE PREMIERS, "Farmer John"
17 ? AND THE MYSTERIANS, "96 Tears"
18 THE SEEDS, "Pushin' Too Hard"
19 THE SHADOWS OF KNIGHT, "Gloria"
20 THE STANDELLS, "Dirty Water"

PUNK ROCK RECORDS THAT MADE THE BRITISH TOP 20 BEFORE IT WAS FASHIONABLE

The chart position for each single follows the date on which it first hit that slot.

1   "God Save the Queen," THE SEX PISTOLS, June 4, 1977 (4)
2   "Pretty Vacant," THE SEX PISTOLS, July 9, 1977 (6)
3   "Do Anything You Wanna Do," EDDIE AND THE HOT RODS, August 13, 1977 (9)
4   "Gary Gilmore's Eyes," THE ADVERTS, September 27, 1977 (18)
5   "Holidays in the Sun," THE SEX PISTOLS, October 22, 1977 (8)
6   "Angels with Dirty Faces," SHAM 69, May 13, 1978 (19)
7   "My Way"/"No One Is Innocent," THE SEX PISTOLS with RONALD BIGGS, July 8, 1978 (7)
8   "If the Kids Are United," SHAM 69, July 29, 1978 (9)
9   "Top of the Pops," THE REZILLOS, August 12, 1978 (17)
10 "Hong Kong Garden," SIOUXSIE AND THE BANSHEES, August 26, 1978 (7)
11 "Ever Fallen in Love," THE BUZZCOCKS, September 23, 1978 (12)
12 "Hurry Up Harry," SHAM 69, October 14, 1978 (10)
13 "Public image," PUBLIC IMAGE LTD., October 21, 1978 (9)
14 "Germ Free Adolescence," X-RAY SPEX, November 4, 1978 (19)
15 "Tommy Gun," THE CLASH, December 2, 1978 (20)

THE 10 BEST PUNK NAMES
Of Individuals—Bands Too Numerous to Mention

1 STIV BATORS (The Dead Boys)
2 LAURA LOGIC (Essential Logic)
3 TORY CRIMES (The Clash)
4 LUX INTERIOR (The Cramps)
5 JOHNNY ROTTEN (The Sex Pistols)
6 RAT SCABIES (The Damned)
7 JOE STRUMMER (The Clash)
8 POLY-STYRENE (X-ray Spex)
9 ARI UP (The Slits)
10 SID VICIOUS (The Sex Pistols)

·◀❙❙▶·

LENNY KAYE CHOOSES THE MOST INSANE NOVELTY RECORDS

32 ***The Spider and the Fly***, BOBBY CHRISTIAN AND THE ALLEN SISTERS
Caught in the web, emphasis on the *B*.

53 ***Delicious***, JIM BACKUS AND FRIEND
Post-Magoo and pre-*Gilligan's Island*. One of the many contagious laughter records to have dotted the landscape of recorded sound (see Large Larry's "Are You Ticklish?") and the theme song of Village Oldies.

14 ***The Out Crowd***, THE SQUARES
"Horace, are you going out with Freda the librarian? I hear she's brilliant." "Oh, Melvin, she's brilliant but she's not a genius!" *A* is for Artie Resnick.

26 ***Stickball***, P. VERT
Nostalgia of our time. Like stickball, and basketball, and playing in the streets. And you had a little girl, and she was your love. Because love between two people. . . . Mrs. Bruno, can Tony come out and play?

61   ***Flying Saucer,*** BUCHANAN AND GOODMAN
This is John Cameron-Cameron at the scene of the first (and
still best) break-in record. The outer space disc jockey cues up
. . . The Clatters! A fairly accurate representation of what Top
Forty radio was like in the flush opening years of rock and roll.

40   ***Ambrose (Part Five),*** LINDA LAURIE
A boy, a girl, a subway tunnel. Just keep walkin'.

8   **"Oliver Cool,"** OLIVER COOL
The swingingest superego in school, the role he was born to
play. And with some lovely gooping.

76   ***Transfusion,*** NERVOUS NORVUS
So this twin-pipe papa goes out for a cruise and he's tooling
down the highway doing ninety-five and the road skids to the
sound of epic crash. Mr. Norvus was also known as DJ Jimmy
Drake.

19   ***Roaches,*** THE COURT JESTERS
Doo-wop takes on a very real urban problem, offering advice
("Don't leave your food on the table!") and wry observation
("Crawling up the wall").

27   ***Fluffy,*** GLORIA BALSAM
Who among us could resist a wet nose? The aural equivalent of
Come Back, Little Sheba includes some notes only dogs can
hear.

99   ***Psycho,*** JACK KITTEL
La luna beckons. Napoleon XIV is taken away, Fred Blassie
("Pencil Neck Geek") is a pro wrestler, but Jack Kittel simply
is, peeling the layers of madness like an onion, garnishing the
hamburger of his mind. Pass the fries.

LENNY KAYE *is best known as the guitarist of The Patti Smith Group, but he has
also been a rock critic for* Rolling Stone *and other publications, a record producer
(The Sidewinders, Nuggets), and a solo artist, under his own name as well as the
celebrated Link Cromwell pseudonym. Kaye is a record collector with omnivorous
rock and roll tastes but with a special passion for a cappella and novelty sides.*

BOBBY PICKETT'S FAVORITE NOVELTY RECORDS

1   "The Monster Mash"
2   "Deteriorata"
3   "Ahab, the Arab"
4   "Purple People Eater"
5   "Shaving Cream"
6   "Star Drek"
7   "Silly Drug Songs"
8   "Dragnet" (The first all-talk novelty song I remember hearing.)
9   "Banana Boat Song"
10 "Flying Saucer"
11 "I Love Your Toes"
12 "Junkfood Junkie"

BOBBY "BORIS" PICKETT *had a trend-setting hit in the summer of 1962 with "The Monster Mash" but is best known as a television and film actor. He now lives in New York City.*

-◄▮▮►-

ROCK YUKS
The 10 Best Rock Laughs

1   "Wipe Out," THE SURFARIS
2   "I Put a Spell on You," SCREAMIN' JAY HAWKINS
3   "Anarchy in the U.K.," THE SEX PISTOLS
4   "Bob Dylan's 115th Dream," BOB DYLAN
5   "Little Girl," THE SYNDICATE OF SOUND
6   "Rip Van Winkle," THE DEVOTIONS
7   "These Boots Are Made for Walkin'," NANCY SINATRA
8   "Big Yellow Taxi," JONI MITCHELL
9   "Ob–La–Di, Ob–La–Da," THE BEATLES
10 "Do the Freddie," FREDDIE AND THE DREAMERS

TWENTY-EIGHT:
I AM NOT A JUVENILE DELINQUENT

OLD AGE

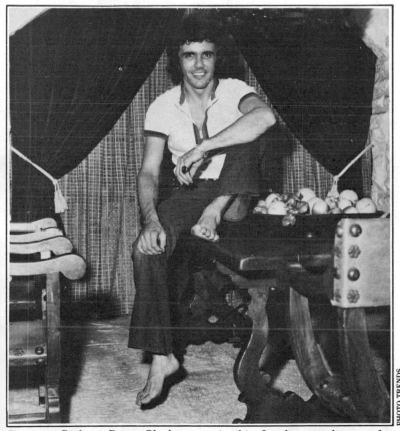

Rags to Riches: Dave Clark poses in his London penthouse after announcing the breakup of the Dave Clark Five in August 1970.

LIP READERS
Rock Stars Who Have Complained of Hearing Loss

1 ROGER DALTREY
2 JOHN ENTWISTLE
3 JERRY GARCIA
4 FELIX PAPPALARDI
5 PETE TOWNSHEND (repeatedly)
6 FRANKIE VALLI
7 BRIAN WILSON

·◀▮▶·

AGES OF 20 MALE ROCK STARS IN 1984

1	DAVID BOWIE	37	11	JOHN LYDON	28
2	JOHNNY BURNETTE	50	12	FRANKIE LYMON	42
3	ERIC CLAPTON	39	13	ELVIS PRESLEY	49
4	EDDIE COCHRAN	46	14	LLOYD PRICE	51
5	SAM COOKE	49	15	OTIS REDDING	43
6	ALAN FREED	62	16	LOU REED	40
7	BUDDY HOLLY	48	17	BOB SEGER	38
8	MICK JAGGER	41	18	ROD STEWART	39
9	BILLY JOEL	35	19	GENE VINCENT	49
10	JOHN LENNON	44	20	JOHNNY WINTER	40

·◀▮▶·

AGES OF 30 FEMALE ROCK STARS IN 1984

1	JOAN ARMATRADING	34	10	LULU	36
2	RITA COOLIDGE	39	11	MELISSA MANCHESTER	33
3	JULIE DRISCOLL	37	12	LINDA McCARTNEY	43
4	CASS ELLIOTT	41	13	CHRISTINE McVIE	41
5	CONNIE FRANCIS	46	14	BETTE MIDLER	39
6	ARETHA FRANKLIN	42	15	JONI MITCHELL	41
7	JANIS IAN	33	16	MARIA MULDAUR	41
8	JANIS JOPLIN	41	17	STEVIE NICKS	36
9	GLADYS KNIGHT	40	18	LAURA NYRO	37

19	MICHELLE PHILLIPS	40	25	CARLY SIMON	39
20	BONNIE RAITT	35	26	GRACE SLICK	45
21	MARTHA REEVES	43	27	DONNA SUMMER	36
22	MINNIE RIPERTON	36	28	RONNIE SPECTOR	37
23	LINDA RONSTADT	38	29	DUSTY SPRINGFIELD	45
24	DIANA ROSS	40	30	TANYA TUCKER	26

·◄❙▶·

30 OVER 40
In 1980

1	BRIAN AUGER	41	17	KRIS KRISTOFFERSON	44
2	GINGER BAKER	41	18	JOHN LENNON	40
3	JERRY BUTLER	41	19	LITTLE ANTHONY GOURDINE	40
4	JUDY COLLINS	41			
5	JOEY DEE	40	20	RICK NELSON	40
6	DION DiMUCCI	41	21	ROY ORBISON	44
7	DR. JOHN	40	22	BOBBY PICKETT	40
8	DON EVERLY	43	23	DAVE PRATER	43
9	PHIL EVERLY	41	24	CLIFF RICHARD	40
10	ADAM FAITH	40	25	SMOKEY ROBINSON	40
11	MARVIN GAYE	41	26	JIMMY RUFFIN	41
12	BUDDY GUY	44	27	NEIL SEDAKA	41
13	RUDOLPH ISLEY	41	28	ALLEN TOUSSAINT	42
14	JORMA KAUKONEN	40	29	BILL WYMAN	40
15	EDDIE KENDRICKS	40	30	FRANK ZAPPA	40
16	BEN E. KING	42			

·◄❙▶·

10 ROCKERS AGED 45 TO 49
In 1980

1	CHUCK BERRY	49*	4	JERRY LEE LEWIS	45
2	LONNIE DONEGAN	49	5	LITTLE RICHARD	48
3	RONNIE HAWKINS	46	6	RAY MANZAREK	45

7	JOHN MAYALL	47		9	CARL PERKINS	48
8	SAM MOORE	45		10	JOE TEX	47

*Disputable—by authors

19 ROCKERS OVER 50
In 1980

1	CHET ATKINS	56		11	B. B. KING	55
2	CHUCK BERRY	54*		12	ALEXIS KORNER	52
3	JAMES BROWN	52		13	JOHNNY OTIS	59
4	PAPA JOHN CREACH	63		14	LES PAUL	57
5	BO DIDDLEY	52		15	JOHNNIE RAY	53
6	FATS DOMINO	52		16	TINY TIM	50
7	LEE DORSEY	56		17	JOE TURNER	69
8	BILL HALEY	53		18	MUDDY WATERS	65
9	SCREAMIN' JAY HAWKINS	51		19	LINK WRAY	50
10	ALBERT KING	57				

*Disputable—by Berry

OLDEST SURVIVING GROUPS

1   **THE FOUR TOPS,** since 1953
    Originally formed in the pre-Presley fifties.
2 and 3 **THE DELLS,** since 1953; **THE ISLEY BROTHERS,** since 1956
    Both of these groups had hits in the fifties and survive today
    with the original membership more or less intact, making those
    who follow here look like pikers.
4   **THE MIRACLES,** since 1956
    All but one of the original male members remain—but without
    Smokey, does it really make much difference?
5   **THE KINKS,** since 1962
    Two out of four.

6   **THE ROLLING STONES,** since 1962
Four out of five original members are still with the group.

7   **THE PRETTY THINGS,** since 1963
Two original members—Phil May and Dick Taylor, who was in
The Stones before Bill Wyman, if you can imagine that—are
on the group's most recent album.

8   **THE SEARCHERS,** since 1963
The band is complete, though they didn't record between about
1967 and 1979, at least not for the U.S. market.

9   **THE WHO,** since 1964
Three out of four remain.

10   **THE GRATEFUL DEAD,** since 1965
Personnel changes on the fringes of the band are too numb-
ingly numerous to enumerate.

11   **THE BEE GEES,** since 1965
All they've lost is hair.

-◄▐▶-

WHERE ARE THEY NOW?
Rock Retirements

1   PETE BEST (The Beatles), baker
2   DAVE CLARK (The Dave Clark Five), businessman
3   CHRIS DREJA (The Yardbirds), photographer
4   TOMMY FACENDA (The Blue Caps), fireman
5   LONNIE JOHNSON, chef
6   LAURA NYRO, mother
7   GENE PITNEY, marina owner
8   DEAN TORRANCE (Jan and Dean), graphic artist
9   DOUG YULE (The Velvet Underground), carpenter

ROCK SONGS RECORDED BY FRANK SINATRA
With Original Artists

1 "Are You Lonesome Tonight?" ELVIS PRESLEY
2 "Bad, Bad Leroy Brown," JIM CROCE
3 "Bang Bang," SONNY AND CHER
4 "For Once in My Life," STEVIE WONDER
5 "Goin' Out of My Head," LITTLE ANTHONY AND THE IMPERIALS
6 "Goody, Goody," FRANKIE LYMON AND THE TEENAGERS
7 "If," THE PARAGONS
8 "Isn't She Lovely?" STEVIE WONDER
9 "Just the Way You Are," BILLY JOEL
10 "Love Me Tender," ELVIS PRESLEY
11 "Mrs. Robinson," SIMON AND GARFUNKEL
12 "Oh, Babe, What Would You Say?" HURRICANE SMITH
13 "Song Sung Blue," NEIL DIAMOND
14 "Sunny," BOBBY HEBB
15 "Yesterday," THE BEATLES
16 "You Are the Sunshine of My Life," STEVIE WONDER

TWENTY-NINE: TIME

COURTESY STEVE BONNER

Eddie Cochran, the original composer of "Summertime Blues," seen performing onstage in 1958.

LOOKED AT MY WATCH, IT WAS QUARTER TO FOUR . . .

1 "11:59," BLONDIE
2 "5:15," THE WHO
3 "5 O'Clock in the Morning," CREME AND GODLEY
4 "Five O'Clock World," THE VOGUES
5 "In the Midnight Hour," WILSON PICKETT
6 "It Only Takes a Minute," TAVARES
7 "Minute by Minute," THE DOOBIE BROTHERS
8 "Nine to Five," THE KINKS
9 "No Time Like the Right Time," THE BLUES PROJECT
10 "Quarter to Three," GARY "U.S." BONDS
11 "Reelin' & Rockin'," CHUCK BERRY
12 "Rock Around the Clock," BILL HALEY AND HIS COMETS
13 "Six O'Clock," THE LOVIN' SPOONFUL
14 "Time," THE MIGHTY CLOUDS OF JOY
15 "Time Has Come Today," THE CHAMBERS BROTHERS
16 "Time Is on My Side," THE ROLLING STONES
17 "Time Is Tight," BOOKER T. AND THE MGs
18 "Twelve Thirty (Young Girls Are Coming to the Canyon)," THE MAMAS AND THE PAPAS
19 "25 or 6 to 4," CHICAGO
20 "Wake Up Little Susie," THE EVERLY BROTHERS

-◄▮▶-

DON'T STOP
Best Songs Longer Than 10 Minutes

1 "By the Time I Get to Phoenix," ISAAC HAYES, 18:40
2 "Alice's Restaurant Massacre," ARLO GUTHRIE, 18:30
3 "In Held 'Twas I Suite," PROCOL HARUM, 17:51
4 "Sister Ray," THE VELVET UNDERGROUND, 17:00
5 "Papa Was a Rolling Stone," THE TEMPTATIONS, 11:45

6   "No More Tears (Enough Is Enough)," DONNA SUMMER and BARBRA STREISAND, 11:44
7   "Going Home," THE ROLLING STONES, 11:35
8   "The End," THE DOORS, 11:35
9   "Desolation Row," BOB DYLAN, 11:18
10 "Listen to the Lion," VAN MORRISON, 11:05
11 "I Heard It through the Grapevine," CREEDENCE CLEARWATER REVIVAL, 11:05
12 "Disco Inferno," THE TRAMMPS, 10:54

-◄❚❙▶-

How LONG HAS THIS BEEN GOING ON?
20 Songs under 10—but More Than 6—Minutes Long

1   "Jungle Land," BRUCE SPRINGSTEEN, 9:33
2   "Madame George," VAN MORRISON, 9:25
3   "Free Bird," LYNYRD SKYNYRD, 9:08
4   "Dance, Dance, Dance (Yowsah, Yowsah, Yowsah)," CHIC, 8:50
5   "Move on Up," CURTIS MAYFIELD, 8:50
6   "Won't Get Fooled Again," THE WHO, 8:31
7   "Stairway to Heaven," LED ZEPPELIN, 7:55
8   "Bo Diddley," THE ANIMALS, 7:36
9   "Stuck inside of Mobile with the Memphis Blues Again," BOB DYLAN, 7:31
10 "Wake Up Everybody," HAROLD MELVIN AND THE BLUE NOTES, 7:30
11 "Cortez the Killer," NEIL YOUNG, 7:29
12 "You Can't Always Get What You Want," THE ROLLING STONES, 7:28
13 "Living for the City," STEVIE WONDER, 7:26
14 "Thank You for Talkin' to Me Africa," SLY AND THE FAMILY STONE, 7:14
15 "Layla," DEREK AND THE DOMINOS, 7:10
16 "Hey Jude," THE BEATLES, 7:06

17   "Racing in the Street," BRUCE SPRINGSTEEN, 6:52
18   "Why D'Ya Do It," MARIANNE FAITHFULL, 6:45
19   "What'd I Say," RAY CHARLES, 6:25
20   "Like a Rolling Stone," BOB DYLAN, 6:00

HONORABLE MENTION: Although *Electric Ladyland* lists no time for it, Jimi Hendrix' "Voodoo Chile" is somewhere around 8:00.

-◄❚❚►-

THEY OFTEN CALL ME SPEEDO
15 Songs Less Than 2 Minutes—but More Than 90 Seconds—Long

1   "Now I Wanna Sniff Some Glue," THE RAMONES, 1:34
2   "Hello There," CHEAP TRICK, 1:39
3   "Why Don't We Do It in the Road?" THE BEATLES, 1:42
4   "Odds and Ends," BOB DYLAN, 1:43
5   "Twenty Flight Rock," EDDIE COCHRAN, 1:43
6   "Dayton, Ohio, 1903," RANDY NEWMAN, 1:47
7   "Not Fade Away," THE ROLLINGS STONES, 1:48
8   "Yakety Yak," THE COASTERS, 1:50
9   "The Letter," THE BOX TOPS, 1:50
10   "Shut Down," THE BEACH BOYS, 1:50
11   "David Watts," THE KINKS, 1:52
12   "My Way of Giving," THE SMALL FACES, 1:52
13   "Let It Rock," CHUCK BERRY, 1:53
14   "Who Slapped John?" GENE VINCENT, 1:56
15   "White Riot," THE CLASH, 1:58

QUICK ONES

10 Songs Less than 90—but More Than 60—Seconds Long

1 "Tommy's Holiday Camp," THE WHO, 1:01
2 "Threshold," THE STEVE MILLER BAND, 1:04
3 "Nightmares," THE J. GEILS BAND, 1:14
4 "Steadfast, Loyal and True," ELVIS PRESLEY, 1:15
5 "Some Kind-a Earthquake," DUANE EDDY, 1:17
6 "Hobo's Blues," PAUL SIMON, 1:21
7 "Hound Dog," JERRY LEE LEWIS, 1:24
8 "Tutti-Frutti," THE MC5, 1:27
9 "Father of Night," BOB DYLAN, 1:28
10 "Judy Is a Punk," THE RAMONES, 1:30

·◄▐▐►·

WHAM, BAM, THANK YOU, MA'AM

8 Songs Less Than 1 Minute Long

1 "There's a Riot Goin' On," SLY AND THE FAMILY STONE, 0:00*
2 "Miracle Cure," THE WHO, 0:11
3 "Her Majesty," THE BEATLES, 0:23
4 "Field Day for the Sundays," WIRE, 0:26
5 "Interludings," ROD STEWART, 0:40
6 "Straight Line," WIRE, 0:42
7 "My Mummy's Dead," JOHN LENNON, 0:48
8 "The Commercial," WIRE, 0:48

*Or so says the record sleeve.

DAVID McGEE PICKS THE ESSENTIAL CHRISTMAS ALBUMS

1   ***Elvis' Christmas Album,*** ELVIS PRESLEY
    This contains Presley's definitive recording of "Blue Christ-
    mas"; a tough, tasty Leiber-Stoller blues, "Santa Claus Is Back
    in Town"; and some stirring, more meditative moments, such
    as "(There'll Be) Peace in the Valley (For Me)" and "I Believe."

2   ***Elvis Sings the Wonderful World of Christmas,*** ELVIS
    PRESLEY
    By turns stately and reflective, low-down and rocking, Elvis
    turns in one bravura performance after another. Where do its
    virtues begin? Try the ironic treatment of Charles Brown's
    Christmas blues classic, "Merry Christmas, Baby," fueled by
    Presley's rousing, slightly lascivious vocal and James Burton's
    stinging guitar solos. Or try any of several altogether breath-
    taking ballad performances, particularly the first three cuts on
    side two, one of which ("If I Get Home on Christmas Day"
    may well be the King's best recorded vocal.

3   ***Phil Spector's Christmas Album***
    A grand, masterful stroke that is the ultimate rock statement
    in Christmas albums. Most of Spector's famed troupe of artists
    are present here, turning in exceptional performances all
    around, most of them on such Christmas standards as "Jingle
    Bells" and "Bells of St. Mary's." Of special note: Darlene
    Love's vocal on "Christmas (Baby Please Come Home)." And
    if there's any doubt about Spector's sentimental side, listen to
    his spoken coda at the end of side two.

4   ***Someday at Christmas,*** STEVIE WONDER
    A gem from first cut to last, with Wonder in top form vocally
    The rewards here are many, in both standard ("Ave Maria"
    and original material (none composed by Wonder, however)
    The socially conscious title track makes the album.

5   ***The Season for Miracles,*** SMOKEY ROBINSON AND THE
    MIRACLES

A mellow outing graced by Smokey's subtle interpretation of "Deck the Halls" and a bossa nova-cum-R&B arrangement of Stevie Wonder's "I Can Tell When Christmas Is Near."

6 **Merry Christmas: The Supremes**

A pop delight from 1965. In addition to an ingratiating, languid treatment of "Silver Bells," The Supremes turn in a blockbuster performance on a little-recognized classic, "Little Bright Star." Harvey Fuqua's Phil Spector-influenced production presents a grand challenge for Diana Ross, and she responds with one of the best overall album performances of her early career.

7 **Jackson 5 Christmas Album**

This strikes a neat balance between lighthearted seasonal fare ("Frosty the Snowman" is a standout) and more sentimental tunes along the lines of "Have Yourself a Merry Little Christmas." Young Michael Jackson's interpretation of "Give Love on Christmas Day" is a revelation.

8 **Soul Christmas,** various artists

Not in print but worth searching for. A compilation, the album features exemplary performances by Joe Tex, Booker T. and the MGs, Clarence Carter, Carla Thomas, Solomon Burke, and King Curtis, among others. Otis Redding's mordant rendering of "White Christmas" conjures up an image of a Christmas dream that is so bleak it might have given Irving Berlin second thoughts about having written the song in the first place.

9 **Rhythm & Blues Christmas,** various artists

Another compilation, this one contains ten songs recorded between 1949 and 1967. It includes one of the indisputably great Christmas sides in Clyde McPhatter and the Drifters' 1954 recording of "White Christmas," noteworthy in part for McPhatter's shattering solo on the chorus, which Elvis copped, almost note for note, on his first Christmas album.

10 **Christmas Gift 'Rap,** various artists

This features The Temptations, The Supremes, Stevie Wonder, and Smokey Robinson and the Miracles singing songs

from their respective Christmas albums. No higher recommen
dation could be given.

11　*Happy Holidays to You,* THE WHISPERS
Impassioned, sensitive vocalizing by one of the finest young
black groups around. The title song and "This Christmas,"
written by Donny Hathaway, are particularly memorable.

HONORABLE MENTION:

1　*The Ventures' Christmas Album*
Guaranteed to bring a smile. Each song begins with the firs
few bars of a popular rock song of the mid-1960s, when thi
album was recorded. Lennon-McCartney's "I Feel Fine"

inexplicably worked into "Rudolph the Red-Nosed Reindeer"
must be heard to be believed. Collector's item.

2   ***The Beach Boys' Christmas Album***
A fairly nondescript collection, to be sure, but notable for
Brian Wilson's lovely song "Christmas Day," which also
features Al Jardine's first recorded vocal solo. It also contains
the hit single, "Little Saint Nick," another Wilson original.

3   ***Holiday for Teens,*** PAUL AND PAULA
Though forever linked with one of rock's most tepid eras (the
pre-Beatles sixties), Paul and Paula (particularly the latter)
were not without talent, as this record amply demonstrates.
The open-minded will find much to admire in the tasty, bluesy
treatments of several standards as well as in the scintillating
guitar and sax work throughout. Most of all, Paula's vocals are
surprisingly hard-edged, a fortunate development in light of
Paul's faceless crooning. Charlie McCoy is the uncredited
harmonica player on "I'll Be Home for Christmas."

4   ***The New Possibility*** and ***Christmas with John Fahey***
John Fahey's solo guitar recordings of inestimable beauty and
eccentricity. A Christmas message with a difference.

5   ***A Charlie Brown Christmas,*** VINCE GUARALDI TRIO
Guaraldi's evocative, lyrical soundtrack for the CBS-TV special is the quintessential "mellow" Christmas recording. Floats
like a butterfly, stings like a bee, with musical styles ranging
from neo-impressionism to be-bop.

6   ***Light of the Stable,*** EMMYLOU HARRIS
Harris' Yule offering is yet another vehicle for her pristine,
ethereal vocals. Christmas carols seem to have been written
with Harris in mind. Neil Young, Dolly Parton, and Linda
Ronstadt join in on the title tune.

7   ***Merle Haggard's Christmas Present***
One side of Haggard originals (including "If We Make It
through December," a devastating and all-too-true account of a
blue-collar Christmas) and Christmas standards, of which
"Silver Bells" is top-notch. An unbeatable combination.

8   ***Pretty Paper,*** WILLIE NELSON
     Willie sounds pretty bored, but there is beauty in his ennui if
     you stick with him long enough. An oddly moving album that
     could just as well have been titled *Blue Christmas* for its stark
     vision of the holiday season.
9   ***The 12 Hits of Christmas,*** various artists
     A dozen hits of Yuletides past, from Gene Autry's "Rudolph
     the Red-Nosed Reindeer" to Bobby Helms' "Jingle Bell
     Rock," Brenda Lee's "Rockin' around the Christmas Tree,"
     and "The Chipmunk Song." Also included are the original and
     still-unsurpassed versions of "The Little Drummer Boy" (Harry
     Simeone Chorale) and "Do You Hear What I Hear" (Bing
     Crosby).

DAVID MCGEE, *softball star and sentimentalist par excellence,* writes Record
World's *"New York New York" column and is the publication's assistant managing
editor.*

Thirty:
HITS AND FLOPS

The Supremes in 1968.

ARTISTS WITH THE MOST NUMBER 1 HITS
Through 1980

1	THE BEATLES	20
2	ELVIS PRESLEY	18
3	THE SUPREMES	12
4	THE BEE GEES	9
5	THE ROLLING STONES	8
6	PAUL McCARTNEY AND WINGS	7
7	PAT BOONE	6
8	ELTON JOHN	6
9	STEVIE WONDER	6
10	THE EAGLES	5
11	THE FOUR SEASONS	5

PERFORMERS WITH THE MOST CONSECUTIVE NUMBER 1 HITS
1955–1980

1   **THE SUPREMES,** 6 (1964–1965)
"Where Did Our Love Go," "Baby Love," "Come See about Me," "Stop! In the Name of Love," "Back in My Arms Again," "I Hear a Symphony"

2   **THE BEATLES,** 5 (1965)
"Eight Days a Week," "Ticket to Ride," "Help!" "Yesterday," "We Can Work It Out"

3   **THE JACKSON 5,** 5 (1969–1970)
"I Want You Back," "ABC," "The Love You Save," "I Found That Girl," "I'll Be There"

4   **ELVIS PRESLEY,** 5 (1959–1961)
"A Big Hunk o' Love," "Stuck on You," "It's Now or Never," "Are You Lonesome Tonight?" "Surrender"

5   **ELVIS PRESLEY,** 4 (1957)
     "All Shook Up," "Let Me Be Your Teddy Bear," "Jailhouse
     ~~Rock," "Don't"~~
6   **THE SUPREMES,** 4 (1966–1967)
     "You Can't Hurry Love," "You Keep Me Hangin' On," "Love
     Is Here and Now You're Gone," "The Happening"
7   **THE BEATLES,** 3 (1964; 1969–1970)
     "I Want to Hold Your Hand," "Can't Buy Me Love," "She
     Loves You"; "Come Together"/"Something," "Let It Be,"
     "The Long and Winding Road"

-◄I I►-

THE 40 GREATEST NUMBER 1 HITS

1   "Jailhouse Rock," ELVIS PRESLEY, 1957
2   "Save the Last Dance for Me," THE DRIFTERS, 1960
3   "(I Can't Get No) Satisfaction," THE ROLLING STONES, 1965
4   "He's So Fine," THE CHIFFONS, 1963
5   "Stay," MAURICE WILLIAMS AND THE ZODIACS, 1960
6   "She Loves You," THE BEATLES, 1964
7   "When a Man Loves a Woman," PERCY SLEDGE, 1966
8   "The Loco-Motion," LITTLE EVA, 1962
9   "Reach Out I'll Be There," THE FOUR TOPS, 1966
10   "I Want You Back," THE JACKSON 5, 1970
11   "Respect," ARETHA FRANKLIN, 1967
12   "You've Lost That Lovin' Feeling," THE RIGHTEOUS
     BROTHERS, 1965
13   "Little Star," THE ELEGANTS, 1958
14   "Suspicious Minds," ELVIS PRESLEY, 1969
15   "Family Affair," SLY AND THE FAMILY STONE, 1971
16   "Heartbreak Hotel," ELVIS PRESLEY, 1956
17   "You Send Me," SAM COOKE, 1957
18   "Quarter to Three," GARY "U.S." BONDS, 1961
19   "The Duke of Earl," GENE CHANDLER, 1962
20   "That'll Be the Day," THE CRICKETS, 1957

21   "I Get Around," THE BEACH BOYS, 1964
22   "House of the Rising Sun," THE ANIMALS, 1964
23   "Everyday People," SLY AND THE FAMILY STONE, 1969
24   "My Girl," THE TEMPTATIONS, 1965
25   "(Sittin' on) The Dock of the Bay," OTIS REDDING, 1968
26   "Running Scared," ROY ORBISON, 1961
27   "Ticket to Ride," THE BEATLES, 1965
28   "Tighten Up," ARCHIE BELL AND THE DRELLS, 1968
29   "Fingertips Pt. 2," STEVIE WONDER, 1963
30   "Yakety Yak," THE COASTERS, 1958
31   "Love Train," THE O'JAYS, 1973
32   "Bad Girls," DONNA SUMMER, 1979
33   "96 Tears," ? AND THE MYSTERIANS, 1966
34   "The Great Pretender," THE PLATTERS, 1956
35   "Hit the Road Jack," RAY CHARLES, 1961
36   "Hound Dog," ELVIS PRESLEY, 1956
37   "Mother-in-Law," ERNIE K-DOE, 1961
38   "You Keep Me Hangin' On," THE SUPREMES, 1966
39   "Kiss and Say Goodbye," THE MANHATTANS, 1976
40   "Midnight Train to Georgia," GLADYS KNIGHT AND THE PIPS, 1973

-◄❚▶-

THE 20 WORST NUMBER 1 HITS

1   "Tammy," DEBBIE REYNOLDS, 1957
2   "Honeycomb," JIMMIE RODGERS, 1957
3   "Why," FRANKIE AVALON, 1960
4   "Hey Paula," PAUL AND PAULA, 1963
5   "Mrs. Brown You've Got a Lovely Daughter," HERMAN'S HERMITS, 1965
6   "Eve of Destruction," BARRY McGUIRE, 1965
7   "Cherish," THE ASSOCIATION, 1966
8   "The Happening," THE SUPREMES, 1967
9   "Honey," BOBBY GOLDSBORO, 1968
10   "Song Sung Blue," NEIL DIAMOND, 1972

11   "I Am Woman," HELEN REDDY, 1972
12   "Top of the World," THE CARPENTERS, 1973
13   "The Loco-Motion," GRAND FUNK RAILROAD, 1974
14   "The Night Chicago Died, PAPER LACE, 1974
15   "My Eyes Adored You," FRANKIE VALLI, 1975
16   "Disco Lady," JOHNNIE TAYLOR, 1976
17   "Disco Duck, Part 1," RICK DEES AND HIS CAST OF IDIOTS,
      1976
18   "Blinded by the Light," MANFRED MANN'S EARTH BAND,
      1977
19   "Play That Funky Music," WILD CHERRY, 1976
20   "MacArthur Park," DONNA SUMMER, 1978

-◄❙❙►-

THE 20 GREATEST 2-SIDED HITS

On all of these records, both sides made the Top Forty

1   "Don't Be Cruel"/"Hound Dog," ELVIS PRESLEY*
2   "I Want to Hold Your Hand"/"I Saw Her Standing There,"
      THE BEATLES** †
3   "I Get Around"/"Don't Worry Baby," THE BEACH BOYS†
4   "Thank You (Falettinme Be Mice Elf Agin)"/"Everybody Is a
      Star," SLY AND THE FAMILY STONE†
5   "Jailhouse Rock"/"Treat Me Nice," ELVIS PRESLEY†
6   "Down on the Corner"/"Fortunate Son," CREEDENCE
      CLEARWATER REVIVAL
7   "The House That Jack Built"/"I Say a Little Prayer,"
      ARETHA FRANKLIN**
8   "Young Blood"/"Searchin'," THE COASTERS**
9   "We Can Work It Out"/"Day Tripper," THE BEATLES** †
10   "Shake"/"A Change Is Gonna Come," SAM COOKE
11   "Night"/"Doggin' Around," JACKIE WILSON
12   "Penny Lane"/"Strawberry Fields Forever," THE
      BEATLES**†

13   "I'm in Love Again"/"My Blue Heaven," FATS DOMINO
14   "(Sweet Sweet Baby) Since You've Been Gone"/"Ain't No Way," ARETHA FRANKLIN
15   "Bird Dog"/"Devoted to You," THE EVERLY BROTHERS**
16   "Surfer Girl"/"Little Deuce Coupe," THE BEACH BOYS
17   "What Am I Living For"/"Hang Up My Rock and Roll Shoes," CHUCK WILLIS
18   "I Want to Walk You Home"/"I'm Gonna Be a Wheel Some Day," FATS DOMINO
19   "Surfin' U.S.A."/"Shut Down," THE BEACH BOYS
20   "Poison Ivy"/"I'm a Hog for You," THE COASTERS

* The only single in rock and roll history with two Number One sides.
**Both sides made the Top Ten.
† The first side listed was a Number One hit.

◄▮▮►

RETREAD ROCK
4 Songs That Have Been Number 1 Hits More Than Once

1   **"The Twist"**
Chubby Checker reached the top spot not only with the same song, but with the same *record*, in 1960 and 1961, the only time that this particular feat has been pulled off.

2   **"Go Away Little Girl"**
Number One with an anchor for Steve Lawrence in 1963 and for Donny Osmond in 1971. Carole King and Gerry Goffin wrote this awful piece of pop fluff, but since they also wrote "The Loco-Motion," maybe they can be forgiven.

3   **"The Loco-Motion"**
This Goffin-King composition was a Number One hit for Little Eva in 1962 and, in a drastically different heavy-metal version, for Grand Funk Railroad in 1974.

4   **"Please Mr. Postman"**
The marvelous Marvelettes took this Motown ditty to the top in 1961; The Carpenters transformed it into California pop tapioca, and it reached Number One again in 1974.

10 NUMBER 1 RECORDS WHOSE ORIGINAL VERSIONS WERE FLOPS

1　**"Rock around the Clock,"** BILL HALEY AND HIS COMETS, 1955
Sonny Dae and His Knights cut the original version of "Rock around the Clock," providing the inspiration for making the hit version, which was, of course, one of the signals that the rock and roll era had kicked off.

2　**"Hanky Panky,"** TOMMY JAMES AND THE SHONDELLS, 1966
"Hanky Panky" was written by New York songwriters Jeff Barry and Ellie Greenwich, who recorded it themselves (as The Raindrops) for the Jubilee label in 1963. Prior to The Shondells' version, "Hanky Panky" had been on at least two singles and The Raindrops' LP without ever making so much as a nudge into the national charts.

3　**"Indian Reservation,"** The Raiders, 1971
Songwriter John D. Loudermilk ("Tobacco Road") did the original of "Indian Reservation" for RCA in 1966. He called it "The Lament of the Cherokee Indian Reservation," and by the time The Raiders picked it up, several other versions had been recorded, notably by The Lewis and Clarke Expedition on a 1967 album and by Don Fardon, who took his version to the Top Twenty in 1968. But the Raiders made it all the way to Number One with the song.

4　**"Without You,"** HARRY NILSSON, 1971
Oddly, Nilsson, most often thought of as a singer/songwriter, has had his biggest hits with songs written by others. (His own tunes fare better in other hands.) "Without You" was originally recorded by Badfinger as a track on their *No Dice* LP, released about a year before Nilsson's hit version.

5　**"My Ding-a-Ling,"** CHUCK BERRY, 1972
This song's history spans twenty years. The original version was by Dave Bartholomew, the man who cowrote Fats Domino's hits. Bartholomew released the song in 1952 on King. In

1954, The Bees (on Imperial) released the very similar "Toy Bell." But none of the early versions showed any national chart action. Ironically, Berry had been performing the song in his live show for years before it was ever recorded.

6   **"Killing Me Softly with His Song,"** ROBERTA FLACK, 1973
Singer Lori Lieberman's producers custom wrote this song for her debut album on Capitol in 1972. Capitol did release the song as a single, but it died. Flack heard it, and her revival put it on top of the charts.

7   **"Mandy,"** BARRY MANILOW, 1974
This was the hit that got Manilow's career off the ground. In its original version, the song was called "Brandy," and it's supposedly about a lost dog, not a lost lover. Co-author Scott English had scraped the song into the Top 100 in 1972, but it peaked at Number Ninety-one after only two weeks.

8   **"Rhinestone Cowboy,"** GLEN CAMPBELL, 1975
Larry Weiss, the writer, did the original version in 1974. Weiss, who also wrote "Bend Me Shape Me" for The American Breed seven years earlier, got a bit of airplay but never made the charts. Ironically, Weiss had just about decided to give up his musical career when Campbell heard his solo album and decided to record "Rhinestone Cowboy."

9   **"Blinded by the Light,"** MANFRED MANN'S EARTH BAND, 1976
"Blinded by the Light" was the first single from Bruce Springsteen's 1973 debut album, but Columbia couldn't get it on the charts. That version is now a valued collector's item, but it was Mann's recording that hit the top.

10   **"It's So Easy,"** LINDA RONSTADT, 1977
Buddy Holly and the Crickets first recorded this Holly-penned number in 1958, but when it was originally released, it didn't have so much as a whiff of success. Yet, by the magic process by which even some unsuccessful "oldies" become famous, Ronstadt's version was instant nostalgia almost twenty years later.

HONORABLE MENTION:

"Hooked on a Feeling," BLUE SWEDE, 1974

B. J. Thomas had already put this song in the Top Five in 1968, but Blue Swede added a genuinely obnoxious opening—"OOBAH-chucka, OOBAH-chucka!"—which spelled the difference between that and a genuine Number One hit. Jonathan King, rarely a man to miss a trick, had also recorded the song in 1971, but his version went nowhere.

-◄❙▮❙►-

PERFORMERS WHO NEVER HAD A NUMBER 1 HIT

1 **JAMES BROWN**
Soul Brother Number One he may be, but the closest the Black Godfather has ever come to being Number One on the pop chart was in 1965, with "I Got You (I Feel Good)," which stalled at Number Three. Five other times, Brown hit the Top Ten, most recently in 1968 with "Say It Loud—I'm Black and I'm Proud," which stopped at Number Ten.

2 **CREEDENCE CLEARWATER REVIVAL**
Creedence had no less than *nine* Top Ten singles; between the spring of 1969 and the end of 1970, five of them spent a total of eight weeks in the Number Two slot. In this period, while such masterful rock and roll as "Proud Mary," "Bad Moon Rising," and "Green River" was being shut out of the top spot, holding sway were such marvelous and memorable discs as Henry Mancini's "Love Theme from Romeo and Juliet," the unforgettable "In the Year 2525" by Zager and Evans, and of course, "I Think I Love You" by TV's Partridge Family.

3 **FATS DOMINO**
Fats scored with no less than eleven Top Ten singles, and although only "Blueberry Hill" and "I'm in Love Again" (both in 1956) made the Top Three, his feat is more impressive because, at the time, rock was having trouble gaining a chart

foothold at all. Domino had four Top Ten records in 1957 and three in 1959, but for some reason he was shut out in 1958.

4   BOB DYLAN

Dylan hit the Top Ten only four times in his pre-Christian career, with his greatest success coming in 1965-1966, when both "Like a Rolling Stone" and "Rainy Day Women #12 & 35" hit Number Two.

5   PETER FRAMPTON

Frampton has had five Top Ten singles, and of course, *Frampton Comes Alive!* was a monstrous 1976 hit, selling more than 10 million copies. Still, it was not until 1977, with "I'm in You" from his follow-up LP, that Frampton got as far as Number Two on the singles listings, and then for only three weeks.

6   THE HOLLIES

The Anglo-harmonizers hit the Top Ten six times in the sixties and seventies without ever coming nearer than Number Two, and then it was with their virtual swan song, "Long Cool Woman (In a Black Dress)," in 1972.

7   MARTHA AND THE VANDELLAS

This must have been the only major Motown group never to top the weekly listings, although "Dancing in the Street" did spend two weeks at Number Two back in 1962. Five other times, Martha and the girls hit the Top Ten without going all the way.

8   THE STYLISTICS

Russell Thompkins Jr. may have been the last of the great falsetto soul singers, but although he led The Stylistics to the Top Ten five times, he never got them further than Number Two, and then for only two weeks in 1974 with "You Make Me Feel Brand New."

9   WAR

One of the original funk bands, and heroes to every lowrider in the San Fernando Valley, War spent two weeks at Number Two with "The Cisco Kid" in 1973 but has never gotten that far since, despite six other Top Ten discs.

10 **DIONNE WARWICK AND THE SPINNERS**
Warwick had nine Top Ten records and The Spinners five, including one Number Two each, before their sole duet, "Then Came You," finally grabbed the top spot in 1974. Since then, however, both have continued to be shut out, although The Spinners came close with "The Rubber-band Man," which hit Number Two in 1976.

11 **THE WHO**
Pete Townshend's prowess as a rock songwriter is widely and justifiably celebrated, but The Who has had only one Top Ten single, "I Can See for Miles," which clocked in at Number Nine in 1967. Just another excuse for guitar demolition, we'd say.

12 **JACKIE WILSON**
Ironically, the two songs for which Jackie Wilson is most remembered, "Lonely Teardrops" and "(Your Love Keeps Lifting Me) Higher and Higher," never got higher than Number Seven and Six, respectively. Wilson came closer with "Night," which made Number Four in 1960, and had a total of six Top Ten singles before being felled by a heart attack onstage in 1976.

THE 15 GREATEST NUMBER 1 ALBUMS
1956-1980 (Greatest-Hits Collections Excluded)

1 *Elvis*, ELVIS PRESLEY, 1956
2 *Revolver*, THE BEATLES, 1966
3 *Meet the Beatles!* 1964
4 *Electric Ladyland*, THE JIMI HENDRIX EXPERIENCE, 1968
5 *Exile on Main St.* THE ROLLING STONES, 1972
6 *There's a Riot Goin' On*, SLY AND THE FAMILY STONE, 1971
7 *Sticky Fingers*, THE ROLLING STONES, 1971
8 *Abbey Road*, THE BEATLES, 1969

9   *Out of Our Heads*, THE ROLLING STONES, 1965
10   *Modern Sounds in Country and Western Music*, RAY
     CHARLES, 1962
11   *Superfly* (soundtrack), CURTIS MAYFIELD, 1972
12   *Green River*, CREEDENCE CLEARWATER REVIVAL, 1969
13   *Sgt. Pepper's Lonely Hearts Club Band*, THE BEATLES, 1967
14   *Songs in the Key of Life*, STEVIE WONDER, 1976
15   *The River*, BRUCE SPRINGSTEEN, 1980

-◄▮►-

THE 10 WORST NUMBER 1 ALBUMS

1   *Briefcase Full of Blues*, THE BLUES BROTHERS, 1979
2   *Seventh Sojourn*, THE MOODY BLUES, 1972
3   *Blood, Sweat and Tears 3*, 1970
4   *Roustabout*, ELVIS PRESLEY, 1965
5   *Get the Knack*, 1979
6   *A Passion Play*, JETHRO TULL, 1973
7   *Chicago VIII*, 1975
8   *Jesus Christ Superstar*, various artists, 1971
9   *Living in the Material World*, GEORGE HARRISON, 1973
10   *4 Way Street*, CROSBY, STILLS, NASH, AND YOUNG, 1971

-◄▮►-

PERFORMERS WHO NEVER HAD A NUMBER 1 ALBUM

1   **THE BEE GEES**
     The Bee Gees tasted ultimate glory only with their contribu-
     tions to the 1978 *Saturday Night Fever* soundtrack. But there,
     they were buttressed by a host of other discophiles. The best
     the Australian trio did on its own was a Number Seven with its
     1967 Beatles-imitation debut, *Bee Gees First*, and a pair of

discoid Number Eights: in 1976, with *Children of the World*, and in 1977, with *Here at Last . . . The Bee Gees . . . Live*.

2 **ARETHA FRANKLIN**

So much for the cream of soul music. With twenty-nine chart albums, Aretha hit the Top Ten six times, and twice made it all the way to Number Two, with *Aretha: Lady Soul* in 1968 and *I Never Loved a Man the Way I Love You* the year before.

3 **MARVIN GAYE**

Despite seventeen chart albums, Gaye only hit Number Two once, with 1973's *Let's Get It On*, and the Top Ten four other times.

4 **GRAND FUNK RAILROAD**

This quintessential heavy-metal band based its success solely on albums. The group had no hit single until 1973's "We're an American Band," despite fifteen chart attempts. Instructively, the *We're an American Band* album broke past the others, getting to Number Two even though the band's days were dwindling.

5 **AL GREEN**

Green has made fourteen albums, but only four have made the Top Ten, despite his stature as the premier soul singer of the seventies. *I'm Still in Love with You* (Number Four in 1972) is still his ranking LP.

6 **THE KINKS**

And what about these guys: Twenty-three chart albums, but only one Top Ten, and that was their *Greatest Hits* collection, which reached Number Nine in 1966.

7 **THE MIRACLES**

Despite twenty-three chart albums with and without Smokey Robinson, and despite the glories of Smokey's voice, the Miracles hit the Top Ten but twice, their greatest success being the second LP of the group's *Greatest Hits* in 1968, which checked in at a paltry Number Seven.

8   **JONI MITCHELL**
     Mitchell's best year was 1974, when both *Court and Spark* and
     the live *Miles of Aisles* hit Number Two. But only one of her
     other nine albums ever made the Top Ten big leagues.

9   **JAMES TAYLOR**
     Taylor has made only eleven albums, five of which have made
     the Top Ten. Yet only *Mud Slide Slim and the Blue Horizon* in
     1971 made it as far as Number Two.

10   **THE TEMPTATIONS**
     The Temptations, with twenty-seven chart albums, reached the
     Top Ten no less than eight times but got as far as Number Two
     only once, with *All Directions* in 1972.

11   **THE VENTURES**
     The Ventures have both Taylor and The Who beaten in this
     sweepstakes, hitting the charts thirty-six times with their
     instrumental rock, on which every beginning electric guitarist
     of the sixties teethed. But they scored only one Top Tenner,
     1963's *The Ventures Play 'Telstar,' 'The Lonely Bull' and
     Others*. And with titles like that, no wonder.

12   **THE WHO**
     Of the group's fourteen albums, seven have made the Top Ten,
     but even *Quadrophenia* and *Who Are You* never slipped past
     Number Two. *Tommy*, original pop opera that it may be, got no
     higher than Number Four, a record matched by *Live at Leeds*.

-◄❙►-

PERFORMERS WITH THE MOST TOP 10 HITS
From 1955 through 1980

1	ELVIS PRESLEY	38	8	ELTON JOHN	17
2	THE BEATLES	33	9	CONNIE FRANCIS	16
3	THE SUPREMES	20	10	PAUL McCARTNEY AND WINGS	16
4	RICKY NELSON	19	11	THE EVERLY BROTHERS	15
5	THE ROLLING STONES	19	12	THE FOUR SEASONS	15
6	PAT BOONE	18	13	THE TEMPTATIONS	15
7	MARVIN GAYE	17			

PERFORMERS WHO NEVER HAD A TOP 10 SINGLE

1 **THE BAND**

One of the reasons Bob Dylan's former backup group never rose to the heights expected of it was its failure to record a major hit single. The closest The Band came (out of nine chart 45s) was "Up on Cripple Creek," which made it to Number Twenty-five in 1969. The group had only one other Top Forty hit ("Don't Do It," which made it to Number Thirty-four in 1972) before breaking up in 1977.

2 **BOBBY BLAND**

Now consider the plight of Bobby "Blue" Bland, who has hit the lists no less than thirty-seven times, made the rhythm & blues or soul Top Ten nineteen times, but never came closer to the pop Top Ten than Number Twenty, which he scored with "Ain't Nothing You Can Do" in 1964.

3 **SOLOMON BURKE**

Twenty-six chart records never netted "King" Solomon anything better than a measly Number Twenty-two in 1965 for the grand "Got to Get You Off My Mind."

4 **THE J. GEILS BAND**

Geils have had seven chart singles, but like The Band, they've never had the one song that could take them all the way—probably some kind of weird tribute to pop radio's anti-electric guitar bias. The band's only Top Twenty shot came in 1974, with "Must of Got Lost," which stopped at Number Twelve.

5 **JIMI HENDRIX**

Hendrix had seven chart singles, but the closest he came to the Top Ten was with Bob Dylan's "All along the Watchtower," which made Number Twenty in 1968.

6 **B. B. KING**

If Geils and The Band have had it hard, consider bluesmaster King, whose singles have made the charts no less than thirty-four times, without ever getting farther than Number

Fifteen, which B. B. achieved with one of his greatest ever, "The Thrill Is Gone," in 1970.

7   **LITTLE WILLIE JOHN**
They say that Little Willie John's version of "Fever" actually outsold Peggy Lee's, but the conservatism of pop radio in 1956 was so great that John's version never got past Number Twenty-four. (Lee's, released in 1958, got to Number One.) Twelve other times, Little Willie John hit the pop rankings, but the highest his soul ever clambered was Number Thirteen in 1960 for the oddly bouncy "Sleep."

8   **PARLIAMENT-FUNKADELIC**
Although these almost identical groups have had no less than thirteen chart singles, they've never made the Top Ten. They came closest with 1976's "Tear the Roof Off the Sucker (Give Up the Funk)" and 1978's "Flash Light," both of which went gold and made it to Number Fifteen and Number Sixteen respectively. It's a different story on the soul charts, of course, where they have had five Top Ten hits and three Number Ones.

-◄❙▶-

PERFORMERS WHO NEVER HAD A TOP 10 ALBUM

1   **THE GRATEFUL DEAD**
Perhaps the ultimate cult band, the San Francisco acid-rock titans have hit the LP charts no less than nineteen times without ever getting further than Number Sixteen, with 1974's *Grateful Dead from the Mars Hotel*. Indeed, only two other Dead albums (*Wake of the Flood*, Number Eighteen in 1973, and *Blues for Allah*, Number Twelve in 1975) have even made the Top Twenty. Some—not even counting us—may count this a blessing.

2   **BUDDY HOLLY**
It is a sad measure of the treatment of Holly's musical legacy

that only three of his albums ever made the U.S. charts at all. *The Buddy Holly Story* climbed to Number Eleven in 1959, soon after his death—but that was the best any of his LPs did.

3 **JAN AND DEAN**

Although their surf-and-hot-rod music never lacked humor (or substantial contributions from their cronies, The Beach Boys), "The Laurel and Hardy of the surf crowd" didn't ever do better than a stingy Number Twenty-two, for *Drag City* in 1964.

4 **JERRY LEE LEWIS**

Okay, Buddy Holly died, The Dead were always a bit boring. But Jerry Lee's piano is still pumping, and boredom leaves the room when he enters. So how come only one of his eighteen chart albums (*The Session*, 1973) has ever made the Top Forty? And then at Number Thirty-seven?!? You figure it out.

5 **JOHN MAYALL**

Mayall has had eighteen chart albums without ever coming closer to the top than Number Twenty-two, in 1970 with *USA Union*. But at least most of his later efforts were dull enough to deserve their obscurity.

6 **WILSON PICKETT**

The Exciting Wilson Pickett checked in at Number Twenty-one in 1966, but it's been downhill from there as far as the Wicked One's album chart success is concerned. Odd, since Pickett was one of the genuine geniuses of soul music.

7 and 8 **TEN YEARS AFTER; CANNED HEAT**

These two hard-rock blues-boogie combos were hot stuff in the late sixties and early seventies, wowing crowds during the rock festival epoch with flashy guitar stunts and a semblance of urban blues purity. But it took a major hit, "On the Road Again," to push *Boogie with Canned Heat* to Number Sixteen in 1968; and Ten Years After, despite lead guitarist Alvin Lee's memorable Woodstock pyrotechnics, never climbed further than Number Fourteen, with 1970's *Cricklewood Green*. Ten Years After charted eleven times, Canned Heat ten times.

9 and 10   THE YARDBIRDS; BUFFALO SPRINGFIELD

Two of the seminal sixties-into-seventies rock bands—the latter spawned Neil Young, CSNY, Poco, and Loggins and Messina; the former, Led Zeppelin, Jeff Beck, Eric Clapton, and Renaissance—never had much luck in their heyday. Of the Yardbirds' six prepsychedelic albums, only *The Yardbirds' Greatest Hits* made the Top Thirty (Number Twenty-eight in 1967). Of Buffalo Springfield's three discs of prototypical California folk / country, the biggest deal was *Last Time Around*, which climbed no further than Number Forty-two in 1968. The next year's first of two anthologies, *Retrospective: The Best of Buffalo Springfield*, could only equal that sorry record.

-◄▮▮►-

LOST IN THE TRANSLATION, PART 1
British Performers Who Never Made the American Singles Charts

All of these performers had at least one Top-Twenty hit in the U.K.

1	THE BARRON KNIGHTS	11	HAWKWIND
2	JEFF BECK	12	THE PRETTY THINGS
3	COLIN BLUNSTONE	13	THE ROCKIN' BERRIE
4	FAMILY	14	SCAFFOLD
5	THE MERSEYBEATS	15	THE SHADOWS
6	MEDICINE HEAD	16	WIZZARD
7	JOHNNY KIDD AND THE PIRATES	17	ROY WOOD
8	JUDGE DREAD	18	ALVIN STARDUST
9	BILLY FURY	19	THE STRAWBS
10	THE HERD		

LOST IN THE TRANSLATION, PART 2
U.K. Number 1 Hits That Never Made the U.S. Charts

1 "Please Don't Tease," CLIFF RICHARD, 1960
2 "Apache," THE SHADOWS, 1960
3 "Wooden Heart," ELVIS PRESLEY, 1961
4 "Dance On," THE SHADOWS, 1962
5 "Summer Holiday," CLIFF RICHARD, 1963
6 "Sweets for My Sweet," THE SEARCHERS, 1963
7 "Little Red Rooster," THE ROLLING STONES, 1964
8 "I'm Alive," THE HOLLIES, 1965
9 "Out of Time," CHRIS FARLOWE, 1966
10 "All or Nothing," THE SMALL FACES, 1966
11 "Lily the Pink," SCAFFOLD, 1968
12 "Ob-La-Di, Ob-La-Da," MARMALADE, 1968
13 "Albatross," FLEETWOOD MAC, 1968
14 "Blackberry Way," THE MOVE, 1968
15 "Voodoo Chile," JIMI HENDRIX, 1970
16 "Coz I Luv You," SLADE, 1971
17 "Metal Guru," T. REX, 1972
18 "See My Baby Jive," WIZZARD, 1973
19 "Skweeze Me, Pleeze Me," SLADE, 1973
20 "I'm the Leader of the Gang (I Am)," GARY GLITTER, 1973
21 "I Love You Love Me Love," GARY GLITTER, 1973
22 "Angel Fingers," WIZZARD, 1974
23 "Tiger Feet," MUD, 1974
24 "Devil Gate Drive," SUZI QUATRO, 1974
25 "Jealous Mind," ALVIN STARDUST, 1974
26 "Everything I Own," KEN BOOTHE, 1974
27 "Down Down," STATUS QUO, 1974
28 "Bye Bye Baby," THE BAY CITY ROLLERS, 1975
29 "Oh Boy," MUD, 1975
30 "Tears on My Pillow," JOHNNY NASH, 1975

31 "D.I.V.O.R.C.E," BILLY CONNOLLY, 1975
32 "I Love to Love," TINA CHARLES, 1976
33 "Mississippi," PUSSYCAT, 1976
34 "Under the Moon of Love," SHOWADDYWADDY, 1976
35 "Don't Cry for Me, Argentina," JULIE COVINGTON, 1976
36 "Chanson d'Amour," THE MANHATTAN TRANSFER, 1977
37 "Show You the Way to Go," THE JACKSONS, 1977
38 "Angelo," BROTHERHOOD OF MAN, 1977
39 "Yes Sir I Can Boogie," BACCARA, 1977

-◄▮▮►-

Songs THAT TOOK A LONG TIME TO HIT

1 **"Dedicated to the One I Love,"** THE SHIRELLES
When this record was originally released in the summer of
1959, it barely made the Top 100 and disappeared after only a
month. Almost two years later, the same record rocketed to
Number Three.

2 **"Does Your Chewing Gum Lose Its Flavor (On the Bed
Post Over Night),"** LONNIE DONEGAN
Dot Records originally released Donegan's skiffle novelty, a
major U.K. smash, in 1959. But it was not until 1961 that the
record went to Number Five on the U.S. charts.

3 **"Get Together,"** THE YOUNGBLOODS
Originally issued as the followup to the minor hit, "Grizzly
Bear," "Get Together" peaked at Number Sixty-two when it
was released in the fall of 1967. But in 1969, a reissue of the
same record soared to Number Five.

4 **"Please Please Me,"** THE BEATLES
Vee-Jay Records first released this single in February 1963.
No sale, not terribly surprising for a British artist's first U.S.
release in those days. They followed this one with "From Me to
You," which was beaten out by Del Shannon's American-made

cover version. It wasn't until exactly a year after the first U.S. release of "Please Please Me" that it made the Top Three—in the wake, of course, of a massive Capitol Records promotional blitz for the band's more current records.

5   **"Space Oddity,"** DAVID BOWIE

Bowie cut this single in the late sixties in England, but it was not until 1972 that RCA first issued it in America. Moreover, it took until 1973 for "Space Oddity" to make the American Top Twenty. This prompted RCA to repackage the album originally titled *David Bowie* as *Space Oddity*. Long ignored, that record also took off for the upper reaches of the charts.

6   **"Sunshine of Your Love,"** CREAM

Cream's initial blast of power-trio pop originally entered the charts in January 1968. It struggled to the Top Forty briefly before dropping out of sight. But in August of the same year, it had a chart revival that took the song all the way to the Top Five.

7   **"There's a Moon Out Tonight,"** THE CAPRIS

Recorded in 1958 and released in obscurity, it was not until 1961 that it placed at Number Three.

-◄❙▶-

ONE-SHOTS
20 TOP 10 RECORDS BY GROUPS WHO NEVER AGAIN MADE THE CHARTS

In the beginning, rock and roll was the music of one-shots, inspired 45s by people who almost deterministically were never heard from again. Perhaps it was better that way; by the seventies, even the former porno starlet Andrea True was able to sustain a small "career," with three followups to her one Top Ten hit, while the typical one-shot was a novelty, such as "Rubber Duckie" by Ernie, the Sesame Street *Muppet. Still, one could fill up a good-sized jukebox with one-shot rock and R&B*

hits from the past two decades. The following are twenty heroic examples of those who lived up to the tradition. Parenthetical numbers following dates indicate chart positions.

1   **"Alley-Oop,"** THE HOLLYWOOD ARGYLES, 1960 (1)
Kim Fowley, who has since perpetrated The Runaways, among other more long-lived entities, had a hand in this. In a way, his entire career has been one long attempt to follow up this zany takeoff on the comic strip caveman, though the closest he has come was "Bumble Boogie" by B. Bumble and the Stingers—but alas, even that had its dreary successors.

2   **"The Book of Love,"** THE MONOTONES, 1958 (5)
One supposes they never found out who wrote it—pity, because if they had, perhaps they'd have found it in them to repeat their success.

3   **"Fire,"** THE CRAZY WORLD OF ARTHUR BROWN, 1968 (2)
Brown was one of the more byzantine products of psychedelia, an eccentric Englishman who actually set himself aflame during his stage shows of that era. Brown has since lapsed into art-rock of an excruciating sort. "Fire" is perhaps most noteworthy as the most successful stateside hit single that producer Pete Townshend (of The Who) has ever had a hand in. The Who's biggest hit, "I Can See for Miles," made it no further than Number Nine and Townshend's other great one-shot production job, Thunderclap Newman's "Something in the Air," stalled at Number Thirty-seven.

4   **"Get a Job,"** THE SILHOUETTES, 1958 (1)
The original "shadada-da" disc, a nonsense lyric with a protest message similar to The Coasters' "Yakety Yak."

5   **"Happy, Happy Birthday Baby,"** THE TUNE WEAVERS, 1957 (5)
The most miserable birthday in rock and roll history, until Lesley Gore's. But where Lesley plays the spoiled brat, The Tune Weavers' nameless chanteuse acts out the tragedy through a letter—succinct and desperate.

6   **"Hold Your Head Up,"** ARGENT, 1972 (5)
       Although Rod Argent's group, which featured former Zombie
       Russ Ballard, would go on to some LP chart success, the band
       never again hit the Hot 100. Predictably enough, since this is
       not exactly heavy metal at its most scintillating.

7   **"In the Summertime,"** MUNGO JERRY, 1970 (3)
       A rather horrible revival of the British skiffle craze. One might
       have known then that the decade wasn't going to match the one
       that preceded it.

8   **"Israelites,"** DESMOND DEKKER AND THE ACES, 1969 (9)
       To this day, the only Top Ten reggae record by a Jamaican—
       transplanted to England, but nonetheless Jamaican. Probably
       lyrically offensive, if a North American could decipher the
       lyrics—fortunately, we can't.

9   **"Just One Look,"** DORIS TROY, 1963 (10)
       In this context, the title seems to say it all.

10   **"Little Star,"** THE ELEGANTS, 1958 (2)
       One of the most haunting vocal group singles ever made. But
       only collectors of extreme rarities have ever heard of the
       followups, none of which even made *Billboard*'s rhythm &
       blues charts.

11   **"Mule Skinner Blues,"** THE FENDERMEN, 1960 (5)
       Pure silliness, a whoop and a crash, and maniacal laughter
       that stops just short of becoming a yodel. I don't know if we
       could have taken any more like this.

12   **"One Summer Night,"** THE DANLEERS, 1958 (7)
       Another grand doo-wop ballad.

13   **"Party Lights,"** CLAUDINE CLARK, 1962 (5)
       Claudine's utter anguish that her mother won't let her cross the
       street to go to that party makes one suspect suicide as the
       reason that this classic was never pursued. Or to quote Van
       Morrison, "Come back, baby, come back."

14   **"Pipeline,"** THE CHANTAY'S, 1963 (4)
       The great surf instrumental comes closer to capturing the
       awesome power of the ocean than any of its brethren, even
       Dick Dale's marvelous "Misirlou."

15   **"Psychotic Reaction,"** THE COUNT FIVE, 1966 (5)
From the heyday of The Yardbirds' rip-offs and garage-band groove, this is the heavyweight champion, the original punk-rock classic. Good-bad, but far from boring.

16   **"Rockin' Chair,"** GWEN McRAE, 1975 (9)
Although McRae—whose husband, George, turned in a great one the year before with "Rock Your Baby"—scored three other R&B chart hits, this predisco dance number is her sole excursion to the Hot 100.

17   **"Sally, Go 'round the Roses,"** THE JAYNETTS, 1963 (2)
The most ominous girl group record ever made—theories abound as to its meaning, which remains forever shrouded in the murk of history.

18   **"Sea of Love,"** PHIL PHILLIPS, 1959 (2)
A tragicomic love lyric set against one of the most absurd crooning backing choruses in rock and roll history, plus former bellhop Phillips' bizarrely bel canto vocal. A followup to this is inconceivable.

19 and 20   **"Sh-Boom,"** THE CHORDS 1954 (5); **"Earth Angel (Wi You Be Mine),"** THE PENGUINS, 1955 (8)
These were the first rhythm & blues records to cross over to the Top Ten of the pop chart—and with good reason, since both are great vocal group discs, the former a rocker, the latter a ballad.

-◄❙▮▶-

JOHN SWENSON PICKS THE 15 MOST BORING CLASSIC ALBUMS

1   *All Things Must Pass*, GEORGE HARRISON
2   *At Carnegie Hall, Volumes I-IV*, CHICAGO
3   *Crosby, Stills and Nash*
4   *Days of Future Passed*, THE MOODY BLUES

5   *John Denver's Greatest Hits*
6   *Diamond Dogs*, DAVID BOWIE
7   *A Gift from a Flower to a Garden*, DONOVAN
8   *Goodbye Yellow Brick Road*, ELTON JOHN
9   *In-a-Gadda-da-Vida*, IRON BUTTERFLY
10   *In the Court of the Crimson King: An Observation by King Crimson*
11   *The Sun Bear Concerts*, KEITH JARRETT
12   *Time Has Come*, THE CHAMBERS BROTHERS
13   *The Wall*, PINK FLOYD
14   *Wheels of Fire*, CREAM
15   *Yessongs*, YES

JOHN SWENSON *has been an editor of* Crawdaddy, Circus, *and* High Times *and has written books on* The Who, The Beatles, *and* Kiss. *He is co-editor (with Dave Marsh) of* The Rolling Stone Record Guide, *which taught him more about boring albums than he cares to recall.*

- ◄ ▌ ► -

RISING TO THE TOP IN ELEVATORS
Rock Repertoires That Have Been Transposed into Muzak

1   THE BEACH BOYS
2   THE BEATLES
3   THE BEE GEES
4   THE DRIFTERS
5   GERRY AND THE PACEMAKERS
6   HERMAN'S HERMITS
7   OTIS REDDING
8   THE RIGHTEOUS BROTHERS
9   SIMON AND GARFUNKEL

THIRTY-ONE:
THE NAME GAME

The MC5.

WHAT'S YOUR NAME?

1   **JESSE BELVIN**
Belvin recorded "So Fine" in 1955 as The Sheiks, doing all the voices himself. He was also responsible for all the voices on the Cliques' 1956 hit, "Girl of My Dreams."

2   **CHER**
Cher recorded "I Love You Ringo," a Beatlemania disc, as Bonnie Jo Mason, for Phil Spector.

3   **AHMET ERTEGUN**
As one of the most important rhythm & blues writers of all time, he used the pseudonym A. Nugetre, a palindrome of his real name. (It's on "Mess Around" by Ray Charles, "Ting-a-Ling" by The Clovers, and "Whatcha Gonna Do" by The Drifters, among others.)

4   **BILL GRAHAM**
A World War II refugee named Wolfgang Wolodia Grajonka, the future promoter picked his new moniker out of the Bronx telephone book.

5   **JAMES BROWN AND HIS FAMOUS FLAMES**
King Records owner Syd Nathan didn't want "Mashed Potatoes" on his label, so they went to Atlantic and cut their hit as Nat Kendricks and the Swans.

6   **JERRY LEIBER and MIKE STOLLER**
These great songwriters used Elmo Glick as a pseudonym. Similarly, Bert Berns often wrote as Bert Russell.

7   **JEREMY SPENCER**
Then guitarist with Fleetwood Mac, Spencer recorded the rockabilly-based "Somebody's Gonna Get Their Head Kicked in Tonight" as Earl Vance and the Valiants.

8   **THE BEACH BOYS**
They recorded "Pamela Jean," a reworked version of Brian Wilson's "Car Crazy Cutie," as The Survivors.

9   **THE OLYMPICS**
The Olympics, of "Western Movies" fame, had a hit with

"Peanut Butter" (later covered by J. Geils) as The Marathons.

10 **RITCHIE VALENS**
He recorded "Fast Freight" in 1959 as Arvee Allens.

-◄❚❘►-

FAMOUS PSEUDONYMS OF THE 1950s
And the Folks Who Made Them Famous

1   JOHNNY ACE (John Marshall Alexander Jr.)
2   THE BIG BOPPER (Jiles Perry Richardson)
3   FREDDY CANNON (Fredrick Anthony Picariello)
4   DAVE "BABY" CORTEZ (David Clowney)
5   KING CURTIS (Curtis Ousley)
6   BOBBY DARIN (Walden Robert Cassotto)
7   BO DIDDLEY (Elias McDaniel)
8   ADAM FAITH (Terrence Nelhams)
9   CONNIE FRANCIS (Constance Franconero)
10 GUITAR SLIM (Eddie Jones)
11 SLIM HARPO (James Moore)
12 PEPPERMINT HARRIS (Harrison Nelson)
13 LITTLE WILLIE JOHN (William J. Woods)
14 ERNIE K-DOE (Ernest Kador)
15 BEN E. KING (Benjamin Nelson)
16 SMILEY LEWIS (Overton Amos Lemmons)
17 PROFESSOR LONGHAIR (Roy Byrd)
18 NERVOUS NORVUS (Jimmy Drake)
19 JOHNNY OTIS (John Veliotcs)
20 LES PAUL (Lester Polfus II)
21 JACK SCOTT (Jack Scafone Jr.)
22 DEE DEE SHARP (Dione La Rue)
23 CONWAY TWITTY (Harold Lloyd Jenkins)
24 RITCHIE VALENS (Richard Valenzuela)
25 GENE VINCENT (Vincent Eugene Craddock)
26 LITTLE WALTER (Marion Walter Jacobs)
27 MUDDY WATERS (McKinley Morganfield)
28 HOWLIN' WOLF (Chester Burnett)

FAMOUS PSEUDONYMS OF THE 1960s
And the Folks Who Made Them Famous

1 MARTY BALIN (Martin Buchwald)
2 CAPTAIN BEEFHEART (Don Van Vliet)
3 GENE CHANDLER (Eugene Dixon)
4 CHUBBY CHECKER (Ernest Evans)
5 CHER (Cherilyn Sarkisian La Pierre Bono Allman)
6 DEREK (Johnny Cymbal)
7 BOB DYLAN (Robert Allan Zimmerman)
8 CASS ELLIOTT (Ellen Naomi Cohen)
9 GEORGIE FAME (Clive Powell)
10 WAYNE FONTANA (Glyn Geoffrey Ellis)
11 DOBIE GRAY (Leonard Victor Ainsworth III)
12 TOMMY JAMES (Thomas Gregory Jackson)
13 LITTLE EVA (Eva Narcissus Boyd)
14 LULU (Marie McDonald McLaughlin Laurie)
15 TAJ MAHAL (Henry Saint-Claire Fredricks Williams)
16 MANFRED MANN (Mike Liebowitz)
17 ED MARIMBA (Artie Tripp III)
18 VAN MORRISON (George Ivan)
19 MICKIE MOST (Michael Peter Hayes)
20 P. J. PROBY (James Marcus Smith)
21 ? of The Mysterians (Rudy Martinez)
22 GENYA RAVAN (Goldie Zelkowitz)
23 JOHNNY RIVERS (John Ramistella)*
24 BOBBY RYDELL (Robert Lewis Ridarelli)
25 MITCH RYDER (Billy Levise)
26 SAM THE SHAM (Sam Samudio)
27 DEL SHANNON (Charles Westover)
28 DUSTY SPRINGFIELD (Mary Isobel Catherine O'Brien)
29 RINGO STARR (Richard Starkey)
30 CAT STEVENS (Steven Demetri Georgiou)
31 DINO VALENTI (Chester Powers)
32 FRANKIE VALLI (Francis Castelluccio)
33 JR. WALKER (Autry DeWalt Jr.)

34   WOLFMAN JACK (Bob Smith)
35   STEVIE WONDER (Steveland Judkins Morris)
36   TAMMY WYNETTE (Wynette Pugh)
37   JESSE COLIN YOUNG (Perry Miller)

*Changed at the suggestion of Alan Freed

-◄❚▶-

FAMOUS PSEUDONYMS OF THE 1970s
And the Folks Who Made Them Famous

1   MARC BOLAN (Marc Feld)
2   DAVID BOWIE (David Robert Hayward-Jones)
3   JIMMY CLIFF (James Chambers)
4   COMMANDER CODY (George Frayne)
5   JESSI COLTER (Miriam Johnson Jennings)
6   ALICE COOPER (Vincent Furnier)
7   ELVIS COSTELLO (Declan Patrick MacManus)
8   KIKI DEE (Pauline Mathews)
9   JOHN DENVER (John Deutschendorf)
10   RICK DERRINGER (Rick Zehringer)
11   BUCK DHARMA (Donald Roeser)
12   DR. JOHN THE NIGHT TRIPPER (Malcolm John Creaux
      Rebennack Jr.)
13   FREDDY FENDER (Baldermar G. Huerta)
14   GARY GLITTER (Paul Gadd)
15   ELTON JOHN (Reginald Dwight)
16   CHAKA KHAN (Yvette Marie Holland)
17   DENNY LAINE (Brian Arthur Haynes)
18   MAGIC DICK (Richard Salwitz)
19   MEAT LOAF (Marvin Lee Aday)
20   FREDDIE MERCURY (Frederick Bulsara)
21   IGGY POP (James Jewell Osterburg)
22   LOU REED (Louis "Butch" Firbank)
23   JOHNNY ROTTEN (John Lydon)
24   LEON RUSSELL (Russell Bridges)
25   SOUTHSIDE JOHNNY (John Lyon)

26   JOE STRUMMER (John Mellor)
27   STEVE TYLER (Steven Tallarico)
28   SID VICIOUS (John Simon Ritchie)
29   JERRY JEFF WALKER (Ronald Crosby)
30   PETER WOLF (Peter Blankenfield)

-◀❚▶-

REAL NAMES OF 15 GREAT DUOS

1   BILLY FORD and LILLIE BRYANT (Billy and Lillie)
2   CHAD STUART and JEREMY CLYDE (Chad and Jeremy)
3   DICK ST. JOHN and DEE DEE SPERLING (Dick and Dee Dee)
4   ROLAND TRONE and CLAUDE JOHNSON (Don and Juan)
5   MARK VOLMAN and HOWARD KAYLAN (Flo and Eddie)
6   JAN BERRY and DEAN TORRANCE (Jan and Dean)
7   MARVIN PHILLIPS and JOE JOSEA (Marvin and Johnny)
8   MICKEY BAKER and SYLVIA ROBINSON (Mickey and Sylvia)
9   PATIENCE and PRUDENCE MCINTYRE (Patience and Prudence)
10   RAY HILDEBRAND and JILL JACKSON (Paul and Paula)
11   FRANCINE BARKER and HERB FEEMSTER (The original
     Peaches and Herb)
12   PETER ASHER and GORDON WALLER (Peter and Gordon)
13   SAM MOORE and DAVE PRATER (Sam and Dave)
14   SHIRLEY PIXLEY and LEONARD LEE (Shirley and Lee)
15   CLYDE BATTON and GARY PAXTON (Skip and Flip)

-◀❚▶-

THE RAMONES' REAL NAMES

1   JEFFREY HYMAN (Joey Ramone)
2   THOMAS ERDELYI* (Tommy Ramone)
3   DOUGLAS COLVIN (Dee Dee Ramone)
4   MARK BELL (Marky Ramone)
5   JOHN CUMMINGS (Johnny Ramone)

*Retired

THE REAL NAMES OF KISS

1 PETER CRISSCOLA (Peter Criss)
2 PAUL FREHLEY (Ace Frehley)
3 GENE KLEIN (Gene Simmons)
4 STANLEY EISEN (Paul Stanley)

25 GREAT NICKNAMES

1 BAD BOY (Clarence Palmer)
2 THE BIG MAN (Clarence Clemons)
3 THE BIG O (Roy Orbison)
4 BONZO (John Bonham)
5 THE BOSS (Bruce Springsteen)
6 THE DUKE OF EARL (Gene Chandler)
7 THE GLIMMER TWINS (Mick Jagger and Keith Richards)
8 THE HAWK (Ronnie Hawkins)
9 THE ICE MAN (Jerry Butler)
10 THE KILLER (Jerry Lee Lewis)
11 THE KING (Elvis Presley)
12 LITTLE MISS SHARECROPPER (LaVern Baker)
13 MR. BLUES (Wynonie Harris)
14 MR. EXCITEMENT (Jackie Wilson)
15 MR. PERSONALITY (Lloyd Price)
16 MR. SOUL (Sam Cooke)
17 THE NURK TWINS (John Lennon and Paul McCartney)
18 PEARL (Janis Joplin)
19 PIGPEN (Ron McKernan)
20 PLONK (Ronnie Lane)
21 THE PRINCE OF WAILS (Johnnie Ray)
22 THE QUEEN OF SOUL (Aretha Franklin, also Carla Thomas)
23 THE ROCKVILLE ROCKET (Gene Pitney)

24 SOUL BROTHER NUMBER ONE, THE GODFATHER OF SOUL, MR. DYNAMITE, THE HARDEST WORKING MAN IN SHOW BUSINESS (James Brown, who else?)

25 TOWSER (Pete Townshend)

-◄▐▐►-

THE BIG LIST

1 ARTHUR "BIG BOY" CRUDUP
2 BIG BILL BROONZY
3 THE BIG BOPPER
4 BIG BROTHER AND THE HOLDING COMPANY
5 BIG DEE ERWIN
6 BIG EDDIE BURNS
7 BIG JOE MCCOY
8 BIG MACEO
9 BIG MAMA THORNTON
10 BIG MAYBELLE
11 "BIG" WALTER HORTON
12 BIG WALTER JACKSON
13 BIG WALTER PRICE
14 BIG YOUTH
15 GENTLE GIANT
16 JOHN "BIG MOOSE" WALKER
17 LONG JOHN BALDRY
18 CLARENCE "BIG MAN" CLEMONS
19 WILBERT "BIG CHIEF" ELLIS
20 YOUNG MARBLE GIANTS

THE LITTLE LIST

1   LITTLE ANTHONY AND THE IMPERIALS
2   LITTLE BROTHER MONTGOMERY
3   LITTLE CAESAR AND THE ROMANS
4   LITTLE ESTHER PHILLIPS
5   LITTLE EVA
6   LITTLE JOE AND THE THRILLERS
7   LITTLE JUNIOR PARKER
8   LITTLE MILTON
9   LITTLE RICHARD
10 LITTLE STEVIE WONDER
11 LITTLE SONNY
12 LITTLE SONNY BROWN
13 LITTLE WALTER
14 LITTLE WILLIE JOHN
15 LITTLE WILLIE LITTLEFIELD
16 PEE WEE CRAYTON
17 SHORTY LONG
18 THE SMALL FACES
19 TINY BRADSHAW
20 TINY TIM

-◄||►-

REAL GUITAR MEN

1   MCHOUSTON "MICKEY"/"GUITAR" BAKER
2   GUITAR CRUSHER
3   JORGEN "MR. GUITAR" INGMANN
4   GUITAR NUBBITT
5   GUITAR SLIM
6   JOHNNY "GUITAR" WATSON

A DOZEN COOL ROCK AND ROLL JOHNNYS

This list was compiled by Andy Edelstein of Relix *magazine.*

1   JOHNNY B. GOODE
2   JOHNNY TOO BAD
3   JOHNNY ROTTEN
4   JOHNNY ANGEL
5   JOHNNY BURNETTE
6   JOHNNY AND THE MOONDOGS
7   JOHNNY RAMONE
8   JOHNNY MELODY
9   JOHNNY AND THE HURRICANES
10 JOHNNY THUNDER(S)
11 JOHNNY KIDD
12 JOHNNY CASH/JOHNNY PAYCHECK

WHAT'S THE UGLIEST PART OF YOUR BODY?

1   "Pretty Little Angel Eyes," CURTIS LEE
2   "Ashtray Heart," CAPTAIN BEEFHEART
3   "Back in My Arms Again," THE SUPREMES
4   "Barefootin'," ROBERT PARKER
5   "Big Leg Emma," FRANK ZAPPA
6   "Boobs a Lot," THE HOLY MODAL ROUNDERS
7   "Brown Eyed Girl," VAN MORRISON
8   "Eyes," MICHAEL HURLEY
9   "Fingertips—Pt. 2," STEVIE WONDER
10 "First I Look at the Purse," THE CONTOURS
11 "Greasy Heart," THE JEFFERSON AIRPLANE
12 "Green Eyed Lady," SUGARLOAF
13 "Hair," THE COWSILLS
14 "Hand of Fate," THE ROLLING STONES

15 "Hearts of Stone," OTIS WILLIAMS AND THE CHARMS
16 "Hot Head," CAPTAIN BEEFHEART
17 "I Want to Hold Your Hand," THE BEATLES
18 "Mystic Eyes," THEM
19 "Noises for the Leg," THE BONZO DOG BAND
20 "Penis Dimension," THE MOTHERS OF INVENTION with THE
     ROYAL PHILHARMONIC ORCHESTRA
21 "King of Hands," ARGENT
22 "Smash Your Head against the Wall," JOHN ENTWISTLE
23 "Stink-Foot," FRANK ZAPPA
24 "This Old Heart of Mine," THE ISLEY BROTHERS
25 "Your Feets Too Big," THE BEATLES

·◄▐▐►·

ROCK NOBILITY

1	JOE "KING" CARRASCO	18	KING HARVEST
2	DUKE AND THE DRIVERS	19	KING PINS
3	THE EARLS	20	KING SOLOMON
4	THE "5" ROYALS	21	KINGFISH
5	FUNKY KINGS	22	THE KINGSMEN
6	THE GENTRYS	23	GLADYS KNIGHT AND THE PIPS
7	SHIRLEY GUNTHER AND THE QUEENS	24	NOBLE KNIGHTS
8	THE JACKS	25	THE NOBLES
9	ALBERT KING	26	PRINCE
10	B. B. KING	27	PRINCE BUSTER
11	BEN E. KING	28	QUEEN
12	CAROLE KING	29	THE ROYAL TEENS
13	EARL KING	30	THE ROYALTONES
14	FREDDIE KING	31	SAM THE SHAM AND THE PHARAOHS
15	KING CRIMSON	32	SCREAMING LORD SUTCH
16	KING CURTIS	33	THE SHADOWS OF KNIGHT
17	KING FLOYD	34	THE SIR DOUGLAS QUINTET
		35	TEEN QUEENS

ROCK AND ROLL DOCTORS

1   DR. WILLIAM ABRUZZI, the doctor at Woodstock
2   "DOC" BERGER, of Southside Johnny and the Asbury Jukes
3   DR. DEMENTO, disc jockey
4   DR. FEELGOOD
5   THE FOUR INTERNS, gospel quartet
6   DR. HOOK AND THE MEDICINE SHOW
7   DR. JOHN THE NIGHT TRIPPER
8   DOC POMUS, songwriter
9   DR. ROBERT, of The Beatles song
10 DR. ROSS, blues singer
11 DR. WEST'S MEDICINE SHOW AND JUNK BAND

-◀▮▶-

50 BIRD GROUPS

In the late forties and through the fifties, after Sonny Til and the Orioles hit with "Crying in the Chapel," it became de rigueur *for black harmony groups to name themselves after various birds. This is a tradition that continues up to the present day with such bands as The Eagles.*

1	ATOMIC ROOSTER	11	CHICKEN SHACK
2	THE BIRDS	12	THE CROWS
3	THE BLACKBYRDS	13	THE DIXIE HUMMINGBIRDS
4	THE BLUEBIRDS	14	DUCKS DELUXE
5	BLUE JAYS	15	THE EAGLES
6	BUDGIE	16	THE FALCONS
7	THE BUZZARDS	17	FEATHERS
8	THE BYRDS	18	THE FIVE OWLS
9	THE CARDINALS	19	THE FLAMINGOS
10	THE CHICKADEES	20	THE FOUR LARKS

21	THE HAWKS	36	THE QUAILTONES
22	HUMMINGBIRD	37	RARE BIRD
23	THE JAYHAWKS	38	THE RAVENS
24	THE LARKS	39	THE ROBINS
25	MALLARD	40	SPARROW
26	THE MEADOWLARKS	41	THE SPARROWS
27	ANN NICHOLS AND	42	THE STARLINGS
	HER BLUEBIRDS	43	STONE THE CROWS
28	SONNY TIL AND THE ORIOLES	44	THE SWALLOWS
29	THE OSPREYS	45	THE SWANS
30	THE PARAKEETS	46	THE SWAN SILVERTONES
31	THE PARROTS	47	TUCKY BUZZARD
32	THE PEACOCKS	48	WHIPPOORWILLS
33	THE PELICANS	49	THE WRENS
34	THE PENGUINS	50	THE YARDBIRDS
35	THE QUAILS		

EMPHASIS ON ARACHNIDS
10 Performers Named after Bugs

1 ADAM AND THE ANTS
2 THE BEATLES
3 B. BUMBLE AND THE STINGERS
4 BUMBLE BEE SLIM
5 THE CRICKETS
6 IRON BUTTERFLY
7 THE ROCHES
8 THE SCORPIONS
9 THE SPIDERS FROM MARS
10 SPYDER TURNER

REAL DOG ACTS

1 BONZO DOG (DOO DAH) BAND
2 BOW WOW WOW
3 BULLDOG
4 THE DINGOES
5 THE FABULOUS POODLES
6 THE HOUNDS
7 THE LAUGHING DOGS
8 THE POINTER SISTERS
9 THE SPANIELS
10 SWAMP DOGG

THE 20 BEST GROUP NAMES

1 THE ROLLING STONES
2 THE CRICKETS
3 THE WHO
4 JOHNNY AND THE HURRICANES
5 THE GRATEFUL DEAD
6 THE MIRACLES
7 LED ZEPPELIN
8 THE BAND
9 THE TEMPTATIONS
10 THEM
11 TALKING HEADS
12 THE BEATLES
13 THE CLASH
14 THE GANG OF FOUR
15 THE KINKS
16 THE VELVET UNDERGR
17 THE FAMOUS FLAMES
18 THE FUGS
19 THE MOTHERS OF INVE
20 THE FALCONS

THE 20 WORST GROUP NAMES

1 IT'S A BEAUTIFUL DAY
2 BOFFALONGO
3 THE SLITS
4 VANILLA FUDGE
5 ULTIMATE SPINACH
6 THE PORK DUKES

7   WIGGY BITS
8   THE SOUTHER, HILLMAN, FURAY BAND
9   JO MAMA
10 JETHRO TULL
11 STYX
12 MOBY GRAPE
13 MASHMAKHAN
14 KLAATU
15 AIR SUPPLY
16 FRIJID PINK
17 STRAWBERRY ALARM CLOCK
18 SUPERTRAMP
19 NEW YORK ROCK AND ROLL ENSEMBLE
20 YES

-◄❙▮❙►-

BANDS NAMED AFTER SONGS

1   JO JO GUNNE, after a song written by Chuck Berry
2   THE STONE PONEYS, from Charley Patton's "Stone Poney
    Blues"
3   THE McCOYS, from The Ventures' instrumental, "McCoy"
4   THE LOVIN' SPOONFUL, from the lyrics of Mississippi John
    Hurt's "Coffee Blues"
5   THE SKYLINERS, from the Charlie Barnett song
6   THE PRETTY THINGS, from the Bo Diddley song, which they
    perform on their first LP
7   THE ROLLING STONES, after Muddy Waters' great blues song
8   DEEP PURPLE, from the classic Bing Crosby song

BANDS NAMED AFTER PLACES

1   AMERICA
2   THE ATLANTA RHYTHM SECTION
3   THE BAY CITY ROLLERS
4   BLACK OAK ARKANSAS
5   BOSTON
6   THE BROOKLYN BRIDGE
7   CHICAGO
8   DETROIT
9   THE DETROIT EMERALDS
10 THE DETROIT WHEELS
11 FLINT
12 THE IRON CITY HOUSEROCKERS
13 JACKSON HEIGHTS
14 KANSAS
15 KOKOMO
16 L.A. EXPRESS
17 THE LEFT BANKE
18 THE LIVERPOOL SCENE
19 THE MANHATTANS
20 THE MC5 (Motor City)
21 THE MEMPHIS HORNS
22 THE MUSCLE SHOALS RHYTHM SECTION
23 NAZARETH
24 NEW YORK CITY
25 THE NEW YORK DOLLS
26 NEW YORK MARY
27 THE NEW YORK ROCK AND ROLL ENSEMBLE
28 THE OHIO PLAYERS
29 THE OHIO EXPRESS
30 OKLAHOMA
31 OREGON
32 THE OZARK MOUNTAIN DAREDEVILS

33 PARIS
34 DAVID PEEL AND THE LOWER EAST SIDE
35 THE RUBBER CITY REBELS
36 SOUTHSIDE JOHNNY AND THE ASBURY JUKES
37 UK
38 UNITED STATES OF AMERICA
39 UTOPIA
40 BOBBY TAYLOR AND THE VANCOUVERS

NUMBER 1 WITH A DILDO
Band Names with Sexual Connotations

1 BEES MAKE HONEY
2 THE BUZZCOCKS
3 CREAM
4 HUMAN SEXUAL RESPONSE
5 ROOT BOY SLIM AND THE SEX CHANGE BAND
6 THE SEX PISTOLS
7 THE SIC F*CKS
8 THE SLITS
9 10CC
10 THE TUBES
11 THE VIBRATORS
12 XTC

Honorable Mention: THE LOVIN' SPOONFUL, STEELY DAN

ALL-TIME BEST ALBUM TITLES

1　*Bringing It All Back Home*, BOB DYLAN
2　*Exile on Main Street*, THE ROLLING STONES
3　*Darkness on the Edge of Town*, BRUCE SPRINGSTEEN
4　*The Young Mod's Forgotten Story*, THE IMPRESSIONS
5　*Rubber Soul*, THE BEATLES
6　*The Otis Redding Dictionary of Soul*
7　*Are You Experienced?* THE JIMI HENDRIX EXPERIENCE
8　*A Whole New Thing*, SLY AND THE FAMILY STONE
9　*Over Under Sideways Down*, THE YARDBIRDS
10　*Too Much Too Soon*, THE NEW YORK DOLLS
11　*Promised Land*, ELVIS PRESLEY
12　*Pretzel Logic*, STEELY DAN

-◄▮▶-

THE ALL-TIME WORST ALBUM TITLES

1　*Aoxomoxoa*, THE GRATEFUL DEAD
2　*Chicago XIV*
3　*Sloppy Seconds*, DR. HOOK AND THE MEDICINE SHOW
4　*Q: Are We Not Men? A: We Are Devo*
5　*The Hissing of Summer Lawns*, JONI MITCHELL
6　*Sir Army Suit*, KLAATU
7　*Fulfillingness' First Finale*, STEVIE WONDER
8　*A Gift from a Flower to a Garden*, DONOVAN
9　*Tormato*, YES
10　*Buddah and the Chocolate Box*, CAT STEVENS

THIRTY-TWO:
THE DICTIONARY OF ROCK
AND ROLL

Screamin' Jay Hawkins is famed for making his stage entrance from a closed coffin.

COURTESY ROLLING STONE

CHRIS BEACHLEY CHOOSES THE 10 BEST BEACH RECORDS

Beach music is not, as one might expect, simply songs about surf and sun, but rather the peculiar mix of pop, rock, and light rhythm & blues that rock fans from the Virginia and Carolina beaches claim as their own special genre. Most of this music is all but unknown outside those areas.

1   "Sixty Minute Man," THE DOMINOES
2   "Ms. Grace," THE TYMES
3   "Thank You John," WILLIE TEE
4   "Summertime's Calling Me," THE CATALINAS
5   "39-21-46," THE SHOWMEN
6   "Green Eyes," THE RAVENS
7   *"A Quiet Place,"* GARNETT MIMMS AND THE ENCHANTERS
8   "Hello Stranger," BARBARA LEWIS
9   "Nip Sip," THE CLOVERS
10 "The Entertainer," TONY CLARKE

CHRIS BEACHLEY *is editor of* It Will Stand, *a magazine that chronicles the beach-music scene.*

-◄❙▐▶-

ROCK AROUND THE BLOCK
Or There Goes the Neighborhood

1   *Abbey Road,* THE BEATLES
2   "Baker Street," GERRY RAFFERTY
3   "Brooklyn Roads," NEIL DIAMOND
4   "Creeque Alley," THE MAMAS AND THE PAPAS
5   "Cypress Avenue," VAN MORRISON
6   "Dead End Street," THE KINKS
7   "Dead Man's Curve," JAN AND DEAN
8   "Desolation Row," BOB DYLAN
9   "Easy Street," EDGAR WINTER GROUP

10   "442 Glenwood Avenue," PIXIES THREE
11   *461 Ocean Blvd.*, ERIC CLAPTON
12   "Funky Broadway," WILSON PICKETT
13   "Funky Street," ARTHUR CONLEY
14   "Heartbreak Road," BILL WITHERS
15   "Lonely Avenue," RAY CHARLES
16   "Love Street," THE DOORS
17   *McLemore Avenue*, BOOKER T AND THE MGs
18   "Main Street," BOB SEGER
19   "Penny Lane," THE BEATLES
20   "Positively 4th Street," BOB DYLAN
21   "Route 66 Theme," NELSON RIDDLE
22   "77 Sunset Strip," DON RALKE
23   "Shakin' Street," THE MC5
24   "South Street," THE ORLONS
25   "Tarkio Road," BREWER AND SHIPLEY
26   *3614 Jackson Highway*, CHER
27   "Thunder Road," BRUCE SPRINGSTEEN
28   "Tobacco Road," THE NASHVILLE TEENS
29   "2120 S. Michigan Avenue," THE ROLLING STONES
30   "2-4-6-8 Motorway," THE TOM ROBINSON BAND

RIOT ON SUNSET STRIP
Songs about Los Angeles

1   "Blue Jay Way," THE BEATLES
2   "Celluloid Heroes," THE KINKS
3   "Coming into Los Angeles," ARLO GUTHRIE
4   "Creeque Alley," THE MAMAS AND THE PAPAS
5   "Dead Man's Curve," JAN AND DEAN
6   "Do You Know the Way to San Jose," DIONNE WARWICK
7   "For What It's Worth" ("Stop, Hey What's That Sound"),
     BUFFALO SPRINGFIELD
8   "Heart of Gold," NEIL YOUNG

9   "Hollywood Dream," THUNDERCLAP NEWMAN
10   "Hollywood Nights," BOB SEGER
11   "Hollywood Swinging," KOOL AND THE GANG
12   "L. A. Woman," THE DOORS
13   "Ladies of the Canyon," JONI MITCHELL
14   "Life in the Fast Lane," THE EAGLES
15   "Los Angeles," X
16   "MacArthur Park," RICHARD HARRIS
17   "Midnight Train to Georgia," GLADYS KNIGHT AND THE PIPS
18   "Trouble Every Day," THE MOTHERS OF INVENTION
19   "Ventura Highway," AMERICA

-◄▮▶-

WEST SIDE STORY
Songs about New York City

1   "Back in the New York Groove," ACE FREHLEY
2   "The Boy from New York City," THE AD LIBS
3   "59th Street Bridge Song (Feelin' Groovy)," SIMON AND
     GARFUNKEL
4   "Harlem Nocturne," THE VISCOUNTS
5   "Living for the City," STEVIE WONDER
6   "Native New Yorker," ODYSSEY
7   "New York City," JOHN LENNON AND THE PLASTIC ONO
     BAND
8   "New York City Serenade," BRUCE SPRINGSTEEN
9   "New York Skyline," GARLAND JEFFREYS
10   "New York State of Mind," BILLY JOEL
11   "New York Tendaberry," LAURA NYRO
12   "New York's a Lonely Town," THE TRADE WINDS
13   "On Broadway," THE DRIFTERS
14   "Rockaway Beach," THE RAMONES
15   "Shattered," THE ROLLING STONES
16   "Spanish Harlem," BEN E. KING
17   "Summer in the City," THE LOVIN' SPOONFUL

18   "Twelve Thirty (Young Girls Are Coming to the Canyon),"
     THE MAMAS AND THE PAPAS
19   "Up on the Roof," THE DRIFTERS
20   "Walk on the Wild Side," LOU REED

-◄▮▮►-

NO MONEY DOWN
The Rock and Roll Used-Car Lot

1   "The Anaheim Azusa and Cucamonga Sewing Circle, Book
     Review and Timing Association," JAN AND DEAN
2   "Brand New Cadillac," THE CLASH
3   "Bucket 'T'," JAN AND DEAN, THE WHO
4   "Cadillac Ranch," BRUCE SPRINGSTEEN
5   "Cherry Cherry Coupe," THE BEACH BOYS
6   "Custom Machine," THE BEACH BOYS
7   "Dead Man's Curve," JAN AND DEAN
8   "Drag City," JAN AND DEAN
9   "Drive My Car," THE BEATLES
10   "Eldorado Slim," LITTLE FEAT
11   "409," THE BEACH BOYS
12   "From a Buick 6," BOB DYLAN
13   "Fun, Fun, Fun," THE BEACH BOYS
14   "G.T.O.," RONNY AND THE DAYTONAS
15   "Hey Little Cobra," THE RIP CHORDS
16   "Hot Rod Lincoln," JOHNNY BOND, COMMANDER CODY AND
     HIS LOST PLANET AIRMEN
17   "Jaguar and the Thunderbird," CHUCK BERRY
18   "Little Deuce Coupe," THE BEACH BOYS
19   "Long Black Limousine," ELVIS PRESLEY
20   "Maybellene," CHUCK BERRY
21   "Mercedes Benz," JANIS JOPLIN
22   "Mustang Sally," WILSON PICKETT
23   "My Mustang Ford," CHUCK BERRY
24   "Racing in the Street," BRUCE SPRINGSTEEN
25   "Schlock Rod, Parts 1 and 2," JAN AND DEAN

26 "Spirit of America," THE BEACH BOYS
27 "Street Machine," THE SUPER STOCKS
28 "Shut Down," THE BEACH BOYS
29 "Three Window Coupe," THE RIP CHORDS
30 "2-4-6-8 Motorway," THE TOM ROBINSON BAND

-◄▌▶-

I'LL CRY IF I WANT TO

1 "Cry Baby," GARNETT MIMMS AND THE ENCHANTERS
2 "Cry Cry Cry," BOBBY BLAND
3 "Cry Like a Baby," THE BOX TOPS
4 "Crying," ROY ORBISON
5 "Crying in the Chapel," SONNY TIL AND THE ORIOLES
6 "Crying in the Rain," THE EVERLY BROTHERS
7 "It's My Party," LESLEY GORE
8 "96 Tears,"? AND THE MYSTERIANS
9 "No Woman No Cry," BOB MARLEY AND THE WAILERS
10 "Teardrops on Your Letter," HANK BALLARD AND THE MIDNIGHTERS
11 "Tears on My Pillow," LITTLE ANTHONY AND THE IMPERIALS
12 "Tracks of My Tears," SMOKEY ROBINSON AND THE MIRACLES

-◄▌▶-

15 SONGS FOR THE DOGS

1 "Black Dog," LED ZEPPELIN
2 "Do the Dog," RUFUS THOMAS
3 "Dogs," THE WHO
4 "Dogs, Part II," KEITH MOON
5 "Doggin' Around," JACKIE WILSON
6 "Get Down," GILBERT O'SULLIVAN
7 "Hey Bulldog," THE BEATLES

8   "Hound Dog," ELVIS PRESLEY
9   "I Wanna Be Your Dog," THE STOOGES
10   "I'm Gonna Buy Me a Dog," THE MONKEES
11   "Martha My Dear," THE BEATLES
12   "Me and You and a Dog Named Boo," LOBO
13   "Old Shep," ELVIS PRESLEY
14   "Walkin' the Dog," RUFUS THOMAS
15   "The Way You Dog Me Around," THE DIABLOS

-◄❙▮►-

Don't BRING ME DOWN

1   "Back in the U.S.A.," CHUCK BERRY
2   "Back in the USSR," THE BEATLES
3   "Crash Landing," JIMI HENDRIX
4   "Dayton Ohio—1903," RANDY NEWMAN
5   "Early Morning Rain," GORDON LIGHTFOOT
6   "Flight 505," THE ROLLING STONES
7   "Glow Girl," THE WHO
8   "The Great Airplane Strike," PAUL REVERE AND THE
     RAIDERS
9   "Sky Pilot," ERIC BURDON AND THE ANIMALS
10   "2-4-2 Fox Trot (The Lear Jet Song)," THE BYRDS
11   "Who's Driving My Plane," THE ROLLING STONES

-◄❙▮►-

Follow THAT DREAM

1   "Bob Dylan's Dream," BOB DYLAN
2   "Bob Dylan's 115th Dream," BOB DYLAN
3   "Daydream," THE LOVIN' SPOONFUL
4   "Dream a Little Dream of Me," CASS ELLIOTT
5   "Dream Lover," BOBBY DARIN
6   "Dream On," AEROSMITH

7   "Dreamin'," JOHNNY BURNETTE
8   "Dreams," THE EVERLY BROTHERS
9   "If I Can Dream," ELVIS PRESLEY
10   "I Dreamed I Saw St. Augustine," BOB DYLAN
11   "I Had Too Much to Dream (Last Night)," THE ELECTRIC PRUNES
12   "In Dreams," ROY ORBISON

-◄▐▐►-

Ebb TIDE

1   "Bermuda Triangle," FLEETWOOD MAC
2   "Catch a Wave," THE BEACH BOYS
3   "Nantucket Sleighride," MOUNTAIN
4   "Oceans Away," PHILIP GOODHAND-TAIT
5   "Pacific Ocean Blue," DENNIS WILSON
6   "Remember (Walkin' in the Sand)," THE SHANGRI-LAS
7   "Ride the Wild Surf," JAN AND DEAN
8   "Sail Away," RANDY NEWMAN
9   "San Francisco Bay Blues," JESSE FULLER
10   "Sea Cruise," FRANKIE FORD
11   "Sink the Bismarck," JOHNNY HORTON
12   "Sloop John B," THE BEACH BOYS
13   "Wooden Ships," JEFFERSON AIRPLANE

Daddy COULD SWEAR, I DECLARE
Songs about Fathers and Sons

1   "Adam Raised a Cain," BRUCE SPRINGSTEEN
2   "Beautiful Boy," JOHN LENNON
3   "Cat's in the Cradle," HARRY CHAPIN
4   "Daddy's Tune," JACKSON BROWNE
5   "The End," THE DOORS

6   "Father and Son," CAT STEVENS
7   "Independence Day," BRUCE SPRINGSTEEN
8   "My Old Man," IAN DURY
9   "Papa Was a Rollin' Stone," THE TEMPTATIONS
10   "Patches," CLARENCE CARTER
11   "Someday Never Comes," CREEDENCE CLEARWATER REVIVAL
12   "Younger Generation," THE LOVIN' SPOONFUL

-◀❙▶-

10 KEY FRAT ROCK HITS

1   "Baby Let Me Bang Your Box," DOUG CLARK AND THE HOT NUTS
2   "Double Shot (Of My Baby's Love)," THE SWINGIN' MEDALLIONS
3   "Farmer John," THE PREMIERS
4   "Last Night," THE MAR-KEYS
5   "Little Latin Lupe Lu," THE RIGHTEOUS BROTHERS, MITCH RYDER AND THE DETROIT WHEELS
6   "Louie Louie," THE KINGSMEN
7   "Quarter to Three," GARY "U.S." BONDS
8   "Respectable," THE OUTSIDERS
9   "Shout," THE ISLEY BROTHERS
10   "You Can't Sit Down," THE DOVELLS

-◀❙▶-

GREAT MAKE-OUT MUSIC

1   "Ooh Baby Baby," SMOKEY ROBINSON AND THE MIRACLES
2   "In the Still of the Nite," THE FIVE SATINS
3   "Under the Boardwalk," THE DRIFTERS
4   "Misty Blue," DOROTHY MOORE
5   "Layla," DEREK AND THE DOMINOS

6   "My Girl," THE TEMPTATIONS
7   "Don't Worry Baby," THE BEACH BOYS
8   "I'm Your Puppet," JAMES AND BOBBY PURIFY
9   "Little Star," THE ELEGANTS
10 "For Your Precious Love," JERRY BUTLER AND THE
    IMPRESSIONS
11 "Love to Love You Baby," DONNA SUMMER
12 "Earth Angel," THE PENGUINS
13 "Cruisin'," SMOKEY ROBINSON
14 "I Only Have Eyes for You," THE FLAMINGOS
15 "Night Moves," BOB SEGER
16 "Soothe Me," SAM AND DAVE
17 "Christo Redentor," HARVEY MANDEL
18 "This I Swear," THE SKYLINERS
19 "Our Day Will Come," RUBY AND THE ROMANTICS
20 "Cupid," SAM COOKE
21 "Do Me," TEDDY PENDERGRASS
22 "Come Softly to Me," THE FLEETWOODS
23 "Sunday Kind of Love," THE HARP-TONES
24 "Daddy's Home," SHEP AND THE LIMELITES
25 "Sweet Dreams," ROY BUCHANAN

-◄❙▶-

DR. FREUD'S BLUES

1   "Acute Schizophrenia Paranoia Blues," THE KINKS
2   "Ah, Ah, Yawa Em Ekat ot Gnimoc Eryeht," NAPOLEON XIV
3   "Cherry Blossom Clinic," THE MOVE
4   "Crackin' Up," BO DIDDLEY
5   "The End," THE DOORS
6   "Excitable Boy," WARREN ZEVON
7   "I'm a Boy," THE WHO
8   "Insane Asylum," WILLIE DIXON
9   "Knockin' around the Zoo," JAMES TAYLOR
10 "Manic Depression," JIMI HENDRIX

11   "Merry Go Round," WILD MAN FISCHER
12   "Mother," JOHN LENNON
13   "Mother and Child Reunion," PAUL SIMON
14   "Mother's Little Helper," THE ROLLING STONES
15   "Nervous Breakdown," EDDIE COCHRAN
16   "19th Nervous Breakdown," THE ROLLING STONES
17   "Paranoid," GRAND FUNK RAILROAD
18   "Paranoid," BLACK SABBATH
19   "Psychotic Reaction," COUNT FIVE
20   "Quadrophenia," THE WHO
21   "Rock Therapy," THE ROCK AND ROLL TRIO
22   "The Rubber Room," PORTER WAGONER
23   "They're Coming to Take Me Away, Ha-Haaa!" NAPOLEON XIV
24   "Transfusion," NERVOUS NORVUS
25   "We Are Normal," THE BONZO DOG (DOO DAH) BAND

-◄▮►-

THE ROCK AND ROLL HAUNTED HOUSE

1   "Ain't Superstitious," HOWLIN' WOLF
2   "Black Magic Woman," FLEETWOOD MAC
3   "Black Widow Spider," DR. JOHN
4   "Cobwebs and Strange," THE WHO
5   "Dinner with Drac (Part 1)," ZACHERLE
6   "Dr. Jekyll and Mr. Hyde," THE WHO
7   "(Don't Fear) The Reaper," BLUE ÖYSTER CULT
8   "Gypsy Eyes," JIMI HENDRIX
9   "The Haunted House," JUMPIN' GENE SIMMONS
10   "Heaven and Hell," THE WHO
11   "I Put a Spell on You," SCREAMIN' JAY HAWKINS
12   "Lon Chaney," GARLAND JEFFREYS
13   "Love Potion No. 9," THE CLOVERS
14   "Monster Mash," BOBBY "BORIS" PICKETT
15   "Monster Party," BILL DOGGETT

16   "Mystery Train," ELVIS PRESLEY
17   "Psycho Killer," TALKING HEADS
18   "The Purple People Eater," SHEB WOOLEY
19   "Rhiannon (Will You Ever Win)," FLEETWOOD MAC
20   "Season of the Witch," DONOVAN
21   "Sweet Exorcist," CURTIS MAYFIELD
22   "Voodoo Chile," THE JIMI HENDRIX EXPERIENCE
23   "Werewolf," THE FRANTICS
24   "Werewolves of London," WARREN ZEVON

-◄❙▮▶-

SONGS ABOUT JOBS

1   "Another Day," PAUL MCCARTNEY
2   "Baby Sitter," BETTY WRIGHT
3   "Clean Up Woman," BETTY WRIGHT
4   "Elevator Operator," SONNY BOY WILLIAMSON II
5   "Factory Girl," THE ROLLING STONES
6   "Gabbin' Blues," BIG MAYBELLE
7   "Ghost Writer," GARLAND JEFFREYS
8   "Handy Man," DEL SHANNON
9   "In the Navy," THE VILLAGE PEOPLE
10   "The Pusher," STEPPENWOLF
11   "Queen of the House," JODY MILLER
12   "Rocket Man," ELTON JOHN
13   "Six Days on the Road," DAVE DUDLEY
14   "So You Want to Be a Rock 'n' Roll Star," THE BYRDS
15   "Taxi," HARRY CHAPIN
16   "Taxman," THE BEATLES
17   "Willie the Pimp," FRANK ZAPPA
18   "WOLD," HARRY CHAPIN
19   "Workin' at the Car Wash Blues," JIM CROCE

DO YOU BELIEVE IN MAGIC?

1 "Black Magic Woman," FLEETWOOD MAC
2 "Do You Believe in Magic," THE LOVIN' SPOONFUL
3 "It's Magic," THE PLATTERS
4 "A Little Bit Like Magic," KING HARVEST
5 "Magic," PILOT
6 "Magic Bus," THE WHO
7 "Magic Carpet Ride," STEPPENWOLF
8 "Magic Is the Night," KATHY YOUNG with THE INNOCENTS
9 "Magic Man," HEART
10 "Magic Moon (Clair De Lune)," THE RAYS
11 "Magic Town," THE VOGUES
12 "Magic Wand," DON AND JUAN
13 "Magic Woman Touch," THE HOLLIES
14 "Mr. Magic Man," WILSON PICKETT
15 "Strange Magic," ELECTRIC LIGHT ORCHESTRA
16 "This Magic Moment," THE DRIFTERS
17 "You Got the Magic," JOHN FOGERTY
18 "You Made Me Believe in Magic," THE BAY CITY ROLLERS
19 "You're Gonna Need Magic," ROY HAMILTON
20 "(You've Got) the Magic Touch," THE PLATTERS

-◄▐▐►-

YOUR MOTHER SHOULD KNOW
Songs of Maternal Advice

1 "Good Enough," BONNIE RAITT
2 "Mama Said," THE SHIRELLES
3 "Mama Told Me Not to Come," RANDY NEWMAN
4 "Mother-in-Law," ERNIE K-DOE
5 "1985," PAUL McCARTNEY
6 "Rolling Stone," MUDDY WATERS

7   "Sherry Darling," BRUCE SPRINGSTEEN
8   "Shop Around," SMOKEY ROBINSON AND THE MIRACLES
9   "Take Time to Know Her," PERCY SLEDGE
10   "That's What Mama Said," BIG WALTER JACKSON
11   "Too Many Fish in the Sea," THE MARVELETTES
12   "You Can't Hurry Love," THE SUPREMES

-◄❙▶-

TOO MUCH MONKEY BUSINESS

1   "Ape Call," NERVOUS NORVUS
2   "Mickey's Monkey," THE MIRACLES
3   "The Monkey Time," MAJOR LANCE
4   "Gorilla You're a Desperado," WARREN ZEVON
5   "Apeman," THE KINKS
6   "Can Your Monkey Do the Dog," RUFUS THOMAS
7   "Monkey Man," THE ROLLING STONES
8   "Harry the Hairy Ape," RAY STEVENS
9   "Gorilla," JAMES TAYLOR
10   "(Theme from) The Monkees," THE MONKEES

-◄❙▶-

MOUNTAIN JAMS

1   "Ain't No Mountain High Enough," MARVIN GAYE and
     TAMMI TERRELL
2   "Billy the Mountain," FRANK ZAPPA AND THE MOTHERS OF
     INVENTION
3   "Black Mountain Side," LED ZEPPELIN
4   "Mountain Jam," THE ALLMAN BROTHERS BAND
5   "Mountain of Love," HAROLD DORMAN
6   "The Mountain's High," DICK AND DEE DEE
7   "Our Mother the Mountain," TOWNES VAN ZANDT
8   "Over the Mountain; Across the Sea," JOHNNIE AND JOE
9   "Rocky Mountain Way," JOE WALSH

10   "Rolling Down a Mountainside," THE MAIN INGREDIENT
11   "There Is a Mountain," DONOVAN
12   "Walkin' with a Mountain," MOTT THE HOOPLE

-◄❙❙▶-

NIGHT MOVES

1   "All Day and All of the Night," THE KINKS
2   "Because the Night," PATTI SMITH
3   "Drive All Night," BRUCE SPRINGSTEEN
4   "A Hard Day's Night," THE BEATLES
5   "Here Comes the Night," THEM
6   "In the Midnight Hour," WILSON PICKETT
7   "In the Still of the Nite," THE FIVE SATINS
8   "Night Moves," BOB SEGER
9   "Night Rally," ELVIS COSTELLO
10   "Night Time," THE STRANGELOVES
11   "Oh, What a Night," THE DELLS
12   "One Night of Sin," SMILEY LEWIS
13   "Something in the Night," BRUCE SPRINGSTEEN
14   "Such a Night," DR. JOHN
15   "There's a Moon Out Tonight," THE CAPRIS
16   "Till the End of the Day," THE KINKS
17   "Tonite, Tonite," THE MELLO-KINGS
18   "Tonight's the Night," ROD STEWART
19   "Walkin' after Midnight," PATSY CLINE
20   "Wild Night," VAN MORRISON

-◄❙❙▶-

TALKING ABOUT YOU
Songs about Musicians and Their Audiences

1   "All of My Friends Were There," THE KINKS
2   "Apple Scruffs," GEORGE HARRISON
3   "Blonde in the Bleachers," JONI MITCHELL

4   "Mr. Soul," BUFFALO SPRINGFIELD
5   "Play That Fast Thing (One More Time)," ROCKPILE
6   "The Punk Meets the Godfather," THE WHO
7   "Rock 'n' Roll Fantasy," THE KINKS
8   "Sally Simpson," THE WHO
9   "Sugar Magnolia," THE GRATEFUL DEAD
10   "Superstar," BETTE MIDLER
11   "Sweet Little Sixteen," CHUCK BERRY
12   "Talk to You," THE SMALL FACES
13   "Watching the Wheels," JOHN LENNON
14   "What's Your Name," LYNYRD SKYNYRD

-◄▮▶-

ROCK BY NUMBERS

0   "Love Minus Zero/No Limit," BOB DYLAN
1   "One," THREE DOG NIGHT
2   "It Takes Two," MARVIN GAYE and KIM WESTON
3   "Quarter to Three," GARY "U.S." BONDS
4   "Four Strong Winds," IAN AND SYLVIA, NEIL YOUNG, BOBBY BARE
5   "Obviously Five Believers," BOB DYLAN
6   "Six O'Clock," THE LOVIN' SPOONFUL
7   "7 Rooms of Gloom," THE FOUR TOPS
8   "Eight Days a Week," THE BEATLES
9   "Riot in Cell Block No. 9," THE CLOVERS
10   "Tenth Avenue Freeze-Out," BRUCE SPRINGSTEEN
11   "7-11," GONE ALL STARS
12   "Twelve Thirty (Young Girls Are Coming to the Canyon)," THE MAMAS AND THE PAPAS
13   "13 Questions," SEATRAIN
14   "Number Fourteen," LOVE
15   "Fifteen Years Ago," CONWAY TWITTY
16   "Sweet Little Sixteen," CHUCK BERRY
17   "Seventeen," BOYD BENNETT AND HIS ROCKETS

18   "I'm Eighteen," ALICE COOPER
19   "19th Nervous Breakdown," THE ROLLING STONES
20   "20-75," WILLIE MITCHELL

-◄❚▶-

20 GREAT PARENTHETICAL THOUGHTS

All of these are actual chart records.

1   "Easy Comin' Out (Hard Goin' In)," WILLIAM BELL
2   "Free Me from My Freedom/Tie Me to a Tree (Handcuff Me)," BONNIE POINTER
3   "Don't Nobody Live Here (By the Name of Fool)," DENISE LASALLE
4   "Jackie Wilson Said (I'm in Heaven When You Smile)," VAN MORRISON
5   "(If Loving You Is Wrong) I Don't Want to Be Right," LUTHER INGRAM
6   "(For God's Sake) Give More Power to the People," THE CHI-LITES
7   "I Never Loved a Man (The Way I Love You)," ARETHA FRANKLIN
8   "It's Only Rock and Roll (But I Like It)," THE ROLLING STONES
9   "My My Hey Hey (Out of the Blue)"/"Hey Hey My My (Into the Black)," NEIL YOUNG
10   "Most Likely You Go Your Way (And I'll Go Mine)," BOB DYLAN
11   "I Don't Want Nobody to Give Me Nothing (Open Up the Door, I'll Get It Myself) (Part 1)," JAMES BROWN
12   "The Shoop Shoop Song (It's in His Kiss)," BETTY EVERETT
13   "Without the One You Love (Life's Not Worth While)," THE FOUR TOPS
14   "Inner City Blues (Make Me Wanna Holler)," MARVIN GAYE
15   "(Your Love Keeps Lifting Me) Higher and Higher," JACKIE WILSON

16 "Life during Wartime (This Ain't No Party . . . This Ain't No Disco . . . This Ain't No Foolin' Around)," TALKING HEADS
17 "Your Good Thing (Is about to End)," MABLE JOHN
18 "Uptight (Everything's Alright)," STEVIE WONDER
19 "Ain't Gonna Bump No More (With No Big Fat Woman)," JOE TEX
20 "Sittin' on a Time Bomb (Waitin' for the Hurt to Come)," THE HONEY CONE

-◄▮▶-

THE 20 GREATEST PARTY RECORDS

1 "Having a Party," SAM COOKE
2 "Dancing in the Street," MARTHA AND THE VANDELLAS
3 "Reelin' and Rockin'," CHUCK BERRY
4 "Quarter to Three," GARY "U.S." BONDS
5 "Jailhouse Rock," ELVIS PRESLEY
6 "C'mon Everybody," EDDIE COCHRAN
7 "Ain't Nothin' but a House Party," THE SHOW STOPPERS
8 "Rip It Up," LITTLE RICHARD
9 "Wang Dang Doodle," KOKO TAYLOR
10 "Livin' for the Weekend," THE O'JAYS
11 "Good Rockin' Tonight," ELVIS PRESLEY
12 "Wild Night," VAN MORRISON
13 "Let the Good Times Roll," SHIRLEY AND LEE
14 "Seven Day Weekend," GARY "U.S." BONDS
15 "Let's Go, Let's Go, Let's Go," HANK BALLARD AND THE MIDNIGHTERS
16 "Tear the Roof Off the Sucker (Give Up the Funk)," PARLIAMENT
17 "We're an American Band," GRAND FUNK RAILROAD
18 "Born to Be Wild," STEPPENWOLF
19 "Splish Splash," BOBBY DARIN
20 "I Want to Take You Higher," SLY AND THE FAMILY STONE

WORST PARTIES ON RECORD

1 "Party Lights," CLAUDINE CLARK
2 "Happy Birthday," THE TUNE WEAVERS
3 "It's My Party," LESLEY GORE
4 "The Tracks of My Tears," THE MIRACLES
5 "Across the Street," LENNY O'HENRY
6 "The Wallflower," ETTA JAMES
7 "I Don't Want to Spoil the Party," THE BEATLES
8 "Get Off of My Cloud," THE ROLLING STONES

-◄❙▮❙►-

RAINY DAYS AND MONDAYS

1 "Crying in the Rain," THE EVERLY BROTHERS
2 "Early Morning Rain," GORDON LIGHTFOOT
3 "Have You Ever Seen the Rain," CREEDENCE CLEARWATER
   REVIVAL
4 "I Wish It Would Rain," THE TEMPTATIONS
5 "It Might as Well Rain until September," CAROLE KING
6 "Just Walking in the Rain," THE PRISONAIRES
7 "Let It Rain," ERIC CLAPTON
8 "Rain," THE BEATLES
9 "Rain Dance," THE GUESS WHO
10 "Rain on the Roof," THE LOVIN' SPOONFUL
11 "Rainin' in My Heart," SLIM HARPO
12 "Raining in My Heart," BUDDY HOLLY
13 "Rains Came," THE SIR DOUGLAS QUINTET
14 "Rainy Day Women #12 & 35," Bob Dylan
15 "Rainy Night in Georgia," BROOK BENTON
16 "Rhapsody in the Rain," LOU CHRISTIE
17 "Rhythm of the Rain," THE CASCADES
18 "Walking in the Rain," THE RONETTES
19 "When It Rains, It Really Pours," BILLY "THE KID" EMERSON
20 "Who'll Stop the Rain," CREEDENCE CLEARWATER REVIVAL

REFLECTIONS

1   "Go to the Mirror Boy," THE WHO
2   "Inside Looking Out," THE ANIMALS
3   "I'll Be Your Mirror," THE VELVET UNDERGROUND
4   "Look at Yourself," URIAH HEEP
5   "Mirror Image," BLOOD, SWEAT, AND TEARS
6   "Mirror Man," CAPTAIN BEEFHEART
7   "Mirror of Love," THE KINKS
8   "Mirror Star," THE FABULOUS POODLES
9   "Nowhere to Run," MARTHA AND THE VANDELLAS
10 "Room Full of Mirrors," THE JIMI HENDRIX EXPERIENCE

-◄▮►-

GREAT SCIENCE-FICTION ROCK

1   "Bionic Man," THE FABULOUS POODLES
2   "Crown of Creation," THE JEFFERSON AIRPLANE
3   "CTA 102," THE BYRDS
4   "The Eggplant That Ate Chicago," DR. WEST'S MEDICINE SHOW AND JUNK BAND
5   "Flying Saucers Rock and Roll," BILLY LEE RILEY AND THE LITTLE GREEN MEN
6   "Here Come the Martian Martians," JONATHAN RICHMAN AND THE MODERN LOVERS
7   "I Love the Night," BLUE ÖYSTER CULT
8   "It Came Out of the Sky," CREEDENCE CLEARWATER REVIVAL
9   "King Kong," FRANK ZAPPA
10 "Looking Out My Back Door," CREEDENCE CLEARWATER REVIVAL
11 "Martian Hop," THE RAN-DELLS
12 "Mr. Spaceman," THE BYRDS
13 "Pure and Easy," THE WHO
14 "Purple People Eater," SHEB WOOLEY

15 "Rocket Man," ELTON JOHN
16 "Space Oddity," DAVID BOWIE
17 "Supersonic Rocket Ship," THE KINKS
18 "Telstar," THE TORNADOES
19 "This Time Tomorrow," THE KINKS
20 "2000 Light Years from Home," THE ROLLING STONES

7 COME 11

1 "7 and 7 Is," LOVE
2 "7 Day Fool," ETTA JAMES
3 "7 Day Weekend," GARY "U.S." BONDS
4 "7 Days," CLYDE McPHATTER
5 "7-11," GONE ALL STARS
6 "7 Letters," BEN E. KING
7 "7 Little Girls Sitting in the Back Seat," PAUL EVANS
8 "7 Minutes to Heaven," THE PONI-TAILS
9 "7 Rooms of Gloom," THE FOUR TOPS
10 "7 Years," THE IMPRESSIONS
11 "7th Son," JOHNNY RIVERS

HERE COMES THE SUN

1 "Ain't No Sunshine," BILL WITHERS
2 "Don't Let the Sun Catch You Crying," GERRY AND THE PACEMAKERS
3 "Don't Let the Sun Go Down on Me," ELTON JOHN
4 "Good Day Sunshine," THE BEATLES
5 "Here Comes the Sun," THE BEATLES
6 "I'll Follow the Sun," THE BEATLES
7 "Please Mr. Sun," TOMMY EDWARDS
8 "Red Rubber Ball," THE CYRKLE
9 "Sun," THE DELL-VIKINGS

10   "The Sun King," THE BEATLES
11   "The Sunshine of Your Love," CREAM
12   "Sunny," BOBBY HEBB
13   "Sunny Afternoon," THE KINKS
14   "Sunny Skies," JAMES TAYLOR
15   "Under the Sun, Moon and Stars," JIMMY CLIFF

-◄❙▶-

BOB DALLEY PICKS THE TOP 10 SURF SONGS

1   "Wipe Out," THE SURFARIS
2   "Pipeline," THE CHANTAY'S
3   "Mr. Rebel," EDDIE AND THE SHOWMEN
4   "Goofy Foot," THE LIVELY ONES
5   "Penetration," THE PYRAMIDS
6   "Tall Cool One," THE MARKETTS
7   "Baja," THE ASTRONAUTS
8   "Golash," THE INTREPIDS
9   "Bustin' Surfboards," THE TORNADOES
10   "Let's Go Trippin'," DICK DALE AND HIS DEL-TONES

BOB DALLEY *writes about surf music for* Goldmine.

-◄❙▶-

THUMBS UP AND OUT

1   "Big Joe and Phantom 309," TOM WAITS
2   "Hitch Hike," MARVIN GAYE
3   "Hitchhiker's Hero," THE ATLANTA RHYTHM SECTION
4   "Kansas City," WILBERT HARRISON
5   "King of the Road," ROGER MILLER
6   "Me and Bobby McGee," JANIS JOPLIN
7   "Ridin' My Thumb to Mexico," JOHNNY RODRIGUEZ
8   "Sweet Hitch-Hiker," CREEDENCE CLEARWATER REVIVAL
9   "Take It Easy," THE EAGLES
10   "Yankee Lady," BREWER AND SHIPLEY

ON THE ROAD AGAIN
10 Famous Songs about Touring

1 "The Load-Out," JACKSON BROWNE
2 "Lodi," CREEDENCE CLEARWATER REVIVAL
3 "Postcard," THE WHO
4 "Sheraton Gibson," PETE TOWNSHEND
5 "Starfucker," THE ROLLING STONES
6 "Stay with Me," THE FACES
7 "Travellin' Band," CREEDENCE CLEARWATER REVIVAL
8 "Travellin' Man," RICKY NELSON
9 "Turn the Page," BOB SEGER
10 "We're an American Band," GRAND FUNK RAILROAD

-◄❙❙►-

GREAT SONGS ABOUT TRAINS

1 "Draw Your Brakes," SCOTTY
2 "Express," B. T. EXPRESS
3 "Hey, Porter," JOHNNY CASH
4 "It Takes a Lot to Laugh, It Takes a Train to Cry," BOB DYLAN
5 "Lonesome Train," ROBERT GORDON and LINK WRAY
6 "Love Train," THE O'JAYS
7 "Midnight Train to Georgia," GLADYS KNIGHT AND THE PIPS
8 "Mystery Train," ELVIS PRESLEY, LITTLE JUNIOR PARKER
9 "Night Train," JAMES BROWN
10 "People Get Ready," THE IMPRESSIONS
11 "Station Man," FLEETWOOD MAC
12 "Train Kept A-Rollin'," THE ROCK AND ROLL TRIO

THE WORLD THROUGH A WINDSHIELD
Truck Driving Anthems

1   "Convoy," C. W. McCall
2   "Detour," DUANE EDDY
3   "Detroit City," BOBBY BARE
4   "Diesel on My Tail," DEL REEVES, BUCK OWENS
5   "Drugstore Truck Drivin' Man," THE BYRDS
6   "Phantom of 309," TOM WAITS
7   "Six Days on the Road," DAVE DUDLEY
8   "30,000 Pounds of Bananas," HARRY CHAPIN
9   "Truckin'," THE GRATEFUL DEAD
10 "Wake Me, Shake Me," THE COASTERS
11 "White Line Fever," THE FLYING BURRITO BROTHERS
12 "Willin'," LITTLE FEAT

-◄❙❘►-

NOT FADE AWAY
Songs about Breaking Up

1   "Backstreets," BRUCE SPRINGSTEEN
2   "(Best Part of) Breakin' Up," THE RONETTES
3   "Break-Up," JERRY LEE LEWIS
4   "Break Up to Make Up," THE STYLISTICS
5   "Breaking Up Is Hard to Do," NEIL SEDAKA
6   "Bye Bye Love," THE EVERLY BROTHERS
7   "Come and Get These Memories," MARTHA AND THE VANDELLAS
8   "Goodbye Babe," THE CASTAWAYS
9   "Hats Off to Larry," DEL SHANNON
10 "High Fidelity," ELVIS COSTELLO
11 "I Can See for Miles," THE WHO
12 "(I Know) I'm Losing You," THE TEMPTATIONS
13 "Kiss Me Baby," THE BEACH BOYS

14   "Loan Me a Dime," BOZ SCAGGS
15   "Most Likely You Go Your Way and I'll Go Mine," BOB
     DYLAN
16   "Mr. Blue," THE FLEETWOODS
17   "Suspicious Minds," ELVIS PRESLEY
18   "There Goes My Baby," THE DRIFTERS
19   "Time Is on My Side," THE ROLLING STONES
20   "Tragic," THE SHEPPARDS
21   "Walk Away Renee," THE LEFT BANKE
22   "Where Did Our Love Go," THE SUPREMES
23   "You Keep Me Hangin' On," THE SUPREMES
24   "You're Gonna Miss Me," THE 13TH FLOOR ELEVATORS
25   "You've Lost That Lovin' Feelin'," THE RIGHTEOUS
     BROTHERS

-◄❚▶-

GOODNIGHT SONGS

1   "Goodnight," THE BEATLES
2   "Goodnight Irene," JERRY LEE LEWIS
3   "Goodnight My Love," JESSE BELVIN
4   "Goodnight Sweetheart, Goodnight," THE FLAMINGOS
5   "Goodnite Sweetheart Goodnite," THE SPANIELS
6   "I Don't Want to Go Home," SOUTHSIDE JOHNNY AND THE
     ASBURY JUKES
7   "See You Later, Alligator," BILL HALEY AND HIS COMETS
8   "Thank You and Goodnight," THE ANGELS
9   "Turn Off the Light," TEDDY PENDERGRASS
10   "Wake Up Little Susie," THE EVERLY BROTHERS

THIRTY-THREE:
TOP OF THE POPS

The legendary Drifters had many hits besides "On Broadway" including "Save the Last Dance for Me" (1960), "Up On the Roof" (1963), and "Under the Boardwalk" (1964).

For the authors, one of the great incentives in a project such as The Book of Rock Lists is the opportunity to inflict on the unsuspecting reader personal opinions about the greatest and most essential records of all time. We were preparing a list of 100 essential albums and a similar number of singles when it dawned on us that picking between Lesley Gore's "It's My Party" and "Farmer John" by The Premiers for the 100th best single was not just silly, it was a symptom of insanity. Therefore, we chose to do something even crazier. What you are about to read is a list of not 100 but 1000 crucial rock and roll singles—and about 600 albums.

These selections are meant to serve as a bottom line of the best that is available in the kinds of music represented in The Book of Rock Lists. The criteria for inclusion are spelled out in the introductions to each of this chapter's two sections. These criteria are, we realize, inadequate (especially in the case of albums), but we needed some objective base to keep us from diving totally off the deep end. Those who have read the morass of information contained in this volume will naturally understand that the omission of Never Mind the Bollocks, Here's The Sex Pistols is ultimately trivial, since every rational man and woman of our times has already purchased this classic, or made an equally objective decision not to. These lists are for you pikers out there with a single shelf of records; now you know what those of us whose collections dominate our living rooms, bedrooms, and occasionally, kitchen walls go through every day.

ORIGINAL ALL-TIME GREATEST TOP 40 HITS

The following lists represent the cream of the crop of the Top For singles of the rock and roll era, 1955-1980—forty records per year, except for 1955, when things got started rather slowly, wit cover battles and pop banality dominating what little primordia rock and R&B actually showed up. The rankings, of course, represent the subjective judgment of the editors as to the relative *merits of these records, artistically and historically. Though the editors are familiar with watching angels dance on pinheads, the rankings are obviously not meant to be absolute: It is for someone more enlightened than we to determine the empirical criteria by which it might be finally ascertained that The Jarmels' "A Little Bit of Soap" is really one notch better than Bobby Bland's "Turn on Your Love Light," though both are quite clearly superior to, say, The Dovells' "Bristol Stomp." Get the picture?* Yes we see.

Volume 1   1955

1 "Tutti-Frutti," LITTLE RICHARD
2 "Maybellene," CHUCK BERRY
3 "Speedoo," THE CADILLACS
4 "When You Dance," THE TURBANS
5 "Black Denim Trousers," THE CHEERS
6 "I Hear You Knocking," SMILEY LEWIS
7 "Rock around the Clock," BILL HALEY AND HIS COMETS
8 "The Great Pretender," THE PLATTERS
9 "At My Front Door," THE EL DORADOS
10 "Only You (And You Alone)," THE PLATTERS
11 "See You Later Alligator," BILL HALEY AND HIS COMETS
12 "Sixteen Tons," TENNESSEE ERNIE FORD
13 "My Boy Flat-Top," BOYD BENNETT AND HIS ROCKETS
14 "Teen Age Prayer," GLORIA MANN
15 "Cry Me a River," JULIE LONDON
16 "Daddy-O," BONNIE LOU
17 "Burn That Candle," BILL HALEY AND HIS COMETS
18 "He," AL HIBBLER
19 "Nuttin for Christmas," JOE WARD
20 "April in Paris," COUNT BASIE

Volume 2—1956

1 "Heartbreak Hotel," ELVIS PRESLEY
2 "Roll over Beethoven," CHUCK BERRY
3 "Fever," LITTLE WILLIE JOHN

4   "Rip It Up," LITTLE RICHARD
5   "Blue Suede Shoes," CARL PERKINS
6   "I'm in Love Again"/"My Blue Heaven," FATS DOMINO
7   "Love Is Strange," MICKEY AND SYLVIA
8   "Why Do Fools Fall in Love," FRANKIE LYMON AND THE TEENAGERS
9   "Be-Bop-A-Lula," GENE VINCENT AND HIS BLUE CAPS
10   "In the Still of the Nite," FIVE SATINS
11   "Don't Be Cruel"/"Hound Dog," ELVIS PRESLEY
12   "Blue Monday," FATS DOMINO
13   "Long Tall Sally"/"Slippin' and Slidin'," LITTLE RICHARD
14   "Stranded in the Jungle," THE CADETS
15   "Let the Good Times Roll," SHIRLEY AND LEE
16   "Since I Met You Baby," IVORY JOE HUNTER
17   "Blueberry Hill," FATS DOMINO
18   "Jim Dandy," LaVERN BAKER
19   "I'll Be Home," THE FLAMINGOS
20   "My Prayer," THE PLATTERS
21   "When My Blue Moon Turns to Gold Again," ELVIS PRESLEY
22   "Honky Tonk (Parts 1 & 2)," BILL DOGGETT
23   "When My Dreamboat Comes Home," FATS DOMINO
24   "Treasure of Love," CLYDE McPHATTER
25   "I Want You, I Need You, I Love You," ELVIS PRESLEY
26   "One in a Million," THE PLATTERS
27   "Love, Love, Love," THE CLOVERS
28   "I Want You to Be My Girl," FRANKIE LYMON AND THE TEENAGERS
29   "My Baby Left Me," ELVIS PRESLEY
30   "Born to Be with You," THE CHORDETTES
31   "Eddie My Love," THE TEEN QUEENS
32   "Ivory Tower," OTIS WILLIAMS
33   "I Walk the Line," JOHNNY CASH
34   "The Flying Saucer (Parts 1 and 2)," BUCHANAN AND GOODMAN
35   "See Saw," THE MOONGLOWS
36   "Seven Days," CLYDE McPHATTER

37   "Singing the Blues," GUY MITCHELL
38   "Out of Sight, Out of Mind," THE FIVE KEYS
39   "Transfusion," NERVOUS NORVUS
40   "Young Love," SONNY JAMES

Volume 3—1957

1   "Whole Lot of Shakin' Going On," JERRY LEE LEWIS
2   "That'll Be the Day," THE CRICKETS
3   "School Day," CHUCK BERRY
4   "Jailhouse Rock," ELVIS PRESLEY
5   "Peggy Sue," BUDDY HOLLY
6   "Little Darlin'," THE DIAMONDS
7   "Great Balls of Fire," JERRY LEE LEWIS
8   "You Send Me," SAM COOKE
9   "Keep a Knockin'," LITTLE RICHARD
10   "Searchin' "/"Young Blood," THE COASTERS
11   "Come Go with Me," THE DELL-VIKINGS
12   "C.C. Rider," CHUCK WILLIS
13   "Oh Boy!" THE CRICKETS
14   "Lucille," LITTLE RICHARD
15   "The Stroll," THE DIAMONDS
16   "Without Love (There Is Nothing)," CLYDE McPHATTER
17   "I'm Walkin'," FATS DOMINO
18   "All Shook Up," ELVIS PRESLEY
19   "Rock and Roll Music," CHUCK BERRY
20   "Jenny, Jenny," LITTLE RICHARD
21   "Wake Up, Little Susie," THE EVERLY BROTHERS
22   "Little Bitty Pretty One," THURSTON HARRIS
23   "Tonite, Tonite," THE MELLO-KINGS
24   "Susie-Q," DALE HAWKINS
25   "Bye Bye Love," THE EVERLY BROTHERS
26   "Let Me Be Your Teddy Bear," ELVIS PRESLEY
27   "Party Doll," BUDDY KNOX
28   "At the Hop," DANNY AND THE JUNIORS
29   "Silhouettes," THE RAYS

30   "Jingle Bell Rock," BOBBY HELMS
31   "Stood Up," RICKY NELSON
32   "Sittin' in the Balcony," EDDIE COCHRAN
33   "Bony Moronie," LARRY WILLIAMS
34   "Too Much," ELVIS PRESLEY
35   "Tear Drops," LEE ANDREWS AND THE HEARTS
36   "Mr. Lee," THE BOBBETTES
37   "You Can Make It if You Try," GENE ALLISON
38   "Raunchy," BILL JUSTIS
39   "Short Fat Fannie," LARRY WILLIAMS
40   "Lotta Lovin'," GENE VINCENT AND HIS BLUE CAPS

Volume 4—1958

1   "Johnny B. Goode," CHUCK BERRY
2   "Little Star," THE ELEGANTS
3   "For Your Precious Love," JERRY BUTLER AND THE
      IMPRESSIONS
4   "Rave On," BUDDY HOLLY
5   "Maybe," THE CHANTELS
6   "Good Golly, Miss Molly," LITTLE RICHARD
7   "Yakety Yak," THE COASTERS
8   "Rumble," LINK WRAY AND HIS RAY MEN
9   "Lonely Teardrops," JACKIE WILSON
10   "Carol," CHUCK BERRY
11   "Summertime Blues," EDDIE COCHRAN
12   "The Book of Love," THE MONOTONES
13   "Hang Up My Rock and Roll Shoes," CHUCK WILLIS
14   "Maybe Baby," THE CRICKETS
15   "Rock and Roll Is Here to Stay," DANNY AND THE JUNIORS
16   "Endless Sleep," JODY REYNOLDS
17   "Sweet Little Sixteen," CHUCK BERRY
18   "It's Only Make Believe," CONWAY TWITTY
19   "La Bamba," RITCHIE VALENS
20   "Stagger Lee," LLOYD PRICE
21   "Wear My Ring around Your Neck," ELVIS PRESLEY

22   "C'mon Everybody," EDDIE COCHRAN
23   "Willie and the Hand Jive," JOHNNY OTIS
24   "I Wonder Why," DION AND THE BELMONTS
25   "High School Confidential," JERRY LEE LEWIS
26   "Rebel-'Rouser," DUANE EDDY
27   "Ten Commandments of Love," THE MOONGLOWS
28   "Talk to Me, Talk to Me," LITTLE WILLIE JOHN
29   "Rockin' Robin," BOBBY DAY
30   "Tears on My Pillow," LITTLE ANTHONY AND THE IMPERIALS
31   "Whole Lotta Lovin'," FATS DOMINO
32   "Charlie Brown," THE COASTERS
33   "Don't You Just Know It," HUEY "PIANO" SMITH AND THE
      CLOWNS
34   "A Lover's Question," CLYDE MCPHATTER
35   "What Am I Living For," CHUCK WILLIS
36   "Get a Job," THE SILHOUETTES
37   "We Belong Together," ROBERT AND JOHNNY
38   "I Cried a Tear," LAVERN BAKER
39   "Do You Want to Dance," BOBBY FREEMAN
40   "Bird Dog"/"Devoted to You," THE EVERLY BROTHERS

Volume 5—1959

1   "What'd I Say," RAY CHARLES
2   "There Goes My Baby," THE DRIFTERS
3   "Back in the U.S.A.," CHUCK BERRY
4   "Sea Cruise," FRANKIE FORD
5   "Kansas City," WILBERT HARRISON
6   "Almost Grown," CHUCK BERRY
7   "A Teenager in Love," DION AND THE BELMONTS
8   "Say Man," BO DIDDLEY
9   "That's Why (I Love You So)," JACKIE WILSON
10   "Love Potion No. 9," THE CLOVERS
11   "I'm Ready," FATS DOMINO
12   "Dance with Me," THE DRIFTERS
13   "Hushabye," THE MYSTICS

14 "Come Softly to Me," THE FLEETWOODS
15 "Red River Rock," JOHNNY AND THE HURRICANES
16 "Dream Lover," BOBBY DARIN
17 "Mary Lou," RONNIE HAWKINS
18 "Since I Don't Have You," THE SKYLINERS
19 "Sweet Nothin's," BRENDA LEE
20 "Raw-Hide," LINK WRAY AND HIS RAY MEN
21 "I Only Have Eyes for You," THE FLAMINGOS
22 "It Doesn't Matter Anymore," BUDDY HOLLY
23 "I Want to Walk You Home"/"I'm Gonna Be a Wheel Some Day," FATS DOMINO
24 "So Fine," THE FIESTAS
25 "Everybody Likes to Cha Cha Cha," SAM COOKE
26 "Where or When," DION AND THE BELMONTS
27 "Tall Cool One," THE WAILERS
28 "('Til) I Kissed You," THE EVERLY BROTHERS
29 "Mr. Blue," THE FLEETWOODS
30 "Talk That Talk," JACKIE WILSON
31 "Sleep Walk," SANTO AND JOHNNY
32 "You Got What It Takes," MARV JOHNSON
33 "(Now and Then There's) A Fool Such as I," ELVIS PRESLEY
34 "Personality," LLOYD PRICE
35 "Only Sixteen," SAM COOKE
36 "Shimmy, Shimmy, Ko-Ko-Bop," LITTLE ANTHONY AND THE IMPERIALS
37 "(If You Cry) True Love, True Love," THE DRIFTERS
38 "You're So Fine," THE FALCONS
39 "Sea of Love," PHIL PHILLIPS WITH THE TWILIGHTS
40 "Mack the Knife," BOBBY DARIN

Volume 6—1960

1 "Stay," MAURICE WILLIAMS AND THE ZODIACS
2 "Only the Lonely (Know How I Feel)," ROY ORBISON

3   "Money (That's What I Want)," BARRETT STRONG
4   "Will You Love Me Tomorrow," THE SHIRELLES
5   "New Orleans," GARY "U.S." BONDS
6   "This Magic Moment," THE DRIFTERS
7   "He Will Break Your Heart," JERRY BUTLER
8   "Walking to New Orleans"/"Don't Come Knockin'," FATS
     DOMINO
9   "Are You Lonesome Tonight?" ELVIS PRESLEY
10   "A Thousand Stars," KATHY YOUNG with THE INNOCENTS
11   "Baby What You Want Me to Do," JIMMY REED
12   "Save the Last Dance for Me," THE DRIFTERS
13   "I Count the Tears," THE DRIFTERS
14   "Doggin' Around," JACKIE WILSON
15   "Shop Around," THE MIRACLES
16   "Georgia on My Mind," RAY CHARLES
17   "Lonely Weekends," CHARLIE RICH
18   "Fannie Mae," BUSTER BROWN
19   "A Fool in Love," IKE AND TINA TURNER
20   "Think," JAMES BROWN
21   "Wonderful World," SAM COOKE
22   "Mountain of Love," HAROLD DORMAN
23   "Lonely Teenager," DION
24   "Sleep," LITTLE WILLIE JOHN
25   "There's Something on Your Mind, Part 2," BOBBY MARCHAN
26   "Ooh Poo Pah Doo—Part II," JESSIE HILL
27   "The Twist," CHUBBY CHECKER
28   "I'm Sorry," BRENDA LEE
29   "Tonight's the Night," THE SHIRELLES
30   "Cathy's Clown," THE EVERLY BROTHERS
31   "I'm Hurtin'," ROY ORBISON
32   "My Girl Josephine," FATS DOMINO
33   "Rockin' around the Christmas Tree," BRENDA LEE
34   "Finger Poppin' Time," HANK BALLARD AND THE
     MIDNIGHTERS
35   "Burning Bridges," JACK SCOTT

36   "Alley-Oop," THE HOLLYWOOD ARGYLES
37   "Chain Gang," SAM COOKE
38   "You Talk Too Much," JOE JONES
39   "Walk—Don't Run," THE VENTURES
40   "Angel Baby," ROSIE AND THE ORIGINALS

Volume 7—1961

1   "Stand by Me," BEN E. KING
2   "The Wanderer," DION
3   "Quarter to Three," GARY "U.S." BONDS
4   "Running Scared," ROY ORBISON
5   "Runaway," DEL SHANNON
6   "Hit the Road Jack," RAY CHARLES
7   "Spanish Harlem," BEN E. KING
8   "Gypsy Woman," THE IMPRESSIONS
9   "It's Gonna Work Out Fine," IKE AND TINA TURNER
10   "Please Mr. Postman," THE MARVELETTES
11   "But I Do," CLARENCE "FROG MAN" HENRY
12   "Travelin' Man"/"Hello Mary Lou," RICKY NELSON
13   "Mother-in-Law," ERNIE K-DOE
14   "Let the Four Winds Blow," FATS DOMINO
15   "A Little Bit of Soap," THE JARMELS
16   "Turn on Your Love Light," BOBBY BLAND
17   "Mama Said," THE SHIRELLES
18   "Cupid," SAM COOKE
19   "Little Egypt (Ying-Yang)," THE COASTERS
20   "There's No Other (Like My Baby)," THE CRYSTALS
21   "School Is Out," GARY "U.S." BONDS
22   "Ya Ya," LEE DORSEY
23   "Daddy's Home," SHEP AND THE LIMELITES
24   "Runaround Sue," DION
25   "I Like It like That, Part 1," CHRIS KENNER
26   "The Mountain's High," DICK AND DEE DEE

27 "I Don't Want to Cry," CHUCK JACKSON
28 "Last Night," THE MAR-KEYS
29 "Gee Whiz (Look at His Eyes)," CARLA THOMAS
30 "Hide Away," FREDDY KING
31 "Marie's the Name His Latest Flame"/"Little Sister," ELVIS PRESLEY
32 "Every Beat of My Heart," GLADYS KNIGHT AND THE PIPS
33 "(I Wanna) Love My Life Away," GENE PITNEY
34 "Bristol Stomp," THE DOVELLS
35 "Barbara-Ann," THE REGENTS
36 "My True Story," THE JIVE FIVE
37 "Peppermint Twist—Part 1," JOEY DEE AND THE STARLITERS
38 "I Know (You Don't Love Me No More)," BARBARA GEORGE
39 "Dedicated to the One I Love," THE SHIRELLES
40 "Let's Twist Again," CHUBBY CHECKER

Volume 8—1962

1 "The Loco-Motion," LITTLE EVA
2 "Up on the Roof," THE DRIFTERS
3 "Twist and Shout," THE ISLEY BROTHERS
4 "Duke of Earl," GENE CHANDLER
5 "He's a Rebel," THE CRYSTALS
6 "Having a Party," SAM COOKE
7 "Party Lights," CLAUDINE CLARK
8 "I'll Try Something New," THE MIRACLES
9 "Do You Love Me," THE CONTOURS
10 "You Really Got a Hold on Me," THE MIRACLES
11 "Big Girls Don't Cry," THE FOUR SEASONS
12 "Green Onions," BOOKER T. AND THE MG'S
13 "He's Sure the Boy I Love," THE CRYSTALS
14 "Twistin' the Night Away," SAM COOKE
15 "Lovers Who Wander," DION
16 "Bring It on Home to Me," SAM COOKE
17 "You Beat Me to the Punch," MARY WELLS

18   "Soul Twist," KING CURTIS
19   "Wild Weekend," THE REBELS
20   "Night Train," JAMES BROWN
21   "Return to Sender," ELVIS PRESLEY
22   "Soldier Boy," THE SHIRELLES
23   "Uptown," THE CRYSTALS
24   "What's So Good about Good-by," THE MIRACLES
25   "Tell Him," THE EXCITERS
26   "Jamie," EDDIE HOLLAND
27   "You'll Lose a Good Thing," BARBARA LYNN
28   "It Might as Well Rain until September," CAROLE KING
29   "Don't Make Me Over," DIONNE WARWICK
30   "Seven Day Weekend," GARY "U.S." BONDS
31   "Village of Love," NATHANIEL MAYER
32   "Half Heaven—Half Heartache," GENE PITNEY
33   "I Need Your Loving," DON GARDNER AND DEE DEE FORD
34   "Beechwood 4-5789," THE MARVELETTES
35   "I Can't Stop Loving You," RAY CHARLES
36   "Don't Play That Song (You Lied)," BEN E. KING
37   "Lover Please," CLYDE MCPHATTER
38   "What's Your Name?" DON AND JUAN
39   "Any Day Now (My Wild Beautiful Bird)," CHUCK JACKSON
40   "Something's Got a Hold on Me," ETTA JAMES

Volume 9—1963

1   "Da Doo Ron Ron," THE CRYSTALS
2   "He's So Fine," THE CHIFFONS
3   "Louie Louie," THE KINGSMEN
4   "Be My Baby," THE RONETTES
5   "Prisoner of Love," JAMES BROWN
6   "On Broadway," THE DRIFTERS
7   "Surfin' Bird," THE TRASHMEN
8   "Heat Wave," MARTHA AND THE VANDELLAS
9   "Shut Down"/"Surfin' U.S.A.," THE BEACH BOYS

10   "One Fine Day," THE CHIFFONS
11   "Then He Kissed Me," THE CRYSTALS
12   "(Today I Met) The Boy I'm Gonna Marry," DARLENE LOVE
13   "Fingertips—Pt. 2," STEVIE WONDER
14   "Donna the Prima Donna," DION
15   "Baby, I Love You," THE RONETTES
16   "Sally, Go 'Round the Roses," THE JAYNETTES
17   "The Monkey Time," MAJOR LANCE
18   "Another Saturday Night," SAM COOKE
19   "Foolish Little Girl," THE SHIRELLES
20   "Can I Get a Witness," MARVIN GAYE
21   "Baby Work Out," JACKIE WILSON
22   "Mama Didn't Lie," JAN BRADLEY
23   "Pipeline," THE CHANTAY'S
24   "Walking the Dog," RUFUS THOMAS
25   "Be True to Your School"/"In My Room," THE BEACH BOYS
26   "Why Do Lovers Break Each Other's Hearts," BOBB B. SOXX
     AND THE BLUE JEANS
27   "Hello Stranger," BARBARA LEWIS
28   "You Don't Own Me," LESLEY GORE
29   "Just One Look," DORIS TROY
30   "I Will Follow Him," LITTLE PEGGY MARCH
31   "Hitch Hike," MARVIN GAYE
32   "Surf City," JAN AND DEAN
33   "What Kind of Fool (Do You Think I Am)," THE TAMS
34   "Don't Say Nothin' Bad (About My Baby)," THE COOKIES
35   "My Boyfriend's Back," THE ANGELS
36   "Twenty Four Hours from Tulsa," GENE PITNEY
37   "That's the Way Love Is," BOBBY BLAND
38   "Wipe Out," THE SURFARIS
39   "Walk Like a Man," THE FOUR SEASONS
40   "Killer Joe," THE ROCKY FELLERS

Volume 10—1964

1 "You've Lost That Lovin' Feelin'," THE RIGHTEOUS BROTHERS
2 "She Loves You," THE BEATLES
3 "I Get Around"/"Don't Worry Baby," THE BEACH BOYS
4 "Baby Love," THE SUPREMES
5 "Leader of the Pack," THE SHANGRI-LAS
6 "Under the Boardwalk," THE DRIFTERS
7 "Dancing in the Street," MARTHA AND THE VANDELLAS
8 "I Want to Hold Your Hand"/"I Saw Her Standing There," THE BEATLES
9 "Where Did Our Love Go," THE SUPREMES
10 "Time Is on My Side," THE ROLLING STONES
11 "The House of the Rising Sun," THE ANIMALS
12 "Goin' Out of My Head," LITTLE ANTHONY AND THE IMPERIALS
13 "You Really Got Me," THE KINKS
14 "Fun, Fun, Fun," THE BEACH BOYS
15 "Walking in the Rain," THE RONETTES
16 "Every Little Bit Hurts," BRENDA HOLLOWAY
17 "Keep on Pushing," THE IMPRESSIONS
18 "Chapel of Love," THE DIXIE CUPS
19 "Sha La La," MANFRED MANN
20 "Oh, Pretty Woman," ROY ORBISON
21 "Dead Man's Curve," JAN AND DEAN
22 "The Shoop Shoop Song (It's in His Kiss)," BETTY EVERETT
23 "All Day and All of the Night," THE KINKS
24 "My Guy," MARY WELLS
25 "The Way You Do the Things You Do," THE TEMPTATIONS
26 "Hold What You've Got," JOE TEX
27 "You Never Can Tell," CHUCK BERRY
28 "Ain't Nothing You Can Do," BOBBY BLAND
29 "Out of Sight," JAMES BROWN
30 "Remember (Walkin' in the Sand)," THE SHANGRI-LAS
31 "I Only Want to Be with You," DUSTY SPRINGFIELD

32   "Baby I Need Your Loving," THE FOUR TOPS
33   "Viva Las Vegas," ELVIS PRESLEY
34   "Keep Searchin' (We'll Follow the Sun)," DEL SHANNON
35   "Do Wah Diddy Diddy," MANFRED MANN
36   "When You Walk in the Room," THE SEARCHERS
37   "She's Not There," THE ZOMBIES
38   "Farmer John," THE PREMIERS
39   "Hi-Heel Sneakers," TOMMY TUCKER
40   "Tobacco Road," THE NASHVILLE TEENS

Volume 11—1965

1   "(I Can't Get No) Satisfaction," THE ROLLING STONES
2   "Like a Rolling Stone," BOB DYLAN
3   "A Change Is Gonna Come"/"Shake," SAM COOKE
4   "Ticket to Ride," THE BEATLES
5   "In the Midnight Hour," WILSON PICKETT
6   "Papa's Got a Brand New Bag—Part 1," JAMES BROWN
7   "The Tracks of My Tears," SMOKEY ROBINSON AND THE
      MIRACLES
8   "Positively 4th Street," BOB DYLAN
9   "Get Off of My Cloud," THE ROLLING STONES
10   "Mr. Tambourine Man," THE BYRDS
11   "My Girl," THE TEMPTATIONS
12   "It's My Life," THE ANIMALS
13   "Stop! In the Name of Love," THE SUPREMES
14   "Land of 1000 Dances," CANNIBAL AND THE HEADHUNTERS
15   "Uptight (Everything's Alright)," STEVIE WONDER
16   "Help Me, Rhonda," THE BEACH BOYS
17   "Day Tripper"/"We Can Work It Out," THE BEATLES
18   "Nowhere to Run," MARTHA AND THE VANDELLAS
19   "Do You Believe in Magic," THE LOVIN' SPOONFUL
20   "Ooo Baby Baby," SMOKEY ROBINSON AND THE MIRACLES
21   "Tired of Waiting for You," THE KINKS
22   "For Your Love," THE YARDBIRDS

23   "Jenny Take a Ride," MITCH RYDER AND THE DETROIT WHEELS
24   "Wooly Bully," SAM THE SHAM AND THE PHARAOHS
25   "I've Been Loving You Too Long (To Stop Now)," OTIS REDDING
26   "Crying in the Chapel," ELVIS PRESLEY
27   "Shotgun," JR. WALKER AND THE ALL STARS
28   "People Get Ready," THE IMPRESSIONS
29   "Help!" THE BEATLES
30   "I Can't Help Myself," THE FOUR TOPS
31   "Rescue Me," FONTELLA BASS
32   "Hurt So Bad," LITTLE ANTHONY AND THE IMPERIALS
33   "She's about a Mover," THE SIR DOUGLAS QUINTET
34   "I'll Be Doggone," MARVIN GAYE
35   "We Gotta Get Out of This Place," THE ANIMALS
36   "Lies," THE KNICKERBOCKERS
37   "Shakin' All Over," THE GUESS WHO
38   "New York's a Lonely Town," THE TRADE WINDS
39   "Here Comes the Night," THEM
40   "Since I Lost My Baby," THE TEMPTATIONS

Volume 12—1966

1   "Reach Out I'll Be There," THE FOUR TOPS
2   "Try a Little Tenderness," OTIS REDDING
3   "When a Man Loves a Woman," PERCY SLEDGE
4   "Hold On! I'm a-Coming," SAM AND DAVE
5   "Gimme Some Lovin'," THE SPENCER DAVIS GROUP
6   "96 Tears," ? AND THE MYSTERIANS
7   "It's a Man's, Man's, Man's World," JAMES BROWN
8   "19th Nervous Breakdown," THE ROLLING STONES
9   "I Fought the Law," THE BOBBY FULLER FOUR
10   "Devil with a Blue Dress On"/"Good Golly Miss Molly," MITCH RYDER AND THE DETROIT WHEELS
11   "Good Lovin'," THE YOUNG RASCALS
12   "Knock on Wood," EDDIE FLOYD

13   "I'm Your Puppet," JAMES AND BOBBY PURIFY
14   "I Want You," BOB DYLAN
15   "Hungry," PAUL REVERE AND THE RAIDERS
16   "Summer in the City," THE LOVIN' SPOONFUL
17   "Pretty Flamingo," MANFRED MANN
18   "Mustang Sally," WILSON PICKETT
19   "Ain't Too Proud to Beg," THE TEMPTATIONS
20   "Have You Seen Your Mother, Baby, Standing in the
     Shadow," THE ROLLING STONES
21   "(I'm a) Road Runner," JR. WALKER AND THE ALL STARS
22   "You Keep Me Hangin' On," THE SUPREMES
23   "Paperback Writer," THE BEATLES
24   "Holy Cow," LEE DORSEY
25   "Gloria," THE SHADOWS OF KNIGHT
26   "Walk Away Renee," THE LEFT BANKE
27   "Psychotic Reaction," COUNT FIVE
28   "Double Shot (of My Baby's Love)," THE SWINGIN'
     MEDALLIONS
29   "Barefootin'," ROBERT PARKER
30   "Cool Jerk," THE CAPITOLS
31   "What Becomes of the Broken Hearted," JIMMY RUFFIN
32   "Let's Go Get Stoned," RAY CHARLES
33   "This Old Heart of Mine (Is Weak for You)," THE ISLEY
     BROTHERS
34   "Eight Miles High," THE BYRDS
35   "Hey Joe," THE LEAVES
36   "Tell It Like It Is," AARON NEVILLE
37   "Love Makes the World Go Round," DEON JACKSON
38   "Don't Mess with Bill," THE MARVELETTES
39   "Talk Talk," MUSIC MACHINE
40   "Stop Stop Stop," THE HOLLIES

Volume 13—1967

1 "Respect," ARETHA FRANKLIN
2 "Soul Man," SAM AND DAVE
3 "I Can See for Miles," THE WHO
4 "Penny Lane"/"Strawberry Fields Forever," THE BEATLES
5 "(Your Love Keeps Lifting Me) Higher and Higher," JACKIE WILSON
6 "Sweet Soul Music," ARTHUR CONLEY
7 "I Heard It through the Grapevine," GLADYS KNIGHT AND THE PIPS
8 "Ruby Tuesday"/"Let's Spend the Night Together," THE ROLLING STONES
9 "Cold Sweat," JAMES BROWN
10 "Good Vibrations," THE BEACH BOYS
11 "I Never Loved a Man (The Way I Love You)," ARETHA FRANKLIN
12 "I Second That Emotion," SMOKEY ROBINSON AND THE MIRACLES
13 "The Letter," THE BOX TOPS
14 "Ain't No Mountain High Enough," MARVIN GAYE and TAMMI TERRELL
15 "Funky Broadway," WILSON PICKETT
16 "Soul Finger," THE BAR-KAYS
17 "For What It's Worth (Stop, Hey What's That Sound)," BUFFALO SPRINGFIELD
18 "The Hunter Gets Captured by the Game," THE MARVELETTES
19 "Brown Eyed Girl," VAN MORRISON
20 "Groovin'," THE YOUNG RASCALS
21 "Wild Honey," THE BEACH BOYS
22 "Chain of Fools," ARETHA FRANKLIN
23 "Tramp," OTIS REDDING and CARLA THOMAS
24 "I Found a Love—Part 1," WILSON PICKETT
25 "So You Want to Be a Rock 'n' Roll Star," THE BYRDS
26 "I Was Made to Love Her," STEVIE WONDER

27 "Expressway to Your Heart," SOUL SURVIVORS
28 "Boogaloo Down Broadway," FANTASTIC JOHNNY C
29 "The Love I Saw in You Was Just a Mirage," SMOKEY
    ROBINSON AND THE MIRACLES
30 "(You Make Me Feel like a) Natural Woman," ARETHA
    FRANKLIN
31 "A Whiter Shade of Pale," PROCOL HARUM
32 "Somebody to Love," THE JEFFERSON AIRPLANE
33 "Nobody but Me," THE HUMAN BEINZ
34 "Friday on My Mind," THE EASYBEATS
35 "Memphis Soul Stew," KING CURTIS
36 "When I Was Young," THE ANIMALS
37 "Judy in Disguise (With Glasses)," JOHN FRED AND HIS
    PLAYBOY BAND
38 "(I Wanna) Testify," PARLIAMENT
39 "Western Union," THE FIVE AMERICANS
40 "Light My Fire," THE DOORS

Volume 14—1968

1   "Jumpin' Jack Flash," THE ROLLING STONES
2   "Dance to the Music," SLY AND THE FAMILY STONE
3   "I Heard It Through the Grapevine," MARVIN GAYE
4   "Everyday People," SLY AND THE FAMILY STONE
5   "(Sittin' on) The Dock of the Bay," OTIS REDDING
6   "All along the Watchtower," JIMI HENDRIX
7   "People Got to Be Free," THE YOUNG RASCALS
8   "Magic Bus," THE WHO
9   "Hey Jude"/"Revolution," THE BEATLES
10 "Cry Like a Baby," THE BOX TOPS
11 "Abraham, Martin and John," DION
12 "Fire," THE CRAZY WORLD OF ARTHUR BROWN
13 "Never Give You Up," JERRY BUTLER
14 "I Wish It Would Rain," THE TEMPTATIONS
15 "Ain't Nothing Like the Real Thing," MARVIN GAYE and
    TAMMI TERRELL

16   "If I Can Dream," ELVIS PRESLEY
17   "I Thank You," SAM AND DAVE
18   "Mighty Quinn (Quinn the Eskimo)," MANFRED MANN
19   "There Is," THE DELLS
20   "Tighten Up," ARCHIE BELL AND THE DRELLS
21   "Ramblin' Gamblin' Man," BOB SEGER
22   "Who's Making Love," JOHNNIE TAYLOR
23   "Sunshine of Your Love," CREAM
24   "Hey, Western Union Man," JERRY BUTLER
25   "Son of a Preacher Man," DUSTY SPRINGFIELD
26   "Slip Away," CLARENCE CARTER
27   "Ain't No Way," ARETHA FRANKLIN
28   "Stay in My Corner," THE DELLS
29   "Love Child," DIANA ROSS AND THE SUPREMES
30   "La-La-Means I Love You," THE DELFONICS
31   "Do You Know the Way to San Jose," DIONNE WARWICK
32   "Cowboys to Girls," THE INTRUDERS
33   "The House That Jack Built," ARETHA FRANKLIN
34   "Born to Be Wild," STEPPENWOLF
35   "I Can't Stop Dancing," ARCHIE BELL AND THE DRELLS
36   "Midnight Confessions," THE GRASS ROOTS
37   "Angel of the Morning," MERRILEE RUSH
38   "Love Makes a Woman," BARBARA ACKLIN
39   "Hold Me Tight," JOHNNY NASH
40   "Yummy Yummy Yummy," THE OHIO EXPRESS

Volume 15—1969

1   "I Want You Back," THE JACKSON 5
2   "Suspicious Minds," ELVIS PRESLEY
3   "Bad Moon Rising," CREEDENCE CLEARWATER REVIVAL
4   "Honky Tonk Women," THE ROLLING STONES
5   "Only the Strong Survive," JERRY BUTLER
6   "Fortunate Son," CREEDENCE CLEARWATER REVIVAL
7   "Something in the Air," THUNDERCLAP NEWMAN
8   "The Thrill Is Gone," B. B. KING

9 "My Whole World Ended (The Moment You Left Me),"
   DAVID RUFFIN
10 "Hot Fun in the Summertime," SLY AND THE FAMILY STONE
11 "Pinball Wizard," THE WHO
12 "Proud Mary," CREEDENCE CLEARWATER REVIVAL
13 "Get Back"/"Don't Let Me Down," THE BEATLES
14 "Someday We'll Be Together," DIANA ROSS AND THE
   SUPREMES
15 "Build Me Up Buttercup," THE FOUNDATIONS
16 "I Can't Get Next to You," THE TEMPTATIONS
17 "It's Your Thing," THE ISLEY BROTHERS
18 "The Chokin' Kind," JOE SIMON
19 "Soul Deep," THE BOX TOPS
20 "Black Pearl," THE CHECKMATES LTD.
21 "Up on Cripple Creek," THE BAND
22 "The Ballad of John and Yoko," THE BEATLES
23 "What Does It Take (To Win Your Love)," JR. WALKER AND
   THE ALL STARS
24 "Friendship Train," GLADYS KNIGHT AND THE PIPS
25 "Too Busy Thinking about My Baby," MARVIN GAYE
26 "What's the Use of Breaking Up," JERRY BUTLER
27 "Polk Salad Annie," TONY JOE WHITE
28 "Backfield in Motion," MEL AND TIM
29 "Let a Woman Be a Woman—Let a Man Be a Man," DYKE
   AND THE BLAZERS
30 "Nothing but a Heartache," THE FLIRTATIONS
31 "My Cherie Amour," STEVIE WONDER
32 "Let's Work Together (Part 1)," WILBERT HARRISON
33 "Whole Lotta Love," LED ZEPPELIN
34 "I Can Hear Music," THE BEACH BOYS
35 "Israelites," DESMOND DEKKER AND THE ACES
36 "Mendocino," THE SIR DOUGLAS QUINTET
37 "One," THREE DOG NIGHT
38 "Cissy Strut," THE METERS
39 "In the Ghetto," ELVIS PRESLEY
40 "Sugar, Sugar," THE ARCHIES

Volume 16—1970

1 "Who'll Stop the Rain"/"Travelin' Band," CREEDENCE CLEARWATER REVIVAL
2 "Instant Karma (We All Shine On)," JOHN LENNON
3 "All Right Now," FREE
4 "Domino," VAN MORRISON
5 "If I Were Your Woman," GLADYS KNIGHT AND THE PIPS
6 "Bridge over Troubled Water," SIMON AND GARFUNKEL
7 "Give Me Just a Little More Time," CHAIRMEN OF THE BOARD
8 "Thank You (Falettinme Be Mice Elf Agin)"/"Everybody Is a Star," SLY AND THE FAMILY STONE
9 "Band of Gold," FREDA PAYNE
10 "ABC," THE JACKSON 5
11 "Signed, Sealed, Delivered I'm Yours," STEVIE WONDER
12 "Make It with You," BREAD
13 "The Tears of a Clown," SMOKEY ROBINSON AND THE MIRACLES
14 "Lola," THE KINKS
15 "Ain't No Mountain High Enough," DIANA ROSS
16 "Patches," CLARENCE CARTER
17 "Kentucky Rain," ELVIS PRESLEY
18 "Don't Play That Song," ARETHA FRANKLIN
19 "Summertime Blues," THE WHO
20 "See Me, Feel Me," THE WHO
21 "Lookin' Out My Back Door"/"Long as I Can See the Light," CREEDENCE CLEARWATER REVIVAL
22 "I Hear You Knocking," DAVE EDMUNDS
23 "The Letter," JOE COCKER
24 "Engine Number 9," WILSON PICKETT
25 "Ooh Child," THE FIVE STAIRSTEPS
26 "Precious Precious," JACKIE MOORE
27 "I'll Be There," THE JACKSON 5
28 "Your Song," ELTON JOHN
29 "Groove Me," KING FLOYD

30   "It's a Shame," THE SPINNERS
31   "The Love You Save," THE JACKSON 5
32   "War," EDWIN STARR
33   "Come and Get It," BADFINGER
34   "Yellow River," CHRISTIE
35   "After Midnight," ERIC CLAPTON
36   "Rainy Night in Georgia," BROOK BENTON
37   "Only Love Can Break Your Heart," NEIL YOUNG
38   "Mama Told Me (Not to Come)," THREE DOG NIGHT
39   "Psychedelic Shack," THE TEMPTATIONS
40   "Spill the Wine," ERIC BURDON AND WAR

Volume 17—1971

1   "Won't Get Fooled Again," THE WHO
2   "Have You Seen Her," THE CHI-LITES
3   "Family Affair," SLY AND THE FAMILY STONE
4   "What's Going On," MARVIN GAYE
5   "Maggie May," ROD STEWART
6   "Let's Stay Together," AL GREEN
7   "Have You Ever Seen the Rain"/"Hey Tonight," CREEDENCE CLEARWATER REVIVAL
8   "Wild Night," VAN MORRISON
9   "Brown Sugar," THE ROLLING STONES
10   "It's Too Late"/"I Feel the Earth Move," CAROLE KING
11   "Bring the Boys Home," FREDA PAYNE
12   "You Are Everything," THE STYLISTICS
13   "Spanish Harlem," ARETHA FRANKLIN
14   "Tired of Being Alone," AL GREEN
15   "Clean Up Woman," BETTY WRIGHT
16   "Just My Imagination (Running Away with Me)," THE TEMPTATIONS
17   "(For God's Sake) Give More Power to the People," THE CHI-LITES
18   "Whatcha See Is Whatcha Get," THE DRAMATICS
19   "Mercy Mercy Me (The Ecology)," MARVIN GAYE

20 "Respect Yourself," THE STAPLE SINGERS
21 "Smiling Faces Sometimes," THE UNDISPUTED TRUTH
22 "Imagine," JOHN LENNON
23 "Inner City Blues (Make Me Wanna Holler)," MARVIN GAYE
24 "Eighteen," ALICE COOPER
25 "Liar," THREE DOG NIGHT
26 "Never Can Say Goodbye," THE JACKSON 5
27 "Trapped by a Thing Called Love," DENISE LASALLE
28 "Black Dog," LED ZEPPELIN
29 "Looking for a Love," THE J. GEILS BAND
30 "Want Ads," HONEY CONE
31 "Got to Be There," MICHAEL JACKSON
32 "Blue Money," VAN MORRISON
33 "Theme from 'Shaft,' " ISAAC HAYES
34 "It Don't Come Easy," RINGO STARR
35 "Mr. Big Stuff," JEAN KNIGHT
36 "Drowning in the Sea of Love," JOE SIMON
37 "Me and Bobby McGee," JANIS JOPLIN
38 "Timothy," THE BUOYS
39 "Do You Know What I Mean," LEE MICHAELS
40 "American Pie—Parts 1 & 2," DON MCLEAN

Volume 18—1972

1 "Tumbling Dice," THE ROLLING STONES
2 "Layla," DEREK AND THE DOMINOS
3 "Papa Was a Rollin' Stone," THE TEMPTATIONS
4 "Freddie's Dead," CURTIS MAYFIELD
5 "All the Young Dudes," MOTT THE HOOPLE
6 "Back Stabbers," THE O'JAYS
7 "I Can See Clearly Now," JOHNNY NASH
8 "I'm Still in Love with You," AL GREEN
9 "Don't Do It," THE BAND
10 "You're So Vain," CARLY SIMON
11 "Look What You Done for Me," AL GREEN

12   "Slippin' into Darkness," WAR
13   "If You Don't Know Me by Now," HAROLD MELVIN AND THE
      BLUE NOTES
14   "Starting All Over Again," MEL AND TIM
15   "Mother and Child Reunion," PAUL SIMON
16   "(If Loving You Is Wrong) I Don't Want to Be Right,"
      LUTHER INGRAM
17   "Betcha by Golly, Wow," THE STYLISTICS
18   "Super Fly," CURTIS MAYFIELD
19   "Join Together," THE WHO
20   "Rock and Roll Lullaby," B. J. THOMAS
21   "Could It Be I'm Falling in Love," THE SPINNERS
22   "The World Is a Ghetto," WAR
23   "I Wanna Be Where You Are," MICHAEL JACKSON
24   "You Wear It Well," ROD STEWART
25   "I Saw the Light," TODD RUNDGREN
26   "Oh Girl!" THE CHI-LITES
27   "School's Out," ALICE COOPER
28   "I'll Be Around," THE SPINNERS
29   "Stay with Me," THE FACES
30   "I'm Stone in Love with You," THE STYLISTICS
31   "Long Cool Woman (In a Black Dress)," THE HOLLIES
32   "Rocket Man," ELTON JOHN
33   "Rockin' Robin," MICHAEL JACKSON
34   "Why Can't We Live Together," TIMMY THOMAS
35   "The City of New Orleans," ARLO GUTHRIE
36   "Brandy (You're a Fine Girl)," LOOKING GLASS
37   "Diary," BREAD
38   "I'll Take You There," THE STAPLE SINGERS
39   "Garden Party," RICK NELSON
40   "Back Off Boogaloo," RINGO STARR

Volume 19—1973

1   "Drift Away," DOBIE GRAY
2   "Let's Get It On," MARVIN GAYE

3   "Superstition," STEVIE WONDER
4   "Call Me (Come Back Home)," AL GREEN
5   "You're So Vain," CARLY SIMON
6   "Midnight Train to Georgia," GLADYS KNIGHT AND THE PIPS
7   "Could It Be I'm Falling in Love," THE SPINNERS
8   "You Are the Sunshine of My Life," STEVIE WONDER
9   "Kodachrome," PAUL SIMON
10   "You Turn Me On, I'm a Radio," JONI MITCHELL
11   "Stir It Up," JOHNNY NASH
12   "Love Train," THE O'JAYS
13   "Brother Louie," THE STORIES
14   "Right Place Wrong Time," DR. JOHN
15   "Do It Again," STEELY DAN
16   "One of a Kind (Love Affair)," THE SPINNERS
17   "The Cisco Kid," WAR
18   "Rockin' Roll Baby," THE STYLISTICS
19   "Knockin' on Heaven's Door," BOB DYLAN
20   "Stuck in the Middle with You," STEALERS WHEEL
21   "Armed and Extremely Dangerous," FIRST CHOICE
22   "Live and Let Die," PAUL MCCARTNEY AND WINGS
23   "I Can't Stand the Rain," ANN PEEBLES
24   "Angel," ARETHA FRANKLIN
25   "That Lady (Part 1)," THE ISLEY BROTHERS
26   "The Love I Lost (Part 1)," HAROLD MELVIN AND THE BLUE
     NOTES
27   "Neither One of Us (Wants to Be the First to Say Goodbye),"
     GLADYS KNIGHT AND THE PIPS
28   "We're an American Band," GRAND FUNK RAILROAD
29   "I'll Always Love My Mama (Part 1)," THE INTRUDERS
30   "Misdemeanor," FOSTER SYLVERS
31   "No More Mr. Nice Guy," ALICE COOPER
32   "Give It to Me," THE J. GEILS BAND
33   "Soul Makossa," MANU DIBANGO
34   "Love Jones," THE BRIGHTER SIDE OF DARKNESS
35   "Hello It's Me," TODD RUNDGREN
36   "I Believe in You (You Believe in Me)," JOHNNIE TAYLOR

37   "Natural High," BLOODSTONE
38   "Ramblin Man," THE ALLMAN BROTHERS BAND
39   "Walk on the Wild Side," LOU REED
40   "Frankenstein," EDGAR WINTER

Volume 20—1974

1   "Overnight Sensation (Hit Record)," THE RASPBERRIES
2   "Living for the City," STEVIE WONDER
3   "You Make Me Feel Brand New," THE STYLISTICS
4   "Sweet Home Alabama," LYNYRD SKYNYRD
5   "Jet," PAUL MCCARTNEY AND WINGS
6   "Then Came You," THE SPINNERS AND DIONNE WARWICK
7   "You Ain't Seen Nothing Yet," BACHMAN-TURNER OVERDRIVE
8   "Rock Your Baby," GEORGE MCCRAE
9   "I Can Help," BILLY SWAN
10   "You Haven't Done Nothin'," STEVIE WONDER
11   "Must of Got Lost," THE J. GEILS BAND
12   "Let's Get Married," AL GREEN
13   "Mighty Love, Part 1," THE SPINNERS
14   "Put Your Hands Together," THE O'JAYS
15   "I've Got to Use My Imagination," GLADYS KNIGHT AND THE PIPS
16   "It's Only Rock 'n' Roll (But I Like It)," THE ROLLING STONES
17   "TSOP (The Sound of Philadelphia)," MFSB
18   "Come and Get Your Love," REDBONE
19   "Band on the Run," PAUL MCCARTNEY AND WINGS
20   "Rock the Boat," THE HUES CORPORATION
21   "Rikki Don't Lose That Number," STEELY DAN
22   "When Will I See You Again," THE THREE DEGREES
23   "Don't You Worry 'Bout a Thing," STEVIE WONDER
24   "Let's Put It All Together," THE STYLISTICS
25   "My Mistake (Was to Love You)," MARVIN GAYE and DIANA ROSS

26   "Doo Doo Doo Doo Doo (Heartbreaker)," THE ROLLING
     STONES
27   "Sideshow," BLUE MAGIC
28   "Lookin' for a Love," BOBBY WOMACK
29   "Whatever Gets You Thru the Night," JOHN LENNON
30   "Keep On Smilin'," WET WILLIE
31   "Free Man in Paris," JONI MITCHELL
32   "Until You Come Back to Me (That's What I'm Gonna Do),"
     ARETHA FRANKLIN
33   "I Shot the Sheriff," ERIC CLAPTON
34   "Help Me," JONI MITCHELL
35   "The Bitch Is Back," ELTON JOHN
36   "Everlasting Love," CARL CARLTON
37   "Waterloo," ABBA
38   "Love's Theme," LOVE UNLIMITED ORCHESTRA
39   "For the Love of Money," THE O'JAYS
40   "Beach Baby," FIRST CLASS

Volume 21—1975

1   "Born to Run," BRUCE SPRINGSTEEN
2   "Bad Luck (Part 1)," HAROLD MELVIN AND THE BLUE NOTES
3   "Shame, Shame, Shame," SHIRLEY AND COMPANY
4   "Lady Marmalade," LABELLE
5   "Why Can't We Be Friends," WAR
6   "Third Rate Romance," THE AMAZING RHYTHM ACES
7   "One of These Nights," THE EAGLES
8   "Jive Talkin'," THE BEE GEES
9   "My Little Town," SIMON AND GARFUNKEL
10   "Fame," DAVID BOWIE
11   "Boogie On Reggae Woman," STEVIE WONDER
12   "This Will Be," NATALIE COLE
13   "Stand by Me," JOHN LENNON
14   "It Only Takes a Minute," TAVARES
15   "Philadelphia Freedom," ELTON JOHN

16   "I'm on Fire," THE DWIGHT TWILLEY BAND
17   "Fly, Robin, Fly," SILVER CONVENTION
18   "18 with a Bullet," PETE WINGFIELD
19   "You're No Good," LINDA RONSTADT
20   "Miracles," THE JEFFERSON STARSHIP
21   "Blue Eyes Crying in the Rain," WILLIE NELSON
22   "Young Americans," DAVID BOWIE
23   "Pick Up the Pieces," THE AVERAGE WHITE BAND
24   "Never Can Say Goodbye," GLORIA GAYNOR
25   "Gone at Last," PAUL SIMON
26   "When Will I Be Loved," LINDA RONSTADT
27   "Shining Star," EARTH, WIND, AND FIRE
28   "Nights on Broadway," THE BEE GEES
29   "Rockin' All over the World," JOHN FOGERTY
30   "Black Water," THE DOOBIE BROTHERS
31   "Let's Do It Again," THE STAPLE SINGERS
32   "You Are So Beautiful," JOE COCKER
33   "Black Superman—'Muhammad Ali,'" JOHNNY WAKELIN
      AND THE KINSHASA BAND
34   "Lyin' Eyes," THE EAGLES
35   "Baby That's Backatcha," SMOKEY ROBINSON
36   "The Hustle," VAN McCOY
37   "Doctor's Orders," CAROL DOUGLAS
38   "How Long," ACE
39   "Rockin' Chair," GWEN McCRAE
40   "Ballroom Blitz," SWEET

      Volume 22—1976

1   "Wake Up, Everybody (Part 1)," HAROLD MELVIN AND THE
      BLUE NOTES
2   "Love to Love You Baby," DONNA SUMMER
3   "She's Gone," HALL AND OATES
4   "Rhiannon (Will You Ever Win)," FLEETWOOD MAC
5   "Tonight's the Night (Gonna Be Alright)," ROD STEWART

6   "The Boys Are Back in Town," THIN LIZZY
7   "Love Is the Drug," ROXY MUSIC
8   "(Don't Fear) The Reaper," BLUE ÖYSTER CULT
9   "Hurt," ELVIS PRESLEY
10   "Sara Smile," HALL AND OATES
11   "Turn the Beat Around," VICKI SUE ROBINSON
12   "Don't Go Breaking My Heart," ELTON JOHN and KIKI DEE
13   "Young Hearts Run Free," CANDI STATON
14   "Right Back Where We Started From," MAXINE NIGHTINGALE
15   "Take It to the Limit," THE EAGLES
16   "50 Ways to Leave Your Lover," PAUL SIMON
17   "Silly Love Songs," PAUL McCARTNEY AND WINGS
18   "Golden Years," DAVID BOWIE
19   "I Love Music (Part 1)," THE O'JAYS
20   "Hold Back the Night," THE TRAMMPS
21   "I Want You," MARVIN GAYE
22   "Only Love Is Real," CAROLE KING
23   "Shannon," HENRY GROSS
24   "Tear the Roof Off the Sucker (Give Up the Funk),"
     PARLIAMENT
25   "Kiss and Say Goodbye," THE MANHATTANS
26   "Fool to Cry," THE ROLLING STONES
27   "Livin' for the Weekend," THE O'JAYS
28   "You Sexy Thing," HOT CHOCOLATE
29   "The Rubberband Man," THE SPINNERS
30   "Theme from 'Mahogany' (Do You Know Where You're Going
     To)," DIANA ROSS
31   "Fooled Around and Fell in Love," ELVIN BISHOP
32   "That's Where the Happy People Go," THE TRAMMPS
33   "Misty Blue," DOROTHY MOORE
34   "Good Hearted Woman," WILLIE NELSON and WAYLON
     JENNINGS
35   "Love Hangover," DIANA ROSS
36   "Lowdown," BOZ SCAGGS
37   "I'll Be Good to You," BROTHERS JOHNSON

38   "December, 1963 (Oh, What a Night)," THE FOUR SEASONS
39   "You Don't Have to Be a Star (To Be in My Show)," MARILYN
      McCOO AND BILLY DAVIS JR.
40   "Let Your Love Flow," THE BELLAMY BROTHERS

Volume 23—1977

1   "Go Your Own Way," FLEETWOOD MAC
2   "More Than a Feeling," BOSTON
3   "I Wish," STEVIE WONDER
4   "Rich Girl," HALL AND OATES
5   "Don't Stop," FLEETWOOD MAC
6   "New Kid in Town," THE EAGLES
7   "The First Cut is the Deepest," ROD STEWART
8   "Whispering/Cherchez la Femme/Se Si Bon," DR. BUZZARD'S
      ORIGINAL "SAVANNAH" BAND
9   "Sir Duke," STEVIE WONDER
10   "Nobody Does It Better," CARLY SIMON
11   "Maybe I'm Amazed," PAUL McCARTNEY AND WINGS
12   "The Killing of Georgie (Parts 1 and 2)," ROD STEWART
13   "Lido Shuffle," BOZ SCAGGS
14   "Dreams," FLEETWOOD MAC
15   "I Feel Love," DONNA SUMMER
16   "Dancing Queen," ABBA
17   "Tryin' to Love Two," WILLIAM BELL
18   "Here Come Those Tears Again," JACKSON BROWNE
19   "Got to Give It Up, Pt. 1," MARVIN GAYE
20   "Luckenbach, Texas (Back to the Basics of Love)," WAYLON
      JENNINGS
21   "Hotel California," THE EAGLES
22   "Gettin' Ready for Love," DIANA ROSS
23   "Angel in Your Arms," HOT
24   "Jet Airliner," THE STEVE MILLER BAND
25   "Heard It in a Love Song," THE MARSHALL TUCKER BAND
26   "You Light Up My Life," DEBBY BOONE

27 "Don't Leave Me This Way," THELMA HOUSTON
28 "Swayin' to the Music (Slow Dancin')," JOHNNY RIVERS
29 "Fly Like an Eagle," STEVE MILLER BAND
30 "You Make Me Feel Like Dancing," LEO SAYER
31 "The Things We Do for Love," 10CC
32 "Car Wash," ROSE ROYCE
33 "Smoke from a Distant Fire," THE SANFORD/TOWNSEND BAND
34 "Hot Line," THE SYLVERS
35 "Handy Man," JAMES TAYLOR
36 "Cat Scratch Fever," TED NUGENT
37 "Life in the Fast Lane," THE EAGLES*
38 "The King Is Gone," RONNIE MCDOWELL
39 "Send in the Clowns," JUDY COLLINS
40 "Black Betty," RAM JAM

*Penalized ten spots for rancid ideology.

Volume 24—1978

1   "Stayin' Alive," THE BEE GEES
2   "Disco Inferno," THE TRAMMPS
3   "Because the Night," THE PATTI SMITH GROUP
4   "Three Times a Lady," THE COMMODORES
5   "Last Dance," DONNA SUMMER
6   "Prove It All Night," BRUCE SPRINGSTEEN
7   "Dance, Dance, Dance (Yowsah, Yowsah, Yowsah)," CHIC
8   "Just What I Needed," THE CARS
9   "Running on Empty," JACKSON BROWNE
10 "Useta Be My Girl," THE O'JAYS
11 "Imaginary Lover," THE ATLANTA RHYTHM SECTION
12 "My Best Friend's Girl," THE CARS
13 "Night Fever," THE BEE GEES
14 "Miss You," THE ROLLING STONES
15 "What's Your Name," LYNYRD SKYNYRD

16 "One Nation under a Groove—Part One," FUNKADELIC
17 "Life's Been Good," JOE WALSH
18 "Who Are You," THE WHO
19 "Jack and Jill," RAYDIO
20 "It's a Laugh," HALL AND OATES
21 "Close the Door," TEDDY PENDERGRASS
22 "Slip Slidin' Away," PAUL SIMON
23 "King Tut," STEVE MARTIN
24 "Breakdown," TOM PETTY AND THE HEARTBREAKERS
25 "Werewolves of London," WARREN ZEVON
26 "Baby Hold On," EDDIE MONEY
27 "Turn to Stone," ELECTRIC LIGHT ORCHESTRA
28 "Macho Man," THE VILLAGE PEOPLE
29 "I Love the Nightlife (Disco 'Round)," ALICIA BRIDGES
30 "Native New Yorker," ODYSSEY
31 "Baker Street," GERRY RAFFERTY
32 "Too Much, Too Little, Too Late," JOHNNY MATHIS AND
DENIECE WILLIAMS
33 "Beast of Burden," THE ROLLING STONES
34 "Two Tickets to Paradise," EDDIE MONEY
35 "Don't Let Me Be Misunderstood," SANTA ESMERALDA
36 "Short People," RANDY NEWMAN
37 "Street Corner Serenade," WET WILLIE
38 "Hot Child in the City," NICK GILDER
39 "Fool (If You Think It's Over)," CHRIS REA
40 "It's a Heartache," BONNIE TYLER

Volume 25—1979
1 "Hot Stuff," DONNA SUMMER
2 "Reunited," PEACHES AND HERB
3 "What a Fool Believes," THE DOOBIE BROTHERS
4 "Good Times," CHIC
5 "Rock with You," MICHAEL JACKSON
6 "Ring My Bell," ANITA WARD
7 "Tusk," FLEETWOOD MAC

8	"I Want You to Want Me," CHEAP TRICK
9	"Heart of Glass," BLONDIE
10	"Ain't No Stoppin' Us Now," McFADDEN AND WHITEHEAD
11	"Pop Muzik," M
12	"Rapper's Delight," THE SUGARHILL GANG
13	"Roxanne," POLICE
14	"We Are Family," SISTER SLEDGE
15	"Cruisin'," SMOKEY ROBINSON
16	"Bad Girls," DONNA SUMMER
17	"Crazy Little Thing Called Love," QUEEN
18	"Is She Really Going Out with Him?" JOE JACKSON
19	"You're Only Lonely," J. D. SOUTHER
20	"Let's Go," THE CARS
21	"Dreaming," BLONDIE
22	"Found a Cure," ASHFORD AND SIMPSON
23	"Cruel to Be Kind," NICK LOWE
24	"Still," THE COMMODORES
25	"Minute by Minute," THE DOOBIE BROTHERS
26	"I Was Made for Lovin' You," KISS
27	"Wait for Me," HALL AND OATES
28	"Fool in the Rain," LED ZEPPELIN
29	"One Way or Another," BLONDIE
30	"Working My Way Back to You"/"Forgive Me, Girl," THE SPINNERS
31	"Knock on Wood," AMII STEWART
32	"Don't Stop 'Til You Get Enough," MICHAEL JACKSON
33	"Don't Do Me Like That," TOM PETTY AND THE HEARTBREAKERS
34	"Send One Your Love," STEVIE WONDER
35	"Dream Police," CHEAP TRICK
36	"Lead Me On," MAXINE NIGHTINGALE
37	"I Wanna Be Your Lover," PRINCE
38	"Boogie Wonderland," EARTH, WIND, AND FIRE
39	"Gold," JOHN STEWART
40	"Don't Let Go," ISAAC HAYES

Volume 26—1980

1   "Hungry Heart," BRUCE SPRINGSTEEN
2   "Refugee," TOM PETTY AND THE HEARTBREAKERS
3   "The Wanderer," DONNA SUMMER
4   "Another Brick in the Wall," PINK FLOYD
5   "Love Stinks," THE J. GEILS BAND
6   "Funkytown," LIPPS, INC.
7   "(Just Like) Starting Over," JOHN LENNON/YOKO ONO
8   "Masterblaster," STEVIE WONDER
9   "Off the Wall," MICHAEL JACKSON
10   "Call Me," BLONDIE
11   "Lookin' for Love," JOHNNY LEE
12   "Special Lady," RAY GOODMAN AND BROWN
13   "On the Radio," DONNA SUMMER
14   "Let Me Be the Clock," SMOKEY ROBINSON
15   "Turning Japanese," THE VAPORS
16   "We Live for Love," PAT BENATAR
17   "Brass in Pocket," PRETENDERS
18   "Tired of Toein' the Line," ROCKY BURNETTE
19   "Train in Vain," THE CLASH
20   "Shining Star," THE MANHATTANS
21   "Tide is High," BLONDIE
22   "Whip It," DEVO
23   "Come Back," THE J. GEILS BAND
24   "Hold On to My Love," JIMMY RUFFIN
25   "Let My Love Open the Door," PETE TOWNSHEND
26   "De Do Do Do, De Da Da Da," THE POLICE
27   "Late in the Evening," PAUL SIMON
28   "Lady," THE WHISPERS
29   "Against the Wind," BOB SEGER AND THE SILVER BULLET
     BAND
30   "Upside Down," DIANA ROSS
31   "Lovely One," THE JACKSONS
32   "Celebration," KOOL AND THE GANG
33   "She's Out of My Life," MICHAEL JACKSON

34 "How Does It Feel to Be Back," DARYL HALL AND JOHN OATES

35 "Coming Up," PAUL McCARTNEY

36 "Drivin' My Life Away," EDDIE RABBIT

37 "And the Beat Goes On," THE WHISPERS

38 "Boulevard," JACKSON BROWNE

39 "Stand by Me," MICKEY GILLEY

40 "All Night Long," JOE WALSH

·◄▮▶·

TOP 40 CHARTMAKERS

These lists include forty albums from each year, beginning in 1963, that made Billboard's *Top 100 chart. Taken together, they are meant to suggest the outlines of a basic rock collection. Because the lists are restricted to the Top 100, there are some glaring omissions (especially in the early sixties and late seventies), but these make their own point. (The rankings within each list, of course, represent the editors' judgment of the albums' relative merit.)*

The list of albums from 1956 to 1962 is included as one entry because so few LPs were charted in those years. Prior to 1963, the Billboard *album chart was not nearly so broadly based; in 1963, which roughly coincides with the beginning of album-oriented rock's importance, the stereo and monaural rankings were combined into a single chart, which provides a nice historical breaking point.*

1956–1962

1 *Here's Little Richard,* 1957

2 *Elvis,* ELVIS PRESLEY, 1956

3 *The Buddy Holly Story,* 1959

4 *The Genius of Ray Charles,* 1960

5 *Elvis Presley,* 1956

6 *Modern Sounds in Country and Western Music,* RAY CHARLES, 1962

7   *Sam Cooke Sings*, 1958
8   *A Date with Elvis*, ELVIS PRESLEY, 1959
9   *Genius + Soul = Jazz*, RAY CHARLES, 1961
10   *For LP Fans Only*, ELVIS PRESLEY, 1959
11   *The Genius Sings the Blues*, RAY CHARLES, 1961
12   *Ricky*, RICKY NELSON, 1957
13   *King Creole*, ELVIS PRESLEY, 1958
14   *$1,000,000.00 Worth of Twang*, DUANE EDDY, 1961
15   *Jimmy Reed at Carnegie Hall*, 1961
16   *Do the Twist*, RAY CHARLES, 1961
17   *Crying*, ROY ORBISON, 1962
18   *Quarter to Three*, GARY "U.S." BONDS, 1961
19   *Ritchie Valens*, 1959
20   *Alan Freed's Memory Lane*, various artists, 1959
21   *Have "Twangy" Guitar—Will Travel*, DUANE EDDY, 1959
22   *Green Onions*, BOOKER T. AND THE MGs, 1962
23   *Oldies but Goodies* (original sound), various artists, 1959
24   *The Everly Brothers*, 1958
25   *Twistin' the Night Away*, SAM COOKE, 1962
26   *Here's the Man*, BOBBY BLAND, 1962
27   *His Hand in Mine*, ELVIS PRESLEY, 1961
28   *Loco-Motion*, LITTLE EVA, 1962
29   *Twist and Shout*, THE ISLEY BROTHERS, 1962
30   *Only Love Can Break a Heart*, GENE PITNEY, 1962
31   *Oldies but Goodies, Vol. 3* (original sound), various artists,
      1961
32   *Baby It's You*, THE SHIRELLES, 1962
33   *Let There Be Drums*, SANDY NELSON, 1962
34   *A Date with the Everly Brothers*, 1960
35   *Surfin' Safari*, THE BEACH BOYS, 1962
36   *Doin' the Twist at the Peppermint Lounge*, JOEY DEE AND THE
      STARLITERS, 1962
37   *The Genius Hits the Road*, RAY CHARLES, 1960
38   *Walk Don't Run*, THE VENTURES, 1960
39   *The Bobby Darin Story*, 1961
40   *Sherry*, THE FOUR SEASONS, 1962

1963

1   *Surfin' U.S.A.*, THE BEACH BOYS
2   *The James Brown Show*
3   *The Freewheelin' Bob Dylan*
4   *On Stage*, CHUCK BERRY
5   *Reminiscing*, BUDDY HOLLY
6   *In Dreams*, ROY ORBISON
7   *Little Stevie Wonder the 12 Year Old Genius*
8   *Prisoner of Love*, JAMES BROWN
9   *Little Deuce Coupe*, THE BEACH BOYS
10   *Baby Workout*, JACKIE WILSON
11   *The Impressions*
12   *Oldies but Goodies Vol. 5* (original sound), various artists
13   *Surfer Girl*, THE BEACH BOYS
14   *Ingredients in a Recipe for Soul*, RAY CHARLES
15   *Shut Down* (Capitol), various artists
16   *Under the Boardwalk*, THE DRIFTERS
17   *Call on Me*, BOBBY BLAND
18   *Little Town Flirt*, DEL SHANNON
19   *Night Beat*, SAM COOKE
20   *Big Girls Don't Cry*, THE FOUR SEASONS
21   *Surfer's Choice*, DICK DALE
22   *Foolish Little Girl*, THE SHIRELLES
23   *Surf City (And Other Swingin' Cities)*, JAN AND DEAN
24   *The Motortown Review, Volume One* (Motown), various artists
25   *Ring of Fire*, JOHNNY CASH
26   *Wipe Out*, THE SURFARIS
27   *Jan and Dean Take Linda Surfin'*
28   *Telstar*, THE TORNADOES
29   *The Patsy Cline Story*
30   *Golden Goodies, Vol. 6* (Roulette), various artists
31   *Murray the "K's" 1962 Golden Gassers* (Scepter), various artists

32   *The Ventures Play "Telstar" "The Lonely Bull" and Others*
33   *Blood, Sweat and Tears*, JOHNNY CASH
34   *Golden Goodies, Vol. 1* (Roulette), various artists
35   *The Chiffons*
36   *Pipeline*, THE CHANTAY'S
37   *Release Me*, ESTHER PHILLIPS
38   *Cry Baby*, GARNETT MIMMS AND THE ENCHANTERS
39   *Two Lovers*, MARY WELLS
40   *Ruby Baby*, DION

1964

1   *The Rolling Stones*
2   *The Beatles' Second Album*
3   *All Summer Long*, THE BEACH BOYS
4   *12 × 5*, THE ROLLING STONES
5   *Meet The Beatles!*
6   *Meet The Temptations*
7   *Pure Dynamite*, JAMES BROWN
8   *You Really Got Me*, THE KINKS
9   *Something New*, THE BEATLES
10   *The Animals*
11   *The Greatest Live Show on Earth*, JERRY LEE LEWIS
12   *Shut Down—Vol. 2*, THE BEACH BOYS
13   *The Impressions Keep on Pushing*
14   *Glad All Over*, DAVE CLARK FIVE
15   *Another Side of Bob Dylan*
16   *Introducing The Beatles*
17   *The Manfred Mann Album*
18   *Ain't That Good News*, SAM COOKE
19   *Louie Louie*, THE KINGSMEN
20   *Where Did Our Love Go*, THE SUPREMES
21   *A Hard Day's Night*, THE BEATLES
22   *The Fabulous Ronettes Featuring Veronica*
23   *It Hurts to Be in Love*, GENE PITNEY

24   *Surfin' Bird*, THE TRASHMEN
25   *Needles and Pins*, THE SEARCHERS
26   *16 Big Hits, Vol. 1* (Motown), various artists
27   *The Dave Clark Five Return!*
28   *Northern Journey*, IAN AND SYLVIA
29   *Dawn (Go Away)*, THE FOUR SEASONS
30   *The Kingsmen—Vol. 2*
31   *The Never Ending Impressions*, THE IMPRESSIONS
32   *Um, Um, Um, Um, Um, Um*, MAJOR LANCE
33   *Drag City*, JAN AND DEAN
34   *Johnny Rivers at the Whisky a GoGo*
35   *The Dusty Springfield Album*
36   *This Is Us*, THE SEARCHERS
37   *Pick Hits of the Radio Good Guys* (Laurie), various artists
38   *Ride the Wild Surf*, JAN AND DEAN
39   *Here We a-Go-Go Again*, JOHNNY RIVERS
40   *Bitter Tears*, JOHNNY CASH

1965

1   *Highway 61 Revisited*, BOB DYLAN
2   *Rubber Soul*, THE BEATLES
3   *The Rolling Stones, Now!*
4   *The Beach Boys Today*
5   *Beatles VI*, THE BEATLES
6   *Having a Rave Up with The Yardbirds*
7   *Out of Our Heads*, THE ROLLING STONES
8   *The Temptations Sing Smokey*
9   *Beatles '65*, THE BEATLES
10   *Mr. Tambourine Man*, THE BYRDS
11   *Bringing It All Back Home*, BOB DYLAN
12   *On Tour*, THE ANIMALS
13   *Otis Blue/Otis Redding Sings Soul*
14   *The Early Beatles*
15   *Help!* (soundtrack), THE BEATLES

16   *Kinks-Size*, THE KINKS
17   *December's Children (And Everybody's)*, THE ROLLING STONES
18   *You've Lost That Lovin' Feelin'*, THE RIGHTEOUS BROTHERS
19   *Them*
20   *Do You Believe in Magic*, THE LOVIN' SPOONFUL
21   *Animal Tracks*, THE ANIMALS
22   *Going to a-Go-Go*, THE MIRACLES
23   *For Your Love*, THE YARDBIRDS
24   *Just Once in My Life*, THE RIGHTEOUS BROTHERS
25   *Temptin' Temptations*, THE TEMPTATIONS
26   *People Get Ready*, THE IMPRESSIONS
27   *Summer Days (and Summer Nights)*, THE BEACH BOYS
28   *Papa's Got a Brand New Bag*, JAMES BROWN
29   *Back to Back*, THE RIGHTEOUS BROTHERS
30   *The Four Tops—Vol. 2*
31   *Kinks Kinkdom*, THE KINKS
32   *Goin' Out of My Head*, LITTLE ANTHONY AND THE IMPERIALS
33   *More Hits by The Supremes*
34   *Right Now*, THE RIGHTEOUS BROTHERS
35   *Having a Wild Weekend*, THE DAVE CLARK FIVE
36   *The Zombies*
37   *Some Blue Eyed Soul*, THE RIGHTEOUS BROTHERS
38   *Kinda Kinks*, THE KINKS
39   *Hang On Sloopy*, THE McCOYS
40   *Here They Come*, PAUL REVERE AND THE RAIDERS

1966

1   *Blonde on Blonde*, BOB DYLAN
2   *Revolver*, THE BEATLES
3   *Aftermath*, THE ROLLING STONES
4   *Otis Redding Dictionary of Soul*
5   *Over Under Sideways Down*, THE YARDBIRDS
6   *Up-Tight*, STEVIE WONDER
7   *The Exciting Wilson Pickett*

8   *Soul and Inspiration*, THE RIGHTEOUS BROTHERS
9   *Animalization*, THE ANIMALS
10 *Hold On! I'm a-Comin'*, SAM AND DAVE
11 *On Top*, THE FOUR TOPS
12 *Pet Sounds*, THE BEACH BOYS
13 *Hums of The Lovin' Spoonful*
14 *Supremes a Go-Go*, THE SUPREMES
15 *Fifth Dimension*, THE BYRDS
16 *The Young Rascals*
17 *Crying Time*, RAY CHARLES
18 *The Soul Album*, OTIS REDDING
19 *Yesterday . . . and Today*, THE BEATLES
20 *East-West*, THE PAUL BUTTERFIELD BLUES BAND
21 *Love*
22 *Jenny Take a Ride*, MITCH RYDER AND THE DETROIT WHEELS
23 *Gloria*, SHADOWS OF KNIGHT
24 *Animalism*, THE ANIMALS
25 *The Sounds of Silence*, SIMON AND GARFUNKEL
26 *When a Man Loves a Woman*, PERCY SLEDGE
27 *Breakout*, MITCH RYDER AND THE DETROIT WHEELS
28 *Go Ahead and Cry*, THE RIGHTEOUS BROTHERS
29 *Wild Thing*, THE TROGGS
30 *I Got You (I Feel Good)*, JAMES BROWN
31 *Turn! Turn! Turn!* THE BYRDS
32 *Just Like Us!* PAUL REVERE AND THE RAIDERS
33 *Bus Stop*, THE HOLLIES
34 *Sunshine Superman*, DONOVAN
35 *The Spirit of '67*, PAUL REVERE AND THE RAIDERS
36 *The Fugs*
37 *Got Live if You Want It!* THE ROLLING STONES
38 *Spinout*, ELVIS PRESLEY
39 *96 Tears*, ? AND THE MYSTERIANS
40 *Midnight Ride*, PAUL REVERE AND THE RAIDERS

1967

1 *Are You Experienced?* THE JIMI HENDRIX EXPERIENCE
2 *Live in Europe*, OTIS REDDING
3 *Sgt. Pepper's Lonely Hearts Club Band*, THE BEATLES
4 *Between the Buttons*, THE ROLLING STONES
5 *I Never Loved a Man the Way I Love You*, ARETHA FRANKLIN
6 *Buffalo Springfield Again*
7 *Cold Sweat*, JAMES BROWN
8 *Wild Honey*, THE BEACH BOYS
9 *The History of Otis Redding*
10 *Disraeli Gears*, CREAM
11 *Younger than Yesterday*, THE BYRDS
12 *Aretha Arrives*, ARETHA FRANKLIN
13 *Reach Out*, THE FOUR TOPS
14 *Fresh Cream*
15 *The Doors*
16 *The Supremes Sing Holland-Dozier-Holland*
17 *Absolutely Free*, THE MOTHERS OF INVENTION
18 *United*, MARVIN GAYE and TAMMI TERRELL
19 *Gimme Some Lovin'*, THE SPENCER DAVIS GROUP
20 *How Great Thou Art*, ELVIS PRESLEY
21 *Soul Men*, SAM AND DAVE
22 *Moby Grape*
23 *Smiley Smile*, THE BEACH BOYS
24 *In a Mellow Mood*, THE TEMPTATIONS
25 *Happy Jack*, THE WHO
26 *Flowers*, THE ROLLING STONES
27 *The Wicked Pickett*, WILSON PICKETT
28 *I Was Made to Love Her*, STEVIE WONDER
29 *Magical Mystery Tour*, THE BEATLES
30 *King and Queen*, OTIS REDDING and CARLA THOMAS
31 *Buffalo Springfield*
32 *With a Lot o' Soul*, THE TEMPTATIONS
33 *Surrealistic Pillow*, THE JEFFERSON AIRPLANE
34 *Groovin'*, THE YOUNG RASCALS

35   *Happy Together*, THE TURTLES
36   *Procol Harum*
37   *Stop! Stop! Stop!* THE HOLLIES
38   *Live at the Garden*, JAMES BROWN
39   *Bee Gees' First*, THE BEE GEES
40   *The Youngbloods*

1968

1   *Beggar's Banquet*, THE ROLLING STONES
2   *Electric Ladyland*, THE JIMI HENDRIX EXPERIENCE
3   *The Who Sell Out*
4   *The Beatles*
5   *John Wesley Harding*, BOB DYLAN
6   *Music from Big Pink*, THE BAND
7   *Aretha: Lady Soul*, ARETHA FRANKLIN
8   *Axis: Bold as Love*, JIMI HENDRIX
9   *Elvis* (TV Soundtrack), ELVIS PRESLEY
10   *The Dock of the Bay*, OTIS REDDING
11   *Sweetheart of the Rodeo*, THE BYRDS
12   *Aretha Now*, ARETHA FRANKLIN
13   *"Live" at the Apollo Vol. 2*, JAMES BROWN
14   *We're Only in It for the Money*, THE MOTHERS OF INVENTION
15   *Mr. Fantasy*, TRAFFIC
16   *Truth*, THE JEFF BECK GROUP
17   *Wish It Would Rain*, THE TEMPTATIONS
18   *Creedence Clearwater Revival*
19   *The Midnight Mover*, WILSON PICKETT
20   *Magic Bus—The Who on Tour*
21   *Traffic*
22   *Special Occasion*, THE MIRACLES
23   *You're All I Need*, MARVIN GAYE and TAMMI TERRELL
24   *Waiting for the Sun*, THE DOORS
25   *The Crazy World of Arthur Brown*, ARTHUR BROWN
26   *Steppenwolf*

27 *Shine on Brightly*, PROCOL HARUM
28 *Last Time Around*, BUFFALO SPRINGFIELD
29 *Cry Like a Baby*, THE BOX TOPS
30 *The Notorious Byrd Brothers*, THE BYRDS
31 *I Can't Stand Myself When You Touch Me*, JAMES BROWN
32 *Wheels of Fire*, CREAM
33 *Cheap Thrills*, BIG BROTHER AND THE HOLDING COMPANY
34 *Love Child*, DIANA ROSS AND THE SUPREMES
35 *Crown of Creation*, THE JEFFERSON AIRPLANE
36 *There Is*, THE DELLS
37 *Johnny Cash at Folsom Prison*
38 *In the Groove*, MARVIN GAYE
39 *I'm in Love*, WILSON PICKETT
40 *Reflections*, DIANA ROSS AND THE SUPREMES

1969

1   *Abbey Road*, THE BEATLES
2   *Let It Bleed*, THE ROLLING STONES
3   *Green River*, CREEDENCE CLEARWATER REVIVAL
4   *The Band*
5   *Tommy*, THE WHO
6   *Bridge over Troubled Water*, SIMON AND GARFUNKEL
7   *With a Little Help from My Friends*, JOE COCKER
8   *The Ice Man Cometh*, JERRY BUTLER
9   *Smash Hits*, THE JIMI HENDRIX EXPERIENCE
10 *Second Winter*, JOHNNY WINTER
11 *Stand!* SLY AND THE FAMILY STONE
12 *Willy and the Poorboys*, CREEDENCE CLEARWATER REVIVAL
13 *Led Zeppelin II*
14 *From Elvis in Memphis*, ELVIS PRESLEY
15 *Bayou Country*, CREEDENCE CLEARWATER REVIVAL
16 *Ice on Ice*, JERRY BUTLER
17 *Aretha Franklin: Soul '69*
18 *Beck-Ola*, THE JEFF BECK GROUP

19   *Everybody Knows This Is Nowhere*, NEIL YOUNG
20   *Dusty in Memphis*, DUSTY SPRINGFIELD
21   *Love Man*, OTIS REDDING
22   *The Soft Parade*, THE DOORS
23   *Joe Cocker!*
24   *It's Our Thing*, THE ISLEY BROTHERS
25   *Goodbye*, CREAM
26   *Time Out for Smokey Robinson and the Miracles*
27   *M. P. G.*, MARVIN GAYE
28   *Live and Well*, B. B. KING
29   *Volunteers*, THE JEFFERSON AIRPLANE
30   *My Cherie Amour*, STEVIE WONDER
31   *Happy Sad*, TIM BUCKLEY
32   *Johnny Winter*
33   *Blind Faith*
34   *Led Zeppelin*
35   *Completely Well*, B. B. KING
36   *For Once in My Life*, STEVIE WONDER
37   *Puzzle People*, THE TEMPTATIONS
38   *Uncle Meat*, THE MOTHERS OF INVENTION
39   *Dimensions*, THE BOX TOPS
40   *From Memphis to Vegas/From Vegas to Memphis*, ELVIS PRESLEY

1970

1   *Layla*, DEREK AND THE DOMINOS
2   *Moondance*, VAN MORRISON
3   *John Lennon/Plastic Ono Band*
4   *Live at Monterey*, OTIS REDDING and THE JIMI HENDRIX EXPERIENCE
5   *Signed Sealed and Delivered*, STEVIE WONDER
6   *I Want You Back*, THE JACKSON 5
7   *Bitches Brew*, MILES DAVIS
8   *The Band of Gypsys*, THE JIMI HENDRIX EXPERIENCE

9   *Woodstock* (soundtrack), various artists
10 *Get Yer Ya-Ya's Out!* THE ROLLING STONES
11 *Eric Clapton*
12 *Spirit in the Dark*, ARETHA FRANKLIN
13 *Cosmo's Factory*, CREEDENCE CLEARWATER REVIVAL
14 *His Band and the Street Choir*, VAN MORRISON
15 *Gasoline Alley*, ROD STEWART
16 *Morrison Hotel*, THE DOORS
17 *Patches*, CLARENCE CARTER
18 *In Philadelphia*, WILSON PICKETT
19 *Mad Dogs and Englishmen*, JOE COCKER
20 *Let It Be*, THE BEATLES
21 *Live Peace in Toronto 1969*, THE PLASTIC ONO BAND
22 *Live at Leeds*, THE WHO
23 *Indianola Mississippi Seeds*, B. B. KING
24 *Kiln House*, FLEETWOOD MAC
25 *Stage Fright*, THE BAND
26 *Pendulum*, CREEDENCE CLEARWATER REVIVAL
27 *After the Gold Rush*, NEIL YOUNG
28 *Lola vs. PowerMan and the Money go round*, THE KINKS
29 *Hey Jude*, THE BEATLES
30 *ABC*, THE JACKSON 5
31 *This Girl's in Love with You*, ARETHA FRANKLIN
32 *The James Gang Rides Again*
33 *Eric Burdon Declares "War,"* ERIC BURDON AND WAR
34 *Atom Heart Mother*, PINK FLOYD
35 *On Tour (With Eric Clapton)*, DELANEY AND BONNIE AND
    FRIENDS
36 *Diana Ross*
37 *Sex Machine*, JAMES BROWN
38 *Idlewild South*, THE ALLMAN BROTHERS BAND
39 *Led Zeppelin III*
40 *No Dice*, BADFINGER

1971

1 *Who's Next*, THE WHO
2 *There's a Riot Goin' On*, SLY AND THE FAMILY STONE
3 *Sticky Fingers*, THE ROLLING STONES
4 *Every Picture Tells a Story*, ROD STEWART
5 *Imagine*, JOHN LENNON
6 *Led Zeppelin IV*
7 *What's Going On*, MARVIN GAYE
8 *Al Green Gets Next to You*
9 *A Nod Is as Good as a Wink to a Blind Horse*, THE FACES
10 *One Dozen Roses*, SMOKEY ROBINSON AND THE MIRACLES
11 *The London Howlin' Wolf Sessions*
12 *The Stylistics*
13 *Live at the Regal*, B. B. KING
14 *Rainbow Bridge* (soundtrack), JIMI HENDRIX
15 *Tapestry*, CAROLE KING
16 *At Fillmore East*, THE ALLMAN BROTHERS BAND
17 *Blue*, JONI MITCHELL
18 *The Cry of Love*, JIMI HENDRIX
19 *Tupelo Honey*, VAN MORRISON
20 *I Think We're All Bozos on This Bus*, THE FIRESIGN THEATRE
21 *Elvis Country*, ELVIS PRESLEY
22 *Gonna Take a Miracle*, LAURA NYRO
23 *Aretha Live at Fillmore West*, ARETHA FRANKLIN
24 *Nilsson Schmilsson*, HARRY NILSSON
25 *Long Player*, THE FACES
26 *Pearl*, JANIS JOPLIN
27 *(For God's Sake) Give More Power to the People*, THE
    CHI-LITES
28 *Shaft* (soundtrack), ISAAC HAYES
29 *Morning After*, THE J. GEILS BAND
30 *Music*, CAROLE KING
31 *Love It to Death*, ALICE COOPER
32 *Where I'm Coming From*, STEVIE WONDER
33 *Surf's Up*, THE BEACH BOYS

34   *Super Bad*, JAMES BROWN
35   *Live at Fillmore West*, KING CURTIS
36   *Lost in the Ozone*, COMMANDER CODY AND HIS LOST PLANET
     AIRMEN
37   *All Day Music*, WAR
38   *Killer*, ALICE COOPER
39   *Maybe Tomorrow*, THE JACKSON 5
40   *Madman Across the Water*, ELTON JOHN

1972

1   *Exile on Main Street*, THE ROLLING STONES
2   *Talking Book*, STEVIE WONDER
3   *Super Fly* (soundtrack), CURTIS MAYFIELD
4   *Saint Dominic's Preview*, VAN MORRISON
5   *I'm Still in Love with You*, AL GREEN
6   *For the Roses*, JONI MITCHELL
7   *Back Stabbers*, THE O'JAYS
8   *Let's Stay Together*, AL GREEN
9   *Music of My Mind*, STEVIE WONDER
10   *Paul Simon*
11   *Never a Dull Moment*, ROD STEWART
12   *Young, Gifted and Black*, ARETHA FRANKLIN
13   *Hendrix in the West*, JIMI HENDRIX
14   *Eat a Peach*, THE ALLMAN BROTHERS BAND
15   *All Directions*, THE TEMPTATIONS
16   *I Can See Clearly Now*, JOHNNY NASH
17   *Trouble Man* (soundtrack), MARVIN GAYE
18   *Can't Buy a Thrill*, STEELY DAN
19   *Street Corner Symphony*, THE PERSUASIONS
20   *Rock of Ages*, THE BAND
21   *"Live"—Full House*, THE J. GEILS BAND
22   *The World Is a Ghetto*, WAR
23   *Something/Anything?* TODD RUNDGREN
24   *Everybody's in Show-Biz*, THE KINKS
25   *Amazing Grace*, ARETHA FRANKLIN

26   *Ben*, MICHAEL JACKSON
27   *No Secrets*, CARLY SIMON
28   *The Rise and Fall of Ziggy Stardust and the Spiders from Mars*, DAVID BOWIE
29   *L.A. Midnight*, B. B. KING
30   *Mardi Gras*, CREEDENCE CLEARWATER REVIVAL
31   *Got to Be There*, MICHAEL JACKSON
32   *Round 2: The Stylistics*
33   *A Lonely Man*, THE CHI-LITES
34   *All the Young Dudes*, MOTT THE HOOPLE
35   *Machine Head*, DEEP PURPLE
36   *Will the Circle Be Unbroken*, THE NITTY GRITTY DIRT BAND
37   *Beatitude: Respect Yourself*, THE STAPLE SINGERS
38   *The Kink Kronikles*
39   *Some Time in New York City*, JOHN AND YOKO/PLASTIC ONO BAND with ELEPHANT'S MEMORY
40   *Honky Château*, ELTON JOHN

1973

1   *Innervisions*, STEVIE WONDER
2   *Mott*, MOTT THE HOOPLE
3   *The Spinners*
4   *Call Me*, AL GREEN
5   *Quadrophenia*, THE WHO
6   *Let's Get It On*, MARVIN GAYE
7   *Pat Garrett and Billy the Kid* (soundtrack), BOB DYLAN
8   *Lynyrd Skynyrd (Pronounced Leh-nerd Skin-nerd)*
9   *Masterpiece*, THE TEMPTATIONS
10   *Band on the Run*, PAUL MCCARTNEY AND WINGS
11   *There Goes Rhymin' Simon*, PAUL SIMON
12   *Sound Track Recordings from the Film 'Jimi Hendrix,'* JIMI HENDRIX
13   *Houses of the Holy*, LED ZEPPELIN
14   *Still Alive and Well*, JOHNNY WINTER

15   *Countdown to Ecstasy*, STEELY DAN
16   *In the Right Place*, DR. JOHN
17   *Rockin' Roll Baby*, THE STYLISTICS
18   *Mind Games*, JOHN LENNON
19   *Ship Ahoy*, THE O'JAYS
20   *Goat's Head Soup*, THE ROLLING STONES
21   *Brothers and Sisters*, THE ALLMAN BROTHERS BAND
22   *Ladies Invited*, THE J. GEILS BAND
23   *Imagination*, GLADYS KNIGHT AND THE PIPS
24   *Goodbye Yellow Brick Road*, ELTON JOHN
25   *The Dark Side of the Moon*, PINK FLOYD
26   *A Letter to Myself*, THE CHI-LITES
27   *Hey Now Hey (The Other Side of the Sky)*, ARETHA FRANKLIN
28   *Livin' for You*, AL GREEN
29   *3 + 3*, THE ISLEY BROTHERS
30   *The Blues Ridge Rangers*
31   *Bloodshot*, THE J. GEILS BAND
32   *For Everyman*, JACKSON BROWNE
33   *Drift Away*, DOBIE GRAY
34   *American Graffiti* (soundtrack), various artists
35   *Time Fades Away*, NEIL YOUNG
36   *All American Boy*, RICK DERRINGER
37   *Neither One of Us*, GLADYS KNIGHT AND THE PIPS
38   *Doing It to Death*, THE J.B.'S
39   *Soul Makossa*, MANU DIBANGO
40   *Made in Japan*, DEEP PURPLE

1974

1   *461 Ocean Boulevard*, ERIC CLAPTON
2   *Al Green Explores Your Mind*
3   *Veedon Fleece*, VAN MORRISON
4   *It's Only Rock 'n' Roll*, THE ROLLING STONES
5   *Fulfillingness' First Finale*, STEVIE WONDER
6   *Late for the Sky*, JACKSON BROWNE

7   *It's Too Late to Stop Now*, VAN MORRISON
8   *Nightmares . . . and Other Tales from the Vinyl Jungle*, THE J. GEILS BAND
9   *Second Helping*, LYNYRD SKYNYRD
10   *I Can Help*, BILLY SWAN
11   *Rock 'n' Roll Animal*, LOU REED
12   *Before the Flood*, BOB DYLAN with THE BAND
13   *Walls and Bridges*, JOHN LENNON
14   *Dancing Machine*, THE JACKSON 5
15   *AWB*, THE AVERAGE WHITE BAND
16   *Court and Spark*, JONI MITCHELL
17   *Odds and Sods*, THE WHO
18   *Caught Up*, MILLIE JACKSON
19   *Heart Like a Wheel*, LINDA RONSTADT
20   *Mighty Love*, THE SPINNERS
21   *Let's Put It All Together*, THE STYLISTICS
22   *Nightbirds*, LABELLE
23   *Blue Magic*
24   *Feats Don't Fail Me Now*, LITTLE FEAT
25   *Small Talk*, SLY AND THE FAMILY STONE
26   *That Nigger's Crazy*, RICHARD PRYOR
27   *Pussy Cats*, HARRY NILSSON
28   *On the Beach*, NEIL YOUNG
29   *Let Me in Your Life*, ARETHA FRANKLIN
30   *When the Eagle Flies*, TRAFFIC
31   *Good Old Boys*, RANDY NEWMAN
32   *Pure Smokey*, SMOKEY ROBINSON
33   *Wrap Around Joy*, CAROLE KING
34   *Pretzel Logic*, STEELY DAN
35   *Red*, KING CRIMSON
36   *Secret Treaties*, BLUE ÖYSTER CULT
37   *Rags to Rufus*, RUFUS featuring CHAKA KHAN
38   *Claudine* (soundtrack), GLADYS KNIGHT AND THE PIPS
39   *There Won't Be Anymore*, CHARLIE RICH
40   *Starless and Bible Black*, KING CRIMSON

1975

1 *Born to Run*, BRUCE SPRINGSTEEN
2 *The Basement Tapes*, BOB DYLAN
3 *Horses*, PATTI SMITH
4 *Siren*, ROXY MUSIC
5 *Still Crazy after All These Years*, PAUL SIMON
6 *Blood on the Tracks*, BOB DYLAN
7 *The Who by Numbers*
8 *To Be True*, HAROLD MELVIN AND THE BLUE NOTES
9 *Midnight Lightning*, JIMI HENDRIX
10 *Fleetwood Mac*
11 *Zuma*, NEIL YOUNG
12 *Al Green Is Love*
13 *John Fogerty*
14 *Tonight's the Night*, NEIL YOUNG
15 *Wake Up Everybody*, HAROLD MELVIN AND THE BLUE NOTES
16 *Red Headed Stranger*, WILLIE NELSON
17 *Rock 'n' Roll*, JOHN LENNON
18 *Daryl Hall and John Oates*
19 *Crash Landing*, JIMI HENDRIX
20 *Country Life*, ROXY MUSIC
21 *Young Americans*, DAVID BOWIE
22 *Love to Love You Baby*, DONNA SUMMER
23 *A Quiet Storm*, SMOKEY ROBINSON
24 *Today*, ELVIS PRESLEY
25 *Really Rosie*, CAROLE KING
26 *Survival*, THE O'JAYS
27 *Gratitude*, EARTH, WIND, AND FIRE
28 *Inseparable*, NATALIE COLE
29 *Is It Something I Said?* RICHARD PRYOR
30 *That's the Way of the World*, EARTH, WIND, AND FIRE
31 *Promised Land*, ELVIS PRESLEY
32 *Let's Do It Again* (soundtrack), THE STAPLE SINGERS
33 *Schoolboys in Disgrace*, THE KINKS
34 *Why Can't We Be Friends?* WAR

35   *Family Reunion*, THE O'JAYS
36   *More American Graffiti* (soundtrack), various artists
37   *In the City*, TAVARES
38   *Supernatural*, BEN E. KING
39   *Lou Reed Live*
40   *High on You*, SLY STONE

1976

1   *The Sun Sessions*, ELVIS PRESLEY
2   *Songs in the Key of Life*, STEVIE WONDER
3   *"Live" Bullet*, BOB SEGER AND THE SILVER BULLET BAND
4   *A Night on the Town*, ROD STEWART
5   *Full of Fire*, AL GREEN
6   *Night Moves*, BOB SEGER AND THE SILVER BULLET BAND
7   *The Pretender*, JACKSON BROWNE
8   *Hejira*, JONI MITCHELL
9   *Boston*
10   *Bigger Than Both of Us*, DARYL HALL AND JOHN OATES
11   *One More from the Road*, Lynyrd Skynyrd
12   *Agents of Fortune*, BLUE ÖYSTER CULT
13   *The Clones of Dr. Funkenstein*, PARLIAMENT
14   *Live!* BOB MARLEY AND THE WAILERS
15   *Coney Island Baby*, LOU REED
16   *Dr. Buzzard's Original "Savannah" Band*
17   *Stretchin' Out in Bootsy's Rubber Band*, BOOTSY COLLINS
18   *Jailbreak*, THIN LIZZY
19   *Bicentennial Nigger*, RICHARD PRYOR
20   *The Royal Scam*, STEELY DAN
21   *Desire*, BOB DYLAN
22   *Hotel California*, THE EAGLES
23   *Wings at the Speed of Sound*
24   *Station to Station*, DAVID BOWIE
25   *Viva! Roxy Music*
26   *Small Change*, TOM WAITS
27   *Wired*, JEFF BECK

28 *Hardcore Jollies*, FUNKADELIC
29 *Thoroughbred*, CAROLE KING
30 *Rastaman Vibration*, BOB MARLEY AND THE WAILERS
31 *Mothership Connection*, PARLIAMENT
32 *The Outlaws*, WAYLON JENNINGS, WILLIE NELSON, TOMPALL GLASER, JESSI COLTER
33 *I Want You*, MARVIN GAYE
34 *Smokey's Family Robinson*, SMOKEY ROBINSON
35 *Cry Tough*, NILS LOFGREN
36 *The Roaring Silence*, MANFRED MANN'S EARTH BAND
37 *Where the Happy People Go*, THE TRAMMPS
38 *Car Wash* (soundtrack), various artists
39 *The Manhattans*
40 *Diana Ross*

1977

1   *Saturday Night Fever* (soundtrack), various artists
2   *My Aim Is True*, ELVIS COSTELLO
3   *Street Survivors*, LYNYRD SKYNYRD
4   *In Color*, CHEAP TRICK
5   *Chic*
6   *Rough Mix*, PETE TOWNSHEND with RONNIE LANE
7   *Low*, DAVID BOWIE
8   *Disco Inferno*, THE TRAMMPS
9   *Rumours*, FLEETWOOD MAC
10 *Rocket to Russia*, THE RAMONES
11 *Feelin' Bitchy*, MILLIE JACKSON
12 *Tom Petty and the Heartbreakers*
13 *All 'n' All*, EARTH, WIND, AND FIRE
14 *This Time It's for Real*, SOUTHSIDE JOHNNY AND THE ASBURY JUKES
15 *Teddy Pendergrass*
16 *Monkey Island*, THE J. GEILS BAND
17 *The Beatles at the Hollywood Bowl*
18 *Once upon a Time*, DONNA SUMMER

19 *Aja*, STEELY DAN
20 *Peter Gabriel*
21 *Heroes*, DAVID BOWIE
22 *Don't Let Me Be Misunderstood*, SANTA ESMERALDA starring LEROY GOMEZ
23 *Beauty on a Back Street*, HALL AND OATES
24 *Funkentelechy vs. the Placebo Syndrome*, PARLIAMENT
25 *Are You Serious?* RICHARD PRYOR
26 *Islands*, THE BAND
27 *Talking Heads: 77*
28 *One of the Boys*, ROGER DALTREY
29 *Animals*, PINK FLOYD
30 *I Remember Yesterday*, DONNA SUMMER
31 *JT*, JAMES TAYLOR
32 *Baby It's Me*, DIANA ROSS
33 *Twilley Don't Mind*, THE DWIGHT TWILLEY BAND
34 *Little Criminals*, RANDY NEWMAN
35 *Deep in My Soul*, SMOKEY ROBINSON
36 *Before We Were So Rudely Interrupted*, THE ANIMALS (the original)
37 *Ahh . . . the Name Is Bootsy, Baby!* BOOTSY'S RUBBER BAND
38 *True to Life*, RAY CHARLES
39 *Spectres*, BLUE ÖYSTER CULT
40 *Time Loves a Hero*, LITTLE FEAT

1978

1 *Darkness on the Edge of Town*, BRUCE SPRINGSTEEN
2 *This Year's Model*, ELVIS COSTELLO
3 *Easter*, THE PATTI SMITH GROUP
4 *Heaven Tonight*, CHEAP TRICK
5 *Parallel Lines*, BLONDIE
6 *The Cars*
7 *The Last Waltz* (soundtrack), various artists
8 *You're Gonna Get It!* TOM PETTY AND THE HEARTBREAKERS
9 *C'est Chic*

10   *Wavelength,* VAN MORRISON
11   *Excitable Boy,* WARREN ZEVON
12   *Running on Empty,* JACKSON BROWNE
13   *Wanted,* RICHARD PRYOR
14   *Who Are You,* THE WHO
15   *Sanctuary,* THE J. GEILS BAND
16   *Plastic Letters,* BLONDIE
17   *Life Is a Song Worth Singing,* TEDDY PENDERGRASS
18   *More Songs about Buildings and Food,* TALKING HEADS
19   *Street Hassle,* LOU REED
20   *Natural High,* THE COMMODORES
21   *Skynyrd's First and . . . Last,* LYNYRD SKYNYRD
22   *Some Girls,* THE ROLLING STONES
23   *But Seriously Folks,* JOE WALSH
24   *Stranger in Town,* BOB SEGER AND THE SILVER BULLET BAND
25   *Bootsy? Player of the Year,* BOOTSY'S RUBBER BAND
26   *Eddie Money*
27   *Waylon and Willie,* WAYLON JENNINGS and WILLIE NELSON
28   *Macho Man,* THE VILLAGE PEOPLE
29   *One Nation under a Groove,* FUNKADELIC
30   *One-Eyed Jack,* GARLAND JEFFREYS
31   *David Gilmour*
32   *Stardust,* WILLIE NELSON
33   *Minute by Minute,* THE DOOBIE BROTHERS
34   *Misfits,* THE KINKS
35   *Get It Out 'cha System,* MILLIE JACKSON
36   *Motor-Booty Affair,* PARLIAMENT
37   *Dr. Buzzard's Original "Savannah" Band Meets King Penett*
38   *Waiting for Columbus,* LITTLE FEAT
39   *Peter Gabriel*
40   *2 Hot!* PEACHES AND HERB

1979

1   *Bad Girls,* DONNA SUMMER
2   *Damn the Torpedoes,* TOM PETTY AND THE HEARTBREAKERS

3   *Armed Forces*, ELVIS COSTELLO
4   *Off the Wall*, MICHAEL JACKSON
5   *Cheap Trick at Budokan*
6   *Journey Through the Secret Life of Plants*, STEVIE WONDER
7   *Risque*, CHIC
8   *Tusk*, FLEETWOOD MAC
9   *The Wall*, PINK FLOYD
10   *In Through the Out Door*, LED ZEPPELIN
11   *Rust Never Sleeps*, NEIL YOUNG AND CRAZY HORSE
12   *Eat to the Beat*, BLONDIE
13   *Candy-O*, THE CARS
14   *Uncle Jam Wants You*, FUNKADELIC
15   *Mingus*, JONI MITCHELL
16   *Here, My Dear*, MARVIN GAYE
17   *Fear of Music*, TALKING HEADS
18   *Teddy*, TEDDY PENDERGRASS
19   *Low Budget*, THE KINKS
20   *Van Halen II*
21   *McFadden and Whitehead*
22   *Look Sharp!* JOE JACKSON
23   *Labour of Lust*, NICK LOWE
24   *We Are Family*, SISTER SLEDGE
25   *Outlandos d'Amour*, POLICE
26   *The Kids Are Alright* (soundtrack), THE WHO
27   *Prince*
28   *Big Fun*, SHALAMAR
29   *Wave*, THE PATTI SMITH GROUP
30   *Where There's Smoke . . .* SMOKEY ROBINSON
31   *Dire Straits*
32   *Deguello*, ZZ TOP
33   *Stay Free*, ASHFORD AND SIMPSON
34   *Every 1's a Winner*, HOT CHOCOLATE
35   *Identify Yourself*, THE O'JAYS
36   *Joe's Garage, Act I*, FRANK ZAPPA
37   *Live Rust*, NEIL YOUNG AND CRAZY HORSE
38   *Lodger*, DAVID BOWIE

39   *Midnight Magic*, THE COMMODORES
40   *Dream Police*, CHEAP TRICK

1980

1   *The River*, BRUCE SPRINGSTEEN
2   *The Wanderer*, DONNA SUMMER
3   *London Calling*, THE CLASH
4   *Hotter Than July*, STEVIE WONDER
5   *Warm Thoughts*, SMOKEY ROBINSON
6   *Zenyatta Mondatta*, THE POLICE
7   *Peter Gabriel*
8   *Empty Glass*, PETE TOWNSHEND
9   *Love Stinks*, THE J. GEILS BAND
10   *Dirty Mind*, PRINCE
11   *Triumph*, THE JACKSONS
12   *Get Happy*, ELVIS COSTELLO
13   *Hold Out*, JACKSON BROWNE
14   *Common One*, VAN MORRISON
15   *Black Market Clash*, THE CLASH
16   *Scary Monsters*, DAVID BOWIE
17   *Double Fantasy*, JOHN LENNON/YOKO ONO
18   *Real People*, CHIC
19   *Kurtis Blow*
20   *Pretenders*
21   *Beat Crazy*, THE JOE JACKSON BAND
22   *Uprising*, BOB MARLEY AND THE WAILERS
23   *Bad Luck Streak in Dancing School*, WARREN ZEVON
24   *Making Movies*, DIRE STRAITS
25   *Big Fun*, SHALAMAR
26   *Sacred Songs*, DARYL HALL
27   *Anytime, Anyplace, Anywhere*, THE ROSSINGTON COLLINS
     BAND
28   *Ray, Goodman and Brown*
29   *Seconds of Pleasure*, ROCKPILE
30   *Black Sea*, XTC

31   *Taking Liberties*, ELVIS COSTELLO
32   *The Whispers*
33   *One-Trick Pony*, PAUL SIMON
34   *Women and Children First*, VAN HALEN
35   *New Clear Days*, THE VAPORS
36   *Scream Dream*, TED NUGENT
37   *The Up Escalator*, GRAHAM PARKER AND THE RUMOUR
38   *Voices*, DARYL HALL and JOHN OATES
39   *Blow Fly's Party*, BLOW FLY
40   *Back in Black*, AC/DC

THIRTY-FOUR:
SEALED WITH A KISS

"THE 10 COMMANDMENTS OF LOVE"
The Moonglows, 1958

1 "Thou shall never love another"
2 "Stand by me all the while"
3 "Take happiness with the heartaches"
4 "Go through life wearing a smile"
5 "Thou shall always have faith in me in everything I say and do"
6 "Love me with all your heart and soul until our life on earth is through"
7 "Come to me when I am lonely"
8 "Kiss me when you hold me tight"
9 "Treat me sweet and gentle"
10 * . . .

*There is no tenth commandment of love.

SELECTED BIBLIOGRAPHY

BEECHER, JOHN, and JONES, MALCOLM, eds. *The Buddy Holly Story*. New York: MCA Records, 1979.

DALTON, DAVID, and KAYE, LENNY. *Rock 100*. New York: Grosset and Dunlap, 1977.

DAVIES, HUNTER. *The Beatles: The Authorized Biography*. 2d ed., rev. New York: McGraw-Hill, 1978.

DEFOE, B. GEORGE, and DEFOE, MARTHA, eds. *Volume: International Discography of the New Wave*. New York: One Ten Records, 1980.

ERRIGO, ANGIE, and LEANING, STEVE. *The Illustrated History of Rock Album Art*. London: Octopus Books, 1979.

FRAME, PETE. *Rock Family Trees*. New York: Quick Fox, 1980.

GAMBACCINI, PAUL, ed. *Critic's Choice Top 200 Albums*. New York: Omnibus, 1978.

GOLDROSEN, JOHN. *Buddy Holly: His Life and Music*. New York: Quick Fox/Music Sales, 1979.

GREEN, JONATHON, ed. *The Book of Rock Quotes*. New York: Omnibus Press, 1977.

GROSS, MICHAEL, and JAKUBOWSKI, MAXIM, eds. *Rock Yearbook, 1981*. New York: Delilah Books/Grove Press, 1980

HARDY, PHIL, and LAING, DAVE. *The Encyclopedia of Rock*. Vols. 1–3. Frogmore, England: Panther Books, 1976.

HARRIS, SHELDON. *Blues Who's Who*. New Rochelle, New York: Arlington House, 1979.

HENDERSON, DAVID. *Jimi Hendrix: Voodoo Child of the Aquarian Age*. New York: Doubleday, 1978.

HOPKINS, JERRY, and SUGARMAN, DANNY. *No One Here Gets Out Alive*. New York: Warner Books, 1980.

JENKINSON, PHILIP, and WARNER, ALAN. *Celluloid Rock: Twenty Years of Movie Rock*. London: Lorrimer Publishing, 1974.

JØRGENSEN, ERNST; RASMUSSEN, ERIK; and MIKKELSEN, JOHNNY. *Elvis Recording Sessions*. Oslo, Norway: Jee Publications, 1977.

LEAF, DAVID. *The Beach Boys and the California Myth*. New York: Grosset and Dunlap, 1978.

LICHTER, PAUL. *The Boy Who Dared to Rock: The Definitive Elvis*. New York: Dolphin/Doubleday, 1978.

LOGAN, NICK, and WOFFINDEN, BOB. *The Illustrated Encyclopedia of Rock*. New York: Harmony Books, 1977.

MACKEN, BOB; FORNATALE, PETER; and AYERS, BILL. *The Rock Music Source Book*. New York: Anchor Books/Doubleday, 1980.

MARCHBANK, PEARCE, and MILES. *The Illustrated Rock Almanac*. London: Paddington Press, 1977.

MARSH, DAVE. *Born to Run: The Bruce Springsteen Story*. New York: Delilah Books/Doubleday, 1979.

MARSH, DAVE, and SWENSON, JOHN, eds. *The Rolling Stone Record Guide*. New York: Rolling Stone Press/Random House, 1979.

MARTIN, GEORGE, with HORNSBY, JEREMY. *All You Need Is Ears*. New York: Macmillan, 1979.

MATLIN, LEONARD, ed. *TV Movies*. 2d ed., rev. New York: Signet Books, 1980.

McCABE, PETER, and SCHONFIELD, ROBERT D. *Apple to the Core*. New York: Pocket Books, 1976.

MILLER, JIM, ed. *The Rolling Stone Illustrated History of Rock and Roll*. 2d ed., rev. New York: Rolling Stone Press/Random House, 1980.

MUIR, EDDIE, ed. *"Wild Cat": A Tribute to Gene Vincent*.

MUIR, EDDIE, and SCOTT, TONY. *Eddie Cochran*.

NITE, NORM N. *Rock On: The Illustrated Encyclopedia of Rock and Roll*. Vol. 1. New York: T.Y. Crowell, 1978. Vol. 2. Popular Library, 1977.

NUGENT, STEPHEN, and GILLETT, CHARLIE, eds. *Rock Almanac: Top Twenty American and British Singles and Albums of the Fifties, Sixties and Seventies*. New York: Anchor Books/Doubleday, 1978.

OSBORNE, JERRY, and HAMILTON, BRUCE. *Presleyana*. Chicago: Follett Books, 1980.

RINZLER, ALAN. *Bob Dylan: The Illustrated Record*. New York: Harmony Books, 1978.

SANTELLI, ROBERT. *Aquarius Rising: The Rock Festival Years*. New York: Delta Books, 1980.

SCADUTO, ANTHONY *Bob Dylan: An Intimate Biography*. New York: Signet Books/New American Library, 1973.

SCHAFFNER, NICHOLAS. *The Beatles Forever*. New York: McGraw-Hill Paperbacks, 1977.

SOLOMON, CLIVE. *Record Hits: The British Top Fifty*. New York: Omnibus Press, 1977.

STAMBLER, IRWIN. *The Encyclopedia of Pop, Rock, and Soul*. New York: St. Martin's Press, 1977.

STOKES, GEOFFREY. *The Beatles*. New York: Rolling Stone Press/Times Books, 1980.

TAYLOR, DEREK. *As Time Goes By*. San Francisco: Straight Arrow Books, 1973.

WHITBURN, JOEL. *Joel Whitburn's Top Pop Artists and Singles 1955–1978*. Menomonee Falls, Wisconsin: Record Research, 1979. Supp. 1973–1979.

WORTH, FRED. L. *Thirty Years of Rock 'n' Roll Trivia*. New York: Warner Books, 1980.

YORK, WILLIAM., ed. *Who's Who in Rock Music*. Seattle: Atomic Press, 1978.

ZALKIND, RONALD. *Contemporary Music Almanac 1980/81*. New York: Schirmer Books, 1980.

Circus, Crawdaddy, Creem, Fabulous Magazine, Goldmine, Guitar Magazine, Guitar Player, Living Blues, Melody Maker, Musician, the *National Enquirer, New Musical Express, Performance, Playboy, Rolling Stone, Trouser Press, Who Put the Bomp?*